# RELEVANT TOPICS IN EATING DISORDERS

Edited by **Ignacio Jáuregui-Lobera**

**Relevant Topics in Eating Disorders**
Edited by Ignacio Jáuregui-Lobera

**Published by InTech**
Janeza Trdine 9, 51000 Rijeka, Croatia



**Publishing Process Manager** Dragana Manestar

**Technical Editor** Teodora Smiljanic

**Cover Designer** InTech Design Team

Additional hard copies can be obtained from orders@intechopen.com

Relevant Topics in Eating Disorders, Edited by Ignacio Jáuregui-Lobera
p. cm.
ISBN 978-953-51-0001-0

For EU product safety concerns:
IN TECH d.o.o., Prolaz Marije Krucifikse Kozulić 3, 51000 Rijeka, Croatia,
info@intechopen.com or visit our website at intechopen.com.

# Meet the editor

Dr Ignacio Jáuregui-Lobera, MD, PhD, MSc, is Director of the Behavioural Sciences Institute and Associate Professor of the Pablo de Olavide University in Seville (Spain). He is psychiatrist, family practitioner and psychologist, and since 1993 he is working in the field of eating disorders, overweight and obesity. He is member of the Academy for Eating Disorders (USA) and the Spanish Association for the Study of Eating Disorders. He has published five books about eating disorders as well as different articles on the same field of study. He is Coordinator of the Editorial Board of the journal Nutrición Hospitalaria and member of the Royal Academy of Medicine of Seville (Spain).

# Contents

# Preface

Eating disorders are common, frequently severe, and often devastating pathologies. Biological, psychological, and social factors are usually involved in these disorders in both the aetiopathogeny and the course of disease. Besides the patients, families are also disturbed by the disorder. Among sociocultural aspects, the figures from epidemiological studies need to be revised as well as the gender topics. What are the key variables in the development of eating disorders? Age, gender, biological factors, specific types of personality, westernization, physical activity, etc., could be some adequate answers, but the interaction among those possible variables might better explain the problem of the development of each particular eating disorder.

This book includes different studies about the core concepts of eating disorders, from general topics to some different modalities of treatment. Sandra Torres et al. give us a complete overview of epidemiological data, which has yielded conflicting findings and interpretations. The chapter by Pilar Ramos et al. brings the main points about the pernicious pattern established among weight, image, and body control during adolescence as key variables in the development of eating disorders. The role of some psychosocial factors as well as the role of some biological influences is explained by Ana Sepúlveda & María Calado, Paolo Cotrufo et al., Arantzazu Rodríguez-Fernández & Alfredo Goñi, and Janas-Kozik, respectively. These chapters are a good framework on some etiopathogenic elements involved in eating disorders.

A very relevant part of this book highlights some clinical and therapeutic issues from both psychosocial and biological points of view. Thus, the need of training programs focused on emotion regulation skills (Ohmann & Popow), the neuropsychology of eating disorders (Camacho Ruiz et al.), the relationship with food in eating disorders (Arlene Leite Nunes) and the cardiovascular complications in eating disorders (Jáuregui-Garrido & Jáuregui-Lobera) are relevant clinical facets of eating disorders. With respect to the treatment, Moria Golan, Escobar-Koch et al., Rosenvinge & Pettersen, and Kroon Van Diest & Perez, summarize such important fields as an integrative model of treatment, the patients' point of view, a comprehensive model of recovery, and some ideas about prevention.

The book ends with the relevant topic of nutrition in eating disorders. The nutritional evaluation of eating disorders (Inmaculada Ruiz Prieto) is followed by nutritional treatment (Patricia Bolaños Ríos). Both chapters include some new technologies in order to improve the nutritional management of these disorders as well as the nutritional education focused on the patients and the families. Finally, the chapter of enteral nutrition as a life-saving treatment is developed by Maria Gabriella Gentile.

Professionals such as psychologists, nurses, doctors, and nutritionists, among others, may be interested in this book.

**Ignacio Jáuregui-Lobera**
Pablo de Olavide University and Institute of Behavioral Science Dr. Jauregui SCP,
Seville,
Spain

# Part 1

## General Topics, Concepts

1

# The Epidemic of Anorexia Nervosa: Myth or Reality?

Sandra Torres[1], Marina Guerra[1], Filipa Vieira[1],
Kylee Miller[3], António Roma-Torres[2] and Isabel Brandão[2]
[1]*Faculty of Psychology and Educational Sciences - University of Porto*
[2]*Department of Psychiatry, Hospital of S. João, Porto*
[3]*School of Education, University of North Carolina*
[1,2]*Portugal*
[3]*USA*

## 1. Introduction

Anorexia nervosa (AN) is an eating disorder (ED) characterized by a severe weight loss due to inadequate food intake, and has associated significant medical and psychological sequelae (Bulik et al. 2005; Torres & Guerra, 2007). Despite the fact that AN was only recognized as a mental disorder during the 20th century, there are a great number of studies about this disease. A mixture of curiosity and concern justifies this attention given by both researchers and the community at large.

One of the most explored areas in AN research is the epidemiology, specifically, the estimation of the prevalence and incidence of the disease. The incidence measures the strength of occurrence of a disease and is defined as the number of new cases in the population over a specific period of time (usually 1 year). It is commonly expressed in terms of cases per 100 000 persons in the population per year. The prevalence is the total number of cases in the population, and is calculated for a specific point in time (point prevalence) or period of time (period prevalence). This rate indicates the percentage of the population that presents with the disease (Garb, 1996; Hoek, 2006).

The application of epidemiological methods to ED research began approximately 40 years ago and was motivated by the speculation of a marked increase in AN. The hypothesis in growth of AN has been bolstered by the increase in hospital admission rates, which have been variously defined as a 'slight rise' (Russell, 1985) to an 'epidemic scenario' (Epstein, 1986, as cited in Williams & King, 1987). Conversely, other researchers argue that there is no evidence to support an increased rate of this pathology (e.g. Fombonne, 1995; Williams & King, 1987).

Several methodological limitations are the basis of these inconsistent findings which should be considered when we intend to discern whether or not the rates of AN increase over time.

In this chapter we will analyze relevant, published epidemiological studies in order to better determine the extent of this eating pathology. Relevant articles in English and Portuguese were collected from PubMed and reviewed, independent of publication year and the sample studied. Metaanalytic studies were also included. Key search terms relating to epidemiology and ED were used. Follows is a review the main obstacles in this field, as we believe they strongly contribute to the main discrepancies found in the results.

## 2. Obstacles in the study of epidemiology

In spite of considerable efforts, researchers have faced several methodological problems in the study of incidence and prevalence of AN. These obstacles draw into question the validity of many studies and have left fundamental questions unanswered (Hoek & Hoehen, 2003; Hoek, 2006). These difficulties can be grouped into three broad categories: 1) sample selection; 2) definition of a case; and 3) detection of cases.

### 2.1 Sample selection

AN is an uncommon disease. In order to attain a larger number of people with AN, some studies selected samples from persons at increased risk of having an ED, such as students. Likewise, data on patients attending hospital services have also attracted researchers' attention (Patton & King, 1991). Consequently, there are a variety of samples studied, including graduate and undergraduate students, participants recruited from health settings (either primary health care or mental health services), as well as people from the community (Heatherton et al. 1995). These different criteria implemented in sample selection limit the ability to compare data between studies and generalize the outcomes to the general population.

Furthermore, it should be noted that there is a little use of randomized samples in the reviewed research. Considering the existence of risk groups for ED, sampling procedures should be carefully defined, to increase validity and reliability (Heatherton et al., 1995).

### 2.2 Definition of a case

For these reasons it is important to understand the diagnostic criteria applied in the definition of a "case" of AN in epidemiological studies. Review of these studies clearly reveals variation in diagnostic criteria between studies and countries, as well as over time.

Obviously, these differences can produce fluctuations in prevalence rates. On the other hand, even when the diagnostic criteria are defined, the researchers may use different degrees of accuracy in criteria application (Fombonne, 1995). Regardless of the discussion on advantages/disadvantages of being flexible in the application of diagnostic criteria in clinical settings, it must be stressed that the non-uniformity of their use interferes in the counting of cases, and consequently, represents a serious obstacle in the definition of a trend (increasing, decreasing, or constant) in the epidemiology of AN.

Some authors have argued for the use of homogeneous criteria in epidemiology research, specifically adapted for the study setting. Szmuckler (1985, p.144) justifies this need: "Criteria for the diagnosis of AN developed in a hospital setting achieves a reasonable degree of precision, but in a community setting, distinctions between those affected and those unaffected become less clear. With features such as weight loss and the characteristic psychopathology, the evidence points to graded severities".

Sharing this point of view, several epidemiological studies have included partial AN cases (formally considered as an ED not otherwise specified) in their analyses, arguing that they can also provide useful information about causal factors (Hardy & Dantchev, 1989; Heatherton et al., 1995; Patton et al., 1990; Råstam et al., 1989). More recently, Dellava et al. (2011) have illustrated the impact of using broad diagnostic criteria for AN on results. Specifically, that inclusion of individuals with more 'normal' BMIs may disguise key underlying factors for a BMI characteristic of AN. As such, interpretation of cited outcomes warrants some caution, as the relationship between full and partial syndromes is not clearly known.

### 2.3 Detection of cases

The difficulty in detecting cases is another practical problem which underlies the epidemiology of ED. One issue that contributes to this is the compatibility of AN with the cultural value placed on slimness. In occidental societies, this disease may not be detected, particularly during its early stages, because of its semblance to non-pathological dieting. Both dieting and exercise constitute well accepted behaviors of everyday lifestyles which are heavily promoted by media (Jones et al., 1980).

Another problem that hinders the detection of cases, mainly in research focused on hospital records, is the resistance of individuals with AN to seek treatment (Hoek, 2006). Due to the egosyntonic nature of symptoms, people with this disease often desire to maintain a low weight and, for this reason, avoid professional help (Preti et al., 2009). Thus, the number of patients that seek treatment does not correspond to the actual number of cases existing in the community.

On the other hand, community surveys also face problems that limit the detection of cases. The major difficulty is related to the relatively low base rate of the disorder, which requires large study samples in order to obtain an accurate measure of incidence and prevalence (Wakeling, 1996). Other great obstacles are inherent in the use of self-report measures, and understandable for several reasons. First, assessment instruments are developed according to diagnostic criteria defined in clinical settings, and thus not adequately adapted to community settings, as previously reported. Second, these studies depend on participants' self-reported answers to identify core symptoms of the disease, some of which are difficult to identify and interpret. For example, the amount of food eaten and disturbances in the way in which one's body weight or shape is experienced are two subjective and complex issues to assess. Third, data from self-report measures may be easily biased due to outliers or missing answers (Fairburn & Beglin, 1990). Similarly, the literature reveals that ED are over-represented in non-respondent participants which leads to a low prevalence estimation (Santonastaso et al., 1996). In a low prevalence pathology, as with AN, it is not necessary to have a wide range of missing data to distort the epidemiological data (Hardy & Dantchev, 1989).

In conclusion, the singular use of these assessment methodologies presents some gaps. In the following sections we will analyze the methodological options adopted by several authors to balance these limitations.

To this point we have discussed the main obstacles in achieving reliable epidemiological data in AN. It could sound peculiar starting, rather than ending, this chapter focusing on the limitations of the studies in this domain. However, the purpose of this approach is to prepare the reader to critically analyze the studies that will be hereafter described, and to better understand the inherent difficulties that make comparisons of the outcomes a difficult task.

## 3. Types of studies

As a result of over 40 years in epidemiological research of ED, it is possible to find a great variety of study designs. Describing each of them would be an exhaustive task, and probably futile for the reader. Therefore, in this section we propose to highlight several studies that have been recognized by the research community as central; and also consider the multiplicity of achieved results and/or methodology implemented. These will be presented alongside a historical background about epidemiological studies in AN.

We will begin with the studies implemented with clinical samples, splitting them between those which found evidence of an increase in cases of AN and those which contradict this trend. Secondly, we will review the research developed with non-clinical samples: studies with students and community surveys. We will stress the different methodologies as well as main conclusions.

### 3.1. Studies with clinical samples

The first analyses in the study of the epidemiology of AN were on the rates of hospital-based services, centered on the assumption that most of the individuals with this disease would be referred to health units at some point-in-time (Wakeling, 1996). Following this clinic-based methodology some researchers concentrated analyses to psychiatric units, while others adopted a more comprehensive approach, exploring general hospital reports in a circumscribed area in order to find cases of AN that could have been treated by other medical specialties.

With the aim of providing a clear overview of the studies reviewed in this field, particularly those which concern incidence rates, specific data from each are synthesized in tables, which can be consulted in the Appendix. Tables 1 and 2 display the incidence results, and describe the studies that report an increase in the incidence (table 1) and those that do not confirm this trend (table 2), respectively. For convention, incidence rates are estimated for a period of one year, unless otherwise specified. Table 3 presents the prevalence rates obtained from clinical samples. In the following sections we will briefly discuss these tables, concentrating on the most relevant outcomes provided.

#### 3.1.1 Indicators of an increase of AN

Historically, Theander (1970) was a pioneer in analyzing the hospital admission data, including both psychiatric and general medical services. He evaluated the incidence of AN in Sweden over the period from 1930 to 1960 and noted a sharp increase in incidence during those three decades. In subsequent years other researchers have followed his line of inquiry in greater depth, analyzing psychiatric records from several hospitals (Jones et al., 1980; Kendell et al., 1973). Commensurate with Theander's (1970) results, it was reported that the number of cases of AN had increased the decades between 1960 and 1980.

Several explanations have been assigned to this event, most of them relating to the value placed on diet: 1) the concern about losing weight had been rising in the population; 2) the significant growth of the weight-loss industry; and 3) the popularity of books about diets. However, the validity of this conclusion is questionable, as the increase in reported cases of AN could also reflect a more efficient means of case detection, reflected in the increase of articles published since 1970 (Jones et al., 1980).

Thenceforward, studies were developed in an attempt to control confounding variables that could contribute to an apparent increase of this disease. One of many such studies was developed by Willi and Grossmann (1983) in a 20-year retrospective study that found a significant increase (.38 to 1.12 per 100 000) in cases of AN between 1956 and 1975, in Switzerland (see table 1 in Appendix). The authors surmised that this increase was not attributable to the use of non-standardized diagnostic criteria, or from hospitalization of the most severe cases in the first sampling periods of the study.

Another study, by Eagles et al. (1999), assessed the possible causes of the 5.3% increase in the incidence rates in Scotland between 1965 and 1991, as reported in an earlier work by Eagles et al. (1995). Eagles et al. (1999) concluded that this rise was not due to an increase of extreme cases presenting to specialist services. Despite this result, the hypothesis that people with AN are becoming more readily identified due to growth in professional awareness is still openly stressed by several authors (Eagles et al., 1999; Munk-Jørgensen et al., 1995; Pawluck & Gorey, 1998).

Of all studies described in table 1, the works developed in Rochester, Minnesota should be highlighted as well. They provide prospective data in 55-year trends on the incidence of AN within a single community, using consistent methodology. The researchers screened approximately 30 diagnostic terms referring to undetected cases in the epidemiological archives at the Mayo Clinic, and in medical records from other healthcare providers in the surrounding geographic area. The first analysis reported on a 45-year period (1935-1979) and suggested surprisingly high incidence rates (overall age- and sex-adjusted of 7.3 per 100 000 person-years). No significant long-term trend in rates was ascertained in this study. Instead, it was suggested the existence of different trends according to specific age groups (Lucas et al., 1988).

A closer look at specific age ranges revealed the population most at-risk was also responsible for the spike in incidence rates up through 1984 (Lucas et al., 1991). A peak incidence was observed in people between the ages of 15 and 19, which contributed to the remarkable increase in incidence rates for women between the periods of 1950-1954 (7.0/ 100 000 per years) and 1980-1984 (26.3/ 100 000 per years). It is noted that the incidence rates for 20-year-old women remained constant. Lucas et al. hypothesized that this increase would not continue, or if it were to persist it would do so on a lesser scale. They were convinced that AN had reached its peak in the early 1980s, with evidence that while the milder forms of the disease in adolescents had been increasing, the more severe forms of the disease had remained constant. These authors also noted a cyclic trend in the incidence rate which coincided with changing fashion and idealized body image, which may affect the more vulnerable subjects.

These results were replicated by Lucas et al. (1999) using updated incidence rates, and adding the new cases diagnosed with AN from 1985 through 1989. The upward trend in incidence rates was still observed in adolescents 15- to 19-year-old, as well as a noted rise among 10- to 14-year-old females between 1950 and 1989. The overall age-adjusted incidence rate was 15.0/ 100 000 per years among females, and 1.5/100.000 per years among males.

A comparative analysis of the previous 50 years' research has revealed continuance of the linear increase for 15 to 24-year-old females, possibly because of the vulnerability of this age group to social and psychological pressures (Lucas et al., 1999). In 1985 the estimated prevalence of AN among 15 to 19-year-old girls in Rochester was 0.48% (Lucas et al., 1991). This makes AN a relatively common disorder among young females (Lucas et al., 1999). In males the scenario was reportedly quite different. As the occurrence of AN in males was both rare and constant over the 55-year period, Lucas et al. (1999) stressed that sex and age groups must be considered separately.

The quality of Lucas' team's studies has been recognized throughout the scientific community, as they addressed some of the limitations frequently identified in epidemiological studies. Fombonne (1995) applauded the prospective nature, consistent diagnostic criteria, and the relatively large sample of cases obtained within and across these three studies. Additionally, he enhanced the estimation of adjusted and standardized rates. Despite these strengths, Fombonne pointed out several limitations, such as overlapping age groups, and the need to control for the differential migration into the area of study.

### 3.1.2 Indicators against the increase of AN

In our point of view, the majority of research invalidating the increase of AN date from a more recent period (see Appendix- table 2). One of the first studies we found in this vein was published in 1987 and observed a rise in the number of first-time psychiatric admissions in England, between 1972 and 1981. From the authors' analysis of the age-period-cohort effect, Williams and King (1987) concluded that this was not a significant increase in cases of AN.

These authors argued that longitudinal incidence data are subject to these three effects. Specifically, they suggested that the age effect is related with possible changes in the structure's population, such as the rise in the number of citizens in a specific age group, relative to the rest of population. The period effect is associated with specific characteristics inherent in the study period. For example, if vigilance with regard to the detection of AN had increased in some period, or if the methods of case detection had improved, or if the diagnostic criteria had changed during said time, these particularities would influence the number of the detected cases. The cohort effect is connected to the community's features, in other words, it is the result of being born in a particular time and place. This effect makes the community members susceptible to cultural influences typical for that period, such as the emphasis on slimness.

Examination of data on patients admitted to psychiatric facilities in the Williams and King (1987) study revealed that the upward trend in incidence rates was due to an increase of young women in the population (age effect). Another factor that may have contributed to this apparent increase was the rise in readmissions of women with anorexia. In light of these findings, Williams and King argued that the idiom "epidemic" was inappropriate to describe the trend in the incidence of AN.

Later, in New Zealand, Hall and Hay (1991) controlled for the additional effect of the availability of services. Using clinical interviews, another case detection method described by Williams and King (1987), results suggest that the number of patients with AN increased when the treatments became more accessible. When they controlled for the age effect it was found that the morbidity of this disease had not increased. Consequently, the goal of treatment dispersion was established.

Some years later, Hoek et al. (1995) improved upon this case detection method in a continuation of his investigations from the mid '80s (Hoek, 1991). This schema was implemented with primary care and general practitioners who were trained by the researchers to observe core symptoms in ED. Clinicians were provided guidelines, which included strategies to circumvent the common obstacle of disease-denial on the part of the patient. With this methodology, a representative sample of the Dutch population, roughly 1%, was assessed for AN symptomology.

In the baseline study (1985-1986), Hoek (1991) observed a point prevalence of 18.4/ 100 000 and an incidence of 6.3/ 100 000 cases per year, without defining an evolutionary trend[1]. In the three subsequent years, Hoek et al. (1995) observed a higher incidence rate of 8.1/ 100 000 cases per years. However, an overall analysis of these and other studies led the authors to conclude that there was insufficient evidence of an increasing risk of AN during the 1980s compared to the 1970s.

Commensurate with these studies, more recent research by Currin et al. (2005) also reported a stable increase in the incidence of AN between 1988 and 2000. Currin et al. limited their search for new cases of AN to primary care services in the UK. They estimated an age- and sex-adjusted incidence rate of 4.7/ 100 000 for the year 2000. When compared with the work of Turnbull et al. (1996), it was similarly concluded that the incidence of AN remained stable from 1988-1993 with an incidence rate of 4.2/ 100 000 cases in 1993. Currin et al. (2005) concluded that this disease remained remarkably consistence over the 12 years of the study duration.

In summation, after thorough review of the clinical research, we consider a position either for or against the increase in incidence of AN as speculative. The research, despite inclusion of longitudinal data sets[2], presents several limitations. In addition to the obstacles discussed earlier, two additional problems warrant discussion. The first being selection bias: the cases described in medical reports only represent self-selected people who seek treatment. According to previous studies, only 60% of individuals with AN were admitted to hospitals (Joergensen, 1992), and one-third of the people who meet stringent diagnostic criteria were treated in mental health facilities (Hoek, 2006). Thus, it is likely that the rates calculated from medical record reviews constitute an underestimation of the disease within the community (Hoek, 2006).

Secondly, information from medical histories is not standardized and varies by site. This may limit the availability of relevant and necessary information about core eating disorder-related symptoms (Fombonne, 1995). Few researchers have broached this limitation (Eagles et al., 1995).

---

[1] For this reason Hoek's (1991) study was not included in tables 1 or 2, as these tables are organized according to incidence trends. Results are presented in table 3, with prevalence rates.

[2] Dating back to 1930 (Fombonne, 1995).

In addition to these limitations, few studies have examined the incidence of AN over long periods of time, within a defined geographic region(s), and using standardized methodologies (e.g., assessment tools, diagnostic criteria, etc; Eagles et al., 1995; Lucas et al., 1999). Furthermore, the analysis of incidence trends over the last ten years using said methodology is even more scarce. One of the studies which implemented these criteria was conducted over a 40 -year period (1956-1999), in Switzerland (Milos et al., 2003). This study showed oscillations in incidence rates over the duration of data collection[3]. For instance, between the 1960's and 1970's there was a significant increase in reported rates of AN, but since then the rates have remained stable. In the authors' opinion, whether this punctual increase in rates reflects changes in society's response to AN or true changes in incidence is an unanswered question. The validity and reliability of this research are widely accepted in research community, and a gold-standard for eating-disorders research (Pike, 2004).

### 3.2 Studies with non-clinical samples

This section will focus on epidemiological studies of AN conducted on non-treatment-seeking samples. These include research on students as well as community-wide surveys. Results are summarized in tables 4 and 5 in the Appendix, respectively.

It is noted that the studies with non-clinical samples appear to favor using *prevalence* data of AN, opposed to the *incidence* rates reported in clinic-based research. This distinction may be due to the necessity of conducting research in a specific geographic area, with prolonged access to patients over several years, and less financial resources; all of which are necessary for analysis of trends in incidence rates.

#### 3.2.1 Studies with student samples

Research with student samples have primarily adopted three distinct approaches: 1) use of the *key informant*, which requires the collaboration of school personnel for release of demographic and health information (e.g., student's weight); 2) *research based on self-report questionnaires*, which allows gathering data on a large scale and the ability to parse-out the more severe cases; and 3) the *two-stage survey*, in which the students undergo initial screening with a self-report questionnaire and researcher-identified high-risk subjects are subsequently interviewed in person to assess eating disorder-related symptoms. The two-stage process is the most commonly accepted method (Patton et al., 1990).

##### 3.2.1.1 The key informant method

This method is the most economical in terms of time, personnel, and financial resources; however, it presents rather significant problems. The first is the sole, observable, criteria of weight loss, a limitation inherent to the field of ED research (Patton & King, 1991). Assessment is also subject to the buy-in and motivation of the informant, all of which may present bias.

With so many confounding variables, it is no wonder that we have few studies implementing this approach. The one most cited in the literature is that by Crisp et al. (1976), conducted in England. Data was collected from nine groups of school girls who

[3] For this reason this study is presented both in table 1 and 2, according to the results for each time period.

attended both public and private institutions. Informants included both teachers and health professionals who were trained to identify cases of AN. In the majority of cases, identified students had previously been referred to and/or received medical attention.

Prevalence reported was roughly 1 girl with anorexia per 200 female students. The number of cases detected differed greatly between schools; and private schools presented higher rates than their public counterparts (1% versus 0.2%, respectively). It should be noted that this prevalence rate was similar to the incidence rates reported by Joergensen (1992) (see Appendix - table 3). It was concluded that AN is a common and serious disease within the English, female, school-aged population, and broke ground for other population-based inquiries.

Despite the large number of girls surveyed (N=12391), Szmukler (1985) criticized Crisp and colleagues' convenience sampling, and argued that participant selection was made based on school personnel's knowledge of student's medical outcomes.

#### 3.2.1.2 Studies based on self-report questionnaires

This method allows for sampling greater numbers of people than does the use of key informants. It is also easier to obtain informed consent, expedient, and generally well accepted by participants. Here, too, we are confronted with the limitations of using a single instrument for assessment, such as the frequent false positives and high rates of missing answers, as previously discussed in section 2.3 of this chapter. Beyond these, the relative paucity of external validation data about self-report-screening questionnaires limits their generalizability (Keski-Rahkonen et al., 2006).

In the United States, Haetherton et al. (1995) tested the efficacy of mailed self-report questionnaires. They sent the "Eating Disorder Inventory" (Garner et al., 1982) via post to randomly selected students from a college in the Northeastern US. No cases of AN were identified using this method. Similar methodology was also used in Portugal, with estimated rates of AN between 0% (Dixe, 2007; Machado et al., 2004) and 0.4% (Carmo et al., 1996) in females. This is somewhat lower compared to rates reported using other data collection techniques.

In brief, self-report questionnaires provide relevant data about the population's eating patterns, but the interpretation of results requires some caution. The two-stage survey, which utilizes an interview, emerged with the intent to overcome these shortcomings.

#### 3.2.1.3 Two- and three-stage survey

The need for both screening (via self-report) and diagnostic steps (via clinical interview) by qualified individuals is now widely accepted in the research community. Several studies report a substantial number of individuals scoring above the measure's cutoff points which places them in an at-risk category, but that subsequent diagnostic criteria for AN are not met (Johnson- Sabine et al., 1988; Whitaker et al., 1990).

Despite the thoroughness of the two-stage survey, its efficacy is still dependent on the quality of the instrument used (Fairburn & Beglin, 1990). Clinical interviews are a commonly used tool to control for this limitation; minimizing false positives and reaching a more complete analysis of eating behavior changes (Heatherton et al., 1995). To decrease the high number of subjects incorrectly labeled as not having AN symptomology (false negatives) (Rodríguez-Cano et al., 2005) and to control for the predisposition of people with

AN to hide their symptomology (Peláez Fernández et al., 2007), it is highly important for researchers to use control groups. The control groups are deemed "not at-risk" by receiving scores below clinical cut-off on the questionnaire of choice.

In persons with AN, the two-stage survey has been implemented in female adolescents –the population group most at-risk. The first published studies employing a two-stage survey on teenage girls had two common outcomes: 1) a reduction in the number in detected cases of AN, and 2) the frequent corroboration of partial AN syndrome, compared to studies using treatment-seeking samples. In fact, several surveys did not identify any anorexic participants from among the study participants (Jonhson-Sabine et al., 1988; Mann et al., 1983; Patton et al., 1990), as shown table 4 (see Appendix).

Subsequent double-stage prevalence studies, with identification of false negatives, have shown higher prevalence rates. Specifically, at the beginning of the century in Spain, the estimated prevalence of AN in female students between the ages of 12 and 18, was 0.45% (Rojo et al., 2003). A study completed only four years later in the same country, however, reported a decreased incidence of 0.33%, likely due to the inclusion of females up to 21 years of age (Peláez Fernández et al., 2007). In Portugal, female students between 12 and 23-years-old, have a purported prevalence rate of 0.39% (Machado et al., 2007) - similar to that reported by Peláez Fernández et al. (2007).

Higher prevalence rates have also been reported in studies using so-called "three-stage" surveys. These employ the two-stage model with the addition of a third stage –a review of medical records for a defined geographical area, on the same age-group as in the first two phases. One of the precursors to the three-stage survey was work done by Råstam et al. (1989). Their work has attracted attention not only because of the high prevalence rates reported, but also for the innovative methods applied to at-risk group selection (the first stage). Their methodology began with a review of school health records for individual growth charts from all 15-year-old residents in Göteborg (Sweden) enrolled in school. In addition, students completed a brief questionnaire covering topics including food interests, desire to lose weight, and menstrual irregularities. Results from these two procedures were examined by one clinician. After review, school nurses confirmed the weight of the students who presented symptoms compatible with a diagnosis of AN; and reported others students, not detected in this first phase, who might raise suspicion of suffering from this disease. In the second stage, the selected high-risk group of students underwent a neuropsychological examination and their parents were interviewed by the same clinician. The third stage in the identification process included a search of the town's pediatric and child psychiatric clinics for any additional cases that may have been overlooked in the schools. The analysis of medical case registers were conducted with same-age peers who resided in the same geographic area. The prevalence of AN in this study for girls 15-years-old or younger was 0.7%. This result is nearly double those estimated by the two-stage process. This rate is, however, comparable to the key informant methodology reported by Crisp et al. (1976). Råstam et al. (1989), hypothesized that peak incidence of AN may occur around the age of 14.

Rathner and Messner (1993), as well as Santonastaso et al., (1996), are two more current groups to employ the three-stage model. Rathner and Messner (1993) reported an impressive 1.3% population prevalence in female students aged 15-20 years. These authors proclaimed the advantages of the three-stage procedure: "In our own study this stage led to the detection of a new case and shows that some cases may be missed even with a rigorous two-stage procedure and the application of various indices. The results of our third stage suggest that (...) all subjects of a pre-defined sub-risk group should be interviewed and, additionally, that a case-register stage should always be added to any further studies" (Rathner & Messner, 1993, p.182).

Despite this suggestion the three-stage methodology did not propagate. At present, the two-stage screening approach is the most widely used procedure in epidemiological studies, also having been adopted in community survey use. Even so, they too have their limitations. The poor response rates, the low sensitivity, lack of specificity in the screening instruments, and the small number of the interviewed participants considered sub- risk, are some of the more common methodological problems cited (Hoek, 2006).

### 3.2.2 Studies with community samples

Community surveys have proliferated in the last decade. The main reason for this phenomenon is the recognition that they provide a more accurate prevalence rate of AN. Clinical samples represent only a minority of the people with AN existing in the community. On the other hand, population-based data may be useful in adjusting the more meaningful features of ED, which may differ from clinical to community setting. In addition, whether the fluctuation over the incidence rates is due to cohort-effects is another issue that may be clarified in these studies.

In addition to quantifying the occurrence of AN, population studies can also provide data on the distribution of the age-of-onset, natural course, and medical outcomes of this disease (Faravelli et al., 2006; Hudson et al., 2007). For this reason, *lifetime prevalence* is often reported. It represents the proportion of persons in a sample of the population that at some point in their life (up to the time of assessment) have experienced a disorder. Considering that point- and period-prevalence only include cases identified at a specific period of time it is expected that lifetime prevalence identifies a larger number of cases and, consequently, presents a higher rate (Robins et al., 1984). Lifetime prevalence rates observed in various studies with community samples can be seen in table 5 (see Appendix).

One interesting finding that emerges from the analysis is the emphasized importance of the interview in the more current publications. The two-stage methodology continues to be implemented (cf. Hudson et al., 2007; Lahortiga-Ramos et al., 2005) but in some cases the interview is integrated in the first stage of the screening (cf. Faravelli et al., 2006; Preti et al., 2009). Other works have adopted the clinical interview as a main procedure, applying it to the whole sample (cf. Favaro et al., 2003).

Three main features can be identified as differentiating factors among community-based surveys. One of them is the geographic area covered. Most of the studies select participants from a limited geographic area, most often in an urban area (cf. Faravelli et al., 2006; Favaro et al., 2003; Lahortiga-Ramos et al., 2005; Robins et al., 1984); while others use larger, nationally representative community samples (cf. Ghaderi & Scott, 2001; Götestam & Agras, 1995; Hudson et al., 2005; Preti et al., 2009; Wade et al., 2006).

A second differentiating factor is the gender of the participants included in samples. While studies with female participants are most common, it is possible to find studies with both genders, though they rarely estimate sex-adjusted incidence/prevalence rates. These rates are sensitive to this criterion, as AN is overrepresented in female population. Lifetime prevalence rates in female population-based surveys often achieve higher values, between 1% (Hudson et al., 2997; Preti et al., 2009) and 2.0% (Favaro et al., 2003; Wade et al., 2009), compared to studies with both sexes (0.5.%; Faravelli et al., 2006; Preti et al., 2009) and, particularly, with the rates estimated for males (0.3%; Hudson et al., 2007).

The third factor to be considered is the age of the selected sample. Despite the variability in the participants' age range of reviewed studies in Table 5 (see Appendix), a large number of community studies excluded individuals younger than 18-years-old. This is of concern, as these adolescents are the subset of the population most at risk to develop AN. Hence, the reported prevalence rates might be considered lower-bound estimates of existent frequencies (Preti et al., 2009).

Data on the incidence trends of AN as measured in community samples are narrow and limited to short periods of time (less than two years). As observed in prevalence reports, the rates calculated on incidence are significantly higher than the majority of values cited in studies using case registers: 120/ 100 000 (Ghaderi & Scott, 2001) to 200/ 100 000 per year (Lahortiga-Ramos et al., 2005). The latter, higher rate may be due to: 1) the sample used (e.g., population-based; only females between 13 and 22 years of age); 2) time between baseline and follow-up (18 months); and/or 3) high response rates.

The relatively high incidence of AN found in these studies is consistent with other research pointing to an increase in the prevalence across time, particularly in the second half of the 20th century (Bulik et al., 2006; Preti et al., 2009). Nevertheless, the observed changes in cultural responses to AN over the last decades may have played a role in this increase. In addition to the easier access to specialized health services, the larger social awareness to confront this disorder and a decrease of the associated stigma, both should also be considered (Pawluck & Gorey, 1998). In fact, current cases of initial-diagnosis of AN tend to occur in mid-adolescence (Lahortiga-Ramos et al., 2005). Despite this, data may reflect a precocious appearance of the disease, and may also be due to an earlier detection of this pathology provided for an increased attention by the media.

As previously stated, community studies are useful to better understand the symptoms, the course, and the outcomes of AN. Analyzing the symptoms, there is a broad consensus about the over-representation of the full-blown and sub-threshold ED featured in the community. Lifetime prevalence rates of partial AN[4] in female samples were, on average, around 2.5% (Favaro et al., 2003; Wade et al. 2006).

Regarding the course and outcome, it seems that patients tend to migrate between different diagnostic categories of ED, despite that a great percentage of them (roughly 50%) experience substantial symptom recovery over the course of the disorder (Faravelli et al., 2006; Wade et al. 2006). It is likely that the outcome is not solely due to treatment, given that the use of health services among those affected remains low (Faravelli et al., 2006; Hudson et al., 2007; Preti et al., 2009).

---

[4] Subjects who share many of the features of patients with anorexia nervosa, but fail to meet strict diagnosis criteria.

## 4. Conclusion

The question of whether the incidence of AN is on the rise has been considerably debated and, using Pike's (2004, p.259) words, finding an answer to this question remains "a Herculian task". As a result of various sampling and assessment procedures, data from epidemiological studies have yielded conflicting findings and interpretations (Currin et al., 2005; Fombonne, 1995; Hoek, 2006; Hoek & van Hoeken, 2003; Hudson et al., 2007). The great disparity of estimates is a result of both complex disease and complex domains of study. Consequently, even the most robust future studies will likely be unable to eliminate all the methodological biases stated throughout this chapter (Pike, 2004).

The majority of metaanalytic studies reported an average prevalence rate for females with AN at 0.3% (Hoek, 1993, 2006; Hoek & van Hoeken, 2003; Hsu, 1996). The registered incidence rates peaked at 8/ 100 000 (0.008%) per year (Hoek, 2006). However, the recent population-based studies evidence an underestimation of true incidence rates. Researchers have reported substantial lifetime prevalence rates in females - near 2.0% - (Favaro et al., 2003; Wade et al., 2009), suggesting that, at the present, AN is a relatively common disease among adolescent girls and young women.

If this is true, when did AN start rising, and does this constitute an epidemic? The answers to these questions are approached using long-term studies (Lucas et al., 1999; Milos et al., 2004) and meta-analyses (Hoek, 2006; Hoek & van Hoeken, 2003; Hsu, 1996). These authors observed that the incidence of AN increased significantly during the 1960s and 1970s in females 12- to 25-years-old, despite not registering at epidemic proportions. Since that period the rates have remained fairly constant, suggesting that the incidence of AN has plateaued.

The period ruled by the increase of new cases may be characterized by the impact of environmental risk factors, which led to the increased rates until saturation. As Milos et al. (2004, p.255) argued: "If we assume that people need to have a vulnerability for developing AN, and there is a limited number of people with such vulnerabilities, we can expect that the effects of media-promoted beauty ideals will reach a peak in the sense of saturation effect and then a plateau".

Therefore, it makes sense that this increase has been registered in younger people, because these individuals are more vulnerable to socio-cultural influences during adolescence.

It should be noted that this interesting conclusion is only valid for severe cases, given that it derives from the analysis of treatment-seeking samples. The evolution of the number of cases with less severity, or those who are not in treatment, is unknown.

However, in our opinion, some signals of a slight increase in less severe cases among young females are given by recent data from robust community studies. Some researchers have suggested an increased prevalence of AN during the second half of the 20th century (Bulik et al., 2006; Hoek & Van Hoeken, 2003; Preti et al., 2009). However, this increase has not been reflected in an increase in the number of cases of AN in hospital records (Milos et al., 2004). This may mean that while the majority of cases are not seeking treatment and are likely the less severe cases of AN. Besides this fact, population-based surveys have revealed significant lifetime prevalence rates of partial AN, around 2.5%, and a point prevalence of 0.7% (Favaro et al., 2003; Wade et al., 2006), which may translate to an increase of cases with less pronounced symptoms. The fervent concern with body image and the desire to be thinner that has been reported in normal-weight female students (e.g. Afifi-Soweid et al.,

2002; Carmo et al., 1996; Neighbors & Sobal, 2007) may, in addition, contribute to the development of less severe forms of AN and sub-threshold ED.

It should be noted that the possible increase of partial syndromes should not be undervalued. Subclinical ED is equally alarming, particularly in adolescence, presenting a milieu of physical and mental problems during early adulthood (Johnson et al., 2002).

Future studies focusing on long-term, single, and large population-based epidemiological procedures to sample multiple regions and using standardized assessment methods, will surely help to clarify if partial syndromes and less severe cases of AN are in increasing trend. A good example of this type of survey was recently implemented in Europe, with the involvement of six countries (cf. Preti et al., 2009). The data obtained with the use of this methodology can provide more information about the evolution and distribution of different categories of ED within communities. It is important, however, to consider the presence of different profiles (e.g., purging in the absence of binge eating) and question the validity of the existing assessment tools (Wade, 2007).

Another challenge for new epidemiological research is the identification of etiological and risk factors in the development of AN. In this field, the study of groups with less common presentations of the disease might be particularly fruitful (Wakeling, 1996). Actually, some advances in the study of males, as well as Blacks and Asians, have been done in the last decade. For males, the recent incidence rate were estimated to be below 1.0/ 100 000 cases per year (Lucas et al., 1999; Currin et al., 2005) and the lifetime prevalence was at 0.3% (Hudson et al., 2007). Nevertheless, the studies with these populations are quite scarce. The same dearth in data is seen with transcultural studies, which are few and report contradictory data. Some such studies have verified an increase of AN in non-Western cultures (e.g. Nadaoka et al., 1996; Nakamura et al., 2000) but others have not (e.g. Hoek et al., 2005). This subset of inquiry has great potential for progress.

Despite great advancements in the study of the epidemiology of AN, there is still a long way to go to reach its full potential. Trends in AN could generate much useful information about the range of the disease, the adjustment of current classification, and its etiology. Cumulatively, the emerging outcomes may be useful in planning health services.

## 5. Summary

A substantial controversy exists as to whether or not AN is increasing. The strength of comparative studies are weakened by differences in the study-related methodologies. Aware of this limitation, we broached the question in the title of this chapter: is the increase in AN a myth or reality? Firstly, is important to clarify if there is indeed an increase in AN. The most recent studies suggest that the incidence of severe cases had increased over the past century, peaking in the 1970s, with a plateau from then to present day. Females 12- to 25-years-old were the largest contributing contingent in the growing expression of this disease. Considering that partial syndromes of AN have been achieving significant prevalence rates in recent studies, along with prevailing body dissatisfaction amongst the general population, it is possible that less severe forms of AN have been increasing during the 21st century. Determining if AN is an epidemic, is surely the less ambiguous part of the question to answer. General population-based epidemiological surveys have reported higher prevalence rates when compared to studies using other samples, but even that, does not constitute an epidemic. Nevertheless, it is possible to conclude that AN is relatively common among young females.

## 6. Appendix

| Reference | City/ Country | Source of case detection | Diagnostic criteria | Study period | Sample used to calculate the incidence | Incidence (per 100 000 population) | Total number of cases |
|---|---|---|---|---|---|---|---|
| Theander (1970) | South of Sweden | Medical records | Clinical | 1931-1940<br>1941-1950<br>1951-1960 | All (♀) | 0.08<br>0.19<br>0.45<br>Per year=0.24 | N(♀)=94 |
| Kendell et al. (1973) | (a) Monroe (USA)<br>(b) Camberwell (England)<br>(c) Northeast of Scotland | Psychiatric case register | Clinical | Areas:<br>(a) 1960-1969<br>(b) 1965-1971<br>(c) 1966-1969 | All(♀)<br><br>♀ (15-34 years) | (a) USA- 0.37<br>(b) England- 0.66<br>(c) Scotland- 1.60<br><br>(a) USA- 0.8<br>(b) England- 4.1<br>(c) Scotland- 10.8 | N(♀)=28 |
| Jones et al. (1980) | Monroe (USA) | Psychiatric case register and medical records | Clinical | 1960-1969<br><br>1970-1976 | All (♀+♂)<br>All (♀)<br>♀ (15-24 years)<br>All (♀+♂)<br>All (♀)<br>♀(15-24 years) | 0.35<br>0.49<br>0.55<br>0.64<br>1.16<br>3.26 | N(♀)=16<br><br>N(♀)=29 |
| Willi & Grossmanan (1983) | Zurich (Switzerland) | Medical: pediatric and psychiatric records (public and private health services) | Clinical | 1956-1958<br>1963-1965<br>1973-1975 | All (♀) | 0.38<br>0.55<br>1.12 | N(♀)=10<br>N(♀)=17<br>N(♀)=38 |
| Szmukler et al. (1986) | Northeastern Scotland | Psychiatric case register | Russell | 1978-1982 | All (♀+♂) | 4.06 | N(♀)=120 (estimated) |
| Eagles et al. (1995) | Northeastern Scotland | Hospital and primary care records | Clinical | 1965-1991 | All (♀) | Average annual increase: 5.3% | N(♀)= 287 |
| Lucas et al. (1988) | Rochester, Minnesota (USA) | Medical records of possible eating disorder | DSM-III-R/ Russell | 1935-1949<br>1950-1964<br>1965-1979 | All (♀)<br>10-19 years (♀)<br>10-19 years (♀)<br><br>Age- and gender-adjusted | 52.4<br>21.6<br>48.6<br><br>7.3 | 1935-1979:<br>N(♀)=128<br>N(♂)= 12 |

♀ - Females; ♂ - Males
* Values calculated considering all diagnoses of eating disorders

Table 1. Studies in the clinical setting which estimate an increase in the incidence of anorexia nervosa

| Reference | City/ Country | Source of case detection | Diagnostic criteria | Study period | Sample used to calculate the incidence | Incidence (per 100 000 population) | Total number of cases |
|---|---|---|---|---|---|---|---|
| Lucas et al. (1991) | Rochester, Minnesota (USA) | Medical records of possible eating disorder | DSM-III-R/ Russell | <br>1935-1984<br>1950-1954<br>1980-1984 | Age- and gender-adjusted<br><br><br>Age- and gender-adjusted | <br>14.6<br>7.0<br>26.3<br>8.2 | 1935-1984:<br>N(♀)= 166<br>N(♂)= 15 |
| Lucas et al. (1999) | Rochester, Minnesota (USA) | Medical records of possible eating disorder | DSM-III-R/ Russell | 1935-1989 | Age- and gender-adjusted<br>Age- and gender-adjusted | 15.0<br>8.3 | N(♀)= 193<br>N(♂)= 15 |
| Møller-Madsen & Nystrup (1992) | Denmark (nationwide) | Nationwide psychiatric case register | ICD-8 | 1970-1989 | All (♀+♂)*<br>1970<br>1988<br>1989<br>♀ (15-24 years)*<br>1970<br>1987<br>1989 | <br>0.42<br>1.36<br>1.17<br><br>3.37<br>11.96<br>8.97 | Total<br>N(♀)= 844<br>N(♂)= 71<br>15-24 years:<br>N(♀)= 536<br>N(♂)= 30 |
| Joergensen (1992) | Fyn County (Denmark) | National register of psychiatric admissions, local hospital records, and registers of psychiatric outpatients | DSM-III-R | 1977-1986 | All (♀)<br>♀ (10-24 years) | 3.25<br>11.0 | N(♀)= 87<br>N(♂)= 6 |
| Pagsberg & Wang (1994) | Bornholm County (Denmark) | National register of psychiatric admissions, local hospital records, and personal contact with physicians from the health care system | ICD-10 | 1970- 1989 | All (♀)<br>1970-1984<br>1985-1989<br>♀ (10-24 years)<br>1970-1984<br>1985-1989 | <br>2.8<br>13.7<br><br>11.9<br>57.1 | N(♀)= 29<br>N(♂)= 1 |
| Milos et al. (2004) | Zurich (Switzerland) | Medical records | DSM-III-R | 1963-1965<br><br>1973-1975 | Total (♀+♂)<br>♀ (12-25 years)<br>Total (♀+♂)<br>♀ (12-25 years) | 0.55<br>6.79<br>1.12<br>16.75 | N(♀+♂) = 17<br><br>N(♀+♂) = 38 |

♀ - Females; ♂ - Males
* Values calculated considering all diagnoses of eating disorders

Table 1. (cont.) Studies in the clinical setting which estimate an increase in the incidence of anorexia nervosa

| Reference | City/ Country | Source of case detection | Diagnostic criteria | Study period | Sample used to calculate the incidence | Incidence (per 100 000 population) | Total number of cases |
|---|---|---|---|---|---|---|---|
| Williams & King (1987) | London (England) | Psychiatric admissions register | Unspecified | 1972-1981 | All (♀) | Between 1.4 and 2.0 | Unspecified |
| | | | | | ♀ (10-64 years) | Average annual increase: 2% | |
| Nielsen (1990) | Denmark (nationwide) | Nationwide psychiatric admissions register | ICD-8 | 1973-1987 | All (♀) | 1.90 | N(♀)= 744 |
| | | | | | All (♂) | 0.17 | N(♂)= 63 |
| Willi et al. (1990) | Zurich (Switzerland) | Medical and psychiatric records (public and private health services) | Clinical | | ♀ (12-25 years) | | |
| | | | | 1956-1958 | | 0.38 | N(♀)= 10 |
| | | | | 1963-1965 | | 0.55 | N(♀)= 17 |
| | | | | 1973-1975 | | 1.12 | N(♀)= 38 |
| | | | | 1983-1985 | | 1.43 | N(♀)= 48 |
| Hall & Hay (1991) | Wellington (New Zealand) | Interview in the first admission of patients with eating disorders | DSM-III | 1977-1986 | All (♀+♂) | 5.0 | N(♀)= 162<br>N(♂)= 8 |
| | | | | | ♀ (15-29 years) | 33.9 | |
| Hoek et al. (1995) | Netherlands (nationwide) | General medical practitioners were trained to diagnose eating disorders | DSM-III-R and DSM-IV | 1985-1989 | All (♀+♂) | 8.1 | N(♀)=55<br>N(♂)= 5 |
| | | | | | All (♀) | 14.7 | |
| | | | | | ♀ (15-19 years) | 79.6 | |
| Turnbull et al. (1996) | England | Primary care registers | Clinical | 1988 | ♀ (10-39 years) | 18.5 | Unspecified |
| | | | | 1994 | ♀ (10-39 years) | 18.1 | N(♀)=100 |
| | | | | | Age- and gender-adjusted | 4.2 | |
| Currin et al. (2005) | England | Primary care registers | Clinical | 2000 | ♀ (10-39 years) | 20.1 | N(♀)=51 |
| | | | | | Age- and gender-adjusted | 4.7 | |
| Milos et al. (2004) | Zurich (Switzerland) | Medical records | DSM-III-R | 1983-1985 | Total (♀+♂)<br>♀ (12-25 years) | 1.43<br>16.44 | N(♀+♂) = 48 |
| | | | | 1993-1995 | Total (♀+♂)<br>♀ (12-25 years) | 1.17<br>19.72 | N(♀+♂) = 41 |

♀ - Females; ♂ - Males

Table 2. Studies in the clinical setting which **do not** estimate an increase in the incidence of anorexia nervosa

| Reference | City/ Country | Source of case detection | Diagnostic criteria | Study period | Sample size | Sample used to calculate the prevalence | Prevalence | Total number of cases |
|---|---|---|---|---|---|---|---|---|
| Duddle (1973) | Manchester (England) | Psychiatric evaluation of students admitted to the University Student Health Center | Clinical (Dally, 1969) | 1966-1972 | 638 (♀ + ♂) | Undergraduate students | Not estimate<br>1966/67- 0 cases<br>1968- 1 case<br>1969- 2 cases<br>1970- 7 cases<br>1971- 13 cases | Duddle (1973) |
| Meadows et al. (1986) | Leicester (England) | Records from to General Hospitals<br>Two-stage study (EAT + interview) | Eating Attitudes Test (EAT) and DSM-III | Unspecified | 584 (♀) | ♀ (18-22 years) | Not estimate<br>1 case | Meadows et al. (1986) |
| Kutcher, Whitehouse & Freeman (1985) | Scotland | Psychiatric case register | DSM-III | Unspecified | 146 (♀ + ♂) | Psychiatric patients (♀+♂) | *Point prevalence:* 3.6% | N(♀)=5 |
| Culberg & Engström-Lindberg (1988) | Nacka (Sweden) | Request information from multiple care givers (medical and non-medical) | DSM-III | 1984-1985 | 4651 (♀ + ♂) | All (♀+♂)<br>♀ (16-24 years)<br>♂ (16-24 years) | *Period prevalence* (2 years):<br>22/ 100 000<br>258/ 100 000<br>21/ 100 000 | N(♀)=16<br>N(♂)= 1 |
| Lucas et al. (1988) | Rochester, Minnesota (USA) | Medical records review for comorbid diagnoses | DSM-III-R/ Russell | 1935-1979 | 30 628 (♀ + ♂) | Age- and gender-adjusted<br>(♀) age-adjusted<br>(♂) age-adjusted | *Lifetime prevalence:*<br>113.1/ 100 000<br>203.9/ 100 000<br>16.9/ 100 000 | 1935-1979:<br>N(♀)=128<br>N(♂)= 12 |
| Lucas et al. (1991) | Rochester, Minnesota (USA) | Medical records review for comorbid diagnoses | DSM-III-R/ Russell | 1985 | 32 353 (♀ + ♂) | Age- and gender-adjusted<br>age-adjusted (♀)<br>♀ (15-19 years)<br>age-adjusted (♂) | *Lifetime prevalence:*<br>149.5/ 100 000<br>269.9/ 100 000<br>480.3/ 100 000<br>22.5/ 100 000 | 1985:<br>N(♀)= 99<br>N(♂)= 6 |

♀ - Females; ♂ - Males

Table 3. Prevalence studies of anorexia nervosa in the clinical setting

| Reference | City/ Country | Source of case detection | Diagnostic criteria | Study period | Sample size | Sample used to calculate the prevalence | Prevalence | Total number of cases |
|---|---|---|---|---|---|---|---|---|
| Hoek (1991) | Netherlands (nationwide) | General practitioners were trained to diagnose eating disorders | DSM-III-R | 1985 | 151 781 (♀ + ♂) | All (♀ e ♂) | *Point prevalence* 18.4/ 100 000 | N(♀ e ♂)=28 |
| Nielsen (1990) | Denmark (nationwide) | Nationwide register of psychiatric admissions | ICD-8 | 1973-1987 | 300 000 (♀ + ♂) | All (♀)<br>♀ (15-19 years)<br>All (♂) | *Average prevalence per year:*<br>6.7/ 100 000<br>34.7/ 100 000<br>0.6/ 100 000 | N(♀)= 744<br><br>N(♂)= 63 |
| Joergensen (1992) | Fyn County (Denmark) | National register of psychiatric admissions, local hospital records, and registers of psychiatric outpatients | DSM-III-R | 1977-1986 | 540 000 (♀ + ♂) | ♀ (15-19 years) | *Over the total period:* 120/ 100 000 | N(♀)= 87<br>N(♂)= 6 |

♀ - Females; ♂ - Males

Table 3. (cont.) Prevalence studies of anorexia nervosa in the clinical setting

| Reference | City/ Country | Case detection method | Diagnostic criteria | Study period | Sample size | Sample used to calculate the prevalence | Prevalence | Total number of cases |
|---|---|---|---|---|---|---|---|---|
| Crisp et al. (1976) | England | Key informant (teachers and school medical officers) in both public and private institutions | Clinical | 1972-1974 | 12 391 (♀) | Schoolgirls | *Over the total period:*<br>Private schools- 1%<br>Public schools- 0.2%<br>All schools -4.6/1000 | N(♀)= 57 |
| Button & Whitehouse (1981) | England | Two-stage (EAT + interview) | Clinical | Unspecified | 578 (♀ + ♂) College students | ♀ + ♂ (16 years and older) | 1/578 | N(♀)= 1<br>N(♂)= 0 |
| Mann et al. (1983) | London (England) | Two-stage (EAT + interview) | Clinical | 1982 | 262 (♀) (2 schools) | ♀ (15 years) | 0% | N(♀)= 0 |
| Johnson-Sabine et al. (1988) | London (England) | Two-stage (EAT + interview) | Clinical | Unspecified | 1010 (♀) | ♀ (14-16 years) | 0% | N(♀)= 0 |
| Råstam et al. (1989) | Gottembourg (Sweden) | Three-stage (questionnaires and growth charts + interview + case register) | DSM-III and DSM-III-R | 1985 | 4291 (♀ + ♂) | ♀ e ♂ (15 years) | *Period prevalence:*<br>♀ - 0.7%<br>♂- 0.09% | N(♀)= 14<br>N(♂)= 3 |
| Patton et al. (1990) | London (England) | Two-stage (EAT + interview); 12 months of follow-up | Russell | Unspecified | 176 (♀) | ♀ (14-17 years) | 0% | N(♀)= 0 |
| Whitaker et al. (1990) | New Jersey (USA) | Two-stage (ESI and EAT + interview) | DSM-III | 1984 | 5596 (♀ + ♂) | ♀ (14-17 years) | *Lifetime prevalence:*<br>0.2% | N(♀)= 12<br>N(♂)= 0 |
| Rathner & Messner (1993) | Italy | Three-stage (EAT and ANIS + interview+ case register) | DSM-III-R | Unspecified | 517 (♀) | ♀ (11-20 years)<br>♀ (11-14 years)<br>♀ (15-20 years) | *Point prevalence:*<br>0.58%<br>0.0%<br>1.3% | N(♀)= 4 |
| Wlodarczyk-Bisaga & Dolan (1996) | Poland | Two-stage (EAT + interview); 10 months of follow-up | DSM-III-R | Unspecified | 747 (♀) | ♀ (14-16 years) | 0% | N(♀)= 0 |
| Carmo et al., (1996) | Lisbon and Tagus Valley (Portugal) | Questionnaire developed to assess diagnosis criteria (29 secondary state schools) | DSM-III-R | Unspecified | 2422 (♀) | ♀ (10-21 years) | 0.4% | N(♀)= 9 |
| Santonastaso et al. (1996) | Italy | Three-stage (EAT and IMC + interview + case register and 1 year follow-up) | DSM-IV | Unspecified | 359 (♀) | ♀ (16 years) | 0% | N(♀)= 0 |

♀ - Females; ♂ - Males

Table 4. Epidemiological studies of anorexia nervosa with student samples

| Reference | City/ Country | Case detection method | Diagnostic criteria | Study period | Sample size | Sample used to calculate the prevalence | Prevalence | Total number of cases |
|---|---|---|---|---|---|---|---|---|
| Rojo et al. (2003) | Valencia (Spain) | Two-stage (EAT-40 + interview) | DSM-IV | 1998-1999 | 544 (♀ + ♂) | ♀ + ♂ (12-18 years)<br>♀ (12-18 years)<br>♂ (12-18 years) | Period prevalence:<br>0.22%<br>0.45%<br>0.0% | N(♀)= 1<br>N(♂)= 0 |
| Machado et al. (2004) | Minho (Portugal) and Galicia (Spain) | EDI + Questionnaire from COST Action B6 | DSM-IV | Unspecified | College Students (♀):<br>Portugal- 486<br>Spain – 595 | Both samples (♀)<br>(17-44 years) | 0% | N(♀)= 0 |
| Dixe (2007) | Central area of Portugal | EDI + Questionnaire | DSM-IV | Unspecified | High school and undergraduate students:<br>1388 (♀ + ♂) | ♀ + ♂<br>(14-25 years) | 0% | N(♀)= 0<br>N(♂)= 0 |
| Machado et al. (2007) | Portugal | Two-stage (EDE-Q + Interview EDE) | DSM-IV | Unspecified | 2028 (♀)<br>(Public school system) | ♀ (12-23 years) | 0.39% | N(♀)= 8 |
| Peláez Fernandez et al. (2007) | Madrid (Spain) | Two-stage (EAT-40 and EDE-Q + Interview EDE) | DSM-IV | 2001-2002 academic year | 1545 (♀ + ♂)<br>(Public and private schools) | ♀ (12-21 years)<br>♂ (12-21 years) | 0.33%<br>0.0% | N(♀)= 3<br>N(♂)= 0 |

♀ - Females; ♂ - Males

Table 4. (cont.) Epidemiological studies of anorexia nervosa with student samples

| Reference | City/ Country | Case detection method | Diagnostic criteria | Study period | Sample size | Sample used to calculate the rate | Prevalence/ Incidence | Total number of cases |
|---|---|---|---|---|---|---|---|---|
| Robins et al. (1984) | USA:<br>(a) New Heaven<br>(b) Baltimore<br>(c) St Louis | Household survey<br>(*"Diagnostic Interview Schedule"* applied by lay interviewers) | DSM-III | 1981-1982 | (♀ + ♂)<br>(a) 3058<br>(b) 3481<br>(c) 3004 | ♀ + ♂<br>(18-65 years) | *Lifetime prevalence:*<br>0.03%<br>0.1%<br>0.1% | Unspecified |
| Götestam & Agras (1995) | Norway | Self-report questionnaire send by mail | DSM-III-R | 1992 | 1849 (♀) | ♀ (18-59 years)<br>♀ (18-29 years)<br><br>♀ (18-59 years)<br>♀ (18-29 years) | *Lifetime prevalence:*<br>0.43<br>0.88<br><br>*Point prevalence:*<br>0.27%<br>0.35% | N(♀)= 8<br><br>N(♀)= 5 |
| Ghaderi & Scott (2001) | Sweden | Questionnaire (survey for eating disorders) | DSM-IV | 1999 (2-year follow-up study) | 1122 (♀) | ♀ (20-32 years) | *1-year incidence:*<br>120/ 100 000 | N(♀)= 1 |
| Favaro et al. (2003) | Padova (Italy) | Clinical Interview for DSM-IV (SCID) | DSM-IV | Unspecified | 934 (♀) | ♀ (18-25 years) | *Lifetime prevalence:*<br>2.0% | N(♀)= 19 |
| Lahortiga-R. et al. (2005) | Navarra (Spain) | Two-stage (EDI + Interview) | DSM-IV | 18 months follow-up | 2734 (♀) | ♀ (13-22 years) | *Incidence per year:*<br>200/ 100 000 | N(♀)= 8 |
| Bulik et al. (2006) | Sweden | Telephone interview of twins; and analysis of two additional sources of information (hospital discharge registry and cause-of-death registry) | DSM-IV | 4- year period ending in 2022 | 31 406 individual twins (♀ + ♂) | Twins born between January 1, 1935 and December 32, 1958 | *Overall prevalence (3 sources):*<br>*1.20% (♀)* | N(♀)= 253 |
| Faravelli et al. (2006) | Sesto Fiorentino (Italy) | Three-phase / two-wave design (interview by general practitioner + re-interview by psychiatrist + re-interview with EDE) | DSM-IV | Unspecified | 2355 (♀ + ♂) | ♀ + ♂<br>(14 years and older) | *Lifetime prevalence:*<br>0.42% | N(♀ + ♂)= 9 |
| Wade et al. (2006) | Australia | Telephone interview to twins (EDE) | DSM-IV | 2001-2003 | 1002 individual twins (♀) | ♀ (28-39 years) | *Lifetime prevalence:*<br>1.9% | N(♀)= 19 |
| Hudson et al. (2007) | USA | Household survey<br>(face-to-face interview: SCID) | DSM-IV | 2001-2003 | 2980 (♀ + ♂) | ♀ (18 years and older)<br>♂ (18 years and older) | *Lifetime prevalence:*<br>0.9%<br>0.3%<br>*Period Prevalence (year):*<br>0% | Unspecified |
| Preti et al. (2009) | Belgium, France, Germany, Italy, Netherlands, and Spain | Household survey<br>(Two-phase interview: general psychiatric interview + SCID) | DSM-IV | 2001-2003 | 4139 (♀ + ♂) | ♀+♂ (18 years and older)<br>♀ (18 years and older)<br>♂ (18 years and older) | *Lifetime prevalence:*<br>0.48%<br>0.93%<br>0.0% | N(♀)= 22<br>N(♂)= 0 |

♀ - Females; ♂ - Males

Table 5. Epidemiological studies of anorexia nervosa with community samples

## 7. References

Afifi-Soweid, R. A., Kteily, M. B., & Shediac-Rizkallah, M. C. (2002). Preoccupation with weight and disordered eating behaviors of entering students at a university in Lebanon. *International Journal of Eating Disorders,* Vol.32, No.1, (July 2002), pp. 52-57, ISSN 0276-3478

Bulik, C. M., Reba, L., Siega-Riz, A., & Reichborn-Kjennerud, T. (2005). Anorexia Nervosa: Definition, Epidemiology, and Cycle of Risk. *International Journal of Eating Disorders,* No.37, Supplement, (April 2005), pp. S2-S9, ISSN 0276-3478

Bulik, C. M., Sullivan, P. F., Tozzi, F., Furberg, H., Lichtenstein, P., Pedersen, N. L. (2006). Prevalence, Heritability, and Prospective Risk Factors for Anorexia Nervosa. *Archives of General Psychiatry,* Vol. 63, No.3, (March 2006), pp. 305-312, ISSN 0003-990X

Button, E. J., & Whitehouse, A. (1981). Subclinical anorexia nervosa. *Psychological Medicine,* Vol.11, No.3, (August 1981), pp. 509-516, ISSN 0033-2917

Carmo, I., Reis, D., Varandas, P., Bouça, D., Padre Santo, D., Neves, A., et al. (1996). Prevalence of Anorexia Nervosa: A Portuguese Population Study. *European Eating Disorders Review, Vol.*4, No.3, (September 1996), pp. 157-170, ISSN 1099-0968

Crisp, A. H., Palmer, R. L., & Kalucy, R. S. (1976). How common is Anorexia Nervosa? A prevalence study. *The British Journal of Psychiatry,* Vol.128, No.6, (June 1976), pp. 549-554, ISSN 0007-1250

Culberg, J., & Engström-Lindberg, M. (1988). Prevalence and incidence of eating disorders in a suburban area. *Acta Psychiatrica Scandinavica,* Vol.78, No.3, (September 1988), pp. 314-319, ISSN 0001-690X

Currin, L., Schmidt, U., Treasure, J., & Jick, H. (2005). Time trends in eating disorder incidence. *The British Journal of Psychiatry,* Vol.186, No.2, (February 2005), pp. 132-135, ISSN 0007-1250

Dellava, J. E., Thornton, L. M., Lichtenstein, P., Pedersen, N. L., & Bulik, C. M. (2011). Impact of broadening definitions of anorexia nervosa on sample characteristics. *Journal of Psychiatric Research,* Vol.45, No.5, (May 2011), pp. 691-698, ISSN 0022-3956

Dixe, M. A. (2007). Prevalência das doenças do comportamento alimentar. *Análise Psicológica,* Vol.25, No.4, (October 2007), pp. 559-569, ISSN 0870-8231

Duddle, M. (1973). An increase of anorexia nervosa in a university population. *The British Journal of Psychiatry,* Vol.123, No.577, (December 1973), pp. 711-712, ISSN 0007-1250

Eagles, J. M., Easton, E. A., Nicoll, K. S., Johnston, M. I., & Millar, H. R. (1999). Changes in the presenting features of females with anorexia nervosa in Northeast Scotland, 1965-1991. *International Journal of Eating Disorders,* Vol.26, No.3, (November 1999), pp.289-294. ISSN 0276-3478

Eagles, J. M., Johnston, M. I., Hunter, D., Lobban, M., & Millar, H. R. (1995). Increasing incidence of anorexia nervosa in the female population of Northeast Scotland. *American Journal of Psychiatry,* Vol.152, No.9, (September 1995), pp.1266-1271, ISSN 0002-953X

Fairburn, C. G., & Beglin, S. J. (1990). Studies of the epidemiology of bulimia nervosa. *American Journal of Psychiatry,* Vol.147, No.4, (April 1990), pp. 401-408, ISSN 0002-953X

Faravelli, C., Ravaldi, C., Truglia, E., Zucchi, T., Cosci, F., & Ricca, V. (2006). Clinical epidemiology of eating disorders: Results from the Sesto Fiorentino Study.

*Psychotherapy and Psychosomatics*, Vol.75, No.6, (October 2006), pp.376-383, ISSN 0033-3190

Favaro, A., Ferrara, S., & Santonastaso, P. (2003). The spectrum of eating disorders in young women: A prevalence study in a general population sample. *Psychosomatic Medicine*, Vol.65, No.4, (July-August 2003), pp. 701-708, ISSN 1534-7796

Fombonne, E. (1995). Anorexia nervosa: No evidence of an increase. *The British Journal of Psychiatry*, Vol.166, No.4, (April 1995), pp. 462-471, ISSN 0007-1250

Garb, J. L. (1996). *Understanding Medical Research: A practitioner's guide*. Little, Brown and Company, ISBN 0316291692, Boston, USA

Garner, D. M., Olmstead, M. P., Bohr, Y., & Garfinkel, P. E. (1982). The Eating Attitudes Test: Psychometric features and clinical correlates. *Psychological Medicine*, Vol.12, No.4, (November 1982), pp. 871-878, ISSN 0033-2917

Ghaderi, A., & Scott, B. (2001). Prevalence, incidence and prospective risk factors for eating disorders. *Acta Psychiatrica Scandinavica*, Vol.104, No.2, (August 2001), pp. 122-130, ISSN 0001-690X

Götestam, K. G., & Agras, W. S. (1995). General population-based epidemiological study of eating disorders in Norway. *International Journal of Eating Disorders*, Vol.18, No.2, (September 1995), pp. 119-126, ISSN 0276-3478

Hall, A., & Hay, P. (1991). Eating disorder patient referrals from a population region 1977-1986. *Psychological Medicine*, Vol.21, No.3, (August 1991), pp. 697-701, ISSN 0033-2917

Hardy, P., & Dantchev, N. (1989). Épidemiologie dês troubles des conduites alimentaires. *Confrontations Psychiatriques*, Vol.31, No.22 (January 1989), pp. 133-163, ISSN 0153-9329

Heatherton, T. F., Nichols, P., Mahamedi, F., & Keel, P. (1995). Body weight, dieting, and eating disorder symptoms among college students, 1982 to 1992. *American Journal of Psychiatry*, Vol.152, No.11, (November 1995), pp. 1623-1629, ISSN 0002-953X

Hoek, H. W. (1991). The incidence and prevalence of anorexia nervosa and bulimia nervosa in primary care. *Psychological Medicine*, Vol.21, No.2, (May 1991), pp. 455-460, ISSN 0033-2917

Hoek H. W. (2006). Incidence, prevalence and mortality of anorexia nervosa and other eating disorders. *Current Opinion in Psychiatry*, Vol.19, No.4, (July 2006), pp. 389-394, ISSN 0951- 7367

Hoek, H. W., Bartelds, A. I., Bosveld, J. F., Graaf, Y., Limpens, V. E., Maiwald, M., et al. (1995). Impact of urbanization on detection rates of eating disorders. *American Journal of Psychiatry*, Vol.152, No.2, (September 1995), pp. 1272-1278, ISSN 0002-953X

Hoek, H. W., & van Hoeken, D. (2003). Review of the prevalence and incidence of eating disorders. *International Journal of Eating Disorders*, Vol.34, No.4, (December 2003), pp. 383-396, ISSN 0276-3478

Hoek, H. W., Van Harten, P. N., Hermans, K. M. E., Katzman, M. A., Matroos, G. E., & Susser, E. S. (2005). The incidence of anorexia nervosa on Curacao. *American Journal of Psychiatry*, Vol.162, No.4, (April 2005), pp.748-752, ISSN 0002-953X

Hsu, L. K. G. (1996). Epidemiology of the eating disorders. *The Psychiatric Clinics of North America*, Vol.19, No.4, (December 1996), pp. 681-700, ISSN 0193-953X

Hudson, J. I., Hiripi, E., Pope, H. G, & Kessler, R. C. (2007). The prevalence and correlates of eating disorders in the national comorbidity survey replication. *Biological Psychiatry*, Vol.61, No.3, (February 2007), pp. 348-358, ISSN 0006-3223

Joergensen, J. (1992). The epidemiology of eating disorders in Fyn County, Denmark, 1977-1986. *Acta Psychiatrica Scandinavica*, Vol.85, No.1, (January 1992), pp. 30-34, ISSN 0001-690X

Jones, D. J., Fox, M. M., Babigian, H. M., & Hutton, H. E. (1980). Epidemiology of anorexia nervosa in Monroe County, New York: 1960-1976. *Psychosomatic Medicine*, Vol.42, No.6, (November 1980), pp. 551-558, ISSN 1534-7796

Johnson, J. G., Cohen, P., Kasen, S., & Brook, J. S. (2002). Eating disorders during adolescence and the risk for physical and mental disorders during early adulthood. *Archives of General Psychiatry*, Vol.59, No.6, (June 2002), pp. 545-552, ISSN 0003-990X

Jonhson-Sabine, E., Wood, K., Patton, G., Mann, A., & Wakeling, A. (1988). Abnormal eating attitudes in London schoolgirls - a prospective epidemiological study: Factors associated with abnormal response on screening questionnaires. *Psychological Medicine*, Vol.18, No.3, (August 1988), pp. 615-622, ISSN 0033-2917

Keski-Rahkonen, A., Sihvola, E., Raevuori, A., Kaukoranta, J., Bulik, C.M., Hoek, H.W. et al. (2006). Reliability of self-reported eating disorders: Optimizing population screening. International Journal of Eating Disorders, Vol.39, No.8, (December 2006), pp. 754-762, ISSN 0276-3478

Kendell, R. E., Hall, D. J., Hailey, A., & Babigian, H. M. (1973). The epidemiology of anorexia nervosa. *Psychological Medicine*, Vol.3, No.2, (May 1973), pp. 200-203, ISSN 0033-2917

Kutcher, S. P., Whitehouse, A. M., & Freeman, C. P. (1985). "Hidden" eating disorders in Scottish psychiatric inpatients. *American Journal of Psychiatry*, Vol.142, No.12, (December 1985), pp. 1475-1478, ISSN 0002-953X

Lahortiga-Ramos, F., De Irala-Estévez, J., Cano- Prous, A., Gual-García, P., Martínez-González, M. A. & Cervera-Enguix, S. (2005). Incidence of eating disorders in Navarra (Spain). *European Psychiatry*, Vol.20, No.2, (March 2005), pp. 179-185, ISSN 0924-9338

Lucas, A. R., Beard, C. M., O'Fallon, W. M., & Kurland, L. T. (1988). Anorexia nervosa in Rochester, Minnesota: A 45-year study. *Mayo Clinic Proceedings*, Vol.63, No.5, (May 1988), pp. 433-442, ISSN 0025-6196

Lucas, A. R., Beard, C. M., O'Fallon, W. M., & Kurland, L. T. (1991). 50-year trends in the incidence of anorexia nervosa in Rochester, Minn.: A population-based study. *American Journal of Psychiatry*, Vol.148, No.7, (July 1991), pp. 917-922, ISSN 0002-953X

Lucas, A. R., Crowson, C. S., O'Fallon, W. M., & Melton, L. J. (1999). The ups and downs of anorexia nervosa. *International Journal of Eating Disorders*, Vol.26, No.4, (December 1999), pp. 397-405, ISSN 0276-3478

Machado, P.P., Fernandez, M. L., Gonçalves, S., Martins, C., Otero, M. C., Machado, B. C., et al. (2004). Eating related problems amongst Iberian female college students. *International Journal of Clinical and Health Psychology*, Vol.4, No.3, (September 2004), pp. 495-504, ISSN 1697-2600

Machado, P., Machado, B., Gonçalves, S., & Hoek, H. (2007). The prevalence of eating disorders not otherwise specified. *International Journal of Eating Disorders*, Vol.40, No.3, (April 2007), pp. 212-217, ISSN 0276-3478

Mann, A. H., Wakeling, A., Wood, K., Monck, E., Dobbs, R., & Szmukler, G. (1983). Screening for abnormal eating attitudes and psychiatric morbidity in an unselected population of 15-year-old schoolgirls. *Psychological Medicine*, Vol.13, No.3, (August 1983), pp. 573-580, ISSN 0033-2917

Meadows, G. N., Palmer, R. L., Newball, E. U., & Kenrick, J. M. (1986). Eating attitudes and disorder in young women: A general practice based survey. *Psychological Medicine*, Vol.16, No.2, (May 1986), pp. 351-357, ISSN 0033-2917

Milos, G., Spindler, A., Schnyder, U., Martz, J., Hoek, H., & Willi, J. (2004). Incidence of severe anorexia nervosa in Switzerland: 40 years of development. *International Journal of Eating Disorders*, Vol.35, No.3, (April 2004), pp. 250–258, ISSN 0276-3478

Møller-Madsen, S., & Nystrup, J. (1992). Incidence of anorexia nervosa in Denmark. *Acta Psychiatrica Scandinavica*, Vol.86, No.3, (September 1992), pp. 197-200, ISSN 0001-690X

Munk-Jørgensen, P., Møller-Madsen, S., Nielsen, S., & Nystrup, J. (1995). Incidence of eating disorders in psychiatric hospitals and wards in Denmark, 1970-1993. *Acta Psychiatrica Scandinavica*, Vol.92, No.2, (August 1995), pp. 91-96, ISSN 0001-690X

Nadaoka, T., Oiji, A., Takahashi, S., Morioka, Y., Kashiwakura, M., & Totsuka, S. (1996). An epidemiological study of eating disorders in a northern area of Japan. *Acta Psychiatrica Scandinavica*, Vol.93, No.4, (April 1996), pp. 305-310, ISSN 0001-690X

Nakamura, K., Yamamoto, M., Yamazaki, O., Kawashima, Y., Muto, K., Someya, T., et al. (2000). Prevalence of anorexia nervosa and bulimia nervosa in a geographically defined area in Japan. *International Journal of Eating Disorders*, Vol.28, No.2, (September 2000), pp. 173-180, ISSN 0276-3478

Neighbors, L. A. & Sobal, J. (2007). Prevalence and magnitude of body weight and shape dissatisfaction among university students. *Eating Behaviors*, Vol.8, No.4, (December 2007), pp. 429-439, ISSN 1471-0153

Nielsen, S. (1990). The epidemiology of anorexia nervosa in Denmark from 1973 to 1987: A nationwide register study of psychiatric admission. *Acta Psychiatrica Scandinavica*, Vol.81, No.6, (June 1990), pp. 507-514, ISSN 0001-690X

Pagsberg, A. K., & Wang, A.-R. (1994). Epidemiology of anorexia nervosa and bulimia nervosa in Bornholm County, Denmark, 1970-1989. *Acta Psychiatrica Scandinavica*, Vol.90, No.4, (October 1994), pp. 259-265, ISSN 0001-690X

Patton, G. C., Johnson-Sabine, E., Wood, K., Mann, A. H., & Wakeling, A. (1990). Abnormal eating attitudes in London schoolgirls - a prospective epidemiological study: Outcome at twelve month follow-up. *Psychological Medicine*, Vol.20, No.2, (May 1990), pp. 383-394, ISSN 0033-2917

Patton, G. C., & King, M. B. (1991). Epidemiological study of eating disorders: Time for a change of emphasis. *Psychological Medicine*, Vol.21, No.2, (May 1991), pp. 287-291, ISSN 0033-2917

Pawluck, D. E., & Gorey, K. M. (1998). Secular trends in the incidence of anorexia nervosa: Integrative review of population-based studies. *International Journal of Eating Disorders*, Vol.23, No.4, (May 1998), pp. 347-352, ISSN 0276-3478

Peláez Fernández, M. A., Labrador, F. J., & Raich, R. M (2007). Prevalence of eating disorders among adolescent and young adult scholastic population in the region of Madrid (Spain). *Journal of Psychosomatic Research*, Vol.62, No.6, (June 2007), pp. 681-690, ISSN 0022-3999

Pike, K. M. (2004). Solving the complex puzzle of the incidence of anorexia nervosa one piece at a time. *International Journal of Eating Disorders*, Vol.35, No.3, (April 2004), pp. 259-261, ISSN 0276-3478

Preti, A., Girolamo, G. D., Vilagut, G., Alonso, J., Graaf, R. D., Bruffaerts, R., et al. (2009) The epidemiology of eating disorders in six European countries: Results of the ESEMeD-WMH project. *Journal of Psychiatric Research*, Vol.43, pp. 1125–1132, ISSN 0022-3956

Rathner, G., & Messner, K. (1993). Detection of eating disorders in a small rural town: An epidemiological study. *Psychological Medicine*, Vol.23, No.1, (February 1993), pp.175-184, ISSN 0033-2917

Råstam, M., Gilbert, C., & Garton, M. (1989). Anorexia Nervosa in a Swedish urban region: A population-based study. *British Journal of Psychiatry*, Vol.155, No.5, (November 1989), pp. 642-646, ISSN 0007-1250

Robins, L.N., Helzer, J.E., Weissman, M.M., Orvaschel, H., Gruenberg, E., Burke, J.D., et al. (1984). Lifetime prevalence of specific psychiatric disorders in three sites. *Archives of General Psychiatry*, Vol.41, No.10, (October 1984), pp. 949-95, ISSN 0003-990X

Rodríguez-Cano, T., Beato-Fernández, L., & Belmonte-Llario, A. (2005). New contributions to the prevalence of eating disorders in Spanish adolescents: Detection of false negatives. *European Psychiatry*, Vol.20, No.2, (March 2005), pp. 173-178, ISSN 0924-9338

Rojo, L., Livianos, L., Conesa, L., García, A., Domínguez, A., Rodrigo, G., et al. (2003). Epidemiology and risk factors of eating disorders: a two-stage epidemiologic study in a Spanish population aged 12-18 years. *International Journal of Eating Disorders*, Vol.34, No.3, (November 2003), pp. 281-291, ISSN 0276-3478

Russell, G. F. M. (1985). The changing nature of anorexia nervosa: An introduction to the conference. *Journal of Psychiatric Research*, Vol.19, No.2-3, pp. 101-109, ISSN 0022-3956

Santonastaso, P., Zanetti, T., Sala, A., Favaretto, G., Vidotto, G., & Favaro, A. (1996). Prevalence of eating disorders in Italy: A survey on a sample of 16-year-old female students. *Psychotherapy and Psychosomatics*, Vol.65, No.3, (February 2010), pp. 158-162, ISSN 1423-0348

Szmukler, G. I. (1985). The epidemiology of anorexia nervosa and bulimia. *Journal of Psychiatry Research*, Vol.19, No.2-3, pp. 143-153, ISSN 0022-3956

Theander, S. (1970). Anorexia nervosa: A psychiatric investigation of 94 female patients. *Acta Psychiatrica Scandinavica Suppl.*, Vol.45. No.S214, (June 1970), pp. 5-194, ISSN 0001-690X

Turnbull, S., Ward, A., Treasure, J., Jick, H., & Derby, L. (1996). The demand for eating disorder care: An epidemiological study using the General Practice Research Database. *British Journal of Psychiatry*, Vol.169, No.6, (December 1996), pp. 705-712, ISSN: 0007-1250

Torres, S. & Guerra, M. P. (2007). Psicologia da Saúde e Anorexia Nervosa [Health Psychology and Anorexia Nervosa], In: *Psicologia da Saúde: Contextos e Áreas de*

*Intervenção,* J. C. Teixeira, (Ed.), pp. 187-233, Climpesi Editores, ISBN 978-972-796-275-4, Lisboa, Portugal.

Wade, T. D. (2007). Epidemiology of eating disorders: creating opportunities to move the current classification paradigm forward. *International Journal of Eating Disorders,* Vol.40, No.S3, pp. S27-S30, (November 2007), ISSN 0276-3478

Wade, T. D., Bergin, J. L., Tiggemann, M., Bulik, C. M., & Fairburn, C. G. (2006). Prevalence and long-term course of lifetime eating disorder in an adult Australian twin cohort. *Australian and New Zealand Journal of Psychiatry,* Vol.40, No.2, (February 2006), pp. 121-128, ISSN 0004-8674

Wakeling, A. (1996). Epidemiology of anorexia nervosa. *Psychiatry Research,* Vol.62, No.1, (April 1996), pp. 3-9, ISSN 0165-1781

Whitaker, A., Johnson, J., Shaffer, D., Rapoport, J. L., Kalikow, K, Walsh, B. T., et al. (1990). Uncommon troubles in young people: Prevalence estimates of selected psychiatric disorders in a nonreferred adolescent population. *Archives of General Psychiatry,* Vol.47, No.5, (May 1990), pp. 487-496, ISSN 0003-990X

Willi, J., Giacometti, G., & Limacher, B. (1990). Update on the epidemiology of anorexia nervosa in a defined region of Switzerland. *American Journal of Psychiatry,* Vol.147, No.11, (November 1990), pp. 1514-1517, ISSN 0002-953X

Willi, J., & Grossmann, S. (1983). Epidemiology of anorexia nervosa in a defined region of Switzerland. *American Journal of Psychiatry,* Vol.140, No.5, (May 1983), pp. 564-567, ISSN 0002-953X

Williams, P., & King, M. (1987). The "epidemic" of anorexia nervosa: Another medical myth? *The Lancet,* Vol.329, No.8526, (January 1987), pp. 205-207, ISSN 0140-6736

Wlodarczyk-Bisaga, K., & Dolan, B. (1996). A two-stage epidemiological study of abnormal eating attitudes and their prospective risk factors in Polish schoolgirls. *Psychological Medicine,* Vol.26, No.5, (September 1996), pp. 1021-1032, ISSN 0033-2917

# 2

# Key Variables in the Development of Eating Disorders During the Adolescence: Implications for Sex Differences

Pilar Ramos[1], Francisco Rivera[2] and Carmen Moreno[1]
[1]*University of Seville, Department of Developmental and Educational Psychology,*
[2]*University of Huelva, Department of Clinical, Experimental and Social Psychology,*
*Spain*

## 1. Introduction

Eating disorders such as anorexia or bulimia are associated with unsuitable behavior, cognition and emotions, which could have negative consequences for a person's well-being and health. These risks frequently appear during adolescence, as this developmental stage is characterized by physiological, emotional, cognitive, and above all, social changes that lead to a greater concern for physical appearances. The propensity of adolescents to be unhappy with their body image has been stated in many studies, in which case, the adolescent can go so far as to create distorted perceptions of his/her own body. In short, this population shows major discrepancy between the subjective measurements of their body shape (contributed by the subjects) and the real measurements assessed with objective methods, this leading to a larger proportion of eating disorders (Conley & Boardman, 2007; Gardner, 1996; Martin & Gentry, 1997). Perceiving oneself as «obese» when this is not the case indicates a cognitive problem that can be explained by learning imposed by social and cultural pressures. Thus, the self-perception of one's body becomes a decisive factor for the development of an eating disorder, which is, in turn, more important than body weight itself (Barker & Galambos, 2003; Bessenoff & Snow, 2006; Cash & Deagle, 1997).

The most common behavior that follows this body dissatisfaction is to go on some type weight-loss diet. Most diets reduce the daily energy intake below the recommended quantities. If, in addition to the above, there is a lack of medical surveillance that usually accompanies such diets, it is easy to understand the serious, health-related danger linked to this type of diet (Eisenberg et al., 2005; Larson et al., 2009; Neumark-Sztainer et al., 2007). One system young people erroneously use to control their weight is to skip breakfast (Cho et al., 2003; Niemeier et al., 2006; Timlin et al., 2008), a practice that is somewhat more usual than skipping lunch or supper (Woodruff et al., 2008). In fact, excluding breakfast or having an inadequate or insufficient breakfast is a relatively frequent eating habit among adolescents (Alexy et al., 2010; Woodruff et al., 2008).

Although several studies have demonstrated the relationship existent among the Body Mass Index (BMI), body image and weight control during adolescence, this has not been performed systematically with regards to the differences between boys and girls. Some authors state that the concern for body image differs depending on the gender; that is to say, while boys are concerned with having a muscular body image, girls have beauty ideals that are inseparable from thinness, in most cases below a healthy size (Barker & Galambos, 2003; Espinoza et al., 2010; McArthur et al., 2005; Neumark-Sztainer et al., 1999).

Concretely, although girls have a more correct BMI than boys, girls show greater prevalence when it comes to suffering misperceptions of their body image and this creates a greater number of behaviors dedicated to control their weight (Ivarsson et al., 2006; Larson et al., 2009; Ramos, Rivera et al., 2010). For example, the percentage of adolescents who skip breakfast is higher among girls than among boys; that percentage, in many studies, is more than double (Mullie et al., 2006; Rampersaud et al., 2005; Vereecken et al., 2009; Woodruff et al., 2008; Wu et al., 2006).

Therefore, considering that the BMI represents the physiological aspect of body changes during adolescence, the perception of one's body image represents the cognitive component, the satisfaction with this image corresponds to the emotional component and the behavior of dieting, together with skipping breakfast, is the behavioral component. This work seeks to learn how these components interrelate differently in adolescent boys and girls. In addition to learning the systemic relationship among those four components, this work seeks to learn how these variables interact, with a score for the young people's bio-psycho-social adjustment, and also differentiating between boys and girls (see Figure 1).

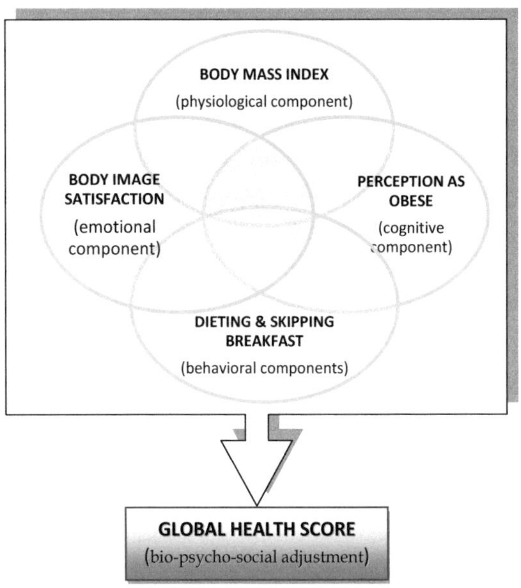


Fig. 1. General approach of the model presented in this study.

## 2. Method

### 2.1 Participants

This paper is classified within the 2006 edition of the international study, *Health Behaviour in School-aged Children* (HBSC). The participants in this study are a representative sample of the adolescent population in Spain. The same was selected with a random multi-stage sampling, stratified by conglomerates, bearing in mind -in addition to the age of the adolescents- the geographical area (region of the country), habitat (rural and urban) and type of education centre (public or private). The resulting sample from this selection process was made up of a total of 6945 Spanish adolescents. Table 1 describes the details of this sample.

| | *13-14 años* | | *15-16 años* | | *17-18 años* | | *Total* | |
|---|---|---|---|---|---|---|---|---|
| | N | % | N | % | N | % | N | % |
| Boys | 1212 | 17.5% | 1260 | 18.1% | 876 | 12.6% | 3348 | 48.2% |
| Girls | 1341 | 19.3% | 1430 | 20.6% | 826 | 11.9% | 3597 | 51.8% |
| Total | 2553 | 36.8% | 2690 | 38.7% | 1702 | 24.5% | 6945 | 100.0% |

Table 1. Sample description by sex and age.

### 2.2 Measures

The HBSC questionnaire collects information about the adolescents based upon various topics related to their lifestyles, their positive health and the contexts in which they grow up. Given the detailed information provided, the following paragraphs only cite references to papers that validate the instruments used in this work.

The *Body Mass Index* (BMI) was used, calculating the formula weight/height$^2$. To understand the body image of the adolescents, the two items described below were used. Firstly, participants were asked about their *perception of body image*, a measurement created by the international HBSC protocol, with five possible answer options (too thin / a little thin / I am an appropriate size / a little fat / too fat). For this study, this measurement was used as a quantitative, 5-point scale, ordering the answer values from too thin to too fat so that the measurement indicated the degree of perceived obesity. Secondly, the subjects were asked about their *satisfaction with their body image*, for which the sub-scale of feelings and attitudes toward one's body, belonging to the *Body Investment Scale,* was used (Orbach & Mikulincer, 1998). This sub-scale is made up of 6 items (I feel frustrated with my physical appearance / I am satisfied with my appearance / I hate my body / I feel comfortable with my body / I reject my body / I like my appearance despite my defects), with 5 answer options, ranging from 1 - very much disagree - to 5 - very much agree. The sub-scale presented a Cronbach alpha in this sample of .88. On the other hand, to explore the behavior of dieting, a measurement was used that was created by the international HBSC protocol. With this measurement, the adolescents were asked whether, at that moment, they were on any type of diet or doing anything to lose weight. Also, they were asked how many days of the week they had more than a glass of milk or a piece of fruit for breakfast, with a possible respond ranging from 0 to 7 days a week.

As an indicator of the bio-psycho-social health level of the adolescents, the *Global Health Score* (GHS) was used. This measurement was created from 20 items related to life satisfaction, perception of health, quality of life related to health and psychosomatic problems. This is a typified score that a good reliability and validity criteria (Ramos, Moreno et al., 2010). This score assesses the physical, psychological and social state of the adolescents, following the most broadly accepted definition of health at the moment; in other words, the definition outlined by the World Health Organization (WHO, 1948).

### 2.3 Procedure

The international coordination of the HBSC study indicates that there are three basic conditions that must be complied with during the data collection procedure. Firstly, it must be the students themselves who respond to the questionnaire; secondly, the anonymity of the answers must be strictly guaranteed and, lastly, the administration of the questionnaires must be carried out within the school context.

In those geographical areas where there was more than one official language, a bilingual questionnaire was used. The questions in one of the two official languages was on one side of the questionnaire and translated into the other language on the other side, so that each student could freely choose the language they felt more comfortable with to complete the questionnaire.

Using the aforementioned measurements (BMI, perception of obesity, satisfaction with body image, dieting, skipping breakfast and GHS) two structural equation models were performed; one for boys and the other for girls. To perform these models, the statistical program EQS 6.1 was used. The parameters were obtained by means of the Maximum Verisimilitude method and the scores were provided using the regression system. The FIT coefficient taken into consideration to evaluate the accuracy of the measuring model was: $\chi 2$ (chi-square). Being that to evaluate the adjustment, the chi-square test alone should not be used because it is affected by the sample size, the following relative adjustment indicators were calculated: Root Mean-Square Error of Approximation (RMSEA), Bentler-Bonett Non-Normed Fit Index (BBNNFI) and incremental indexes (CFI, IFI and MFI). These accuracy adjustment indexes are considered acceptable when the incremental indexes (CFI, IFI and MFI) are greater than .85 (ideally above .90), the BBNNFI is between .90 and .95 (ideally above .95) and the error indexes (RMSEA) are less than .08 (ideally below .05).

Prior to showing the result of the structural equation models, the relationship between the various variables included in the models was assessed, differentiating boys and girls (using the statistical program SPSS 15.0). To understand the relationship between the quantitative variables (BMI, perception of obesity, satisfaction with body image, skipping breakfast and GHS), the Pearson correlation was used. To understand the relationship between the quantitative variables and the categorical variable (dieting) the chi-square test was used as a statistical significance test, while the *phi* coefficient was used to assess the effect size, with the following intervals: from 0 to .09, insignificant; from .10 to .29, low effect size; from .30 to .49, medium effect size; and over .50, large effect size.

## 3. Results

Table 2 shows the comparison of measurements between boys and girls for the different scale variables included in the study. Specifically, were obtained statistically significant differences and low effect sizes (between 0.22 and 0.44) for all of the variables analyzed. It was observed that girls have lower GHS, smaller BMI, perceive themselves as fatter, are less satisfied with their body image and skip breakfast more often.

With regards to dieting behavior, while 18.4% of the girls diet to lose weight, for boys, it was only 9.8%: $\chi^2(1, N = 6917) = 105.33$, $p < .001$, $\Phi = .12$.

| | | N | M | SD | Sig. | d' Cohen |
|---|---|---|---|---|---|---|
| Global Health Score | Boys | 3348 | 0.04 | 0.78 | <.001 | 0.37 |
| | Girls | 3597 | -0.25 | 0.78 | | |
| Body Mass Index | Boys | 3348 | 21.18 | 3.41 | <.001 | 0.23 |
| | Girls | 3597 | 20.44 | 3.10 | | |
| Perception of body as obese | Boys | 3348 | 2.06 | 0.76 | <.001 | -0.34 |
| | Girls | 3597 | 2.33 | 0.79 | | |
| Satisfaction with body image | Boys | 3348 | 3.03 | 0.83 | <.001 | 0.44 |
| | Girls | 3597 | 2.64 | 0.92 | | |
| Skipping breakfast | Boys | 3348 | 1.58 | 2.15 | <.001 | -0.22 |
| | Girls | 3597 | 2.07 | 2.33 | | |

Table 2. Comparison of measurements between boys and girls for the different scale variables.

On the other hand, Table 3 shows the Pearson correlation between the different quantitative variables. This table shows that all the variables correlate with each other, in which case, the correlation coefficients equal or greater than 0.10. Moreover, the size of the correlations indicates interesting sex differences. For example, the correlation between the GHS and perceiving one's body image as obese is more than twice as high for girls ($r$ = .26) than for boys ($r$ = .12). Furthermore, the correlation between the perception of obesity and satisfaction with one's body image is twice as high for girls ($r$ = .50) when compared to boys ($r$ = .25). Lastly, the correlation between the GHS and skipping breakfast is greater for girls ($r$ = .23) than for boys ($r$ = .18).

| | | I | II | III | IV | V |
|---|---|---|---|---|---|---|
| Boys | I. Global Health Score | - | | | | |
| | II. Body Mass Index | -.15 | - | | | |
| | III. Perception of body as obese | -.12 | .50 | - | | |
| | IV. Satisfaction with body image | .43 | -.23 | -.25 | - | |
| | V. Skipping breakfast | -.18 | .11 | .11 | -.16 | - |
| Girls | I. Global Health Score | - | | | | |
| | II. Body Mass Index | -.18 | - | | | |
| | III. Perception of body as obese | -.26 | .52 | - | | |
| | IV. Satisfaction with body image | .48 | -.30 | -.50 | - | |
| | V. Skipping breakfast | -.23 | .10 | .16 | -.20 | - |

Table 3. Matrix of correlations between the different quantitative variables, for boys and girls.

Table 4 shows the relationship between the categorical variable for dieting and all other variables included in the scale. All of the comparisons are statistically significant ($p < .001$) and have appreciable effect sizes (greater than 0.2), both for boys and for girls. In some comparisons, the effect size is large (greater than 0.9), as is the case of the relationship between dieting and the perception of body image as being obese for boys ($d$ = 1.03) and for girls ($d$ = 1.02). The same holds true for the relationship with satisfaction with their body image for girls ($d$ = 0.93).

With regards to the sex differences, in some cases the effect sizes are considerably greater for girls when compared to boys. Specifically, the effect size of the relationship between the GHS and the dieting behavior is almost twice as great for girls ($d$ = 0.47) as for boys ($d$ = 0.29). Likewise, the effect size of the relationship between dieting and being unsatisfied with one's body image is greater for girls (boys 0.70, girls 0.93), it is the same for the relationship between dieting and skipping breakfast (boys 0.23, girls 0.30).

| | | Without dieting | | | With dieting | | | | |
|---|---|---|---|---|---|---|---|---|---|
| | | *N* | *M* | *SD* | *N* | *M* | *SD* | Sig. | *d* |
| Global Health Score | Boys | 3004 | 0.06 | 0.76 | 326 | -0.16 | 0.83 | <.00 | 0.29 |
| | Girls | 2926 | -0.18 | 0.76 | 661 | -0.54 | 0.79 | <.00 | 0.47 |
| Body Mass Index | Boys | 3004 | 20.91 | 3.22 | 326 | 23.61 | 4.03 | <.00 | 0.82 |
| | Girls | 2926 | 20.05 | 2.90 | 661 | 22.17 | 3.37 | <.00 | 0.71 |
| Perception of body as obese | Boys | 3004 | 1.99 | 0.73 | 326 | 2.74 | 0.72 | <.00 | 1.03 |
| | Girls | 2926 | 2.19 | 0.75 | 661 | 2.94 | 0.64 | <.00 | 1.02 |
| Satisfaction with body image | Boys | 3004 | 3.08 | 0.80 | 326 | 2.52 | 0.91 | <.00 | 0.70 |
| | Girls | 2926 | 2.79 | 0.86 | 661 | 1.98 | 0.90 | <.00 | 0.93 |
| Skipping breakfast | Boys | 3004 | 1.53 | 2.13 | 326 | 2.02 | 2.31 | <.00 | 0.23 |
| | Girls | 2926 | 1.94 | 2.27 | 661 | 2.63 | 2.48 | <.00 | 0.30 |

Table 4. Comparison of measurements between dieting behavior and the other scale variables for boys and girls.

To conclude, two structural equation models were performed; one for girls and the other for boys. The following variables were included in both models: GHS, BMI, perception of one's body as obese, satisfaction with one's body image, dieting and skipping breakfast. Both structural equation models presented good indexes of fitness for boys, $\chi^2$ (5, $N$ = 3348) = 41.85, $p < .001$, CFI = .98, IFI = .98, MFI = .99, BBNNFI = .94, RMSEA = .05; and for girls, $\chi^2$ (8, $N$ = 3597) = 56.96, $p < .001$, CFI = .99, IFI = .99, MFI = .99, BBNNFI = .97, RMSEA = .04).

Both in the case of boys and girls, certain bi-varied relationships demonstrated previously wane in the structural equation models. Such is the case for the relationship between BMI and GHS and the relationship between dieting and skipping breakfast. In these cases, there continues to be a relationship between both variables but in an indirect way through other variables, such as perception and satisfaction with one's body image.

On one hand, the influence of the BMI is evidenced through the perception of body image. Moreover, for boys, the BMI influences satisfaction with one's body image. In fact, one aspect, in the case of girls, that highlights the indirect influence of the BMI on satisfaction with body image, through the perception of one's body image, is that the coefficient is higher for girls ($\beta$ = -.50, $p < .001$) than for boys ($\beta$ = -.18, $p < .001$). Therefore, the perception of obesity entails poorer satisfaction with one's body image in the case of girls when compared with boys. This data is logical if the coefficient for the influence of the BMI on body satisfaction is observed; it is significant in the case boys ($\beta$ = -.15, $p < .001$) but nonexistent in the case of girls.

On the other hand, there are also sex differences when it comes to the influence of body satisfaction on the behavior of dieting. Concretely, Figure 2 shows that this influence is higher for girls ($\beta$ = -.21, $p < .001$) than for boys ($\beta$ = -.14, $p < .001$).

**BOYS:**

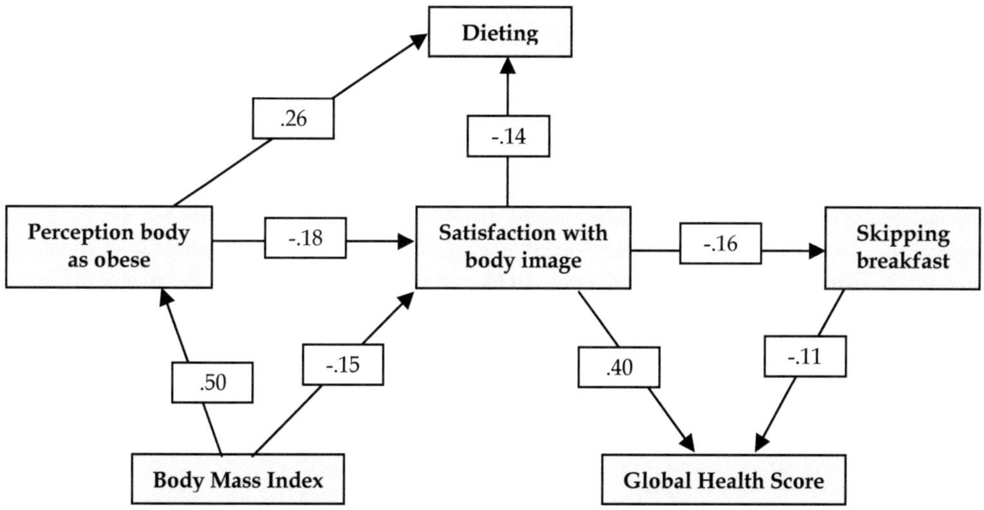


**GIRLS:**

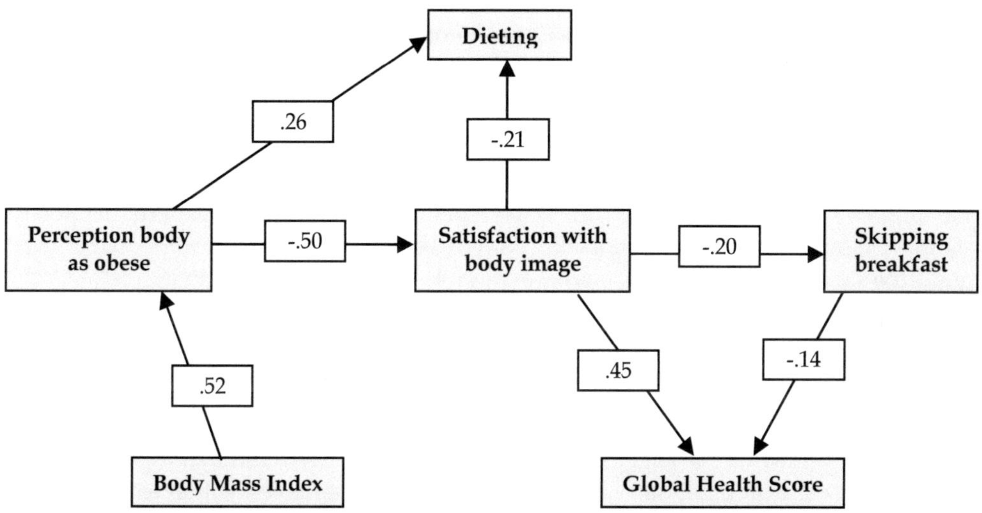


Fig. 2. Standardized estimates of the model parameters for boys and girls.

In conclusion, it can be seen that the main variable of both models is satisfaction with body image. On one hand, this variable is influenced by the perception of one's body image and the BMI (in the girls this influence would be indirect). On the other hand, body satisfaction influences other variables such as the behavior of dieting, skipping breakfast and the GHS. Thus, body satisfaction can be seen as the nexus of both models. In fact, the adjustment variable measured with the GHS is determined, for the most part, by satisfaction with body image (for boys $\beta = .40$, $p < .001$; for girls $\beta = .45$, $p < .001$). Despite the fact that the behavior of skipping breakfast also influences GHS, this influence is much lower (for boys $\beta = -.11$, $p < .001$; for girls $\beta = -.14$, $p < .001$) than it obtain through of body satisfaction.

## 4. Discussion

The results of this study show that the four components related to eating disorders (*physiological*: BMI, *cognitive*: perception of one's body as obese, *emotional*: satisfaction with one's body image and *behavioral*: dieting and skipping breakfast) entail a decrease in the Global Health Score (GHS) for adolescents, this being understood from a broad and integrative point of view, as is recommended by the World Health Organization with the bio-psycho-social paradigm. The bi-varied tests (Pearson correlation and Student *t* test) demonstrate that all the variables included in this research are related to the GHS in adolescents. However, when those variables are included in the global model, some maintain a direct relationship with the GHS while others have an indirect influence, especially in term of satisfaction with one's body image. In short, it has been seen that the BMI ceases to have a direct relationship on health and begins having an indirect influence through the perception that young people have of their body image, which in turn influences their satisfaction with their body image, which, in the end, is a variable that has a high correlation with the GHS.

On the other hand, body image also becomes the nexus between the BMI and the behaviors of dieting and skipping breakfast. Therefore, during adolescence, what makes the young people adopt certain behaviors to control their weight is not so much their real weight (BMI) but the self-perception of their body and the satisfaction they have with their figure. These results are coherent with the discoveries found by other experts who show the mediator role of body image on weight control behaviors and real weight, which takes second place (e.g., Isik et al., 2005; Fan et al., 2010).

Thus, it has been demonstrated that during adolescence certain variables related to the physiological (BMI), cognitive (perception of obesity), emotional (body satisfaction) and behavioral (weight control) components show a dangerous relationship pattern that persists in both boys and girls. This relationship pattern between the various components orbits around the satisfaction with body image, a variable related to the emotion associated with the subjective image of the body figure. This emotional component is shown to play a more central role by influencing behaviors that are potentially dangerous for health (such as dieting without a high BMI or skipping breakfast on a daily basis), as well as its influence on the bio-psycho-social health of the young people (GHS).

These results allow us to suggest the need to impact even more on the emotional component, along with other more cognitive or behavioral variables, within eating disorder prevention programs, as well as on intervention programs for young people with anorexia or bulimia. These suggestions are in the line with those outlined by Stice et al. (2003) with regards to weight control programs; they stressed the importance of increasing body satisfaction in young people. Likewise, Rotenberg et al. (2004) demostrated the difficulty of modifying aspects related to the subjective state of mind by induction, despite achieving changes in the cognitive area with regards to body image.

So, bearing in mind the high indexes of being overweight and obesity currently seen in a large number of young people in developed countries (Currie et al., 2008), the primary prevention of dissatisfaction with body image in young people is difficult to solve (Vander, 2011). Faced with this, the solution could lie in integrated models or paradigms, with an inter-behavioral and interdisciplinary philosophy (Orleans, 2004; Prochaska et al., 2008;

Pronk et al., 2004; Solomon & Kington, 2002), that includes, in a single intervention, the promotion of healthy eating habits that avoid excessive weight, the standard practice of physical exercise, the elimination of unhealthy weight control behaviors and the promotion of the self-acceptation and self-esteem starting from non-physical criteria. Following the recommendations established by Neumark-Sztainer (2009) deriving from the results of the project *Eating Among Teens* (EAT), it is important to pay attention to family comments referring to body weight and behaviors aimed at weight control carried out within this context (e.g., Neumark-Sztainer et al., 2010), it is equally important to intervene with regards to weight control and the body image of friends (e.g., Eisenberg & Neumark-Sztainer, 2010). Moreover, without overlooking the macro-systemic dimension of this subject, according to the ecological theory of Bronfenbrenner (1979), it is necessary to intervene with regards to the danger of the implicit ideas of today's society that prioritizes physical beauty as one of the main standards of personal value (e.g., Grammas & Schwartza, 2009; Levine & Murnen, 2009).

At the same time, this study also demonstrates clear indicators of the less favorable role girls play when compared with boys, in the risk of developing eating disorders. Girls, despite having a lower BMI than boys, perceive themselves as more obese; they are more unsatisfied with their body image; they diet more frequently and skip breakfast more often. All these aspects make it understandable that adolescent girls present bio-psycho-social health scores (GHS) that are lower than their male peers.

One of the clearest sex differences can be seen in the greater bi-varied relationship in girls, with the poorest score for health and dieting on the one hand, and skipping breakfast on the other. These results make sense when considering that girls carry out this type of weight control behavior with less real necessity that boys, since their BMI is better adjusted. Therefore, it is logical that these weight control behaviors lead to a greater decrease in their bio-psycho-social well-being. In the global model, the relationship between dieting and poorer GHS is weaker; however, the relationship between skipping breakfast and poorer GHS persists, both for boys and girls. This could be explained from a strictly biological point of view, due the influence of fasting on physical health, by means of variations in heart rhythm and an increase in parasympathetic activity (Pivik el al., 2006). When fasting is prolonged more than normal, a mechanism leads to a decrease in insulin and an increase in cortisol and catecholamines seeking to maintain blood sugar at an acceptable level. These metabolic changes response as fatigue that not only interferes in physical and muscular performance, but also in various cognitive aspects: lack of concentration, decrease in the capacity for locution or expression, memory, creativity and problem solving, in addition to the consequent despondency and moodiness (Gretchen, 1995; Pereira et al., 2011; Rampersaud et al., 2005).

This study also demonstrates that although there is a correlation in both sexes between perception and satisfaction with one's body image, in the case of girls, this correlation is almost triple the statistic found for boys. That is to say, the perception of obesity by girls is linked more strongly with poorer satisfaction with body image. This data explains the fact that the influence of real weight (BMI) on the satisfaction with one's body image occurs in the case of boys but not in the case of girls, in whom this influence is indirect through body perception. In addition, to fully understanding the most dangerous circle surrounding girls, this study demonstrates that the influence of body satisfaction on the behavior of dieting is greater for girls than for boys. Therefore, we are faced with a clear position of risk for adolescent girls when compared with their male peers. In short, girls, despite having a more appropriate real weight, have a greater perception of obesity, are more unsatisfied with their body image, diet more often to lose weight and skip breakfast more frequently. Likewise, for girls, these weight control behaviors are accompanied by poorer bio-psycho-social health indicators, when compared with boys. Lastly, considering the central role of body satisfaction demonstrated in the global models, for girls—contrary to boys— body satisfaction is less influenced by their real weight, is more influenced by the self-perception and has more influence in dieting behavior. It is therefore necessary to stress the necessity of intervening in the cognitive-emotional patterns of adolescent girls with regards to their weight and body image.

These discoveries, which demonstrate the clear unfavorable role of girls as opposed to boys, are coherent with the findings of other researchers, who coincide in the greater concern girls have of body image (e.g., Kanaan & Afifi, 2010). As Harter (2006) summarizes, many girls worship an ideal of thinness, overestimate the preferences of boys for slender female bodies, see themselves as fatter than other girls and negatively compare themselves with the models of women on display in the media. At the same time, girls are more vulnerable to certain negative thought patterns found in depression, such as self-blame, a negative social comparison, hyper-vigilance to potential stress and brooding (that is to say, an obsession about the future consequences of their hypothetical decisions) (Andrews & Thompson, 2009; Hyde et al., 2008). These gender differences predispose girls to a greater risk of developing eating disorders, depression, self-mutilation, low self-esteem and unnecessary interventions of cosmetic surgery (Ruble et al., 2006). Therefore, following the logic suggested by Perry and Pauletti (2011), it is recommended that future research dedicates more attention to the biological, cognitive and social factors responsible for the differential sensitivity of boys and girls to specific contexts and experiences.

## 5. Conclusion

The variables related to weight, image and body control during adolescence show a clearly pernicious relationship pattern. This relationship pattern between the various key variables in the development of eating disorders orbits around satisfaction with body image—a variable related to the emotion associated with the subjective image of the body figure, which nevertheless has been demonstrated to be more important than other more objective variables (BMI), thus influencing behaviors that are potentially dangerous for health (such as dieting when the BMI is not high, or skipping breakfast), as well as influencing the bio-psycho-social health of the young people.

On the other hand, there is a clear position of risk in adolescent girls when compared with their male peers. In short, girls, despite having a more appropriate real weight, perceive themselves as fat more frequently, are more unsatisfied with their body image, diet to lose weight and skip breakfast more often. Additionally, for girls, these weight control behaviors are accompanied by poorer bio-psycho-social health indicators, when compared with boys. Lastly, bearing in mind the important role of body satisfaction demonstrated in the global models, for girls —contrary to boys— body satisfaction is less influenced by their real weight; receives more influence self-perception and influences the behavior of dieting more strongly.

## 6. Acknowledgment

We would like to thank Spain's Ministry of Health, Social Affairs and Equal for its support and financing of this study. Likewise, we would like to thank the interns who participated in this study to collect and code the data. Lastly, we would like to thank the 375 schools and some 22,000 Spanish adolescents who agreed to complete the questionnaire for the study.

## 7. References

Alexy, U., Wicher, M., & Kersting, M. (2010). Breakfast trends in children and adolescents: frequency and quality. *Public Health Nutrition,* Vol. 13, No. 11, pp. 1795-1802, ISSN 1475-2727

Andrews, P. W., & Thompson, J. A. (2009). The bright side of being blue: Depression as an adaptation for analyzing complex problems. *Psychological Review,* Vol. 116, No. 3, pp. 620–654, ISSN 0033-295X

Barker, E. & Galambos, N. (2003). Body Dissatisfaction of Adolescent Girls and Boys: Risk and Resource Factors. *The Journal of Early Adolescence,* Vol. 23, No. 2, pp. 141-165, ISSN 1552-5449

Bessenoff, G. & Snow, D. (2006). Absorbing Society's Influence: Body Image Self-Discrepancy and Internalized Shame. *Sex Roles,* Vol. 54, No. 9-10, pp. 727-731, ISSN 1573-2762

Bronfenbrenner, U. (1979). *The ecology of human behavior,* Harvard University Press, ISBN 0-674-22456-6, Cambridge, MA

Cash, T.F. & Deagle, E.A. (1997). The nature and extent of body-image disturbances in anorexia nervosa and bulimia nervosa: A meta-analysis. *International Journal of Eating Disorders,* Vol. 22, No. 2, pp. 107–126, ISSN 1098-108X

Cho, S., Dietrich, M., Brown, C.J., Clark, C.A. & Block, G. (2003). The effect of breakfast type on total daily energy intake and body mass index: Results from the third national health and nutrition examination survey (NHANESIII). *Journal of the American College of Nutrition,* Vol. 22, No. 4, pp. 296–302, ISSN 1541-1087

Conley, A. & Boardman, J.D. (2007). Weight overestimation as an indicator of disordered eating behaviors among young women in the United States. *International Journal of Eating Disorders,* Vol. 40, No. 5, pp. 441–445, ISSN 1098-108X

Currie, C., Roberts, C., Morgan, A., Smith, R., Settertobulte, W., Samdal, O., & Rasmussen, B. (2008). *Inequalities in young people's health: International report from the HBSC 2005/06 survey,* WHO Regional Office for Europe, ISBN 978-92-890-7195-6, Copenhague, Denmark

Eisenberg, M.E. & Neumark-Sztainer, D. (2010). Friends' dieting and disordered eating behaviors among adolescents five years later: findings from Project EAT. *Journal of Adolescent Health,* Vol. 47, No. 1, pp. 67-73, ISSN 1054-139X

Eisenberg, M. E., Neumark-Sztainer, D., Story, M. y Perry, C. (2005). The role of social norms and friends' influences on unhealthy weight-control behaviors among adolescent girls. *Social Science and Medicine,*Vol. 60, No. 6, pp. 1165-1173, ISSN 0277-9536

Espinoza, P., Penelo, E., & Raich, R.M. (2010). Disordered eating behaviors and body image in a longitudinal pilot study of adolescent girls: what happens 2 years later?. *Body Image,* Vol. 7, No. 1, pp. 70-73, ISSN 1740-1445

Fan, Y.O., Li, Y.P., Liu, A.L., Hu, X., Ma, G., & Xu, G. (2010). Association between body mass index, weight control concerns and behaviors, and eating disorder symptoms among non-clinical Chinese adolescents. *BMC Public Health*, Vol. 10, No. 1, pp. 314-325, ISSN 1471-2458

Gardner, R. (1996). Methodological issues in assessment of the perceptual component of body image disturbance. *British Journal of Psychology*, Vol. 87, No. 2, pp. 327-337, ISSN 2044-8295

Grammas, D.L. & Schwartz, J.P. (2009). Internalization of messages from society and perfectionism as predictors of male body image. *Body Image*, Vol. 6, No. 1, pp. 31-36, ISSN 1740-1445

Gretchen, M. (1995). The impact of breakfast especially ready-to-eat cereals on nutrient intake and health of children. *Nutrition Research*, Vol. 15, No. 4, pp. 595-613, ISSN 0271-5317

Harter, S. (2006). The self, In: *Handbook of child psychology: Vol. 3. Social, emotional, and personality development*, W. Damon & R. M. Lerner (Series Eds.) & N. Eisenberg (Vol. Ed.), (6th ed.), PP. 505–570). John Wiley & Sons, ISBN 978-0-471-27287-8, Hoboken, NJ

Hyde, J.S., Mezulis, A.H., & Abramson, L.Y. (2008). The ABCs of depression: Integrating affective, biological, and cognitive models to explain the emergence of the gender difference in depression. *Psychological Review*, Vol. 115, No. 2, pp. 291–313, ISSN 0033-295X

Isik, B.I., Orsel, S., Akdemir, A., & Ozbay, M.H. (2005). The relationship between dieting and body image, body ideal, self-perception, and body mass index in Turkish adolescents. *International Journal of Eating Disorders*, Vol. 37, No. 2, pp. 150-155, ISSN 1098-108X

Ivarsson, T., Svalander, P., Litlere, O., & Nevonen, L. (2006). Weight concerns, body image, depression and anxiety in Swedish adolescents. *Eating Behaviors*, Vol. 7, No. 2, pp. 161-175, ISSN 1471-0153

Kanaan, M.N. & Afifi, R.A. (2010). Gender differences in determinants of weight-control behaviours among adolescents in Beirut. *Public Health Nutrition*, Vol. 13, No. 1, pp. 71-81, ISSN 1475-2727

Larson, N.I., Neumark-Sztainer, D., & Story, M. (2009). Weight Control Behaviors and Dietary Intake among Adolescents and Young Adults: Longitudinal Findings from Project EAT. *Journal of the American Dietetic Association*, Vol. 109, No. 11, pp. 1869-1877, ISSN 0002-8223

Levine, M.P. & Murnen, S.K. (2009). "Everybody Knows That Mass Media are/are not [pick one] a Cause of Eating Disorders": A Critical Review of Evidence for a Causal Link Between Media, Negative Body Image, and Disordered Eating in Females. *Journal of Social and Clinical Psychology*, Vol. 28, No. 1, pp. 9-42, ISSN 0736-7236

Martin, M., & Gentry, J. (1997). Stuck in the Model Trap: The Effects of Beautiful Models in Ads on Female Pre-Adolescents and Adolescents. *Journal of Advertising*, Vol. 26, No. 2, pp. 19-33, ISSN 0091-3367

McArthur, L., Holbert, D., & Peña, M. (2005). An Exploration of the attitudinal and perceptual dimensions of body image among male and female adolescents from six latin american cities. *Adolescence*, Vol. 40, No. 160, pp. 801-817, ISSN 0001-8449

Mullie, P., Clary, P., de Ridder, D., Deriemaeker, P., Duvigneaud, N., Hebbelinck, M., Grivegnée, A.R., & Autier, P. (2006). Breakfast frequency and fruit and vegetable consumption in Belgian adolescents: A cross-sectional study. *Nutrition & Food Science*, Vol. 36, No. 5, pp. 315-326, ISSN 0034-6659

Neumark-Sztainer, D., Bauer, K.W., Friend, S., Hannan, P.J., Story, M., & Berge, J.M. (2010). Family weight talk and dieting: how much do they matter for body dissatisfaction and disordered eating behaviors in adolescent girls? *Journal of Adolescent Health*, Vol. 47, No. 3, pp. 270-276, ISSN 1054-139X

Neumark-Sztainer, D., Wall, M., Haines, J., Story, M., & Eisenberg, M.E. (2007). Why does dieting predict weight gain in adolescents? Findings from project EAT-II: A 5-year longitudinal study. *Journal of the American Dietetic Association*, Vol. 107, No. 3, pp. 448-455, ISSN 0002-8223

Neumark-Sztainer, D. (2009). Preventing obesity and eating disorders in adolescents: What can health care providers do? *Journal of Adolescent Health, Vol.* 44, No. 3, pp. 206-213, ISSN 1054-139X

Neumark-Sztainer, D., Story, M., Falkner, N., Beuhring, T., & Resnick, M. (1999). Sociodemographic and Personal Characteristics of Adolescents Engaged in Weight Loss and Weight/Muscle Gain Behaviors: Who Is Doing What?. *Preventive Medicine*, Vol. 28, No. 1, pp. 40-50, ISSN 0091-7435

Niemeier, H., Raynor, H., Lloyd-Richardson, E., Rogers, M., & Wing, R. (2006). Fast Food Consumption and Breakfast Skipping: Predictors of Weight Gain from Adolescence to Adulthood in a Nationally Representative Sample. *Journal of Adolescent Health*, Vol. 39, No. 6, pp. 842-849, ISSN 1054-139X

Orleans, C.T. (2004). Addressing multiple behavioral health risks in primary care. Broadening the focus of health behavior change research and practice. *American Journal of Preventive Medicine*, Vol. 27, No. 1, pp. 1-3, ISSN 0749-3797

Pereira, M.A., Erickson, E., McKee, P., Schrankler, K., Raatz, S., Lytle, L., & Pellegrini, A. (2011). Breakfast Frequency and Quality May Affect Glycemia and Appetite in Adults and Children. *Journal of Nutrition*, Vol. 141, No. 1, pp. 163-168, ISSN 1541-6100

Perry, D.G. & Pauletti, R.E. (2011). Gender and Adolescent Development. *Journal of Research on Adolescence*, Vol. 21, No. 1, pp. 61-74, ISSN 1532-7795

Pivik, R.T., Dykman, R.A., Tennal, K., & Gu, Y. (2006). Skipping breakfast: Gender effects on resting heart rate measures in preadolescents. *Physiology & Behavior*, Vol. 89, No. 2, pp. 270-280, ISSN 0031-9384

Prochaska, J.J., Spring, B., & Nigg, C.R. (2008). Multiple health behavior change research: An introduction and overview. *Preventive Medicine*, Vol. 46, No. 3, pp. 181-188, ISSN 0091-7435

Pronk, N.P., Peek, C.J., & Goldstein, M.G. (2004). Addressing multiple behavioral risk factors in primary care. A synthesis of current knowledge and stakeholder dialogue sessions. *American Journal of Preventive Medicine*, Vol. 27, No. 1, pp. 4-17, ISSN 0749-3797

Rampersaud, G.C., Pereira, M.A., Girard, B.L., Adams, J., & Metzl, J.D. (2005). Breakfast habits, nutritional status, body weight, and academic performance in children and adolescents. *Journal of the American Dietetic Association*, Vol. 105, No. 5, pp. 743-760, ISSN 0002-8223

Rotenberg, K.J., Taylor, D., & Davis, R. (2004). Selective mood- induced body image disparagement and enhancement effects: Are they due to cognitive priming or subjective mood? *International Journal of Eating Disorders*, Vol. 35, No. 3, pp. 317-332, ISSN 1098-108X

Ruble, D. N., Martin, C. L., & Berenbaum, S. A. (2006). Gender development, In: *Handbook of child psychology: Vol. 3. Social, emotional and personality development*, W. Damon & R. M. Lerner (Series Eds.) & N. Eisenberg (Vol. Ed.), (6th ed.), pp. 858–932. John Wiley & Sons, ISBN 978-0-471-27287-8, Hoboken, NJ

Solomon, S. & Kington, R. (2002). National efforts to promote behavior-change research: Views from the Office of Behavioral and Social Sciences Research. *Health Education Research*, Vol. 17, No. 5, pp. 495-499, ISSN 1465-3648

Stice, E., Trost, A., & Chase, A. (2003). Healthy weight control and dissonance-based eating disorder prevention programs: Results from a controlled trial. *International Journal of Eating Disorders*, Vol. 33, No. 1, pp. 10-21, ISSN 1098-108X

Timlin, M.T., Pereira, M.A., Story, M., & Neumark-Sztainer, D. (2008). Breakfast eating and weight change in a 5-year prospective analysis of adolescents: Project EAT (eating among teens). *Pediatrics*, Vol. 121, No. 3, pp. 638-645, ISSN 0031-4005

Vander, J.S. (2011). Unhealthy weight control behaviors among adolescents. *Journal of Health Psychology*. Retrieved from <http://hpq.sagepub.com/content/early/2011/06/06/1359105311409787.abstract>

Vereecken, C., Dupuy, M., Rasmussen, M., Kelly, C., Nansel, T. R., Al Sabbah, H., Baldassari D, Jordan MD, Maes L, Niclasen BV, Ahluwalia N; HBSC Eating & Dieting Focus Group. (2009). Breakfast consumption and its socio-demographic and lifestyle correlates in schoolchildren in 41 countries participating in the HBSC study. *International Journal of Public Health*, Vol. 54, No. 2, pp. 180-190, ISSN 1661-8564

Woodruff, S.J., Hanning, R.M., Lambraki, I., Storey, K.E., & McCargas, L. (2008). Healthy Eating Index-C is compromised among adolescents with body weight concerns, weight loss dieting, and meal skipping. *Body Image*, Vol. 5, No. 4, pp. 404-408. ISSN 1740-1445

World Health Organization (1948). *WHO Constitution*. Geneva: World Health Organization.

Wu, T.Y., Rose, S.E., & Bancroft, J.M. (2006). Gender Differences in Health Risk Behaviors and Physical Activity Among Middle School. *Journal of School Nursing*, Vol. 22, No. 1, pp. 25-31, ISSN 1546-8364

# Part 2

## Etiopathogenic Factors

# 3

# Westernization: The Role of Mass Media on Body Image and Eating Disorders

Ana R. Sepúlveda[1] and María Calado[2]
[1]*School of Psychology, Autonomous University of Madrid, Madrid,*
[2]*Department of Psychiatry, Meixoeiro Hospital of Vigo, Vigo,*
*Spain*

## 1. Introduction

This chapter aims to illustrate the relationship between sociocultural globalisation and body image - globalising mechanisms appear to disseminate the Western standard of female and male beauty. Thus, the combination of ubiquitous messages for eating behaviours and beauty in both advertising and mass media programming may lead to confusion and body image dissatisfaction amongst many young people. The aim is to examine the framework of causality of culturally-induced manifestations of eating and body image disorders by gender and, in particular, to examine the role that the mass media plays in the development of male and female body attitudes regarding ideal body images and how this may in turn have an impact on their mental health.

## 2. The concept of body dissatisfaction in the literature and its association with mass media effects

Body image is a construct determined by a series of individual and socio-cultural factors that intervenes decisively in several aspects of our lives in Western society. Amongst the broader socio-cultural determinants of body image development are ideal body representations transmitted through various socialisation agents such as the mass media, which clearly stands out as spokespeople for these cultural values. Thus, it can be argued that the mass media not only reinforces cultural stereotypes but also strengthens gender behaviour patterns. From a multidimensional perspective, body image is formed through the dynamic interaction of several of these sociocultural and individual factors; the alteration of one of these necessarily affects the rest of the factors in the cycle (Calado, 2010, 2011). A model of body image development by gender is described in Figure 1.

The mass media serves as a mediating structure between individuals and their bodies by sending a powerful message to society: only a determined physical stereotype of beauty is valued. Reiterated by other primary agents of socialisation, such as families, peers and schools, the idea is taken seriously mainly by young women. This issue has been addressed through the analysis of gender as a main factor in the social construction of body image (Calado, 2011). From a gender sociocultural perspective, different perceptive (body

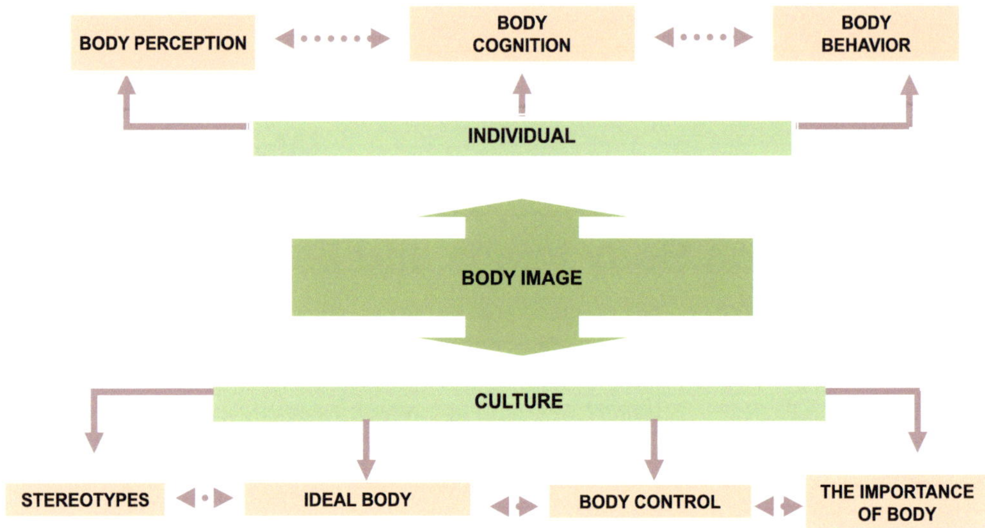


Fig. 1. Model of factors contributing to the development of body image amongst young people by gender (Adapted from Calado, 2011)

functioning), cognitive (thoughts about the body, nutrition or situations that interfere in life), affective and behavioural (affective-sexual relations and behaviours) processes in society are generated, which will affect the formation of a positive or negative body image. The differences regarding the gender body standard go beyond physical appearance as both body representations lead to two very different ways of appreciating the body.

Socialisation agents such as television, internet, cinema and printed media project the idea that ideal body images can be reached through body control and change and that it is solely up to a person's resolve to realise these ideals. This implies moving from the representation of ideal bodies to providing information on how to achieve them. However, in many cases the images presented as ideal prove to be unachievable (unless through aggressive methods such as cosmetic surgery) as they have probably, prior to their publication, been airbrushed and retouched, and thus become unreal.

The variable that continues to be unalterable in content analysis of body control in women is weight. Obesity stereotypes tend to include the belief that weight is controllable (Blaine & McElroy, 2002; Crandall & Martínez, 1996) and overweight people tend to be portrayed as greedy, weak and lazy, whilst miracle weight-loss results are normalised by experts (Blaine & McElroy, 2002). Recent criticism in this direction led to weight loss advice stressing more the importance of health, which was thus associated with thinness (Calado, 2010). Wiseman et al. (1992) found that since 1981 joint weight loss and exercise magazine articles had increased indicating a possible cultural redefinition of methods for weight loss. Previous studies had reported articles based solely on dieting as a weight loss mechanism (Garner et al., 1980; Toro et al., 1989).

Finally, the association between an ideal body and social values must be pointed out. Ideal body shapes are associated with personality traits and positive values, enhancing even more their desirability. The beauty ideal becomes a value in itself and trends that move in different directions are frowned upon. Thin women are therefore associated with wealth, health, control and beauty, whilst being fat is associated negatively with weakness, laziness, lack of control and unhealthy lifestyles. These dynamics lead to the attribution of positive values, including being more intelligent, friendlier and more determined, to thinner people on television (Fouts & Burggraf, 1999).

Several studies have discussed the relationship between mass media and the development of body dissatisfaction from the assumption that the ideal of beauty can deeply impact a person's body attitudes and behaviours (Grabe et al., 2008; Groesz et al., 2002). Thus, aesthetic standards based on the ideal stereotype of thin women and muscular men, may lead to conform idealised cultural values and are considered possible determinants of body image dissatisfaction. These cultural values are unique in that persons are apparently subject to powerful and continuous reinforcing mechanisms through exposure to consistent, reiterative and persuasive thin-ideal images (Blaine & McElroy, 2002; Cusumano & Thompson, 1997; Hogan & Strasburger, 2008; Wiseman et al., 1992).

Existing research reflects a complex reality in which the debate continues as to whether these forms of mass media imply a cause and effect relation or if they are a correlation relationship. The majority of findings are provided by correlational research on the relationship between exposure frequency to the thin ideal and body dissatisfaction (Cusumano & Thompson, 1997; Grabe et al., 2008). These studies showed that reading fashion and fitness magazines, exposure to television music videos and access to specific content through internet or social network websites, such as Facebook or Twitter (Cusumano & Thompson, 1997; Hatoum & Belle, 2004; Hogan & Strasburger, 2008), were associated with body dissatisfaction amongst adolescents due to reiterative exposure to idealised beauty images and, in turn, triggered the desire to lose weight because of this influence. Furthermore, several experimental investigations have suggested that exposure to thin media images led to an increase in body dissatisfaction (Grabe et al., 2008; Groesz et al., 2002). The meta-analysis of 25 experimental studies by Groesz et al. (2002) showed that participants were significantly more dissatisfied with their bodies after viewing thin-idealised models than after viewing average-sized models, plus-sized models, or inanimate objects

However, the majority of society is exposed to reinforcing messages by the mass media that may cause body image dissatisfaction and does not develop unhealthy attitudes and/or behaviours. The question, therefore, would be to ask what individual factors may be working as translators of these social messages that function as risk factors for disordered eating behaviours. In other words, what psychological processes are triggered in a person by which he or she becomes more vulnerable to the group of beliefs, values and attitudes received by socialising agents.

Longitudinal studies are crucial for distinguishing causal risk factors in order to demonstrate whether the exposure to mass media precedes and predicts the development of disturbed body image and disordered eating. There are less published studies that suggest that early exposure to the thin-ideal can predict an increase in body image dissatisfaction. Dohnt and Tiggemann (2006) interviewed a sample of 97 girls aged 5 to 8 years to study how they incorporated the desire for thinness and satisfaction with appearance, and the relationship of this association with their self-esteem. A year later, the variable watching appearance-focused television programmes predicted an increase of appearance dissatisfaction and, subsequently, the girls' desire for thinness was found to precede temporarily low self-esteem. Thus, it appears that a greater exposure to music television shows and appearance-focused magazines leads to a stronger level of dieting awareness. This is consistent with another study by Harrison and Hefner (2006), in which greater overall television exposure predicted both a thinner ideal adult body shape and a higher level of disordered eating in a sample of girls aged 7 to 12 years. In an older sample of college-aged women, Aubrey (2006) studied the total exposure to sexually objectifying television and magazines and found that the exposure to the media predicted levels of self-objectification (defined as the attributes applied to one´s physical self-concept) a year later, especially in women with low self-esteem. According to Aubrey, the exposure to mass media could be associated with an increase in viewers' definitions of their physical selves in terms of externally perceivable traits (i.e. body appearance) rather than internal traits (i.e. body control). One explanation for this process is that exposure to televised objectification cultivates a particular view of the self, a view that emphasises the importance of physical appearance.

## 3. The association of the effects of the mass media with the Westernisation of the body image according to gender

It appears that sociocultural factors may affect female and male adolescents differently; whilst exposure to the muscular ideal has been associated with greater body dissatisfaction in male adolescents, females have reported the desire to be thinner (Farquhar & Wasylkiw, 2007; Hatoum & Belle, 2004).

Research has frequently assessed weight as a body dissatisfaction indicator for women, such as studies on Miss America pageants and Playboy centrefolds. In most cases researchers agree that the ideal body weight for women has decreased progressively over the last 30 years (Garner et al., 1980; Silverstein et al., 1986; Spitzer et al., 1999). This trend is also apparent in television and cinema, which represent women as thinner than the social norm (Fouts & Burggraf, 2000; Fouts & Vaughan, 2002).

Less attention is paid to male body representations, although this has been gradually changing in recent years. Historically, male ideal body images have been associated with muscle bulk, such as the lead actor of the iconic film *Rambo*. There is less of a consensus in published studies on this topic, but there appears to have been an increase in the desire amongst men for muscularity as reported by Leit et al., (2001) in their review of Playgirl models and by Spitzer and colleagues (1999) in male models.

Images that are represented by the media tend to transmit and reinforce dominant cultural ideologies as well as reject representations that question these stereotypes. Calado (2011) shows that these stereotyped body messages generate discrimination dynamics regarding gender roles and the ideal body image (Figure 2), and convey false ideas of reaching this ideal through processes of body transformation and of social success associated with specific body images, as well as possibly trigger unhealthy behaviours.

The objectification of women is based on an ideal of youth and thinness, and the objectification of men is based on thinness as well, but also muscularity and fitness. The reemphasising of these ideals creates the false idea that ideal body images are atemporal, static and immutable, resulting in an unbalance and selection of certain body shapes and exclusion and invisibility of others. This leads, as mentioned previously, to a homogenisation of the ideal body by gender.

Amongst the sociocultural factors that most influence negatively female and, progressively more, male body image perceptions are stereotypical ideal body representations transmitted through different socialisation agents and most notably the mass media. The mass media appears to exercise powerful social learning processes by means of negative and positive reinforcement of mechanisms of beliefs and behaviours. However, these mechanisms tend towards homogenisation through stereotyped and single-viewed notions regarding beauty and the rejection of reality, that is to say, heterogeneous and made up ethnicities, ages and shapes.

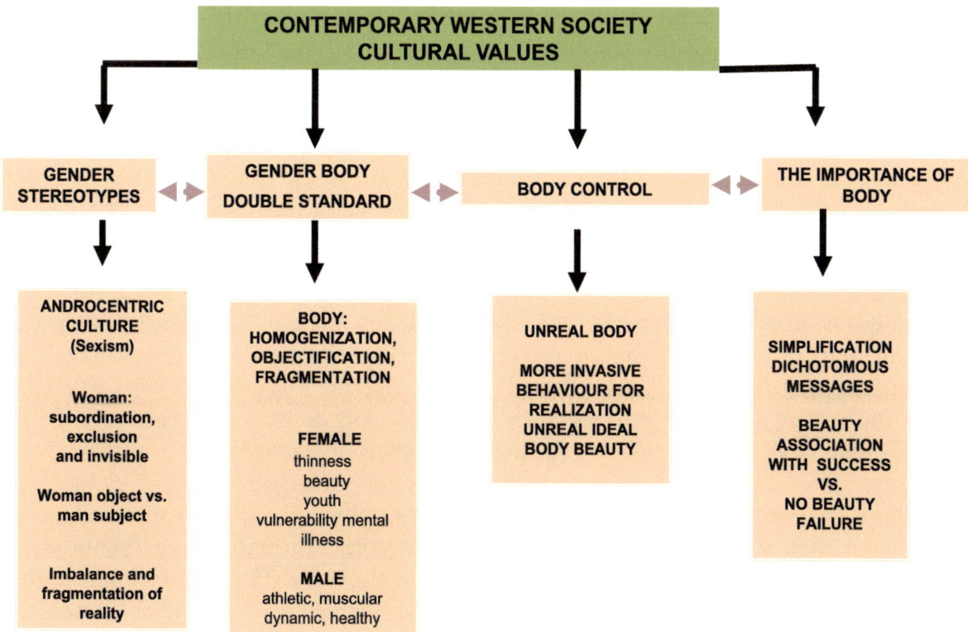


Fig. 2. Sociocultural messages influential in shaping body image (Adapted from Calado, 2011)

The spread of these rigid, stereotyped and dichotomic messages conveys an oversimplified, homogeneous and incomplete picture of reality, allowing for further associations between low self-esteem and body dissatisfaction. An example of this can be found in the television programme Extreme Makeover where participants and viewers are led to believe that their self-esteem can only improve if they have previously undergone a radical transformation of their body image (Cocimano, 2004). The association between a certain type of body, personality traits and success is also reinforced by the mass media through the portrayal and glorification of celebrities. The constant emphasis on the association between celebrities and their body image (by the mass media) reaffirms the belief that success can only be obtained if accompanied by an ideal body. These associations have been studied by Plaza (2005), who examined 519 celebrities in women's magazines and found that they were usually attributed with positive values such as professionalism and the ability to work hard. Life experience, however, was relegated to a lesser issue as most celebrities were under 30 years of age. Once again, the youth versus maturity dichotomy can be observed.

On the other hand, sociocultural beauty standards do not flow in parallel for both genders. This asymmetry has been reported in studies that have assessed the parts of the body which are of most concern to men and women. In this respect, gender differences regarding content and structure of the dimensions associated with the body are relevant. Men tended to be more concerned about their bodily strength (chest, arms or muscles), whilst women were more concerned about their weight (body shape satisfaction or size of breasts) (Blowers et al., 2003). The impossibility of attaining either of these body ideals triggered emotions such as fear, depression or anxiety.

Another differentiating gender element linked to body image is the aging experience, or rather, the double standard for aging. Halliwell and Dittmar (2003) found attitudes towards aging in women to be centred mainly on the physical aspect of their bodies and thus, aging was considered negative as physical attraction decreased and became disassociated with the social value of youth. On the other hand, for men, aging had a negative impact on their physical ability, whilst changes in their appearance were seen as more neutral or even as positive. Social beliefs of masculinity underline traits such as ability, autonomy, energy and self-control, all of which supposedly increase through aging. Therefore, men may view aging as a process that enhances their appeal and, although they also expressed negative attitudes towards body aging, these were not as marked as in the female sample.

Women tend to interiorise their role as body-objects and value themselves regarding their physical appearance; in comparison, men appear to focus more on the aspects of their body associated with function and thus may present higher self-esteem. The prevailing social conditions appear to lead women towards associating their self-worth with their body satisfaction, whilst this synergy does not appear to apply to men. Furthermore, the link between body and self-esteem may influence women to consider as secondary other personal aspects, such as intellectual, artistic or social skills, generating a global single factored self-esteem associated with their self-perceived physical appearance (Calado, 2011). Martínez-Benlloch (2001) has argued that gender content (masculinity/femininity) is expressed in the manner that they are assumed at adolescence. Boys are inclined to focus their self-worth on variables such as self-control, personal power, competitiveness and physical functioning (a dynamic picture of the body), and girls tend to associate their self-worth with weight concerns, sexual attraction and body objectification.

These sociocultural influences appear to have functioned as a protective factor for body image disorders in men. However, there appears to be recent trend suggesting a progressive inversion. Halliwell and Dittmar (2003) in their study of a male sample reported significant differences regarding ages. Younger males, who were more effected by sociocultural body image pressures, exhibited behaviours aimed at changing parts of their bodies they were dissatisfied with, whereas differences by age were not found in the female sample. This fact suggests that levels of concern amongst men may increase in the future. Overall, it seems that the body can be shaped to fit particular ideals and beliefs as a personal project.

An up-to-date review by López-Guimera et al. (2010) has accumulated evidence that the mass media are an extremely important source of information and reinforcement in relation to the nature of the thin beauty ideal and how to attain it. However, less evidence was found for the processes implicated in this relationship, though these are deserving of further research. These authors have postulated that there are at least three processes that convey the relationship between the media, body dissatisfaction and disordered eating: internalisation of the thin beauty ideal, social comparison and activation of the thinness schema. Moreover, social and family support play a crucial role in the awareness and reinforcement of the thin beauty ideal and disordered eating behaviours, which could work as a protective factor for low awareness and internalisation of the thin-schema (López-Guimera et al., 2010).

## 4. Homogenisation processes of the body ideal regarding physical beauty in different cultures

Body image research has argued that body gender stereotypes change from one culture to another and over time. Thus, ideal beauty would be different for every culture as every culture establishes standards that are adopted by varying expressions according to the historic period of the society (Frith et al., 2006). These beauty standards generate anomalous concerns and behaviours linked to body image and directed at obtaining these ideals.

There are diverse practices of beauty across cultures. For example, in China, until fairly recently, an attribute of female beauty was having small feet, leading to the bandaging of young girls' feet in order to stunt growth. This practice was initiated when the girl was between the ages of four and seven, and was widespread for over a thousand years. In Myanmar, a long neck is associated with beauty. Paduang women wear coiled brass neck rings to the point of not being able to remove them because of bone and tissue deformation. In Sumatra, teeth filing was a common practice. Across Africa, skin scarification - where decorative designs are cut into the skin to emphasise beauty as well as ethnic origins - has been practised for centuries. Moreover, some African cultures have seen the deliberate fattening of women as a sign of beauty, fertility, health and prosperity. Amputation and mutilation have been practiced amongst the Mongoni tribe in Malawi. In Arabic culture, henna has been used for centuries on special occasions to decorate the body with bold geometric designs. There are many more examples, perhaps as many as cultures with their own beauty ideals. Traditional African, Asian and Arabic cultures have been cited as examples where, at the very least, thinness was not emphasised as a requirement for feminine beauty (Calado 2011; Soh et al. 2006). However, even across cultures, to attain these ideals of beauty at times implied subjecting oneself to risk behaviours or practices, mainly as regards the female gender.

However, because of globalising dynamics and global access to Western socialising agents' messages, there appears to be an increasing trend in ideal body image homogenisation regarding gender. That is, there appears to be an increasing belief that the beauty ideal has become stable.

These social agents have exported a Eurocentric concept of beauty to the rest of the world. Historically, even the Eurocentric beauty standard regarding ideal body shape has changed in the last 50 years, moving from more voluptuous female shapes to extremely stick-thin body shapes, such the British model Twiggy in the 1960s, and this has never really yielded to a more normal average-sized female body (Frith et al., 2006). Indeed, the stereotypes of a thin body ideal for women and a muscular body ideal for men may also facilitate a full range of unhealthy weight loss practices to control the body image (Gandarillas et al., 2003; Grogan, 2006; Perez-Gaspar et al., 2000), which may lead to idealised cultural values. Body image dissatisfaction and disordered eating have apparently influenced more severely women and this has been associated with the etiology of several psychological and psychiatric disorders. Body dissatisfaction increases the drive for thinness and dieting; and dieting is the greatest risk factor for the development of an eating disorder. Adolescent females, who diet only moderately, are five times more likely to develop an eating disorder than those who do not diet, and those who diet severely are 18 times more likely to develop an eating disorder (Patton et al., 1999). In terms of psychiatric cases, a number of epidemiological studies have presented similar eating disorders prevalence rates, around 4.5% in Western countries (Favaro et al., 2003; Gandarillas et al., 2003; Perez-Gaspar et al., 2000), although this rate may be higher if subclinical cases are included (approximately 8%).

Across cultures, Asian and black women are increasingly considered beautiful when they meet Eurocentric ideals in terms of body shape, skin color and hair texture and, unsurprisingly, cosmetic surgery and health care products have become a ready solution. China, Japan and South Korea are amongst the top seven countries where cosmetic surgery is performed, along with the United States, India, Brazil and Mexico (Haas *et al.*, 2008). According to the American Society of Plastic Surgery, approximately 11.7 million cosmetic surgical and nonsurgical procedures were performed in 2007. This is a 457% increase since 1997. Globally, almost $13.2 billion was spent on cosmetic surgical procedures in 2007 (Haas et al. 2008). Many Asian women opt for surgery in order to copy the chins, big eyes or high-bridged noses of popular Western actresses. Evidence suggests that this leaning towards a Westernised appearance starts at an early age; dark haired Asian women now play with blonde-haired Barbie dolls when children. Ultimately, older Caucasian females also undergo one form or another of cosmetic surgery to address aging in their quest for youth. Other forms of body intervention are performed by all ages, mainly lipoplasty and breast augmentation (Haas et al. 2008). Men have also become targets of these beauty messages, although the intensity and number of advertisements seem to pale into insignificance when compared to women. Nevertheless, this homogenisation of beauty across gender, culture and ethnicity is a trend that allows for mechanisms of social control by cosmetic industries, which also accumulate high profits from the transmission of these messages (Hesse-Biber et al. 2006). Moreover, Haas et al. (2008) reviewed the reasons for undergoing cosmetic surgery and found that these were mainly motivated by psychological and psychosocial factors and, in some cases, psychiatric disorders. Recently, increasing eating disorders rates have also been reported in non-Western societies, such as the Middle East (Nobakht & Dezhkam, 2000), China (Huon et al. 2002) and Japan (Chisuwa & O'Dea, 2010), although the prevalence rates are still far below those in Western countries.

The case of Fiji is an outstanding example of global-marketing of beauty standards and how these have affected traditional culture norms previously immune to body disturbance and disordered eating. Fijian culture traditionally holds a robust and rounded body image as the norm for females and males. In contrast, a slim body was considered unhealthy. Only three years after the arrival of television in 1995, dominated by Western broadcast programmes and films, Fijian society noted a drastic increase in eating disorders and general dissatisfaction with physical appearance. In other words, these disorders had not been recorded (or did not exist) until the advent of televised media on the islands (Becker, 2004). Other examples could be considered illustrative cases, although the methodology is more limited and the results debatable. In the case of Iran, the country banned Western media after the fall of the Sha and, therefore, Iranians were not exposed to the thin body beauty. In a particular study, female and male Iranian college students were compared with their American counterparts. As expected, the Iranian female students scored considerably higher than the U.S. participants when asked to assess their body-esteem, while men, from both countries, scored higher than the women (Akiba, 1998). These results suggest that the current access to Western mass media has had a more significant impact amongst the female population. Another study carried out by Nasser (1994) confirmed that unhealthy eating behaviours and the desire to be thinner were emerging in Egyptian culture amongst secondary school students in opposition to values traditionally placed on rounded female bodies. Lastly, Caradas et al. (2001) conducted research in South Africa in order to compare body image issues amongst white and black girls. Their findings indicated that the prevalence of abnormal eating attitudes was equally common in schoolgirls from different ethnic backgrounds.

Certainly, Westernisation and globalising values have permeated the majority of non-Western cultures and established body image ideals and eating behaviours. As regards the media, it is fairly easy to see that a significant number of Western television programmes have been adapted to different countries (Asian, Latin American, etc) and dubbed in various languages. Publicity tends to be more local for cooperate reasons, but these advertisements are also, in many cases, generic commercials believed to appeal to a variety of countries and are, consequently, aired and dubbed all over Western Europe. The same can be said for printed media that either offer different versions of globalised magazines (*Hello, Cosmopolitan,* etc) or publish magazines that imitate in form and content Western publications.

In this context, it is also important to assess the degree of acculturation regarding over-exposure to idealised images within the African-American, Asian-American and Latin-American communities. There has been less research assessing body dissatisfaction or eating disorders in minority groups. Clinical criteria developed for Caucasian populations do not effectively map illnesses for non-Western samples, thus, information is still uncertain and scarce. Several studies, however, confirmed as a result of ethnicity and cultural conflict was significantly related to body dissatisfaction and maladaptive eating attitudes (Alegria et al., 2007; Cummins & Lehman, 2007; Hesse-Biber et al., 2004). The study by Akan and Grilo (1995) reported that Caucasians had greater levels of disordered eating and dieting behaviours and attitudes and greater body dissatisfaction than Asian-Americans and African-Americans who differed little on these measures. Likewise, a history of being teased about weight and size was associated with unhealthy eating behaviours and body dissatisfaction in Caucasians but not in Asian-Americans. A further study that compared a Caucasian and an African-American female sample suggested the latter group had appearance concerns over the issues of hair and skin, specifically to straighten their hair and try to achieve lighter skin tones, in an attempt to integrate aspects of both cultures into their lives (Hesse-Biber et al., 2004). In contradiction of these findings, however, another study found that African-American and Latin-American women differed little from Caucasian women in terms of body dissatisfaction and eating-disordered features (Hrabosky & Grilo, 2007). Recently, a rigorous eating disorder study carried out by Alegria et al. (2007) of Latin Americans in the United States found elevated rates for binge eating but low prevalence of anorexia nervosa. Specifically, foreign birth was associated with a decreased risk of binge eating and those who spent more than 70% of their lifetime in the U.S. reported the highest rate for an eating disorder. In short, findings suggest that there exists some support for the risk effect of acculturation and racial differences regarding eating and body image.

## 5. Exploring trends in male body dissatisfaction, appropriate instrument measure and its association with mass media effects

A relatively new direction of research in this field is the growing impact of body image concerns amongst males and, consequently, increasing male body dissatisfaction (Plaza, 2005). Thus, men may have found a certain protection from eating pathologies due to the fact that physical appearance has historically been attributed as a value to women, whilst men have been valued for other aspects of their lives such as work and intelligence (Calado, 2011). Male body image disorders have been invisible and apparently non-existent until recently as they would have challenged sociocultural preconceptions regarding gender roles (Spitzer et al. 1999). However, since the beginning of the present century this scenario has changed with increasing pressure on men to conform to ideal body images as well.

The stereotypes of mass media for males have been revised from heroes and male celebrities to muscular athletes and actors. Television and magazines now offer new categories that describe the ideal physical appearances men should aspire to and which are associated with certain lifestyles. All these categories have in common the imitation of messages linked to the association of celebrities, their physical appearance and success. Not very long ago it would have been unthinkable to define men in terms solely of body exhibition and objectification; metrosexuals, for example, describes heterosexual males who assume traditional female attributes such as wearing cosmetics. The most famous representative is perhaps the footballer David Beckham. In fact, socialising agents and other actors realise that they have tapped into a new market, that these new models are accepted and imitated as ideal images (Farquhar & Wasylkiw, 2007; Leit et al., 2001; McCreary & Sasse, 2000; Spitzer *et al.* 1999). As in the case of women, men are now faced with ideal stereotypes based solely on their physical appearance but which promise success and wider social acceptance if obtained. Again, these stereotypes are unreal and in most cases unattainable if not through aggressive interventions on one's body and behaviour.

Several studies assessed the impact on men's health of mass media exposure to male beauty ideals (Farquhar & Wasylkiw, 2007; Hospers & Jansen, 2005; McCreary & Sasse, 2000). Findings report increasing pressure for men to attain slender and muscular bodies through extreme weight control behaviours such as over-exercise and anabolic steroid use (Hatoum & Belle, 2004). Likewise, Hatoum and Belle (2004) identified a link between magazine exposure to this type of content and concerns regarding bodybuilding, fitness, excessive protein supplement use and cosmetic surgery aimed at enhancing muscularity.

Moreover, men who try to obtain a muscular and athletic beauty ideal may trigger issues such as increasing concerns about their appearance and possibly new forms of disorders linked to body image such as body dysmorphic disorder (BDD). This disorder is characterised by intense obsession with his or her appearance and body image and the attempt to fix the perceived flaws through excessive exercise. This disorder has become increasingly noted and there is a growing interest, specifically, in muscle dysmorphia, which is more frequently present amongst men (Murray et al., 2010; Veale et al., 2003). Muscle dysmorphia disorder has been considered since its inception as a type of "reverse anorexia," or "bigorexia." It is classified under several different categories, as a manifestation of BDD or obsessive compulsive disorder or as a new form of eating disorder (Murray et al., 2010). Excessive concern and obsessive thoughts regarding physical appearance, symptoms of anxiety and depression, altered behaviour of social and working life, direct people suffering from this disorder towards related rituals such as excessive weightlifting, a meticulous diet, and anabolic steroids used for aesthetic purposes. Recent research suggests a strong conceptual similarity with anorexia nervosa (Murray et al., 2010). For example, weightlifters that are not identified with the disorder spend forty minutes a day worrying about the development of their musculature, unlike the five hours spent by men with bigorexia.

Pope et al., (2005) compared men with muscle dysmorphia to men with BDD without muscle dysmorphia, finding similarities in demographic features and a number of non-muscle related body areas of concern. However, those with muscle dysmorphia were significantly more likely to lift weights excessively, diet and engage in anabolic steroid abuse. They also had a poorer quality of life and were significantly more likely to have attempted suicide. These findings may also suggest that bigorexia is similar to an eating disorder spectrum. Similarly, higher levels of body fat dissatisfaction in conjunction with muscle dissatisfaction were also uniquely predictive of eating pathology amongst men (Tylka et al. 2005).

Ricciardelli and colleagues (2007) systematically reviewed the literature related to body image concerns, disordered eating and other behaviours associated with increasing muscle size amongst men from different cultural groups. They concluded that there was no consistent pattern that could summarise the nature of body image concerns in males across the different cultures. There is also no consistent finding related to moderating variables that mediate the relationship between the effects of acculturation, body change strategies and disordered eating. The majority of studies reviewed have been conducted with minority groups of males living in Western countries like the U.S. and using non-standardised and non-validated measures amongst males.

It is noteworthy to point out several shortcomings in the methodology of these studies. Most utilised administered self-report questionnaires designed for and validated in samples of females, which may not be appropriate for measuring the nature of men's body dissatisfaction and a possible eating psychopathology. In this regard, several new self-report instruments specific for assessing body image disturbance amongst the male population have been recently developed. Table 1 presents an updated review of some new instruments developed for assessing body image in male samples.

The majority of these tools were developed and validated in samples in the United States, and very few translated or validated in other countries. It is, therefore, possible that research illustrating the differences in eating disorder psychopathology between muscle dysmorphia and anorexia nervosa may have drawn premature or invalid conclusions because of the insensitivity of the measures in detecting men's body image and eating concerns (Murray et al. 2010; Ricciardelli et al. 2007).

## 6. Recommendations for health promotion: towards a positive body image

The next step after obtaining a bigger picture of the global trend in body image and eating concerns over the last decades is to question whether this complex context can be altered. The effects of globalisation go beyond economics with digital mass media and new technologies exporting Western cultural standards around the world. This theoretical perspective suggests that modifying the context may also be able to change the psychological distress associated with body image disturbance (Calado, 2011).

| Year | Author/ Country | Instrument | Description | Sample |
|---|---|---|---|---|
| 2000 | Edwards & Launder (Wales, UK) | Swansea Muscularity Attitudes Questionn. (SMAQ). | 20 items on a 7-point Likert scale. Grouped: Drive for muscularity and Positive attributes of muscularity. | 303 male students. |
| 2000 | McCreary & Sasse (Canada) | Drive for Muscularity Scale (DSM). | 15 items on a 6-point Likert scale. Grouped: Muscularity-oriented body image and Muscularity behaviour. | 197 male and female college-age. |
| 2002 | Mayville et al. (U.S.) | Muscle Appearance Satisfaction Scale (MASS). | 19 items on a 5-point Likert scale. Grouped: Bodybuilding Dependence, Muscle Checking, Substance Use, Injury and Muscle Satisfaction. | 372 male weightlifters. |
| 2004 | Hildebrand et al. (U.S.) | Muscle Dysmorphic Disorder Inventory (MDDI). | 13 items on a 5-point Likert scale. Grouped in 3 subscales: Drive for Size (DFS), Appearance Intolerance (AI), and Functional impartment (FI) | 237 male weightlifters |
| 2004 | Hildebrand et al. (U.S.) | Bodybuilder Image Grid–Original(BIG-O). | Figure-rating scale of 30 male figures that vary in body fat and musculature. | 237 male weightlifters |
| 2005 | Tylka et al. (U.S.) | Male Body Attitudes Scale (MBAS). | 24 items on a 6-point Likert scale. Grouped: Muscularity, Low body fat and Height | 294 undergraduate men |
| 2010 | Hildebrand et al. (U.S.) | Male Body Checking Questionnaire (MBCQ) | 19 items on a 5-point Likert scale. Grouped: Global muscle checking, Chest and shoulder checking, Other-comparative checking, Body testing. | 196 undergraduate men |

Table 1. Instruments of assessment body image disturbances in male sample

What appears to be true is that an effective society should aim to endorse measures that create healthy environments, which in turn promote health rather than concentrate resources solely on dealing with treatment. The World Health Organisation (2004) argues that individual health programmes rarely have a long-term impact on health problems. However, the majority of programmes carried out in this direction have targeted risk populations with the hope of reducing later cases, instead of addressing the root causes of these disorders. The question is whether individual interventions have the capacity to modify health risks or unhealthy lifestyles and habits. Hesse-Biber et al. (2006) argue that it is important to take into account the sociocultural, political and economic context as well as the psychological process, in order to understand how an individual operates in a given social context. All of these approaches analysed together provide a holistic explanation of the impact of socialcultural pressure in body image and eating disorders.

Studying both the social as well as the psychological factors can help determine why some people develop body image and eating disorders and others do not. Solutions cannot be found in the separation of the private life and public sphere of individuals. In the case of women, as long as they are focused on their appearance, the public space they are allowed to occupy will be limited. Hesse-Biber et al. (2006) emphasise that efforts must be made to change our current anthropocentric thinking. Changes that allow for a healthier society regarding eating behaviours, body image and social self-esteem should be sought through holistic interventions. This point of view is important as depending on the perspective adopted, researchers can tailor the indexes that in turn assess programme outcomes.

Furthermore, it is surprising that regardless of the evidence suggesting a strong association between social agents and body image and eating disorders, the corresponding authorities have been lax when considering implementing initiatives aimed at addressing these attitudes and behaviours. Efforts carried out in most western countries, such as Spain, aimed at promoting positive body images, have been few and weak. Moreover, when compared to the resources the different socialising agents have to respond to these interventions (i.e. the cosmetics industry via mass advertising campaigns can override most public health campaigns).

The steps that have been taken by all concerned in the direction of promoting healthy and positive body images and preventing disorders are clearly insufficient. Hence, a clear association should be made between research, public policy and good practice, so to establish clear directives for interventions and programmes. However, although this task will not be easy given the amount of economic interests vested in body appearance in Western society, robust awareness campaigns are required since at present there does not appear to be many public policies that protect and promote a common good associated with a positive body image. The argument for or against image regulations and sociocultural pressure is not a specific topic in the arena of public health. Nevertheless, as in other fields of research and treatment, there is an increasing awareness of these issues by various organisations, professionals in the field of health and education and patients and their relatives, who are willing to support initiatives that lead to health promotion. But the underlying question that remains is whether or not society as a whole is in agreement. Are the actors involved concerned enough to agree to change? And are industries that profit from increased body awareness and obsessions willing to adopt measures for change?

On the other hand, the implementation of assessment procedures for adopted health promotion measures would require a common focus and language (Calado, 2011). This would also call for the collaboration of different sectors with the required conceptual and practical know-how in the area of health, research and society. Furthermore, this collaboration would allow the development of previously proposed health determinants and individual indicators that could provide information on the effects of possible measures to be implemented. Establishing specific indicators is essential for an evaluation of interventions in priority problems with the aim of finding solutions. The results of promoting health through scientific research are particularly important. This means that we are able to learn from previous positive and negative experiences, and to replicate those projects, programmes and plans that have proven most cost-effective. Taking into account the changing nature of reality, follow-up monitoring is an essential procedure in determining not only the degree of acceptance and compliance with those measures but also future courses of action.

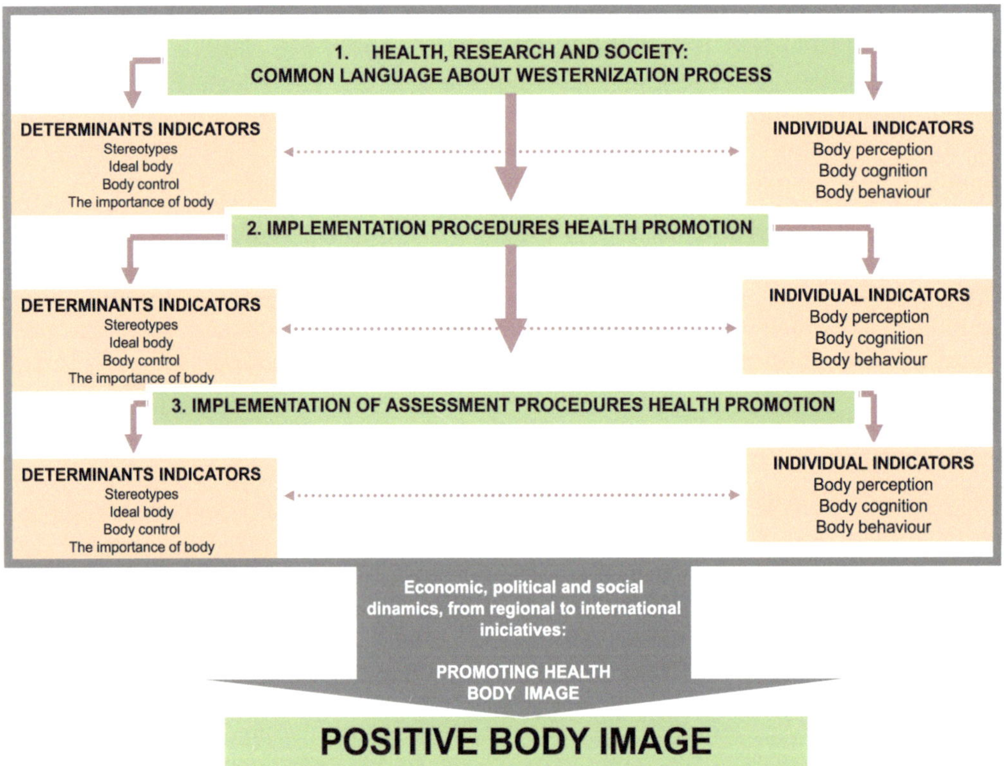


Fig. 3. Promoting health for a positive body image.

The discussion of solutions should involve regional, national and international initiatives, and it should include economic, political and social aspects of social dynamics. This perspective, therefore, underlines the idea that the concept of prevention and health promotion in relation to body image should be seen as dynamic and multidimensional. This implies a starting point that considers not only gender but also other factors such as age or ethnicity, which have not been as frequently addressed. We must consider that to date the majority of prevention programmes at individual level have not reflected the characteristics of ethnic and cultural minorities, and differences in terms of social status or habitat, such as large cities, urban or rural areas.

Finally, it is necessary that the media takes an active part in promoting a positive and healthy body image. Media advocacy requires an integrated approach drawing from community-based strategies and combining them with innovative media technology to target public policy debate and decisions (Hesse-Biber et al. 2006) and gender equity (Calado, 2011).

## 7. Conclusion

This chapter suggests that mainly social factors can provide a powerful theoretical framework through which to assess the influence of mass media messages of thinness on women and men. The Western thin and muscular ideals are facilitated by cosmetic, fashion, diet and mass media industries, which are crucial structural elements of current global markets. Even if these standards by gender do not have the same impact on everyone, the majority of our populations feel the restrain in one way or another. However, these economic and consumption interests are likely responsible for maintaining unrealistic body ideals, endorsing self-improvement and self-control and influencing the social-economic status of most women and men of different races, classes and ethnicities.

The chapter has offered an overview of the situation of body image in Western societies and highlighted ways of addressing the problems outlined and, more importantly, the steps that need to be taken to create a society free of unhealthy gender-specific body image standards. In conclusion, all these considerations suggest that if certain harmful aspects of lifestyle that contribute to negative body images and eating behaviours are to be altered, it is necessary to carry out social interventions to change personal motivations that can lead to disorders. There is a need, therefore, for a social and health sciences approach, advocating a biopsychosocial model, where psychological distress would be the result of complex interaction between biological, psychological and social variables. The goal would be the acquisition of good health linked to a positive body image in women and men, and understood as the ability to function satisfactorily in different social contexts without interferences associated with body image.

## 8. References

Akan, G. E. & Grilo, C. M. (1995). Sociocultural influences on eating attitudes and behaviors, body image, and psychological functioning: A comparison of African- American, Asian-American, and Caucasian college women. *International Journal of Eating Disorders,* 18, 181–187.

Akiba, D. (1998). Cultural variations in body esteem: how young adults in Iran and the United States view their own appearances. *Journal of Social Psychology,* 138, 539-40.

Alegria, M., Woo, M., Cao, Z., Torres, M., Meng, X.L. & Striegel-Moore, R. (2007). Prevalence and correlates of eating disorders in Latinos in the United States. *International Journal of Eating Disorders,* 40, S15-21.

Aubrey, J. S. (2006). Effects of sexually objectifying media on self-objectification and body surveillance in undergraduates: Results of a 2-year panel study. *Journal of Communication,* 56, 366-386.

Becker, A. E. (2004). Television, disordered eating, and young women in Fiji: negotiating body image and identity during rapid social change. *Culture, Medicine and Psychiatry,* 28, 533-559.

Blaine, B., & McElroy, (2002). Selling stereotypes: weight loss infomercials, sexism, and weightism. *Sex Roles,* 46, 345-351.

Blowers, L.C., Loxton, N. J., Flesser, M.G., Occhipinti, S. & Dawe, S. (2003) The Relationship between socio-cultural pressure to be thin and body dissatisfaction in preadolescent girls. *Eating Behaviors,* 4, 229–244.

Calado, M. (2010). *Guía de psicoeducación y autoayuda en trastornos alimentarios*. Pirámide, Madrid.

Calado (2011). *Liberarse de las apariencias: Género e imagen corporal*. Madrid: Pirámide

Caradas, A.A., Lambert, E.V & Charlton, K.E. (2001). An ethnic comparison of eating attitudes and associated body image concerns in adolescent South African schoolgirls. *Journal of Human Nutrition and Dietetics*, 14, 111-120.

Chisuwa, N. & O'Dea, J. (2010). Body image and eating disorders amongst Japanese adolescents. A review of the literature. *Appetite*, 54, 5-15.

Cocimano, G. (2004). *Los mutantes de la cirugía estética. El credo de las apariencias*. Letralia: tierra de letras. 116. Retrieved from http://www.letralia.com/116/articulo04.htm.

Crandall, C. S., & Martínez, R. (1996). Culture, ideology, and antifat attitudes. *Personality and Social Psychology Bulletin*, 22, 1165-1176.

Cusumano, D. L., & Thompson, J. K. (1997). Body image and body shape ideals in magazines: Exposure, awareness, and intenalization. *Sex Roles*, 37 (9-10), 701-721.

Cummins, L. & Lehman, J. (2007). Eating disorders and body image concerns in asian american women: assessment and treatment from a multicultural and feminist perspective. *Eating Disorders*, 15, 217-230.

Dohnt, H., & Tiggemann, M. (2006). The contribution of peer and media influences to the development of body satisfaction and self-esteem in young girls: A prospective study. *Developmental Psychology, 42*, 929-936.

Edwards, S., & Launder, C. (2000). Investigating muscularity concerns in male body image: development of the Swansea Muscularity Attitudes Questionnaire. *International Journal of Eating Disorders*, 28, 120-124.

Favaro, A., Ferrara, S. & Santonastaso, P. (2003). The spectrum of eating disorders in young women: a prevalence study in a general population sample. *Psychosomatic Medicine*, 65, 701-8

Farquhar, J. C. & Wasylkiw, L. (2007). Media images of men: Trenes and consequences of body conceptualization. *Psychology of Men and Masculinity*, 8, 145-160.

Fouts, G., & Burggraf, K. (1999). Television situation comedies: Female body images and verbal reinforcements. *Sex Roles*, 40 (5/6), 473-481.

Fouts, G., & Burggraf, K. (2000). Television situation comedies: Female weight, male negative comments and audience reactions. *Sex Roles*, 42 (9/10), 925-932.

Fouts, G., & Vaughan, K. (2002). Television situation comedies: male weight, negative references, and audience reactions. *Sex Roles*, 46 (11/12), 439-442.

Frith, K., Shaw, P. & Cheng, H. (2006). The construction of beauty: a cross-cultural analysis of women's magazine advertising. *Journal of Communication*, 55, 56-70.

Gandarillas, A., Zorrilla, B., Sepulveda, A. R., & Munoz, E. (2003). *Trastornos del Comportamiento Alimentario: prevalencia de casos clínicos en mujeres adolescentes de la Comunidad de Madrid*. (vol. 85) Documentos Técnicos de Salud Pública; Instituto de Salud Publica, Madrid.

Garner, D. M., Garfinkel, P. E., Schwartz, D., & Thompson, M. (1980). Cultural expectations of thinness in women. *Psychological Reports*, 47, 483-491.

Grabe, S., Ward, L. M., & Hyde, J. S. (2008). The role of the media in body image concerns among women: A meta-analysis of experimental and correlational studies. *Psychological Bulletin*, 134, 460-476.

Groesz, L. M., Levine, M. P., & Murnen, S. K. (2002). The effect of experimental presentation of thin media images on body satisfaction: a meta-analytic review. *International Journal of Eating Disorders*, 31, 1-16.

Grogan, S. (2006). Body image and health: contemporary perspectives. *Journal of Health Psychology*, 11, 523-530.

Haas, C.F., Champion, A. & Secor, D. (2008). Motivating factors for seeking cosmetic surgery: a synthesis of the literature. *Plastic Surgical Nurses*, 28, 177-82.

Halliwell, E., & Dittmar, H. (2003). A qualitative investigation of women's and men's body image concerns and their attitudes toward aging. *Sex Roles*, 49, 675-684.

Harrison, K., & Hefner, V. (2006). Media exposure, current and future body ideals, and disordered eating among preadolescent girls: A longitudinal panel study. *Journal of Youth and Adolesence*, 35, 153-163.

Hatoum, I. D. & Belle, D. (2004). Mags and abs: media consumption and bodily concerns in men. *Sex Roles*, 51, 397-407.

Hesse-Biber, S., Howling, S. A., Leavy, P., & Lovejoy, M. (2004). Racial identity and the development body image issues among African American adolescent girls. *The Qualitative Report*, 9, 49-79.

Hesse-Biber, S., Leavy, P., Quinn, C.E., & Zoino, J. (2006). The mass marketing of disordered eating and eating disorders: the social psychology of women, thinness and culture. *Women's Studies International Forum*, 29, 208-224.

Hildebrandt, T., Langenbucher, J. & Schlundt, D.G. (2004). Muscularity concerns among men: development of attitudinal and perceptual measures. *Body Image*, 2, 169 -181.

Hildebrandt, T., Walker, D.C., Alfano, L., Delinsky, S. & Bannon, K. (2010). Development and validation of a male specific body checking questionnaire. *International Journal of Eating Disorders*, 43, 77-87.

Hogan, M. J. & Strasburger, V. C. (2008). Body image, eating disorders, and the media. *Adolescent Medicine - State of the Art Reviews*, 19, 521-546.

Hospers, H. J. & Jansen, A. (2005). Why homosexuality is a risk factor for eating disorders in males. *Journal of Social and Clinical Psychology*, 24, 1188-1201.

Hrabosky, J. I., & Grilo C.M. (2007). Body image and eating disordered behavior in a community sample of Black and Hispanic women. *Eating Behavior*, 8, 106-114.

Huon, G.F., Mingyi, Q., Oliver, K. & Xiao, G. (2002). A large-scale survey of eating disorder symptomatology among female adolescents in the People's Republic of China. *International Journal Eating Disorders*, 32, 192-205.

Leit, R. A., Pope, H. G., & Gray, J. J. (2001). Cultural expectations of muscularity in men: The evolution of Playgirl centerfolds. *International Journal of Eating Disorders*, 29 (1), 90-93.

López-Guimera, G., Levine, M. P., Sánchez-Carracedo, D., & Fauquet, J. (2010). Influence of Mass Media on Body Image and Eating Disordered Attitudes and Behaviors in Females: A Review of Effects and Processes. *Media Psychology*, 13, 387-416.

Martinez-Benlloch, I. (Coord.) (2001). *Genero, desarrollo psico-social y trastornos de la imagen corporal. Colección de estudios 71*. Instituto de la Mujer. Ministerio de Trabajos y Asuntos Sociales, Madrid

Mayville, S.B, Williamson, D.A, White, M. A, Netemeyer, R.G, & Drab, D.L. (2002). Development of the Muscle Appearance Satisfaction Scale. *Assessment*, 9, 351-360.

McCreary, D. R., & Sasse, D. K. (2000). Exploring drive for muscularity in adolescent boys and girls. *Journal of American College Health*, 48, 297-304.

Murray, S. B., Rieger, E., Touyz, S. W., & De la Garza García Lic Y. (2010). Muscle dysmorphia and the DSM-V conundrum: where does it belong? A review paper. *International Journal of Eating Disorders*, 43, 483-491.

Nasser, M. (1994). Screening for abnormal eating attitudes in a population of Egyptian secondary school girls. *Social Psychiatry and Psychiatric Epidemiology*, 29, 25-30.

Nobakht, M. & Dezhkam, M. (2000). An epidemiological study of eating disorders in Iran. *International Journal Eating Disorder*, 28, 265-71.

Patton, G.C., Selzer, R., Coffey, C., Carlin, J.B., & Wolfe, R. (1999). Onset of adolescent eating disorders: population based cohort study over 3 years. British Medical Journal, 318, 765-768.

Perez-Gaspar, M., Gual, P., Irala-Estevez, J., Martinez-Gonzalez, M. A., Lahortiga, F., & Cervera, S. (2000). Prevalence of eating disorders in a representative sample of female adolescents from Navarra (Spain). *Medicina Clinica*, 114, 481-486.

Plaza, J. F. (2005). *Modelos de varón y mujer en las revistas femeninas para adolescentes: la representación de los famosos*. Fundamentos, Madrid.

Pope, C.G., Pope, H.G., Menard, W., Fay, C., Olivardia, R. & Phillips, K. (2005). Clinical features of muscle dysmorphia among males with body dysmorphic disorder. *Body Image*, 2, 395–400.

Ricciardelli, L.A., McCabe, M.P., Williams, R.J. & Thompson, J.K. (2007). The role of ethnicity and culture in body image and disordered eating among males. *Clinical Psychology Review*, 27, 582-606.

Silverstein, B., Perdue, L., Peterson, B., Vogel, L., & Fantini, D.A. (1986). Possible causes of the thin standard of bodily attractiveness for women. International *Journal of Eating Disorders*, 5, 907-916.

Soh, NL., Touyz, S. & Surgenor, L. (2006). Eating and body image disturbances across cultures: a review. *European Eating Disorder Review*, 14, 54-65.

Spitzer, B. L., Henderson, K. A., & Zivian, M. T. (1999). Gender differences in population versus media body sizes: a comparison over four decades. *Sex Roles*, 40 (7), 545-565.

Toro, J., Cervera, M., & Pérez, P. (1989). Body shape publicity and anorexia nervosa. *Social Psychiatry and Psychiatric Epidemiology*, 23, 132-136.

Tylka, T. L., Bergeron, D., & Schwartz, J. P. (2005). Development and evaluation of the Male Body Attitudes Scale (MBAS). *Body Image*, 2,161-175.

Veale, D., Kinderman, P., Riley, S. & Lambrou, C. (2003). Self-discrepancy in body dysmorphic disorder. *British Journal Clinical Psychology*, 42, 157-169.

Wiseman, C. V., Gray, J. J., Mosimann, J. E., & Ahrens, A. H. (1992). Cultural expectations of thinness in women: An update. *International Journal of Eating Disorders*, 11, 85-89.

World Health Organization (WHO) (2004). *Promoción de la salud mental. Conceptos, evidencia emergente, práctica*. WHO, Ginebra.

# 4

# Biological Gender, Sexual Orientation and Gender Role in Eating Disorders

Paolo Cotrufo, Mara Iannaccone and Stefania Cella
*Observatory on Eating Disorders, Department of Psychology,*
*Second University of Naples,*
*Italy*

## 1. Introduction

Richard Morton, an English physician, provided the first medical description of an eating disorder, disordered man in 1689 (Morton, 1694). The patient was described as "The Son of the Reverend Minister Steele." At the age of 16, he began to fast. Morton attributed his "want of appetite" to "studying too hard" as well as to the "passions of his mind": Morton prescribed him to abandon his studies and move to the country. The doctor was successful with his patient, who followed his advices.

During the last century, information on eating disorders in men has been mostly limitated to single-case reports (Falstein et al., 1956; Leger et al., 1969; Beumont et al., 1972). Only since the late 1980, researchers have reported some studies of moderate sample size (Pope et al., 1986; Schneider & Agras, 1987; Fichter & Daser, 1987).

Yet, despite eating pathologies have been traditionally associated with females, they are not rare among males: it is estimated, in fact, that 5-10% of anorexia nervosa patients (Oyebode et al., 1998) and 10-15% of bulimia nervosa patients are men (Carlat & Camargo, 1991). Hoek et al. (2003) found a 0.8 incidence rate (female: male ratio = 27:1) for bulimia and below a 0.5 incidence rate for anorexia in a population of 100,000 subjects. However, eating disorders may be increasing among males: compared to the past, in fact, other studies point out a prevailing upward trend (Carlat et al., 1997; Nelson et al., 1999; Kjelsas et al., 2004).

So, researches examining both sexes have been conducted to investigate the peculiar features - if any - of anorexia in men, and gender differences in eating pathologies. The onset of the disorder, that Hilde Bruch (1973) believed to occur at an earlier stage in male subjects, is actually similar to that in females (Fichter et al., 1985; Crisp et al., 1986). Forman-Hoffman et al. (2008) have found that the eating disorders age of onset in males appeared to have a single peak at about the age of 14. Patients with older ages of onset, unlike those with younger ages of onset, reported lower percentage of mean matched population weight and a longer period of disorder. This study, according to the authors, confirmed the results of previous studies carried out on female samples.

Similar clinical pictures for male and female patients with eating disorders have been described (Hall et al., 1985; Crisp et al., 1986; Braun et al., 1999). Olivardia et al. (1995), in a study designed to assess the characteristics of eating-disordered men, concluded that eating psychopathologies appear to display noticeably similar features in affected individuals of both genders. However, differences have also been found.

Males are more preoccupied by food, weight, and show more hyperactivity, more achievement orientation and more sexual anxiety than females (Fichter et al., 1985). In a review on bulimia nervosa in men, Carlat & Camargo (1991) have found higher prevalence of premorbid obesity, homosexuality and asexuality, and less concern with strict weight control in bulimic males than females.

Therefore, homosexuality appears to be more frequent among men, especially among those who develop bulimia nervosa (Carlat et al., 1997; Grabhorn et al., 2003). Furthermore, males with an eating disorder differ from females because there is the occurrence of a stronger psychiatric comorbidity and a higher rate of suicide attempts (Bramon-Bosch et al., 2000).

Higher rates of premorbid obesity and overweight result to be more common in males than in females (Sharp et al., 1994; Fernández -Aranda et al., 2004), as well as a higher perfectionism and interpersonal distrust (Joiner et al., 2000). As Lewinsohn et al. (2002) have indicated in their study, excessive exercising is more frequent in men than in women. Moreover, the absolute proportion of individuals wanting or having sought treatment is very low in both groups but, at comparable levels of problematic eating behaviors, females are more likely to have sought treatment than males.

In addition to eating pathology, men may show signs of "muscle dysmorphia" or "reverse anorexia" (Harvey & Robinson, 2003). This disorder is characterized by the drive to increase their muscle mass, which may cause distress, body dissatisfaction, and feeling of ineffectiveness, occupational dysfunction, impaired social activities and relationship. Although the studies aimed at monitoring comorbidity between reverse anorexia and eating disorders highlight the resemblance of some traits (Davis & Scott-Robertson, 2000; Olivardia et al., 2000; Goldfield et al., 2006), no studies are available up to date which can explain this similarity in empirical terms. Conceptually, reverse anorexia is included in the body dysmorphic disorder, and the concern for not being muscular enough may be determined by a distorted perception of one's own body image (H.G. Pope et al., 1997; Olivardia et al., 2001; C.G. Pope et al., 2005). Even though there are no epidemiologic works indicating the spreading of this disorder (Olivardia, 2001), it is believed that 5% of males who do body building suffer from reverse anorexia (Pope et al., 1997) and that 9% of the subjects with body dysmorphism focus their feeling of ineffectiveness on muscles (Pope et al., 2000).

Even if the most relevant researchers on this disorder, as Pope and Olivardia, finally believe those features closer to dysmorphism than to eating disorders, the relevance in reverse anorexia patients psychopathology of the drive to increase their muscular mass could be considered the proper "reverse" of the anorectic drive for thinness. Consequently, the cultural bond between muscle mass and virility, if compared with the bond between thinness and the lack of feminine body shape, could open, in our opinion, a fertile topic of research and theoretical investigation on the importance of gender, sexual orientation, sexual impairments on body identity features.

## 2. Sexual orientation and eating disorders in male population

The studies mentioned so far have shown that features such as homosexuality and asexuality may be distinctive of male eating disorders, so, these topics have attracted researchers increasing attention. The emphasis on sexual orientation suggests that there may be an association with eating psychopathologies. In literature, ample evidence supports this suggestion: in fact, among the studies of eating-disordered men, those that report sexual orientation of subjects show that a considerable number of these men are homosexual, bisexual or asexual.

Anorexic and bulimic males report greater problems in terms of sexual isolation, sexual inactivity and conflictual homosexuality than anorexic and bulimic females (Herzog et al., 1984).

Five of the 9 male patients with bulimia nervosa, described by Robinson & Holden (1986), showed atypical sexuality, while only a little evidence of increased homosexuality or "sexual conflict" in 15 male bulimic patients, was found by Pope et al. (1986). Nevertheless, the definition of "homosexual activity" as at least one homosexual experience to orgasm within the preceding five years, which study assessment was based on, could be considered only partially adequate.

In their study, Fichter & Daser (1987) have found that male and female anorexia nervosa patients share more features in common than dissimilarities on symptomatology. However, they observed that anorexic men also show several signs of disturbed psychosexual and gender identity development. Therefore, the authors concluded males with uncertain gender identity have a remarkably higher risk of developing an eating disorder during adolescence than males with a less indefinite gender identity.

A comparison between a sample of 15 bulimic male subjects and one of 15 bulimic female subjects has highlighted a statistically significant difference about marriage and sexual preference. Most females, in fact, were married and most males declared a homosexual or bisexual preference (Schneider & Agras, 1987). Therefore, sexual identity concerns seem to be a distinctive feature of males with eating disorders (Farrow, 1992).

Carlat et al. (1997) carried out a research on 135 subjects diagnosed with an eating pathology: 42% of the bulimic male patients were identified as homosexuals or bisexuals, and 58% of the anorexic patients were identified as asexual.

### 2.1 Studies on natural samples of homosexual males

The findings of clinical samples researches have lead to further investigations on the bond between sexual orientation and increased risk for eating disorder symptoms in natural samples, in order to hypothesize the why and how of the higher eating disorders prevalence among gay and bisexual males.

Homosexual orientation is associated with dysfunctional eating patterns and higher rates of body dissatisfaction (French et al., 1996); furthermore, it appears to be a specific risk factor for eating disorder psychopathology in males (Russel & Keel, 2002).

A research study carried out by Yelland & Tiggemann (2003) compared a group of 52 homosexual males with a control group of heterosexual males and a group of 55 heterosexual females. The outcomes showed concern about physical appearance and psychological characteristics typically associated with eating disorders, which made the sample of homosexual males more similar to heterosexual females than to the control males.

Moreover, homosexuals showed higher values than controls with regard to the drive to increase muscle mass.

Kaminski et al. (2005) have used, for their study, a self-report instrument specifically designed to assess men's eating attitudes and behaviors, exercise, and body image (Male Eating Behavior and Body Image Evaluation). The authors found gay men to be more likely to experience poor body image and related eating disorders symptomatology than straight men.

In a study on sexually active male adolescents, Ackard et al. (2008) found eating disorder symptoms were more prevalent among males who reported a greater number of sexual partners, irrespective of gender of sex partner, and those who reported having male sexual partners.

According to some authors, attending to a gay recreational group is related to lower levels of eating disturbance, so, it may be considered as a protective factor against eating problems (Williamson & Spence, 2001). Actually, Feldman & Meyer (2007) have showed that the participation in the gay community is significantly associated to higher subclinical eating disorders' prevalence.

In conclusion, several empirical studies confirm homosexuality to be a risk factor *per se* in the development of an eating disorder in males. The most recurrent explanation for this findings is that gay are more worried about their look and, therefore, less satisfied with their bodies and more vulnerable to eating problems in order to attract other men. In fact, men give more importance to physical beauty than women, when choosing their mate. So, the homosexual man who has to attract another man is more preoccupied about his physical appearance (Siever, 1994). In this supposition gay culture and gay communities have also been implicated, as within these great emphasis is placed upon the importance of physical attractiveness. Males may feel themselves pressured to conform to this value that, increasing vulnerability to body dissatisfaction, could make them more prone to eating pathologies (Beren et al., 1996; Yelland & Tiggeman, 2003; Hospers & Jansen, 2005).

## 3. Sexual orientation and eating disorders in female population

Researches aiming to investigate the relationship between sexual orientation and eating pathology in female population have produced heterogeneous and unclear results.

First, lesbians appear to be less exposed to risk of eating disorder symptoms. Homosexual women's greater body satisfaction and lower concern with weight and appearance may contribute to their lower rates of eating disorders (Siever, 1994). As support to this assumption, some researches revealed fewer dysfunctional eating attitudes and behaviors in homosexual women than in heterosexuals (Schneider et al., 1995; Lakkis et al., 1999; Strong et al., 2000).

Herzog et al. (1992) found that homosexual women were less concerned with weight than heterosexual woman, they were more satisfied with their bodies, had a significantly higher body weight ideal and consequently a lower drive for thinness. Similarly, heterosexual females showed greater concern with their weight and physical appearance, higher anxiety about being overweight, and more dieting behavior (Gettleman & Thompson, 1993). Brand et al. (1992) reported higher concern with body weight and dieting in heterosexual women and homosexual men. Actually, in this study, gender was more strongly related to body satisfaction than was sexual orientation. Lesbians and heterosexual women, in fact, showed more body dissatisfaction and reported greater frequency of dieting than gay or heterosexual men. A comparison between samples of heterosexual, homosexual and bisexual males and females has showed major differences between homosexual and heterosexual males with regard to body dissatisfaction, the resort to compensatory strategies and binge eating episodes. The sample of homosexual females showed lower body dissatisfaction than heterosexuals, even though they were not less likely to report dieting, binge eating or unhealthy weight control behaviors (French et al., 1996).

Lesbian subcultures have been described to downplay the importance of physical attractiveness and traditional ideals of beauty (Striegel-Moore, 1990). Within this context, one hypothesis has been that lesbians generally do not suffer from body image problems or disordered eating because they are not vulnerable to cultural pressures to be thin as most heterosexual women do (Brown, 1987). Some researchers argue that lesbians may be subject to less pressure with regard to their physical attractiveness and, consequently, are less dissatisfied with their bodies (Brown, 1987; Barron, 1998) and less vulnerable to eating disorders than heterosexual women (Siever, 1994). LaTorre and Wendenburg (1983) found that women who reported same-sex sexual experiences were generally more satisfied with both their sexual activities and activities and their bodies than were women who only reported heterosexual experiences. By contrast, emphasis on appearance has been thought to put homosexual males at risk from body dissatisfaction and eating problems (Carlat & Camargo, 1991; Herzog et al., 1992; Siever, 1994; Russell & Keel, 2002).

These evidences support a model where lesbianism might be seen as a protective factor against disordered eating attitudes. Other studies, conversely, have found no major differences between hetero- and homosexual women concerning body dissatisfaction (Beren et al., 1996; Striegel-Moore et al., 1990), with regard to the presence of dysfunctional eating attitudes and behaviors (Streigel-Moore et al., 1990; Beren et al., 1996; Share & Mintz, 2002; Moore & Keel, 2003) or in rates of eating disorders (French et al., 1996). For example, Heffernan (1996) reported that lesbians were not significantly different from heterosexual women in attitudes concerning body weight and appearance or dieting. In addition, no bulimia nervosa prevalence differences, among lesbians and heterosexual women, were found, but binge eating disorder resulted more frequent.

In contrast, Striegel-Moore et al. (1990) found a stronger association between body esteem and self-esteem in homosexual women and higher rates of bingeing in homosexual women compared to heterosexuals. Particularly, lesbian undergraduates students reported lower self-esteem, higher interpersonal distrust and difficulties in identifying their own emotions, than heterosexual students did. Body esteem was found to be related more closely with self-esteem in lesbians, than in heterosexual students. Similar results have been found by Wichstrøm (2006): a same-sex sexual experience, among a natural female population increased the prevalence of bulimic symptoms in a 5-year follow-up.

These findings seem to support the hypothesis that lesbian experience is associated with greater body dissatisfaction and abnormal eating behaviors.

## 4. Body dissatisfaction, abnormal eating behaviors and eating disorder attitude in homo and heterosexuals

Starting from these considerations, we have conducted a study to assess the body satisfaction, the presence of abnormal eating behaviors and the presence of eating disorders psychological characteristics in a natural population of homosexuals and heterosexuals, both male and female (Cella et al., 2010).

We screened 110 homosexuals (85 males and 25 females) and 121 heterosexuals (85 males and 36 females), aged 18-50, by means of: a) an *ad hoc* socio-demographic schedule; b) the *Eating Disorders Inventory 2* (Garner, 1991); c) the *Eating Disorders Inventory 2 – Symptom Checklist* (Garner, 1991); d) The *Body Uneasiness Test* (Cuzzolaro et al., 2000).

Overall, the results obtained appear to be similar to those reported in the literature. No significant differences have emerged between hetero- and homosexual females with respect to the presence of dysfunctional eating attitudes and behaviors (Table 1, 2). Conversely, in the homosexual male sample, higher concern is expressed about body image and those psychological features the literature often considers being related to, or indicators of, a risk factor for ED onset. Furthermore these features make the sample of homosexual males more similar to the group of females (homo- and heterosexuals) than to the heterosexual males (Schneider et al., 1995). Despite having a lower BMI, homosexual men show a higher body dissatisfaction, drive for thinness and ineffectiveness than the sample of heterosexual males; moreover they show a smaller ability to recognise and distinguish feelings and emotions, a lower ability in the impulse regulation and a higher social insecurity (Table 2). Regarding to

| | | Average scores | | | |
|---|---|---|---|---|---|
| | p | **Homosexual men (N=85)** | **Heterosexual men (N=85)** | **Homosexual women (N=25)** | **Heterosexual women (N=36)** |
| **Age** | .841 | 27.54 | 28.75 | 28.68 | 27.94 |
| **Body Mass Index** | **.001** | 24.02 | 25.89 | 26.93 | 23.43 |
| | | N (%) | | | |
| **Socioeconomic background** | .192 | | | | |
| Low | | 56 (67%) | 47 (55.3%) | 12 (48%) | 25 (71.4%) |
| High | | 27 (32.5%) | 38 (44.7%) | 13 (52%) | 10 (28.6%) |
| **Abnormal eating behaviors** | | | | | |
| Diet | .163 | 22 (26.5%) | 22 (26.2%) | 12 (48%) | 12 (33.3%) |
| Binge eating | .139 | 45 (54.2%) | 51 (60%) | 10 (40%) | 16 (45.7%) |
| Compensatory Strategies | **.002** | 12 (14.6%) | 0 | 4 (16%) | 3 (8.6%) |
| Weight control | .504 | 45 (58.4%) | 53 (64.6%) | 6 (26.1%) | 11 (31.4%) |
| **Drive for thinness ≥ 14** | **.019** | 8 (9.4%) | 2 (2.5%) | 3 (12%) | 7 (19.4%) |
| **Cut-off GSI** | **.000** | 29 (34.5%) | 10 (11.8%) | 11 (44%) | 14 (38.9%) |

Table 1. Socio-demographic characteristics and eating behaviors of the male homosexual (N=85), male heterosexual (N=85), female homosexual (N=25) and female heterosexual (N=36) sample

dysfunctional eating behaviors, they show a higher trend towards the binge eatings and the use of strategies to compensate weight gain than heterosexuals (Table 1). In all these areas they do not show any major differences from both groups of hetero- and homosexual women. Unlike the data reported in the literature (Feldman & Meyer, 2007), this sample showed no difference as a consequence of being or not being members of an association of homosexuals. The presence or absence of a stable relationship appears, furthermore, as an important variable in differentiating the homosexual men with a greater body image concern, which may lead to disordered eating. The results indicate that homosexual men not engaged in a sentimental relationship, if compared to those who are engaged, show higher concern for their physical appearance, higher levels of avoidance behaviors related to the body image and feelings of detachment and alienation in relation to their body, deeper feelings of ineffectiveness, lower capacity to accurately recognise and distinguish feelings and emotional states and a lower ability in the impulse regulation (Table 3). It seems plausible that the presence of a stable relationship may lead these individuals towards a

| | | Average scores | | | |
|---|---|---|---|---|---|
| | p | Homosexual men (N=85) | Heterosexual men (N=85) | Homosexual women (N=25) | Heterosexual women (N=36) |
| **EDI 2 scales** | | | | | |
| Drive for thinness | **.000**[a] | 4.38 | 2.09 | 6.52 | 6.42 |
| Bulimia | **.001**[a] | 2.55 | .93 | 3.04 | 2.75 |
| Body dissatisfaction | **.001**[b] | 5.34 | 5.13 | 9.20 | 8.66 |
| Ineffectiveness | **.000**[a] | 4.72 | 2.08 | 6.24 | 4.78 |
| Perfectionism | .861 | 4.17 | 3.68 | 3.88 | 4.00 |
| Interpersonal distrust | .422 | 4.05 | 3.56 | 4.28 | 3.03 |
| Interoceptive awareness | **.000**[a] | 5.73 | 2.05 | 4.48 | 4.17 |
| Maturity fears | .588 | 6.02 | 5.42 | 4.80 | 5.25 |
| Asceticism | .846 | 3.62 | 3.75 | 4.20 | 3.92 |
| Impulse regulation | **.000**[a] | 6.09 | 2.89 | 5.88 | 3.36 |
| Social insecurity | **.002**[c] | 5.14 | 3.44 | 6.44 | 5.97 |
| **BUT scales** | | | | | |
| Weight Phobia | **.000**[a] | 1.48 | .86 | 1.74 | 1.76 |
| Body Image Concern | **.000**[a] | 1.20 | .74 | 1.56 | 1.55 |
| Compulsive Self Monitoring | **.000**[a] | 1.24 | .59 | 1.03 | 1.10 |
| Avoidance | **.002**[a] | .66 | .23 | .74 | .45 |
| Depersonalization | **.000**[a] | .79 | .31 | .97 | .75 |
| Global Severity Index | **.000**[a] | 1.0 | .57 | 1.27 | 1.34 |

[a]= homosexual men = homosexual women = heterosexual women ≠ heterosexual men
[b]= homosexual women = heterosexual women ≠ homosexual men= heterosexual men
[c]= heterosexual men ≠ homosexual women = heterosexual women; homosexual men = homosexual women = heterosexual women

Table 2. The comparison between male homosexual (N=85), male heterosexual (N=85), female homosexual (N=25) and female heterosexual (N=36) sample in the individual Eating Disorders Inventory 2 (EDI-2) and Body Uneasiness Test (BUT) scales

greater acceptance of their body image and to a lower suffering related to the uneasiness this may generate. From this point of view, homosexual relationship may promote satisfaction and acceptance of one's own body; is an alternative explanation possible? It could be possible to hypothesize that subjects who experience greater body image satisfaction and who show lower concern with their own body weight and shape, tend to be more interpersonally oriented and likely to have a sexual partner and to engage a stable relationship. Actually, considering the homosexual women, no differences emerged with respect of these variables.

Our findings seem to support the hypothesis, therefore, that homosexual orientation is associated with greater body dissatisfaction and abnormal eating behaviors in males, in particular among those who claimed they were not in a stable sentimental relationship.

Our hypothesis, from a psychodynamic point of view, is that the biological gender is not a risk factor per se, as reported in the literature, but rather the feminine component of the sexuality. Obviously, the femininity is present, in different proportion, in every subject, both male and female, both homo and heterosexual. This topic although suggested in theoretical terms (Cotrufo, 2005), has not been the subject of reliable empirical studies and, in our opinion, would require further analysis. Moreover, future studies might benefit from research on the relationship between sexual orientation and eating disorders, which considered the subjects' femininity/masculinity as variables independent of gender and sexual orientation.

| | | Average scores | |
|---|---|---|---|
| | p | **Sentimental relationship (N=18)** | **No sentimental relationship (N=63)** |
| **EDI 2 scales** | | | |
| Drive for thinness | .265 | 2.67 | 4.90 |
| Bulimia | .096 | .94 | 2.86 |
| Body dissatisfaction | .070 | 2.94 | 5.79 |
| Ineffectiveness | **.024** | 2.00 | 5.37 |
| Perfectionism | .267 | 2.72 | 4.63 |
| Interpersonal distrust | .261 | 2.67 | 4.46 |
| Interoceptive awareness | **.027** | 2.39 | 6.67 |
| Maturity fears | .295 | 4.39 | 6.32 |
| Asceticism | .115 | 2.56 | 4.00 |
| Impulse regulation | **.026** | 2.89 | 6.90 |
| Social insecurity | .396 | 3.89 | 5.63 |
| **BUT scales** | | | |
| Weight Phobia | .199 | 1.02 | 1.63 |
| Body Image Concern | **.023** | .58 | 1.40 |
| Compulsive Self Monitoring | .901 | 1.00 | 1.30 |
| Avoidance | **.034** | .22 | .80 |
| Depersonalization | **.028** | .29 | .94 |
| Global Severity Index | .064 | .61 | 1.21 |

Table 3. Influence of a "sentimental relationship" on the individual Eating Disorders Inventory 2 (EDI 2) and Body Uneasiness Test (BUT) scales in the male homosexual sample (N=85)

## 5. Gender role orientation and eating disorders: the role of masculinity and femininity

As widely described, women are more vulnerable to develop eating disorders than men (Hoek et al., 2003) and, traditionally, disordered eating has been considered as a "women's matter" (Pritchard, 2008).

The prevalence of this disease in males, therefore, is much lower than that found in females: the proportion reported in recent studies is almost one anorexic male every twenty-seven females (Hoek et al., 2003). However, numerous empirical contributions, in the literature, suggest that if you take into consideration only the homosexual males, rates rise significantly. As a consequence, a discrete series of studies aimed to understand and deepen the relationship between eating pathology and sexual orientation. Our personal contribution of research fits into this line of study, confirming most of the previous empirical evidence: there is a greater vulnerability of gay men towards eating disturbances.

Unlike biological gender, some researchers, interested in considering the relationship between sex-role orientation and eating psychopathology, are starting to suggest that gender differences in disordered eating behaviors might be best explained by the constructs of masculinity and femininity. However, studies on gender role orientation and eating disorders have not produced conclusive results. In general, femininity was associated with high levels of eating psychopathology, whereas masculinity was negatively related to abnormal eating behaviors and attitudes. In a study of interest, carried out by Meyer et al. (2001) on a group of 100 university students (40 homosexuals and 60 heterosexuals), the results showed - for the whole sample and for the group of homosexuals alone - significant correlations between the scores obtained at the EAT and the "Femininity" scale of the Bem Sex Role Inventory (Bem, 1974), and between the "masculinity" scale and healthy eating behaviors. The authors hypothesize that, unlike the masculine attitude, femininity is an important risk factor in the onset of an eating disorder, and that previous findings among homosexual groups may have been mystified by levels of femininity. Similarly, Johnson et al. (1996) found students with higher levels of self-rated social desirability and lower levels of masculinity reported higher levels of eating problems. Regarding clinical populations, research on associations between eating disturbances and gender role orientation also provides similar results. Femininity emerged as the main trait of gender identity in subjects with eating disorders, in contrast to androgynous (high scores on masculinity and femininity scales) or undifferentiated (low scores on masculinity and femininity) scales showed by male and female subjects without eating disorders (Behar et al., 2002, 2003). Eating disordered women described themselves more often as feminine (Steiger et al., 1989) and scored significantly lower on the masculinity items on the Bem Sex Role Inventory than controls (Sitnick & Katz, 1984). A meta-analytic review showed that women and men with eating disorders reported higher levels of femininity and lower of masculinity than normal controls. However, the relationship between gender role orientation and eating pathologies was small and the studies reviewed were quite heterogeneous methodologically, i.e. in terms of diagnostic criteria of anorexia or bulimia nervosa and inclusion of clinical (small samples) and nonclinical populations (mainly college students) (Murnen & Smolak, 1997). Other authors have analysed the role of femininity in eating disorders with largely similar results (Cotrufo et al., 2007).

However, some studies do not support the view that femininity is a risk factor for the development of an eating pathology. For example, in a study, carried out by Lewis & Johnson (1985) normal control women scored higher than bulimic patients on the femininity scale, so the bulimic participants did not show more feminine self concepts than healthy women. However, when subjects were classified into the four gender role types suggested by Bem (1977), the authors found more bulimic women in the "undifferentiated" category and more normals into the "androgynous" category. They concluded that this pattern could be an indicator of low self-esteem or bulimic patients' difficulties with self-definition. Similarly, in a study carried out on 68 women with anorexia nervosa and 123 women with bulimia nervosa (Hepp et al., 2005), a negative relationship between masculinity and Drive for Thinness, Bulimia and Body Dissatisfaction Eating Disorder Inventory scales was, while femininity was not associated with unhealthy eating attitudes and behaviors. However, when masculine and feminine traits were considered together, in term of the four gender role orientation categories suggested by Bem (1977), subjects with high levels of "androgyny" reported lower levels of eating disorder symptomatology than "undifferentiated" individuals, who showed higher levels of symptoms. Similarly, Behar et al. (2001) found more "androgynous" women in the control group (with no eating disorders) if compared with the eating disordered sample.

Other types of relationships between sex-role orientation and eating disorders have also been reported. In some studies, a higher masculinity is associated with higher levels of abnormal eating attitudes and behaviors (Cantrell & Ellis, 1991; Pritchard, 2008), and not in others (Williams & Ricciardelli, 2001).

Results reported in the literature on gender role orientation and eating pathology are rather contradictory and a comprehensive interpretation of those remains difficult. Methodological and theoretical heterogeneity across studies suggest the need for more accurate theorizing and more careful operational definitions (Murnen & Smolak, 1997).

## 6. Eating disorders and gender identity disorders

If it is true that it is not homosexuality *per se* that acts as a risk factor in developing an eating disorder, but rather the feminine component of sexuality, we should expect to find an association between femininity and eating disorder symptoms, regardless of biological gender, or sexual orientation of the subject. Consequently, it would be acceptable to assume a greater vulnerability to eating disorders in men who experience a strong and persistent identification with the opposite sex and who live a constant discomfort with their biological sex or sense of alienation from the sexual role of that sex, in other words in those men who suffer from a gender identity disorder (American Psychiatric Association, 2000).

The evidence of a possible coexistence between gender identity disorders and eating disorders comes from published single case studies (Fernández-Aranda et al. 2000; Hepp & Milos, 2002).

For example, Winston et al. (2004) have reported two cases of anorexia nervosa and gender identity disorder in biological males who accessed to an eating disorders service.

Vocks et al. (2008) have carried out one of the few existing studies (on a moderate sample size), to our knowledge, to discover whether individuals with a gender identity disorder (88 male-to-female transsexuals and 43 female-to-male transsexuals) differ from controls of both sexes (56 males and 116 female) and from eating-disordered individuals (62 females) in terms of eating and body image disturbances. The authors found that male-to-female transsexuals reported a higher degree of disturbed eating behavior and body image than controls of both sexes. In this regard and in contrast to male-to-female transsexuals, female-to-male transsexuals did not differ from female controls but only from male controls.

Male-to-female transsexuals performed more body checking than did female-to-male transsexuals; however, no further differences emerged between the two groups. Finally, both male-to-female transsexuals and female-to-male transsexuals showed a significantly lower degree of body image and eating disorder pathologies on each scale compared to the females with eating disorders.

Starting from those evidences, the authors have hypothesized that people with a gender identity disorder, especially male-to-female transsexuals, have a significantly higher risk of developing an eating disorder. So, it would be desirable to verify, through further studies, if these data can be confirmed, in particular datum if the indication that biological male individuals with gender identity disorders are at enhanced risk of developing eating disturbances can be empirically confirmed. Since literature on eating disorders reports a relationship between femininity and eating disorder pathology in individuals without gender identity disorder, in our opinion, it would be interesting to examine if there is an association between gender role orientation and eating disorders in individuals with gender identity disorder too.

## 7. Conclusion

Is it possible to attempt a discussion of the data we have reported?

Can these empirical evidences be included in a theoretical construct, which may give these figures a meaning?

The empirical evidence of a positive correlation between femininity and eating disorders symptoms is, in our opinion, full of implications and also provides relevant insights from a theoretical perspective.

What is it that links eating disorders and feminine sexuality? Is the hypotheses of the thinness has female ideal body shape promoted by media sufficient to give us an answer?

Is the social-cultural role progression of women involved, since the beginning of '900? Can we argue a reaction of the femininity, starting from the feminist movement in '60s, years of the great increasing of eating disorders incidence, which modify the female ideal body shape?

In a recent study, we described the importance of pubertal body transformation (Cotrufo et al., 2007) especially for female, in the eating disorders onset: it could be the "embodied" femininity itself that causes distress?

In our opinion, the answer could be the rejection of femininity/passivity, and the failure, by contemporary adolescents, of identification process in their mothers that seems to be the core of eating disorders. It is possible that this relationship is also true for males, because there is not always correspondence between psychological sex and anatomical sex: the first is not the simple cast of the second. It may be that anorexia is a disease of the femininity, rather than a disease of the female gender (Cotrufo, 2005).

## 8. References

Ackard, D.M.; Fedio, G.; Neumark-Sztainer, D. & Britt, H.R. (2008). Factors associated with disordered eating among sexually active adolescent males: gender and number of sexual partners. *Psychosomatic Medicine*, Vol. 70, No. 2, (February 2008), pp. 232-238, ISSN 0033-3174

American Psychiatric Association (2000). *Diagnostic and statistical manual of mental disorders* (4th edition), American Psychiatric Publishing, Inc., ISBN 978-0890420256, Washington, DC

Barron, N. (1998). Living into my body, In: *Looking queer: Body image and identity in lesbian, bisexual, gay, and transgender communities,* D. Atkins, (Ed.), 5–15, Harrington Press, ISBN 978-1560239314, New York

Behar, R.; De la Barrera, M. & Michelotti, J. (2001). Gender identity and eating disorders. *Revista médica de Chile,* Vol. 129, No. 9, (September 2001), pp. 1003-11, ISSN 0034-9887

Behar, R.; De la Barrera, M. & Michelotti, J. (2002). Femininity, masculinity, androgyny and eating behaviours. *Revista médica de Chile,* Vol. 130, No. 9, (September 2002), pp. 964-75, ISSN 0034-9887

Behar, R.; De la Barrera, M. & Michelotti J. (2003). Clinical characteristics and gender identity among eating disordered patients subtypes. *Revista médica de Chile,* Vol. 131, No. 7, (July 2003), pp. 748-58, ISSN 0034-9887

Bem, S.L. (1974). The measurement of psychological androgyny. *Journal of Consulting and Clinical Psychology,* Vol. 42, No. 2, (April 1974), pp. 155–162, ISSN 0022-006X

Bem, S.L. (1977). On the utility of alternative procedures for assessing psychological androgyny. *Journal of Consulting and Clinical Psychology,* Vol. 45, No. 2, (April 1977), pp. 196–205, ISSN 0022-006X

Beren, S.E.; Hayden, H.A.; Wilfley, D.E. & Grilo, C.M. (1996). The influence of sexual orientation on body dissatisfaction in adult men and women. *International Journal of Eating Disorders,* Vol. 20, No. 2, (September 1996), pp. 135–141, ISSN 0276-3478

Beumont, P. J. V.; Beardwood, C. J. & Russell, G. F. M. (1972). The occurrence of the syndrome of anorexia nervosa in male subjects. *Psychological Medicine*, Vol. 2, No. 3, (August 1972), pp. 216–231, ISSN 0033-2917

Bramon-Bosch, E.; Troop, N. A. & Treasure, J. L. (2000). Eating disorders in males: a comparison with female patients. *European Eating Disorders Review,* Vol. 8, No. 4, (August 2000), pp. 321-328, ISSN 1072-4133

Brand, P.A.; Rothblum, E. D. & Solomon, L. J. (1992). A comparison of lesbians, gay men, and heterosexuals on weight and restrained eating. *International Journal of Eating Disorders,* Vol. 11, No. 3, (April 1992), pp. 253-259, ISSN 0276-3478

Braun, D.L.; Sunday, S.R.; Huang, A. & Halmi, K.A. (1999). More males seek treatment for eating disorders. *International Journal of Eating Disorders,* Vol. 25, No. 4, (May 1999), pp. 415-424, ISSN 0276-3478

Brown, L. (1987). Lesbians, weight and eating: New analyses and perspectives, In: *Lesbian psychologies: Explorations and challenges,* Boston Lesbian Psychologies Collective (Eds.), 294-309, University of Illinois Press, ISBN 978-025-2014-04-8, Chicago

Bruch, H. (1973). *Eating Disorders, Obesity, Anorexia Nervosa and the Person Within,* Basic Books, New edition (25 May 1979), ISBN 978-046-5017-82-9, New York

Cantrell, P.J. & Ellis, J.B. (1991). Gender role and risk patterns for eating disorders in men and women. *Journal of Clinical Psychology,* Vol. 47, No. 1, (January 1991), pp. 53–57, ISSN 0021-9762

Carlat, D.J. & Camargo, C.A. (1991). Review of bulimia nervosa in males. *The American Journal of Psychiatry,* Vol. 148, No. 7, (July 1991), pp. 831-843, ISSN 0002-953X

Carlat, D.J.; Camargo, C.A. & Herzog, D.B. (1997). Eating disorders in males: a report on 135 patients. *The American Journal of Psychiatry,* Vol. 154, No. 8, (August 1997), pp. 1127-1132, ISSN 0002-953X

Cella, S.; Iannaccone, M.; Ascione, R. & Cotrufo, P. (2010). Body dissatisfaction, abnormal eating behaviours and eating disorder attitude in homo and heterosexuals. *Eating and Weight Disorders,* Vol. 15, No. 3, (September 2010), pp. 180-185, ISSN 1124-4909

Cotrufo, P. (2005). *Anoressia del sessuale femminile. Dal caos alla costituzione del limite,* Franco Angeli, ISBN 88- 464- 6858-9, Milano

Cotrufo, P.; Cella, S.; Cremato, F. & Labella, A.G. (2007). Eating disorders attitude and abnormal eating behaviours in a sample of 11-13 year-old school children: The role of pubertal body transformation. *Eating and Weight Disorders,* Vol. 12, No. 4, (December 2007), pp. 154-60, ISSN 1124-4909

Crisp, A.H.; Burns, T. & Bhat, A.V. (1986). Primary anorexia nervosa in the male and female: a comparison of clinical features and prognosis. *British Journal of Medical Psychology,* Vol. 59, No. 2, (June 1986), pp. 123-132, ISSN 0007-1129

Cuzzolaro, M.; Vetrone, G.; Marano, G. & Battacchi, M. (2000). Body Uneasiness Test, BUT, In: *Repertorio delle scale di valutazione in psichiatria,* Conti, L. (Ed.), 1759-1761, SEE, ISBN 88-8465-014-3, Firenze

Davis, C. & Scott-Robertson, L. (2000). A psychological comparison of females with anorexia nervosa and competitive male bodybuilders: body shape ideals in the extreme. *Eating Behaviors,* Vol. 1, No. 1, (September 2000), pp. 33-46, ISSN 1471-0153

Falstein, E. I.; Feinstein, S. C. & Judas, I. (1956). Anorexia nervosa in the male child. *American Journal of Orthopsychiatry,* Vol. 26, No. 4, (October 1956), pp. 751–772, ISSN 0002-9432

Farrow, J.A. (1992). The adolescent male with an eating disorder. *Pediatric Annals,* Vol. 21, No. 11, (November 1992), pp. 769-774, ISSN 0090-4481

Feldman, M.B. & Meyer, I.H. (2007). Eating disorders in diverse lesbian, gay, and bisexual populations. *International Journal of Eating Disorders,* Vol. 40, No. 3, (April 2007), pp. 218-226, ISSN 0276-3478

Fernández -Aranda, F.; Peri, J. M.; Navarro, V.; Badla-Casnovas, A.; Turon-Gil, V. & Vallejo-Ruiloba, J. (2000). Transsexualism and anorexia nervosa: A case report. *Eating Disorders*, Vol. 8, (n .d.), pp. 63-66, ISSN 1064-0266

Fernández -Aranda, F.; Aitken, A.; Badı´a, A.; Gime´nez, L.; Solano, R.; Collier, D.; Treasure, J. & Vallejo, J. (2004). Personality and Psychopathological Traits of Males with an Eating Disorder. *European Eating Disorders Review*, Vol. 12, No. 6, (November 2004), pp. 367-374, ISSN 1072-4133

Fichter, M. M.; Daser, C. & Postpischil, F. (1985). Anorexic syndromes in the male, *Journal of psychiatric research*, Vol. 19, No. (2-3), (n. d.), pp. 305-13, ISSN 0022-3956

Fichter, M. M. & Daser, C. (1987). Symptomatology, psychosexual development and gender identity in 42 anorexic males. *Psychological Medicine*, Vol. 17, No. 2, (May 1987), pp. 409–418, ISSN 0033-2917

Forman-Hoffman, V.L.; Watson, T.L. & Andersen, A.E. (2008). Eating disorder age of onset in males: distribution and associated characteristics. *Eating and Weight Disorders*, Vol. 13, No. 2, (June 2008), pp. 28-31, ISSN 1124-4909

French, S.A.; Story, M.; Remafedi, G.; Resnick, M.D. & Blum, R.W. (1996). Sexual orientation and prevalence of body dissatisfaction and eating disordered behaviors: a population-based study of adolescents. *International Journal of Eating Disorders*, Vol. 19, No. 2, (March 1996), pp. 119 - 126, ISSN 0276-3478

Garner, D.M. (1991). *Eating Disorder Inventory – 2. Professional manual*. Odessa, FL: Psychological Assessment Resources.

Gettelman, T.E. & Thompson, J.K. (1993). Actual differences and stereotypical perceptions in body image and eating disturbance: A comparison of male and female heterosexual and homosexual samples. *Sex Roles*, Vol. 29, No. 7-8, (n.d.), pp. 545–562, ISSN 0360-0025

Goldfield, G.S.; Blouin, A.G. & Woodside, D.B. (2006). Body image, binge eating, and bulimia nervosa in male bodybuilders. *Canadian Journal of Psychiatry*, Vol. 51, No. 3, (March 2006), pp. 160-168, ISSN 0706-7437

Grabhorn, R.; Köpp, W.; Gitzinger, I.; von Wietersheim, J. & Kaufhold, J. (2003). Differences between female and male patients with eating disorders--results of a multicenter study on eating disorders (MZ-Ess). *Psychotherapie, Psychosomatik, medizinische Psychologie*, Vol. 53, No. 1, (January 2003), pp. 15-22, ISSN 0937-2032

Hall, A.; Delahunt, J. W. & Ellis, P. M. (1985). Anorexia nervosa in the male, clinical features and follow-up on nine patients. *Journal of Psychiatric Research*, Vol. 19, No. 2-3, (n.d), pp. 315- 321, ISSN 0022-3956

Harvey, J.A. & Robinson, J.D. (2003). Eating disorders in men: Current considerations. *Journal of Clinical Psychology in Medical Settings*, Vol. 10, No. 4, (n.d), pp. 297–306, ISSN 1068-9583

Heffernan, K. (1996). Eating disorders and weight concern among lesbians. *International Journal of Eating Disorders*, Vol. 19, No. 2, (March 1996), pp. 127 - 138, ISSN 0276-3478

Hepp, U. & Milos., G. (2002), Gender Identity disorder and eating disorder. *International Journal of Eating Disorders*, Vol. 32, No.4, (December 2002), pp. 473-478, ISSN 0276-3478

Hepp, U.; Spindler, A. & Milos, G. (2005). Eating disorder symptomatology and gender role orientation. *International Journal of Eating Disorders*, Vol. 37, No. 3, (April 2005), pp. 227-33, ISSN 0276-3478

Herzog, D.B.; Norman, D.K.; Gordon, C. & Pepose, M. (1984). Sexual conflict and eating disorders in 27 males. *The American Journal of Psychiatry*, Vol. 141, No. 8, (August 1984) pp. 989-990, ISSN 0002-953X

Herzog, D.B.; Newman, K.A.; Warshaw, M. & Yeh, C. (1992). Body image satisfaction in homosexual and heterosexual women. *International Journal of Eating Disorders*, Vol. 11, No. 4, (May 1992), pp. 391–396, ISSN 0276-3478

Hoek, H.W. & Van Hoeken, D. (2003). Review of the prevalence and incidence of eating disorders. *International Journal of Eating Disorders*, Vol. 34, No. 4, (December 2003), pp. 383-396, ISSN 0276-3478

Hospers, H.J. & Jansen., A. (2005). Why homosexuality is a risk factor for eating disorder in males. *Journal of Social and Clinical Psychology*, Vol. 24, No. 8, (December 2005), pp. 1188- 1201, ISSN 0736-7236

Johnson, M.E.; Brems, C. & Fischer, P. (1996). Sex role conflict, social desirability, and eating-disorder attitudes and behaviors. *Journal of General Psychology*, Vol. 123, No. 1, (January 1996), pp. 75–87, ISSN 0022-1309

Joiner, T. E.; Katz, J. & Heatherton, T. F. (2000). Personality features differentiate late adolescent females and males with chronic bulimic symptoms. *International Journal of Eating Disorders*, Vol. 27, No. 2, (March 2000), pp. 191–197, ISSN 0276-3478

Kaminski, P.L.; Chapman, B.P.; Haynes, S.D. & Own, L. (2005). Body image, eating behaviors, and attitudes toward exercise among gay and straight men. *Eating Behaviors*, Vol. 6, No. 3, (June 2005), pp. 179 - 187, ISSN 1471-0153

Kjelsas, E.; Bjornstrom, G. & Gotestam, K.G. (2004). Prevalence of eating disorders in female and male adolescents (14-15 years). *Eating behaviors*, Vol. 5, No. 1, (January 2004), pp. 13-25, ISSN 1471-0153

Lakkis, J.; Ricciardelli, L.A. & Williams, R.J. (1999). The role of sexual orientation and gender related-traits in disordered eating. *Sex Roles*, Vol. 41, No. 1-2, (July 1999), pp. 1-16, ISSN 0360-0025

LaTorre, R.A. & Wendenburg, K. (1983). Psychological characteristics of bisexual, heterosexual and homo-sexual women. *Journal of Homosexuality*, Vol. 9, No. 1, (n.d), pp. 87-97, ISSN 0091-8369

Leger, J. M.; Blanchinet, J. & Vallat, J. N. (1969). In the light of two cases of mental anorexia in boys, can an important role be attributed to the father's personality for the onset of this illness?. *Annales Medico-Psychologiques*, Vol. 2, No. 1, (n.d), pp. 101–108.

Lewinsohn, P.M.; Seeley, J.R.; Moerk, K.C. & Striegel- Moore, R.H. (2002). Gender differences in eating disorder symptomps in young adults. *International Journal Eating Disorders*, Vol. 32, No. 4, (December 2002), pp. 426-440, ISSN 0276-3478

Lewis, L.D. & Johnson, C. (1985). A comparison of sex role orientation between women with bulimia and normal controls. *International Journal of Eating Disorders*, Vol. 4, No. 3, (August 1985), pp. 241–257, ISSN 0276-3478

Meyer, C.; Blissett, J. & Oldfield, C. (2001). Sexual orientation and eating psychopathology: The role of masculinity and femininity. *International Journal of Eating Disorders*, Vol. 29, No. 3, (April 2001), pp. 314–318, ISSN 0276-3478

Moore, F. & Keel, P.K. (2003). Influence of sexual orientation and age on disordered eating attitudes and behaviors in women. *International Journal of Eating Disorders*, Vol. 34, No. 3, (November 2003), pp. 370 - 374, ISSN 0276-3478

Morton R. (1694), *Phthisiologia or a Treatise of Consumptions*, Smith & Walford, London.

Murnen, S.K. & Smolak, L. (1997). Femininity, masculinity, and disordered eating: A meta-analytic review. *International Journal of Eating Disorders*, Vol. 22, No. 3, (November 1997), pp. 231–242, ISSN 0276-3478

Nelson, W.L.; Hughes, H.M.; Katz, B. & Searight, H.R. (1999). Anorexic eating attitudes and behaviors of male and female college students. *Adolescence*, Vol. 34, No. 135, (n. d.), pp. 621-633, ISSN 0001-8449

Olivardia, R. (2001). Mirror, mirror on the wall, who's the largest of them all? The features and phenomenology of muscle dysmorphia. *Harvard Review of Psychiatry*, Vol. 9, No. 5, (September-October, 2001), pp. 254-259, ISSN 1067-3229

Olivardia, R.; Pope, H.G. Jr; Mangweth, B. & Hudson J. (1995). Eating disorders in college men. *The American Journal of Psychiatry*, Vol. 152, No. 9, (September 1995), pp. 1279-85, ISSN 0002-953X

Olivardia, R.; Pope, H.G. Jr & Hudson, J. I. (2000). Muscle dysmorphia in male weightlifters: A case - control study. *American Journal of Psychiatry*, Vol. 157, No. 8, (August 2000), pp. 1291-1296, ISSN 0002-953X

Oyebode, F.; Boodhoo, J.A. & Schapira, K. (1998). Anorexia nervosa in males. Clinical features and outcome. *International Journal of Eating Disorders*, Vol. 7, No. 1, (January 1998), pp. 121-124, ISSN 0276-3478

Pope, C.G.; Pope, H.G.; Menard, W.; Fay, C.; Olivardia, R. & Phillips, K.A. (2005). Clinical features of muscle dysmorphia among males with body dysmorphic disorder. *Body Image*, Vol. 2, No. 4, (December 2005), pp. 395-400, ISSN 1740-1445

Pope, H. G.; Hudson, J. I. & Jonas, J. M. (1986). Bulimia in men: A series of 15 cases. *Journal of Nervous and Mental Disease*, Vol. 174, No. 2, (February 1986), pp. 117–119, ISSN 0022-3018

Pope, H.G. Jr; Gruber, A.J.; Choi, P.; Olivardia, R. & Phillips, K.A. (1997). Muscle Dysmorphia. An underrecognized form of body dysmorphic disorder. *Psychosomatics*, Vol. 38, No. 6, (November-December, 1997), pp. 548-557, ISSN 0033-3182

Pope, H.G. Jr; Olivardia, R. & Phillips, K. (2000). *The Adonis Complex: The Secret Crisis of Male Body Obsession* (1ST edition), Free Press, ISBN 978-0684869100, New York

Pritchard, M. (2008). Disordered Eating in Undergraduates: Does Gender Role Orientation Influence Men and Women the Same Way?. *Sex Roles,* Vol. 59, No. 3-4, (n.d.), pp.282-289, ISSN 0360-0025

Robinson, P. H. & Holden, N. L. (1986). Bulimia nervosa in the male: a report of nine cases. *Psychological Medicine*, Vol. 16, No. 4, (November 1986), pp. 795-803, ISSN 0033-2917

Russell, C.J. & Keel, P.K. (2002). Homosexuality as a specific risk factor for eating disorders in men. *International Journal of Eating Disorders*, Vol. 31, No. 3, (April 2002), pp. 300-306, ISSN 0276-3478

Schneider, J.A. & Agras, W.S. (1987). Bulimia in males: A matched comparison with females. *International Journal of Eating Disorders*, Vol. 6, No. 2, (March 1987), pp. 235-242, ISSN 0276-3478

Schneider, J.A.; O'Leary, A. & Jenkins, S.R. (1995). Gender, sexual orientation and disordered eating. *Psychology and Health*, Vol. 10, No. 2, (February 1995), pp. 113-128, ISN 0887-0446

Share, T.L. & Mintz, L.B. (2002). Differences between lesbians and heterosexual women in disordered eating and related attitudes. *Journal of Homosexuality*, Vol. 42, No. 4, (n.d), pp. 89-106, ISN 0091-8369

Sharp, C.W.; Clark, S.A.; Dunan, J.R.; Blackwood, D.H. & Shapiro, C.M. (1994). Clinical presentation of anorexia nervosa in males: 24 new cases. *International Journal of Eating Disorders*, Vol. 15, No. 2, (March 1994), pp.125-134, ISSN 0276-3478

Siever, M. (1994), Sexual orientation and gender as factors in socioculturally acquired vulnerability to body dissatisfaction and eating disorders. *Journal of Consulting and Clinical Psychology*, Vol. 62, No. 2, (April 1994), pp.252-260, ISSN 0022-006X

Sitnick, T. & Katz, J.L. (1984). Sex role identity and anorexia nervosa. *International Journal of Eating Disorders*, Vol. 3, No. 3, (Spring 1984), pp. 81–87, ISSN 0276-3478

Steiger, H.; Fraenkel, L. & Leichner, P.P. (1989). Relationship of body-image distortion to sex-role identifications, irrational cognitions, and body weight in eating-disordered females. *Journal of Clinical Psychology*, Vol. 45, No. 1, (January 1989), pp. 61–65, ISSN 0021-9762

Striegel-Moore, R. H.; Tucker, N. & Hsu, J. (1990). Body image dissatisfaction and disordered eating in lesbian college students. *International Journal of Eating Disorders*, Vol. 9, No. 5, (September 1990), pp. 493-500, ISSN 0276-3478

Strong, S.M.; Williamson, D.A.; Netemeyer, R.G. & Geer, J.H. (2000). Eating disorder symptoms and concerns about body differ as a function of gender and sexual orientation. *Journal of Social and Clinical Psychology*, Vol. 19, No. 2, (Summer 2000), pp. 240 - 255, ISSN 0736-7236

Vocks, S.; Stahn, C. & Loenser, K. (2008). Eating and Body Image Disturbances in Male-to-Female and Female-to- Male Transsexuals, *Archives of sexual behavior*, Vol. 38, No.3, (June 2008), pp. 364-77, ISSN 0004-0002

Wichstrøm, L. (2006). Sexual orientation as a risk factor for bulimic symptoms. *International Journal of Eating Disorders*, Vol. 39, No. 6, (September 2006), pp. 448-453, ISSN 0276-3478

Williams, R.J. & Ricciardelli, L.A. (2001). Sex-role traits and the comorbidity of symptoms of disordered eating and problem drinking. *Eating behaviors*, Vol. 2, No. 1, (Spring 2001), pp. 67-77, ISSN 1471-0153

Williamson, I. & Spence, K. (2001). Towards an understanding of risk factors for eating disturbance amongst gay men. *Health Education*, Vol. 101, No. 5, (October 2001), pp. 217–227, ISSN 0965-4283

Winston, A.P.; Acharya, S.; Chaudhuri, S. & Fellowes, L. (2004). Anorexia nervosa and gender identity disorder in biologic males: a report of two cases. *International Journal of Eating Disorders*, Vol. 36, No. 1, (July 2004), pp.109-113, ISSN 0276-3478

Yelland, C. & Tiggemann, M. (2003). Muscularity and the gay ideal: body dissatisfaction and disordered eating in homosexual men. *Eating Behaviors*, Vol. 4, No. 2, (August 2003), pp. 107-116, ISSN 1471-0153

# 5

# Risk of Eating Disorders and Physical Self-Concept in Adolescence

Arantzazu Rodríguez-Fernández and Alfredo Goñi
*University of The Basque Country, Spain*

## 1. Introduction

Recent years have witnessed an intensification in the study of factors associated with eating disorders (EDs), mainly due to increased social concern regarding these problems. For 30 years now, these types of problems have become increasingly frequent; so much so, in fact, that it can now be said (Schur et al., 2000) that more than half of all adolescents feel dissatisfied with their bodies. This has given rise to a multitude of studies on the epidemiological scope of these disorders, the personality traits which influence their development and sustained presence and the factors which may intervene in their prevention.

The numerous factors which predispose a person to eating disorders include: the psycho-physiological changes of adolescence, being aged between 14 and 20, having certain personality traits, being female and belonging to Western culture (Striegel-Moore, 1997; Toro, 2004; Garner, 1998). However, the construct most frequently considered as predictor of a greater predisposition to anorexia nervosa (AN) or bulimia nervosa (BN), as a factor in their subsequent sustained presence and even as a prerequisite for the development of any kind of eating disorder is low self-esteem and, in particular, dissatisfaction with one's own body shape (Gual et al., 2002; Fairburn et al., 1998; Toro, 2004).

A chapter such as this one, dedicated to studying the relationship between EDs and physical self-concept during adolescence, cannot afford to overlook body image, a construct which is strongly associated with EDs and closely linked to physical self-concept. We will therefore take a moment to explain the term *body image* and to explore its similarities and differences in relation to *physical self-concept.*

## 2. Body image

One's body image is formed from diverse information provided by different sensorial receptors (visual, tactile and coenesthetic), collected gradually over time. It can be evoked in a single whole and is commonly associated with significant emotional responses resulting from its aesthetic assessment (Toro, 2004).

Interest in appearance and body image has, over recent years, reached an all-time high, but is not exclusive to either our society or our modern era. In pre-Columbian cultures artificial cranial deformation was seen as a symbol of beauty and, more recently, during the 19th and early 20th centuries, it was common for women to wear corsets in order to enlarge their busts and reduce their waists, despite the fact that habitual use of this garment resulted in the deformation of the thoracic cavity. Examples of concern over body image in non-Western cultures include neck stretching (i.e. the wearing of hard metal neck rings to give the appearance of an elongated neck), earlobe elongation and lip plates (used to stretch the lower lip), practices all typical of certain African tribes, which aim to enhance the beauty of the wearer (de la Serna, 2004).

### 2.1 Definition

As is often the case with scientific terms, the notion *body image* poses a fair degree of conceptual complexity, and no consensus has yet been reached regarding its definition, how it should be assessed or how its alterations or distortions are manifested (Baile, 2003).

The first references to body image and the alterations associated with it, can be found in medical studies in the field of neurology from the beginning of the 20th century. During the 1920s, Henry Head proposed that individuals all construct a model or image of themselves, and that this image constitutes a standard with which they compare body movements. Hence the term *body schema* came into use (Fisher, 1990). Some time later, in 1935, Schilder proposed the following definition of body image:

> *"the picture of our own body which we form in our mind, i.e. the way in which our body is represented to ourselves" (Schilder, 1935, p.46).*

Later on, this definition was expanded to include emotional and attitudinal aspects (Kolb, 1959); and some years later, two aspects of body image were identified (Slade & Russell, 1973): adequate body estimation and feelings and attitudes towards one's own body. Given that behaviour is related to physical self-concept and degree of body satisfaction (for example, the avoidance of situations in which one is obliged to show one's naked body or attempts to change one's physical body shape), the behavioural component was finally added to the perceptive and cognitive-affective ones (Cash & Pruzinsky, 1990; Thompson, 1990). Consequently, body image is formed by three different components:

- The perceptual component: the accuracy with which one perceives the size of different body segments, or one's body as a whole. Perceptual alterations can result in either overestimation (perception of one's body as being bigger than it really is) or underestimation (perception of one's body as being smaller than it really is).
- The subjective component (cognitive-affective): degree of body satisfaction. This refers to attitudes, feelings, thoughts and valuations (satisfaction, concern or anxiety) generated by either one's body as a whole or by any of its parts, its weight or any other aspect of one's physical appearance.
- The behavioural component: behaviours provoked by one's perception of one's body and associated feelings (e.g. avoiding situations involving nudity, purchasing clothes which hide certain parts of one's body, exhibition, avoidance of exhibition, checking one's body, attempts to change one's physical shape, etc.).

As a result of this conceptual complexity, several different definitions exist which vary as regards the emphasis they place on each of the three components. A comprehensive view of the concept, however, is offered by the following definition:

> *"... it is a complex construct which includes the perception we have of our whole body, each of its parts and its movement and limits, the subjective experience of attitudes, thoughts, feelings and assessments we make, and the way in which we behave as a result of our thoughts and feelings" (Raich, 2000, p.25).*

After taking into account different contributions, Baile (2003) also attempts a definition, which includes all prior knowledge regarding body image, defining it as follows:

> *"a complex psychological construct which refers to how self-perception of one's body / appearance generates a mental representation, consisting of a perceptive body schema and its associated emotions, thoughts and behaviours" (Baile, 2003, p.58).*

However, a review of over one hundred papers on body image leads to the conclusion that:

> *"the concept of body image has yet to be conclusively defined and the task of measuring alterations in body image in an objective manner is still a formidable challenge" (Skrzypek et al., 2001, p.216).*

### 2.2 Factors which influence body dissatisfaction

It is broadly accepted that dissatisfaction with one's body image and its distortions are not the result of a single cause, but are rather due to a range of different factors (Toro, 2004). The list of risk factors considered is extensive, with some of the principal ones being social-cultural pressure from the media, family and interpersonal relationships (Rodríguez & Goñi, 2009), and certain personal characteristics such as gender, diverse physical-biological aspects, cognitive distortions and even physical-sporting activity (Rodríguez & Goñi, 2009; Esnaola & Rodríguez, 2009). The following sections analyse those factors which have been studied in most detail.

#### 2.2.1 Social-cultural factors

One of the factors, which most influences alterations in body image, is the cultural concept of beauty which prevails in each society. Every culture establishes its own stereotype of beauty and ugliness, which changes over time. Thus, in certain intellectual circles, an excessive concern over musculature, body shape or sport has been viewed for years as something typical of the less intellectually or culturally enlightened segments of society. Nowadays, however, the cultural pressure of the female model of slimness, the muscular prototype of masculinity and, in both cases, the stigmatisation of obesity (all factors associated with possible eating disorders) is well documented (Acosta & Gómez, 2003).

But how is this cultural pressure transmitted? The mass media play a key role in the propagation and exaltation of aesthetic stereotypes. Publicity invades everything; manifestations of body aesthetics are a constant presence in the film world, the fashion world, television shows and adverts, etc. Only perfect bodies are valid for selling products; today, more than ever, an image has more selling power than a thousand words (Gervilla, 2002). However, some studies have found that the influence exerted by fashion magazines is much more pernicious for body image, because since it is information that the subject him or herself has made an effort to obtain, its processing is more intentional and therefore more profound (Harrison & Cantor, 1997; Tiggemann, 2003); the same cannot be said for television, where messages appear incidentally, rendering their processing and influence less intense.

Reference groups constitute another powerful transmitter of society's prevailing body ideals. It is in primary groups, such as family and peers, that reference values for body image are created, with the family being the first socialisation context and a powerful risk factor for dissatisfaction, through two mechanisms (Kearney-Cooke, 2002): a) modelling, through which parents transmit their attitudes and values to their children, including negative attitudes and values regarding body image (Rieves & Cash, 1996; Hill & Franklin, 1998); and b) parents' verbal messages about their children's image, appearance or weight (Striegel-Moore & Kearney-Cook, 1994).

Nevertheless, in some cases, negative comments about body image from friends can become even more important than those messages received from one's own family, since it has been found that frequent peer interactions involving discussions of weight, body shape or diets are more closely associated with traits typical of EDs or body dissatisfaction (Barr-Taylor et al., 1998).

All these influences contribute to ensuring that the socially-accepted body image is internalised as the chosen aesthetic model, and this model plays a vital role in body satisfaction/dissatisfaction: when the discrepancy between the desired body image and one's own physical appearance is minimal, one tends to feel satisfied with one's body. However, if the discrepancy between the desired body and one's own is too great, body dissatisfaction arises.

### 2.2.2 Personal factors

In addition to social-cultural factors, certain personal characteristics also facilitate the appearance and sustained presence of body image alterations. The following sections analyse the most important of these: gender, age-related physical and biological changes, cognitive distortions and even physical-sporting activity, among others.

**Gender**

Concern about body image is not exclusive to women; there are also many men who feel dissatisfied and concerned about their physical appearance, and indeed the number of these men has tripled over the last 25 years (Pope et al., 2000). In relation to gender differences, it has been observed that men assess their physique in terms of strength (chest, shoulders, biceps and muscular strength), while women express concerns related to weight and the shape of certain body parts (hips, thighs, buttocks, etc.).

These results indicate the presence of a gender-based double body standard, which causes a predominance of bigorexia among men and renders the prevalence of AN and BN significantly higher (90% in fact) among women (American Psychiatric Association [APA], 2003).

**Physical and biological aspects**

As regards physical and biological aspects, during puberty the body undergoes major changes, and difficulties accepting these changes often give rise to concern over physical appearance. Thus, a rejection of the physical and biological changes typical of the early years of puberty may become a risk factor for developing a distortion in physical self-concept at a later stage.

Girls who develop earlier than their friends and classmates often experience more problems in relation to body image, since the majority of them consider the changes they observe in their own bodies (such as, for example, developing breasts and broadening hips) to be grotesque, or fattening, rather than as proof of the fact that they are reaching adulthood. Moreover, the changes which take place in their bodies go against the aesthetic model of the female body: broadening hips and thighs as opposed to narrow hips and slender thighs. For their part, boys who take longer to grow than their peers often end up deeply scarred by their concern over being small and puny, missing those traits typically associated with masculinity (Raich, 2000).

**Cognitive distortions**

Although we are all immersed in the same culture, not everyone is influenced in the same way by social-cultural pressure; much the same is true also of other influences, such as the family or social context in which each individual exists and develops. Why is this? What makes some people more capable than others of resisting these influences?

People with body image disorders develop beliefs about their physical appearance and its implications, which influence their thinking, emotions and behaviour. These beliefs are formed during early adolescence, when self-identity and physical development change rapidly. As Ellis (Ellis & Maclaren, 2005) asserts, we feel how we think; how one feels and acts will depend on how one interprets facts and events. In other words, feelings depend on one's own interpretations, judgments and thoughts.

Raich (2000) recounts a series of psychological experiments, which demonstrate how people behave in accordance with what they believe they are like and others react to them in accordance with how they show themselves to be. Thus, a group of actors had a hideous scar painted on their faces just before going to an interview. However, at the end of the make-up session the scar was removed without their knowing it, so that when they arrived at the interview they believed their faces were still disfigured. Following the interview, the actors claimed to have noted the interviewers' unease over the traumatic scars they had (or thought they had) on their faces; the same interviewers also reported not having liked the person interviewed very much, because they seemed to have a complex about their physical appearance. The conclusion that can be drawn from this experimental situation is clear: when faced with a real situation or event, the most important thing is how one judges, interprets or understands one's own possibilities; depending on this, individuals will feel and act in a certain way.

**Physical-sporting activity**

Sportsmen and women constitute a special group as regards altered body image perception. Those who habitually engage in sporting activity may have a higher risk of developing EDs due to the sports environment itself, which not only may precipitate this type of disorder in a predisposed individual (or exacerbate an already existing symptom), but may even legitimise it (Wilmore, 1991). Indications and signs of these alterations in the elite sportsmen and women of certain disciplines are often ignored, and are, on occasions, even considered natural. The emphasis on obtaining a fat-free body and the acceptance of the need to engage in excessive physical exercise in the world of top-level competition may make an existing eating disorder harder to diagnose, and consequently more difficult to treat (Thompson, 1990).

In short, it is currently widely accepted that the causes of body image alterations do not stem from a single factor, but are rather the result of multiple factors such as culture, family, interpersonal relationships and personal characteristics such as gender, physical and biological aspects, personality, cognitive distortions and physical activity, etc. Delimiting and analysing the possible causes of body alterations is a basic exercise which will help us gain a better understanding of these disorders and will provide us with information which can be used to ensure more effective interventions.

## 3. Eating disorders

Eating disorders are serious psychological disturbances which involve abnormal eating habits (APA, 2003) and which may be fatal in between 4% and 20% of cases (Cruz et al., 2002). Although there are many different subtypes, the two most common EDs are AN and BN. In Spain alone, the Health Ministry sets the prevalence rate at 1.5% of the population; in other words, 500,000 Spaniards would be diagnosed with AN, BN or one of their subtypes, a figure which rises sharply to 8 million adolescents and young adults in the United States. In both cases, the rate is particularly high among adolescent girls and young women, with a proportion of 9 to 1 in comparison with men.

### 3.1 Risk factors for eating disorders

Exploring the factors which influence the origin, development and sustained presence of EDs is of enormous theoretical and social interest. It is also a controversial and complex task due, firstly, to the numerous underlying causes, and secondly to the fact that it is not always easy to distinguish between the risk indicators of an eating disorder and the indicators of normal habits designed to look after one's appearance, since both are closely linked to each other and the dividing line between them is often very fine.

In AN, some authors (Lucas; and Plog & Pircke, as cited in Chinchilla, 1994; Toro, 2004) highlight both biological vulnerability (genetic, biochemical and anatomical-physiological) and psychological and social vulnerability (family, friends, culture) as key factors in determining personality changes, which prompt diet behaviour. Others (Chinchilla, 1995, 2002), however, offer a more exhaustive analysis of all possible factors (see chart 1), dividing them into: a) predisposing factors (those that are found in the initial stage and which facilitate the appearance of the disorder, but which are not an inevitable sign of its development); b) precipitating factors (precursor behaviours which increase the risk of development when they interact with trigger factors) and c) sustained presence factors (in this phase factors which foster the perpetuation of the disorder interact with diverse defence mechanisms).

BN is also divided into these factors (see chart 2), although it is generally accepted that the etiopathogenesis of this disorder has not been fully explored and is multi-factorial in nature (Chincilla, 2002). Of all of these factors, we will focus on those used subsequently for studying the relationship between physical self-concept and eating disorders, namely: body mass index, gender, age, personality traits and physical-sporting activity.

| ANOREXIA NERVOSA | | |
|---|---|---|
| **Predisposing F.** | **Precipitating F.** | **Sustained presence F.** |
| - Genetic vulnerability (hypothalamic decrease and neuronal transmission).<br>- Age (12-25 years old).<br>- Being female.<br>- Affective disorder.<br>- Obesity.<br>- Medium-low social level.<br>- Low self-esteem.<br>- Family members with affective disorders, addictions or eating disorders.<br>- Maternal obesity.<br>- Social-cultural pressure.<br>- Early stressful situations.<br>- Family concern about appearance and/or diet.<br>- Parental dependency.<br>- Incomplete personal identity.<br>- Overprotective or strict family.<br>- Difficulty attaining independence.<br>- Certain professions (dancers, models, gymnasts).<br>- Certain psychological traits (perfectionism, negativism, isolation, subordination, self-sacrifice, mood swings). | - Body changes during adolescence.<br>- Separations, deaths and family conflicts.<br>- Parental breakups.<br>- First sexual experiences.<br>- Rapid weight increase.<br>- Criticism about one's body.<br>- Disease resulting in weight loss.<br>- Disfiguring injury.<br>- Increase in physical activity.<br>- Life events.<br>- Families which try to prevent children from growing up.<br>- Sporting activity.<br>- School and marriage.<br>- Dieting.<br>- Stress affecting the endocrine functions. | - Consequences of starvation.<br>- Altered family interactions.<br>- Social isolation.<br>- Anorexic thoughts.<br>- Excessive physical attitude.<br>- Iatrogenesis.<br>- Hypothalamic alternations.<br>- Tendency to be hard workers, anxious to achieve professional success.<br>- Being responsible and determined to fulfil obligations.<br>- Alexithymia.<br>- Attitudes to food mediated more by external than internal influences.<br>- Reduction of carbohydrates and fat.<br>- Hyperactivity.<br>- Concern about food-centred thoughts.<br>- Severe mood swings.<br>- Difficulty identifying feelings. |

Source: Chinchilla, 1995; Chinchilla, 2002; Toro & Vilardel, 1987.

Chart 1. Predisposing, precipitating and sustained presence factors of anorexia nervosa.

### 3.1.1 Body mass index

Body weight is related to the onset of ED symptoms; a high body mass index tends to be associated with the desire to lose weight and achieve a slimmer body (Schur et al., 2000; Richard et al., 1990) and also prospectively predicts body dissatisfaction and the beginning of bulimic pathology and binging (Vogeltanz-Holm et al., 2000).

According to data obtained from the non-clinical adolescent population (Goñi & Rodríguez, 2004), the existing relationships among diverse ED-linked symptoms, thoughts and behaviours and body mass index are notable. Those with a higher body mass index are not only disgusted by their physical appearance and want to lose weight, they also have a higher frequency of eating disorder personality traits and behaviours; in specific terms, those with a higher body mass index also tend to score higher in *drive for thinness*, as well as in *body dissatisfaction, negative self-assessment* and *interpersonal distrust.* Coinciding with the findings of other studies (Toro, 2004), *perfectionism,* on the other hand, is higher in thinner subjects and lower in subjects with either normal or above-normal weight.

| BULIMIA NERVOSA | | |
|---|---|---|
| **Predisposing F.** | **Precipitating F.** | **Sustained presence F.** |
| - Family history of psychiatric problems.<br>- Addictive behaviours.<br>- Mood disorders in first degree relatives.<br>- High ED morbidity in the family.<br>- Predisposition to obesity.<br>- Disorganised or conflictive families.<br>- Emotional dependency.<br>- Neurobiological alternations (serotonin/ noradrenalin / dopamine, etc.)<br>- Alterations in insulin secretion.<br>- Body dissatisfaction.<br>- Obsession with obesity.<br>- Low self-esteem.<br>- Prior mood disorder.<br>- Social phobia.<br>- Addictive behaviours.<br>- Borderline personality.<br>- Perfectionism.<br>- Social-cultural factors. | - Following a strict diet.<br>- Prior anorexia nervosa.<br>- Being overweight.<br>- Body dissatisfaction.<br>- Concern about weight. | - Persistence of predisposing factors.<br>- Seriousness of predisposing factors.<br>- Body dissatisfaction.<br>- Concern about weight.<br>- Continued behavioural alteration of eating regulation mechanisms by alternate abstinence, binging and vomiting. |

Source: Chinchilla, 1995; Chinchilla, 2002; Toro & Vilardel, 1987.

Chart 2. Predisposing, precipitating and sustained presence factors of bulimia nervosa.

### 3.1.2 Adolescence and gender

It is during adolescence, when individuals have to adapt to major changes in their bodies, changes which often go against the socially-accepted stereotype of beauty (broadening hips, thighs and buttocks), that physical self-esteem runs the risk of deteriorating more among girls than among boys (Franzoi & Shields, 1984), giving rise to EDs. It is therefore hardly surprising that AN, BN and other subtypes of clinical pathologies occur most frequently in the female population, with 15 to 24-year-old girls and young women being the main risk group (Toro & Vilardell, 1987).

### 3.1.3 Personality traits

Personality traits are another important factor associated with body image rejection and the disorders derived from this. Different personality patterns exist for each type of alteration associated with body image (AN and BN as opposed to bigorexia). The aetiology of bigorexia seems to be related to a narcissistic personality, in which the individual in question is interested almost exclusively in him or herself. It sometimes arises as a means of compensating fears of homosexuality and seeking self-affirmation, with having a muscular body ending up becoming an end in itself. At risk individuals tend to be insecure, with low self-esteem, who feel themselves to be unattractive to the opposite sex, a situation which leads to a regime of uncontrolled exercise.

Traits such as perfectionism, hyperactivity, shyness, negativism, isolation, a tendency towards self-sacrifice, mood swings and subordination have often been related to the onset of AN and BN. During the first part of the 20th century, detailed descriptions were drafted of the personality of certain anorectic patients (DuBois, 1949), and a short time later, more studies were published attesting to the "abnormal" characteristics of these patients' personalities (Dally, 1969). Over recent years, Cloninger's model of temperamental dimensions has been related to eating disorders, particularly AN (Casper, 1990). Cloninger (1988) proposed a personality model with four temperamental dimensions, which are the consequence of either genetic inheritance or early-learned behaviour. These dimensions are: a) harm avoidance, or the ability to cope with potentially harmful life events; b) reward dependence, understood as the tendency to establish or easily make responses conditional upon reinforcement signals (approval, help, etc,); novelty seeking or excitability of the response to new stimuli; and d) persistence, understood as the tendency to sustain certain behaviour as a means of resisting frustration.

Casper (1990) was the first researcher to exhaustively assess these four dimensions in patients suffering from AN, finding that, in comparison with control subjects, they scored very low in novelty seeking but very high in harm avoidance and reward dependence (although this latter result was not statistically significant). These conclusions have since been confirmed by subsequent studies (Bulik et al., 1995; Klump et al., 2000) and have been related to cognitive factors such as ineffectiveness, perfectionism and interpersonal distrust (Vervaet et al., 2003).

But it is David Garner (1998), currently one of the world's leading experts in these types of psychopathology, who has most thoroughly explored the personality traits of EDs, focusing particularly on drive for thinness, ineffectiveness, perfectionism, interpersonal distrust, interoceptive awareness, maturity fears, asceticism, impulse regulation and social insecurity. All these traits form part of what is currently perhaps the most important instrument used for diagnosing EDs: the Eating Disorders Inventory (EDI). The following is a brief description of each one.

Drive for thinness, or a desire to lose weight, is the psychopathological core and driving force behind those behaviours aimed at ensuring a slimmer figure: hypo-caloric diet for individuals with AN and vomiting for those suffering from BN. The principal personality traits of these patients are an incessant search for thinness (Bruch, 1973) and an exaggerated fear of weight gain (Russell, 1970), driven by an internalisation of the prevailing aesthetic model of the ideal body shape (Toro, 2004). Nevertheless, not all ED patients experience this drive or impulse; those diagnosed as atypical (20%) claim not to feel any drive for thinness and insist that their low food intake is due to a lack of appetite or gastric alternations.

It was Bruch (1973) who first described the feeling of ineffectiveness as one of the disturbances underlying EDs. Since then, this trait has been present in the majority of clinical explanations (Garner & Bemis, 1985; Wagner et al., 1987). However, and despite the fact that ineffectiveness has always been understood as something very similar to negative self-assessment or low self-esteem, Garner (1998) sees it as a construct which, while being similar to both, nevertheless goes one step further in that it also includes feelings of emptiness and loneliness.

As regards perfectionism (very common in eating disorders, particularly AN), clinical experience shows a close association with body dissatisfaction, since patients want everything they do or have (including their bodies) to be seen by others as perfect. These individuals are overwhelmed by a constant desire to ensure that their personal results are always the best and wage a fierce battle to achieve perfection in everything that they do (Bruch, 1973). They end up believing that only the very highest personal performance levels are acceptable. They are also convinced that the other people in their immediate environment, such as parents, teachers, friends or relatives, all expect nothing less than exceptional results from them (Garner, 1998). This personality trait has recently been put to the test, with the results being contradictory. Some authors (Bastiani et al., 1995; Szabò & Terre Blanche, 1997) have concluded that this personality trait has nothing whatsoever to do with EDs, since it fails to improve following the patient's treatment and recovery. Others, by contrast (Casper, 1990; Toro, 2004) claim that: a) perfectionism is sensitive to the condition of the disease; b) some aspects of perfectionism represent a transitory state associated with the clinical state; and c) studies which demonstrate the opposite can assert only that perfectionism does not improve with the elimination of inanition, and should not dismiss the possibility that it may have developed after the ED.

Distrust in social relationships is another variable closely associated with eating disorders. This interpersonal distrust is characterised by a notable lack of interest in establishing intimate relationships and by a clear difficulty in expressing thoughts and feelings (Garner, 1998; Gismero, 2001). Moreover, between 24% and 55% of anorexic patients also suffer from some kind of social anxiety disorder (Toro, 2004). Studies exist which show that those with a high level of body dissatisfaction experience more difficulties in their relationships with others (Chinchilla, 2002; Gismero, 2001). Indeed, some even claim that in certain cases, the need to keep people at arm's length is a trigger factor for some types of ED (Johnson & Connors, 1987).

In 1974, reference was made to the deep-rooted distrust of all sensations originating from inside the organism (interoceptive awareness) felt by patients suffering from AN. This distrust was termed *intra-psychic paranoia* (Selvini-Palazzoli, 1974), and is a character trait often referred to as *alexithymia* due to the difficulty experienced by patients in identifying and describing their feelings, or due to a way of thinking severely conditioned by concerns over bodily symptoms. In this sense, it was recently found that the anomalous eating responses of ED patients are in fact the result of difficulties in correctly interpreting emotional states (Toro, 2004) and are found in over 70% of cases (Zonnevijille-Bendek et al., 2002).

Research carried out into the personality trait known as maturity fears is a little ambiguous. While some authors (Garner, 1998) argue that this trait is closely associated with body dissatisfaction because the psychopathological core of these patients is a fear of the adult body, other authors defend a totally different hypothesis, claiming that the biographies of these subjects show adolescents who were too mature for their age, with high levels of responsibility, reflection or competitiveness (Chinchilla, 2002).

However, personality traits vary from one gender to the other, and in accordance with the type of eating disorder in question. It is generally accepted that people with AN are calmer, more indifferent, more organised and more methodical than those suffering from BN, and within this specific type of pathology, bulimic and anorectic patients are more excitable, curious, impulsive and untidy than restrictive anorectic patients (Toro, 2004). As regards gender, it has been found that men diagnosed with EDs have a greater tendency to avoid problems and harm, and are more reward dependent and more perfectionist than their female counterparts. Moreover, while for adolescent girls the main character trait for ED risk is drive for thinness, for adolescent boys it is problem avoidance (García-Grau et al., 2004; Woodside, 2004).

### 3.1.4 Physical-sporting activity

It is of special interest to clarify whether sport is really a trigger factor in EDs or merely a means of weight control used by those with a prior history of eating disorders, thus resulting in a higher concentration of these pathologies among the sporting population.

It has been shown that some types or forms of physical activity may have negative health consequences (Beumont et al., 1994), one of these consequences being the development of an ED. There are various reasons for proposing sport as a factor for the risk or sustained presence of eating disorders: a) physical hyperactivity is one of the criteria established by the World Health Organization (WHO, 1992) in the International Classification of Mental and Behavioural Disorders 10 (ICD-10) for diagnosing an ED when it occurs in conjunction with significant weight loss (BMI $\leq$ 17.5); b) having recourse to physical exercise and sporting activity as a means of weight control may result in excessive exercising or exercise which wears or reduces specific body areas (Mansfield & McGinn, 1993); c) excessive or compulsive physical activity contributes decisively not only to the pathogenesis of EDs, but also to their sustained presence (Davis et al., 1994); and d) some authors have identified sport as a risk factor for eating disorders, especially among women and in relation to certain specific types of sport (Pope et al., 1997).

Also, a higher prevalence of EDs has been found among sportsmen and women than among the general population (Toro, 2004). The prevalence figures estimated by Wilmore & Costill (1998) are 50% for elite sportswomen, while for the general population it is around 1%, and Houtkooper (2000) estimates that between 1% and 39% of sportsmen and women present symptoms related to eating disorders. Some authors (Sundgot-Borgen, 2001; Sundgot-Borgen & Torstveit, 2004) even claim that the indications and signs of these alterations in the elite sportsmen and women of certain disciplines are often ignored, and are, on occasions, even considered natural. Those sports in which, in addition to performance, body image is also valued, those with weight categories or those which highlight the importance of a fat-free body are the ones which most push athletes towards developing some kind of ED (de la Serna, 2004; Dosil & Díaz, 2002).

On the other hand, however, it has been shown that one consequence of EDs is an increase in sporting activity as subjects reduce their weight and food intake (Davis et al., 1997), and that sports which require strict weight control are chosen by those individuals who already possess certain personality traits which render them susceptible to EDs (Eisler & le Grance, 1990; Leon, 1984). In this sense, it has been found that the relationship between sport and the risk of some kind of eating disorder is mediated by an important factor: the sportsman or woman's own eating history (Vasquez et al., 1997), since in 93% of the cases studied, subjects claimed to have had eating problems prior to taking up sport.

Moreover, some consider sport to be an effective means of preventing these pathologies. These studies sustain that EDs have no relationship with physical activity (Meadows, 2005) or, specifically, with a high number of exercise hours per week (Kjelsas & Augestad, 2004). Furthermore, some authors defend sport as a means of strengthening body image (Esnaola, 2005). Also, the symptoms of EDs seem to be more closely related to feelings of obligation (i.e. being obliged to engage in physical exercise), rather than to the actual amount of exercise carried out (Seigel & Hetta, 2001).

In short, the fact that athletes who engage in sports which place greater emphasis on the need to have a low body weight in order to compete are apparently at greater risk of developing alterations in the perception of their body image, may be explained by a prior (perhaps latent) alteration in eating behaviour or by a risk of such an alteration; in other words, these individuals are attracted to this type of sporting activity precisely because they provide them with a need to control their weight. This seems to imply that the individual in question already suffers from an ED (or at least demonstrates a certain attitude) before taking up the sport in question (Sacks, 1990).

A more conciliatory, middle-of-the-road theory, was proposed some years ago by Epling et al. (1983). These authors suggested that physical activity and food intake are closely interlinked, and that a reduction in food intake prompts an increase in physical activity, and that this, in turn, prompts a further reduction in the amount of food consumed. Thus, a vicious circle is established in which one factor fosters the emergence of the other.

Today, the question of the causal relationship between sport and EDs continues to be a complicated issue requiring further clarification (Pierce et al., 1993). To this end, it is important to clearly define the population studied, in order to facilitate comparisons between results, thus obtaining reliable data regarding the real prevalence of these disorders. Clustering criteria should include important data such as the way in which physical activity is measured (subjective or objective), whether or not the activity in question is an individual or team sport, the age of the sample group and other variables associated with EDs. If these indications are followed, then reliable data will be obtained regarding the true effects of sport on AN and BN, and which traits of sporting activity are linked to this type of pathology.

## 4. Physical self-concept and EDs

It is clear that EDs are pathologies typical of adolescence, which have become increasingly serious over recent years due to rising incidence and prevalence rates. This rise is partly due to social pressure to achieve the aesthetic model of thinness, which results in increasingly common cases of body dissatisfaction, and is strengthened a priori by certain factors such as age, gender and personality traits. Nevertheless, the body dissatisfaction involved in EDs has been associated exclusively with the body image each individual has of him or herself. And bearing in mind that body image is only one part of physical self-concept directly affected by physical appearance (Stein, 1996), the doubt arises as to what relationship exists between physical self-concept and all its facets with the possible development of AN or BN during this crucial developmental stage.

However, before examining the possible relationship between physical self-concept and the risk of developing AN or BN, it is important to clarify what is actually understood by physical self-concept, what its connection is with body image and what differences exist between the two constructs.

We could define physical self-concept as "the concept one has of one's body traits and / or physical appearance, physical fitness, strength and physical-sporting abilities" (Esnaola, 2005, p.134). This definition is based on a four-dimensional theory (Esnaola, 2005; Goñi et al., 2006) developed from Fox's model (1988) which divides physical self-concept into the following four dimensions (see figure 1):

- *Physical ability* (athletic and sporting skills in Fox's model): perception of the qualities ("I'm good"; "I have qualities") and abilities ("I feel competent"; "I feel self-assured") required for engaging in sport; ability to learn new sports; personal security and predisposition to sport.
- *Physical fitness:* physical condition and fitness; stamina and physical energy; confidence in one's physical condition.
- *Physical attractiveness:* perception of one's own physical appearance; security and satisfaction regarding one's own image.
- *Strength:* regarding oneself and/or feeling strong, able to lift weights, secure in engaging in exercises which require strength and a predisposition to carry out such exercises.

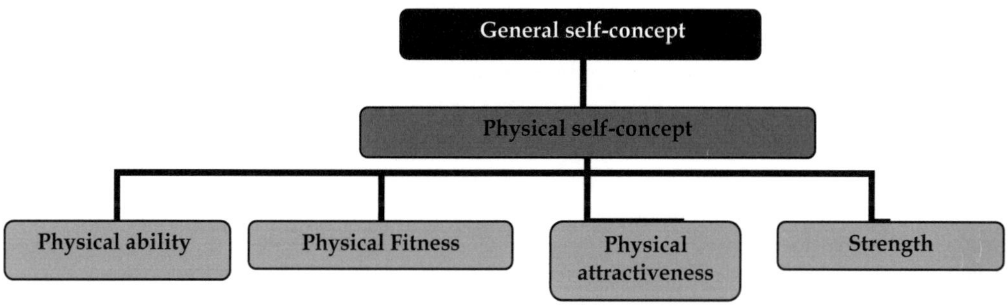


Fig. 1. Model of physical self-concept by Esnaola (2005) and Goñi et al. (2006)

Physical self-concept is a construct which does not function in an isolated manner, but rather works as just one element in a hierarchical, multidimensional system of general self-concept (see figure 2). Indeed, research carried out to date involving both young people / adolescents (Harter, 1987, 1988 1989) and adults (Adams, 1977) highlights the importance of physical self-concept in global self-concept; and within this construct, these studies underscore the importance of the sub-dimensions physical ability and physical attractiveness (Moreno, 1997). This domain seems to be so important that it has even been termed the "public self" (Harter, 1990).

The general trend appears to be to focus on physical appearance as the principal domain of the general self, especially during adolescence, between the ages of 11 and 15 (Atienza et al., 2004; Trent et al., 1994) and for both boys and girls (Pastor, 1998). Any differences found are attributed to the different way in which society treats attractive subjects with greater physical abilities (i.e. such individuals are generally more popular, receive preferential treatment and are more frequently praised for their physical qualities than their less attractive counterparts). As regards the weight of each of the facets of physical self-concept within the physical self, despite the fact that some authors have observed that physical ability, strength or physical fitness play a key role as domains of physical self-concept, it is attractiveness which is most closely related to physical self-concept, and even to general self-concept or self-esteem in both adolescents and adults (Maïano et al., 2004; Klomsten et al., 2004; Asçi et al., 1999).

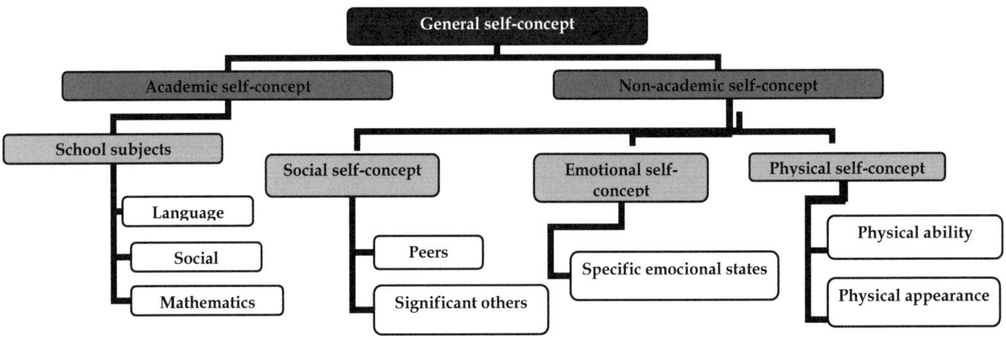


Fig. 2. Self-concept model by Shavelson, Hubner and Stanton (1976)

Since the 1960s, research into body image has received a great deal of attention, particularly from the field of psychology, psychiatry, medicine in general and even sociology. It is considered a crucial concept for explaining key aspects of personality, such as self-esteem or self-concept, as well as the social integration of adolescents. One can therefore say that body image has been explored mainly from both a clinical and psychosocial perspective (de Gracia et al., 1999). On the other hand, the study of physical self-concept is located within a predominantly social-educational or social-psychological research tradition (Jackson, 1992), due to its focus on identifying relationships with other dimensions of self-concept and on analysing its relations with affective (psychological wellbeing, self-esteem, anxiety, etc.) and behavioural characteristics (healthy habits, social skills, sporting activity, etc.).

In addition to being two constructs, which have been studied from different research traditions, there are also other aspects which distinguish body image from physical self-concept.

- The term physical self-concept encompasses a broader range of notions than body image. Although there are various different models of physical self-concept, it is made up by at least four more specific dimensions: physical fitness, sporting skill/ability, strength and physical attractiveness (Esnaola, 2005; Fox & Corbin, 1989; Goñi, et al., 2006). Some authors (Marsh et al., 1994) even claim that a greater number of dimensions is required (strength, obesity, physical activity, stamina, sporting skill / ability, coordination, health, appearance and flexibility) to provide a full idea of the concept. It can therefore be said that physical self-concept encompasses the term body image.
- Body image is defined as a construct with a multidimensional structure which includes self-perceptions, thoughts, feelings and actions related to one's own body, mainly as regards appearance (Cash & Pruzinsky, 1990); there is a certain degree of overlap between body image and the physical attractiveness dimension (perception of one's own physical appearance, security about and satisfaction with one's own image) of physical self-concept.

- However, it is also true that body image is a broader concept than that of physical attractiveness, since according to these same authors (Cash & Pruzinsky, 2002), body image includes experiences relating to the body's functioning (the perception and experience of all kinds of sensations, how we experience the aging process) and level of capacity (kinaesthesia, physical health, etc.).

One general framework, which has been used as a basis for research into the relationship between self-concept and body image distortion, is the self-discrepancy theory proposed by Higgins et al. (1985). This theoretical approach provides a model for analysing the differences between real self-concept (how one sees oneself) and ideal self-concept (ideal attributes that one would like to have; a self-assessment one carries out in relation to certain goals), which may be related to the onset or development of body image alterations. Thus, when the individual fails to achieve their ideal body image, a self-discrepancy occurs which may be the origin of body dissatisfaction (Marsh et al., 2007; Lau et al., 2004).

However, although body image and physical self-concept have mainly been analysed from different yet complementary perspectives, an undeniable relationship nevertheless exists between them. What have been put to the test, however, are a) the interrelationship between body image and general self-concept, and b) the relationship between physical self-concept and body dissatisfaction, with significant correlations being found in both cases.

In relation to the first case, we know that breakdowns in the development of self-concept contribute to alterations in body image, which in turn foster certain weight-related attitudes and behaviours characteristic of eating disorders. In other words, individuals with many negative and few positive ideas about themselves are more vulnerable to cultural messages about weight and body shape, and this vulnerability contributes to the development of the attitudes and behaviours typical of EDs (Stein & Corte, 2007). As regards the second case, i.e. the relationship between body dissatisfaction and physical self-concept, the only three studies carried out in this field all found a clear association between the two variables in both adolescents and university students (Esnaola, 2005; Goñi & Rodríguez, 2004; Goñi & Rodríguez, 2007). We can therefore assume that physical self-concept is a good indicator of possible eating disorders, since dissatisfaction with one's own body (the principal symptom of EDs) is clearly related not only to general self-concept, but also to poor physical self-concept (Esnaola, 2005; Goñi & Rodríguez, 2007), although the scope of this relationship has yet to be explored in any depth. Consequently, perhaps the most novel contribution of this chapter is its review of the results obtained both in these studies and in other more recent ones whose findings will be presented here for the first time, offering a much more enriching overview of the whole issue.

Therefore, the first questions that need to be asked are whether or not physical self-concept is related to the risk of suffering from some kind of ED during adolescence and, if so, how? In order to respond to these questions, an empirical study was conducted on a sample of 880 adolescents and young adults aged between 12 and 23, as well as a total of 48 patients clinically diagnosed in the Eating Disorder Treatment Unit of a hospital in the Basque Country (Spain). The level of physical self-concept was assessed using the Physical Self-Concept Questionnaire (CAF), validated and published in Spanish (Goñi et al., 2006). The probability of suffering from an ED was examined by assessing the presence or absence of eight clinically relevant symptoms which normally accompany AN and BN. These symptoms were assessed using the Eating Disorders Inventory-2 (EDI-2), by Garner (1998).

The CAF questionnaire follows the four-dimensional model outlined above and examines both physical self-concept in each of the four dimensions (physical ability, physical fitness, physical attractiveness and strength) and general perception of physical self-concept. The psychometric properties of this questionnaire are more than acceptable, with the reliability coefficients (Cronbach's alpha) being $\alpha = .84$ for the ability scale, $\alpha = .88$, for fitness, $\alpha = .87$ for physical attractiveness and $\alpha = .83$ for strength. These four components explain 61.34% of the variance of the questionnaire, with a total reliability of $\alpha = .92$. For its part, the alpha coefficient for the general physical self-concept scale is .87.

Outside the clinical field, the EDI-2 is used to help diagnose EDs because it offers a fast method of detecting subjects with sub-clinical EDs or who are at risk of developing a disorder of this type. The result of the inventory should not, however, be used as a substitute for a diagnosis carried out by a mental health professional. This questionnaire is a very common instrument also in the field of clinical research, because it enables the results of different sample groups to be compared and provides interesting descriptive information about said groups. The internal consistency (or reliability) coefficient for the questionnaire is between .83 and .93 for the population suffering from eating disorders, although in the normal population, the alpha indexes for each scale are between .70 and .93. The instrument assesses feelings, attitudes and behaviours characteristic of individuals diagnosed with EDs, such as:

- *Drive for thinness.* Assesses the clinical manifestation of an intense drive to become thinner, or a strong fear of becoming fat, two feelings always present in patients suffering from EDs and a key factor in their diagnosis. The items refer to concern about weight, dieting and fear of weight gain.
- *Bulimia.* Assesses the tendency towards or presence of thoughts related to uncontrolled binging.
- *Body dissatisfaction.* Measures the degree of dissatisfaction with one's general body shape or with certain body parts which typically concern patients with EDs.
- *Ineffectiveness or negative self-assessment.* Assesses feelings of general inadequacy, insecurity, emptiness, self-loathing and having no control over one's life. Conceptually, ineffectiveness is similar to low self-esteem or negative self-assessment, but in this case it goes one step further to include also the feeling of loneliness and emptiness.
- *Perfectionism.* Assesses subjects' conviction that they must always attain perfect performance levels, or do better than they are currently doing, and the degree to which they themselves believe and think others believe that nothing but the very best results are acceptable.
- *Interpersonal distrust.* Assesses subjects' general feelings of alienation and their scarce interest (or total disinterest) in forming close relationships. It also examines subjects' difficulty expressing their thoughts and feelings.
- *Interoceptive awareness.* Assesses difficulties in recognising and responding appropriately to sensations stemming from inside the body (feelings, the sensations of hunger and satiety, etc.).
- *Maturity fears.* Assesses subjects' fear of becoming adults, with all that that entails, and their desire to return to the security of childhood.

The correlations extracted with bilateral significance for the five measures of physical self-concept and the eight measures of ED behaviours and personality traits are shown in table 1.

The results indicate that physical attractiveness is the component of the physical self that correlates most closely with the risk of developing an eating disorder, since it has the highest inverse relationship levels with both body dissatisfaction and drive for thinness. In other words, a poor perception of one's own physical attractiveness is more closely associated with high body dissatisfaction and a greater drive for thinness. The results also reveal that a high level of physical attractiveness serves as a moderate protective factor against BN. Something similar can be observed if we focus on the personality traits typical of individuals suffering from EDs, since low physical ability and low physical attractiveness levels have the greatest degree of interconnection with the risk of developing an eating disorder.

Of all the scales designed to assess eating disorders, ineffectiveness is the one with the highest correlations with all the dimensions of physical self-concept, probably due to the fact that this measure represents a construct that is very similar to that of general self-concept. These correlations are slightly higher than those found for body dissatisfaction, whose values oscillate between $r$ =-.398 for physical ability, and $r$ = -.600 for the global measure of physical self-concept. This means that body dissatisfaction goes slightly beyond a simple assessment of physical attractiveness, since the correlations between the two ($r$ = -.574) are lower than for the global physical self.

Finally, it is worth mentioning that drive for thinness was found to have a very weak association with physical ability ($r$ = -.109) and physical fitness ($r$ = -.184), and no association whatsoever with strength ($r$ = .014). This leads us to conclude that drive for thinness and weight loss behaviours are mainly prompted by subjects' desire to achieve greater physical attractiveness. Although it is true that general physical self-concept has very similar relationships to attractiveness with drive for thinness, it is also true that some authors have found a major overlap between the global assessment of the perceived physical self and the assessment of the more specific dimension of physical attractiveness. In other words, despite the absence of any correlation of note between drive for thinness and physical ability, fitness or strength, the association found with general physical self-concept seems only logical, since individuals tend to bestow considerable importance on physical attractiveness within physical self-concept.

However, correlation analyses are often inadequate for providing an in-depth exploration of the relationship between two variables. Since this is a case in point, the decision was made to divide the whole sample group up in accordance with the level of physical self-concept (low vs. medium/high). This would enable a comparison to be carried out between the different results obtained for each of the EDI scales, based on a T-student mean comparison analysis (see table 2). The results indicate that it is individuals with low physical self-concept levels who always score highest in all the measures of typical ED symptoms assessed using Garner's EDI-2 (1998). In other words, those who perceive themselves as having a poor physical self are those who have greater body dissatisfaction, a higher drive for thinness, a greater number of typically bulimic behaviours and more pronounced personality traits typical of those with EDs (ineffectiveness, perfectionism, interpersonal distrust, interoceptive awareness and maturity fears). Similarly, the data also indicate that the greatest differences due to physical self-concept levels were found for body dissatisfaction.

| | | Ability | Fitness | Attractiveness | Strength | General physical self-concept |
|---|---|---|---|---|---|---|
| Drive for thinness | r Pearson | -.109*** | -.184*** | -.362*** | .014 | -.342*** |
| | p (bil) | .002 | .000 | .000 | .677 | .000 |
| Bulimia | r Pearson | -.252*** | -.223*** | -.222*** | -.103*** | -.215*** |
| | p (bil) | .000 | .000 | .000 | .003 | .000 |
| Body dissatisfaction | r Pearson | -.398*** | -.438*** | -.574*** | -.176*** | -.600*** |
| | p (bil) | .000 | .000 | .000 | .000 | .000 |
| Ineffectiveness | r Pearson | -.471*** | -.424*** | -.433*** | -.283*** | -.499*** |
| | p (bil) | .000 | .000 | .000 | .000 | .000 |
| Perfectionism | r Pearson | .056 | .133*** | .051 | .049 | .055 |
| | p (bil) | .108 | .000 | .142 | .156 | .113 |
| Interpersonal distrust | r Pearson | -.398*** | -.347*** | -.344*** | -.201*** | -.377*** |
| | p (bil) | .000 | .000 | .000 | .000 | .000 |
| Interoceptive awareness | r Pearson | -.381*** | -.343*** | -.372*** | -.200*** | -.386*** |
| | p (bil) | .000 | .000 | .000 | .000 | .000 |
| Maturity fears | r Pearson | -.168*** | -.112*** | -.130*** | -.067 | -.161*** |
| | p (bil) | .000 | .001 | .000 | .053 | .000 |

*** $p < .001$

Table 1. Correlations between self-concept and EDs in a non-clinical sample group

| | | n | M | SD | t | p |
|---|---|---|---|---|---|---|
| Drive for thinness | low PSC | 169 | 5.78 | 4.963 | 8.246 | **.000*** ** |
| | medium/high PSC | 662 | 3.03 | 3.522 | | |
| Bulimia | low PSC | 169 | 2.99 | 3.180 | 6.576 | **.000*** ** |
| | medium/high PSC | 663 | 1.53 | 2.403 | | |
| Body dissatisfaction | low PSC | 169 | 13.75 | 6.569 | 16.703 | **.000*** ** |
| | medium/high PSC | 663 | 5.73 | 5.286 | | |
| Ineffectiveness | low PSC | 169 | 10.74 | 7.588 | 14.135 | **.000*** ** |
| | medium/high PSC | 663 | 4.11 | 4.743 | | |
| Perfectionism | low PSC | 169 | 6.44 | 5.643 | 2.818 | **.005** ** |
| | medium/high PSC | 663 | 5.45 | 3.584 | | |
| Interpersonal distrust | low PSC | 169 | 6.76 | 5.077 | 9.464 | **.000*** ** |
| | medium/high PSC | 663 | 3.53 | 3.636 | | |
| Interoceptive awareness | low PSC | 169 | 8.60 | 6.481 | 10.574 | **.000*** ** |
| | medium/high PSC | 662 | 4.16 | 4.373 | | |
| Maturity fears | low PSC | 169 | 8.67 | 4.330 | 4.751 | **.000**** ** |
| | medium/high PSC | 663 | 6.96 | 3.548 | | |

** $p < .01$; *** $p < .001$

Table 2. Eating disorders in accordance with physical self-concept (PSC)

The variability of ED behaviours and traits was also examined in accordance with the general measure of physical self-concept, with the results showing significantly higher levels of all of them in the group with low general physical self-concept. However, two stand out from the rest: body dissatisfaction, for being the trait with the greatest variation between one degree of self-concept and the other, and negative self-assessment, for being the variable in which the second greatest differences were observed.

In short, we can affirm that physical self-concept is indeed associated with eating disorders, since the data repeatedly indicate that low physical self-concept correlates with a greater number of psychological behaviours and traits typical of individuals suffering from EDs. Low physical self-concept therefore poses a significantly greater risk of developing AN or BN than normal or higher-than-average physical self-concept.

### 4.1 Gender and age

Another interesting question to explore is whether the risk of EDs associated with physical self-concept is similar for everyone throughout the entire adolescent period, or whether associated risk factors also exist, and if so, what these factors are. The data shown in tables 3 to 6 help answer this question. The results fail to confirm differences between the two genders in four out of the eight scales studied (table 3). Nevertheless, both drive for thinness and body dissatisfaction are significantly higher among adolescent girls than among adolescent boys, while boys were found to have a greater number of typically bulimic behaviours, a greater degree of perfectionism and more maturity fears. This means that adolescent girls do indeed have a more intense desire to be thin than boys, and experience a greater degree of body dissatisfaction.

| | GENDER | n | M | SD | T | p |
|---|---|---|---|---|---|---|
| **Drive for thinness** | Male | 428 | 2.83 | 3.243 | -5.655 | **.000*** ** |
| | Female | 403 | 4.39 | 4.559 | | |
| **Bulimia** | Male | 428 | 2.01 | 2.605 | 2.025 | **.043*** |
| | Female | 404 | 1.64 | 2.675 | | |
| **Body dissatisfaction** | Male | 428 | 6.31 | 6.029 | -4.921 | **.000*** ** |
| | Female | 404 | 8.47 | 6.664 | | |
| **Ineffectiveness** | Male | 428 | 5.38 | 6.420 | -.371 | .711 |
| | Female | 404 | 5.54 | 5.652 | | |
| **Perfectionism** | Male | 428 | 6.40 | 4.415 | 5.569 | **.000*** ** |
| | Female | 404 | 4.85 | 3.580 | | |
| **Interpersonal distrust** | Male | 428 | 4.42 | 4.337 | 1.683 | .093 |
| | Female | 404 | 3.93 | 3.988 | | |
| **Interoceptive awareness** | Male | 428 | 4.97 | 4.885 | -.511 | .609 |
| | Female | 403 | 5.15 | 5.500 | | |
| **Maturity fears** | Male | 428 | 7.61 | 3.863 | 2.448 | **.015*** |
| | Female | 404 | 6.98 | 3.668 | | |

** $p < .01$; *** $p < .001$

Table 3. Eating disorders in accordance with gender

More conclusive are the results for the variability of the risk of EDs in accordance with age range during adolescence. As shown in table 4, the desire to lose weight (drive for thinness) remains stable throughout all adolescence, with similar indexes for both 12-year-olds and 18-year-olds.

Nevertheless, in the other measures studied, body dissatisfaction, bulimic behaviours, ineffectiveness (or negative self-assessment), perfectionism, interpersonal distrust, interoceptive awareness and maturity fears, the values increase as adolescence progresses.

| | AGE | n | M | SD | F | p |
|---|---|---|---|---|---|---|
| **Drive for thinness** | From 12 to 14 | 474 | 3.45 | 3.809 | 1.858 | .157 |
| | From 15 to 17 | 261 | 3.97 | 4.175 | | |
| | Over 18 | 96 | 3.23 | 4.466 | | |
| **Bulimia** | From 12 to 14 | 475 | 1.30 | 2.228 | 32.789 | **.000*** ** |
| | From 15 to 17 | 261 | 2.19 | 2.568 | | |
| | Over 18 | 96 | 3.47 | 3.722 | | |
| **Body dissatisfaction** | From 12 to 14 | 475 | 6.03 | 5.948 | 31.336 | **.000*** ** |
| | From 15 to 17 | 261 | 8.42 | 6.125 | | |
| | Over 18 | 96 | 11.02 | 7.579 | | |
| **Ineffectiveness** | From 12 to 14 | 475 | 4.07 | 4.246 | 79.414 | **.000*** ** |
| | From 15 to 17 | 261 | 5.61 | 4.897 | | |
| | Over 18 | 96 | 11.90 | 10.662 | | |
| **Perfectionism** | From 12 to 14 | 475 | 5.27 | 3.263 | 104.211 | **.000*** ** |
| | From 15 to 17 | 261 | 4.50 | 3.306 | | |
| | Over 18 | 96 | 10.65 | 5.883 | | |
| **Interpersonal distrust** | From 12 to 14 | 475 | 3.37 | 3.389 | 47.446 | **.000*** ** |
| | From 15 to 17 | 261 | 4.38 | 3.816 | | |
| | Over 18 | 96 | 7.67 | 6.303 | | |
| **Interoceptive awareness** | From 12 to 14 | 474 | 4.05 | 4.111 | 53.352 | **.000*** ** |
| | From 15 to 17 | 261 | 5.18 | 4.889 | | |
| | Over 18 | 96 | 9.70 | 7.674 | | |
| **Maturity fears** | From 12 to 14 | 475 | 7.09 | 3.663 | 6.704 | **.001** ** |
| | From 15 to 17 | 261 | 7.21 | 3.318 | | |
| | Over 18 | 96 | 8.61 | 5.096 | | |

** $p < .01$; *** $p < .001$

Table 4. Eating disorders in accordance with age

Given that the results of the multiple comparisons reveal the existence of significant differences for all aforementioned variables between all three age groups, we can conclude that the risk of developing an ED varies throughout adolescence, being strongest in the 18-23 age range, despite the fact that the desire to be thin remains stable through the whole of this developmental stage.

The close relationship between physical self-concept and risk of developing some kind of eating disorder has already been mentioned in previous sections. It is therefore important to verify whether physical self-concept also differs in accordance with gender or age (tables 5 and 6, respectively). In relation to gender, adolescent boys tend to have a higher level of physical self-concept than adolescent girls in all components: physical ability, physical fitness, attractiveness and strength, as well as general physical self.

| | GENDER | N | M | SD | T | p |
|---|---|---|---|---|---|---|
| Ability | Male | 428 | 25.98 | 6.818 | 830 | .000*** |
| | Female | 404 | 23.29 | 6.714 | | |
| Fitness | Male | 428 | 25.81 | 7.233 | 830 | .000*** |
| | Female | 404 | 22.02 | 7.130 | | |
| Attractiveness | Male | 428 | 24.76 | 6.883 | 830 | .000*** |
| | Female | 404 | 22.07 | 7.571 | | |
| Strength | Male | 428 | 23.15 | 6.148 | 830 | .000*** |
| | Female | 404 | 19.69 | 6.442 | | |
| General physical self-concept | Male | 428 | 26.68 | 6.870 | 830 | .000*** |
| | Female | 404 | 23.47 | 7.442 | | |

*** $p < .001$

Table 5. Physical self-concept in accordance with gender

| | AGE | n | M | SD | F | p |
|---|---|---|---|---|---|---|
| Ability | From 12 to 14 | 475 | 25.96 | 6.889 | 31.831 | .000*** |
| | From 15 to 17 | 261 | 23.98 | 6.754 | | |
| | Over 18 | 96 | 20.21 | 4.971 | | |
| Fitness | From 12 to 14 | 475 | 25.29 | 7.683 | 23.145 | .000*** |
| | From 15 to 17 | 261 | 22.92 | 7.324 | | |
| | Over 18 | 96 | 20.29 | 3.916 | | |
| Attractiveness | From 12 to 14 | 475 | 24.71 | 7.593 | 24.896 | .000*** |
| | From 15 to 17 | 261 | 22.69 | 7.223 | | |
| | Over 18 | 96 | 19.32 | 3.841 | | |
| Strength | From 12 to 14 | 475 | 22.19 | 6.982 | 11.787 | .000*** |
| | From 15 to 17 | 261 | 21.13 | 6.220 | | |
| | Over 18 | 96 | 18.77 | 3.567 | | |
| General physical self-concept | From 12 to 14 | 475 | 26.48 | 7.397 | 34.717 | .000*** |
| | From 15 to 17 | 261 | 24.51 | 7.222 | | |
| | Over 18 | 96 | 20.05 | 4.191 | | |

*** $p < .001$

Table 6. Physical self-concept in accordance with age

Much clearer is the connection between physical self-concept and EDs, in accordance with age, since as reflected in table 6, the pattern of the results is similar in both cases throughout adolescence. Thus, although the risk of EDs increases with age, reaching its highest point between the ages of 18 and 23, physical self-concept reaches its highest values between the ages of 12 and 14, and then gradually decreases until it reaches its lowest point between the ages of 18 and 23.

This, in addition to corroborating the relationship between physical self-concept and EDs, also demonstrates how physical self-concept may be both a predisposing factor, and an important preventive factor to be borne in mind when trying to protect adolescents against the risk of developing AN or BN. By improving the four dimensions of the physical self, we can improve general physical self-concept, thus reducing the probability of adolescents suffering from some kind of ED.

This strengthening of physical self-concept is particularly important between the ages of 15 and 23, when the risk of EDs becomes higher. However, this does not mean that we should overlook the fact that good prevention work should begin long before the pathology starts to develop. Moreover, bearing in mind that the body changes typical of adolescence are one of the variables which have most frequently been proposed as precursors to body dissatisfaction and eating pathologies, the best option would be to begin prevention work from an early age, even before the age of 12.

### 4.2 Body mass index

Another factor which is often considered to be one of the basic aspects underlying EDs is body mass index (i.e. the proportion between a subject's weight and height). It is no coincidence that the World Health Organisation establishes a BMI of less than 17.5 (severely underweight) as an informal criterion for the diagnosis of AN. Hence it is important to explore whether this index mediates the relationship between physical self-concept and eating disorders; in other words, whether those with a higher body mass index have a poorer physical self and a higher number of ED symptoms associated with the perceived physical self.

The results both for the personality traits and eating disorder behaviours measured using the EDI questionnaire and for the five measures of physical self-concept are presented in tables 7 and 8. The data show significant differences in all the ED measures, with the exception of perfectionism and maturity fears. All confirm that the higher the body mass index, the greater the number of eating disorder symptoms detected in the adolescent.

However, these differences do not appear in all groups and nor is there a clear pattern which remains constant for all scales. Thus, while bulimic behaviours seem to be higher among those whose weight / height ratio is within normal limits, in comparison with those with a lower BMI, differences were found both between the normal weight and severely underweight groups, and between the overweight group and the three other BMI groups in relation to body dissatisfaction and drive for thinness.

As regards the relationship between BMI and physical self-concept (table 8), the results reveal that those with a higher BMI report having a lower self-concept of their physical ability, fitness, physical attractiveness and strength, as well as a lower physical self-concept understood in its more general sense.

| | | n | M | SD | F | p |
|---|---|---|---|---|---|---|
| | Severely underweight | 81 | 2.32 | 3.40 | | |
| **Drive for thinness** | Underweight | 268 | 3.17 | 3.59 | 8.115 | **.000*** ** |
| | Normal | 375 | 3.73 | 4.05 | | |
| | Overweight | 51 | 5.51 | 4.76 | | |
| | Severely underweight | 81 | 1.41 | 2.10 | | |
| **Bulimia** | Underweight | 269 | 1.49 | 2.38 | 5.663 | **.001** ** |
| | Normal | 375 | 2.25 | 2.93 | | |
| | Overweight | 51 | 2.35 | 2.72 | | |
| | Severely underweight | 81 | 5.90 | 5.39 | | |
| **Body dissatisfaction** | Underweight | 269 | 5.88 | 5.69 | 13.517 | **.000*** ** |
| | Normal | 375 | 8.28 | 6.64 | | |
| | Overweight | 51 | 10.37 | 6.11 | | |
| | Severely underweight | 81 | 4.84 | 4.80 | | |
| **Ineffectiveness** | Underweight | 269 | 4.43 | 4.90 | 8.164 | **.000*** ** |
| | Normal | 375 | 6.24 | 6.94 | | |
| | Overweight | 51 | 8.18 | 6.79 | | |
| | Severely underweight | 81 | 5.26 | 3.35 | | |
| **Perfectionism** | Underweight | 269 | 5.48 | 3.34 | 2.514 | .057 |
| | Normal | 375 | 6.08 | 4.70 | | |
| | Overweight | 51 | 4.75 | 4.60 | | |
| | Severely underweight | 81 | 4.31 | 3.71 | | |
| **Interpersonal distrust** | Underweight | 269 | 3.41 | 3.49 | | |
| | Normal | 375 | 4.63 | 4.68 | 8.201 | **.000*** ** |
| | Overweight | 51 | 6.18 | 4.49 | | |
| | Severely underweight | 81 | 4.67 | 4.51 | | |
| **Interoceptive awareness** | Underweight | 268 | 4.35 | 4.47 | 4.846 | **.002** ** |
| | Normal | 375 | 5.76 | 5.78 | | |
| | Overweight | 51 | 6.29 | 5.29 | | |
| | Severely underweight | 81 | 7.81 | 3.81 | | |
| **Maturity fears** | Underweight | 269 | 7.14 | 3.68 | 1.963 | .118 |
| | Normal | 375 | 7.31 | 3.76 | | |
| | Overweight | 51 | 8.39 | 4.57 | | |

** $p < .01$; *** $p < .001$

Table 7. Eating disorders in accordance with BMI

| | | n | M | SD | F | P |
|---|---|---|---|---|---|---|
| Ability | Severely underweight | 81 | 25.17 | 5.500 | 9.987 | .000*** |
| | Underweight | 269 | 25.76 | 7.210 | | |
| | Normal | 375 | 23.91 | 6.726 | | |
| | Overweight | 51 | 20.57 | 6.709 | | |
| Fitness | Severely underweight | 81 | 26.10 | 5.905 | 20.285 | .000*** |
| | Underweight | 269 | 25.50 | 7.678 | | |
| | Normal | 375 | 23.06 | 7.152 | | |
| | Overweight | 51 | 18.00 | 6.073 | | |
| Attractiveness | Severely underweight | 81 | 24.32 | 7.285 | 18.503 | .000*** |
| | Underweight | 269 | 25.23 | 7.179 | | |
| | Normal | 375 | 22.44 | 6.963 | | |
| | Overweight | 51 | 18.07 | 6.517 | | |
| Strength | Severely underweight | 81 | 18.86 | 6.373 | 5.031 | .002** |
| | Underweight | 269 | 21.05 | 6.449 | | |
| | Normal | 375 | 21.69 | 6.357 | | |
| | Overweight | 51 | 22.43 | 6.090 | | |
| General physical self-concept | Severely underweight | 81 | 27.16 | 7.059 | 22.445 | .000*** |
| | Underweight | 269 | 26.65 | 6.820 | | |
| | Normal | 375 | 24.03 | 7.213 | | |
| | Overweight | 51 | 18.96 | 6.570 | | |

** $p < .01$; *** $p < .001$

Table 8. Physical self-concept in accordance with BMI

In short, as a general pattern, physical self-concept and EDs are associated with body mass index. Moreover, if we bear in mind the correlation found between the physical self and ED symptoms, we can indeed conclude that adolescents with a higher body mass index have a poorer physical self-concept and are at greater risk of EDs, in the sense that they have a greater number of traits and behaviours defined as symptoms of EDs.

### 4.3 Physical-sporting activity

To date, the relationship between physical-sporting activity and physical self-concept has been widely corroborated (Goñi & Rodríguez, 2004; Goñi & Rodríguez, 2007; Esnaola, 2005; Ruiz de Azúa, 2007), but it still remains to be seen whether the relationship between these two variables is connected in any way to the probability of developing an ED.

In order to test this hypothesis, we first took only those four traits most closely linked to EDs, namely drive for thinness, bulimic behaviours, body dissatisfaction and ineffectiveness, evaluated, as in all other cases, by the EDI-2 questionnaire. Secondly, subjects were divided into two groups, low physical self-concept and medium/high physical self-concept, in each of the dimensions of the physical self, in accordance with the scores obtained in said dimensions.

| | | | EDI scales | | | | | | | |
|---|---|---|---|---|---|---|---|---|---|---|
| | | | DT | | Bul | | BD | | In | |
| | | | M | (SD) | M | (SD) | M | (SD) | M | (SD) |
| ABILITY | Low | Spor | 6.17 | (5.30) | 2.17 | (2.72) | 10.50 | (5.97) | 8.81 | (6.60) |
| | | Habit | 5.45 | (5.35) | 3.65 | (3.49) | 13.37 | (7.12) | 12.73 | (8.42) |
| | Med/High | Spor | 4.83 | (4.67) | 1.33 | (1.89) | 8.64 | (6.62) | 5.24 | (4.59) |
| | | Habit | 3.74 | (4.55) | 1.56 | (2.49) | 6.63 | (6.20) | 4.49 | (5.11) |
| | p | Phy_Act | **.000*** ** | | **.001** ** | | .554 | | .123 | |
| | | Ph Self | **.001** ** | | **.000*** ** | | **.000*** ** | | **.000*** ** | |
| | | Ph Self * Ph Act | .860 | | **.000*** ** | | **.000*** ** | | **.000*** ** | |
| FITNESS | Low | Spor | 5.59 | (4.97) | 2.49 | (2.70) | 11.67 | (7.61) | 9.31 | (6.44) |
| | | Habit | 7.29 | (6.26) | 2.63 | (3.57) | 12.03 | (6.98) | 9.63 | (7.12) |
| | Med/High | Spor | 5.21 | (4.96) | 1.19 | (1.85) | 8.06 | (5.25) | 5.12 | (4.66) |
| | | Habit | 3.36 | (4.07) | 1.70 | (2.54) | 6.74 | (6.37) | 4.89 | (5.91) |
| | p | Phy_Act | **.016*** | | .758 | | **.026*** | | **.002** ** | |
| | | Ph Self | **.000*** ** | | **.000*** ** | | **.000*** ** | | **.000*** ** | |
| | | Ph Self * Ph Act | .559 | | .738 | | .238 | | .242 | |
| ATTRACTIVENESS | Low | Spor | 8.06 | (5.61) | 2.14 | (2.65) | 14.10 | (7.28) | 11.00 | (6.60) |
| | | Habit | 8.78 | (5.93) | 2.56 | (3.12) | 14.38 | (7.48) | 8.77 | (5.60) |
| | Med/High | Spor | 4.35 | (4.30) | 1.48 | (2.11) | 7.62 | (5.09) | 5.03 | (4.40) |
| | | Habit | 3.14 | (3.89) | 1.72 | (2.66) | 6.38 | (5.85) | 5.08 | (6.32) |
| | p | Phy_Act | **.037*** | | .950 | | **.002** ** | | **.000*** ** | |
| | | Ph Self | **.000*** ** | | **.004** ** | | **.000*** ** | | **.000*** ** | |
| | | Ph Self * Ph Act | .071 | | .258 | | .549 | | .107 | |
| STRENGTH | Low | Spor | 6.21 | (5.52) | 1.92 | (2.56) | 9.88 | (6.46) | 7.91 | (6.31) |
| | | Habit | 4.57 | (5.64) | 1.94 | (2.67) | 9.18 | (6.86) | 7.83 | (7.36) |
| | Med/High | Spor | 4.09 | (3.66) | 1.27 | (1.73) | 8.61 | (6.35) | 4.77 | (4.09) |
| | | Habit | 3.68 | (4.12) | 1.80 | (2.79) | 6.75 | (6.54) | 4.51 | (5.44) |
| | p | Phy_Act | **.000*** ** | | .335 | | **.000*** ** | | **.000*** ** | |
| | | Ph Self | **.004** ** | | .575 | | **.000*** ** | | **.000*** ** | |
| | | Ph Self * Ph Act | **.044*** | | .654 | | .173 | | .375 | |

*p<.05, **p<.01, ***p<.001

Legend: DT= Drive for thinness; Bul= Bulimia; BD= Body dissatisfaction; In= Ineffectiveness; Spor= Sporadic; Habit= Habitual; Phy_Act= Physical activity; Ph Self= Physical self-concept; Ph Act= Physical activity.

Table 9. EDs in accordance with physical self-concept and physical activity

The data available confirm that, in the majority of cases, the frequency of physical activity does indeed seem to explain the variation observed in the scores obtained for the different behaviours and ideas associated with EDs at a physical self-concept level (table 9), with the general rule being that assiduous physical exercise reduces the risk of AN or BN, except as regards the number of bulimic behaviours according to self-concept in physical ability, where the risk increases.

Also, the risk of EDs varies in accordance with the level obtained in all facets of the perceived physical self, since seeing oneself in a positive light results in a significant reduction in body dissatisfaction, behaviours characterised as bulimic, drive for thinness and ineffectiveness or negative self-assessment. The only exception to this lies in the bulimia scale in relation to the strength dimension, where current data are unable to confirm the existence of statistical differences.

Various interactions have been found between the effect of the frequency of physical-sporting activity and the level of physical self-concept, specifically that of low physical ability with bulimia, body dissatisfaction and ineffectiveness; this behavioural pattern is also followed by drive for thinness in accordance with strength, since frequent physical activity in lower self-concept levels leads to a greater probability of a strong desire to lose weight.

In short, we can conclude that among those with low self-concept, habitual physical-sporting activity is associated with a greater risk of eating disorders.

### 4.4 Physical self-concept and EDs in the clinical population

However, these affirmations based on a sample group with no prior diagnosis of EDs could not be considered complete until further research had been carried out to establish whether or not they hold up when the population analysed are clinical patients (table 10) previously diagnosed with EDs by qualified staff at the Eating Disorder Unit of a hospital located in the Basque Country (Spain). To this end, a total of 48 patients participated in the study. All were adolescent girls aged between 12 and 22.

The results obtained for patients diagnosed with EDs enable further clarification of the previous affirmations. The correlations continue to be negative, thus confirming that the poorer the concept each individual has of her physical self, the greater the probability of suffering from an ED (with this probability being understood as the presence of a greater number of traits which define this type of psychopathology) and vice versa. Moreover, all the correlations oscillate between moderate and high, with those observed between body dissatisfaction and the physical attractiveness dimension ($r$ = .725) and general physical self-concept ($r$ = .770) being particularly worth noting.

Nevertheless, four important differences were found in the sample of patients with EDs: a) again, the component strength had the lowest relationship indexes, but unlike with the general population, where its correlations were not significant, in this case they did correlate statistically with a moderate level of interrelation; b) despite the fact that physical attractiveness was found in this case to correlate more closely with the majority of behaviours, traits and attitudes, these correlations were lower than those of general physical self-concept and physical fitness; c) although in the non-clinical sample group perfectionism was not associated with any dimension of physical self-concept, in the group of adolescents

| | | Ability | Fitness | Attractiveness | Strength | General Physical Self-concept |
|---|---|---|---|---|---|---|
| **Drive for thinness** | Pearson r | -.258 | **-.414**** | **-.375**** | **-.348**** | **-.682***** |
| | p (bil) | .077 | .003 | .009 | .015 | .000 |
| **Bulimia** | Pearson r | **-.302*** | **-.393**** | -.187 | **.314*** | **-.456**** |
| | p (bil) | .037 | .006 | .203 | .030 | .001 |
| **Body dissatisfaction** | Pearson r | **-.456**** | **-.591***** | **-.725***** | .139 | **-.770***** |
| | p (bil) | .001 | .000 | .000 | .347 | .000 |
| **Ineffectiveness** | Pearson r | -.158 | **-.650***** | **-.491***** | **-.304*** | **-.452**** |
| | p (bil) | .282 | .000 | .000 | .036 | .001 |
| **Perfectionism** | Pearson r | **.579***** | .269 | **.601***** | .271 | **.482**** |
| | p (bil) | .000 | .064 | .000 | .063 | .001 |
| **Interpersonal distrust** | Pearson r | **-.615***** | **-.679***** | **-.313*** | **-.303*** | -.153 |
| | p (bil) | .000 | .000 | .030 | .036 | .299 |
| **Interoceptive awareness** | Pearson r | -.051 | **-.621***** | **-.482**** | -.197 | **-.587***** |
| | p (bil) | .731 | .000 | .001 | .179 | .000 |
| **Maturity fears** | Pearson r | **-.465**** | **-.401**** | -.242 | **-.540***** | -.139 |
| | p (bil) | .001 | .005 | .097 | .000 | .347 |

*** $p < .001$; *** $p < .01$

Table 10. Correlations between self-concept and EDs in a clinical sample group

with EDs, high correlations were found between perfectionism and physical ability, physical attractiveness and general physical self-concept, a finding which confirms that individuals with EDs are extremely perfectionist and want their perceived physical self, not just their attractiveness level, to be perfect; and d) unlike in the non-clinical population, in which drive for thinness had a weak correlation with physical fitness, here the correlation is moderate/high.

## 5. Physical self-concept and risk of developing EDs: conclusions

The results presented in this chapter confirm that sustained by previous research (Goñi & Rodríguez, 2004, 2007), i.e. that EDs are negatively associated with physical self-concept in all its dimensions, particularly in relation to physical attractiveness, which is revealed as the dimension most closely linked to the four behaviours and thoughts most commonly present in EDs: drive for thinness, bulimia, body dissatisfaction and ineffectiveness (or negative self-assessment).

It is logical to think that EDs occur always in individuals with a low physical self-concept, or the opposite, i.e. that physical self-concept drops when an ED develops. Whatever the case is, ED patients' assessment of their physical self is much lower than that of the normal population. However, it was necessary to demonstrate this idea, and indeed, the obtained results confirm it. When subjects were divided into two groups in accordance with physical self-concept (low vs. medium/high), significant differences were found for all ED symptoms in accordance with the all the dimensions of physical self-concept. We can therefore conclude that individuals who assess their physical attributes negatively have a greater potential risk of suffering from AN or BN at some point in the future.

However, although the various studies which have examined the relationship between physical self-concept and EDs in the non-clinical population (i.e. in those with no prior clinical diagnosis) have repeatedly reached these same conclusions, no studies had hitherto focused on this relationship in the clinical population, which is why the data presented here are totally unprecedented.

Again, a negative relationship is observed between the dimensions of the perceived physical self and ED symptoms, but in this case, the correlations are closer, with strength being the dimension with the lowest relationship indexes, although these indexes are still significant (unlike in the non-clinical population). Despite the fact that among patients with EDs the level of association between perceived physical attractiveness and ED symptoms is higher than among the normal population, it is physical fitness and general physical self-concept which are most closely related to eating disorder symptoms. All this prompts an important question, the answer to which is vital for establishing the risk factors for these pathologies and for planning effective prevention programmes. It is a question which, to date, has also been impossible to answer: is the development of AN or BN what makes poor self-perception spread to other areas of the physical self, or is the opposite true, i.e. that an ED arises not when self-assessment of one's physical attractiveness is negative (something which is very common among the normal, non-clinical population), but when the individual in question begins to perceive themselves negatively in all aspects of their physical self?

Diverse authors have tried to explain why only a small part of the total population ends up developing eating disorders, when around 75% claim to feel dissatisfied with their physical appearance (an important risk factor); and many have defended the idea of restrictive dieting as a mediating and trigger factor (Garner, 1998; Heilbrun & Witt, 1990; Toro, 2004). However, in light of the data presented here, perhaps the answer to this question lies elsewhere. If the results obtained in this study (in the clinical population the highest correlations with ED symptoms are found mainly in low general physical self-concept and low physical fitness, more than in low physical attractiveness) are considered in conjunction with the fact that the percentage of ED diagnoses is surprisingly higher among sportsmen and women than among the normal population (Houtkooper, 2000; Toro, 2004; Wilmore & Costill, 1998), then we can conclude that perhaps, one of the trigger factors may also be perceiving oneself as physically incompetent. In any case, we must not forget that this reflection is only a hypothesis which requires further empirical support.

What is clear, however, is that low physical self-concept is a clear risk factor for developing some kind of ED. Both in the non-clinical population (i.e. those with no previous diagnosis of AN or BN) and the clinical sample group, the relationship found between the components of the perceived physical self and the symptoms of EDs provides a glimpse of how we can work to reduce the risk or severity of these pathologies, i.e. by improving the four facets of physical self-concept. Learning to accept one's own physical attractiveness and assessing that attractiveness more positively will help reduce eating disorder behaviours aimed at achieving a body image more in keeping with the current stereotype of beauty. Moreover, fostering physical ability and physical fitness will also make it possible to reduce, if not avoid, those personality traits which underlie these types of psychological alterations.

However, physical self-concept is not the only risk factor associated with EDs. It can be said that the risk of suffering from EDs (measured using the responses provided to the EDI questionnaire) is mediated by social-personal variables such as age, gender, body mass index and engagement in physical-sporting activity. It can also be stated that the risk of EDs is greater among adolescent girls than among adolescent boys, among 15-23-year-olds than among 12-14-year-olds and among those who engage in physical activity sporadically than among those who exercise regularly.

In relation to gender, the implications of the data presented here are important for the diagnosis, prevention and treatment of EDs. Although until now, EDs have been considered as pertaining exclusively to women with a set of clearly-defined personality traits, recently the situation seems to have changed somewhat. The increase in incidence rates in both the male and female populations has blurred some of the personality traits which, until recently, were considered distinctive of anorectic or bulimic patients. This makes the early detection of possible future cases even more difficult, since the warning bells now focus only on behaviours such as starvation, vomiting or restrictive dieting, i.e. behaviours which occur once the pathology has already fully developed.

In the association between gender and EDs, physical self-concept also plays a key role, since adolescent girls tend to have a poorer physical self and a greater risk of EDs than their male counterparts. What remains to be clarified is a key question in this gender-physical self-concept-ED trinomial: is it gender that determines whether or not an individual has a poorer physical self-concept, and does this in turn increase the risk of developing an ED? Attempts are currently being made to answer this question using structural equations modelling (SEM), which offers an approach to the study of causal relations.

Of special relevance also is the relationship found between body mass index and risk of ED associated with low physical self-concept. Individuals who are overweight perceive themselves physically in a poorer light in all the dimensions of the physical self, and as weight is reduced, so these self-perceptions improve; physical performance and ability increase, as do physical fitness and perceived strength, and subjects see themselves as more attractive. The psychological implication of this is clear: within healthy limits, body weight control strengthens self-concept in all these physical facets (ability, fitness, attractiveness and strength), meaning that, thanks to the aforementioned connection with behaviours and traits typical of EDs, the probability of developing AN or BN is significantly reduced.

As regards age, if all three variables (EDs, physical self-concept and age) are borne in mind, then the relationship between improved physical self-concept and EDs is observed to be related to age. Thus, while the risk of suffering from EDs tends to increase throughout adolescence, physical self-concept is associated with a considerable reduction in this risk, with those reporting low physical self-concept having a considerably higher risk of developing an ED than their counterparts in the medium/high group.

Improvement of and education about physical self-concept is therefore a good method of fighting against EDs, because it seems to significantly reduce the growing effect of age on these pathologies; however, it is not and should not be the only method used. The fact that, as time goes by, seeing oneself as less physically attractive is associated with an increasing risk of EDs may indicate the presence of another uncontrolled variable which has a negative effect on this relationship. Therefore, education about self-concept should always be accompanied by a diverse range of other methods which aim to cover as many variables as possible linked to EDs.

One good method may be to engage in regular physical-sporting activity, since the data presented here show that physical activity is a modulating variable of the risk of developing eating disorders. This may be due to the fact that engaging in regular exercise improves all the dimensions of the physical self (Esnaola, 2005; Goñi et al., 2004), helping individuals see themselves as more able, fitter, more attractive and physically stronger, all dimensions of physical self-concept which are inversely linked to the risk of developing eating disorders.

## 6. References

Acosta, M. V., & Gómez, G. (2003). Insatisfacción corporal y seguimiento de dieta. Una comparación transcultural entre adolescentes de España y México. *Revista Internacional de Psicología Clínica y de la Salud, 3*(1), (January 2003), pp. 9-21, ISSN 1697-2600

Adams, G. (1977). Physical attractiveness research. *Human Development, 20,* (July 1977), pp. 217-239, ISSN 0018-716X.

American Psychiatric Association [APA] (2003). *Diagnostic and statistical manual of mental disorders* (4th ed-TR), American Psychiatric Pub, ISBN 0890420254, Washington DC

Asçi, F. H., Asçi, A., & Zorba, E. (1999). Cross-cultural validity and reliability of Physical Self-Perception Profile. *International Journal of Sport Psychology, 30,* (May 1977), pp. 399-406, ISSN 0047-0767

Atienza, F. L., Balaguer, I., & Moreno, Y. (2004). El perfil de autopercepciones para niños: Análisis de la validez factorial y la fiabilidad de la versión castellana. *Psicothema, 16* (3), (July, 2004), pp. 461-467, ISSN 0214-9915

Baile, J. I. (2003). ¿Qué es la imagen corporal? *Cuadernos del Marqués de San Adrián. Revista de Humanidades, 16*(3), (June 2003),pp. 53-70, ISSN 1579-4806

Barr-Taylor, C., Sharpe, T., Shisslak, C., Bryson, S., Estes, L. S., Gray, N., McKnight, K. M., Crago, M., Kraemer, H. C., & Killen, E. D. (1998). Factors associated with weight concerns in adolescent girls. *International Journal of Eating Disorders, 24,* (January 1998), pp. 31-42, ISSN 0276-3478

Bastiani, A. M., Rao, R., Weltzin, T., & Kaye, W. H. (1995). Perfectionism in anorexia nervosa. *International Journal of Eating Disorders, 17*(2), (March 1995), pp. 147-152, ISSN 0276-3478

Beumont, P. J. V., Arthur, B., Russell, J. D., & Touyz, S. W. (1994). Excessive physical activity in dieting disorder patients: Proposals for a supervised exercise program. *International Journal of Eating Disorders, 15*(1), (January 1994), pp. 21-36, ISSN 0276-3478

Bruch, H. (1973). *Eating disorders: Obesity, anorexia nervosa and the person within,* Basic Books, ISBN 0-465-01-82-7, New York

Bulik, C. M., Sullivan, P. F., Weltzin, T. E., & Kaye, W. H. (1995). Temperament in eating disorders. *International Journal of Eating Disorders, 17*(3), (April, 1995), pp. 251-261, ISSN 0276-3478

Cash, T. F., & Pruzinsky, T. (1990). *Body images: Development, deviance and change,* Guilford, ISBN 0444880747, New York

Cash, T. F., & Pruzinsly, T. (2002). *Body image: A handbook of theory, research, and clinical practice,* Guilford, ISBN 1-57230-777-3, New York

Casper, R. C. (1990). Personality features of women with good outcome from restricting anorexia nervosa. *Psychosomatic Medicine, 52*, (March, 1990), pp. 156-170, ISSN 0033-3174

Chinchilla, A. (1994). *Anorexia nerviosa y bulimia nerviosa,* Ergon, ISBN 978-84-86754-25-9, Madrid

Chinchilla, A. (1995). *Guía teórico-práctica de los trastornos de la conducta alimentaria: Anorexia nerviosa y bulimia nerviosa,* Masson, ISBN 978-84-458-0317-2, Barcelona

Chinchilla, A. (2002). *Trastornos de la conducta alimentaria: anorexia y bulimia nerviosas, obesidad y atracones,* Masson, ISBN 84-458-1241-6, Barcelona

Cloninger, C. R. (1988). A unified biosocial theory of personality and its role in the development of anxiety states: A reply to commentaries. *Psychiatry Development, 6*(2), (April 1988), pp. 83-120, ISSN 0262-9283

Cruz, S., Maganto, C., & Echebarría, A. (2002). Autoconcepto e imagen corporal en adolescentes. In *Investigaciones en psicología clínica,* C. Maganto (Ed.), 147-172, Ibaeta Psicología, ISBN 978-84-600-9816-4, San Sebastián

Dally, P. (1969). *Anorexia nervosa,* Grune and Stratton, New York

Davis, C., Katzman, D. K., Kaptein, S., Kirsh, C., Brewer, H., Kalmbach, K., et al. (1997). The prevalence of high-level exercise in the eating disorders: Etiological implications. *Comprehensive Psychiatry, 38*(6), (December 1997), pp. 321-326, ISSN 0010-440X

Davis, C., Kennedy, S. H., Ravelski, E., & Dionne, M. (1994). The role of physical activity in the development and maintenance of eating disorders. *Psychological Medicine, 24*(4), (october 1994), pp. 957-967, ISSN 0033-2917

de Gracia, M., Marcó, M., Fernández, M., & Juan, J. (1999). Autoconcepto físico, modelo estético e imagen corporal en una muestra de adolescentes. *Psiquis, 20*(1), (January 1999), pp. 15-26, ISSN 0210-8348

de la Serna, I. (2004). Anorexia y vigorexia. *Monografías de Psiquiatría 16(2),* (April 2004), pp. 3-15, ISSN 0214-4220

Dosil, J., & Díaz, O. (2002). Valoración de la conducta alimentaria y de control de peso en practicantes de aeróbic. *Revista de Psicología del Deporte, 11*(2), (June 2002), pp. 183-195, ISSN 1132-239X

DuBois, F. S. (1949). Compulsion neurosis with cachexia (anorexia nervosa). *American Journal of Psychiatry, 106*(2), (August 1949), pp. 107-115, ISSN 1535-7228

Eisler, I., & le Grance, D. (1990). Excessive exercise and anorexia nervosa. *International Journal of Eating Disorders, 9*(1), (January 1990), pp. 27-46, ISSN 0276-3478

Ellis, A., & MacLaren, C. (2005). *Rational emotive behaviour therapy: A therapist's guide.* Impact Publishers, ISBN 1886230617, California

Epling, W. F., Pierce, W. D., & Stefan, L. (1983). A theory of activity-based anorexia. *International Journal of Eating Disorders, 3*(1), (Autum 1983), pp. 27–46, ISSN 0276-3478

Esnaola, I. (2005). Autoconcepto físico y satisfacción corporal en mujeres adolescentes según el deporte practicado. *APUNTS. Educación Física y Deportes, 80,* (April 2005), pp. 5-12, ISSN 1577-4015

Esnaola, I. (2005). *Elaboración y validación del cuestionario Autokontzeptu Fisikoaren Itaunketa (AFI) de autoconcepto físico.* Universidad del País Vasco, ISBN 978-84-8373-752-1, Bilbao

Esnaola, I., & Rodríguez, A. (2009). La imagen corporal y el autoconcepto físico. In *El autoconcepto físico. Psicología y educación,* A. Goñi (Ed.), pp. 60-79, Pirámide, ISBN 978-84-368-2246-5, Madrid

Fairburn, C. G., Doll, H. A., Welch, S. L., Hay, P. J., Davies, B. A., & O'Connor, M. E. (1998). Risk factor s for binge eating disorder: A community-based, case-control study. *Archives of General Psychiatry, 55,* (May 1998), pp. 425-432, ISSN 0003-990X

Fisher, S. (1990). The evolution of psychological concepts about the body. In *Body Images: Development, deviance and change,* T. F. Cash & T. Pruzinsky, T. (Eds.), 77- 103, The Guilford, ISBN 0444880747, New York

Fox, K. R. (1988). The self-esteem complex and youth fitness. *Quest, 40*(3) (December 1988), pp. 230-246, ISSN 1750-9696

Fox, K. R., & Corbin, C. B. (1989). The Physical Self-Perception Profile: Development and preliminary validation. *Journal of Sports and Exercise Psychology, 11,* (December 1989), pp. 408-430, ISSN 0895-2779

Franzoi, S. L., & Shields, S. A. (1984). The Body Esteem Scale: Multidimensional structure and sex differences in a college population. *Journal of Personality Assessment, 48(2),* (March 1984), pp. 173-178, ISSN 0022-3891

García-Grau, E., Fusté, A., & Miró, A. (2004). Coping style and vulnerability to eating disorders in adolescent boys. *European Eating Disorders Review, 12,* (January/February 2004), pp. 61-67, ISSN 1099-0968

Garner, D. M. (1998). *EDI. Inventario de trastornos de la conducta alimentaria. Manual.* TEA, ISBN 8471745364, Madrid

Garner, D. M., & Bemis, K. M. (1985). Cognitive therapy for anorexia nervosa. In *Handbook of psychotherapy for anorexia nervosa and bulimia,* D. M. Garner & P. E. Grafinkel (Eds.), pp. 107-146, Guilford, ISBN 0898626420, New York

Gervilla, E. (2002). La tiranía de la belleza, un problema educativo hoy. La estética del cuerpo como valor y como problema. *Teoría de la Educación, 14,* (2002), pp. 185-206, ISSN 1138-9737

Gismero, E. (2001). Evaluación del autoconcepto, la satisfacción con el propio cuerpo y las habilidades sociales en la anorexia y bulimia nerviosas. *Clínica y Salud, 12*(3), (september 2001), pp. 289-304, ISSN 1130-5274

Goñi, A., Ruiz de Azúa, S. & Rodríguez, A. (2006). *Cuestionario de Autoconcepto Físico.* EOS, ISBN 8497271971, Madrid

Goñi, A., & Rodríguez, A. (2004). Eating disorders, sport practice and physical self-concept in adolescents. *Actas Españolas de Psiquiatría, 32(1),* (January/February 2004), pp. *29-36,* ISSN 1139-9287

Goñi, A., & Rodríguez, A. (2007). *Variables associated with the risk of eating disorders in adolescence. Salud Mental, 30(4),* (July/August, 2007), pp. *16-23,* ISSN 0195-3325

Gual, P., Pérez-Gaspar, M., Martínez-González, M. A., Lahortiga, F., Irala-Estévez, J., & Cervera, S. (2002). Self-esteem, personality and eating disorders: Baseline assessment of a prospective population-based cohort. *International Journal of Eating Disorders, 31,* (April 2002), pp. 261-273, ISSN 0276-3478

Harrison, K., & Cantor, J. (1997). The relationship between media consumption and eating disorders. *Journal of Communication, 47,* (March 1997), pp. 40-67, ISSN 1460-2466

Harter, S. (1987). The determinants and mediational role of global self-worth in children. In *Contemporary issues in developmental psychology,* N. Endler (Ed.), pp. 219-242, Wiley, ISBN 0030084210, New York

Harter, S. (1988). *Manual for the Self-Perception Profile for Adolescents,* University of Denver, Denver

Harter, S. (1989). Causes, correlates and the functional role of global self-worth: a life span perspective. In *Perceptions of competence and incompetence across the life span,* J. Kolligan (Ed.), pp. 43-70, Yale University Press, New Haven

Harter, S. (1990). Self and identity development. In *At the threshold: The developing adolescent,* S. Feldman & G. Elliot (Eds.), pp. 352-387, Harvard University, ISBN 0-674-05035-5, Cambridge

Heilbrun, A. B., & Witt, N. (1990). Distorted body image as a risk factor in anorexia nervosa: Replication and clarification. *Psychological Reports, 66,* (March 1990), pp. 407-416, ISSN 0033-2941

Higging, E. T., Kleian, R., & Strauman, T. (1985). Self-concept discrepancy theory: A psychological model for distinguishing among different aspects of depression and anxiety. *Social Cognition, 3*(1), (January 1985), pp. 51-76, ISSN 0278-016X

Hill, A. J., & Franklin, J. A. (1998). Mothers, daughters, and dieting: Investigating the transmission of weight control. *British Journal of Clinical Psychology, 37,* (February 1998), pp. 3-13, ISSN 2044-8260

Houtkooper, L. (2000). Eating disorders and disordered eating in athletes. In *Clinical sports nutrition,* L. Burke & V. Deakin (Eds.), 210-240, McGraw-Hill, ISBN 0070277206, New York

Jackson, L. A. (1992). *Physical appearance and gender: Sociobiological and sociocultural perspectives.* University of New York, ISBN 079140823X, Albany

Kearney-Cooke, A. (2002). Familial influences on body image development. In *Body Image. A handbook of theory, research and clinical practice,* T. F. Cash & T. Pruzinsky (Eds.), 99-107, Guilford, ISBN 1-57230-777-3, New York

Kjelsas, E., & Augestad, L. B. (2004). Gender, eating behavior, and personality characteristics in physically active students. *Scandinavian Journal of Medicine and Science Sports, 14,* (August, 2004), pp. 258-268, ISSN 1600-0838

Klomsten, A. T., Skaalrik, E. M., & Espnes, O. A. (2004). Physical self-concept and sports: Do gender differences still exist? *Sex Roles, 50* (1-2), (January 2004), pp. 119-127, ISSN 0360-0025

Klump, K. L., Bulik, C. M., & Pollice, C., Halmi, K. A., et al. (2000). Temperament and character in women with anorexia nervosa. The *Journal of Nervous and Mental Disease, 188,* (September 2000), pp. 559-567, ISSN 0022-3018

Arieti, S. (1959). *American Handbook of Psychiatry.* Basic Books, ISBN 9780465001514, New York

Lau, Patrick W. C., Lee, A., Ransdell, L., Yu, C. W. & Sung, R.Y. T. (2004). The association between global self-esteem, physical self-concept and actual versus ideal body size rating in Chinese primary school children. *International Journal of Obesity, 28* (2), (February 2004), pp. 314-319, ISSN 0307-0565

Leon, G. R. (1984). Anorexia nervosa and sports activities. *Behavior Therapist, 7*(1), (January 1984), pp. 9-10, ISSN 0005-7894

Maïano, C., Ninot, G., & Bilard, J. (2004). Age and gender effects on global self-esteem and physical self-perception in adolescents. *Journal of Youth and Adolescence, 3*(4), (June 2004), pp. 307-316, ISSN 0047-2891

Mansfield, A., & McGinn, B. (1993). Pumping irony: The muscular and the feminine. In *Body matters,* S. Scott & D. Morgan (Eds.), 49-68, Falmer, ISBN 9781850009429, London

Marsh, H. W., Hau, K. T., Sung, R. Y. T & Yu, C. W. (2007). Childhood obesity, gender, actual-ideal body image discrepancies, and physical self-concept in Hong Kong children : Cultural differences in the value of moderation. *Developmental Psychology, 43*(3), (May 2007), pp. 647-662, ISSN 0012-1649

Marsh, H. W., Richards, G. E., Johnson, S., Roche, L., & Tremayne, P. (1994). Physical Self-Description Questionnaire: psychometric properties and a multitrait-multimethod analysis of relation to existing instruments. *Journal of Sport and Exercise Psychology, 16*(3), (March 1994), pp. 270-305, ISSN 1469-0292

Meadows, S. M. (2005). Correlates in the development of eating disorders among adolescent males. *Dissertation Abstracts International, 65*(7-B), 3716

Moreno, Y. (1997). *Propiedades psicométricas del Perfil de Autopercepción Física (PSPP).* Universidad de Valencia, Valencia

Pastor, Y. (1998). *Estudio de la influencia del autoconcepto multidimensional sobre el estilo de vida saludable en la adolescencia media.* Doctoral thesis. Valencia: Universidad de Valencia

Pierce, E. F., Daleng, M. L., & McGowan, R. W. (1993). Scores on exercise dependence among dancers. *Perceptual and Motor Skills, 76*(2), (April 1993), pp. 531-535, ISSN 0031-5125

Pope, H. G., Gruber, A., Choi, P. Y., Olivardia, R., & Phillips, J. (1997). Muscle dysmorphia: An underrecognized form of body dysmorphic disorder. *Psychosomatics, 38*(6), (December 1997), pp. 548-557, ISSN 0033-3182

Pope, H.G., Phillips, K.A., & Olivardia, R. (2000). *The Adonis complex: The secret crisis of male body obsession*. The Free Press, ISBN 978-0684869100, Sydney

Raich, R. M. (2000). *Imagen corporal. Conocer y valorar el propio cuerpo.* Pirámide, ISBN 978-84-368-1442-2, Madrid

Richard, K. J., Thompson, J. K., & Coovert, M. (1990). Development of body image and eating disturbance. Unpublished manuscript.

Rieves, L., & Cash, T. F. (1996). Social developmental factors and women's body-image attitudes. *Journal of Social Behavior and Personality, 11*, (1996), pp. 63-78, ISSN 0301-2212

Rodríguez, A., & Esnaola, I. (2009). Los trastornos de la conducta alimentaria y el autoconcepto físico. In *El autoconcepto físico. Psicología y educación,* A. Goñi (Ed.), 173-192, Pirámide, ISBN 978-84-368-2246-5, Madrid

Rodríguez, A., & Goñi, A. (2009). Vulnerabilidad del autoconcepto físico a los influjos socioculturales. In *El autoconcepto físico. Psicología y educación,* A. Goñi (Ed.), 224-247, Pirámide, ISBN 978-84-368-2246-5, Madrid.

Ruiz de Azúa, S. (2007). *El autoconcepto físico: Estructura interna, medida y variabilidad.* Universidad del País Vasco, ISBN 978-84-8373-916-7, Bilbao

Russell, G. F. M. (1970). Anorexia nervosa: Its identity as an illness and its treatment. In *Modern trends in psychological medicine,* J. H. Price (Ed.), 131-164, Butterworths, ISBN 8445812416, London

Sacks, M. H. (1990). Psychiatry and sports. *Annals of Sports Medicine, 5*, (January 1990), pp. 47-52, ISSN 0734-1997

Schilder, P. (1935). *Image and appearance of the human body*. Kegan Paul, Trench Trubner and Co, ISBN 0415191327, London

Schur, E. A., Sanders, M., & Steiner, H. (2000). Body dissatisfaction and dieting in young children. *International Journal of Eating Disorders, 27*(1), (January 2000), pp. 74-82, ISSN 0276-3478

Seigel, K., & Hetta, J. (2001). Exercise and eating disorders symptoms among young females. *Eating and Weight Disorders, 6*(1), (March 2001), pp. 32-39, ISSN 1590-1262

Selvini-Palazzoli, M. (1974). *Self-starvation: From the intrapsychic to the transpersonal approach*. Chaucerm, ISBN 0903137801, London

Shavelson, R. J., Hubner, J. J., & Stanton, J. C. (1976). Self-concept: Validation of construct interpretations. *Review of Educational Research, 46*, (summer 1976), pp. 407-441, ISSN 0034-6543

Skrzypek, S., Wehmeier, P. & Remschmidt, H. (2001). Body image assessment using body size estimation in recent studies on anorexia nervosa. *European Child and adolescent Psychiatry, 10*(4), (December 2001), pp. 215-221, ISSN 1018-8827

Slade, P. D., & Russell, G. F. M. (1973). Awareness of body dimensions in anorexia nervosa: Cross-sectional and longitudinal studies. *Psychological Medicine, 3*(2), (June 1973), pp. 188-199, ISSN 0033-2917

Stein, K. F., & Corte, C. (2007). Identity impairment and the eating disorders: content and organization of the self-concept in women with anorexia nervosa and bulimia nervosa *Eating Disorders Review, 15*(1), (Janaury/February 2007), pp. 58–69, ISSN 1099-0968

Stein, R. J. (1996). Physical self-concept. In *Handbook of self-concept: Developmental, social and clinical considerations*, B. A. Bracken (Ed.), 374-394, John Wiley and Sons, ISBN 978-0-471-59939-5, Oxford

Striegel-Moore, R. H. (1997). Risk factors for eating disorders. In *Adolescent nutritional disorders: Prevention and treatment*, M. S. Jacobson & J. M. Rees (Eds.), 98-109, Academy of Sciences, ISBN 1573310212, New York

Striegel-Moore, R. H., & Kearney-Cook, A. (1994). Exploring parents' attitudes and behaviors about their children's physical appearance. *International Journal of Eating Disorders, 15*(4), (May 1994), pp. 377-385, ISSN 0276-3478

Sundgot-Borgen, J., & Torstveit, M. K. (2004). Prevalence of eating disorders in elite athletes is higher than the general population. *Clinical Journal of Sport Medicine, 14*(1), (January 2004), pp. 25-32, ISSN 1536-3724

Szabò, C. P., & Terre Blanche, M. J. (1997). Perfectionism in anorexia nervosa. *The American Journal of Psychiatry, 14*, (January 1997), pp. 132-140, ISSN 1535-7228

Thompson, J. K. (1990). *Body image disturbance: Assessment and treatment*. Pergamon Press, ISBN 0205144829, New York

Tiggemann, M. (2003). Media exposure, body dissatisfaction and disordered eating: television and magazines are not the same! *European Eating Disorders Review, 11*, (March 2003), pp. 418-430, ISSN 1072-4133

Toro, J. (2004). *Riesgos y causas de la anorexia nerviosa*. Ariel, ISBN 978-84-344-0910-1, Barcelona

Toro, J., & Vilardell, E. (1987). *Anorexia nerviosa*. Martínez-Roca, ISBN 9788427011359, Barcelona

Trent, L. M. Y., Rusell, G., & Cooney, G. (1994). Assessment of self-concept in early adolescence. *Australian Journal of Psychology, 46*(1), (January 1994), pp. 21-28, ISSN 1742-9536

Vásquez, R., Ángel, L. A., García, J., Martínez, L. M., & Chavarro, K. (1997). Conducta alimentaria en deportistas. *Revista Colombiana de Psiquiatría, 26(2),* (April/June 1997), pp. 115-127, ISSN 0034-7450

Vervaet, M., Audenaert, K., & van Heeringen, C. (2003). Cognitive and behavioural characteristics are associated with personality dimensions in patients with eating disorders. *European Eating Disorders Review, 11,* (June 2003), pp. 363-378, ISSN 1072-4133

Vogeltanz-Holm, N., Wonderlich, S. A., Lewis, B. A., Wilsnack, S. C., Harris, T. R., Wilsnack, R. W., & Kristjanson, A. F. (2000). Longitudinal predictors of binge eating, intense dieting, and weight concerns in a national sample of women. *Behavior Therapy, 31,* (spring 2000), pp. 221-235, ISSN 0221-0235

Wagner, S., Halmi,, K. A., & Maguire, T. V. (1987). The sense of personal ineffectiveness in patients with eating disorders: One construct or several? *International Journal of Eating Disorders, 6*(14), (July 1987), pp. 495-505, ISSN 0276-3478

Wilmore, J. H. (1991). Eating and weight disorders in the female athlete. *International Journal of Sport Nutrition 1(2),* (June 1991), pp. 104-117, ISSN 1526-484X

Wilmore, J. H., & Costill, L. (1998). *Fisiología del esfuerzo y del deporte.* Paidolibo, ISBN 9788480199162, Barcelona

Woodside, D. B. (2004). Assessing and treating men with eating disorders. *Psychiatric Times, 21,* (March 2004), pp. 1-6, ISSN 0893-2905

Zonnevijille-Bendek, M., van Goozen, S. & Cohen-Kettenis, P. (2002). Do adolescent anorexia nervosa patients have deficits in emotional functioning? *European Child and Adolescent Psychiatry, 11*(1), (August 2002), pp. 38-42, ISSN 1018-8827

6

# Orexigenic and Anorexigenic Peptides in Restrictive Type of Anorexia Nervosa

Małgorzata Janas-Kozik[1,2], Małgorzata Stachowicz[3], Adam Janas[4], Ireneusz Jelonek[2], Krzysztof Krysta[1] and Irena Krupka-Matuszczyk[1]

[1]*Department and Clinic of Psychiatry and Psychotherapy, Medical University of Silesia Katowice,*
[2]*Department of Child and Adolescents Psychiatry and Psychotherapy, Ward John Paul II Pediatric Center Sosnowiec,*
[3]*Department of Molecular Biology, Medical University of Silesia Sosnowice,*
[4]*Students Scientific Association, Department and Clinic of Psychiatry and Psychotherapy, Medical University of Silesia Katowice,*
*Poland*

## 1. Introduction

### 1.1 Subtypes of Anorexia Nervosa (AN)

Current diagnostic criteria distinguish between two subtypes of Anorexia Nervosa (AN): the restrictive anorexia nervosa (AN-R) and binge/purging anorexia nervosa (AN-B), according to DSM-IV (APA, 1994). These two subtypes may be differentiated by various kind of anorexigenic-orexigenic dysregulation. Among other symptoms, AN is a disorder characterized by abnormal eating behavior and by weight changes which are reflected in multiple endocrine and metabolic abnormalities. Among them, dysregulation of anorexigenic and orexigenic signaling seem to play a prominent role. A number of orexigenic peptides have been identified such as ghrelin, neuropeptide Y, and melanin-concentrating hormone.

### 1.2 Ghrelin – the orexigenic peptide

Ghrelin is a 28-amino acid peptide discovered by Kojima et al. in 1999 (Kojima et al., 1999). Its biological activity depends on the post- translational acylation of serine 3 with octanoic acid. Ghrelin is mainly secreted by A-like cells in the fundus of stomach, but it is also produced in small quantities in the hippocampus, pancreas, intestines, male gonads, placenta and pituitary gland (Lazarczyk et al., 2003). It is known that ghrelin influences the motility in the gastrointestinal system, secretion of hydrochloric acid and endo- and exogenous pancreas functions (Murray et al., 2003;ang Broglio et al., 2001). It stimulates the secretion of such hormones as growth hormone, cortisol, prolactin, aldosterone, and adrenocorticotropic hormone (Lazarczyk et al., 2203; Murray et al., 2003; Broglio et al., 2001; Wren et al., 2000; Warzecha et al., 2006; Dembinski et al., 2005). It also influences the cardiovascular system by reducing blood pressure and increasing cardiac output (Kojima et al., 1999). Ghrelin affects the proliferation of cancer cells, and it is known that resistance to ghrelin can be responsible for cancer cachexia (Ziegman et al., 2003). The highest increase of the plasma ghrelin concentration is observed before food intake. After feeding the ghrelin plasma level decreases within 2 h (Neary et al., 2003). Starvation and/or malnutrition results in an increase of ghrelin level (Ziegman et al., 2003).

### 1.3 Orexin A (OXA, hypocretine-1) – the orexigenic peptide

Orexin A (OXA, hypocretine-1) has been isolated from rat hypothalamus and named for its ability to stimulate feeding when injected into the brain (Sakurai et al., 1998 and Kirchgessner 2002). Orexin A is expressed in the lateral hypothalamic area, which has been described as the "feeding center", and this peptide was initially characterized as an orexigenic (appetite-stimulating) factor (Mieda et al., 2002). Orexin A can rapidly cross the brain - blood barrier to reach the brain from the blood. Although no saturable transport system was found for orexin A, its fast rate of entry is probably explained by simple diffusion facilitated by a high degree of lipophilicity (Kastin et al., 1999).

### 1.4 Leptin (LEP)– the anorexigenic peptide

The main anorexigenic peptide is leptin, of which the primary source is adipose cells. Leptin regulates energy balance throughout the body by controlling processes involved in energy intake and utilization (Myers 2004 and Hebebrand et al., 2007). Underweight AN patients have consistently been found to have significantly lower plasma leptin concentrations compared to normal weight controls (Grinspoon et al., 1996; Casaneuva et al., 1997; Ferron et al. 1997; Lob et al., 2003). LEP is a protein product of a OB (obese) gene. LEP comes in two types: free and bound with plasma protein, each having its own function in the system. Free LEP controls fat tissue mass, while LEP bound with soluble receptor form controls energy expenditure. The leptin receptor (OB-R) is a product of the OB-R gene located on chromosome 1 (1p31).

## 2. Participants

Thirty females suffering from AN-R of the restrictive type (AN-R) were included in the study (M age: 17 ± 1.59; range 14 - 20 years; SD: 1,59). They were diagnosed as AN-R according to DSM IV and ICD 10 criteria (APA, 1994 and ICD-10, 1998). They had a ≥15% body weight loss and their body mass index (BMI) was below 17.5 kg/m$^2$. The mean duration of the disease before admission to the hospital, established by interviews with the patients and their families, was 11.5 ± 7 months. All the patients were hospitalized for up to 3 months in the Child and Adolescent Psychiatry and Psychotherapy Ward at the John Paul II Pediatric Center in Sosnowiec.

During hospitalization the patients received treatment including a normocaloric diet (2300 kcal/d: 98.4 kcal/d of protein, 75 kcal/d of fat, and 376 kcal/d of carbohydrates), supervised meal consumption (the meals were provided 5 times a day) and cognitive-behavioral psychotherapy (CBT). CBT was performed by a team of psychiatrist, psychologist and a nurse. It was based on the constant number and time of meals. An individual system of positive and negative reinforcements was introduced. A positive reinforcement was given for an increase and a negative reinforcement for a decrease in body weight. Those patients who reached a

BMI of 16.5 kg/m2 were allowed to leave the hospital for weekends. Psychotherapy was performed for 45 minutes twice a week on an individual basis by one psychologist and 60 minutes twice a week in group mode by two psychologists. When a BMI of 17 kg/m2 was reached the patient was discharged from the hospital and ambulatory treatment was started. The patients were examined once a month and their weight was checked by a nurse and psychiatrist. AN-R patients did not take medicaments, only occasionally they have taken anxiolytic drugs because they had single symptoms of anxiety and depressive syndrome but depression and obsessive compulsive disorder were excluded.

The control group consisted of 20 healthy schoolgirls from Silesian colleges (M age:18.5; range 18.0-19.0 years; SD = 0.3), a mean BMI of 21.4 (range 17.6-25.7, SD = 2.1). None were suffering from any psychiatric disorder, including eating disorders or receiving any drugs. Their daily intake of food over the past year had per day a mean of 2100-2300 kcal. This information was gained from each girl during a clinical interview which contained eating disorder symptoms and behaviors and during psychiatric, neurological and physical examinations. The protocol of the study was approved by the Local Bioethics Committee and written informed consent to participate in the study was obtained from all those participants and their parents.

## 3. Laboratory methods

Blood was collected by the method described by Baranowska et al (2005). Venous blood samples were collected in the fasting state (between 8-9 a.m.) into Vacutainer tubes containing EDTA (1mg/ml of blood). The blood samples were gently shaken and then transferred to centrifuge tubes containing aprotinin (0.6TIU/ml of blood). They were centrifuged at 1,600 x g for 15 minutes at 4°C. The plasma collected was immediately frozen and kept at -70°C. The orexin A plasma level was measured by commercial radioimmunoassay kits (Phoenix Pharmaceuticals. Mountain View, California). Buffer A, a 1% water solution of trifluoroacetic acid and buffer B, a 60% solution of acetonitrol in a 1% solution of trifluoroacetic acid were used, as well as chromatography columns, for the extraction (SEP-PAK C-18. Waters Associates). The leptin plasma level was measured by commercial enzymoimmunological assay (Leptin Sandwich ELISA, DRG Instruments GmbH Deutschland) using a ELISA counter (DRG Elisa MAT 2000). Plasma orexin A levels were determined by means of LKB Wallac Clini Gamma 1272 gamma counter. The minimal detectable quantity was 0.001 ng/ml. Procedures recommended by Phoenix Peptide for extraction were followed. Plasma ghrelin levels were determined by radioimmunoassay (RIA, Linco Research, Inc.) using the LKB Wallac Cinigamma 1272 gamma counter. The procedure was done according to the manufacturer's instructions. The minimal detectable quantity was 93 pg/ml The AN-R patients' blood was sampled four times: at admission and after 2, 3 and 6 months of therapy. The control participants have blood drawn only once.

## 4. Statistical analysis

### 4.1 Ghrelin

All the values are presented as the mean ± SD. Statistical analysis was carried out by the Student's t-test. The Spearman's correlation was calculated using the Microsoft Excel 6.0 software. The $p < 0.05$ was accepted as the essential level of statistical significance.

### 4.2 Orexin A (OXA, hypocretine-1) and leptin (LEP)

Calculations were performed using the Statistica version 7.1 statistical package. The Shapiro-Wilk test was used to determine the normality of data distribution. The level of statistical significance was determined at $p < 0.05$. As the BMI results showed normal distribution, the ANOVA test for repeated measurements was used. To compare BMI parameters between periods of time, the LSD (least significant differences) - post hoc test was used. The non-paired t-test was used for comparison between patients and control participants. As the leptin and orexin A values did not show a normal distribution, the nonparametric Friedman test was performed in order to detect differences between multiple measurements. The mean range- post hoc test was used to compare leptin and orexin A parameters during the period of study. The non-parametric Mann-Whitney test was used for comparison between patients and control participants. The non-parametric Spearman's test was used to investigate any correlation between leptin or orexin A levels with BMI, or any reciprocal correlation between leptin and orexin A. When leptin levels were transformed into logarithmic values, as lg10, and the BMI was expressed as a BMI SDS (z-score), the Pearson test was used to assess the correlation between these parameters (Maliński, 2004 and Maliński et al., 1999).

## 5. Results

### 5.1 Ghrelin

#### 5.1.1 Body mass index (BMI)

The BMI before the therapy calculated for all 30 AN-R patients was 15.1 kg/m$^2$ ± 1.4. After 3 months of treatment BMI increased to 17.2kg/m$^2$ ± 1.1 and a further increase was noted after 6 months of the therapy to 17.7 kg/m$^2$ ± 1.8. The BMI in the control group was 21.4 kg/m$^2$ ± 2.1. A statistically significant difference between BMI of AN-R patients and BMI of the control group was noted before the therapy, after 3 and 6 months of therapy compared with the control group ($p<0.001$, t-Student test).

#### 5.1.2 The total ghrelin plasma level

The total ghrelin plasma level before therapy was 6652.1± 2152.7 pg/ml, after 3 months of treatment the total ghrelin plasma level decrease to 3858.5± 1331.8 pg/ml and after 6 months of treatment the total ghrelin plasma level decrease too and was 3187.4± 1348.2 pg/ml. The total ghrelin plasma level in the control group was 4855± 1421.4 pg/ml. A statistically significant difference between the total ghrelin plasma level of AN-R patients and the total ghrelin plasma level of the control group was noted before therapy, after 3 and 6 months of therapy compared with the control group, $p=0.002$; $p=0.015$ and $p<0.001$, respectively (t-Student test) .

#### 5.1.3 Correlation between the BMI and the total ghrelin plasma level

There was no correlation between BMI and the total ghrelin plasma level in AN-R patients (n=30) before therapy ($R= - 0,14$, $p=0,47$, Spearman correlation ). Also in the control group no correlation between BMI and the total ghrelin plasma level was observed ($R=0,15$; $p=0,50$).

#### 5.1.4 Correlation between the total ghrelin plasma level change and BMI change in AN-R patients

A change of the BMI is understood as the difference between the BMI before and after 6 months of the therapy (BMI 6 - BMI 0). A change of the total ghrelin plasma level is the difference between the total ghrelin plasma level before and after 6 months of the therapy (Ghrelin 6 - Ghrelin 0). BMI change and the total ghrelin plasma level change before and after 3 months of the therapy did not show statistically significant correlation (R=-0.304; p=0.1011). BMI change and the total ghrelin plasma level change before and after 6 months of the therapy correlated in statistically significant relation (R = - 0.52; p=0.0054).

#### 5.1.5 Correlation between duration of disorder and the total ghrelin plasma level and BMI

There was no statistically significant correlation between the AN-R duration and either the total ghrelin plasma level (R = 0.10; p=0.58) or BMI change (R =-0.25; p=0.18) (Janas-Kozik et al, 2007).

### 5.2 Orexin A (OXA, hypocretine-1)

#### 5.2.1 The orexin A (OXA) plasma level

The mean OXA plasma level before the therapy for all 30 AN-R patients was 0.04 ng/ml ± 0.05, significantly lower than in control group (0.08 ng/ml ± 0.10) (p= 0.039, Mann-Whitney test). After 2, 3, and 6 months of treatment the OXA plasma levels significantly decreased: 0.02 ng/ml ± 0.03, 0.01 ng/ml ± 0.01, 0.01 ng/ml ± 0.01, respectively (p<0.001, Friedman test). A significant decrease of OXA plasma level was observed after 3 and 6 months of therapy compared to baseline (NIR- post hoc test, p<0.001)

#### 5.2.2 Body mass index (BMI) for orexin A (OXA) and leptin (LEP) plasma level

The mean BMI before the therapy for all 30 AN-R patients was 14.8 kg/m$^2$ ± 1.3. A statistically significant difference between BMI of AN-R patients and BMI of the control group was noted (non paired t-Student test, p<0.001). After 2 and 3 months of treatment BMI increased to 15.7 kg/m$^2$ ± 1.1 and 17.1 kg/m$^2$ ± 1.1, respectively. A further increase to 17.7 kg/m$^2$ ± 1.1 was noted after 6 months of the therapy. The increase of BMI in the described above periods of time, when measurements were done, i.e. after 2, 3 and 6 months of therapy was statistically significant, (ANOVA test F=29.51; p< 0.001). A statistically significant difference between BMI of AN-R patients and BMI of the control group was noted before the therapy, after 2, 3 and 6 months of therapy compared with the control group (p<0.001, non paired t-Student test).

#### 5.2.3 Correlation between the change of BMI and the change of orexin A (OXA) plasma level

There was no correlation between BMI and OXA plasma level in AN-R patients before the therapy and after 2, 3 and 6 months of the therapy ( R= 0.06, p=0.759; R=0.01, p=0.967;

R= 0.33, p=0.077; R= -0.01, p=0.98; respectively; the Spearman correlation). There was no correlation between BMI and OXA plasma level in control group (R=0.32, p= 0.171).

#### 5.2.4 Correlation between a change of BMI and the orexin A (OXA) plasma level

Change of BMI and change of OXA plasma levels compared to baseline did not show statistically significant correlations (2 months: R = - 0.12, p = 0.514; 3 months: R = - 0.25, p = 0.177; 6 months: R = -0.25, p = 0.174, Spearman correlation).

### 5.3 The leptin (LEP)

#### 5.3.1 The leptin (LEP) plasma level

The mean LEP plasma level before the therapy for all 30 AN-R patients was 1,00± 0.73 ng/ml while the LEP plasma level in the control group was 14.00 ± 11.99 ng/ml. After 2, 3 and 6 months of treatment LEP plasma levels in AN-R patients were 4.53 ± 4.74 ng/ml, 6.96 ± 5.58 ng/ml, 8.27 ± 6.94 ng/ml, respectively. Statistically significant increase of LEP plasma levels in investigated periods of time was observed ($p<0.001$, the Friedman test), although even after 6 months of therapy the LEP levels in patients made slightly more than a half of control participants values

#### 5.3.2 Correlation between the BMI and the leptin (LEP) plasma level

There was no correlation between BMI and LEP plasma level in AN-R patients before the therapy and after 2 and 3 months of the therapy ( R= 0.22; p=0.239; R=0.22; p=0.240; R=0.16, p=0.387, respectively; the Spearman correlation). There was, however a correlation between BMI and LEP plasma level in AN-R patients after 6 months of the therapy (R= 0.59; $p < 0.001$). There was no correlation between BMI and LEP plasma level in control group (R=0.20, p=0.402).

#### 5.3.3 Correlation between the change change of BMI and the change of leptin (LEP) plasma level

A change of the BMI and LEP was expressed as a difference between the BMI and LEP values after 2, 3 and 6 months of the therapy compared to baseline. Change of BMI and LEP plasma levels showed statistically significant correlation (2 months: R = 0.54, p = 0.002; 3 months: R = 0.52, p = 0.003; 6 months R = 0.76, $p <0.001$; the Spearman correlation).

### 5.4 Correlation between leptin (LEP) and orexin A (OXA) plasma levels

Before the therapy a statistically significant negative correlation between OXA and LEP levels in patients with AN-R was observed (R= - 0.38, p=0.039; the Spearman correlation). There was no correlation between LEP and OXA after 2 and 3 and 6 months of the therapy (R= 0.24; p=0.203, R=0.33; p=0.076, R=0.07, p=0.699, respectively). There was no correlation between OXA plasma levels and LEP plasma levels in the control group (R=0.06, p=0.806). In patients suffering from AN-R, no statistically significant correlation between duration of the illness and LEP or OXA plasma levels was found (R= -0.03, p= 0.868, R=0.19, p=0.309, respectively, the Spearman correlation). (Janas-Kozik et al, 2011)

## 6. Discussion

### 6.1 The total ghrelin plasma level study in patients of suffering from anorexia nervosa

Ghrelin is the most sensitive determinant of the nutrition state. Secretion of ghrelin is strongly related to food intake. The hypothalamic-pituitary-suprarenal axis is activated when access to food is limited and during the stress. The secretion of ghrelin mobilizes mechanisms counteracting states of energy deficits, stimulates searching for food and influences memory of information connected with eating (Ziegman et al. 2003; Inui, 2001; Wu et al.,2004). The secretion of ghrelin increases during starvation and during expecting a meal (Murray et al., 2003). In ghrelin study before the therapy BMI was significantly lower in the restricting anorectic patients (AN-R) patients (15.1 kg/m$^2$ ± 1.4.) compared with the control group (21.4 kg/m$^2$ ± 2.1; $p<0.001$). After 3 and 6 months of cognitive-behavioral therapy, increase of BMI was observed in AN-R patients (17.2kg/m$^2$ ± 1.1 and 17.7 kg/m$^2$ ± 1.8., respectively) but during the therapy the BMI was always significantly lower in AN-R patients compared with the control group (21.4 kg/m$^2$ ± 2.1).

In ghrelin study before the therapy in patients suffering from AN-R the total ghrelin plasma level was significantly higher (6652.1± 2152.7 pg/ml ) compared with the control group (4855± 1421.4 pg/ml; $p=0.002$). This observation has been confirmed by other scientists (Otto et al., 2001; Nedvikova et al., 2003; Tanaka et al., 2203; Toole et al., 2003). After 3 and 6 months of therapy the total ghrelin plasma level in AN-R patients was significantly lower compared with the control group (3858.5± 1331.8 pg/ml; $p=0.015$ and 3187.4± 1348.2 pg/ml; $p<0.001$, respectively).

We suggest that in AN-R patients before the therapy ghrelin plays a role of the orexigenic peptide and informs CNS (central nervous system) about deficit of energy when the BMI is low. We observe that after 3 months of therapy in AN-R patients ghrelin stops playing this role, because its level dramatically decreases compared with the control group (3858.5 ± 1331.8 pg/ml; 4855± 1421.4 pg/ml, respectively, $p=0.002$). After 3 months of the therapy the BMI is low ( 17.2kg/m$^2$ ± 1.1) and the total ghrelin plasma level decreases in AN-R patients (the total ghrelin plasma level before the therapy was 6652.1± 2152.7 pg/ml and the total ghrelin plasma level after 3 months the therapy was 3858.5± 1331.8 pg/ml). It is interesting that after 6 months of the observation BMI is still low (17.7 kg/m$^2$ ± 1.8.) and the total ghrelin plasma level is still decreasing in AN-R patients (3187.4± 1348.2 pg/ml) compared with the control group (4855± 1421.4 pg/ml). No correlation was observed between BMI and the total ghrelin plasma level both in AN-R patients before therapy (R= -0,14, p=0,47) and in the control group (R=0,15; p=0,50) analyzed separately. However, there was a statistically significant negative correlation between the total ghrelin plasma level change and BMI change in AN-R patients after 6 months of therapy ($R = -0.52$; $p=0.0054$). We suggest that in AN-R patients ghrelin does not send "correct" information to CNS about state of the organism feeding. We think that in AN-R patients ghrelin is rather responsible for model of eating behavior (for regularly and normocaloric diet), but is not responsible for stimulation of food intake. Our results show that 6 months of the therapy is sufficient to form a new habits connected with food intake. Before the therapy the higher total ghrelin plasma level (6652.1± 2152.7 pg/ml) is observed in AN-R patients comparing to the control group (4855± 1421.4 pg/ml ) in our study (Janas-Kozik et al. 2007).

Nedvikowa (2003) and Toole (2003) suggest that such a significant increase of the total ghrelin plasma level in AN-R patients can be a result of compensating mechanisms in poor eating habits. According to Otto et al. (2001) ghrelin is a peripheral hormone related to appetite and food intake and informs CNS about a necessity of activating a metabolic variant which saves more energy. In AN-R patients there is no statistically significant correlation between BMI change and duration of AN-R (R =-0.25; p=0.18) and between the total ghrelin plasma level and duration of the disorder (R = 0.10; p=0.58). We suggest that the therapy is very important regardless of the duration of the Anorexia Nervosa (Janas-Kozik et al., 2007).

Two forms of ghrelin hav e been found, acylated ghrelin and desacyl ghrelin. Plasma desacyl ghrelin concentration accounts for more than 90% of total circulating ghrelin (Hosoda et al., 2000). Acylated ghrelin produces stimulatory effects on food intake. Physiological role of desacyl ghrelin is not well known. Some studies even showed that desacyl ghrelin decrease food intake and delay gastric empting in mice and rats (Asakawa et al., 2005 and Chen CY et al., 2005). Further study is required to determine whether desacyl ghrelin is biologically active and binds to an as-yet-unidentified receptor ( hosoda et al., 2006). The role of acylated and desacyl ghrelin in anorexia has to be analyzed separately. It might give an explanation why total ghrelin level in anorexia decreased below the level of healthy participants after 3 and 6 months of therapy (Janas-Kozik et al., 2007).

### 6.2 Orexin A (OXA) plasma level in patients suffering from anorexia nervosa

In the present study, orexin A levels before treatment were significantly lower in the AN-R patients compared to control group, similarly as in our previous paper (Janas-Kozik et al., 2006). In the course of treatment and with subsequent weight gain, orexin A levels showed a further decline. A reduction of orexin A levels during AN realimentation was also found in a recent study of Bronsky et al (2010). However, their results differ with those of ours in that their baseline orexin A levels were higher than in healthy control participants. In our study baseline orexin A plasma levels was lower compared to control group (0.04 ng/ml ± 0.05; 0.08 ng/ml ± 0.10, respectively). Furthermore, we did not observe a statistically significant correlation between the BMI and orexin A plasma levels before the therapy or after 2, 3 and 6 months of treatment (R= 0.06, p=0.759; R=0.01, p=0.967; R= -0.33, p=0.077; R= -0.01, p=0.98; respectively; the Spearman correlation) and no correlation was also found between changes in orexin A plasma levels and changes in the BMI after 2, 3 and 6 months (2 months: R = -0.12, p = 0.514; 3 months: R = - 0.25, p = 0.177; 6 months: R = -0.25, p = 0.174, Spearman correlation). Generally, the pattern of orexin A levels during treatment of patients with AN-R was similar to that found in our previous paper for ghrelin (Janas-Kozik et al., 2006), however, the baseline orexin A levels were significantly lower compared to the control participants. A number of observations point to an increase in the orexin A level during fasting and weight loss, and a decrease during weight gain. Komaki et al. (2001) reported an increase in orexin A plasma levels in adult fasting, non-obese participants during 10 days of fasting which was followed by a reduction in orexin A plasma levels during subsequent re-feeding. Bronsky et al. (2007) observed a significant increase in orexin A plasma levels after a decrease of BMI from about 28 kg/m$^2$ to 26 kg/m$^2$ in fasting obese children. Also other studies of orexin A plasma levels showed a significant decrease of this peptide in obese, and morbidly obese participants (Adam et al., 2002). These results could be compatible with those obtained in our study with AN-R patients (Janas-Kozik et al., 2011).

### 6.3 Leptin (LEP) plasma level in patients suffering from anorexia nervosa

The results of our study corroborate those of other researchers showing a decrease of leptin levels in patients with AN-R, compared with those in control participants (1.00± 0.73 ng/ml in AN-R patients before the therapy and 14.00 ± 11.99 ng/ml in the control group) and its increase during increment in body weight (Casaneuva et al., 1997 and Hebebrandt et al., 2007). Leptin appears to play an important role in triggering an adaptive response to starvation and a low level of this peptide is connected with stimulating the increase of orexigenic peptides and subsequent weight gain. Holtkamp et al. (2004) suggested that high serum leptin levels at discharge from inpatient treatment may indicate a risk for renewed weight loss and an unfavorable 1 year outcome in AN patients. In our AN-R patients the leptin plasma levels increased significantly after 2, 3 and 6 months of treatment (4.53 ± 4.74 ng/ml, 6.96 ± 5.58 ng/ml, 8.27 ± 6.94 ng/ml, respectively )and there was a statistically significant correlation between the BMI and leptin plasma levels after 6 months of treatment ($R= 0.59$; $p < 0.001$). Changes in the BMI and leptin plasma levels also showed a statistically significant correlation during the 6-month observation period (2 months: $R = 0.54$, $p = 0.002$; 3 months: $R = 0.52$, $p = 0.003$; 6 months $R = 0.76$, $p <0.001$; the Spearman correlation). However, there was no correlation between the change in leptin level after 2 months and the change in BMI after 6 months, compared to baseline. Therefore, our results suggest that changes in leptin levels in the early phase of treatment may not predict body weight gain after 6 months of treatment. The lack of correlation between the BMI and leptin in our control participants may indicate that such a correlation may not hold for participants with a BMI within the normal range (Janas-Kozik et al., 2011).

### 6.4 Correlation between leptin (LEP) and orexin A (OXA) plasma levels

Before treatment, a significant negative correlation between leptin and orexin A plasma levels in our AN-R patients was observed ($R= - 0.38$, $p=0.039$; the Spearman correlation). This means that lower leptin levels were associated with relatively higher levels of orexin A, however, orexin A levels being still in a range lower than that of the control participants. A reciprocal relationship between leptin and orexin effects on hypothalamic neurons was found in a study of Muroya et al.(2004). Also recently, a bidirectional association between plasma concentration of leptin and orexin as regards nicotine craving was demonstrated (von der Goltz et al., 2010). Such inverse correlation between leptin and orexin plasma levels was also found both in obese and non-obese participants (Komaki et al., 2001 and Bronsky et al. 2007). However, in AN-R patients studied by us, such an association was observed only initially and has not hold during the course of treatment (Janas-Kozik et al., 2011). Also Bronsky et al.(2010) did not find such an association during an 8-week realimentation of AN patients. A limitation to our study may be that the participants in the control group had a narrower age range, which did not exactly match the AN-R patients for age. Furthermore, during treatment no records were taken of the symptoms of anorexia such as drive for thinness, strength of appetite or desire for eating as well as of the type of food consumed. Despite these limitations we believe that our study of anorexigenic and orexigenic peptides during treatment of participants with the restrictive type of anorexia nervosa produced some interesting outcomes. We confirmed the results of other studies on the specific pattern of leptin in AN patients, such as baseline low levels and increase during treatment. We also corroborated an effect described by Bronsky et al. (2010), such as a decrease of orexin A levels during anorexia treatment (Janas-Kozik et al, 2011).

## 7. Conclusions

7.1. The total ghrelin plasma level in the restrictive type of anorexia nervosa (AN-R) is connected with the pathological feeding behavior (Janas-Kozik et al., 2007).

7.2. It is not known, which proportion of orexin A in plasma comes from brain and which from gut, and whether or not plasma orexin A is orexigenic (Janas-Kozik et al., 2011).

7.3. In AN-R patients before treatment we found a significant reciprocal correlation between plasma levels of leptin and orexin which may suggest some relationship between these two peptides in AN-R patients (Janas-Kozik et al., 2011).

## 8. References

Adam JA, Menheere PP, van Dielen FM, Soeters PB, Buurman WA, Greve JW.: Decreased plasma orexin-A levels in obese individuals. *Int J Obes Relat Metab Disord* 2002;26:274–6

American Psychiatric Association, Diagnostic and Statistical Manual of Mental Disorder (DSM-IV) APA. Washington D.C. 1994

Asakawa A, Inui A, Fujimiya M, Sakamaki R, Shinfuku N, Ueta Y, Meguid MM, Kasuga M. Stomach regulates energy balance via acylated ghrelin and desacyl ghrelin. *Gut* 2005; 54:18-24

Baranowska B, Wolińska-Witort E, Martyńska L, Chmielowska M, Baranowska-Bik A. Plasma orexin A, orexin B, leptin, neuropeptide Y (NPY) and insulin in obese women. *Neuro Endocrinol Lett* 2005; 26: 293-6

Broglio F, Arvat E, Benso A, Gottero C, Muccioli G, Papotti M, Van der Lely AJ, Deghenghi R, Ghigo E. Ghrelin, a natural Gh secretagogue produced by stomach, induces hyperglycemia and reduces insulin secretion in humans. *J Clin Endocrinol Metab* 2001;86:5083–6

Bronsky J, Nedvidkova J, Krasnicanova H, Vesela M, Schmidtova J, Koutek J,Kellermayer R, Chada M, Kabelka Z, Hrdlicka M, Nevoral J, Prusa R.: Changes of orexin A plasma levels in girls with anorexia nervosa during eight weeks of realimentation. *Int J Eat Disord* Oct 26 2010 e-pub ahead of print

Bronský J, Nedvídková J, Zamrazilová H, Pechová M, Chada M, Kotaska K, Nevoral J, Prusa R.: Dynamic changes of orexin A and leptin in obese children during body weight reduction. *Physiol Res* 2007;56:89–96

Casaneuva FF, Dieguez Popovic V, Peino R, Considine RV, Caro JF. Serum immunoreactive leptin concentrations in patients with anorexia nervosa before and after partial weight recovery. *Biochem Mol Med* 1997; 60: 116-120.

Chen CY, Inui A, Asakawa A, Fujino K, Kato I, Chen CC, Ueno N, Fujimiya M.: Des-acyl ghrelin acts by CRF type 2 receptors to disrupt fasted stomach motility in conscious rats. *Gastroenterology* 2005; 129: 8-25

Dembinski A, Warzecha Z, Ceranowicz P, Bielanski W, Cieszkowski J, Dembinski M, Pawlik WW, Kuwahara A, Kato I, Konturek PC. Variable effect of ghrelin administration on pancreatic development in young rats. Role of insulin-like growth factor-1. *J Physiol Pharmacol* 2005;56: 555–70

Ferron F, Considine RV, Peino R, Lado IG, Dieguez C, Casaneuva FF. Serum leptin concentrations in patients with anorexia nervosa. bulimia nervosa and non-specific eating disorders correlate with the body mass index but are independent of the respective disease. *Clin Endocrinol* 1997; 46: 288-93

Grinspoon S, Gulick T, Askari H, Landt M, Lee K, Anderson E et al. Serum leptin levels in women with anorexia nervosa. *J Clin Endocrinol Metab* 1996; 81: 3861-3863

Hebebrand J, Muller TD, Holtkamp K, Herpertz - Dahlmann B. The role of leptin in anorexia nervosa: clinical implications. *Mol Psychiatry* 2007; 12: 23-35

Hosoda H, Kojima M, Kangawa K: Biological, physiological, and pharmacological aspects of ghrelin. *J Pharmacol Sci.* 2006; 100: 398-410

Hosoda H, Kojima M, Matsuo H, Kangawa K.: Ghrelin and des-acyl ghrelin: two major forms of rat ghrelin peptide in gastrointestinal tissue. *Biochem Biophys Res Commun* 2000; 279: 909-913

Inui A.: Eating behavior in AN - An excess of both orexigenic and anorexigenic signaling? *Mol Psychiatry* 2001; 6: 620-624

Janas-Kozik M, Krupka-Matuszczyk I, Krzystanek M, Tomasik-Krótki J.: Stężenie wybranych peptydów oreksygenicznych w osoczu a aktywność fosfolipazy D w płytkach krwi u chorych z jadłowstrętem psychicznym. *Wiad Lek* 2006;59:307–10

Janas-Kozik M., Krupka-Matuszczyk I., Malinowska-Kołodziej I., Lewin-Kowalik J.: Total ghrelin plasma level in patients with the restrictive type of anorexia nervosa. *Regul Pept* 2007 T.140 No.1-2 p..43-46

Janas-Kozik M., Stachowicz M., Krupka-Matuszczyk I., Szymszal J., Krysta K., Janas A., Rybakowski J.K.: Plasma levels of leptin and orexin A in the restrictive type of anorexia nervosa. *Regulatory Peptides* 168 (2011) 5–9

Kastin A.J, Akerstorm V. Orexin A but not Orexin B rapidly enters brain from blood by simple diffusion. *The Journal of Pharmacology and Experimental Therapeutics* 1999; 289: 219-223

Kirchgessner AL. Orexins in the brain-gut axis. *Endocrine Rev* 2002; 23: 1-15

Klasyfikacja zaburzeń psychicznych i zaburzeń zachowania w ICD-10. Uniwersyteckie Wydawnictwo Medyczne „Vesalius"; IPN, Kraków-Warszawa 1998

Kojima M, Hosoda H, Date Y, Nakazato M, Matsuo H, Kangawa K. Ghrelin is a growth-hormone-releasing acylated peptide from stomach.*Nature* 1996;402:656–60

Komaki G, Matsumoto Y, Nishikata H, Kawai K, Nozaki T, Takii M, Sogawa H, Kubo C: Orexin-A and leptin change inversely in fasting non-obese subjects. *Eur J Endocrinol* 2001;144:645–51

Lazarczyk MA, Lazarczyk M, Grzela T. Ghrelin: a recently discovered gut–brain peptide. *Int J Mol Med* 2003;12:279–87

Lob S, Pickel J, Bidlingmaier M, Schaaf L, Backmund H, Gerlinghoff M, Stalla GK. Serum leptin monitoring in anorectic patients during refeeding therapy. *Exp Clin Endocrinol Diabetes* 2003; 111: 278-82

Maliński M., Szymszal J.: Współczesna statystyka matematyczna w medycynie w arkuszach kalkulacyjnych. Śl. Akad. Med. Katowice 1999

Maliński M.: Weryfikacja hipotez wspomagana komputerowo. Wyd. Politechniki Śl. Gliwice 2004.

Mieda M, Yanagisawa M. Sleep, feeding.and neuropeptides: roles of orexins and orexin receptors *Curr Opin Neurobiol* 2002; 12: 339-345

Muroya S, Funahashi H, Yamanaka A, Kohno D, Uramura K, Nambu T, Shibahara M, Kuramochi M, Takigawa M, Yanagisawa M, Sakurai T, Shioda S, Yada T.: Orexins (hypocretins) directly interact with neuropeptide Y, POMC and glucoseresponsive neurons to regulate Ca 2+ signaling in a reciprocal manner to leptin: orexigenic neuronal pathways in the mediobasal hypothalamus. *Eur J Neurosci* 2004;19:1524–34

Murray C, Kamm M, Bloom S, Emmanuel A. Ghrelin for the gastroenterologist: history and potential. *Gastroenterology* 2003;125:1492–502

Myers MG. Leptin receptor signaling and the regulation of mammalian physiology. *Recent Prog Horm Res* 2004; 59: 287-304

Neary NM, Small CJ, Bloom SR. Gut and mind. *Gut* 2003;52:918–21

Nedvikowa J, Krykorkova I, Bartak V, Papezova H, Gold PW, Alesci S, Pacak K. Loss of meal-induced decrease in plasma ghrelin levels in patients with anorexia nervosa. *J Clin Endocrinol Metab* 2003; 88:1678-1682

Otto B, Cuntz U, Fruehauf E, Wawarta R, Folwaczny C, Riepl RL, Heiman ML, Lehnert P, Fichter M, Tschop M. Weight gain decreases elevated plasma ghrelin concentrations of patients with anorexia nervosa. *Eur J Endocrinol* 2001; 145: 669-673

Sakurai T, Amemiya A, Ishii M, Matsuzaki I, Chemelli RM, Tanaka H, Williams SC, Richardson JA, Kozlowski GP, Wilson S, Arch JR, Buckingham RE, Haynes AC, Carr SA, Annan RS, McNulty DE, Liu WS, Terrett JA, Elshourbagy NA, Bergsma DJ, Yanagisawa M. Orexins and orexin receptors: a family of hypothalamic neuropeptides and G protein-coupled receptors that regulate feeding behavior. *Cell* 1998; 20;92: 573-85

Tanaka M, Nauro T, Yasuhara D, Tatebe Y, Nagai N, Shiiya T, Nkazato M, Matsukura S, Nozoe S.: Fasting plasma ghrelin levels in subtypes of anorexia nervosa. *Psychoneuroendocrinology* 2003;28:829-835

Toole V, Kadem M, Bluet-Pajot MT, Frere D, Foulon C, Bossu C, Dardennes R, Mounier C, Zizzari P, Lang F, Epelbaum J and Estour B.: Balance in ghrelin and leptin levels in anorexia nervosa patients and constitutionally thin women. *J Clin Endocrinol Metab* 2003; 88: 109-116

von der Goltz C, Koopman A, Dinter C, Richter A, Grosshans M, Nakovics H, Wiedemann K, Mann K, Winterer G, Kiefer F.: Orexin and leptin are associated with nicotine craving: a link between smoking, appetite and reward. *Psychoneuroendocrinol* 2010;35:570–7.

Warzecha Z, Dembinski A, Ceranowicz P, Dembinski M, Cieszkowski J, Konturek SJ, Polus A, Pawlik WW, Kuwahara A, Kato I, Konturek PC. Influence of ghrelin on gastric and duodenal growth and expression of digestive enzymes in young mature rats. *J Physiol Pharmacol* 2006;57: 425–37

Wren AM, Small CJ, Ward HL, Murphy KG, Dakin CL, Taheri S,Kennedy AR, Roberts GH, Morgan DG, Ghatei MA, Bloom SR. The novel hypothalamic peptide ghrelin stimulates food intake and growth hormone secretion. *Endocrinology* 2000;141: 4325–8

Wu JT, Kral JG.: Ghrelin. Integrative neuroendocrine peptide in health and disease. *Ann Surg* 2004; 239:464-474

Ziegman J, Elmquist. Minireview: from anorexia to obesity—the yin and yang of body weight control. *Endocrinology* 2003;144:3749–56

# Part 3

# Clinical Facets of Eating Disorders

# 7

# Self Injurious Behavior in Adolescent Girls with Eating Disorders

S. Ohmann and C. Popow
*Dept. of Child and Adolescent Psychiatry, Medical University of Vienna*
*Austria*

## 1. Introduction

Self-injurious behaviour (SIB), repetitive intentional hurting, bruising, cutting, burning, self-poisoning etc. with the intent to cause pain and tissue damage, is observed as comorbid condition in various psychiatric disorders. SIB is frequently but not exclusively encountered in patients with borderline personality, posttraumatic stress, and eating disorders, but it may also occur in otherwise "healthy" persons, and it may be "learned" from peers, especially in the hospital environment (Ohmann et al., 2008). SIB aims at instantaneously reducing inner tensions resulting from anxiety, depression, stress, self-discontentedness etc., at (re)gaining self-control and escaping from numbness and dissociative states, it may serve to fulfil wishes for self-punishment, and there may (rarely) be appellative aspects alerting other people about ones poor psychical state (Favaro & Santonastaso, 1999). SIB is socially not well accepted and must be differentiated from occasional or psychotic self-mutilation and socially accepted habits like piercing and tattooing. SIB does not necessarily imply death wishes (Simeon et al., 1995) and has clearly to be differentiated from (attempted) suicide or parasuicidal gestures (Eberly, 2005). The relationship between SIB and suicidal behaviour is, however, complex.

Depending on the motivational background, Favaro & Santonastaso (1998, 2000) differentiated two dimensions, impulsive and compulsive, of non-suicidal self-injury (NSSI). Depending on the characteristics of the action, Favazza & Simeon (1995) also distinguished between compulsive (hair pulling, nail biting, skin picking, scratching) and impulsive SIB (skin cutting, hitting and burning). Impulsive SIB occurs episodically, is positively connoted, and patients exhibit only little resistance towards their ego-syntonic impulses. Compulsive SIB is habitual, occurs repetitively, and patients exhibit some resistance towards their ego-dystonic urges. Compulsive SIB shares commonalities with obsessive-compulsive disorder (OCD).

Patients with eating disorders (EDs) often present with a combination of obsessive-compulsive and impulsive symptoms (Lacey & Evans, 1986). Considering the effects, extreme starving, repeated vomiting, purging etc. can also be considered as SIB (van der Kolk et al., 1991; Ahrén-Moonga et al., 2008). In the study of Laye-Gindhu & Schonert-Reichl (2005), adolescents considered their eating-disordered behaviour as self-harm.

SIB in patients with EDs tends to be more repetitive, and characterized by little suicidal intent. Some patients exhibit direct (e.g., skin cutting), some indirect self-aggressive behaviour (e.g., severe alcohol abuse) (Favaro & Santonastaso, 2002). SIB in ED patients may be considered as an indicator of psychopathological severity (Newton et al., 1993; Claes et al., 2003), especially if it is related to the frequency or severity of SIB (Claes et al., 2003).

Although suicide is not a primary aim, persons engaged in SIB exhibit a greater risk for suicide-related behaviour in clinical populations (Whitlock et al., 2006, Brunner et al., 2007). SIB is a risk factor for suicide: patients with SIB describe more suicidal ideation and past suicide attempts (Dulit et al., 1994). Persons who later committed or attempted suicide often present with a history of SIB (Hawton, 2005; Hawton et al., 1993; Hawton et al., 1999). Adolescents with suicidal ideation have a 18-fold risk of being engaged in repetitive SIB and a 2-fold increased risk of occasional SIB. Among the various subgroups of SIB, most of them do not imply a high suicidal risk and may be classified as "non-suicidal", but suicide may never be excluded. Therefore adolescents presenting with SIB must always carefully be evaluated for suicidality (Greydanus & Shek, 2009). As concerns SIB and suicide in patients with EDs, BN is more frequently related to suicide attempts (Favaro & Santonastaso, 1996). Patients with EDs who purge and those with comorbid affective, substance use, and cluster B personality disorders (PDs) report more frequently about suicide attempts (Favaro & Santonastaso, 1997; Franko et al., 2004; Milos et al., 2004; Stein et al., 2004).

## 2. Prevalence

The prevalence rate of SIB is high and rising among adolescents (13-40%, Table 1). It is especially high in patients with borderline personality disorder (BPD) and EDs (25-61%) (Skegg, 2005; Zanarini et al., 2006; Bjarehed & Lundh, 2008; Peebles et al., 2011). Associations between SIB and EDs were identified in the 1980s (Pattison & Kahan, 1983; Lacey & Evans 1986; Favazza et al., 1989): there is a high prevalence of SIB among patients with EDs, ranging between 25.4% and 55.2% (Favaro & Santonastaso, 1998; Favaro et al., 2007; Favazza et al., 1989; Lacey, 1993; Welch & Fairburn, 1996; Claes et al., 2001; Claes & Vandereycken, 2007; Paul et al., 2002). The rates vary depending on research methodology, patient selection, assessment procedure and definition of SIB (Claes & Vandereycken, 2007). EDs are considered as one of the most frequently associated diagnoses in SIB patients, ranging up to 54% to 61% (Svirko & Hawton, 2007). This relates especially to female self-injurers (Dulit et al., 1994; Favazza et al., 1989; Herpertz, 1995). 32% of ED outpatients reported that they had injured themselves at least once (Solano et al., 2005).

Svirko & Hawton (2007) described rates of NSSI between 13.6% and 42.1% in patients with restrictive type Anorexia Nervosa (AN-R), between 27.8% and 68.1% for binge eating/purging type Anorexia Nervosa (AN-BP), and between 26% and 55.2% for Bulimia Nervosa (BN). According to Fahy & Eisler (1993), 25.6% of patients with BN and 24% of patients with AN reported that they deliberately hurt themselves in the last year. Similar data were collected by Favara & Santonastaso (1996): 24% of their outpatients with purging type AN (AN-P) and 30% of patients with purging type BN (BN-P) admitted SIB. This contrasts with a report of Stein et al (2004) who identified SIB in only 11% of outpatients with EDs. Favaro & Santonastaso (1999; 2000) reported no significant differences between AN and BN as concerns types of SIB, except for a higher prevalence of suicide attempts and substance/alcohol abuse in patients with BN. Claes et al. (2004a) observed a high correlation between substance/alcohol abuse and SIB among all types of EDs. Nagata et al. (2003) noted that repetitive SIB tended to prevail among patients with EDs and drug abuse compared to

| Publication | Prevalence of combined SIB and ED (%) | Comments |
|---|---|---|
| Fahy & Eisler (1993) | 25.6 (BN)<br>24.0 (AN) | BN, n=67, AN, n=29; 1 year prevalence |
| Favazza & Rosenthal (1993) | 61 (ED/SIB) | metaanalysis |
| Lacey (1993) | 8 (regular cutting)<br>40 (self-damaging & addictive behavior) | BN women, n=112 |
| Herpertz (1995) | 25-45 | psychiatric inpatients (mostly female), n=154 |
| Favara & Santonastaso (1996) | 24 (AN-P)<br>30 (BN) | Outpatients, n=398<br>(cited according to Ross et al., 2009) |
| Favaro & Santonastaso (1998) | 72 | BN, n=125 (BN-P n=100, BN-NP n=25), age=16-41a |
| Favaro & Santonastaso (1999) | 76 (BN-P)<br>61 (BN-NP) | BN, n=175 (BN-P n=139, BN-NP n=36), age=16-50a |
| Favaro & Santonastaso (2000) | 59 (AN-R)<br>68 (AN-BP) | AN, n=236, age 12-49a |
| Claes et al. (2001) | 40-44 | ED inpatients, n=134, mean age=19 |
| Anderson et al. (2002) | 12-46 | BN (BN+SIB n=19, BN+ suicidal behaviour n=28, BN+ no SIB/ no suicidal behaviour n=105) |
| Paul et al., 2002 | 34.6 (life time prev.)<br>21.3 (6 mo prev.)<br>43.3 (BN)<br>35.8 (EDNOS) | Inpatients, women (n=376: AN n=119, BN n=137, EDNOS n=120) |
| Claes & Vandereycken (2003) | 38.6 (26-55)<br>26.1 (AN-R)<br>27.8 (AN-P)<br>55.2 (BN) | ED inpatients, n=70, mean age 22a<br>AN-R, n=23<br>AN-P, n=18<br>BNn=29 |
| Claes et al. (2004a) | 46.5 | ED, at least one form of SIB, n=178 |
| Claes et al. (2004b) | 47 | ED, at least one form of SIB, n=131 |
| Stein et al (2004) | 32 | ED outpatients, n = 150, history of parasuicide; |
| Solano et al. (2005) | 32 | ED outpatients,n=35, lifetime SIB occurrence |
| Claes & Vandereycken (2006) | 45.4 | ED inpatients, n=185, mean age=21a, some form of SIB in their recent history |
| Favaro et al. (2007) | 4.8-13.9 | community sample, n=934 |

| | | |
|---|---|---|
| Claes & Vandereycken (2007a) | 38.6 (BN) | ED n=70, mean age 22a |
| Svirko & Hawton (2007) | 25.4-55.2 (SIB in EDs)<br>54-61 (Eds in SIB) | metaanalysis (1989-2005) |
| Bjarehed & Lundh (2008) | 13-40 | ED adolescents, age = 14<br>cited after Peebles et al., 2011 |
| Favaro et al. (2008) | 33 | N = 95 (BN-P) |
| Muehlenkamp et al. (2009) | 14.5 | N = 131 (BN) |
| Ross et al. (2009) | 13.9 | male and female high school students, n=440, age=12-17a; significantly more desire for thinness, body dissatisfaction and perfectionism in SIB vs. no-SIB students |
| Skarderud & Sommerfeldt (2009) | 13-68 | higher prevalence in BN and AN-B than AN-R; non-systematic literature search (1985-2008) |
| Wright et al. (2009) | 4.5-4.9 | community sample, students, two surveys (1. N=5045; 2. N=805) |
| Claes et al. (2010) | 45 | ED female inpatients, n=177 |
| Peebles et al. (2011) | 40.8 | ED adolescents, n = 1432, age=10-21a |

Abbreviations: AN - anorexia nervosa, AN-B – AN bingeing type, AN-R – AN, restrictive type, AN-P – AN, purging type; BN - bulimia nervosa, BN-P – BN, purging type, BN-NP, BN no-purging type; ED - eating disorder, EDNOS – eating disorder not otherwise specified

Table 1. Prevalence of self injurious behaviour in patients with eating disorders

patients with drug abuse only. Concerning AN subgroups, patients with AN-BP showed more impulsive SIB (e.g., cutting and burning) than patients with AN-R. Claes et al. (2001) reported 44% of female inpatient ED patients to admit at least one form of SIB (mostly hair pulling, scratching, cutting, or bruising) with a mean age at onset of 17.5 years (AN-R 34.3%, AN-P 51.8% and BN 43.6%). According to Cabrera (2011) SIB occurred simultaneously with ED in 48.5 per cent of the patients, later in 40 per cent, and before ED in 11.5 per cent only.

## 2.1 BN and SIB

BN is one of the most frequently associated diagnoses among females with self-mutilating behaviour (Dulit et al., 1994; Favazza et al., 1989; Herpertz, 1995). The co-occurrence of bulimia and SIB is not a simple overlapping of two syndromes: these are two specifically associated entities that share various pathogenic features, but no cause-and-effect relationship. Impulsivity and compulsivity in BN are two distinct coexisting dimensions (Favara & Santonastaso, 1998, 1999). Some symptoms of BN (e.g. purging) can be considered as self-injurious actions. SIB in patients with BN is not only used for releaving tensions but also as an alternative to binge eating and a way to sense one´s body again, to restore reality and identity. Some patients also described their self-injurious behaviour as an irresistible impulse of self-punishment (Favara & Santonastaso, 1998).

Favaro & Santonastaso (1999) reported that patients with BN and impulsive SIB (such as skin cutting and burning) more frequently had a history of sexual abuse and depression, and a higher probability of suicide attempts; whereas patients with BN and compulsive SIB (such as hair pulling and onycophagia) lacked awareness towards emotions and body sensations, showed greater obsessionality, and had a shorter duration of illness.

The term "multi-impulsive" bulimia created by Lacey & Evans (1986) characterizes patients with BN who, in addition to bingeing, vomiting, or purging, have difficulties to control impulsive behaviours (e.g., deliberate and recurrent SIB, alcohol or drug abuse, kleptomania, promiscuous sexual activity, or shop lifting).

### 2.2 AN and SIB

Only a few studies have explored the clinical significance of SIB in patients with AN. Common characteristics of the two disorders are female sex, frequent onset during adolescence, patients perceiving themselves as ineffective and dissatisfied with their body, ascetic, and having urges for self punishment (Favaro & Santonastaso, 2000). Both belong to the spectrum of obsessive-compulsive disorders (Hollander & Wong, 1995), and both aim at controlling body functions (Slade 1982; Cross, 1993; Favazza, 1998; Fairburn et al, 1999).

AN-BP patients seem to be more similar to BN than to AN-R (Garfinkel et al., 1980; Garner et al., 1985). Impulsive SIB (skin cutting and burning) and suicide attempts are therefore more frequently observed in AN-BP than in AN-R patients (Da Costa & Halmi, 1992; Favaro & Santonastaso, 1997).

Adolescents with AN who perceive themselves as overweight exhibit a 3-fold increased risk for repetitive SIB. The two core symptoms of AN, distorted body image and low body mass index (BMI), are correlated with repetitive SIB (Brunner et al., 2007). The presence of more than one type of SIB in patients with AN relates to a greater need of controlling the body, and to greater difficulties in accepting treatment (Favaro & Santonastaso, 2000).

## 3. Functions of SIB in EDs

"Problem behaviours" (e.g., alcohol and substance misuse, ED, and SIB) co-occur, aiming at decreasing negative affect, especially during periods of emotional distress. "Emotional cascades" originate when an individual intensely ruminates on negative affect, thus increasing its magnitude. Engaging in dysregulated behaviours distracts from rumination (Selby et al., 2008). Dysregulated behaviours relate to various personal risk factors, and the ability to intensively perceive negative affect., and may be utilized to experientially avoid negative feelings. According to the principles of the Acceptance and Commitment Therapy (ACT; Hayes et al., 1999), experiential avoidance is defined as the process of avoiding, escaping or otherwise altering unwanted private events (e.g., thoughts, feelings, memories) and the contexts that elicit them. SIB and binge eating are focused distracters. They shift attention away from cues eliciting negative affect, reduce physiological arousal and facilitate the regulation of mood (Linehan 1993; Chapman et al., 2006; Kingston et al., 2010).

A few studies have identified common effects and functionalities of SIB in EDs: SIB serves as a rapid affect regulating strategy for high and low arousal states (Claes et al., 2010), and as a resource of self-help against bodily or emotional discomfort. Although this effect may be short-lived, patients may prefer the physical to the emotional pains (Paul et al., 2002). SIB relieves inner tensions, stops dissociation, and is used for self-stimulation or self-punishment. SIB may help gaining self-affirmation and attention, but it my also result in defective appearance and unattractiveness because of its scars and traces (Vanderlinden & Vandereycken, 1997).

It is still unknown whether affect regulation is the most important function of SIB in patents with various EDs, and if this holds true for all types of SIB. Claes et al. (2010) studied the change of affect before and after various forms of SIB in female inpatients with EDs. 45% of the patients practiced at least one type of NSSI, cutting and scratching being preferred over bruising and burning. The affect regulating function was confirmed for all types of NSSI except bruising. Positively valuated low-arousal affect states increased and negatively valuated high-arousal affect states decreased after NSSI. The increase in positive affect after NSSI was significantly related to the frequency of NSSI and the numbers of functions attributed to NSSI. The affective valence and the level of arousal changed consistently across all types of NSSI. Positively connoted states of low arousal (e.g. "relieved") significantly increased, and negatively connoted states of high arousal (e.g. "anger" or "anxiety") significantly decreased. Scratching, bruising, cutting, and burning were positively (increase positive affect) and negatively (decrease negative affect) reinforced. The change in positive affect after SIB was correlated with the monthly frequency of SIB, the planning of NSSI, and the number of functions attributed to the different SIB methods. Finally the authors found a positive association between the increase in positive affect and the number of reasons given for scratching, bruising, or cutting: the more functions attributed to a particular SIB method, the higher was the increase in positive affect.

## 4. Relationships between EDs and SIB

The relationships between SIB and EDs are complex, and not categorical but a continuum (Favaro & Santonastaso, 2002). Empirical data suggest that EDs and SIB are, in fact, interrelated (Claes et al., 2001).

Community-based research in adolescents supports a significant relationship between EDs and SIB (Brunner et al., 2007). Ross et al. (2009) found a NSSI prevalence of 13.9% in students. Students engaging in NSSI compared to non-NSSI students completed the Eating Disorders Inventory: NSSI students showed significantly more eating pathology than their non-NSSI peers. They also reported about poor introspective awareness, difficulties regulating impulses and affect, feelings of ineffectiveness, distrust, and social insecurity, bulimic inclinations and dissatisfaction with their bodies. Students who continued or had stopped NSSI reported comparable rates of eating pathology. Regardless of gender, students engaging in NSSI showed more disturbed psychological and behavioural traits that are commonly found in persons with EDs. They also thought more about and engaged more in bingeing. In agreement with current theories, bingeing - like SIB – seems to provide a more indirect but concrete way to fight and relieve feelings of distress. Both behaviours represent body actions that deal with overwhelming affect.

SIB in ED patients has been related to neuroticism and conscientiousness, and negatively to extraversion and openness (Claes et al., 2004a).

Peebles et al. (2011) retrospectively explored the prevalence of SIB in a large clinical sample of adolescents with EDs (n = 1.432 patients aged 10-21a). Adolescents with ED and SIB were more likely to be older, female, to have BN or a longer duration of AN, weighed more, had a history of binge eating, purging, disturbed mood or substance abuse. Bingeing and or purging behaviours were more common in patients with SIB, even in those with ED not otherwise specified (EDNOS) or AN.

EDs and SIB may be manifestations of the same underlying difficulties: both use physical attacks on the body, and are interchangeably used to relieve distress (Cross, 1993). Both, SIB and EDs, are body-focused disorders that share a variety of similar etiological, risk and maintaining factors, thus accounting for their co-occurrence (Muehlenkamp et al., 2009, 2011).

According to the emotion avoidance theories (Muehlenkamp et al., 2009), patients with EDs and SIB attempt to actively cope with negative emotional experiences (Skårderud & Sommerfeldt, 2009). A theoretical model explaining the high co-occurrence of SIB in populations with EDs was recently proposed by Muehlenkamp et al. (2011). Early childhood trauma relates to low self-esteem, psychopathology, body dissatisfaction, and dissociation, all being risk factors for SIB and EDs. Additional factors involved in the ED - SIB association are impulsivity, obsessive-compulsive traits, a self-criticizing cognitive style, increased needs of control, and certain characteristics of the family environment (Svirko & Hawton, 2007).

### 4.1 Affect dysregulation

Failing to regulate negative affect is an important factor for the onset and maintenance of EDs, especially in patients with BN (Agras et al., 2009; Smyth et al., 2007; Waters et al., 2001). Patients with EDs and SIB have a higher incidence of depression compared to patients with EDs without SIB (Anderson et al., 2002; Claes et al., 2003; Favaro & Santonastaso, 1999). Some patients with EDs use SIB to reduce distress and uncomfortable feelings (Favazza & Conterio, 1989; Paul et al., 2002). Since the affective problems precede EDs and SIB, dysregulation of affect could be responsible for the onset of both pathologies, at least in some patients (Ross et al., 2009).

### 4.2 Dissociation

SIB in EDs are associated with higher dissociation scores (Brown et al., 1999; Claes et al., 2003; Paul et al., 2002).This appears to play a role in the ED – SIB association. Dissociation, the unconscious way of escaping from negative affect, is also related to trauma.

### 4.3 Trauma

There is a strong association between (early) childhood sexual trauma (before age 15) and the presence of SIB, but the exact mechanism of the link between childhood sexual abuse and ED and/or SIB is still unclear (Claes & Vandereycken, 2007). Early childhood trauma leads to a negative self-image, decreased self-worth and self-esteem, feelings of incompetence and ineffectiveness. As previously stated, these are all risk factors of SIB and EDs. SIB in EDs was associated with childhood physical and sexual abuse (Dohm et al., 2002), but not with adult sexual abuse (Brown et al., 1999). There is a significantly higher prevalence of childhood sexual abuse in self-injuring patients with EDs compared to non-self-injuring patients with EDs (Tobin & Griffing, 1996).

### 4.4 Impulsivity

Increased impulsivity (trait and state) is an important and causal factor for the association, onset, and maintenance of EDs and SIB (Brown et al., 1999; Claes et al., 2001, 2003; Svirko & Hawton, 2007). The alternative hypothesis that increased impulsivity emerges as a side-effect of ED pathology and in turn leading to SIB (Fessler, 2002) is not very probable because of the timing: SIB may emerge before, after, or at the same time as the ED (Paul et al., 2002). The association between SIB and EDs appears to be more specific than an association between EDs and other impulsive behaviours (Welch & Fairburn, 1996; Favazza & Conterio, 1989).

Impulsive behaviours are a trans diagnostic characteristic of EDs (Favaro et al., 2005) – they are very common, and the co-existence of even more than one type of impulsive behaviours is not uncommon. Various studies have implicated impulsivity as a maintaining factor of bulimic symptoms (Sullivan et al., 1998; Fahy & Eisler, 1993; Engel et al., 2005). Among EDs, impulsive and multi-impulsive subjects have specific temperamental characteristics (high novelty seeking and low persistence) and show increased purging behaviour.

The assumption that impulsive behaviours are specifically associated with binge eating does not hold true. Impulsive behaviours are involved in all four diagnostic subgroups of EDs (AN-R: restricting AN, AN-BP: binge eating/purging AN, BN-P: purging BN, BN-NP: non purging BN) (Favaro et al., 2005). Binge eating, however, significantly predicts the presence and number of impulsive behaviours.

The presence of various types of impulsive behaviours (e.g. SIB, suicide attempts, substance and alcohol abuse, stealing, running away etc.) is correlated with severe eating pathology, fears of maturing, early traumatic experiences and symptoms of other psychiatric disorders.

### 4.5 Obsessive-compulsive disorder, ED and SIB

There is a link between obsessive-compulsive disorder (OCD) and EDs and the two disorders share a specific pathophysiologic background (Sallet et al., 2010). There is also a link between OCD, SIB, and EDs: SIB Patients with EDs and SIB had significantly more obsessive-compulsive thoughts and behaviours compared with ED patients without SIB (Paul et al., 2002). Patients with BN and SIB had significantly more comorbid OCD compared with patients with BN without SIB (Anderson et al., 2002). At present it is not clear if the main link between OCD and SIB is the additional distress caused by the OCD or the SIB background or if there is a common pathophysiologic background for all three disorders (if SIB is considered a disorder and not a symptom).

### 4.6 Impulsive and compulsive SIB

Favaro & Santonastaso (1998, 2000) explored Favazza & Simeon´s (1995) subcategorization of impulsive and compulsive SIB. Using factor analysis, the authors confirmed the two orthogonal symptom dimensions model, finding "impulsive SIB" (skin cutting, burning, suicide attempts, substance/alcohol abuse, and laxative/diuretics abuse), and "compulsive SIB" (hair pulling, severe nail biting, self-induced vomiting). Favaro & Santonastaso (2000), repeated their study in patients with AN and SIB. They again confirmed their two-dimensional model of impulsive vs. compulsive SIB. In AN patients, the compulsive SIB factor included hair pulling and severe nail biting, the impulsive factor included skin cutting and burning and suicide attempts. The authors found that a combination of impulsive and compulsive SIB may be observed occasionally. They also detected a third factor, purging, in this specific group of patients . Substance/alcohol abuse did not load on any factor, probably because of the small number of such patients in the sample. The impulsivity SIB dimension significantly correlated with a temperament factor, novelty-seeking, a trait believed to be related to impulsivity (Cloninger, 1994). Compulsive SIB correlated with the temperament factor, harm avoidance, a trait believed to be related to obsessive-compulsive disorder (Maggini et al., 2000). These results suggest that impulsivity and obsessive-compulsive characteristics are involved in different types of SIB and ED patients.

### 4.7 Self-criticism and self-punishment

Both disorders, SIB and EDs, may be exploited as a means of self-punishment (e.g., Herpertz, 1995; Lacey, 1993; Paul et al., 2002; Favaro & Santonastaso, 2000). Patients with EDs and SIB are generally more self-critical and feel guiltier than patients with EDs who do not harm themselves (Claes et al., 2003). In addition, patients with EDs and SIB express greater body dissatisfaction than those without SIB (Anderson et al., 2002; Solano et al., 2005). This indicates again that patients with EDs and SIB exhibit a self-critiquing cognitive style (Anderson et al., 2002).

### 4.8 Control

Both EDs and SIB view their bodies as a means to control overwhelming affect (Ross et al., 2009). The role of this factor is still unclear because there are no studies providing direct evidence for the need for control being involved in the ED-SIB association (Svirko & Hawton, 2007).

### 4.9 Family environment

Although former interpretations of the "typical ED family" with dysfunctional transactional patterns (eg, Lagos, 1981) did not hold, families of patients with EDs generally are a complicated environment (Fujimori et al., 2011). Patients with EDs and SIB describe their family environment as less cohesive, expressive and more conflictual than those without SIB (Claes et al., 2004b).

Families of patients with EDs showed high emotional over-involvement (60% vs. 3% (controls)) and high criticism (47% vs. 15%) as signs of high levels of expressed emotions (EE) in these families (Kyriacou et al., 2007). Yamaguchi et al (2000) reported that patients with EDs who had overprotective parents (another EE factor) exhibited increased suicidal behaviour. This is an important finding because EE relate to outcome and therapy.

## 5. Pain sensitivity and ED

Pain sensitivity is decreased in patients with EDs (Claes et al., 2001, 2006). Patients with EDs who report about decreased sensation of pain during SIB have a longer history of SIB and a higher prevalence of dissociation and traumatic experience. The presence/absence of pain reported during SIB is not significantly related to the type of ED but to the duration of the disorder: the longer the history of SIB, the less pain is reported. There are significant correlations between pain sensation and other features of EDs, eg, patients with lower body weight / BMI report abut less sensation of pain during cutting.

## 6. Personality disorders and EDs

The presence of a PD is an important factor in patients with EDs that also contributes to SIB (Eberly, 2005). There is a close co-morbidity of EDs and especially borderline, schizoid and obsessive-compulsive PDs. (Godart et al., 2000). The "Practice guideline for the treatment of patients with EDs", edited by the American Psychiatric Association (2006), recommends to routinely assess all patients with EDs for the presence of a PD. In clinical studies on EDs it may be difficult to find out predisposing factors and their consequences in patients with EDs (Ahrén-Moonga et al., 2008).

Halmi (2003) speculated that EDs could play a role in the development of a PD, EDs serving as a mode of expressing difficulties of personality dysfunction at a younger age. This is not very probable because the "roots" of PDs date back to a much earlier developmental stage (Young et al., 2003) and ED psychopathology is considered to be more "reactive". But the "true" origins of EDs are not understood as yet. In contrast Favaro et al. (2005) stated that impulsive or multi-impulsive behaviour in EDs does not necessarily relate to PD because impulsive behaviours usually diminish or disappear with remission of the ED.

There are greater problems, poorer functioning, and protracted courses in patients with ED/PD in comparison to patients with only ED or only PD. This is also true for other, non-ED axis I disorders. Chen et al. (2011) reported that EDs in female patients were associated with poorer global functioning and non-ED axis I and II disorders, especially borderline and avoidant PD, whereas in male patients EDs were more associated with axis II disorders, especially borderline PD.

### 6.1 BPD and EDs

Various studies have examined the relationship between BPD and EDs (e.g. Cassin & von Ranson, 2005; Levitt et al., 2004). Chen et al. (2009) observed EDs in about half of treatment-seeking BPD females. BPD patients with BN were four times as likely to engage in frequent SIB (Dulit et al., 1994). Absence of an ED improves the prognosis of BPD (Zanarini et al., 2004).

Although the prevalence of BPD in patients with AN-BP is similar to those with BN (Braun et al., 1994), cluster B PD psychopathology appears to be higher in patients with BN compared to AN patients (Bulik et al., 2004; Franko et al., 2005; Franko & Keel, 2006; Holderness et al., 1994; Rosenvinge et al., 2000). Previous studies based on diagnostic interviews (Cassin & Ranson, 2005) have reported comorbidity rates for EDs and BPD of around 3% for AN-R, 21% for BN and 9% for binge eating disorder (BED). One-quarter of women with BN also had BPD (Sansone & Levitt, 2005). A low rate of Cluster B PDs was observed in patients who recovered from AN-R (5%) or AN-BP (11%) (Wagner et al., 2006).

There is a strong relationship between BPD and dysregulated eating behaviours such as binge-eating and purging. Although there is still no clear explanation for the mechanisms of this linkage (Selby et al., 2010b), these behaviours occur frequently in individuals with (Cassin & von Ranson, 2005) and without AN and BN (Marino & Zanarini, 2001).

The dysregulation of negative affect is a hallmark of BPD (Selby & Joiner, 2009) and ED (Selby et al., 2008; Selby et al., 2009). Fluctuations of negative affect and difficulties tolerating negative emotions are responsible for dysregulated eating behaviors (Anestis et al., 2007; Anestis et al., 2008; Whiteside et al., 2007). Eating pathology helps to reduce negative affect (Smyth et al., 2007). Fighting negative affect could thus be one of the common underlying pathophysiological mechanisms.

Sensitivity to rejection, the tendency to worry about and to defensively or anxiously expect rejection, and to intensely react to situations where rejection is expected (Downy & Feldman, 1996), plays a role in in both, patients with BPD and with EDs. Dysregulated eating behaviour seems to be related to dysregulation of emotions (Selby et al., 2010b): patients with BPD exhibit high levels of rejection sensitivity leading to problems with emotional dysregulation, and subsequently to dysregulated eating behaviour (Selby et al. 2010).

### 6.2 Relationship between EDs, SIB and suicidal behaviour

The risk of suicide is higher in EDs than in any other psychiatric disorders (Harris & Barraclough, 1994; Franko & Keel, 2006). Particularly AN is associated with high rates of completed suicide (standardized mortality ratio for suicide in these patients range from 1.0 to 5.3; Franko & Keel, 2006). There are two specific risk factors for suicide in ED patients, suicidal ideation and a history of suicidal attempts (Prinstein et al., 2008; Franko & Keel, 2006).

One possible reason for the high risk of suicide in AN is the fact that ED patients are continuously exposed to pain, feelings of incompetence, humiliation and despair. This may reduce the fear of pain and thus increase the risk of suicide. On the other hand, feelings of incompetence and despair may lead to suicidal ideation. Selby et al., (2010 a) identified two potential roads to suicidal behaviour in AN: repetitive exposure to painful and destructive behaviours (e.g., vomiting, use of laxatives, and NSSI) endangers AN-BP patients, and exposure to pain due to starvation endangers AN-R patients.

Preti et al. (2010) found a clear decrease of suicide rates in BN as compared to AN in the last decades (suicide rate (AN) = 0,124 per 100 person-years; standardized mortality ratio = 31.0; suicide rate (BN) = 0,030 per 100 person-years, standardized mortality ratio = 7,5). Inpatients with AN have a higher mortality risk that is related to chronicity and seriousness of the illness leading to hospitalization. Contrasting with these reports, Bulik et al. (1999) found no difference in the suicide mortality rates among the various types of EDs.

Huas et al. (2011) identified 6 factors predicting a high mortality risk in severely affected adult AN inpatients: older age, longer duration of ED, history of suicide attempt, misuse of diuretics, intensity of ED symptoms and desired low BMI at admission). Patients with EDs without suicide attempts have a lower suicidal risk.

There are various studies comparing the different rates of suicide attempts in patients with AN and those with BN. Differences are related to different recruitment strategies and different subtypes of patients with AN that were included (Forcano et al., 2011). Some studies report significant differences (Bulik et al., 1999; Herzog et al., 2000), some report higher rates in BN (Favaro & Santonastaso, 1997, 2000; Nagata et al., 2000; Chen et al., 2009; Ahrén-Moonga et al., 2008), and some in AN (Franko et al., 2004).

Relatively few studies have explored the suicidal risk in relation to the AN subtype. Higher rates were reported for AN-BP compared to AN-R patients (Favaro & Santonastaso, 1997; Bulik et al., 2008; Milos et al., 2004; Youssef et al., 2004; Forcano et al., 2011). "Migration" from AN-R to AN-BP increased the likelihood of a suicide attempt (Foulon et al., 2007). Especially purging behaviours are associated with higher rates of suicide attempts (Franko & Keel, 2006; Tozzi et al., 2006). Patients with AN-BP were reported to possess a higher pain tolerance compared to patients with AN-R (Papezova et al., 2005). Although AN-BP patients exhibit a higher suicidality risk, AN-R individuals still have elevated rates of attempted suicide when compared to the general population (Franko & Keel, 2006). Suicidal behaviour is more frequently observed in binge eating disorder (BED) when compared to obese non-BED control patients (Grucza et al., 2007).

Suicide attempts occur in 3% to 20% of patients with AN (Franko & Keel, 2006). Patients with AN who attempted suicide were characterized in their personality profile by aggressive and impulsive traits, hopelessness, neuroticism, psychasthenia, and external locus of control (Brezo et al, 2006; Grucza et al., 2005; Ahrén-Moonga et al., 2008), as well as by high persistence, low self-directedness and high self-transcendence (Bulik et al., 1999; Bulik et al., 2008).

Some studies suggest that suicide attempts and NSSI are present in more than half of patients with BN (Franko & Keel, 2006; Svirko & Hawton, 2007). Male patients with BN, and especially those who experience analgesia during self-cutting, exhibit a high risk of committing suicide (Matsumoto et al., 2005; Matsumoto et al., 2008). Internalizing personality traits combined with impulsivity increase the probability of suicidal behaviours in patients with BN. Increased ED symptoms and general psychopathology, impulsive behaviours and parental alcohol abuse were identified as risk factors for suicide attempts in patients with BN (Forcano et al., 2009). These patients also scored higher for harm avoidance, and lower for self-directedness, reward dependence and cooperativeness.

Community based studies in adolescents found relationships between ED psychopathology and suicidal ideation, and between SIB and suicide attempts (Miotto et al., 2003; Brunner et al., 2007; Crow et al., 2008; Neumark-Sztainer et al., 1998; Rodriguez-Cano et al., 2006). An association between ED psychopathology and suicidality has been reported across various clinical and community based samples of adolescent patients. Psychosocial pathology is sex dependent in adolescent patients with EDs: ED psychopathology is related to hopelessness and suicidality in adolescent girls, even after controlling for depression/negative affect, whereas ED psychopathology in adolescent boys is related to self-reported history of sexual abuse and various externalizing problems (drug abuse, violence and impulsivity) (Zaitsoff & Grilo, 2010).

### 6.3 Impact of PDs on treatment outcome in EDs

Comorbidity of EDs and BPD has significant implications for the course and outcome of treatment. EDs plus BPD results in more frequent hospitalizations, more severe psychopathology, lower psychosocial functioning and more interpersonal problems (Johnson et al., 1989; Steiger et al., 1994; Wonderlich & Swift, 1990). Comorbid BPD increases the risk of poor response to psychosocial treatment (Coker et al., 1993; Herzog et al., 1991; Johnson et al., 1989; Rossiter et al., 1993; Steiger & Stotland, 1996) and negative outcomes (Johnson et al., 1990; Fichter et al., 1994; Keel & Mitchell, 1997; Steiger & Stotland, 1996; Rosenvinge et al., 2000; Wonderlich & Michell, 1997).

Long-term follow up studies are not consistent and do not unanimously support the findings of short-term studies (Fallon et al., 1991; Norring, 1993; Rowe et al., 2008; Ben-Porath et al., 2009). Grilo et al., (2003) didn´t find a poorer treatment outcome of patients with EDs and comorbid borderline, avoidant, or obsessive-compulsive PD, whereas Wilfey et al. (2000) observed a poorer treatment response for patients with BEDs and comorbid Cluster B psychopathology.

## 7. Clinical correlates predicting SIB in EDs

There are similar predictors of impulsive and compulsive dimensions of SIB in patients with AN and BN (Favaro & Santonastaso, 2002). Childhood sexual abuse, e.g., predicts impulsive SIB in both syndromes (Favaro & Santonastaso, 1998, 1999, 2000, 2008; van der Kolk 1991).

Compulsive SIB is predicted by a shorter duration of illness, and a more accentuated lack of interoceptive awareness in patients with BN; and by younger age, and higher scores on the obsessionality subscale in patients with AN.

Impulsive SIB is predicted by sexual abuse and depression in patients with BN, and by sexual abuse and anxiety in patients with AN (Favaro & Santonastaso, 2000, 2002).

Other significant independent predictors of impulsive SIB were high scores of harm avoidance, and self-transcendence, whereas childhood sexual abuse, the presence of a cluster B personality disorder, and low self-directedness were predictors of suicide attempts (Favaro et al., 2008).

Poor social adaptation and high levels of anxiety are considered predisposing factors in the development of EDs, especially in patients with BN and SIB (Ahrén-Moonga et al., 2008). Wildman et al. (2004) observed that depressive symptoms preceded the onset of both, ED and SIB, in adolescents.

Concomitant impulsive and compulsive SIB is the most important predictor of treatment drop-out in AN patients (Favaro & Santonastaso, 2000), whereas in BN patients, concomitant impulsive and compulsive SIB reduces the risk of treatment drop-out (Favaro & Santonastaso, 1998). This difference was explained by a different role of control: in BN the need for control is ego-dystonic in BN, and ego-syntonic in AN patients (Favaro & Santonastaso, 2000).

## 8. Differences between EDs/SIB and EDs/no SIB patients

SIB in patients with EDs (EDs/SIB) implies higher levels of psychological dysfunction, consisting dissociative experiences (Paul et al., 2002), and increased impulsiveness compared to EDs/no SIB (Claes et al., 2001, 2003). Patients with EDs/SIB exhibit more clinical symptoms of anxiety, depression, and hostility (Paul et al., 2002), and patients with more than one type of SIB exhibit the worst clinical symptomatology (Claes et al., 2003). In another study Claes et al. (2003) found significantly more self-criticism, self-abasement, self-punitiveness and guilt in EDs/SIB compared to EDs/no SIB patinets. EDs/SIB patients exhibit more cluster B (borderline, antisocial) PDs and a more severe history of trauma than EDs/no SIB. SIB patients report more anger than EDs/no SIB patients. ED patients with a history of SIB are more dissatisfied with their bodies compared with EDs/no SIB patients (Claes et al., 2003; Solano et al., 2005).

Claes & Vandereycken (2007a) reported that high levels of dissociation and self-criticism but not impulsiveness distinguished sexually abused EDs/SIB from EDs/no SIB patients . Stein et al. (2004) reported about more lifetime drug abuse, impulse control problems, bipolar symptoms and more out- and inpatient treatment in EDs/SIB compared to EDs/no SIB patients.

Concerning personality traits in ED patients with and without SIB (cutting, burning, hair pulling), patients with EDs/SIB score significantly higher on the neuroticism and lower on the extraversion scales. On subtraits the EDs/SIB patients appeared to be more anxious, more willing to please and less cheerful, efficient and ambitious. Personality traits (except for impulsiveness) were not associated with the frequency or form of SIB or with subtypes of EDs. There was no significant interaction effect between ED subtype and presence/absence of SIB (Claes et al, 2004a).

From a family perspective, significant differences in the family environment were observed in patients with EDs/SIB vs. EDs/no SIB (Claes et al., 2004b): the family environment of EDs/SIB patients was less cohesive, expressive and socially oriented, and more conflictual and disorganized than the families of EDs/no SIB patients. The authors also observed a poorer treatment prognosis in EDs/SIB patients. Paternal care is also important for ED pathology. EDs/SIB patients exhibited more severe ED pathology (more pronounced body dissatisfaction and increased fears of maturing) and reported about less paternal care. More than half of the patients stated that their fathers demonstrated "affectionless control". EDs/no SIB patients mainly had conflicts with their mother whereas EDs/SIB patients were also involved in conflicts with their fathers (Fujimori et al., 2011).

Patients with BN and SIB are more likely affected of comorbid obsessive-compulsive disorder compared to BNs without SIB (Anderson et al., 2002; Fujimori et al., 2011).

Anderson et al. (2002) examined how women with BN/SIB differed from women with BN/no SIB and from women with BN who attempted suicide with lethal intent. BN/SIB women reported significantly more laxative and drug abuse. Women with BN and suicide attempts had the highest rates of overall comorbidity across the three groups. SIB patients scored significantly higher on the self-transcendence scale. BN/SIB women appeared to engage more in drugs abuse (laxatives and illicit drugs). Patients who attempted suicide had the highest rates of axis I and axis II comorbidities. High scores on self-transcendence may signal a greater sense of dissociation and disconnectedness in BN/SIB female patients.

Adolescents with EDs who engage in SIB are more dissatisfied with the shape and size of their body than their non-SIB peers and manifest greater socially related affective problems. Self-injurers who hurt themselves only once also exhibited more severe eating pathology compared with their non-SIB peers. Adolescents who reported to have stopped self-injuring demonstrated similar rates of eating pathology as adolescents who admitted to regularly engage in SIB. The authors concluded that cessation of SIB does not immediately change the ED pathology (Ross et al., 2009).

## 9. Treatment of patients with EDs/SIB

ED/SIB patients are generally difficult to treat (Fujimori et al., 2011). Therapy should address SIB early in the treatment process by finding out predisposing and triggering factors and by teaching alternatives to SIB. Dialectical behaviour therapy (DBT) (Linehan, 1993) is a very efficient treatment program for both disorders, adolescent BPD and EDs (Rathus & Miller, 2002; Fleischhaker et al., 2006; Salbach et al., 2007). DBT was originally developed for chronically suicidal female adult outpatients with BPD. Clinical studies involving adult patients with BPD, BN, and BED show that these patients benefit from DBT (Palmer et al., 2003; Safer et al., 2001; Telch et al., 2001). The program was later modified for adolescents (DBT-A) and includes self-regulatory and cognitive strategies (Miller et al., 1997; Fleischhaker et al., 2006). DBT has significant positive effects on disordered eating, negative mood regulation and depression (Rutherford & Couturier, 2007).

In DBT for eating disorders (DBT-E) changed eating behaviour is considered to be a consequence of stress, traumatisation or difficulties in regulating emotions. The treatment aims at imparting skills to improve regulation of emotions, tolerance to distress, and eating behaviour (Sipos et al., 2011).

Various types of NSSI act as a function of affect regulation in patients with EDs. Therefore treatment of SIB needs to zoom in on this important function (Claes et al., 2010). The authors suggested three helpful strategies:

1. educating the patients on the affect regulating functions of NSSI, enabling patients to understand the functionality of their behaviour;
2. assessing the functionality of affective antecedents and consequences of NSSI, and suggesting alternative, less harmful behaviours for dealing with these irksome affective states; and
3. introducing preventive strategies for dealing with (high-arousal) negative affective states.

Kingston et al. (2010) suggested to reduce experiential avoidance, by suggesting ACT or mindfulness-based interventions, irrespective of the particular pattern of a patients´ harmful behaviours.

Claes et al. (2002b) recommended starting with psycho-education about the medical risks of ED behaviour, and to perform a systematic and detailed functional analysis with the patient, identifying external (situational) and internal (emotional and cognitive) triggers that instigate self-harming behaviours. The functional analysis will uncover the functional significance of the behaviour, hierarchical relationships, and the specific situational or behavioural background. This enables the patient to develop meaningful cognitive strategies and to change affective content. In a second step, the patient is encouraged to experiment with alternative and more effective coping strategies in order to decrease tension and to distract attention. Then, the patients are motivated to expose themselves gradually to the situations and emotional triggers that initially triggered SIB (systematic desensitisation), aiming at extinguishing the self-harming reactions by habituating to threatening stimuli. All major triggering situations have to be mastered following a hierarchical order. Accompanying dissociative reactions have to be identified and fought, employing strategies for reorientation in the here-and-now. Another, essential part of the therapy is cognitive reprocessing of the patient´s irrational thoughts, gradually replacing them by more appropriate cognitions. For some patients also a social skills training program is indicated, teaching how to react appropriately in social situations.

The Self-Injury Questionnaire -Treatment Related (SIQ-TR) by Claes & Vandereycken (2007b) focuses not only on detailed self-monitoring of SIB but also on assessing its situational, cognitive and affective antecedents and consequences. The questionnaire helps getting essential information for therapeutic planning, including a wide range of cognitive, affective, and behavioural interventions. It is crucial to detect the functional meaning of the concerned behaviour. If SIB is linked to dissociative states, it may be a way of "keeping in touch" with the here-and-now reality. If associated with low self-esteem, SIB may express self-criticism as self-punishment. However, independent of the background, the first approach to SIB is to try to replace it by a more adaptive and less harmful behaviour while keeping its functionality. Patients are e.g. taught healthier affect-regulation skills to deal with stressful situations, and "grounding" techniques enabling to escape from dissociative states (Briere & Gil, 1998; Zlotnick et al., 1996). Cognitive strategies are used to correct irrational beliefs about traumatic experiences (e.g., from self-criticism to criticising others; the offender is guilty, not the victim).

Kröger et al. (2010) investigated the effect of an adapted 3-month DBT inpatient program in patients with BPD and comorbid AN/BN who had already failed to respond to ED specific inpatient treatments. At follow-up the remission rate was 54% for BN, and 33% for AN. The mean weight of AN patients was not significantly increased at post-treatment, but it was improved at follow-up. The frequency of binge-eating episodes was reduced in BN patients at post treatment and at follow-up. Self-rated eating-related complaints, psychopathology, and global psychosocial functioning were improved.

Selby et al. (2010b) recommended therapeutic interventions in patients with BPDs and EDs: patients should identify and correct rejection related maladaptive thoughts in order to decrease dysregulation of emotions and subsequently dysregulated eating.

Fujimori et al. (2011) highlighted the importance of the fathers participating in the treatment program. The authors stated that insight into the patient-father relationship might provide a sound basis for treating patients with EDs and SIB.

Salbach et al. (2007) designed and evaluated an inpatient DBT-AN/BN program for adolescents. The program lasts for 12 weeks and consists of three phases (preparation, treatment, transfer of reached goals in everyday life). Restrictive dieting (weight gain < 500 g/week), binge eating and purging are considered as SIB and therefore as the problem with the highest treatment priority. Treatment elements are individual therapy (50 min twice weekly), establishing the objectives of the week (30 min weekly), group-therapy for skills training (90 min once weekly), group-therapy for mindfulness training (50 min once weekly), group-therapy for ED and self-esteem (90 min once weekly), family sessions (50 min once weekly or two weekly), group body therapy (50 min weekly or two weekly), reference group (60 min twice weekly). The treatment plan consists of 4 steps -individual freedom is successively increased depending on the patient´s body weight and her/his ability to adequately eat. The body weight is assessed twice weekly. If patients do not regularly gain weight by 500g/week, day pass and visiting hours are suspended.

## 10. Implications for preventing EDs/SIB

One essential problem in the development of EDs and SIB is bullying by peers or teachers. Effective anti-bullying strategies have been developed (e.g. International Bullying Prevention Association, Kandersteg Declaration Against Bullying in Children and Youth) but these ideas and strategies are not established nationwide as yet.

Another essential problem of patients with EDs and SIB is their difficulty to regulate emotions. Training programs aiming at teaching how to adequate regulate emotions are possibly effective. Such training programs do not exist as yet, their efficacy has to be proven. In addition to focusing on emotion regulation skills, it may be also important to create interventions that increase the skills of individuals in using more abstract and verbal ways to cope with distress (Ross et al., 2009).

There is also a need of trained medical staff, working in the schools, providing early on-site assessment and specific advice for adolescents presenting with eating problems or SIB.

## 11. Limitations of the EDs/SIB research

Most studies of EDs/SIB have several important limitations.

A first limitation of the research in this area is the use of multiple confounding terms and ambiguous definitions of SIB. Many studies used inaccurate definitions of SIB (Fujimori et al., 2011), making study results difficult to interpret. SIB is often synonymously used with self-mutilation, self-harm etc. Self-mutilation includes severe forms of self-harm. Self-harm is a more general term that is often used to refer to suicide attempts and may also include indirect methods of self-damage, such as binge eating, alcohol or drug abuse. Some authors have assumed that SIB is an independent clinical entity that occurs in the context of ED (Pattison & Kahan, 1983; Favazza & Conterio, 1989), whereas others consider SIB and abnormal eating behaviours as symptoms of BPD (Gunderson et al., 1987). In recent years, the significance of diagnostic subtyping of EDs according to DSM IV criteria has been criticised.

Recent research has shown that patients with EDs are better classified if personality (Westen & Harnden-Fischer, 2001), temperament and character (Klump et al., 2000) variables are taken into account. Therefore, classifying EDs on an impulsivity-compulsivity spectrum has been proposed, especially since a high prevalence of SIB has been detected in these patients (Claes et al., 2002a; Favaro & Santonastaso, 1998).

A second limitation concerns control groups: most studies did not compare ED patients with non-ED subjects. This is especially important for evaluating the prevalence of complications and comorbidities, e.g., the prevalence of EDs/SIB.

A third limitation is been the almost exclusive preference of female patents with EDs. EDs for many reasons have a high preference of females. This difference has, unfortunately, led to disregarding the specific aspects of male EDs.

A fourth limitation was to consider only recent acts of SIB. Therefore, the prevalence of EDs/SIB may be underestimated. Ross et al. (2009) recommended examining lifetime prevalence of SIB.

A fifth limitation relates to research on EDs/SIB restricted to clinical samples. Only a few studies have been conducted involving eating pathologies and SIB in community based, non-clinical, adult populations. These studies, however, have limitations: Favazza et al. (1989) found 38% of their sample of university students with SIB admitted having an ED. Whitlock et al. (2006) noted that SIB respondents were significantly more likely to endorse more than one symptom of an ED as compared to their non-SIB peers. Samples of university students reflect a minority and are not representative of this age group. EDs often occur in upper-middle class populations. Community based studies on EDs have to be explored in a large unbiased group with a wide range of ethnicities and socio-economic status.

A sixth limitation is the lack of standardized measures of eating pathology (Ross et al, 2009).

These limitations and the paucity of sound available longitudinal treatment studies involving large patient samples in adolescents leave many questions open and a multitude of research questions that await to be answered.

## 12. Conclusion and core messages

The main EDs and SIB share important predisposing, maintaining and prognostic factors. Patients with EDs and SIB are likely to present with a comorbid Axis II disorder, especially BPD. An important task is to detect patients at high mortality risk. SIB should be addressed early in the treatment process.

The core messages are summarised in Table 2:

1. SIB is frequently observed in patients with EDs (increasing prevalence, 13-40. Some authors consider dieting, bingeing, self-induced vomiting, and purging as SIB
2. Both body focused problem behaviours have common predisposing, maintaining, and prognostic factors, and aim at reducing or avoiding negative affect
3. Main risk factors for SIB are childhood trauma, dysregulation of affect, dissociative, impulsive, obsessive tendencies, , increased self-criticism leading to self-punishment, complicated family environments
4. SIB in ED patients is associated with increased severity of the ED, psychopathologic comorbidity (especially posttraumatic, cluster B personality disorders), body disgust, impulsivity, and suicidality; more difficult treatment, and a poorer prognosis
5. Psychotherapy should aim at first targeting SIB and suicidal behavior (e.g. Dialectic Behavioral Therapy)
6. Possible preventive strategies include teaching of emotion regulation, and stress management

Table 2. Core Messages: Self injurious behaviours (SIB) in adolescent girls with eating disorders (EDs)

## 13 References


Agras, W.S. & Telch, C.F. (1998). The effects of caloric deprivation and negative affect on binge eating in obese binge-eating disordered women. *Behav Ther,* Vol. 29, No. 3, (Summer 1998), pp. 491-503, doi: 10.1016/S0005-7894(98)800-45-2

Ahrén-Moonga, J., Holmgren, S., von Knorring, L. & Klinteberg, B. (2008). Personality traits and self-injurious behaviour in patients with eating disorders. *Eur Eat Disord Rev,* Vol. 16, No. 4, (Jul 2008), pp. 268-75, PMID 18240124

American Psychiatric Association (2006). Treatment of patients with eating disorders. *Am J Psychiatry,* Vol. 163, No. 7, (Jul 2006), pp. 4-54, ISSN 16925191

Anderson, C.B., Carter, F.A., McIntosh, V.V., Joyce, P.R. & Bulik, C.M. (2002). Self-harm and suicide attempts in individuals with bulimia nervosa. *Eat Disord,* Vol. 10, No. 3, (Fall 2002), pp. 227-43, PMID 16864266

Anestis, M.D., Selby, E.A., Fink, E. & Joiner, T.E. (2007). The multifaceted role of distress tolerance in dysregulated eating behaviors. *Int J Eat Disord,* Vol. 40, No. 8, (December 2007), pp. 718-26, PMID 17868125

Anestis, M.D., Peterson, C.B., Bardone-Cone, A.M., Klein, M.H., Mitchell, J.E., Crosby, R.D. et al. (2008). Affective lability and impulsivity in a clinical sample of women with bulimia nervosa: The role of affect in severely dysregulated behaviour. *Int J Eat Disord,* Vol. 42, No. 3, (April 2009), pp. 259-66, PMID 18951460

Ben-Porath, D.D., Wisniewski, L. & Warren, M. (2009). Differential treatment response for eating disordered patients with and without a comorbid borderline personality diagnosis using a dialectical behaviour therapy (DBT)-informed approach. *Eat Disord,* Vol. 17, No. 3, (May-Jun 2009), pp. 225-41, PMID 19391021

Bjärehed, J. & Lundh, L.G. (2008). Deliberate self-harm in 14-year-old adolescents: How frequent is it, and how is it associated with psychopathology, relationship variables, and styles of emotional regulation? *Cogn Behav Ther,* Vol. 37, No. 1, pp. 26-37, PMID 18365796

Braun, D.L., Sunday, S.R. & Halmi, K.A. (1994). Psychiatric comorbidity in patients with eating disorders. *Psychol Med,* Vol. 24, No. 4, (Nov 1994), pp. 859-67, PMID 7892354

Brezo, J., Paris, J., Tremblay, R., Vitaro, F., Zoccolillo, M., Hebert, M. et al. (2006). Personality traits as correlates of suicide attempts and suicidal ideation in young adults. *Psychol Med,* Vol. 36, No. 2, pp. 191-202, PMID 16332283

Briere, J. & Gil, E. (1998). Self-mutilation in clinical and general population samples: prevalence, correlates, and functions. *Am J Orthopsychiatry,* Vol. 68, No. 4, (Oct 1998), pp. 609-20, PMID 9809120

Brown, L., Russell, J., Thornton, C. & Dunn, S. (1999). Dissociation, abuse and the eating disorders: Evidence from an Australian population. *Aust N Z J Psychiatry,* Vol. 33, No. 4, (Aug 1999), pp. 521-8, PMID 10483846

Brunner, R., Parzer, P., Haffner, J., Stehen, R., Roos, J., Klett, M. & Resch, F. (2007). Prevalence and psychological correlates of occasional and repetitive deliberate self-harm in adolescents. *Arch Pediatr Adolesc Med,* Vol. 161, No. 7, (Jul 2007), pp. 641-9, PMID 17606826

Bulik, C.M., Klump, K.L., Thornton, L., Kaplan, A.S., Devlin, B., Fichter, M.M. et al. (2004). Alcohol use disorder comorbidity in eating disorders: a multicenter study. *J C Psychiatry,* Vol. 65, No. 7, (Jul 2004), pp. 1000-6, PMID 15291691

Bulik, C.M., Sullivan, P.F. & Joyce, P.R. (1999).Temperament, character and suicide attempts in anorexia nervosa, bulimia nervosa and major depression. *Acta Psychiatr Scand*, Vol. 100, No. 1, (Jul 1999), pp. 27-32, PMID 10442436

Bulik, C.M., Thornton, L., Pinheiro, A.P., Plotnicov, K., Klump, K.L., Brandt, H. et al. (2008). Suicide attempts in anorexia nervosa. *Psychosom Med*, Vol. 70, No. 3, (Apr 2008), pp. 378-83, PMID 18256339

Cassin, C.E. & von Ranson, K.M. (2005). Personality and eating disorders: a decade in review. *Clin Psychol Rev*, Vol. 25, No. 7, pp. 895-916, PMID 16099563

Cabrera, D. (2011). Understanding eating disorders and cutting. *Addiction Professional*, Vol. 9, No. 2, (Mar-Apr 2011), pp. 22-4

Chapman, A.L., Gratz, K.L. & Brown, M.Z. (2006). Solving the puzzle of deliberate self-harm: The experiential avoidance model. *Behav Res Ther*, Vol. 44, No. 3, (Mar 2006), pp. 371-94, PMID 16446150

Chen, E.Y., Brown, M.Z., Harned, M.S. & Linehan, M.M. (2009). A comparison of borderline personality disorder with and without eating disorders. *Psychiatry Res*, Vol. 170, No. 1, (Nov 30 2009), pp. 86-90, PMID 19796824

Chen, E.Y., McCloskey, M.S., Michelson, S., Gordon, K.H. & Coccaro, E. (2011). Characterizing eating disorders in a personality disorders sample. *Psychiatry Res*, Vol. 185, No. 3, (Feb 28 2011), pp. 427-32, PMID 20667417

Claes, L., Vandereycken, W. & Vertommen, H. (2001). Self-injurious behaviors in eating-disordered patients. *Eat Behav*, Vol. 2, No. 3, (Autumn 2001), pp. 263-72, PMID 15001035

Claes, L., Vandereycken, W. & Vertommen, H. (2002a). Impulsive and compulsive traits in eating disordered patients compared with controls. *Personality and Individual Differences*, Vol. 32, (March 2001), pp. 707-14 , PII: S0191-8869(01)00071-X

Claes, L., Vandereycken, W. & Vertommen, H. (2002b). Therapy-related assessment of self-harming behaviors in eating disordered patients: a case illustration. *Eat Disord*, Vol. 10, No. 3, (Fall 2002), pp. 269-79, PMID 16864269

Claes, L., Vandereycken, W. & Vertommen, H. (2003). Eating-disordered patients with and without self-injurious behaviors: a comparison of psychopathological features. *Eur Eat Disord Rev*, Vol. 11, No. 5, (Apr 2003), pp. 379-96, doi: 10.1002/erv.510

Claes, L., Vandereycken, W. & Vertommen, H. (2004a). Personality traits in eating-disordered patients with and without self-injurious behaviors. *J Pers Disord*, Vol. 18, No. 4, (Aug 2004), pp. 399-404, PMID 15342326

Claes, L., Vandereycken, W. & Vertommen, H. (2004b). Family environment of eating disordered patients with and without self-injurious behaviors. *Eur Psychiatry*, Vol. 19, No. 8, (Dec 2004), pp. 494-8, PMID 15589709

Claes, L., Vandereycken, W. & Vertommen, H. (2006). Pain experience related to self-injury in eating disorder patients. *Eat Behav*, Vol. 7, No. 3, (Aug 2006), pp. 204-13, PMID 16843222

Claes, L. & Vandereycken, W. (2007a). Is there a link between traumatic experiences and self-injurious behaviors in eating-disordered patients? *Eat Disord*, Vol. 15, No. 4, (Jul-Sep 2007), pp. 305-15, PMID 17710568

Claes, L. & Vandereycken, W. (2007b). The Self-Injury Questionnaire-Treatment Related (SIQ-TR): construction, reliability and validity in a sample of female eating disorder patients. In *Psychological tests and testing research trends,* P.M. Goldfarb (Ed.), Nova Science Publishers, ISBN 1-60021-569-6, New York

Claes, L., Klonsky, E.D., Muehlenkamp, J., Kuppens, P. & Vandereycken, W. (2010). The affect-regulation function of nonsuicidal self-injury in eating-disordered patients: which affect states are regulated? *Compr Psychiatry,* Vol. 51, No. 4, (Jul-Aug 2010), pp. 386-92, PMID 20579512

Cloninger, C.R., Przybeck, T. R., Svrakic, D.M. & Wetzel, R.D. (1994). *The Temperament and Character Inventory (TCI): A guide to its development and use.* Center for Psychobiology of Personality, ISBN-10: 0964291703, Washington University, St. Louis, MO

Coker, S., Vize, C., Wade, T. & Cooper, P.J. (1993). Patients with bulimia nervosa who fail to engage in cognitive behavior therapy. *Int J Eat Disord,* Vol. 13, No. 1, pp. 35-40, PMID 8477275

Cross, L. (1993). Body and self in feminine development: Implications for eating disorders and delicate self-mutilation. *Bull Menninger Clin,* Vol. 57, No. 1, (Winter 1993), pp. 41-68, PMID 8443617

Crow, S.C., Eisenberg, M.E., Story, M. & Neumark-Sztainer, D. (2008). Suicidal behaviour in adolescents: relationship to weight status, weight control behaviors, and body dissatisfaction. *Int J Eat Disord,* Vol. 41, No. 1, (Jan 2008), pp. 82-7, doi: 10.1002/eat.20466

DaCosta, M. & Halmi, K.A. (1992). Classifications of anorexia nervosa: Question of subtypes. *Int J Eat Disord,* Vol. 11, No. 4, (May 1992), pp. 305-13, doi: 10.1002/1098-108X(199205)11:4<305::AID-EAT2260110403>3.0CO;2-2

Dohm, F.A., Striegel-Moore, R.H., Wilfley, D.E., Pike, K.M., Hook, J. & Fairburn, C.G. (2002). Self-harm and substance use in a community sample of Black and White women with binge eating disorder or bulimia nervosa. *Int J Eat Disord,* Vol. 32, No. 4, (Dec 2002), pp. 389-400, PMID 12386904

Downy, G. & Feldman, S. (1996). Implications of rejection sensitivity for intimate relationships. *J Pers Soc Psychol,* Vol. 70, No. 6, (Jun1996), pp. 1327-43, PMID 8667172

Dulit, R.A., Fyer, M.R., Leon, A.C., Brodsky, B.S. & Frances, A.J. (1994). Clinical correlates of self-mutilation in borderline personality disorder. *Am J Psychiatry,* Vol. 151, No. 9, (Sep 1004), pp. 1305-11, PMID 8067485

Engel, S.G., Corneliussen, S.J., Wonderlich, S.A., Crosby, R.D., le Grange, D., Crow, S. et al. (2005). Impulsivity and compulsivity in bulimia nervosa. *Int J Eat Disord,* Vol. 38, No. 3, (Nov 2005), pp. 244-51, doi: 10.1002/eat.20169

Fahy, T. & Eisler, I. (1993). Impulsivity and eating disorders. *Br J Psychiatry,* Vol. 162, (Febr 1993), pp. 193-7, PMID 8435689

Fairburn, C.G., Shafran, R. & Cooper, Z. (1999). A cognitive behavioural theory of anorexia nervosa. *Behav Res Ther,* Vol. 37, No. 1, (Jan 1999), pp. 1-13, PMID 9922553

Fallon, B.A., Walsh, B.T., Sadik, C., Saoud, J.B. & Lukasik, V. (1991). Outcome and clinical course in inpatient bulimic women: a 2-year to 9-year follow-up study. *J Clin Psychiatry,* Vol. 52, No. 6, (Jun 1991), pp. 272-78, PMID 2055901

Favaro, A. & Santonastaso, P. (1996). Purging behaviors, suicide attempts, and psychiatric symptoms in 398 eating disordered subjects. *Int J Eat Disord,* Vol. 20, No.1, (Jul 1996), pp. 99-103, PMID 8807357

Favaro, A. & Santonastaso, P. (1997). Suicidality in eating disorders: Clinical and psychological correlates. *Acta Psychiatr Scand*, Vol. 95, No. 6, (Jun 1997), pp. 508-14, PMID 9242846

Favaro, A. & Santonastaso, P. (1998). Impulsive and compulsive self-injurious behavior in bulimia nervosa: prevalence and psychological correlates. *J Nerv Ment Dis*, Vol. 186, No. 3, (Mar 1998), pp. 157-65, PMID 9521351

Favaro, A. & Santonastaso, P. (1999). Different types of self-injurious behavior in bulimia nervosa. *Compr Psychiatry*, Vol. 40, No. 1, (Jan-Feb 1999), pp. 57-60, PMID 9924879

Favaro, A. & Santonastaso, P. (2000). Self-injurious behaviour in anorexia nervosa. *J Nerv Ment Dis*, Vol. 188, No. 8, (Aug 2000), pp. 537-42, PMID 10972574

Favaro, A. & Santonastaso, P. (2002). The spectrum of self-injurious behavior in eating disorders. *Eat Disord*, Vol. 10, No. 3, (Fall 2002), pp. 215-25, PMID 16864265

Favaro, A., Ferrara, S. & Santonastaso, P. (2007). Self-injurious behavior in a community sample of young women: relationship with childhood abuse and other types of self-damaging behaviors. *J Clin Psychiatry*, Vol. 68, No. 1, (Jan 2007), pp. 122-31, PMID 17284140

Favaro, A., Santonastaso, P., Monteleone, P., Bellodi, L., Mauri, M., Rotondo, A., Erzegovesi, S. & Maj, M. (2008). Self-injurious behavior and attempted suicide in purging bulimia nervosa: associations with psychiatric comorbidity. *J Affect Disord*, Vol. 105, No. 1-3, (Jan 2008), pp. 285-9, PMID 17568684

Favaro, A., Zanetti, T., Tenconi, E., Degortes, D., Ronzan, A., Veronese, A. & Santonastaso, P. (2005). The relationship between temperament and impulsive behaviors in eating disordered subjects. *Eat Disord*, Vol. 13, No. 1, (Jan-Feb 2005), pp. 61-70, PMID 16864331

Favazza, A.R. (1998). The coming of age of self-mutilation. *J Nerv Ment Dis*, Vol. 186, No. 5, (May 1998), pp. 259-68, PMID: 9612442

Favazza, A.R. & Conterio, K. (1989). Female habitual self-mutilators. *Acta Psychiatr Scand*, Vol. 79, No. 3, (Mar 1989), pp. 283-89, PMID 2711856

Favazza, A.R., DeRosear, L. & Conterio, K. (1989). Self-mutilation and eating disorders. *Suicide Life Threat Behav*, Vol. 19, No. 4,(Winter 1989), pp. 352-61, PMID 2609364

Favazza, A.R. & Rosenthal, R.J.(1993). Diagnostic issues in self-mutilation. *Hosp Community Psychiatry*, Vol. 44, No. 2, pp.134-140

Favazza, A.R. & Simeon, D. (1995). Self-mutilation. In *Impulsivity and aggression,* E. Hollander & D. Stein (Eds.), pp. 185-200, John Wiley & Sons, ISBN 0471953288, 9780471953289, Sussex, England

Fessler, D.M. (2002). Pseudoparadoxical impulsivity in restrictive anorexia nervosa: A consequence of the logic of scarcity. *Int J Eat Disord*, Vol. 31, No. 4, (May 2002), pp. 376-88, PMID 11948643

Fichter, M., Quadflieg, N. & Rief, W. (1994). Course of multi-impulsive bulimia. *Psychol Med*, Vol. 24, No.3, pp. 591-604, PMID 7991741

Fleischhaker, C., Munz, M., Böhme, R., Sixt, B. & Schulz, E. (2006). Dialectical behaviour therapy for adolescents (DBT-A) - a pilot study on the therapy of suicidal, parasuicidal, and self-injurious behavior in female patients with a borderline disorder. *Z Kinder Jugendpsychiatr Psychother*, Vol. 34, No.1, (Jan 2006), pp. 15-25, PMID 16485610

Forcano, L., Fernández-Aranda, F., Alvarez-Moya, E., Bulik, C., Granero, R., Gratacòs, M., Jiménez-Murcia, S., Krug, I., Mercader, J.M., Riesco, N., Saus ,E., Santamaría, J.J. & Estivill, X. (2009). Suicide attempts in bulimia nervosa: personality and psychopathological correlates. *Eur Psychiatry*, Vol. 24, No. 2, (Mar 2009), pp. 91-7, PMID 19101125

Forcano, L., Álvarez, E., Santamaría, J.J., Jiménez-Murcia, S., Granero, R., Penelo, E., Alonso, P., Sánchez, I., Menchón, J.M., Ulman, F., Bulik, C. & Fernández-Aranda, F. (2011). Suicide attempts in anorexia nervosa subtypes. *Compr Psychiatry*, Vol. 52, No. 4, (Jul-Aug 2011), pp. 352-58, PMID 21683172

Foulon, C., Guelfi, J.D., Kimpan, A., Ades, J., Romo, L., Houdeyer, K. et al. (2007). Switching to the bingeing/purging subtype of anorexia nervosa is frequently associated with suicidal attempts. *Eur Psychiatry*, Vol. 22, No. 8, (Nov 2008), pp. 513-19, PMID 17482799

Franko, D.L., Dorer, D.J., Keel, P.K., Jackson, S., Manzo, M.P. & Herzog, D.B. (2005). How do eating disorders and alcohol use disorders influence each other? *Int J Eat Disord*, Vol. 38, No. 3, (Nov 2005), pp. 200-7, PMID 16216020

Franko, D.L., Keel, P.K., Dorer, D.J., Blais, M.A., Delinsky, S.S., Eddy, K.T. et al. (2004). What predicts suicide attempts in women with eating disorders? *Psychol Med*, Vol. 34, No. 5, (Jul 2004), pp. 843-53, PMID 15500305

Franko, D.L. & Keel, P.K. (2006). Suicidality in eating disorders: occurrence, correlates, and clinical implications. *Clin Psychol Rev*, Vol. 26, No. 6, (Oct 2006), pp. 769-82, PMID 16875766

Fujimori, A., Wada, Y., Yamashita, T., Choi, H., Nishizawa, S., Yamamoto, H. & Fukui, K. (2011). Parental bonding in patients with eating disorders and self-injurious behavior. *Psychiatry Clin Neurosci*, Vol. 65, No. 3, (Apr 2011), pp. 272-9, doi: 10.1111/j.1440-1819.2011.02192.x.

Garfinkel, P.E., Modofsky, H. & Garner, D.M. (1980). The heterogeneity of anorexia nervosa. *Arch Gen Psychiatry*, Vol. 37, No. 9, (Sep 1980), pp. 1036-40, PMID 6932188

Garner, D.M., Garfinkel, P.E. & O'Shaughnessy, M. (1985). The validity of the distinction between bulimia with and without anorexia nervosa. *Am J Psychiatry*, Vol. 142, No. 5, (May 1985), pp. 581-87, PMID 3857011

Godart, N.T., Flament, M.F., Lecrubier, Y. & Jeammet, P. (2000). Anxiety disorders in anorexia nervosa and bulimia nervosa: Co-morbidity and chronology of appearance. *Eur Psychiatry*, Vol. 15, No. 1, (Feb 2000), pp. 38-45, PMID 10713801

Greydanus, D.E. & Shek, D. (2009). Deliberate self-harm and suicide in adolescents. *Keio J Med*, Vol. 58, No. 3, (Sep 2009), pp. 144-51, PMID 19826208

Grilo, C.M., Sanislow, C.A., Shea, M.T. et al. (2003). The natural course of bulimia nervosa and eating disorder not otherwise specified is not influenced by personality disorders. *Int J Eat Disord*, Vol. 34, No. 3, (Nov 2003), pp. 319-30, PMID 12949923

Grucza, R.A., Przybeck, T.R. & Cloninger, C.R. (2005). Personality as a mediator of demographic risk factors for suicide attempts in a community sample. *Compr Psychiatry*, Vol. 46, No. 3, (May-Jun 2005), pp. 214-22, PMID 16021592

Grucza, R.A., Przybeck, T.R. & Cloninger, C.R. (2007). Prevalence and correlates of binge eating disorder in a community sample. *Compr Psychiatry*, Vol. 48, No. 2, (Mar-Apr 2007), pp. 124-31, PMID 17292702

Gunderson, J.G. & Zanarini, M.C. (1987). Current overview of the borderline diagnosis. *J Clin Psychiatry,* Vol. 48, No. 5-14, (Aug 1987), pp. 5-14, PMID 3301824

Halmi, K.A. (2003). Classification, diagnosis and comorbidities of eating disorders: A review. In *Eating disorders.* M. Maj, K. Halmi, J.J.Lopez-Ibor, & N.Sartorius (Eds.), Vol. 1-33, ISBN 0-470-84865-0, Wiley, Hoboken, NJ

Harris, E.C. & Barraclough, B. (1994). Suicide as an outcome for mental disorders. A meta-analysis. *Br J Psychiatry,* Vol. 170, pp. 205-28, (Mar 1997), PMID 9229027

Hawton, K. (2005). *What happens to deliberate self-harm patients in the long term?* Available from http://www.psychiatry.ox.ac.uk/csr/reslongterm.html

Hawton, K., Fagg, J., Platt, S. & Hawkins, M. (1993). Factors associated with suicide after parasuicide in young people. *BMJ,* Vol. 306, No. 6893, (Jun 1993), p. 1641, PMID 8324431

Hawton, K., Houston, K. & Shepperd, R. (1999). Suicide in young people. Study of 174 cases, aged under 25, based on coroners´ and medical records. *Br J Psychiatry,* Vol. 175, (Sep 1999), pp. 271-76, PMID 10645330

Hayes, S.C., Wilson, K. & Strosahl, K. (1999). *Acceptance and commitment therapy: An experiential approach to behaviour change.* Guilford, ISBN-10 1572304812, New York

Herpertz, S. (1995). Self- injurious behavior: Psychopathological and nosological characteristics in subtypes of self-injurers. *Acta Psychiatr Scand,* Vol. 91, No. 1, (Jan 1995), pp. 57-68, PMID 7754789

Herzog, D.B., Greenwood, D.N., Dorer, D.J., Flores, A.T., Ekeblad, E.R., Richards, A. et al. (2000). Mortality in eating disorders: a descriptive study. *Int J Eat Disord,* Vol. 28, No. 1, (Jul 2000), pp. 20-6, PMID 10800010

Herzog, D.B., Keller, M.B., Lavori, P.W. & Sacks, N.R. (1991). The course and outcome of bulimia nervosa. *J Clin Psychiatry,* Vol. 52, No. 10, (Oct 1991), pp. 4-8, PMID 1938989

Holderness, C.C., Brooks-Gunn, J. & Warren, M.P. (1994). Co-morbidity of eating disorders and substance abuse review of the literature. *Int J Eat Disord,* Vol. 16, No. 1, (Jul 1994), pp. 1-34, PMID 7920577

Hollander, E. & Wong, C.M. (1995). Obsessive-compulsive spectrum disorders. *J Clin Psychiatry,* Vol. 56, No. 4, pp. 3-6, PMID 7713863

Huas, C., Caille, A., Godart, N., Foulon, C., Pham-Scottez, A., Divac, S., Dechartres, A., Lavoisy, G., Guelfi, J.D., Rouillon, F. & Falissard, B. (2011). Factors predictive of ten-year mortality in severe anorexia nervosa patients. *Acta Psychiatr Scand,* Vol. 123, No.1, (Jan 2011), pp. 62-70, PMID 20958272

Johnson, C., Tobin, D. & Enright, A. (1989). Prevalence and clinical characteristics of borderline patients in an eating-disordered population. *J Clin Psychiatry,* Vol. 50, No. 1, (Jan 1989), pp. 9-15, PMID 2783416

Johnson, C., Tobin, D.L. & Dennis, A. (1990). Differences in treatment outcome between borderline and nonborderline bulimics at one-year follow-up. *Int J Eat Disord,* Vol. 9, No. 6, (Nov 1990), pp. 617-27, doi: 10.1002/1098-108X(199011)9:6<617::AID-EAT2260090604>3.0CO;2-V

Keel, P.K. & Mitchell, J.E. (1997). Outcome in bulimia nervosa. *Am J Psychiatry,* Vol. 154, No. 3, (Mar 1997), pp. 313-21, PMID 9054777

Kingston, J., Clarke, S. & Remington, B. (2010). Experiential avoidance and problem behavior: a mediational analysis. *Behav Modif,* Vol. 34, No. 2, (Mar 2010), pp. 145-63, PMID 20308355

Klump, K.L., Bulik, C.M., Pollice, C. et al. (2000). Temperament and character in women with anorexia nervosa. *J Nerv Ment Dis*, Vol. 188, No. 9, (Sep 2000), pp. 559-67, PMID 11009328

Kröger, C., Schweiger, U., Sipos, V., Kliem, S., Arnold, R., Schunert, T. & Reinecker, H. (2010). Dialectical behaviour therapy and an added cognitive behavioural treatment module for eating disorders in women with borderline personality disorder and anorexia nervosa or bulimia nervosa who failed to respond to previous treatments. An open trial with a 15-month follow-up. *J Behav Ther Exp Psychiatry*, Vol. 41, No. 4, (Dec 2010), pp. 381-88, PMID 20444442

Kyriacou, O., Treasure J. & Schmidt, U. (2008). Expressed emotion in Eating Disorders assessed via self-report: An examination of factors associated with expressed emotion in carers of people with Anorexia Nervosa in comparison to control families. *Int J Eat Disord*, Vol. 41, No. 1, (Jan 2008), pp. 37-46

Lacey, J.H. (1993). Self-damaging and addictive behaviour in bulimia nervosa. *Br J Psychiatry*, Vol. 163, (Aug 1993), pp. 190-94, PMID 8075910

Lacey, J.H. & Evans, C.D. (1986). The impulsivist: A multi-impulsive personality disorder. *Br J Addict*, Vol. 81, No. 5, (Oct 1986), pp. 641-49, PMID 3539167

Lagos, J.M. (1981). Family therapy in the treatment of anorexia nervosa: theory and technique. Int J Psychiatry Med, Vol. 11, No. 3, pp.291-302

Laye-Gindhu, A. & Shonert-Reichl, K. (2005). Nonsuicidal self-harm among community adolescents: understanding the "whats" and "whys" of self-harm. *Journal of Youth and Adolescence*, Vol. 34, No.5, (Oct 2005), pp. 445-57, doi: 10.1007/s10964-005-7262-z

Levitt, J.L., Sansone, R.A. & Cohn, L. (2004). *Self-harm behaviour and eating disorders*, ISBN-10 0415946980, Brunner-Routledge, New York

Linehan, M. (1993). *Cognitive-behavioral treatment of borderline personality disorder*. Guilford, ISBN-10 0898621836, New York

Marino, M.F. & Zanarini, M.C. (2001). Relationship between EDNOS and its subtypes and borderline personality disorder. *Int J Eat Disord*, Vol. 29, No. 3, (Apr 2001), pp. 349-53, PMID 11262516

Maggini, C., Ampolline, P., Marchesi, C., Gariboldi, S. & Cloninger, C.R. (2000). Relationships between tridimensional personality questionnaire dimensions and DSM-III-R personality traits in Italian adolescents. *Compr Psychiatry*, Vol. 41, No. 6, (Nov-Dec 2000), pp. 426-31, PMID 11086147

Matsumoto, T., Yamaguchi, A., Asami, T., Okada, T., Yoshikawa, K. & Hirayasu, Y. (2005). Characteristics of self-cutters among male inmates: association with bulimia and dissociation. *Psychiatry Clin Neurosci*, Vol. 59, No. 3, (Jun 2005), pp. 319-26, PMID 15896226

Matsumoto, T., Imamura, F., Chibi, Y., Katsumata, Y., Kitani, M. & Takeshima, T. (2008). Analgesia during self-cutting: clinical implications and the association with suicidal ideation. *Psychiatry Clin Neurosci*, Vol. 62, No. 3, (Jun 2008), pp. 355-58, PMID 18588599

Milos, G., Spindler, A., Hepp, U. & Schnyder, U. (2004). Suicide attempts and suicidal ideation: links with psychiatric comorbidity in eating disorder subjects. *Gen Hosp Psychiatry*, Vol. 26, No.2, (Mar-Apr 2004), pp. 129-35, PMID 15038930

Miller, A.L., Rathus, J.H., Linehan, M.M., Wetzler, S. & Leigh, E. (1997). Dialectical behaviour therapy adapted for suicidal adolescents. *Journal of Practical Psychiatry and Behavioral Health*, Vol. 3, pp. 78-86

Miotto, P., De Coppi, M., Frezza, M. & Preti, A. (2003). Eating disorders and suicide risk factors in adolescents: an Italian community-based study. *J Nerv Ment Dis*, Vol. 191, No. 7, (Jul 2003), pp. 437-43, PMID 12891090

Muehlenkamp, J.J., Engel, S.G., Wadeson, A., Crosby, R.D., Wonderlich, S.A., Simonich, H. & Mitchell, J.E. (2009). Emotional states preceding and following acts of non-suicidal self-injury in bulimia nervosa patients. *Behav Res Ther*, Vol. 47, No. 1, (Jan 2009), pp. 83-7, PMID 19027892

Muehlenkamp, J.J., Claes, L., Smits, D., Peat, C.M. & Vandereycken, W. (2011). Non-suicidal self-injury in eating disordered patients: a test of a conceptual model. *Psychiatry Res*, Vol. 188, No. 1, (Jun 30 2011), pp. 102-8, PMID 21216476

Nagata, T., Kawarada, Y., Kiriike, N. & Iketani, T. (2000). Multi-impulsivity of Japanese patients with eating disorders: primary and secondary impulsivity. *Psychiatry Res*, Vol. 94, No. 3, pp. 239-50, PMID 10889288

Nagata, T., Oshima, J., Wada, A., Yamada, H. & Kiriike, N. (2003). Repetitive self-mutilation among Japanese eating disorder patients with drug abuse disorder: comparison with patients with metamphetamine use disorder. *J Nerv Ment Dis*, Vol. 191, No. 5, (May 2003), pp. 319-23, PMID 12819551

Neumark-Sztainer, D., Story, M., Dixon, L.B. & Murray, D.M. (1998). Adolescents engaging in unhealthy weight control behaviors: are they at risk for other health compromising behaviors? *Am J Publ Health*, Vol. 88, No. 6, (Jun 1988), pp. 952-5, PMID 9618628

Newton, J.R., Freeman, C.P. & Munro, J. (1993). Impulsivity and dyscontrol in bulimia nervosa: Is impulsivity an independent phenomenon or a marker of severity? *Acta Psychiatr Scand*, Vol. 87, No. 6, (Jun 1993), pp. 389-94, PMID 8356889

Norring, C. (1993). Borderline personality organization and prognosis in eating disorders. *Psychoanalytic Psychology*, Vol. 10, No. 4, (Fal 1993), pp. 551-72, doi: 10.1037/h0079502

Ohmann, S., Schuch, B., Konig, M., Blaas, S., Fliri, C. & Popow, C. (2008). Self-injurious behavior in adolescent girls. Association with psychopathology and neuropsychological functions. *Psychopathology*,Vol. 41, No. 4, (May 2008), pp. 226-35, doi: 10.1159/000125556

Palmer, R., Birchall, H., Damani, S., Gatward, N., McGrain, L. & Parker, L. (2003). A dialectical behavior therapy program for people with an eating disorder and borderline personality disorder: description and outcome. *Int J Eat Disord*, Vol. 33, No. 3, (Apr 2003), pp. 281-86, PMID 12655624

Papezova, H., Yamamotova, A. & Uher, R. (2005). Elevated pain threshold in eating disorders: physiological and psychological factors. *J Psychiatry Res*, Vol. 39, No. 4, (Jul 2005), pp. 431-38, PMID 15804394

Pattison, E.M. & Kahan, J. (1983). The deliberate self-harm syndrome. *Am J Psychiatry*, Vol. 140, No. 7, (Jul 1983), pp. 867-72, PMID 6859301

Paul, T., Schroeter, K., Dahme, B. & Nutzinger, D.O. (2002). Self-injurious behavior in women with eating disorders. *Am J Psychiatry*, Vol. 159, No. 3, (Mar 2002), pp. 408-11, PMID 11870004

Peebles, R., Wilson, J.L. & Lock, J.D. (2011). Self-injury in adolescents with eating disorders: Correlates and Provider bias. *J Adolesc Health*, Vol. 48, No. 3, (Mar 2011), pp. 310-13, PMID 21338905

Preti, A., Rocchi, M.B., Sisti, D., Camboni, M.V. & Miotto, P. (2010). A comprehensive meta-analysis of the risk of suicide in eating disorders. *Acta Psychiatr Scand*, Vol. 124, No. 1, (Jul 2011), pp. 6-17, PMID 21092024

Prinstein, M.J., Nock, M.K., Simon, V., Aikins, J.W., Cheah, C.S.L. & Spirito, A. (2008). Longitudinal trajectories and predictors of adolescent suicidal ideation and attempts following inpatient hospitalization. *J Consult Clin Psychol*, Vol. 76, No. 1, (Feb 2008), pp. 92-103, PMID 18229987

Rathus, J.H. & Miller, A.L. (2002). Dialectical behaviour therapy adapted for suicidal adolescents. *Suicide Life Threat Behav*, Vol. 32, No. 2, (Summer 2002), pp. 146-57, PMID 12079031

Rodriguez-Cano, T., Beato-Fernandez, L., Belmonte & Llario, A. (2006). Body dissatisfaction as a predictor of self-reported suicide attempts in adolescents: a Spanish community prospective study. *J Adolesc Health*, Vol. 38, No. 6, pp. 684-8, PMID 16730596

Rosenvinge, J.H., Martinussen, M. & Ostensen, E. (2000). The comorbidity of eating disorders and personality disorders: A meta-analytic review of studies published between 1983 and 1998. *Eat Weight Disord*, Vol. 5, No. 2, pp. 52-61, PMID 10941603

Ross, S., Heath, N.L. & Toste, J.R. (2009). Non-suicidal self-injury and eating pathology in high school students. *Am J Orthopsychiatry*, Vol. 79, No. 1, (Jan 2009), pp. 83-92, PMID 19290728

Rossiter, E., Agras, W.S., Telch, C.F. & Schneider, J.A. (1993). Cluster B personality disorder characteristics predict outcome in the treatment of bulimia nervosa. *Int J Eat Disord*, Vol. 13, No. 4, (May 1993), pp. 349-57, PMID 8490637

Rowe, S.L., Jordan, J., McIntosh, V.W., Carter, F.A., Bulik, C.M. & Joyce, P.R. (2008). Impact of borderline personality disorder on bulimia nervosa. *Aust N Z J Psychiatry*, Vol. 42, No. 12, (Dec 2008), pp. 1021-9, PMID: 19016090

Rutherford, L. & Couturier, J. (2007). A review of psychotherapeutic interventions for children and adolescents with eating disorders. *J Can Acad Child Adolesc Psychiatry*, Vol. 16, No. 4, (Nov 2007), pp. 153-7, PMID 18392166

Safer, D.L., Telch, C.F. & Agras, W.S. (2001). Dialectical behaviour therapy for bulimia nervosa. *Am J Psychiatry*, Vol. 158, No. 4, (Apr 2001), pp. 632-4, PMID 11282700

Salbach, H., Klinkowsky, N., Pfeiffer, E., Lehmkuhl, U. & Korte, A. (2007). Dialectical behavior therapy for adolescents with anorexia and bulimia nervosa (DBT-AN/BN) - a pilot study. *Prax Kinderpsychol Kinderpsychiatr*, Vol. 56, No. 2, pp. 91-108, PMID 17410928

Sallet, P.C., de Alvarenga, P.G., Ferrão, Y., de Mathis, M.A., Torres, A.R., Marques, A., Hounie, A.G., Fossaluza, V., do Rosario, M.C., Fontenelle, L.F., Petribu, K. & Fleitlich-Bilyk, B. (2010). Eating disorders in patients with obsessive-compulsive disorder: prevalence and clinical correlates. *Int J Eating Disord*, Vol. 43, No. 4, (May 2010), pp. 315-25

Sansone, R.A. & Levitt, J.L. (2005). Borderline personality and eating disorders. *Eat Disord*, Vol. 13, No. 1, (Jan-Feb 2005), pp. 71-83, PMID 16864332

Selby, E.A., Anestis, M.D. & Joiner, T.E. (2008). Understanding the relationship between emotional and behavioral dysregulation: emotional cascades. *Behav Res Ther*, Vol. 46, No. 5, (May 2008), pp. 593-611, PMID 18353278

Selby, E.A., Anestis, M.D., Bender, T.W. & Joiner, T.E. (2009). An exploration of the emotional cascade model in borderline personality disorder. *J Abnorm Psychol*, Vol. 118, No. 2, (May 2009), pp. 375-87, PMID 19413411

Selby, E.A. & Joiner, T.E. (2009). Cascades of emotion: The emergence of borderline personality disorder from emotional and behavioural dysregulation. *Rev Gen Psychol*, Vol. 13, No. 3, (Sep 1 2009), p. 219, PMID 20161656

Selby, E.A., Smith, A.R., Bulik, C.M., Olmsted, M.P., Thornton, L., McFarlane, T.L., Berrettini, W.H., Brandt, H.A., Crawford, S., Fichter, M.M., Halmi, K.A., Jacoby, G.E., Johnson, C.L., Jones, I., Kaplan, A.S., Mitchell, J.E., Nutzinger, D.O., Strober, M., Treasure, J., Woodside, D.B., Kaye, W.H. & Joiner, T.E. Jr. (2010a). Habitual starvation and provocative behaviors: two potential routes to extreme suicidal behavior in anorexia nervosa. *Behav Res Ther*, Vol. 48, No. 7, (Jul 2010), pp. 634-45, PMID 20398895

Selby, E.A., Ward, A.C. & Joiner, T.E. Jr. (2010b). Dysregulated eating behaviors in borderline personality disorder: are rejection sensitivity and emotion dysregulation linking mechanisms? *Int J Eat Disord*, Vol. 43, No.7, (Nov 1 2010), pp. 667-70, PMID 19806606

Simeon, D., Stein, D.J. & Hollander, E. (1995). Depersonalization disorder and self-injurious behavior. *J Clin Psychiatry*, Vol. 56, No. 4, pp. 36-40, PMID 7713864

Sipos, V., Bohus, M. & Schweiger, U. (2011). Dialectic Behavioral Therapy for Eating Disorders. *Psychother Psychosom Med Psychol*, Vol. 61, No. 2, (Feb 2011), pp. 87-91, PMID 21337287

Skårderud, F. & Sommerfeldt, B. (2009). Self-harm and eating disorders. *Tidsskr Nor Laegeforen*, Vol.129, No.9, (Apr 2009), pp. 877-81, PMID 19415089

Skegg, K. (2005). Self-harm. *Lancet*, Vol. 366, No. 9495, (Oct 22-28 2005), pp. 1471-83, PMID 16243093

Slade, P.D. (1982). Towards a functional analysis of anorexia nervosa and bulimia nervosa. *Br J Clin Psychol*, Vol. 21, No. 3, (Sep 1982), pp. 167-79, PMID 6957251

Smyth, J.M., Wonderlich, S.A., Heron, K.E., Sliwinski, M.J., Crosby, R.D., Mitchell, J.E. & Engel, S.G. (2007). Daily and momentary mood and stress are associated with binge eating and vomiting in bulimia nervosa patients in the natural environment. *J Consult Clin Psychol*, Vol. 75, No. 4, (Aug 2007), pp. 629-38, PMID 17663616

Solano, R., Fernández- Aranda, F., Aitken, A., Lopez, C. & Vallejo, J. (2005). Self-injurious behavior in people with eating disorders. *European Eating Disorders Review*, Vol. 13, No. 1, (Jan/Feb 2005), pp. 3-10, doi: 10.1002/erv.618

Steiger, H. & Stotland, S. (1996). Prospective study of outcome in bulimics as a function of Axis-II comorbidity: long-term responses on eating and psychiatric symptoms. *Int J Eat Dis*, Vol. 20, No. 2, (Sep 1996), pp. 149-61, PMID 8863067

Steiger, H., Thibaudeau, J., Leung, F., Houle, L. & Ghadirian, A.M. (1994). Eating and psychiatric symptoms as a function of axis II comorbidity in bulimic patients. *Psychosomatics*, Vol. 35, No. 1, (Jan-Feb 1994), pp. 41-9, PMID 8134528

Stein, D., Lilenfeld, L.R., Wildman, P.R. & Marcus, M.D. (2004). Attempted suicide and self-injury in patients diagnosed with eating disorders. *Compr Psychiatry*, Vol. 45, No. 6, (Nov-Dec 2004), pp. 447-51, PMID 15526255

Sullivan, P.F., Bulik, C.M. & Kendler, K.S. (1998). Genetic epidemiology of binging and vomiting. *Br J Psychiatry*, Vol. 173, (Jul 1998), pp. 75-9, PMID 9850207

Svirko, E. & Hawton, K. (2007). Self-injurious behaviour and eating disorders: the extent and nature of the association. *Suicide Life Threat Behav*, Vol. 37, No. 4, (Aug 2007), pp. 409-21, NSSI 17896881

Telch, C.F., Agras, W.S. & Linehan, M.M. (2001). Dialectical Behavior Therapy for Binge Eating Disorder. *J Consult Clin Psychol*, Vol. 69, No. 6, (Dec 2001), pp. 1061-5, PMID 11777110

Tobin, D.L. & Griffing, A.S. (1996). Coping, sexual abuse, and compensatory behavior. *Int J Eat Disord*, Vol. 20, No. 2, pp. 143-8, PMID8863066

Tozzi, F., Thornton, L.M., Mitchell, J., Fichter, M.M., Klump, K.L., Lilenfeld, L.R., et al., Collabarative Group. (2006). Features associated with laxative abuse in individuals with eating disorders. *Psychosom Med*, Vol. 68, No. 3, (May-Jun 2006), pp. 470-7, PMID 16738081

van der Kolk, B.A., Perry, J.C. & Herman, J.L. (1991). Childhood origins of self-destructive behavior. *Am J Psychiatry*, Vol. 148, No. 12, pp. 1665-71, PMID 1957928

Vanderlinden, J. & Vandereycken, W. (1997). *Trauma, dissociation, and impulse dyscontrol in eating disorders* (1 edition), Brunner / Mazel, Routledge, ISBN-10 0876308434, New York

Wagner, A., Barbarich-Marsteller, N., Frank, G.K., Bailer, U.F., Wonderlich, S.A. & Crosby, R.D. (2006). Personality traits after recovery from eating disorders: do subtypes differ? *Int J Eat Disord*, Vol. 39, No. 4, pp. 276-84, PMID 16528697

Waters, A., Hill, A. & Waller, G. (2001). Bulimics´ responses to food cravings: Is binge eating a product of hunger or emotional state? *Behav Res Ther*, Vol. 39, No. 8, (Aug 2001), pp. 877-86, PMID 11480829

Welch, S.L. & Fairburn, C.G. (1996). Impulsivity or comorbidity in bulimia nervosa: a controlled study of deliberate self-harm and alcohol and drug misuse in a community sample. *Br J Psychiatry*, Vol. 169, No. 4, (Oct 1996), pp. 451-8, PMID 8894196

Westen, D. & Harnden-Fischer, J. (2001). Personality profiles in eating disorders: rethinking the distinction between axis I and axis II. *Am J Psychiatry*, Vol. 158, No. 4, (Apr 2001), pp. 547-62, PMID 11282688

Whitlock, J., Eckenrode, J. & Silverman, D. (2006). Self-injurious behaviors in a college population. *Pediatrics*, Vol. 117, No. 6, (Jun 2006), pp. 1939-48, PMID 16740834

Whiteside, U., Chen, E., Neighbors, C., Hunter, D., Lo, T. & Larimer, M. (2007). Difficulties regulating emotions: Do binge eaters have fewer strategies to modulate and tolerate negative affect? *Eat Behav*, Vol. 8, No. 2, (Apr 2007), pp. 162-9, PMID 17336786

Wildman, P., Lilenfeld, L.R.R., Marcus, M.D. (2004). Axis I comorbidity onset and parasuicide in women with eating disorders. *Int J Eat Disord*, Vol. 35, No. 2, (Mar 2004), pp. 190-7, PMID 14994356

Wilfley, D., Friedman, M.A., Dounchis, J.Z., Stein, R.I., Welch, R.R. & Ball, S.A. (2000). Comorbid psychopathology in binge eating disorder: relation to eating disorder severity at baseline and following treatment. *J Consult Clin Psychol*, Vol. 68, No. 4, (Aug 2000), pp. 641-9, PMID 10965639

Wonderlich, S.A. & Swift, W.J. (1990). Perceptions of parental relationships in the eating disorders: the relevance of depressed mood. *J Abnorm Psychol*, Vol. 99, No. 4, (Nov 1990), pp. 353-60, PMID 2266209

Wonderlich, S.A. & Mitchell, J.E. (1997). Eating disorders and comorbidity: empirical, conceptual, and clinical implications. *Psychopharmacol Bulletin*, Vol. 33, No. 3, pp. 381-90, PMID 9550882

Yamaguchi, N., Kobayashi, J., Tachikawa, H., Sato, S., Hori, M., Suzuki, T. & Shiraishi, H. (2000). Parental representation in eating disorder patients with suicide. *J Psychosom Res*, Vol. 49, No. 2, (Aug 2000), pp. 131-6, NSSI 11068057

Young, J.E., Klosko, J.S. & Weishaar, M.E. (2003). *Schema Therapy. A Practitioner's Guide*. New York: Guilford Press. ISBN 978-1-57230-838-1

Youssef, G., Plancherel, B., Laget, J., Corcos, M., Flament, M.F. & Halfon, O. (2004). Personality trait risk factors for attempted suicide among young women with eating disorders. *Eur Psychiatry*, Vol. 19, No. 3, (May 2004), pp. 131-9, PMID 15158919

Zaitsoff, S.L. & Grilo, C.M. (2010). Eating disorder psychopathology as a marker of psychosocial distress and suicide risk in female and male adolescent psychiatric inpatients. *Compr Psychiatry*, Vol. 51, No. 2, (Mar-Apr 2010, pp. 142-50, PMID 20152294

Zanarini, M.C., Frankenburg, F.R., Hennen, J., Reich, D. & Silk, K.R. (2004). Axis I comorbidity in patients with borderline personality disorder: 6-year follow-up and prediction of time to remission. *Am J Psychiatry*, Vol. 161, No. 11, (Nov 2004), pp. 2108-14, PMID 15514413

Zanarini, M.C., Frankenburg, F.R. & Ridolfi, M.E. (2006). Reported childhood onset of self-mutilation among borderline patients. *J Pers Disord*, Vol. 20, No. 1, (Feb 2006), pp. 9-15, PMID 16563075

Zimmerman, M. & Matia, J.I. (1999). Axis I diagnostic comorbidity and borderline personality disorder. *Compr Psychiatry*, Vol. 40, No. 4, (Jul-Aug 1999), pp. 245-52, PMID 10428182

Zlotnick, C., Sheat, T., Pearlstein, T., Simpson, E., Costello, E. & Begin, A. (1996). The relationship between dissociative symptoms, alexithymia, impulsivity, sexual abuse and self-mutilation. *Compr Psychiatry*, Vol. 37, No. 1, (Jan-Feb 1996), pp. 12-6, PMID 8770520

# 8

# Neuropsychology of Bulimia Nervosa: New Findings

Esteban Jaime Camacho Ruiz[1], María del Consuelo Escoto Ponce de León[2], Juan Manuel Mancilla Díaz[3], Karina Franco Paredes[4] and Felipe de Jesús Díaz Resendiz[4]

[1]*Unidad Académica Profesional Nezahualcóyotl,*
[2]*Centro Universitario UAEM Ecatepec,*
[1,2]*Universidad Autónoma del Estado de México,*
[3]*Facultad de Estudios Superiores Iztacala,*
*Universidad Nacional Autónoma México,*
[4]*Centro Universitario del Sur,*
*Universidad de Guadalajara,*
*México*

## 1. Introduction

Eating disorders (ED) according to the Diagnostic and Statistical Manual of Mental Disorders, revised text (DSM-IV-RT) produced by the American Psychiatric Association (2000), are classified in anorexia nervosa (AN), bulimia nervosa (BN), and eating disorders not otherwise specified (EDNOS).

The AN is characterized by a refusal to maintain body weight at or above a minimally normal for age and height, intense fear of weight gaining, a change in weight or body shape perception and in post-pubertal women, amenorrhea. On the other hand, the BN is characterized by the presence of recurrent binge eating, use of inappropriate compensatory behaviors repeatedly (in order to prevent weight gain), such as induced vomiting, abuse of laxatives, diuretics, enemas or other drugs, fasting and excessive exercise, and self-worth excessively influenced by weight and body shape besides the presence of depressive symptoms, especially after binge. Sometimes the bulimic behavior is present in patients with AN or people whom carry out restrictive diets, but the BN itself does not produce significant weight loss. What may occur due to induced vomiting, are gastrointestinal problems, severe hypokalemia, hypercholesterolemia (Pauporte & Walsh, 2001), hypernatremia (Crow et al., 2001), hypophosphatemia (Winston & Wells, 2002), impairment in renal fluid and electrolyte balance, with changes that can influence heart function (Andersen, 1985), as well as damage to teeth due to the acidity of vomiting (Daee et al., 2002).

Historically, it has been conceptualized that the BN, like AN, has a socio-cultural origin (Lilenfeld et al., 1998), and twin studies (Wade et al., 1999), reveal an important contribution of genetic factors (between 54 and 83%). The analysis has identified areas on chromosome 10 that may be involved in the onset of BN, in addition, numerous candidate genes for their role in the risk of developing the disorder have been studied (Bulik et al., 2003), on the other hand, biological studies indicate alterations in serotoninergic function in BN patients (Steiger et al., 2005).

BN occurs mainly in adolescents, especially in women, due to different psychological mechanisms, one of them might be the difficult to assume a sexed body (Toro, 1996), although the most possible is the response to social pressure that values thinness as physical attractiveness, which plays an important role in modern societies (Lindberg & Hjern, 2003).

Resarchers suggest that although 1 to 5% of adolescents meet diagnostic criteria for BN, 10 to 50% occasionally use self-induced vomiting or binge eating (Strasburger & Brown, 1998). This disorder occurs primarily in young adults and half of cases develop symptoms before 18 years (Strasburger & Brown, 1998). Similar to AN, BN occurs predominantly in women and less than 1% of men met DSM-IV-RT criteria for this disorder (APA, 2000). The BN is often perceived as an attempt to control, prevent, or minimize the impact of stressful feelings and impulses (Steinberg & Shaw, 1997).

The patients with BN tend to be cognitive and behaviorally impulsive, disorganized, narcissistic and suggestible in nature (Lehoux et al., 2000). In addition, many of them have substance abuse disorders, depression, self-mutilation and impulsive behaviors such as shoplifting or drug abuse (Lledo & Waller, 2000). In view of AN and BN are chronic disorders, with periods of exacerbation and remission of symptoms (Herzog et al., 1999) researchers suggested that the etiological factors involved are present before and during the onset of the disorder, and during remission. It has been proposed that neuropsychological deficits preexist and underlie the etiology of the development of an ED (Silva, 2001), which could explain the high rate of exacerbation and recurrence of symptoms. In fact, treating only the symptoms (e.g. eating habits) and not the underlying problem (e.g. cognitive deficits) is likely to occur relapse (Lena et al., 2004).

Clinical observations have found that patients with ED are unable to focus on cognitive-behavioral skills learned. It has been hypothesized that when there is a specific group of cognitive deficits in a particular severity degree, deficits interfere with the development of self-esteem, assimilation of changes in body image during adolescence, identity formation, interpersonal relationships, and with autonomy, which can reinforce the development of an ED. It is important to note that there is not a single causal factor in the development of AN or BN. In fact, ED are caused by the interaction of multiple factors, however, we know that there are cognitive deficits in patients with ED. When these factors are present in a specific combination and degree of impairment, a cascade of reactions can be driven and can be an important variable in the development of the disease. In addition, the presence of cognitive deficits do not automatically promote the development of an ED, while other protective factors (e.g. adaptive coping and social support) are present, preventing or delaying the development of an ED. It is possible to prevent or intervene in the development and maintenance of an ED, by identifying a cognitive deficit in people who are at high risk or have symptoms of this disorder (Lena et al., 2004).

There is evidence of a relationship between ED and morphological (changes in volume of white matter and gray matter in the brain) and brain function alterations and it has been observed that structural abnormalities are usually reversible with weight gain (Frank et al.,

2004). However, functional abnormalities may be secondary to weight loss and could also reflect underlying primary deficits (Chowdhury & Lask, 2000).

The onset of an ED pathology is characterized by repetitive thoughts associated with body shape and aesthetic evaluation that may result from the influence of the media, wich show thin women who turn out to be more attractive the commercial products and their in turn induce some women to want to be thin, causing changes in their cognitions (Peterson et al., 1999). Within the cognitive impairment in women with ED are distorted beliefs about food, shape and body weight, negative automatic thoughts, dichotomous thinking, representations overarranged about food, weight, and shape, the selective abstraction, overgeneralization, magnification, self-referential ideas and superstitious thinking (García-Camba, 2002). Additionally, it was observed that patients with AN have lower levels of emotional awareness, compared with patients with BN (Bydlowski et al., 2005), although patients with BN have higher impulsivity (Favaro et al., 2005).

Importantly, the characterization of cognitive processes in patients with ED and the interpretation of their behavior in terms of their cognitive structure is a central area for the development of new research. On the other hand, the research related to the neuropsychological assessment of patients with ED has found mixed results, being more abundant those studying attention, moreover, in most cases, no other tests have been used to evaluate cognitive functions additional to attention, and most studies that have measured attention with the Stroop test, have focused on measuring the latency and not the interference.

Due to the increasing number of cases of patients with symptoms of ED it is necessary to characterize the neuropsychological factors such as perseverative thinking, visual memory, selective attention, and executive planning in participants with ED by evaluating both, the time it takes them to answer, and the number of errors committed by people in a paradigm that measures attention as well as the evaluation of the effect of the valence of words related to shape and food.

## 2. Neuropsychology and eating disorders

Neuropsychology is a discipline mainly clinical, which converges between psychology and neurology, and studies the effects of injury, damage or malfunction in the central nervous system structures on the cognitive, psychological, and emotional processes and on the individual behavior (Lezak, 2004). It includes the study of the behavioral expression of lesions in the central nervous system, helping to identify different manifestations of brain dysfunction (Duchesne et al., 2004), and allows us to examine the relationship between behavior and brain function through psychometric tests or qualitative measures in cognitive, sensory-motor, perceptual, and emotional areas.

Neuropsychological investigation of ED began at the end of the decade of the 80 (Ben-Tovim et al., 1989) and has produced mixed results (Mendlewicz et al., 2001; Szmukler et al., 1992) and a significant number of these results support the hypothesis that patients with ED may have underlying cognitive deficits (Braun & Chouinard, 1992). Some studies have methodological limitations, i.e. patient samples have varied in severity of symptoms, different tests were used to measure the same cognitive function; further, studies have weaknesses in the research design itself (not including control group) and include small sample sizes, which leads to low statistical power (Tchanturia et al., 2005).

Some studies indicate that, compared to normal controls, patients with ED have deficits in different neuropsychological domains including verbal and visual memory, visuo spatial ability, attention and executive functions (Bowers, 1994; Camacho et al., 2008; Green et al., 1996; Jones et al., 1991; Kingston et al., 1996; Lauer et al., 1999; Mathias & Kent, 1998; Szmukler et al., 1992). Although these findings consistently indicate that ED are associated with some degree of neuropsychological dysfunction, the specific aspect that is damaged varies between studies, possibly due to variations in methodology. Some studies have found neuropsychological deficits in patients with ED (Palazidou et al., 1990; Touyz et al., 1986). It is possible that other studies with similar findings have not been reported because of the tendency to publish only significant results (Mathias & Kent, 1998).

Among the models that were developed in the area of ED (Vitousek & Orimoto, 1993), one of the most notable advances has been the growth of research that emphasizes cognitive processes and contents. The cognitive model of Vitousek and Orimoto (1993), establishes two cognitive factors that influence the initiation and maintenance of ED: 1) the beliefs of individuals with regard to the shape and the body weight, and 2) the biased processing of information in relation to body shape and weight. On the other hand, cognitive behavioral model of Fairburn et al. (1998) identified 3 factors in the maintenance of AN: 1) dietary restriction increases the sense of self control, 2) starvation promotes dietary restriction, and 3) the extreme concern about shape and weight promote dietary restriction.

Outstandingly, the characterization of cognitive processes in patients with ED and the interpretation of their behavior in terms of their cognitive structure is an important area for the development of new research. Here are some key findings in this area, according to the function evaluated.

### 2.1 Attention and eating disorders

Several studies have found biases in attention in patients with ED. By contrast, other studies have found no attentional biases (see Dobson & Dozois, 2004 and Duchesne et al., 2004 for a review).

Some researchers suggest that negative attitudes and beliefs about food and body shape play a role in ED and suggest the possibility of information processing disturbed in these conditions (Fairburn et al., 1991). In this sense, it is proposed that the attention process in these participants is selective, that is, they attend and respond to those stimuli related to body shape and weight more specifically than people without the disorder, so there is evidence that ED can impair neuropsychological functioning, particularly in the attention processes (Dobson & Dozois, 2004).

It was found that patients with AN have neuropsychological deficits in different domains including verbal and visual memory, visuospatial skills, attention skills and executive functions (Bowers, 1994). On the other hand, a study by Kingston et al. (1996) found that AN patients show deficits on tasks measuring attention, visuospatial skills and memory. In another study, comparing non-restrictive with restrictive eaters, Boon et al. (2000) found that restrictive eaters took less time to recognize stimuli associated with food.

Research on attentional biases in participants with ED, has been made using the Stroop test (Golden, 1994), which has been modified to examine the selective processing of information in various clinical disorders, including ED, in order to evaluate cognitive alterations related to abnormal attitudes about body shape and weight (Ben-Tovim et al., 1989; Channon et al., 1988; Cooper et al., 1992).

It has been observed that patients with AN are slower than control participants in naming the color of words related to food and body (Ben-Tovim et al., 1989). This phenomenon can be described as the interference effect or as the Stroop phenomenon (Stroop, 1935) which is observed particularly in seriously ill patients. Ben-Tovim et al. (1989) found the Stroop effect in patients with AN and BN for words related to food and body shape and weight.

It has been shown that interference for words related to food is more consistent than for words related to the shape and weight (Huon, 1995). By contrast, Sackville et al. (1998) found greater interference for words related to the shape and weight in patients with AN. In this sense, Faunce (2002) hypothesized that patients selectively attend to relevant stimuli for the disorder.

To assess the specificity of the modified Stroop test as an objective measure of the BN, this modified test was administered to patients with BN and two non-clinical control groups (restrictive and not restrictive eaters). Data showed no differences between groups in Stroop effect (Black et al., 1997).

Several studies have shown that patients with ED take longer time to name the color of words related to food, body shape and weight, compared with control participants (Ben-Tovim et al., 1989; Channon et al., 1988; Fairburn et al., 1991; Fassino et al., 2002). Additionally, Cooper and Fairburn (1993) found that in the case of patients with BN, the interference is caused by the frequency of purging and not by the general psychiatric symptoms, however, Black et al. (1997) consider that the differences between bulimic patients and normal controls, do not establish a specific cognitive impairment in these patients.

Jones-Chesters et al. (1998) found that the words associated with food, diet, weight and shape, causing a marked interference and increased latency to name the color of the words in patients with BN compared to control group.

To test that the Stroop effect was restricted to individuals with ED of clinical severity, Cooper et al. (1992) compared four groups: Patients with AN, BN patients, restrictive diet participants and participants with subclinical ED. They found that both groups of patients and the group with subclinical ED, took longer time to name the color of words related to the condition that the restrictive dieters group. Similar results were found by Cooper and Todd (1997), as compared with the control group, both groups, AN and BN, showed a bias in the selective processing of information about food and weight. In another study, comparing groups of AN and BN with groups of restrictive and not restrictive controls, authors found that patients with ED are more selective processing the information related to the figure and the food, and this extends to restrictive control participants (Perpiná et al., 1993).

In a study by Green et al. (1997), they investigated whether concerns about body shape and weight, represented a specific form of anxiety or is regarded as a distinct affective state. Although there was a slowing in naming the color of words related to food, it was not affected by the degree of drive to lose weight. In this sense, there is evidence that the concern about fat, weight and body shape is also present in women without ED. For example, women concerned about weight and are under restrictive diets, show high motivation to lose weight (Garner et al., 1984).

Lovell et al. (1997) conducted a study to investigate whether recovered women with AN or BN have bias towards cognitive aspects of the figure and the food, using a modified Stroop test. They found that BN patients, and AN recovered women were more distracted by concerns about shape, compared with controls and women recovered from BN. No differences were found between groups before and after recovery, i.e. the impairment persisted after clinical recovery.

In a study with a community sample of men and women between 9 and 14 years-old (without ED), it was asked people to name the color of word lists (Stroop-like) related to food, body shape and two sets of neutral words. The results showed a slowing to name the color of words related to food in 11-years-girls but not with words related to the shape. There were no decreases with the 9-years-group (Green & McKenna, 1993). These results can be interpreted in terms of cultural pressures exerted on women to do restrictive diet and achieve an ideal body shape at different stages of development.

In summary, it appears that ED are associated with selective processing of words related to food, weight and shape, observed in some tests designed to assess bias in information processing. Also, with regard to the findings of the Stroop, Huon (1995) argues that it is necessary to establish a theoretical framework for understanding the processes underlying such biases. Vitousek and Hollon (1990) consider that the methods used to examine cognitive biases in anxiety and depression should not only be transferred to the study of ED, besides, these studies require a theoretical foundation that needs to be tested empirically, since without clearly established theories that produce specific hypotheses, models of cognitive processing in patients with ED will be useless (Black et al., 1997). In addition, tests of cognitive processing may be useful to test cognitive theories as they provide a more objective method to assess the processes, compared with self tests. Vitousek and Hollon (1990) have proposed an ED-specific theory based on three premises. The first is that people with this disorder develop elaborate schemes on weight-related issues and its implications for themselves. These patterns influence on perceptions, thoughts, affect and behavior. The second assumption of their model is that the operation of the proposed schemes, promotes ED symptoms in a relatively automatic way. Finally, Vitousek and Hollon suggest that in people with ED, such schemes have the function to simplify, organize and stabilize their experience among themselves and the environment.

## 2.2 Executive functionning and eating disorders

Several authors have found deficits in the functions of planning and problem solving in women with ED (i.e. Tchanturia et al., 2004a, 2004b; Tchanturia et al., 2002). On the other hand, some studies (i.e. Gillberg et al., 2007) found no deficits in executive functions in patients with these disorders.

Green et al. (1996) compared patients with AN and control participants, finding that the AN group showed reaction time and motor speed poorer than control participants. Lauer et al. (1999) investigated the neuropsychological demands of patients with AN and BN before, during, and after treatment that lasted 7 months. It was noted that before treatment, both groups showed deficits in attention and problem solving skills, but found no impairment in memory. At the end of treatment, they found that nearly half of patients still had cognitive deficits. In other study, visuospatial deficits in the AN group were found (Mathias & Kent, 1998). In a trial of executive functions such as abstraction and the use of strategies in patients with AN and using the Wisconsin Card Sorting Test, Fassino et al. (2002) found that patients with AN showed problems of abstraction and thinking flexibility, similar to those seen in patients with obsessive compulsive disorder. Altered body image showed a direct correlation with frontal alterations. On the other hand, Tchanturia et al. (2002), in a controlled study with 30 patients with AN, in which half were patients recovered and the rest still had the disorder, found that patients with AN and recovered showed perceptual and cognitive scores in set variation higher than controls. These results were subsequently confirmed in another sample with AN before and after weight gain (Tchanturia et al., 2004b). In a controlled study, inflexibility in problem-solving tasks set variations in AN patients and BN patients was found (Tchanturia et al. 2004a). In another study, 12 patients with AN and 14 with BN had deficits in problem solving (Lauer et al., 1999). In addition, Fowler et al. (2006) found no deficits in executive functions in 25 patients with AN compared with controls.

### 2.3 Memory and eating disorders

Regarding the evaluation of memory in ED, results have been mixed: Some studies have found deficits in memory (Green et al., 1996; Jones et al., 1991; Kingston et al. 1996; Sebastian et al. 1996; Sherman, et al., 2006), while others have found no such bias (Fowler et al., 2006; Lauer et al., 1999; Touyz et al., 1986). Green et al. (1996) found worsening in working memory in 12 patients with AN compared to control group of 17 participants. This deterioration remained even after regaining weight. In another study, with groups of patients with AN, obese eaters, restrictive and not restrictive eaters, it was found that the first three groups recalled more words related to weight and food and fewer words related to the shape, compared with the group of non-restrictive eaters (King et al., 1991). On the other hand, in a study of 18 patients with AN, there was deterioration in verbal memory compared to the 19 participants without disorder (Sherman, et al., 2006), using the Complex Figure Test Rey (1999). Sebastian et al. (1996) conducted a study comparing patients with ED and a symptomatic (concerned with the weight) and asymptomatic control groups. These authors report a bias in memory for words related to fat, compared with two control groups. These results can be interpreted in the sense that schema activation in participants with ED produces a bias, when participants are exposed to fat-related stimuli.

Based on the literature, the work related to the neuropsychological assessment of participants with ED: a) have obtained different results, being more abundant those studying attention, specifically with the Stroop test, in both, its standard and the modified version, using words related to food and the shape and these versions have not been standardized, b) in most cases, no other tests have been used additionally to assess cognitive aspects in addition to those evaluating the Stroop test, and c) most studies that have measured attention with the Stroop test, have focused on measuring the reaction times but not errors. The results of the implementation of the modified Stroop test provide evidence that the task of mentionning the color of the words, is altered by the semantic content of words related to the concerns of people with ED, consequently, exists competition to name the color and the activation of words whose contents are similar to the participants schemes. In this way, few studies have examined attention bias for words other than those of negative valence. There is evidence that patients with ED exhibit biases in attention to stimuli associated with food, body shape and weight and these biases are not consistently on restrictive diet groups. The neuropsychology of BN has been less studied, although research suggests that may be present cognitive disturbances, including deficits in selective attention and executive functions. Additionally, it is estimated that the prevalence of BN in women ranges from 1% to 3%, while that of AN is 0.5% (Hoek & Hoek, 2003), indicating that although the BN has been less studied, is more prevalent among the population so that their study is relevant from the neuropsychological perspective. The investigation of neuropsychological functioning is of great clinical importance, since alterations in selective attention may be a way that keeps the symptoms of ED. Therefore, it is important to note that the characterization of cognitive processes in ED patients and interpreting their behavior in terms of their cognitive structure is an important area for the development of new research. Therefore, this study aimed to conduct an assessment of perseverative thinking, non-verbal memory, selective attention and executive planning in patients with BN by applying Wisconsin Card Sorting Test (Heaton et al. , 1993), the original Stroop test (Golden, 1994) and modified version, the Rey Complex Figure Test (Rey, 1999) and the of Tower of London Test (Culberston & Zillmer, 1999). Particularly, for the process of attention we used a computer paradigm that records with millisecond precision, the participants' answers to each stimulus presented to them. In the foregoing, it was hypothesized that patients with BN, in contrast to community samples without disorder, may have neuropsychological impairment, specifically in the perseverative thinking, non-verbal memory, selective attention and executive planning.

## 3. Method

### 3.1 Hipotesis

Patients with BN will show poorer neuropsychological performance (lower non-verbal memory capacity, increased perseverative thinking, planning executive poorer, higher latency and interference in attention) compared to participants without ED.

### 3.2 Variables

Verbal memory: It was measured by scores on the reproduction of the figure in the memory section of the Rey Complex Figure Test (1999).

Perseverative thinking: It was measured by the number of perseverative responses (total responses in which the participant continues to responding incorrectly to category in turn: color, shape or number), assessed with the Wisconsin Card Sorting Test (Heaton et al., 1993).

Executive Planning: This variable was measured by the total execution time, total number of movements and total number of violations in the Tower of London Test (Culberston & Zillmer, 1999).

Interference in selective attention: It was measured by the number of errors made by the participants naming the color of the stimulus words, positive and negative, associated with food and body shape in the modified Stroop Test (Camacho et al. 2009) and standard Stroop

Test (Golden, 1994) with three colors. Both paradigms were applied in a computerized version based on E-prime software (Schneider et al., 2002).

Latency in selective attention: It was measured by the scores (milliseconds), obtained by the participants naming the color of the stimulus words, positive and negative, associated with food and body shape of the modified Stroop Test (Camacho et al., 2009) and standard Stroop Test (Golden, 1994) with three colors. Both paradigms were applied in a computerized version of the program based on E-prime (Schneider et al., 2002).

Presence / absence of BN: defined as the presence (or absence) of the disorder, according to the diagnostic criteria of DSM-IV-TR (APA, 2000).

### 3.3 Participants

A total of 64 women, intentionally selected, participated in the study (32 with BN and 32 controls without ED). The mean age of the 32 patients was 21.03 ± 3.81 years old, the body mass index (BMI) mean was 23.64 ± 5.39, and 13.28 ± 1.92 years of mean schooling. The mean age of the 32 control participants was 21.00 ± 3.76 years old, BMI of 21.77 ± 3.17, and 13.25 ± 1.52 years of schooling. The group with BN was selected from ED clinics in the metropolitan area of Mexico City. The control group included 32 women with no history of an ED and was extracted from the community population, matching the disorder group based on their demographic variables (age, sex and schooling). For both groups, tests for the selection and characterization of participants and tests to assess cognitive functions were answered.

### 3.4 Measures

#### 3.4.1 Selection and characterization of participants.

- *Eating Attitudes Test* (Garner & Garfinkel, 1979), identifies the presence of symptoms and concerns characteristic of AN. It consists of 40 items and international cut-off point is greater than 29. It has been validated in Mexico with a reliability of .93 and a cut-off greater or equal to 28, where scores over 28 indicate anorectic symptomatology (Alvarez, 2000).

- *Bulimia Test* (Smith & Thelen, 1984), identifies the presence of symptoms and concerns characteristic of BN. It consists of 36 items and international cut-off point is greater or equal to 102. It has been validated in Mexico with a cut-off point greater or equal to 85, where scores over 85 indicate bulimic symptomatology (Alvarez, 2000).

Interview for Diagnostic of Eating Disorders (Kutlesic et al., 1998), designed for the differential diagnosis of ED according to DSM-IV criteria.

#### 3.4.2 Evaluation of cognitive functionning.

- *Memory Complex Geometric Figures Test* (Rey, 1999). Measures the ability to organize planning for problem solving, memory, and visuo-constructive capability. This test was validated in Mexico, obtaining a reliability of .83 and .78 for the copy to memory (Cortés et al., 1996). In this study, the Test was used in order to assess non-verbal memory. The most common quantitative system for this Test, distinguishes 18 elements, each of which can be scored with a maximum of two points, for a total of 36. Factor analysis showed that 18 perceptual units are grouped consistently in four factors explaining 43.6% of the total variance for copying and 38.6% for memory (Cortés et al., 1996).

- *Wisconsin Card Sorting Test* (Heaton et al., 1993). Measures the ability to make abstract concepts (abstract thinking ability), so as to maintain and change the classification criteria with feedback, namely, the ability to vary the cognitive strategies and skills to develop and maintain an appropriate strategy for problem solving. This test has reliability coefficients of .52 for perseverative errors, 71 for number of errors and .72 for perseverative errors. Factor analysis indicates a three-factor solution explaining 70% of the variance (Heaton et al., 1993). It has shown adequate test-retest reliability for the number of categories completed (.88), number of trials (.74), number of errors (79), number of perseverative answers (68), number of perseverative errors (72 ) and learning to learn (.67, Tate et al., 1998).

- *Tower of London-Drexel* (Culberston & Zillmer, 1999). It is a test originally developed to assess the relationship between attention and performance in sequential actions (Raizner, 2002). It was modified by Culberston and Zillmer (1999) to measure planning and problem solving, behavioral inhibition and impulse control, location of attention, cognitive flexibility, abstract /conceptual reasoning, and behaviors based on rules. The test-retest reliability in an interval of 20 days is acceptable for number of movements and violation of time. Correlations were moderate to high. Factor analysis yielded 5 factors with higher loads in the executive measures, suggesting that it is an useful tool for measuring higher-order problem solving and is more sensitive to the measurement of executive planning, compared with other tests that measure frontal lobe functioning.

- *Computerized Stroop Word Color Test* (Golden, 1994), standard and modified version with stimulus words related to food and body shape. This test evaluates the ability of selective attention, requires that the participant suppress automatic responses in favor of a specific response requested by the evaluator. The test-retest reliability is .86 for the first list (read words), .82 for the second (color naming) and .73 for the third list (color-word; Golden, 1994). This research used the standard version in a computer format for the three lists with one hundred stimuli each. Before each list, instructions for the task were presented to the participant, including three trial exercises that were not counted. Additionally, at the end of the three lists of standard Stroop, participants were presented eight lists with one hundred stimuli words each (food or shape-related), or neutral in two blocks of 400 words each one (Camacho et al., 2009).

### 3.5 Procedure

For BN group, the tests were answered in situ at the clinic where patients were under treatment, in an isolated place (office or cubicle) to avoid interference. For the control sample, tests were applied in the doctor's office.

Stroop Versions were answered with a 14-inch-screen laptop, while the remaining tests were answered in its traditional format.

The sample with ED was recluted from specialized clinics in treatment of ED in Mexico City. Women who agreed to participate were asked to sign informed consent (or their parents if they were under-age) and tests for assessment of cognitive functions and tests for the characterization of participants were answered individually and counterbalanced (the order of application was different for each participant). Height and weight were obtained from records of clinics, based on measurements made by the dietitian or doctor of the clinic and were used to calculate BMI. For the control sample, 50-basic school, 50-high school, and 50-college women, answered the Eating Atitudes Test and Bulimia Test, then, those that did not exceed the cut-off points in both tests, were interviewed by an expert by means of the Interview for Diagnosis of Eating Disorders (Kutlesic et al., 1998), to exclude the presence of an ED. As a result, we selected 32 control women. After being characterized and matched with the BN group, the control group, signed informed consent (or their parents if they are under-age) to participate in the investigation and answered individually and counterbalanced, the tests for the assessment of cognitive functions.

## 4. Results

We identified 32 women with BN and 32 with no disorder. Ages, BMI, and years of education are shown in Table 1. 75% of the sample had at least high school level in both groups.

| Variable | Control ($n$ = 32) | | BN ($n$ = 32) | | $t(62)$ | |
|---|---|---|---|---|---|---|
| | $M$ | ($SD$) | $M$ | ($SD$) | | $p$ |
| Age (years) | 21.00 | (3.76) | 21.03 | (3.81) | 0.07 | n/s |
| BMI (weight in kg./height in meters at square) | 21.77 | (3.17) | 23.64 | (5.39) | 0.10 | n/s |
| Education (years) | 13.25 | (1.52) | 13.28 | (1.92) | 0.03 | n/s |

Table 1. Distribution of groups by age, BMI, and years of education.

Since the groups were matched, t test indicated no statistically significant differences between ages, BMI, or the education level of both groups.

| Variable | Control ($n$ = 32) $M$ ($SD$) | BN ($n$ = 32) $M$ ($SD$) | $t(62)$ |
|---|---|---|---|
| Non-verbal memory (number of recalled elements) | 24.41 (4.32) | 21.22 (5.28) | 2.64** |
| Executive planning | | | |
| Total number of movements | 33.81 (14.47) | 42.28 (16.24) | 2.20* |
| Total execution time (in seconds) | 191.56 (57.30) | 234.44 (88.63) | 2.30* |
| Total number of violations | 0.34 (0.94) | 1.19 (1.62) | 2.56** |
| Perseverative thinking (number of perseverative answers ) | 8.78 (5.43) | 12.38 (8.46) | 2.02* |

Table 2. Comparisons between groups on non-verbal memory, executive planning, and perseverative thinking scales. * $p < .05$; ** $p < .01$.

The results of verbal memory, executive planning, and perseverative thinking scales, are shown in Table 2. In memory scale, statistically significant differences between both groups were found. The group with BN scored lower (fewer items recalled) than the control group.

The results on the scale of executive planning indicate that there were differences in the total number of movements in the total execution time and the total number of violations. It is noted that the group with BN, made more movements and took longer to complete the test, also committed more violations compared with the group without the disorder. Regarding the perseverative thinking, the group with BN showed more perseverative responses compared with control.

For the standard version of Stroop Test, the number of errors and response times are shown in Table 3. There were no differences in the number of errors or response times for each of the lists between the two groups ($p > .05$). The intragroup comparisons showed as expected, the Stroop effect for the control group, $t(62) = 7.28$, $p = .0001$, and for the group with BN, $t(62) = 6.92$, $p = .0001$. This indicates that there is no differential effect for patients and nonpatients with the standard test.

| | Control ($n = 32$) | BN ($n = 32$) | |
|---|---|---|---|
| List | *M* (*SD*) | *M* (*SD*) | *t*(62) |
| Interference[1] | | | |
| Black list | 2.16 (2.10) | 2.34 (3.76) | 0.24 |
| XXXX list | 1.50 (1.52) | 2.41 (2.34) | 1.84 |
| Color list | 1.84 (1.74) | 2.34 (2.06) | 1.05 |
| Latency[2] | | | |
| Black list | 1036.89 (245.17) | 1002.02 (210.75) | 0.61 |
| XXXX list | 964.99 (222.73) | 956.95 (198.73) | 0.15 |
| Color list | 1117.98 (279.05) | 1185.56 (310.84) | 0.10 |

Table 3. Means for the groups in the standard version of Stroop Test. [1]Number of errors for each list. [2]Reaction times for each list in milliseconds.

For the modified version of Stroop Test, the number of errors and reaction times are shown in Table 4. Outstandingly, this modified version in all cases (number of errors and response times) no differences were found between the two groups for lists of neutral words. Statistically significant differences were found for the number of errors in the lists of positive and negative words related to shape, where the BN group made more errors than the control group. It was also noted that the group with BN took longer to respond to both, positive and negative words related to body shape.

Additionally, bivariate intragroup comparisons were made with t test for related samples (Table 4) between each list of stimulus words and their respective neutral word list for each group (control and BN). We found that BN group made more errors in the list of positive words related to body shape and showed higher reaction times in both, positive and negative shape-word lists. Finally, no differences were found in comparisons of the lists in the control group ($p > .05$).

| Word list | | Control ($n$ = 32) $M$ ($SD$) | BN ($n$ = 32) $M$ ($SD$) | $t$(62) |
|---|---|---|---|---|
| Interference[1] | | | | |
| Food positive | | 2.03 (2.16) | 2.88 (3.01) | 1.29 |
| Neutral words | | 2.38 (2.21) | 3.03 (3.53) | 0.89 |
| | $t$[3] | *1.11* | *0.35* | |
| Food negative | | 2.00 (1.80) | 2.78 (2.71) | 1.36 |
| Neutral words | | 2.41 (2.05) | 2.78 (3.05) | 0.58 |
| | $t$[3] | *0.87* | *0.00* | |
| Shape positive | | 2.13 (1.81) | 3.59 (2.76) | 2.52** |
| Neutral words | | 2.50 (2.20) | 2.38 (2.46) | 0.21 |
| | $t$[3] | *1.38* | *4.48**** | |
| Shape negative | | 1.97 (2.13) | 3.50 (3.40) | 2.16* |
| Neutral words | | 2.34 (2.32) | 3.00 (2.55) | 1.08 |
| | $t$[3] | *0.91* | *0.85* | |
| Latency[2] | | | | |
| Food positive | | 1032.17 (194.58) | 1026.51 (224.14) | 0.11 |
| Neutral words | | 1008.63 (182.84) | 998.99 (220.29) | 0.19 |
| | $t$[3] | *1.66* | *1.38* | |
| Food negative | | 1035.83 (199.43) | 1055.41 (230.44) | 0.36 |
| Neutras | | 1017.09 (205.00) | 1029.26 (229.11) | 0.22 |
| | $t$[3] | *1.95* | *1.53* | |
| Shape positive | | 1023.86 (202.12) | 1136.34 (218.86) | 2.14* |
| Neutral words | | 1026.13 (185.33) | 1034.15 (204.09) | 0.17 |
| | $t$[3] | *0.11* | *8.65**** | |
| Shape negative | | 1009.77 (193.04) | 1115.59 (229.50) | 2.00* |
| Neutral words | | 998.02 (172.26) | 997.29 (194.78) | 0.02 |
| | $t$[3] | *0.79* | *5.01**** | |

Table 4. Means for the groups in the modified version of Stroop Test. [1]Number of errors for each list. [2]Reaction times for each list in milliseconds. [3] $t$ test for related samples. * $p < .05$; ** $p < .01$, *** $p < .001$.

## 5. Conclusion

The aim of this study was to evaluate non-verbal memory, perseverative thinking, executive planning, as well as latency and interference in selective attention, in a group of patients with BN. The results indicated deterioration in cognitive functioning in the group with BN.

Regarding the visual delayed memory, patients with BN scored lower (fewer items recalled) than the control group. These results indicate that nonverbal memory problems as measured by the Rey Complex Figure Test (1999), are associated with planning problems which are strategic in nature and in patients with BN, implying a possible weakening processes in strategic memory located in the prefrontal cortex (Sherman et al., 2006). It is likely that the impairment in the memory in patients with BN, can at least partially be attributed to the intense preoccupation with thoughts related to the shape and weight observed in the attention test. An alternative mechanism that could explain the deficits in memory, could be the coexistence of psychological variables not measured in this investigation, such as anxiety and depression. Jones et al. (1991) found that anxiety contributes to a poorer cognitive performance in a sample with AN. However, most studies have not found an association between cognitive performance and depression or anxiety in patients with AN (Green et al., 1996, Kingston et al., 1996, Lauer et al. 1999; Mathias & Kent, 1998), although in this review, we found no studies of BN. In terms of clinical implications, the findings of this study are consistent with the idea that women with BN have difficulty to remember complex and unfamiliar information and the novelity of information can increase the specific cognitive demands. Clinical work with ED patients is based on providing new and complex information in a psychoeducational format, regardless of therapeutic modality. The transmission of such information, should consider the difficulties that women with BN may experience to recall complex information or new. In this sense, the information should be presented so clearly as possible, or more than one time and in different formats (eg verbal, written or video) and should be accompanied by discussion and homework activities between sessions. In the present investigation, results suggest that these difficulties are considered in terms of problems in information processing and not in terms of problems associated with resistance to therapy.

The results on the executive planning scale indicate that there were differences in the total number of movements, in the total execution time, and the total number of violations. It is noted that the group with BN make more movements, it took longer to complete the test, and make more violations in comparison to the group without the disorder. This indicates that the group with BN was deficient in its ability to establish an appropriate strategy to solve problems. These results are consistent with those of Ferraro et al. (1997) who found differences between the group with BN and the control group in executive planning. It is likely that patients who participated in this investigation possess a bad strategy or choose a bad strategy or do not take the time to select a strategy, which could indicate a planning problem. In addition, participants with BN showed cognitive impulsivity. Thus, it can be argued that cognitions and impulsive behaviors in patients with BN, lead to sporadic eating behaviors and out of control. In this sense, it is likely that the impulsive behavior of patients with BN may be a method to achieve independence through self-control; in addition, vomiting and purging behaviors, usually experienced after a binge, could be an effort to reduce anxiety and recover control. Parallel to the mechanisms used by individuals with ED, studies have shown that people with cognitive deficits, have rigid and compensatory strategies, used regardless of the circumstances. It can be postulated that altered dietary patterns are a coping mechanism that can be used by people with neuropsychological deficits as a way to achieve a sense of autonomy and inner control.

Regarding the perseverative thinking, the group with BN showed more perseverative responses compared with control, consistent with those reported by Tchanturia et al. (2005) in the logic that patients with ED have inflexibility on cognitive tasks and inability to change thought patterns. From this perspective, patients with BN have a bias in a skill that is essential for cognitive flexibility and that in these patients, prevents adapting their behavior to changing environmental demands and the use of appropriate strategies for problems solution.

It was observed that patients with BN made more errors on words with positive and negative valence shape-related. These findings are consistent with the results of Cooper and

Fairburn (1993) who found that patients with BN are more concerned with weight and body shape. However, these results contrast with those of Quinton (2004) who found no difference between the BN and control groups. In this sense, it is proposed that patients have knowledge general units or "schemes" that determine which aspects of a situation are more important and what information will be stored and processed. More specifically, cognitive biases are presented for information linked to person concerns (Sebastian et al., 1996). Patients with ED are prone to deny the severity of their disease. This denial can lead to distortion of their answers in the self-report questionnaires, however it is unlikely that the denial of their concerns and symptoms, affect the results produced by the Stroop technique. This is because their performance can only be altered voluntarily, slowing their responses to words related to food and body shape, although the deliberate slowing down would be recorded as an indicator of food-related concern or shape, so is unlikely that a person who seeks to minimize a food problem, adopt the strategy (Ben-Tovim et al., 1989). In this sense, cognitive paradigms offer many advantages for the study of ED, including tests that people are unable to decode, and therefore to alter (Cassin & von Ranson, 2005). Cognitive models of ED have highlighted the role of dysfunctional thinking in relation to body shape and weight in the development and maintenance of the symptoms of these disorders, including the way in the person processes information (Vitousek & Orimoto, 1993). From this perspective, alterations in attention to stimuli related to the shape and weight, found in the present research in participants with BN, represent different forms of bias in information processing, because there is a distortion in the way they perceive and interpret their experiences (Faunce, 2002) because they preferentially attend to body shape related stimuli. Unlike the results reported by Dobson and Dozois (2004) in the logic that patients with BN exhibit biases in attention to words related to food and body shape, in our investigation we found bias for words related the shape only, which also contrasts with the findings of Ben-Tovim et al. (1989) who found no differences between the group with BN and control group with a list of 100 words related to shape, although differences for words related to food were found. Biases for both, words related to shape with positive and negative valence were also found, indicating that patients attend to both, congruent and incongruent words with their own schemes (Vitousek & Orimoto, 1993). In a meta-analysis, Groesz et al. (2002) found that body dissatisfaction among women was higher when they were exposed to images of thin models, compared to exposure to images of women with normal size and / or overweighted. However, this research found in the group with BN, attention bias for both positive and negative words-shape related. This could indicate that there is an activation of thinness schemas in patients with BN and who are highly motivated and cognitively prepared to think about themselves in relation to weight, shape and beauty. It has been suggested that BN is associated with a bias in attention to threats to the ego that are self-directed, so any negative social interactions can cause a perceived threat of isolation and social rejection (Waller et al., 1996). To escape this threat, patients with BN use cognitive strategies that lead to disinhibition of behaviors that would normally inhibited, such as eating. Because body dissatisfaction is a main feature of BN, biases in attention may be due to processes associated with social comparison, based on the shape of others as a way to self-assess their own level of physical attractiveness. Using the model of Williams et al. (1988), which states that attention operates at an automatic level of information processing, one can assume that attention will show a higher tendency towards cognitive biases for relevant schemes. It is likely that people with ED turn their attention to materials related to their own schemes. More specifically, selectively attend to material related to their schemes when different materials are in competition for attention, because this simplifies processing and eliminates the need to address all environmental stimuli.

The standard Stroop Test indicated no differences between groups so that test did not discriminate controls from patients with BN. On the other hand, the lack of overlap between the results of the control group and the group with BN, indicate that the modified Stroop paradigm used in this research, could be a useful tool in neuropsychological characterization of patients with BN as it discriminates between participants with and without BN. It would be important to use this paradigm with other patient groups (e.g. AN) to determine whether the effect is specific for patients with BN. Another comparison group may be women under restrictive diets because they are highly concerned about food, weight and shape, and could show interference in naming color words. It is noteworthy that from the methodological point of view, the choice of words, both, neutral and stimuli, was made based on rigorous methodological criteria, which may contribute to the findings of this research. However, results for the group with BN should be treated with caution due to small sample size, so for further research, we suggested to increase the number of participants with BN.

Research has shown that patients with ED have alexithymic tendencies (Corcos et al., 2000), se we can assume that the neuropsychological deficits found in this research in cognitive areas including executive functions and attention, do not allow patients to develop constructive strategies to solve problems related to social interactions, and may develop maladaptive eating behaviors as a coping mechanism of the conflict in interpersonal development.

Lauer et al. (1999) and Szmukler et al. (1992) explained their findings suggesting that the observed cognitive deficits are a consequence of starvation and can be reversed with proper nutrition. Unfortunately, the hypothesis of malnutrition does not explain the cognitive deficits found in groups with BN. In addition, recent studies indicate that certain cognitive functions do not improve after refeeding or weight gain (Green et al., 1996, Grunwald et al., 2001; Hamsher et al., 1981; Katzman et al., 2001, Kingston et al., 1996; Szmukler et al., 1992), and do not correlate with BMI (Bayless, 2002). Thus, it can be suggested that neuropsychological deficits in various cognitive domains preexist before the development of an ED and are not a consequence of the disorder. It has also been suggested an association between the number of cognitive deficits and a poorer prognosis after treatment (Hamsher et al., 1981; Szmukler et al., 1992).

Some studies show that ED symptoms decrease if the cognitive problem receives treatment (Lena et al., 2004). In these studies, treatment of cognitive deficits, promoted a decrease in symptoms of ED and allowed patients to recover from their abnormal eating patterns. It is likely that cognitive deficits, are the basis for developing an ED, so should be evaluated and incorporated in the treatment of patients with ED, in addition, there is no consensus on whether these abnormalities are related to weight loss, given its focal and asymmetric nature, and the fact that some abnormalities, such as a decrease in gray matter persists despite weight gain. Thus, it is plausible that the observed abnormalities may represent an explanation for the underlying neuropsychological disturbances found in adolescents with ED.

Finally, since the literature reports that ED symptoms in people persist even after recovery from AN or BN (Wagner et al., 2006), it is important to assess cognitive functions before and after treatment, in order to determine whether the biases in these functions remain after recovery. In assessing the effects of cognitive deficits on the development of an ED, it is important for researchers to identify early ED behaviors to minimize the effects of time, and thus, the chronicity of the disorder. Further studies are needed to determine the appropriate follow-up period, which may be specific to an individual, depending on the duration of the disorder and the combination of cognitive deficits.

## 6. Summarising

- This study was conducted to assess perseverative thinking, non-verbal memory, selective attention and executive planning in patients with BN.
- In memory scale, statistically significant differences between both groups were found. The group with BN scored lower (fewer items recalled) than the control group.
- The results on the scale of executive planning indicate that there were differences in the total number of movements in the total execution time and the total number of violations. Participants with BN showed cognitive impulsivity.
- Regarding the perseverative thinking, the group with BN showed more perseverative responses compared with control.
- The BN group made more errors than the control group. It was also noted that the group with BN took longer to respond to both, positive and negative words related to body shape.
- BN group made more errors in the list of positive words related to body shape and showed higher reaction times in both, positive and negative shape-word lists.
- It is likely that the neuropsychological impairment in patients with BN, can at least partially be attributed to the intense preoccupation with thoughts related to the shape and weight observed in the attention test.

## 7. References


Álvarez, G. (2000). *Validación en México de dos instrumentos para detectar trastornos alimentarios: EAT y BULIT*. Tesis de Maestría en Psicología Clínica, Facultad de Psicología, UNAM, México.

American Psychiatric Association. (2000). *Diagnostic and Statistical Manual of Mental Disorders* (4th ed. Text Revised). American Psychiatric Publisher, ISBN-10: 0890420254, Washington, USA.

Andersen, A. E. (1985). *Practical comprehensive treatment of anorexia nervosa and bulimia*. The Johns Hopkins University Press, ISBN-13: 978-0801824425, USA.

Bayless, J. D., Kanz, J. E., Moser, D. J., McDowell, B. D., Bowers, W. A., Andersen, A. E., et al. (2002). Neuropsychological characteristics of patients in a hospital-based eating disorder program. *Annals of Clinical Psychiatry*, Vol.14, No.4 (December 2002), pp. 203–207, ISSN 1573-3238.

Ben-Tovim, D. I., Walker, M. K., Fok, D. & Yap, E. (1989). An adaptation of the Stroop Test for measuring shape and food concerns in eating disorders: A quantitative measure of psychopathology? *International Journal of Eating Disorders*, Vol.8, No.6 (November 1989), pp. 681–687, ISSN 1098-108X.

Black, G. C., Wilson, T., Labouvie, E. & Heffernan, K. (1997). Selective processing of eating disorder relevant stimuli: Does the Stroop Test provide an objective measure of bulimia nervosa? *International Journal of Eating Disorders,* Vol.22, No.3 (November 1997), pp. 329-333, ISSN 1098-108X.

Boon, B., Vogelzang, L. & Jansen, A. (2000). Do restrained eaters show attention toward or away from food, shape and weight stimuli? *European Eating Disorders Review,* Vol.8, No.1 (February 2000), pp. 51-58, ISSN 1099-0868.

Bowers, W. (1994). Neuropsychological impairment among anorexia nervosa and bulimia patients. *Eating Disorders,* Vol.2, No.1 (January 1994), pp. 42-46, ISBN 1532-530X.

Braun, C. M. J. & Chouinard, M. J. (1992). Is anorexia nervosa a neuropsychological disease? *Neuropsychology Review,* Vol.3, No.2 (June 1992), pp. 171-205, ISSN 1573-6660.

Bulik, C. M., Devlin, B., Bacanu, S. A., Thornton, L., Klump, K. L., Fitcher, M. M. et al. (2003). Significant linkage on chromosome 10p in families with bulimia nervosa. *American Journal of Human Genetics,* Vol.72, No.1 (January 2003), pp. 200-207, ISSN 0002-9297.

Bydlowski, S., Corcos, M., Jeammet, P., Paterniti, S., Berthoz, S. & Laurier, C. (2005). Emotion-processing deficits in eating disorders. *International Journal of Eating Disorders,* Vol.37, No.4 (May 2005), pp. 321-329, ISSN 1098-108X.

Camacho, E. J., Escoto, M. C. & Mancilla, J. M. (2008). Neuropsychological evaluation in patients with eating disorders. *Salud Mental,* Vol.31, No.6 (November 2008), pp. 441-446, ISSN 0185-3325.

Camacho-Ruíz, E. J., Mancilla-Díaz, J. M., Escoto-Ponce de León, M. C. & Yáñez-Tellez, M. G. (2009). Design and validation of a computerized stroop-like task to evaluate attentional biases in bulimia nervosa. *Mexican Journal of Behavior Analysis*, Vol.35, No.2 (December 2009), pp. 75-89, ISSN-01 85-4534.

Cassin, S. E. & von Ranson, K. M. (2005). Word lists for testing cognitive biases in eating disorders. *European Eating Disorders Review,* Vol.13, No.3 (June 2005), pp. 216-220, ISSN 1099-0868.

Channon, S., Hemsley, D. & de Silva, P. (1988). Selective processing of food words in anorexia nervosa. *British Journal of Clinical Psychology,* Vol.27, No.3 (September 1988), pp. 259-260, ISSN 0144-6657.

Chowdhury, U. & Lask, B. (2000). Neurological correlates of eating disorders. *European Eating Disorders Review,* Vol.8, No.2 (March 2000), pp. 126-133, ISSN 1099-0868.

Cooper, M. J., Anastasiades, P. & Fairburn, C. G. (1992). Selective processing of eating-, shape-, and weight-related words in persons with bulimia nervosa. *Journal of Abnormal Psychology,* Vol.101, No.3 (August 1992), pp. 352-355, ISSN 0021-843X.

Cooper, M. J. & Fairburn, C. G. (1993). Demographic and clinical correlates of selective information processing in patients with bulimia nervosa. *International Journal of Eating Disorders,* Vol.13, No.1 (January 1993), pp. 109-116, ISSN 1098-108X.

Cooper, M. J. & Todd, G. (1997). Selective processing of three types of stimuli in eating disorders. *British Journal of Clinical Psychology,* Vol.36, No.2 (May 1997), pp. 279-281, ISSN 0144-6657.

Cortés, S. J. F., Galindo, V. M. G. & Salvador, C. J. (1996). La Figura Compleja de Rey: Propiedades psicométricas. *Salud Mental,* Vol.19, No.3 (September 1996), pp. 42-48, ISSN 0185-3325.

Corcos, M., Guilbaud, O., Speranza, M., Paterniti, S., Loas, G., Stephan, P. et al. (2000). Alexithymia and depression in eating disorders. *Psychiatry Research,* Vol.93, No.3 (April 2000), pp.263-266, ISSN 0165-1781.

Crow, S. J., Rosenberg, M. E., Mitchell, J. E. & Thuras, P. (2001). Urine electrolytes as markers of bulimia nervosa. *International Journal of Eating Disorders,* Vol.30, No.3 (November 2001), pp. 279-287, ISSN 1098-108X.

Culberston, W. C. & Zillmer, E. A. (1999). *Tower of London-Drexel (TOL$^{DX}$).* Examiners's manual. Research version. Multi-Health Systems Inc. Canada.

Daee, A., Robinson, P., Lawson, M., Turpin, J. A., Gregory, B. & Tobias, J. D. (2002). Psychologic and physiologic effects of dieting in adolescents. *Southern Medical Journal,* Vol.95, No.9 (September 2002), pp. 1032-1042, ISSN 0038-4348.

Dobson, K. S. & Dozois, D. J. (2004). Attentional biases in eating disorders: A meta-analytic review of Stroop performance. *Clinical Psychology Review,* Vol.23, No.8 (January 2004), pp. 1001-1022, ISSN 0272-7358.

Duchesne, M., Mattos, P., Fontenelle, L. F., Veiga, H., Rizo, L. & Appolinario, J. C. (2004). Neuropsychology of eating disorders: A systematic review of the literature. *Revista Brasileira de Psiquiatria,* Vol.26, No.2 (April 2004), pp. 107-117, ISSN 1516-4446.

Fairburn, C. G., Cooper, P. J., Cooper, M. J., McKenna, F. P. & Anastasiades, P. (1991). Selective information processing in bulimia nervosa. *International Journal of Eating Disorders,* Vol.10, No.4 (July 1991), pp. 415-422, ISSN 1098-108X.

Fairburn, C. G., Shafran, R. & Cooper, Z. (1998). A cognitive behavioural theory of anorexia nervosa. *Behaviour Research and Therapy,* Vol.37, No.1 (January 1998), pp. 1-13, ISBN 0005-7967.

Fassino, S., Piero, Â, A., Abbate, D. G., Leombruni, P., Mortara, P. & Giacomo, R. G. (2002). Attentional biases and frontal functioning in anorexia nervosa. *International Journal of Eating Disorders,* Vol.31, No.3 (April 2002), pp. 274-283, ISSN 1098-108X.

Faunce, G. J. (2002). Eating disorders and attentional bias: A review. *Eating Disorders,* Vol.10, No.2 (April 2002), pp. 125-139, ISSN 1532-530X.

Favaro, A., Zanetti, T., Tenconi, E., Degortes, D., Ronzan, A., Veronese, A. et al. (2005). The relationship between temperament and impulsive behaviors in eating disordered subjects. *Eating Disorders,* Vol.13, No.1 (January 2005), pp. 61-70, ISSN 1532-530X.

Ferraro, F. R., Wonderlich, S. & Jocic, Z. (1997). Performance variability as a new theoretical mechanism regarding eating disorders and cognitive processing. *Journal of Clinical Psychology,* Vol.53, No.2 (February 1997), pp. 117-121, ISSN 1097-4679.

Fowler, L., Blackwell, A., Jaffa, A., Palmer, R., Robbins, T. W., Sahakian, B. J. et al. (2006). Profile of neurocognitive impairments associated with female in-patients with anorexia nervosa. *Psychological Medicine,* Vol.36, No.4 (April 2006), pp. 517-527, ISSN 0033-2917.

Frank, G. K., Bailer, U. F., Henry, S., Wagner, A. & Kaye, W. H. (2004). Neuroimaging studies in eating disorders. *Spectrums,* Vol.9, No.8 (August 2004), pp. 539-548, ISSN 1092-8529.

García-Camba, E. (2002). *Avances en trastornos de la conducta alimentaria. Anorexia nerviosa, bulimia nerviosa, obesidad.* Masson, ISBN: 9788445810682, Spain.

Garner, D. M. & Garfinkel, P. E. (1979). The Eating Attitudes Test: An index of the symptoms of anorexia nervosa. *Psychological Medicine,* Vol.9, No.2 (May 1979), pp. 273-279, ISSN 0033-2917.

Garner, D. M., Olmsted, M. P., Polivy, J. & Garfinkel, P. E. (1984). Comparison between weight-preoccupied women and anorexia nervosa. *Psychosomatic Medicine,* Vol.46, No.3 (May 1984), pp. 255–265, ISSN 1534-7796.

Golden, C. J. (1994). *Stroop. Test de Colores y Palabras.* TEA Ediciones, ISBN: 9788471746542, Spain.

Green, M. W., Elliman, N. A., Rogers, P. J. & Welch, D. A. (1997). Impaired color naming of food and body shape words: Weight phobia or distinct affective state? *International Journal of Eating Disorders,* Vol.21, No.1 (January 1997), pp. 77–82, ISSN 1098-108X.

Green, M. W., Elliman, N. A., Wakeling, A. & Rogers, P. (1996). Cognitive functioning, weight change and therapy in anorexia nervosa. *Journal of Psychiatric Research,* Vol.30, No.5 (September 1996), 401–410, ISSN 0022- 3956.

Green, M. W. & McKenna F. P. (1993). Developmental onset of eating related color-naming interference. *International Journal of Eating Disorders,* Vol.13, No.4 (May 1993), pp. 391–397, ISSN 1098-108X.

Groesz, L. M., Levine, M. P. & Murnen, S. K. (2002). The effect of experimental presentation of thin media images on body satisfaction: A meta-analytic review. *International Journal of Eating Disorders,* Vol.31, No.1 (January 2002), pp. 1–15, ISSN 1098-108X.

Grunwald, M., Ettrich, C., Assmann, B., Dahne, A., Krause, W., Busse, F. et al. (2001). Deficits in haptic perception and right parietal theta power changes in patients with anorexia nervosa before and after weight gain. *International Journal of Eating Disorders,* Vol.29, No.4 (May 2001), pp. 417–428, ISSN 1098-108X.

Hamsher, K. de S., Halmi, K. A. & Benton, A. L. (1981). Prediction of outcome in anorexia nervosa from neuropsychological status. *Psychiatry Research,* Vol.4, No.1 (February 1981), pp. 79–88, ISSN 0165-1781.

Heaton, R. K., Chelune, G. J., Talley, J. L., Kay, G. G. & Curtiss, G. (1993). *Wisconsin Card Sorting Test Manual.* Revised and expanded. Psychological Assesment Resources, USA.

Herzog, D. B., Dorer, D. J., Keel, P. K., Selwyn, S. E., Ekeblad, E. R., Flores, A. T. et al. (1999). Recovery and relapse in anorexia nervosa and bulimia nervosa: A 7.5-year follow-up study. *Journal of the American Academy of Child and Adolescent Psychiatry,* Vol.38, No.8 (August 1999), pp. 829–837, ISSN 0890-8567.

Hoek, H. W. & Hoeken, D. V. (2003). Review of the prevalence and incidence of eating disorders. *International Journal of Eating Disorders,* Vol.34, No.4 (December 2003), pp. 383-396, ISSN 1098-108X.

Huon, G. F. (1995). The Stroop color-naming task in eating disorders. A review of the research. *Eating Disorders,* Vol.3, No.2 (April 1995), pp. 124–132, ISSN 1532-530X.

Jones, B. P., Duncan, C.C., Brouwers, P. & Mirsky, A. F. (1991). Cognition in eating disorders. *Journal of Clinical and Experimental Neuropsychology,* Vol.13, No.5 (October 1991), pp. 711–728, ISSN 1380-3395.

Jones-Chesters, M., Monsell, S. & Cooper, P. J. (1998). The disorder-salient Stroop effect as a measure of psychopathology in eating disorders. *International Journal of Eating Disorders,* Vol.24, No.1 (July 1998), pp. 65–82, ISSN 1098-108X.

Katzman, D. K., Christensen, B., Young, A. R. & Zipursky, R. B. (2001). Starving the brain: Structural abnormalities and cognitive impairment in adolescents with anorexia nervosa. *Seminary of Clinical Neuropsychiatry,* Vol.6, No.2 (April 2001), pp. 146–152, ISSN 1084-3612.

King, G. A., Polivy, J. & Herman, C. P. (1991). Cognitive aspects of dietary restraint: Effects on person memory. *International Journal of Eating Disorders,* Vol.10, No.3 (May 1991), pp. 313–321, ISSN 1098-108X.

Kingston, K., Szmukler, G., Andrewes, D., Tress, B. & Desmond, P. (1996). Neuropsychological and structural brain changes in anorexia nervosa after refeeding. *Psychological Medicine,* Vol.26, No.1 (January 1996), pp. 15–28, ISSN 0033-2917.

Kutlesic, V., Williamson, D. A., Gleaves, D. H., Barbin, J. M. & Murphy-Eberenz, K. P. (1998). The Interview for the Diagnosis of Eating Disorders-IV: Application to DSM-IV diagnostic criteria. *Psychological Assessment,* Vol.10, No.1 (January 1998), pp. 41–48, ISSN 1040-3590.

Lauer, C. J., Gorzewski, B., Gerlinghoff, M., Backmund, H. & Zihl, J. (1999). Neuropsychological assessments before and after treatment in patients with anorexia nervosa and bulimia nervosa. *Journal of Psychiatric Research,* Vol.33, No.2 (March 1999), pp. 129–138, ISSN 0022- 3956.

Lehoux, P. M., Steiger, H. & Jabalpurlawa, S. (2000). State/trait distinctions in bulimic syndromes. *International Journal of Eating Disorders,* Vol.27, No.1 (January 2000), pp. 36–42, ISSN 1098-108X.

Lena, S. M., Fiocco, A. J. & Leyenaar, J. K. (2004). The role of cognitive deficits in the development of eating disorders. *Neuropsychology Review,* Vol.14, No.2 (June 2004), pp. 99–113, ISSN 1573-6660.

Lezak, M. D. (2004). *Neuropsychological assessment.* Oxford University Press, ISBN-10: 0195111214, New York.

Lilenfeld, L., Kaye, W., Greeno, C. G., Merikangas, K.R., Plotnicov, K., Pollice, C. et al. (1998). A controlled family study of restricting anorexia and bulimia nervosa: Comorbidity in probands and disorders in first-degree relatives. *Archives of General Psychiatry,* Vol.55, No.7 (July 1998), pp. 603–610, ISSN 0003-990x.

Lindberg, L. & Hjern, A. (2003). Risk factors for anorexia nervosa: A national cohort study. *International Journal of Eating Disorders,* Vol.34, No.3 (November 2003), pp. 397–408, ISSN 1098-108X.

Lledo, E. P. & Waller, G. (2000). Bulimic psychopathology and impulsive behaviors among nonclinical women. *International Journal of Eating Disorders,* Vol.29, No.1 (January 2000), pp. 71–75, ISSN 1098-108X.

Lovell, D. M., Williams, J. M. & Hill, A. B. (1997). Selective processing of shape-related words in women with eating disorders, and those who have recovered. *British Journal of Clinical Psychology,* Vol.36, No.3 (September 1997), pp. 421–432, ISSN 0144-6657.

Mathias, J. L. & Kent, P. S. (1998). Neuropsychological consequences of extreme weight loss and dietary restriction in patients with anorexia nervosa. *Journal of Clinic and Experimental Neuropsychology,* Vol.20, No.4 (August 1998), pp. 548–564, ISSN 1380-3395.

Mendlewicz, L., Nef, F. & Simon, Y. (2001). Selective handling of information in patients suffering from restrictive anorexia in an emotional Stroop Test and a word recognition. *Neuropsychobiology,* Vol.44, No.2 (August 2001), pp. 59–64, ISSN 0302-282X.

Palazidou, E., Robinson, P. & Lishman, W. A. (1990). Neuroradiological and neuropsychological assessment in anorexia nervosa. *Psychological Medicine,* Vol.20, No.3 (August 1990), pp. 521–527, ISSN 0033-2917.

Pauporte, J. & Walsh, B. T. (2001). Serum cholesterol in bulimia nervosa. *International Journal of Eating Disorders,* Vol.30, No.3 (November 2001), pp. 294–298, ISSN 1098-108X.

Perpiná, C., Hemsley, D., Treasure, J. & de Silva, P. (1993). Is the selective information processing of food and body words specific to patients with eating disorders? *International Journal of Eating Disorders,* Vol.14, No.3 (November 1993), pp. 359–366, ISSN 1098-108X.

Peterson, R., Byus, K. & Gilly, M. (1999). An analysis of the portrayal of female models in television commercial by degree of slenderness. *Journal of Family and Consumer Sciences,* Vol.91, No.1 (February 1999), pp. 83.

Quinton, S. (2004). Processing of five types of 'threat' information in anorexic and bulimic women. *European Eating Disorders Review,* Vol.12, No.3 (May 2004), pp. 184–189, ISSN 1099-0868.

Rey, A. (1999). *Test de Copia y de Reproducción de Memoria de Figuras Geométricas Complejas.* 7ª edición, TEA Ediciones, ISBN 978-84-7174-962-8, Spain.

Sackville, T., Schotte, D. E., Touyz, S. W., Griffiths, R. & Beumont, P. J. (1998). Conscious and preconscious processing of food, body weight and shape, and emotion-related words in women with anorexia nervosa. *International Journal of Eating Disorders,* Vol.23, No.1 (January 1998), pp. 77–82, ISSN 1098-108X.

Schneider, W., Eschman, A. & Zuccolotto, A. (2002). *E-Prime Program.* Psychology Software Tools Inc., Pittsburgh, USA.

Sebastian, S. B., Williamson, D. A. & Blouin, D. C. (1996). Memory bias for fatness stimuli in the eating disorders. *Cognitive Therapy and Research,* Vol.20, No.3 (June 1996), pp. 275–286, ISSN 0147-5916.

Sherman, B. J., Savage, C., Eddy, K., Blais, M., Deckersbach, T., Jackson, S. C. et al. (2006). Strategic memory in adults with anorexia nervosa: Are there similarities to obsessive compulsive spectrum disorders? *International Journal of Eating Disorders,* Vol.39, No.6 (September 2006), pp. 468–476, ISSN 1098-108X.

Silva, G. C. (2001). *Caracterización de un grupo de pacientes con trastornos de la alimentación: estudio descriptivo.* Tesis de maestría, UNAM, México.

Smith, M. C. & Thelen, M. H. (1984). Development and validation of a test for bulimia. *Journal of Consulting and Clinical Psychology,* Vol.52, No.5 (October 1984), pp. 863–872, ISSN 0022-006X.

Steiger, H., Gauvin, L., Engelberg, M. J., Ying Kin, N. M., Israel, M., Wonderlich, S. A. et al. (2005). Mood-and restraint-based antecedents to binge episodes in bulimia nervosa: possible influences of the serotonin system. *Psychological Medicine,* Vol.35, No.11 (November 2005), pp. 1553–1562, ISSN 0033-2917.

Steinberg, B. E. & Shaw, R. J. (1997). Bulimia as a disturbance of narcissism: Self-esteem and the capacity to self-soothe. *Addictive Behaviors,* Vol.22, No.5 (September 1997), pp. 699–710, ISSN 0306-4603.

Strasburger, V. C. & Brown, R. T. (1998). *Adolescent medicine: A practical guide,* 2nd ed. Lippincott-Raven, ISBN 978-0316818759, Philadelphia, USA.

Stroop, J. R. (1935). Studies of interference in serial verbal reactions. *Journal of Experimental Psychology,* Vol.18, No.6 (December 1935), pp. 643–662, ISSN 1076-898X.

Szmukler, G. I., Andrewes, D., Kingston, K., Chen, L., Stargatt, R. & Stanley, R. (1992). Neuropsychological impairment in anorexia nervosa before and after refeeding. *Journal of Clinical and Experimental Neuropsychology,* Vol.14, No.2 (April 1992), pp. 347–352, ISSN 1380-3395.

Tate, R. L., Perdices, M. & Maggiotto, S. (1998). Stability of the Wisconsin Card Sorting Test and the determination of reliability of change in scores. *The Clinical Neuropsychologist,* Vol.12, No.3 (August 1998), pp. 348–357, ISSN 1385-4046.

Tchanturia, K., Anderluh, M.B., Morris, R.G., Rabe-Hesketh, S., Collier, D.A., Sanchez, P. et al. (2004a). Cognitive flexibility in anorexia nervosa and bulimia nervosa. *Journal of the International Neuropsychological Society,* Vol.10, No.4 (July 2004), pp. 513–520, ISBN 1355-6177.

Tchanturia, K., Campbell, I., Morris, R. & Treasure, J. (2005). Neuropsychological studies in anorexia nervosa. *International Journal of Eating Disorders,* Vol.37, No.S1 (April 2005), pp. S72–S76, ISSN 1098-108X.

Tchanturia, K., Morris, R. G., Anderluh, M.B., Collier, D. A., Nikolaou, V. & Treasure, J. (2004b) Set shifting in anorexia nervosa: an examination before and after weight gain, in full recovery and relationship to childhood and adult OCPD traits. *Journal of Psychiatric Research,* Vol.38, No.5 (September 2004), pp. 545–552, ISSN 0022- 3956.

Tchanturia, K, Morris, R. G., Surguladze, S. & Treasure, J. (2002). An examination of perceptual and cognitive set shifting tasks in acute anorexia nervosa and following recovery. *Eating and Weight Disorders,* Vol.7, No.4 (December 2002), pp. 312–315, ISSN 1590-1262.

Toro, J. (1996). *El cuerpo como delito.* Editorial Ariel, ISBN 9788434480230, Spain.

Touyz, S., Beumont, P. & Johnstone, L. (1986). Neuropsychological correlates of dieting disorders. *International Journal of Eating Disorders,* Vol.5, No.6 (September 1986), pp. 1025-1034, ISSN 1098-108X.

Vitousek, K. B. & Hollon, S. D. (1990). The investigation of schematic content and processing in eating disorders. *Cognitive Therapy and Research,* Vol.14, No.2 (April 1990), pp. 191-214, ISSN 1573-2819.

Vitousek, K. B. & Orimoto, L. (1993). Cognitive-behavioral models of anorexia nervosa, bulimia nervosa, and obesity. En: I. K. S. Dobson & P. C. Kendall (eds.). *Psychopathology and cognition.* (pp. 191–242). Academic Press, ISBN 978-0124041752, San Diego, CA.

Wade, T., Neale, M. C., Lake, R. & Martin, N. G. (1999). A genetic analysis of the eating and attitudes associated with bulimia nervosa: Dealing with the problem of ascertainment. *Behavior Genetics,* Vol.29, No.1 (January 1999), pp. 1–10, ISSN 1573-3297.

Wagner, A., Barbarich-Marsteller, N. C., Frank, G. K., Bailer, U. F., Wonderlich, S. A., Crosby, R. et al. (2006). Personality traits after recovery from eating disorders: Do subtypes differ? *International Journal of Eating Disorders,* Vol.39, No.4 (May 2006), pp. 276–284, ISSN 1098-108X.

Waller, G., Watkins, H., Shuck, V. & McManus, F. (1996). Bulimic psychopathology and attentional biases to ego threats among noneating- disordered women. *International Journal of Eating Disorders,* Vol.20, No.2 (September 1996), pp. 169–176, ISSN 1098-108X.

Williams, J. M. G., Watts, F. N., Macleod, C. & Mathews, A. (1988). *Cognitive psychology and emotional disorders*. Willey, ISBN 978-0471944300, USA.

Winston A. P. & Wells, F. E. (2002). Hypophosphatemia following self-treatment for anorexia nervosa. *International Journal of Eating Disorders,* Vol.32, No.2 (September 2002), pp. 245–248, ISSN 1098-108X.

9

# Cardiovascular Complications in Eating Disorders

Beatriz Jáuregui Garrido[1] and Ignacio Jáuregui Lobera[2]
[1]*Department of Cardiology, Universitary Hospital "Virgen del Rocio", Seville,*
[2]*Department of Nutrition and Bromatology. Pablo de Olavide University, Seville,*
*Spain*

## 1. Introduction

Eating disorders (mainly anorexia and bulimia) affect about 5 million persons each year in countries as the United States, and around 3% of young women in western countries have an eating disorder (Becker et al., 1991; Sullivan, 1995). Despite these figures, eating disorders are still not considered a serious type of mental disorder in some countries, resulting in a health care crisis for those currently suffering from these disorders, as well as for their families (Klump et al., 2009). Anorexia nervosa is a severe and potentially fatal disease with high rate of morbidity and mortality. One review has estimated the aggregate mortality rate at 0.56 % per year, or approximately 5.6 % per decade (Sullivan, 1995). At least one third of all deaths in patients with anorexia nervosa are estimated to be due to cardiac causes, mainly sudden death (Isner et al., 1985; Neumärker, 1997; Sharp & Freeman, 1993). Furthermore, the fact that many of these patients are not under medical control leads to the risk of potentially fatal complications, sometimes being underestimated . With respect to anorexia nervosa, it is an eating disorder characterized by a voluntary restriction of the intake, which causes significant weight loss and may reach severe malnutrition and death. Most often affects women (estimated ratio of 10:1) aged between 12 and 25 years, the adolescence being the time of highest risk. It has not been certain whether mortality rates are high for other eating disorders, such as bulimia nervosa and eating disorder not otherwise specified, the latter being the most common eating disorder diagnosis (Kaye, 2009).

Eating disorders are known to result in a variety of potentially serious medical complications. These are usually more severe in patients with anorexia nervosa because of the complications attendant to starvation but many can also be seen in patients with bulimia nervosa, mainly attributed to the purging behaviours in which these patients engage, including self-induced vomiting and laxative abuse (Birmingham & Beumont, 2004).

Cardiovascular complications are common, and they have been reported in up to 80% of the cases, mainly in the form of bradycardia, hypotension, arrhythmias, repolarization abnormalities and sudden death by up to 10% of the cases (Cooke et al., 1994; De Simone et al., 1994; Harris et al., 1993; Isner et al., 1985; Neumärker, 1997; St John Sutton et al., 1985). In recent years special attention has been directed to the QT interval electrocardiographic abnormalities (Higham & Campbell, 1994; Swenne & Larsson, 1999) and changes in myocardial mass and cardiac function detected in the echocardiographic study (Conri et al., 1989; Galetta et al., 2002; Lombardi, 1998; Monmeneu et al., 1999).

Several studies have demonstrated that approximately 30% of deaths in patients with anorexia nervosa are due to cardiac complications (Mont et al., 2003). Data indicates that 80% of patients with an eating disorder have a cardiac complication (Casiero & Frishman, 2006). In fact, food restriction can lead to increased vagal tone, bradycardia, orthostatic hypotension, syncope, arrhythmias, congestive heart failure, and sudden death (Casiero & Frishman, 2006). In addition, mitral valve prolapse has been shown in more than 30% of patients with eating disorders compared to 4% of controls (Johson et al., 1986). Among eating disorder patients, cardiac complications are most common in those with laxative and/or diuretic abuse, and data indicate that, at least at the early stages, cardiac abnormalities are reversible with weight restoration (Mont et al., 2003).

Cardiovascular complications for patients with bulimia nervosa can include arrhythmias, palpitations, orthostatic hypotension, and electrocardiographic disturbances, which may be due to electrolyte imbalances (Katzman et al., 2011; Rome & Ammerman, 2003; Walsh et al., 2000). Patients who engage in self-induced vomiting or diuretic or laxative abuse may also become dehydrated, which can result in dizziness and fainting (Pomeroy & Mitchell, 2002). The abuse of emetics as Ipecac can result in irreversible and potentially fatal cardiomyopathies (Halmi, 2002).

## 2. QT abnormalities and bradycardia

The QT interval is a measure of the time between the start of the QRS complex and the end of the T wave in the heart's electrical cycle. In general, the QT interval represents electrical depolarisation and repolarisation of the left and right ventricles. The duration of the QT interval of the electrocardiogram is a function of the heart rate, and a prolonged QT interval is a biomarker for ventricular tachyarrhythmia and a risk factor for sudden death. Summarizing, the QT interval is a measure of myocardial repolarisation and its length is associated with life threatening ventricular tachycardia (Cooke et al., 1994). The Bazett rate correction formula is commonly used to correct the QT interval for heart rate (QTc). The Bazett formula is convenient and easy to use, but an approximation that may miss or exaggerate abnormalities (Browne et al., 1982). The most commonly used cut-off point for QTc is 440 ms (Vázquez et al., 2003). Figure 1 shows a case of sinus bradycardia.

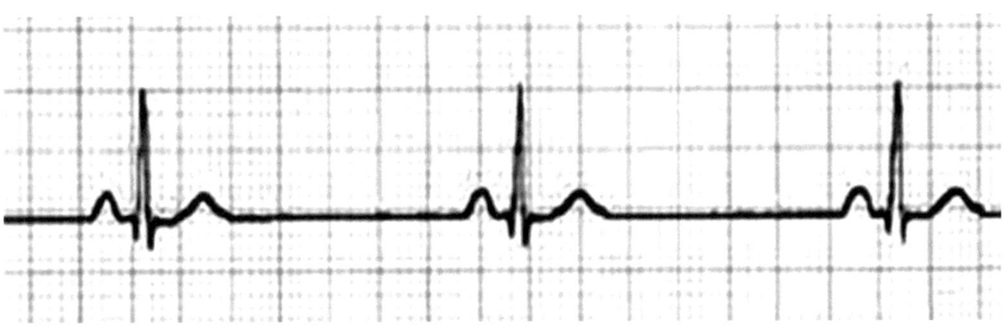

Fig. 1. Sinus bradycardia

With regards to eating disorder patients, QT interval abnormalities have been studied as a marker of sudden death and to assess the effect of refeeding. In fact, it has been proposed that these deaths are a result of cardiac arrhythmias for which a long QT interval on the electrocardiogram is a marker (Isner et al., 1985). Nevertheless, the measurement of the QT interval has a poor predictive value for the recognition of patients who are at particular risk of sudden death. A measured QT interval >600 ms is associated with a significant risk of sudden death (Jackmann et al., 1988), but few patients usually have such long QT intervals. Another QT parameter is the QT dispersion (QTd), which is the difference between the maximum QT and the minimum QT in all derivations. Finally, the dispersion of the corrected QT interval (QTcd) is the difference between the maximum and the minimum QTc interval in the 12 electrocardiographic derivations. The most used cut-off point for the dispersion is 60 ms (Bayés de Luna & Viñolas, 1996; Girola et al., 2001; Hill & Friedman, 1997; Lund et al., 2002; Toivonen, 2002).

Considering the main studies on the QT interval among patients with anorexia nervosa, there are some controversial results. Thus, some studies have not found long QT intervals (Powers et al., 1991; Gottdiener et al., 1978) while others have found long QT intervals (Cooke et al., 1994; Isner et al., 1985; Thurston & Marks, 1974). Apart from methodological problems, these conflicting results could be explained by difficulties in comparison due to the huge variability of the QT interval with heart rate (Cooke et al., 1994). In a recent study, QT and QTc intervals as well as the dispersion intervals QTd and QTcd were longer among anorectic women than in a control group (Vázquez et al., 2003).

In relation with the undernutrition state of anorexia nervosa, arrhythmias, especially bradycardia, are the best-known cardiac disturbances probably as a response to maintain body energy by means of a decrease of cardiac work. There have been different proposed pathogenic mechanisms to explain those disturbances: electrolyte loss, drugs adverse cardiovascular effects, decreased glycogen content in the cardiac cell, myofibril atrophy, interstitial oedema, mitochondrial swelling, and activation of calcium-dependent proteinases. With respect to the pathological basis of a long QT interval in anorexia nervosa there are some proposals too: cardiac muscle is lost in proportion to loss of body mass, but there is no convincing evidence of impairment of ventricular function in these patients, histological studies have not shown myocarditis, abnormalities of the hypothalamus are well described and, finally, a increased autonomic tone has been suggested as a possible mechanism for lengthening the QT interval (Clark & Wildenthal, 1986; Thurston & Marks, 1974; Palossy & Oó, 1977; Powers et al., 1991; Tolnay & von Althen, 1987).

In general, the most frequent findings among anorectic patients have been arrhythmias, bradycardia, atrial extrasystoles, isolated premature ventricular contractions and a significant increase QT and QTc, compared with healthy women of similar age (Panagiotopoulos et al., 2000; Swenne & Larsson, 1999; Vázquez et al., 2003). As a result of these findings, some authors have suggested that weight loss in patients with anorexia nervosa and eating disorders in general is a risk factor for the prolongation and dispersion of the QT interval (Galetta et al., 2002; Swenne & Larsson, 1999). In fact, a significant and negative correlation between QTc and body mass index has been reported (Vázquez et al., 2003). An increase of the QT interval dispersion represents regional differences in myocardial excitability recovery and may lead to and increased arrhythmogenic substrate, with a higher risk for ventricular arrhythmias clinically significant and a higher risk of sudden death. In fact, the increased QT interval and the increased QT dispersion have been associated with higher risk of ventricular arrhythmias in both patients with heart disease and healthy individuals. Thus, the predictive value of the increased QT interval dispersion as a marker of sudden acute ventricular arrhythmia or death has been demonstrated (Harris et al., 1993; Isner et al., 1985). Recently, parameters of QT variability have been proposed as surrogate markers for arrhythmia risk stratification in anorexia nervosa (Koschke et al., 2010). A meta-analysis of heart rate and QT interval alteration in anorexia nervosa showed that bradycardia and relationship between heart rate and body mass index decreases as the disease continues. Moreover QTc interval in anorectic patients was within normal range although significantly longer than in controls (Lesinskiene, et al., 2008).

Considering the subtypes of anorexia nervosa, a significant increase has been found in weight/height ratio and body mass index from malnourished stage to weight restoration, paralleled by a significant decrease in QTd among anorectic patients (restricting type) (Nahshoni, et al., 2007). With respect to bulimia nervosa, compared with the controls, bulimic patients with a history of anorexia nervosa seem to have significantly more signal-averaged electrocardiography abnormalities (Takimoto et al., 2006). Besides the relationship between QT changes and potential fatal arrhythmias, those changes have shown to be related with low resting metabolic rate among chronic anorectic patients (Krantz et al., 2005). Despite the fact that the majority of studies have highlighted the QT disturbances in anorexia nervosa, a prolonged QT interval and QT dispersion have been reported in both anorexia nervosa and bulimia nervosa (Takimoto et al., 2004). In fact, QT and QTd have been shown to be significantly longer in all eating disorder subtypes than in controls. Moreover, QT interval and QTd were significantly correlated with the rate of body weight loss in bulimia nervosa (Takimoto et al., 2004). Figure 2 shows a long QT related to weight loss.

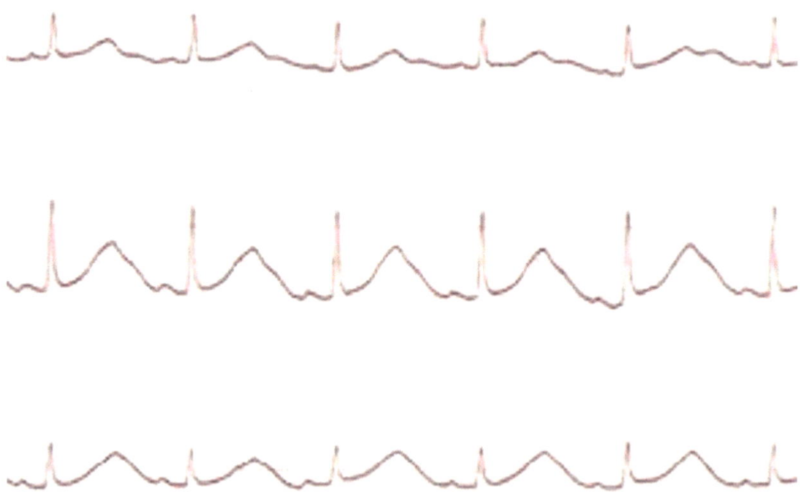

Fig. 2. Long QT interval

### 2.1 QT abnormalities and refeeding

The effect of the reached target weights on QT interval has been demonstrated, with a significant shortening of that interval by means of an adequate refeeding (Cooke et al., 1994). After admission, the QT prolongation and dispersion are usually normalized within the 3 days of refeeding (Swenne, 2000). After refeeding, a significant decrease in QT interval and QT dispersion has been observed as well as a normalization of the heart rate and heart rate variability (Mont et al., 2003). On the other hand, the QT/RR slope has been found significantly enhanced in anorectic patients compared with healthy controls, and this slope returns to normal range values after refeeding. This QT/RR slope seems to be significantly correlated with the body mass index in the patient group (Roche et al., 2005). During the follow-up of these cardiac abnormalities in female adolescents with anorexia nervosa, one year after refeeding a significant decrease in QT, QTc, QTd and QTcd has been reported (Ulger et al., 2006).

## 3. Structural changes

With respect to the cardiac structural changes in eating disorders those referred to the interventricular septum and the left ventricular mass have been the most studied ones. With regards to anorexia nervosa, echocardiography has shown a reduction in the dimensions of the interventricular septum (52% of patients), left ventricular free wall (61%), left atrium (31%) and left ventricular mass (61%) (Silvetti et al., 1998). More recently, by means of tissue Doppler imaging, when compared with control groups, anorectic patients have shown lower left ventricular mass, lower myocardial systolic wave peak of both lateral wall and septum, and comparable early (Em) and atrial (Am) diastolic waves, and Em/Am ratio. On the other hand, the ratio between transmitral peak E-wave and Em has shown significantly greater in anorectic patients than in controls, while no differences have been observed between thin and normal-weight females. In anorectic patients, Sm peak has been significantly related to left ventricular mass indexed, at both septum and lateral wall levels (Galetta et al., 2005). Anorexia nervosa has been associated with a significant reduction in the cyclic variation in the integrated backscatter (IBS) signal of the myocardium, which is also related to left ventricular hypotrophy (Franzoni et al., 2003).

With respect to the ventricular mass, left ventricular chamber dimension and mass seem to be significantly less in women with anorexia nervosa than in either the women of normal weight or the thin women, even after standardisation for body size or after controlling for blood pressure. Nevertheless it seems that there are no substantial changes in the left ventricular shape (De Simone et al., 1994). Some authors have reported a high frequency of mitral valve prolapse due to the disproportion between ventricle and valve among anorectic patients (Conri et al., 1989).

### 3.1 Structural changes and refeeding

Other studies have highlighted that the left ventricular mass index is significantly lower than that in normal subjects as well as the left ventricular end-diastolic and end-systolic volume indexes. Nevertheless, in spite of the reductions in left ventricular mass and volume indexes, left ventricular chamber architecture described as h/R ratio, mass to volume ratio, and short/long left ventricular axis ratio usually is normal. The same applies to the left ventricular afterload assessed as end-systolic meridional and circumferential wall stress. Moreover, among anorectic patients, ejection fraction, percent fractional shortening, and the relationship between end-systolic wall stress and ejection fraction have been all within normal limits. In some patients restudied after a 15% to 20% weight gain, left ventricular mass and volume indexes increased significantly but end-systolic wall stress and ejection fraction did not change (St John Sutton et al., 1985).

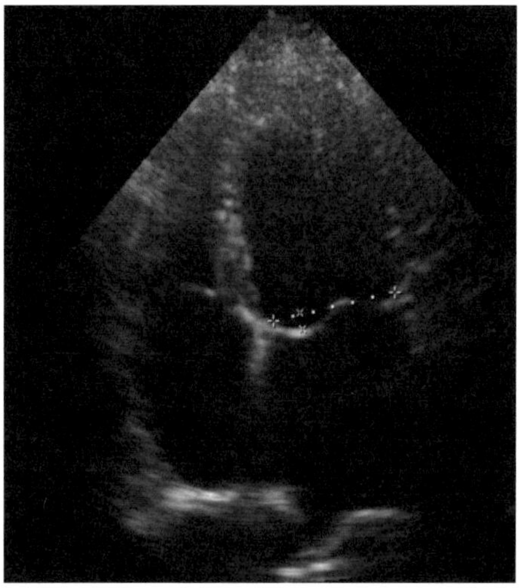

Fig. 3. Mitral valve prolapse

Control echocardiograms of anorectic patients after refeeding have shown an increase in left ventricular diameters and cardiac mass (Ulger et al., 2006). Apart from that, echocardiograms have shown an increase in cardiac output, an improvement in the exercise capacity, and a normalization of the heart rate and heart rate variability after refeeding (Mont et al., 2003). Other authors have reported that cardiac complications of anorexia nervosa are common, usually benign and always reversible after refeeding in hospital (Lupoglazoff et al., 2001). Figure 3 shows a mitral valve prolapse.

## 4. Left ventricular function

In a pioneer study (Gottdiener et al., 1978), the authors found that in spite of the structural changes, left ventricular systolic function, was unimpaired as indicated by normal echocardiographic fractional shortening, and by normal exercise augmentation of ejection fraction determined by radionuclide cineangiography. Another study showed that there was no evidence of arrhythmias at rest, during exercise, or with continuous electrocardiographic recording, concluding that young patients with anorexia nervosa appeared to have essentially normal cardiac function with a reduction in left ventricular muscle mass (Moodie & Salcedo, 1983). It seems that the down-regulation of left ventricular mass per se, like up-regulation of left ventricular mass, is not associated with abnormal left ventricular function (St John Sutton et al., 1985). Other authors have reported similar results (Dec et al., 1987) and a cardiovascular vagal hyperactivity in anorectic patients, which appears to influence the ventricular diastolic dynamics. Heart rate variability and diastolic function analysis have been proposed as useful tools in monitoring anorexia-induced cardiac modifications (Galetta et al., 2003).

Apart from bradycardia, hypotension, tachycardia, a decrease in cardiac chamber size, impaired left ventricular contractility, electrocardiographic changes, pericardial effusion, and mitral valve prolapse, in patients with anorexia nervosa, some previous articles, as the above-mentioned ones have focused on the effects of anorexia nervosa on left ventricular function. However, atrial function in patients with anorexia nervosa has not been studied. The percentage of total transmitral flow contributed by atrial contraction is about 30% (Jovic & Troskot, 1977), which indicates the importance of atrial function in left ventricular filling, and a case of anorexia nervosa as cause of atrial failure has been described (Mizuno et al., 1998).

Cardiac disturbances in anorectic patients are essentially derived from malnutrition and starvation. On a cellular level this leads to diminish the protein synthesis, activation of calcium-dependent proteinases, mitochondrial swelling, decreased glycogen content, interstitial oedema, and myofibrillar atrophy. The physiologic consequences of the malnutrition include decreased contractile force of the ventricle, decreased cardiac output, and decreased diastolic compliance. Clinically, bradycardia, relative hypotension, mitral valve prolapse, and diminished exercise capacity may all be seen in these patients as well as the above mentioned atrial dysfunction (Abel et al., 1979; Fohlin, 1977; Goldberg et al., 1988; Gottdiener et al., 1978; Johnson et al., 1986; Meyers et al., 1986; Monmeneu et al., 1999; Moodie, 1987; Nutter et al., 1979; Tolnai & von Althen, 1987; Warren & Vande Wiele, 1973).

## 5. Electrolyte changes

Eating disorder patients may show varying degrees of dehydration, sodium and chloride depletion, mainly in patients who vomit, potassium deficiency in patients with laxatives abuse, and weaknesses of chlorine, sodium and potassium in patients using diuretics, with different depletions depending on the substance used. With respect to electrolyte disturbances, typical laboratory changes, although not exclusively seen in anorexia nervosa, include hyponatremia, hypokalaemia, and hypochloremia (Baumann et al., 2010).

The presence of the symptoms listed below usually indicates a water loss of about 25% (or more) and indicates a severe situation: oliguria, sunken eyes, dry mucous membranes (dry mouth), shrivelled skin, fever and muscle cramps. Along with this, blood parameters will show an increase of haematocrit value, and increase of the total proteins, increased urine density, and increased urea concentration in urine.

Considering hypochloremia, it would be moderate with a level within a range between 90-95 mEq/L, more severe between 80-90 mEq/L and severe (which would require urgent treatment) an amount of chlorine in blood below 80 mEq/L. The hypochloremia key signs are hypotension and paresis or intestinal ileus.

Hyponatremia is considered moderate when blood sodium levels between 130 and 138 mEq/L, severe with levels between 125 and 130 mEq/L, and very severe when the sodium level is below 125 mEq/L. The characteristic signs are: muscle contractures, muscle aches, muscle fibrillations and sometimes seizures. Hypotension is less common than in hypochloremia, but usual. The accepted normal range is 135-145 mEq/L.

With respect to hypokalaemia, it is moderate between 3-3.5 mEq/L, severe between 2.5 and 3 mEq/L and very severe when less than 2.5 mEq/L. Clinically, there is an hypotonic smooth and striated fibres resulting in severe fatigue, loss of muscle strength and sometimes paralysis. There is frequently hypo- or arreflexia and intestinal paresis, but the worst complication refers to the involvement of the heart muscle. Repolarization abnormalities (prolonged and depressed QT interval, and decreased height of the T wave) are usually found. Nevertheless there is no correlation between potassium levels and specific signs in the ECG. In any case, cardiac or respiratory arrest is the most frequent cause of sudden death. The accepted normal range is 3.4-4.8 mEq/L. The following are the main electrocardiographic changes considering different levels of plasma potassium:

- T-wave flattening or T-wave inversion (Potassium: 3-3.8 mEq/L).
- Long QT interval, prominent U-wave, depression of the ST segment, ventricular extrasystoles (Potassium: 2.3-3 mEq/L).
- Torsades de pointes, ventricular fibrillation (Potassium: < 2.3 mEq/L).

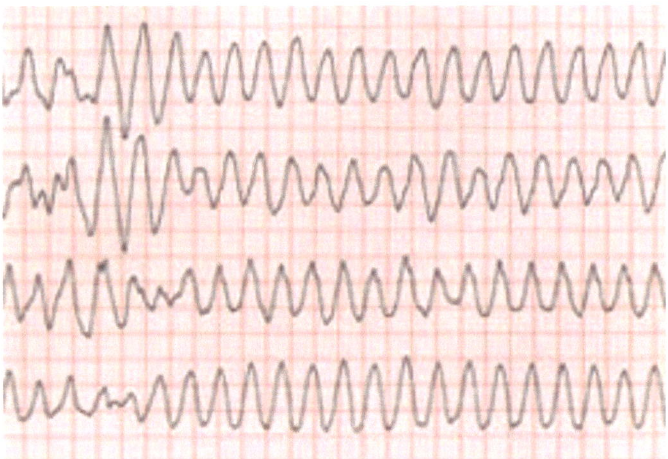

Fig. 4. Ventricular fibrillation

Hypocalcaemia is not frequent among eating disorder patients, hypophosphatemia being more common, especially during refeeding. During refeeding, redistribution from the extracellular to the intracellular space by increasing insulin secretion is found. Another possible, but infrequent finding, is hypoglycaemia. Long restrictive periods lead to the exhaustion of carbohydrates from the last meal, as well as those stored as glycogen. In these situations a syndrome with anxiety, palpitations, sweating, pallor and tachycardia is usual. Many times, this syndrome is labelled as "anxiety attacks" and therefore poorly addressed (Rotellar, 1973; Jáuregui, 2006).

In a cross-sectional, community-based study (Miller et al., 2005) in women with anorexia nervosa, the lowest value for plasma sodium was 122 mEq/L, and 7% of participants had hyponatremia. One participant reported a history of seizures secondary to hyponatremia and none had hypernatremia. The lowest value for plasma potassium was 1.9 mEq/L, and 20% of participants had hypokalaemia, including the 6 women who reported taking potassium supplements. Of the participants with low potassium levels, 48% reported that they regularly purged, whereas the remainder (52%) denied purging. In a previous large study in an outpatient treatment program has reported the absence of hypokalaemia in non-purgers anorectic patients (Rieger et al., 1978). Mean plasma potassium level was lower for the women who reported purging than for those who did not (3.5 vs. 3.7 mEq/L). A history of dysrhythmia was reported by 2% of the women and, in most cases, hypokalaemia was noted as the probable. Serum calcium levels were low in 6% of participants.

The reported serious cardiac abnormalities in patients with anorexia nervosa include dysrhythmias, some of which may be secondary to hypokalaemia (Sharp & Freeman, 1993; Bonne et al., 1993). Screening and monitoring patients with anorexia nervosa for cardiac risk factors and dysfunction is important, and this should include asking patients whether they purge or have histories of hypokalaemia and/or purging behaviours. Monitoring vital signs and performing electrocardiograms and serial measurements of plasma potassium are also important. This is important, as purging may increase the risk of hypokalaemia and subsequent cardiac dysrhythmias, and self-induced vomiting increases the risk of additional complications (Miller et al., 2005). In fact, QT prolongation and ventricular arrhythmia may develop in the setting of severe hypokalaemia, exposing patients to high risk of sudden cardiac event (Facchini et al., 2006).

## 6. Purging behaviours and effects of drugs (laxatives, diuretics, stimulants)

Some studies (e.g., Facchini et al., 2006) have found hypokalaemia only in anorectic patients who vomited. In these patients, serum chloride values were also low. With respect to the causes of this hypokalaemia, anorectic patients who vomit lose hydrogen, chloride and water and develop that hypokalaemia not only because of shift of potassium ion into cells as the result of alkalosis, but also because of increased potassium ion excretion in the urine as the result of reabsorption of hydrogen ion. Moreover, secondary aldosteronism due to the decrease of total body water also causes increase of potassium ion excretion in the urine. Finally, frequent vomiting causes hypokalaemia, which sometimes results in arrhythmia or heart arrest (Koh et al., 1989). Purging behaviours have been related to electrolyte disturbances and, consequently, associated with cardiac disturbances (Fohlin, 1977; Halmi, 1983; Mars et al., 1982; Rajs et al., 1986). In Figure 5, a case presenting hypokalaemia, long QT and *torsades de pointes*, is shown.

Generally, individuals who abuse laxatives may be constipated patients, people engaged in athletic training and eating disorder patients, the latter being the most relevant group. The most frequently abused group of laxatives are of the stimulant class. This may be related to the quick action of stimulants, particularly in individuals with eating disorders, as they may erroneously believe that they can avoid the absorption of calories via the resulting diarrhoea. Medical problems associated with laxative abuse include electrolyte and acid/base changes that can involve the renal and cardiovascular systems and may become life threatening. The renin-aldosterone system becomes activated due to the loss of fluid, which leads to oedema and acute weight gain when the laxative is discontinued. This can result in reinforcing further laxative abuse when a patient feels bloated and has gained weight (Roerig et al., 2010)).

With respect to substance use, a recent study has shown that, in general, eating disorders were associated with greater substance use relative to the control group. Considering the stimulants, across groups, statistically significant differences emerged, the anorectic patients group being more likely to use stimulants (more than 10 times per month) relative to the referent. Those in the anorectic and bulimic groups were more likely to use stimulants (life time use) compared to the control group (Root et al., 2010).

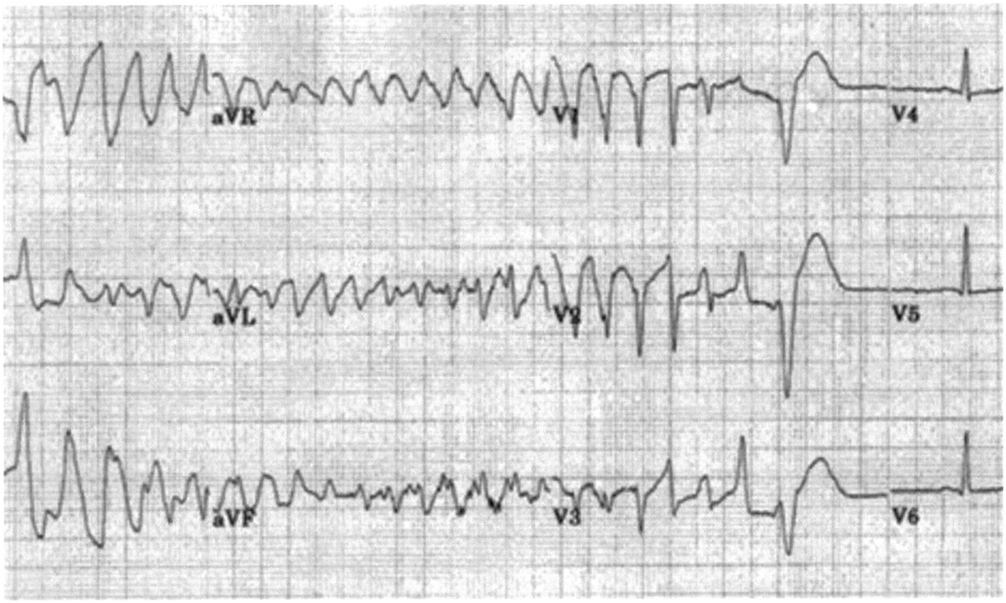


Fig. 5. Hypokalaemia: Long QT interval and torsades de pointes.

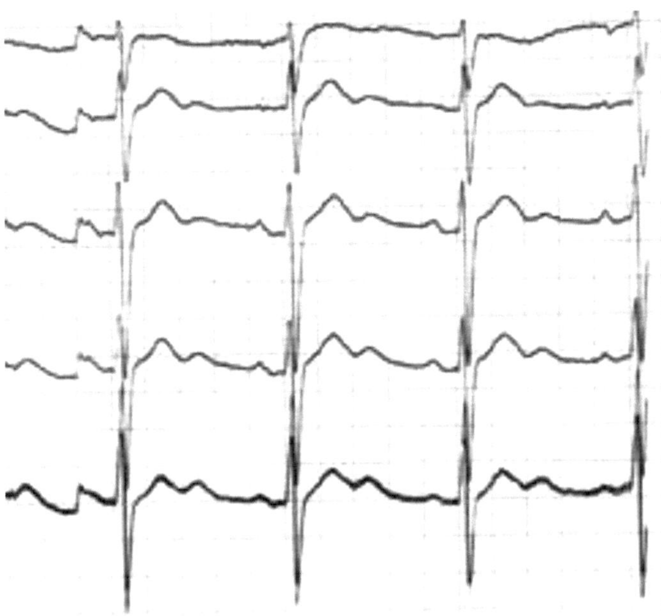

Fig. 6. Prominent U-wave (usual finding in hypokalaemia)

In a pioneer study (Ong et al., 1983), eight patients with bulimia nervosa were given methylamphetamine or placebo intravenously under double blind controlled conditions. In every patient, methylamphetamine reduced self-ratings of hunger and amount of food eaten as measured under laboratory conditions. This finding showed that experimental drugs could modify the food intake of bulimic patients. Although weight loss is among the most commonly cited reasons for using methamphetamine, little is known about the association between eating disorders and treatment outcomes in the population of methamphetamine dependent patients. In a recent study, bulimia nervosa was observed among 2.4% of the participants (methamphetamine dependent adults) (Glasner-Edwards et al., 2011). Apart from weight loss, methamphetamine is frequently used as a recreational drug because of its stimulant effects. Recent studies suggest that methamphetamine use is present in at least 5% of all patients presenting to the emergency room with heart failure and 40% of patients under the age of 45 admitted to the hospital with cardiomyopathy. Chronic use has also been associated with the development of chronic coronary disease as well as cardiomyopathy (Diercks et al., 2008;Karch et al., 1999; Turnipseed et al., 2003; Wijetunga et al., 2004; Yeo et al., 2007).

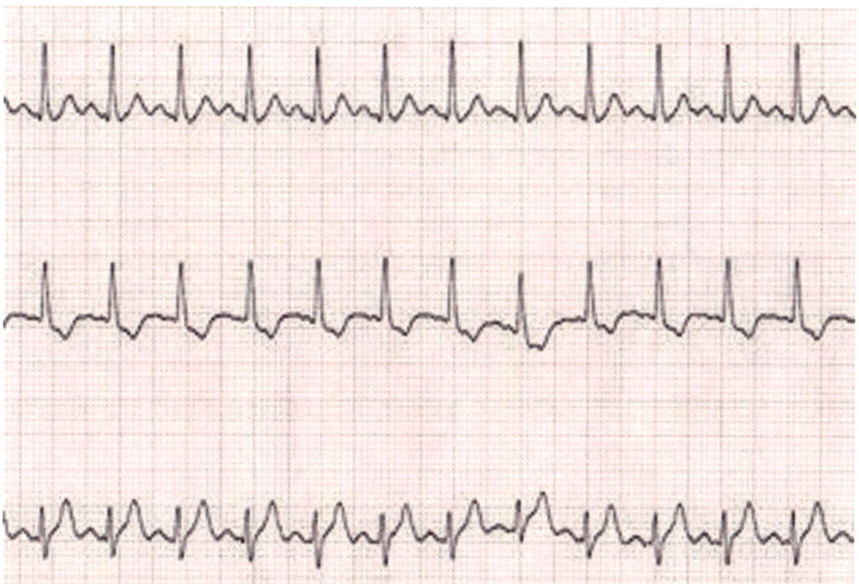

Fig. 7. Stimulants-induced sinus tachycardia

Despite that recovery of left ventricular dysfunction in patients with methamphetamine-induced cardiomyopathy has been described, since the effects of methamphetamine can include myocyte hypertrophy and fibrosis, both relatively irreversible processes, it is likely that some patients will not recover left ventricular function with either appropriate medical therapy or abstinence from methamphetamine (Lopez et al., 2009).

Besides self-inducing vomiting and abuse laxatives, misusing diuretics is the other main cause of hypokalaemia among purging-type eating disorder patients (Greenfeld et al., 1995). Prevalence of hypokalaemia between 4.6-20% of eating disorder patients who purge or abuse diuretics has been reported, and diuretics and laxatives are the most commonly abused purging medications by patients with purging-type eating disorders. In a former study (Mitchell et al., 1985) among bulimic patients, 33.9 % of diuretic abuse and 60.6% of laxative abuse was found, and may be that these figures underestimate the prevalence of diuretic abuse due to the fact that such medication is not only obtained by prescription but is also available in many over-the-counter formulations (92). Again the risk for cardiovascular disturbances is present by means of the relationship between diuretic abuse and hypokalaemia (Mascolo et al., 2011).

## 7. The heart response facing a higher metabolic demand (refeeding syndrome)

Refeeding syndrome has been considered one of the most serious complications related to anorexia nervosa, one which can occur, and possibly prove fatal, with oral as well as enteral and parenteral feeding. The syndrome involves a set of alterations caused by too rapid or unbalanced refeeding in a severely malnourished patient. The main signs and symptoms include sodium and water retention (leading to oedema and possible cardiac failure), hypophosphatemia due to intracellular disturbances (causing generalised systemic problems and a difficulty with energy storage), and the depletion of electrolytes, such as potassium and magnesium, as well as of vitamins (with the associated clinical consequences) and thiamine cofactor, which can lead to Wernicke's syndrome and/or cardiomyopathy. The calorie intake with which the syndrome may occur varies widely among the reported cases (between 10 and 60 kcal/kg/day), while the presence of glucose in the alimentary canal of extremely malnourished patients is a determining factor that can trigger the process (Katzman, 2005; Marinella, 2005; Miller, 2008; O'Connor & Goldin, 2011; Solomon, 1990; Tey et al., 2005).

Refeeding syndrome must be prevented and, therefore, many studies have sought to establish guidelines for medical and nursing care. The recommendations are to achieve a weight gain of approximately 500 g/week and constantly monitor fluid intake. Administration of phosphorus and potassium may be beneficial during the initial weeks of refeeding and the potential value of high-calorie supplements should also be assessed. At all events, the calorie intake should be carefully matched to the initial baseline metabolic rate [7], as should the carbohydrate intake (De Cock et al., 2006; Hearing, 2004; Portsmouth Hospitals NHS Trust, 2007).

Refeeding syndrome consists of cardiovascular, neurologic, and hematologic complications, and can be associated with significant morbidity and mortality. Adverse effects of hypophosphatemia include cardiac failure, muscle weakness, immune dysfunction, and death. Cardiac sequelae are secondary to and occur early in the cascade of events that arise during refeeding. Congestive heart failure results from the decreased ventricular mass and myofibrillar atrophy, causing decreased stroke volume and reduced capacity of the cardiovascular system (Katzman, 2005).

Kohn et al. described acute cardiac complications (arrhythmias, bradycardia, pericardial effusion, hypotension, and cardiac arrest) in anorectic patients during refeeding. These patients developed life-threatening complications associated with refeeding including cardiac arrhythmias documented within the first week of hospitalization.

## 8. Blood pressure changes

Besides de above-mentioned cardiovascular disturbances of eating disorders, another common complication is orthostatic hypotension. Orthostatic heart rate and blood pressure changes are common in anorectic patients on admission to hospital (Shamim et al., 2003). These orthostatic changes place patients with anorexia nervosa at increased risk of syncope. One explanation for the observed orthostatic changes is that starvation leading to low body weight may result in atrophic peripheral muscles, resulting in decreased venous return to the heart.

Recent evidence has shown that normalization of orthostatic pulse changes occurs after approximately 3 weeks of nutritional rehabilitation when patients reach 80% of their ideal body weight. It has been suggested that the resolution of orthostasis can be used as an objective measure of medical stability in patients with anorexia nervosa (Shamim et al., 2003).

## 9. Conclusions

Eating disorders, particularly anorexia nervosa, are life-threatening diseases, with high risk of death due to cardiovascular disturbances. Cardiovascular complications are present promptly, mainly in cases of anorexia nervosa, with more or less severity with regards to structural and functional changes. Cardiovascular complications in eating disorder include bradycardia, QT interval prolongation, orthostatic hypotension, increased vagal tone, mitral valve prolapse (as a consequence of weight loss with an associated reduction in left ventricle mass, resulting in a relatively large mitral valve), possible alterations in myocardial contractility, and reduction in left ventricular wall thickness, among others.

The severity of the eating disorders, specifically the undernourished state, is usually significantly correlated with increased bradycardia and decreased left ventricular force. In this regard, patients with severe sinus bradycardia should be admitted to the hospital in order to monitoring the cardiac function and to gain weight gradually.

Despite the conflicting results about the QT interval alterations, the prolongation of the QT is usually associated with sudden ventricular arrhythmias and death.

Eating disorders may show cardiac abnormalities depending on electrolyte changes associated with purging behaviours and/or drug effects, among other causes.

Orthostatic heart rate and blood pressure changes are common in patients with eating disorders, mainly in cases of anorexia nervosa, and it has been suggested that the resolution of orthostatism could be an objective measure of medical stability.

The main cardiovascular findings among patients with eating disorders are reversible by means of an appropriate refeeding. As a result of this refeeding an increase in cardiac dimensions, ventricular mass, and cardiac output are reached.

Cardiovascular complications in eating disorders may be potentially fatal and they are usually present in early stages of these diseases, being in most cases reversible. An early diagnostic, a prompt treatment, a correct refeeding, and the cardiac monitoring of all patients, are necessary.

## 10. Summarizing

- Cardiovascular complications of eating disorders are common, and they have been reported in up to 80% of the cases, mainly in the form of bradycardia, hypotension, arrhythmias, repolarization abnormalities and sudden death by up to 10% of the cases.
- Despite the conflicting results with respect to QT interval in anorexia nervosa, recent studies show that QT and QTc intervals as well as the dispersion intervals QTd and QTcd are longer among anorectic patients than in controls.
- With respect to bulimia nervosa, bulimic patients with a history of anorexia nervosa seem to have significantly more signal-averaged electrocardiography abnormalities than controls.
- During hospitalization the QT prolongation and dispersion usually normalize within the three days of refeeding.
- The most described structural changes in anorexia nervosa have been the reduction in the dimensions of the interventricular septum, left ventricular free wall, left atrium and left ventricular mass.
- Control echocardiograms of anorectic patients have shown an increase in cardiac output, an improvement in the exercise capacity, and a normalization of the heart rate and heart rate variability after refeeding.
- In spite of the structural changes, left ventricular systolic function usually keeps unimpaired.
- Considering the electrolyte changes, typical laboratory findings in eating disorders include hyponatremia, hypokalaemia and hypochloremia.
- Purging behaviours may increase the risk of hypokalaemia and subsequent cardiac dysrhythmias. Thus, monitoring vital signs and performing electrocardiograms and serial measurements of plasma potassium are relevant.
- Medical problems associated with laxative abuse include electrolyte and acid/base changes that can involve the renal and cardiovascular systems and may become life threatening.
- The chronic use of methamphetamine has been associated with the development of chronic coronary disease as well as cardiomyopathy.
- During refeeding, adverse effects of hypophosphatemia include cardiac failure among others. Cardiac sequelae are secondary to and occur early in the cascade of events that arise during refeeding.
- Orthostatic changes place patients with anorexia nervosa at increased risk of syncope. The normalization of orthostatic pulse changes occurs approximately after three weeks of nutritional rehabilitation when patients reach 80% of their ideal body weight.

## 11. References

Abel, RM., Grimes, JB., Alonso, D., Alonso, M., & Gay, WAJr. (1979). Adverse hemodynamic and ultrastructural changes in dog hearts subjected to protein-calorie malnutrition. *American Heart Journal*, 97, 733-744. ISSN 1097-6744.

Baumann, A., Heitmann, S., Bubendorff, V., & Himmerich, H. (2010). Laboratory changes in anorexia nervosa. *Praxis (Bern 1994)*, 99(11), 661-667. ISSN: 1661-8157.

Bayés de Luna, A., & Viñolas, X. (1996). QT dispersion and heart rate variability. *European Heart Journal*, 17, 165-166. ISSN 1522-9645.

Becker, AE., Grinspoon, SK., Klibanski, A., & Herzog, DB. (1999). Eating disorders. *New England Journal of Medicine*, 340, 1092-1098. ISSN 1533-4406.

Birmingham, CL., & Beumont, P. (2004). *Medical management of eating disorders*. Cambridge University Press, ISBN 9780521727105, New York.

Bodí, V., Monmeneu, JV., Marín, F., Cortés, J., Llobet, E., García, A., Martínez, F., Ponce de León, JC., & Guardiola, M. Dispersión del intervalo QT en pacientes con insuficiencia cardíaca. Determinantes y valor pronóstico. *Revista Española de Cardiología*, 52, 563-569. ISSN 0300-8932.

Bonne, O., Bloch, M., & Berry, E. (1993). Adaptation to severe chronic hypokalaemia in anorexia nervosa: a plea for conservative management. *International Journal of Eating Disorders*, 13, 125-128, ISSN 0276-3478.

Browne, KF., Zipes, DP., Heger, JJ., & Prystowsky, EN. (1982). The influence of the autonomic system on the QT interval in man. *American Journal of Cardiology*, 50, 1099-1103. ISSN 0002-9149.

Casiero, D., & Frishman, WH. (2006). Cardiovascular Complications of Eating Disorders. *Cardiology in Review*, 14(5), 227-31. ISSN 1538-4683.

Clark, AF., & Wildenthal, K. (1986). Disproportionate reduction of actin synthesis in hearts of starved rats. *Journal of Biological Chemistry*, 261, 13168-13172. ISSN 1083-351X.

Conri, C., Roudaut, R., Ducloux, G., Fleury, B., & Moreu, F. (1989). Étude échocardiographique au cours de l'anorexie mentale. *La Presse Médicale*, 18, 806-808. ISSN 0755-4982.

Cooke, RA., Chambers, JB., Singh, R., Todd, GJ., Smeeton, NC., Treasure, J., & Treasure, T. (1994). QT interval in anorexia nervosa. *British Heart Journal*, 72, 69-73. ISSN 0007-0769.

De Cock, A., Mana, F., Velkeniers, B., & Urbain, D. (2006). Hypophosphatemia and refeeding: a corrective or a preventive attitude? *Acta Clinica Belgica*, 61, 134-137. ISSN 0001-5512.

De Simone, G., Scalfi, L., Galderisi, M., Celentano, A., Di Biase, G., Tammaro, P., Garofalo, M., Mureddu, GF., de Divitiis, O., & Contaldo, F. (1994). Cardiac abnormalities in young women with anorexia nervosa. *British Heart Journal*, 71, 287-292. ISSN 0007-0769.

Dec, GW., Biederman, J., & Hougen, TJ. (1987). Cardiovascular findings in adolescent inpatients with anorexia nervosa. *Psychosomatic Medicine*, 49(3), 285-290. ISSN 534-7796.

Diercks, DB., Fonarow, GC., Kirk, JD., Jois-Bilowich, P., Hollander, JE., Weber, JE., Wynne, J., Mills, RM., Yancy, C., & Peacock, WF. (2008). Illicit stimulant use in a United States heart failure population presenting to the emergency department (from the Acute Decompensated Heart Failure National Registry Emergency Module). *American Journal of Cardiology*, 102, 1216-1219. ISSN 0002-9149.

Facchini, M., Sala, L., Malfatto, G., Bragato, R., Redaelli, G., & Invitti, C. (2006). Low-K+ dependent QT prolongation and risk for ventricular arrhythmia in anorexia nervosa. *International Journal of Cardiology*, 106(2), 170-176. ISSN 0167-5273.

Fohlin, L. (1977). Body composition, cardiovascular and renal function in adolescent patients with anorexia nervosa. *Acta Paediatrica Scandinavica Supplement*, 268, 1- 20. ISSN 0300-8843.

Franzoni, F., Galetta, F., Cupisti, A., Rolla, M., Santoro, G., & Pentimone, F. (2003). Ultrasonic tissue characterization of the myocardium in anorexia nervosa. *Acta Paediatrica*, 92(3), 297-300. ISSN 0803-5253.

Galetta, F., Franzoni, F., Cupisti, A., Belliti, D., Prattichizzo, F., & Rolla, M. (2002). QT interval dispersion in young women with anorexia nervosa. *Journal of Pediatrics*, 140, 456-460. ISSN 00223476.

Galetta, F., Franzoni, F., Cupisti, A., Morelli, E., Santoro, G., & Pentimone, F. (2005). Early detection of cardiac dysfunction in patients with anorexia nervosa by tissue Doppler imaging. *International Journal of Cardiology*, 101(1), 33-37. ISSN 0167-5273.

Galetta, F., Franzoni, F., Prattichizzo, F., Rolla, M., Santoro, G., & Pentimone, F. (2003). Heart rate variability and left ventricular diastolic function in anorexia nervosa. *Journal of Adolescent Health*, 32(6), 416-421. ISSN 1054-139X.

Girola, A., Enrini, R., Garbetta, F., Tufano, A., & Caviezel, F. (2001). QT dispersion in uncomplicated human obesity. *Obesity Research*, 9, 71-77. ISSN 1071-7323.

Glasner-Edwards, S., Mooney, LJ., Marinelli-Casey, P., Hillhouse, M., Ang, A., & Rawson, R. (2011). Bulimia nervosa among methamphetamine dependent adults: association with outcomes three years after treatment. *Eating Disorders*, 19(3), 259-269. ISSN 1532-530X.

Goldberg, SJ., Comerci, GD., Feldman, L. (1988). Cardiac output and regional myocardial contraction in anorexia nervosa. *Journal of Adolescent Health Care*, 9, 15- 21. ISSN 1054-139X.

Gottdiener, JS., Gross, HA., Henry, WL., Borer, JS., & Ebert, MH. (1978). Effects of self-induced starvation on cardiac size and function in anorexia nervosa. *Circulation*, 58, 421-433.

Greenfeld, D., Mickey, D., Quinlan, DM., & Roloff, P. (1995) Hypokalemia in outpatients with eating disorders. *American Journal of Psychiatry*, 152, 60–63. ISSN 0002-953X.

Guidelines for the prevention and treatment of adult patients at risk of developing refeeding syndrome. Drug Therapy Guideline No. 46.00. (2007). In: *Refeeding Syndrome Guideline*. NSH.

Halmi, K. (2002). Physiology of anorexia nervosa and bulimia nervosa, In: *Eating disorders and obesity: A comprehensive handbook*, CB Fairburn & KD Brownell, 267-271, Guilford Press, ISBN 1-57230-688-2, New York.

Halmi, KA. (1983). Anorexia nervosa and bulimia. *Psychosomatics*, 24, 11. ISSN 1545-7206

Harris, JP., Kreipe, RE., & Rossbach, CN. (1993). QT prolongation by isoproterenol in anorexia nervosa. *Journal of Adolescent Health*, 14, 390-393. ISSN 1054-139X.

Hearing, SD. (2004). Refeeding syndrome. *British Medical Journal*, 328, 908-909. ISSN 09598138.

Higham, PD., & Campbell, RW. (1994). QT dispersion. *British Heart Journal*, 71, 508-510. ISSN 0007-0769.

Hill, JA., & Friedman, PL. (1997). Measurement of QT interval and QT dispersion. *Lancet*, 349, 894-895. ISSN 0140-6736.

Isner, JM., Roberts, WC., Heymsfield, SB., & Yager, J. (1985). Anorexia nervosa and sudden death. *Annals of Internal Medicine*, 102, 49-52. ISSN 0003-4819.

Jackmann, WM., Friday, KJ., Anderson, JL., Aliot, EM., Clark, M., & Lazzara, R. (1988). The long QT syndromes: a critical review, new clinical observations and a unifying hypothesis. *Progress in Cardiovascular Diseases*, 31, 115-172. ISSN 1532-8643.

Jaúregui I. (2006). *La imagen de una sociedad enferma. Anorexia, bulimia, atracones y obesidad,* Grafema, ISBN 9788493422592, Barcelona.

Johnson, GL., Humphries, LL., Shirley, PB., Mazzoleni, A., & Noonan, JA. (1986). Mitral Valve Prolapse in Patients With Anorexia Nervosa and Bulimia. *Archives of Internal Medicine,* 146(8), 1525-1529. ISSN 0039926.

Jovic, A., & Troskot, R. (1977). Recovery of atrial systolic function after pharmacological conversion of chronic atrial fibrillation to sinus rhythm: a Doppler echocardiography study. *Heart,* 77, 46-49. ISSN 1468-201X.

Karch, SB., Stephens, BG., & Ho, CH. (1999). Methamphetamine-related deaths in San Francisco: demographic, pathologic, and toxicologic profiles. *Journal of Forensic Sciences,* 44, 359-368. ISSN 00221198.

Katzman, DK., Kanbur, NO., & Steinegger, CM. (2010). Medical screening and management of eating disorders in adolescents, In: *The Oxford Handbook of Eating Disorders,* WS Agras, 267-291, Oxford University Press, ISBN 13: 9780195373622, New York:

Katzman, DK. (2005). Medical complications in adolescents with anorexia nervosa: A review of the literature. *International Journal of Eating Disorders,* 37, S52–S59. ISSN 0276-3478.

Kaye, W. (2009). Eating disorders: Hope despite mortal risk. *American Journal of Psychiatry,* 166, 1309-1311. ISSN 0002-953X.

Klump, K., Bulik, C., Kaye, W., Treasure, J., & Tyson, E. (2009). Eating disorders are serious mental illnesses. *International Journal of Eating Disorders,* 42, 97–103. ISSN 0276-3478.

Koh, E., Onishi, T., Morimoto, S., Imanaka, S., Nakagawa, H. & Ogihara, T. (1989). Clinical evaluation of hypokalaemia in anorexia nervosa. *Japanese Journal of Medicine,* 28, 6. ISSN 1881-123X.

Kohn, M., Golden, NH., & Shenker, IR. (1997). Cardiac arrest and delirium: presentations of the refeeding syndrome in severely malnourished adolescents with anorexia nervosa. *Journal of Adolescent Health,* 22, 239. ISSN 1054-139X.

Koschke, M., Boettger, MK., Macholdt, C., Schulz, S., Yeragani, VK., Voss, A., & Bär, KJ. (2010). Increased QT variability in patients with anorexia nervosa--an indicator for increased cardiac mortality? *International Journal of Eating Disorders,* 43(8), 743-750. ISSN 0276-3478.

Krantz, MJ., Donahoo, WT., Melanson, EL., & Mehler, PS. (2005). QT interval dispersion and resting metabolic rate in chronic anorexia nervosa. *International Journal of Eating Disorders,* 37(2), 166-170. ISSN 0276-3478.

Lesinskiene, S., Barkus, A., Ranceva, N., & Dembinskas, A. (2008). A meta-analysis of heart rate and QT interval alteration in anorexia nervosa. *World Journal of Biological Psychiatry,* 9(2), 86-91. ISSN 1814-1412.

Lombardi, F. (1998). The QT interval and QT dispersion: the smaller, the better! *European Heart* Journal, 19, 1279-1281. ISSN 1522-9645.

Lopez, JE., Yeo, K., Caputo, G., Buonocore, M., & Schaefer, S. (2009). Recovery of methamphetamine-associated cardiomyopathy predicted by late gadolinium enhanced cardiovascular magnetic resonance. *Journal of Cardiovascular Magnetic Resonance,* 11, 46. ISSN 0976647.

Lund, K., Perkiomaki, JS., Brohet, C., Elming, H., Zaidi, M., Torp-Pedersen, C., Huicuri, HV., Nygaard, H., & Kirstein Pedersen A. (2002). The prognostic accuracy of different

QT interval measures. *Annals of Nonivasive Electrocardiology*, 7, 10-16. ISSN 1542-474X.

Lupoglazoff, JM., Berkane, N., Denjoy, I., Maillard, G., Leheuzey, MF., Mouren-Simeoni, MC., & Casasoprana, A. (2001). Cardiac consequences of adolescent anorexia nervosa. *Archives des maladies du coeur et des* vaisseaux, 94(5), 494-498. ISSN 1261-694X.

Marinella, MA. (2005). Refeeding syndrome and hypophosphatemia. *Journal of Intensive Care Medicine*, 20, 155-159. ISSN 1525-1489.

Mars, DR., Anderson, NH., & Riggall, FC. (1982). Anorexia nervosa: Adisorder with severe acid-base derangements. *Southern Medical Journal*, 75, 1038. ISSN 0038-4348.

Mascolo, M., Chu, ES., Mehler, PS. (2011). Abuse and clinical value of diuretics in eating disorders therapeutic applications. *International Journal of Eating Disorders*, 44(3), 200-202. ISSN 0276-3478.

Meyers, DG., Starke, H., Pearson, PH., & Wilken, MK. (1986). Mitral valve prolapse in anorexia nervosa. *Annals of Internal Medicine*, 105, 384-386. ISSN 0003-4819.

Miller, KK., Grinspoon, SK., Ciampa, J., Hier, J., Herzog, D., & Klibanski, A. (2005). Medical findings in outpatients with anorexia nervosa. *Archives of Internal* Medicine, 165, 561-566. ISSN 0039926.

Miller, SJ. (2008). Death resulting from overzealous total parenteral nutrition: the refeeding syndrome revisited. *Nutrition in Clinical Practice*, 23, 166-171. ISSN 941-2452.

Mitchell, JE., Hatsukami, D., Eckert, ED., & Pyle, RL. (1985). Characteristics of 275 patients with bulimia. *American Journal of Psychiatry*, 42, 482–485. ISSN 0002-953X.

Mizuno, R., Fujimoto, S., Kimura, Y., Yoshioka, A., Nakano, H., & Dohi, K. (1998). Anorexia nervosa with left atrial failure. *Internal Medicine*, 37(10), 857-860. ISSN 1349-7235.

Mont, L., Castro, J., Herreros, B., Paré, C., Azqueta, M., Magriña, J., Puig, J., Toro, J., & Brugada, J. (2003). Reversibility of Cardiac Abnormalities in Adolescents With Anorexia Nervosa After Weight Recovery. *Journal of the American Academy of Child and Adolescent Psychiatry*, 42(7), 808-813. ISSN 1527-5418.

Moodie, DS., & Salcedo, E. (1983). Cardiac function in adolescents and young adults with anorexia nervosa. *Journal of Adolescent HealthCare*, 4(1), 9-14. ISSN 0197-0070.

Moodie, DS. (1987). Anorexia and the heart. Results of studies to assess effects. *Postgraduate Medicine*, 81, 46-8, 51-52, 55. ISSN 0032-5481.

Nahshoni, E., Weizman, A., Yaroslavsky, A., Toledano, A., Sulkes, J., & Stein, D. (2007). Alterations in QT dispersion in the surface electrocardiogram of female adolescents diagnosed with restricting-type anorexia nervosa. *Journal of Psychosomatic Research*, 62(4), 469-472. ISSN 0022- 3999.

Neumärker, KJ. (1997). Mortality and sudden death in anorexia nervosa. *International Journal of Eating Disorders*, 21, 205-212. ISSN 0276-3478.

Nutter, DO., Murray, TG., Heymsfield, SB., & Fuller, EO. (1979). The effect of chronic protein-calorie undernutrition in the rat on myocardial function and cardiac function. *Circulation Research*, 45, 144-152. ISSN 1524-4571.

O'Connor, G., & Goldin, J. (2011). The refeeding syndrome and glucose load. International Journal of Eating Disorders, 44(2), 182-185. ISSN 0276-3478.

Ong, YL., Checkley, SA., & Russell, GF. (1983). Suppression of bulimic symptoms with methylamphetamine. *British Journal of Psychiatry*, 143, 288-293. ISSN 1472-1465.

Palossy, B., & Oó, M. (1977). ECG alteration in anorexia nervosa. *Advances in Cardiology*, 19, 280-282. ISSN 0065-2326.

Panagiotopoulos, C., McCrindle, BW., Hick, K., & Katzman, DK. (2000). Electrocardiographic findings in adolescents UIT eating disorders. *Pediatrics*, 105, 1100-1105.

Pomeroy, C., & Mitchell, JE. (2002). Medical complications of anorexia nervosa and bulimia nervosa, In: *Eating disorders and obesity: A comprehensive handbook*, CG Fairburn & KD Brownell, 278-285, Guilford Press, ISBN 1-57230-688-2, New York.

Powers, PS., Schocken, DD., Feld, J., Holloway, JD., & Boyd, F. (1991). Cardiac function during weight restoration in anorexia nervosa. *International Journal of Eating Disorders*, 10, 521-530. ISSN 0276-3478.

Rajs, J., Rajs, E., & Lundman, T. (1986). Unexpected death in patients suffering from eating disorders. *Acta Psychiatrica Scandinavica*, 74, 587. ISSN 1600-0447.

Rieger, W., Brady, J., & Weisberg, E. (1978). Hematologic changes in anorexia nervosa. *American Journal of Psychiatry*, 135(8), 984-985. ISSN 0002-953X.

Roche, F., Barthélémy, JC., Mayaud, N., Pichot, V., Duverney, D., Germain, N., Lang, F., & Estour, B. (2005). Refeeding normalizes the QT rate dependence of female anorexic patients. *American Journal of Cardiology*, 95(2), 277-280. ISSN 0002-9149.

Roerig, JL., Steffen, KJ., Mitchell, JE., & Zunker, C. (2010). Laxative abuse: epidemiology, diagnosis and management. *Drugs*, 70(12), 1487-1503. ISSN 0012-6667.

Rome, ES., & Ammerman, S. (2003). Medical complications of eating disorders: An update. *Journal of Adolescent Health*, 33(6), 418-426. ISSN 1054-139X.

Root, TL., Pisetsky, EM., Thornton, L., Lichtenstein, P., Pedersen, NL., & Bulik, CM. (2010). Patterns of co-morbidity of eating disorders and substance use in Swedish females. *Psychological Medicine*, 40(1), 105-115. ISSN 0033-2917.

Rotellar, E. (1973). *ABC de los trastornos electrolíticos*, Jims, ISBN 847092175X, Barcelona.

Shamim, T., Golden, NH., Arden, M., Filiberto, L., & Shenker, IR. (2003). Resolution of vital sign instability: an objective measure of medical stability in anorexia nervosa. *Journal of Adolescent Health*, 32, 73-77. ISSN 1054-139X.

Sharp, CW., & Freeman, CPL. (1993). The medical complication of anorexia nervosa. *British Journal of Psychiatry*, 162, 452-462. ISSN 1472-1465.

Silvetti, MS., Magnani, M., Santilli, A., Di Liso, G., Diamanti, A., Pompei, E., Gambarara, M., Montecchi, F., & Ragonese, P. (1998). The heart of anorexic adolescents. *Giornale Italiano di Cardiologia*, 28(2), 131-139. ISSN 0046-5968.

Solomon, SM., & Kirbi, DF. (1990). The refeeding syndrome. A review. *Journal of Parenteral and Enteral Nutrition*, 14, 90-97. ISSN 0148-6071.

St John Sutton, M., Plappert, T., Crosby, L., Douglas, P., Mullen, J., & Reichek, N. (1985). Effects of reduced left ventricular mass on chamber architecture, load, and function: a study of anorexia nervosa. *Circulation*, 72, 991-1000. ISSN 0009-7322.

Sulllivan, PF. (1995). Mortality in anorexia nervosa. *American Journal of Psychiatry*, 152, 1073-1074. ISSN 0002-953X.

Swenne, I., & Larsson, PT. (1999). Heart risk associated with weight loss in anorexia nervosa and eating disorders: risk factors for QTc interval prolongation and dispersion. *Acta Paediatrica*, 88, 304-309. ISSN 0803-5253.

Swenne, I. (2000). Heart risk associated with weight loss in anorexia nervosa and eating disorders: electrocardiographic changes during the early phase of refeeding. *Acta Paediatrica*, 89(4), 447-452. ISSN 0803-5253.

Takimoto, Y., Yoshiuchi, K., Kumano, H., & Kuboki, T. (2006). Bulimia nervosa and abnormal cardiac repolarization. *Journal of Psychosomatic Research*, 60(1), 105-107. ISSN 0022- 3999.

Takimoto, Y., Yoshiuchi, K., Kumano, H., Yamanaka, G., Sasaki, T., Suematsu, H., Nagakawa, Y., & Kuboki, T. (2004). QT interval and QT dispersion in eating disorders. *Psychotherapy and Psychosomatics*, 73(5), 324-328. ISSN 1423-0348.

Tey, HL., Lim, SC., & Snodgrass, AM. (2005). Refeeding oedema in anorexia nervosa. *Singapore Medical Journal*, 46, 308-310. ISSN 0037-5675.

Thurston, J., & Marks, P. (1974). Electrocardiographic abnormalities in patients with anorexia nervosa. *British Heart Journal*, 36, 719-723. ISSN 0007-0769.

Toivonen, L. (2002). More light on QT interval measurement. *Heart*, 87, 193-194. . ISSN 1468-201X.

Tolnai, S., & von Althen, I. (1987). Calcium-dependent proteolysis in the myocardium rats subjected to stress. *Life Sciences*, 41, 1117-1122. ISSN 0024-3205.

Turnipseed, SD., Richards, JR., Kirk, JD., Diercks, DB., & Amsterdam, EA. (2003). Frequency of acute coronary syndrome in patients presenting to the emergency department with chest pain after methamphetamine use. *Journal of Emergency Medicine*, 24, 369-373. ISSN 0736- 4679.

Ulger, Z., Gürses, D., Ozyurek, AR., Arikan, C., Levent, E., & Aydoğdu, S. (2006). Follow-up of cardiac abnormalities in female adolescents with anorexia nervosa after refeeding. *Acta Cardiologica*, 61(1), 43-49. ISSN 0001-5385.

Vázquez, M., Olivares, JL., Fleta, J., Lacambra, I., & González M. (2003). Alteraciones cardiológicas en mujeres adolescentes con anorexia nerviosa. *Revista Española de Cardiología*, 56(7), 669-673. ISSN 0300-8932.

Walsh, JME., Wheat, ME., & Freund, K. (2000). Detection, Evaluation, and Treatment of Eating Disorders. *Journal of General Internal Medicine*, 15(8), 577-590. ISSN 1525-1497.

Warren, MP., & Vande Wiele, RL. (1973). Clinical and metabolic features of anorexia nervosa. *American Journal of Obstetrics & Gynecology*, 117, 435-49. ISSN 00029378.

Wijetunga, M., Bhan, R., Lindsay, J., & Karch, S. (2004). Acute coronary syndrome and crystal methamphetamine use: a case series. *Hawaii Medical Journal*, 63, 8-13. ISSN 0017-8594.

Yeo, KK., Wijetunga, M., Ito, H., Efird, JT., Tay, K., Seto, TB., Alimineti, K., Kimata, C., & Schatz, IJ. (2007). The association of methamphetamine use and cardiomyopathy in young patients. *American Journal of Medicine*, 120, 165-171. ISSN 0002- 9343.

# 10

# The Relationship with Food in Eating Disorders

Arlene Leite Nunes
*Universidade da Região de Joinville – Univille, Brazil*

## 1. Introduction

Lately, there has been an increasing movement of valorization of *having* in detriment of *being*, in which people are more valued by what they own than by what they are. This, associated with a transformation in the view of the human being and the world, where more and more the appearance has a higher importance, this trend is a fertile ground to increase eating disorders (ED), that are extremely connected to the super valued esthetic model from nowadays (Assumpção, 2004).

ED's constitute in a group of diseases that affect, mainly, female teenagers and young adults, producing strong biological, psychological and social damages and, consequently, propitiating the increase of morbidity and mortality rates in this population (Cordás, 2004).

In terms of magnitude and prevalence, ED's can be considered emergent diseases, typical from post-modern society. It is estimated that, every year, millions of people are affected by some kind of ED. From these, more than 90% are female teenagers (Castro & Goldstein, 1995; Cintra & Fisberg, 2004; Cordás, 2004; Dietz, 1990).

Because of this increasing incidence, these disorders demand prevention and treatment in all possible ways. They are one of the mental disorders that kill the most in the world - whether by malnutrition, heart problems and even suicide. In most cases, the person with the disorder does not consider herself sick, refusing, this way, any treatment, even with the appearance of comorbidities.

In the United States of America, according to Fischer et al. (1995), ED's constitute the third most prevalent non-transmissible chronic disease among teenagers, staying only behind obesity and asthma. Dietz (1990) confirms this claiming that anorexia nervosa (AN) and bulimia nervosa (BN) are among the most prevalent nutritional problems in teenagers. In Brazil, epidemiological data of prevalence of these diseases were not found, according to a revision hold. Nunes et al. (2003), claimed that there are not epidemiological researches about the prevalence of ED's, not only in Brazil, but also in all Latin America.

The two main kinds of ED's, classified as AN and BN, share common characteristics that make them similar, as well as characteristics of their own that make them different. However, the eating patterns that each person with an ED will develop is a singular phenomenon. The kind of food, the frequency of consumption, the ingested amount and other eating characteristics present a specific and individual behavior. It is necessary then, to face each person that manifests these disorders as a unique human being. It is essential to suspend preestablished conceptions about what it is or how an ED should manifest, trying to comprehend the person from her own experiences (Beumont, 2002; DSM-IV-TR, 2002).

The testimony of a twenty-three year old lady, ex-anorectic patient, in an interview to Juste (2004, pp.75) shows us the importance of comprehending ED's: *"What people need to understand is that AN, BN and binge eating are diseases and they need to be treated like that. A girl with AN needs to be taken serious as well as a girl with cancer must be. It's not under her power stop felling fat, vomiting, fasting, as well as it is not under the power of the girl with cancer make her tumor disappear"*.

This testimony is an example of how ED's have not been seen or comprehended with the seriousness they deserve yet, what raises difficulties and delays the search by medical, psychological and nutritional help, fundamental in the case of these disorders. The lack of knowledge and/or acceptance of these disorders as sickness harm even more the person with the disease, what might even lead her to death.

The awareness of some of these theoretical data, as well as the increase of the incidence of these disorders and their seriousness, caused the interest in making a deeper study about this theme. And we did it in a different way: meeting the teenagers with these disorders and listening to them, allowing them to speak.

We observe that, in general, researches have discussed these disorders from approaches that are sometimes interpretative and generalizable. We believe that it is important to comprehend and make a deeper study about ED's from their own experience. Therefore, the present study intended to allow teenagers with ED's to speak, trying to comprehend the meaning of the experience lived by them, attempting to answer the following question "What is the meaning of the experience lived by female teenagers with AN and BN, with emphasis in the aspects related to eating?".

In order to reach it, seven female teenagers were interviewed, all of them diagnosed with AN or BN, according to DSM-IV-TR (2002), they were being taken care in the city of Florianópolis, Santa Catarina, Brazil, aged between 17 to 20.

During the analysis of the interview (that followed the qualitative method, in a phenomenological approach), we tried to identify signification units, categorizing them to reach the general structure of the experience, extracting from this the structure of the lived experience.

This study was hold wishing to comprehend not only what happens in the body of a person, but also what happens in the emotional side: the human being is a whole, so he must be seen and comprehended as a whole. The human being is not just a being that feels. Or just a being that eats. He is a being that feels and eats. Therefore, it is not possible to study ED's isolated from the person that is suffering it, neither the person isolated from his environment. People with AN and BN do not usually have these behaviors only related to food, they relate this way toward life and feelings. They are a whole.

## 2. Methods

This research was characterized as a qualitative research, having a phenomenological approach focusing on the lived experience of female adolescents with ED's.

The research was held in Florianópolis (Santa Catarina, Brazil), involving seven female teenagers diagnosed with ED's, according to DSM-IV-TR (2002), of whom four of them with AN and three of them with BN, aged between 17 and 20 years old, attended in Joana de Gusmão Childhood Hospital, at Regional Medical Clinic and in private clinics. The interviews were conducted from March to May of 2006, until reaching the criterion of saturation, which is the phenomenon that occurs when a number of collected data fail to present something new to the phenomenological understanding (Mucchielli, 1991, as cited in Coppe, 2001).

The inclusion criteria in this study were age, sex and diagnosis of the disorder in question. In addition, participants should allow the understanding of the guiding question, take up the case, communicate without hindrance or limitations, have the consent of parents or guardians to participate and accept the condition of having their interviews recorded.

The interviews were conducted according to a predefined script, consisting of an objective part, trying to collect data for characterization of the interviewees, and a subjective part, with questions that varied according to the course of the interview, trying to capture the lived experience of the interviewees about the ED's. The interviews were conducted by the researcher, at the location where the adolescents received care, and lasted 37 minutes on average, ranging from 23 to 58 minutes.

The interviews were recorded and transcribed verbatim by the researcher. Confidentiality and anonymity were guaranteed for the content in order to preserve the identity of the interviewees who chose a cognomen to be used throughout the interview and signed a Free and Informed Consent Form for participation in this research.

After the transcription, to begin the analysis of the interviews, the steps outlined in the proposal of Amedeo Giorgi were followed (Amatuzzi, 1996; Coppe, 2001; França, 1989; Holanda, 2002, 2003; Martins & Bicudo, 2003; Moreira, 2002), divided in: 1) reading the interview transcripts, with the intention of capturing the sense in all, before the object of research, 2) new reading of the text, with the specific objective of discriminating signification units with a psychological perspective, capturing the moments of sensitive psychological change of each situation, 3) transformation of units in psychological language, in order to reach the most straightforward and explicit expressions as possible to the perceptions contained in the expression of the subject, 4) synthesis of all the signification units, turning them into a consistent report on the experience of the subject, reaching the structure of the experience.

Having finished this step, in order to continue with the analysis of the data, the following methodological paths described by Coppe (2001) were performed: 1) creation of a table containing the identification data of each participant, a description of the signification units and the psychological understanding of each one, allowing us to observe the specific synthesis of each participant, 2) categorization of the signification units in order to comprehend the overall structure of background, then extracting the structure of the lived experience, 3) development of a general synthesis, consisting of the analysis of all reports, to obtain an overview of the material. From this summary, we had a reflexive dialogue, linking empirical and theoretical content that guided our investigation.

The research project was approved by the Ethics Committee in Human Research of Universidade Federal de Santa Catarina[1] (Project No. 013/06) and of Joana de Gusmão Childhood Hospital (Project No. 016/2006).

## 3. The relationship with food in the perception of the adolescents

### 3.1 Brief profile of the adolescents interviewed

Table 1 presents a brief profile of the seven teenagers interviewed, trying to list some information considered important for a better understanding of the phenomenon studied.

The current age of the adolescents interviewed ranged between seventeen and twenty years old. The World Health Organization (WHO, 2005) considers adolescence the period between ten and nineteen years old, but some authors consider that there are many individual variations, influenced by both genetic and sociocultural factors that make age limits of the stages of adolescence approximate. Thus, for these authors, the increasing complexity of the teen phenomenon goes beyond the second decade since the technological development of Western society has led it to an extension of this transitional process. They therefore consider that the final or tardy phase can go up to twenty years of age (Chipkevitch, 1995; Vieira, 2002).

Regarding the type of ED and the treatment phase, of seven adolescents interviewed, four had diagnosis of AN (Gabriela, Carolina, Camila and Paula) and three had diagnosis of BN (Daniela, Helena and Julia). One of them is under treatment, but does not admit she has an ED and is in critical condition (Gabriela), three are under treatment and admit to having an ED (Daniela, Julia and Helena), two are under treatment in the recovery phase (Caroline and Paula) and one is not under treatment, and admits she has an ED and needs treatment (Camila).

| Cognomen | Current age (yrs) | Education | Type of ED | Phase of the ED |
|---|---|---|---|---|
| Daniela | 17 | High School | BN | Under treatment, admits she has ED |
| Gabriela | 17 | 2nd year High School | AN | Under treatment, does not admit she has ED (in critical condition) |
| Helena | 17 | 3rd year High School | BN | Under treatment, admits she has ED |
| Carolina | 19 | Incomplete Higher Education | AN | Under treatment, in recovery phase |
| Julia | 20 | High School | BN | Under treatment, admits she has ED |
| Camila | 20 | Incomplete Higher Education | AN | Stopped treatment, admits she has ED |
| Paula | 20 | Incomplete Higher Education | AN | Under treatment, in recovery phase |

Table 1. Brief profile of the adolescents

[1] Santa Catarina Federal University

With respect to the treatment location, one of them (Gabriela) came from Joana de Gusmão Childhood Hospital (HIJG), four (Daniela, Carolina, Julia and Camilla) from Regional Medical Clinic and two (Helena and Paula) from private clinics. Although the teenagers interviewed were found at the age between seventeen and twenty years old, the disorder manifested between eleven and eighteen years old, and the duration of disorder was between one and nine years. As to education, all of them are between high school and incomplete higher education.

Table 2 presents data related to the anthropometric characteristics of the interviewees, regarding height, weight and body mass index (BMI). One of the most common criteria used in ED's to determine whether a person is below the expected minimum weight is the BMI, calculated as weight in kilograms divided by height in meters$^2$ (DSM-IV-TR, 2002). Although this criterion presents some limitations, it is the most practical and the least costly one to analyze individuals and populations, and thus widely used (Conde & Monteiro, 2006).

According to the WHO (2006) classification criteria, a BMI below 18.50 kg/m$^2$ is already considered underweight, as rates between 17.00 and 18.49 kg/m$^2$ are considered mild underweight, between 16.00 and 16.99 kg/m$^2$ are considered moderate underweight and severe underweight rates below 16.00 kg/m$^2$. The rates between 18.50 and 24.99 kg/m$^2$ are considered normal weight, those above 25 kg/m$^2$, overweight. For diagnostic criteria of ED's, it is considered the BMI less than 17.50 kg/m$^2$ (DSM-IV-TR, 2002).

Based on the data from Table 2, one can see that, of the adolescents diagnosed with AN (Carolina, Paula, Camila and Gabriela), two (Gabriela and Carolina) continue with a BMI below 18.5 kg/ m$^2$, one (Paula ), who is in the process of recovery, presents a normal BMI, and one (Camilla) has no values for not having informed the current weight. Only one (Gabriela) remains below the BMI of 17.50 kg/m$^2$, the teenager who does not admit to having an ED, lying in a state considered serious.

Observing the minimum weight reached, we found that all four adolescents diagnosed with AN (Carolina, Paula, Camila and Gabriela) are found with a BMI below to what is considered normal (18.50 and 24.99 kg/m$^2$). In addition, three of them (Carolina, Paula and Gabriela) have BMI below 16.00 kg/m$^2$, and are thus in a state of severe underweight (WHO, 2006).

It is also interesting to note that when it comes to the maximum weight reached, none of the four (Carolina, Paula, Camila and Gabriela) exceeded the normal BMI, and the highest rate reached was of 23.01 kg/m$^2$, very far from the upper limit of normal weight (24.99 kg/m$^2$). In addition, one of the adolescents (Gabriela), even when she reached her maximum weight, was still below to what is considered normal and within the range of ED's. The maximum BMI reached was 17.35 kg/m$^2$.

By observing the weight loss of these adolescents diagnosed with AN, we found a drop of 20.83 (Carolina) to 44.74% (Gabriela) of weight, and the minimum amount of weight loss was 10 kg (Carolina ) and the maximum was 19 kg (Paula).

With respect to the adolescents diagnosed with BN (Daniela, Julia and Helena), we observed that all of them are currently with normal BMI, and only one (Daniela) had the BMI below normal, when considering the minimum weight. It is noteworthy that the teenager in question was initially diagnosed with AN, who later developed BN, thus confirming the data found in the literature that show that about 70% of people with BN maintain the weight within what is considered normal (Appolinário & Claudino, 2000; Cordás et al., 2004).

Concerning the maximum weight reached, only one of the adolescents (Julia) reached a rate considered overweight (above 25 kg/m²), while the others (Daniela, Helena) had, as well as the adolescents diagnosed with AN, normal BMI, also quite far from the upper limit of normal weight, and the maximum rate achieved was 21.63 kg/m², lower than the one found in the maximum rate of anorexia.

Regarding the weight loss of these adolescents diagnosed with BN, we found a drop of 9.26 (Helena) to 25.76% (Julia) weight, being that the minimum amount of weight loss was 5 kg (Helena) and the maximum was 17 kg (Julia), confirming that there is a significantly greater weight loss in AN rather than in BN (Cordás et al., 2004).

| Cognomen | Height* (m) | Current weight* (kg) | Minimum weight* (kg) | Maximum weight* (kg) | Weight* loss (kg) | Weight* loss (%) | Current BMI* (kg/m²) |
|---|---|---|---|---|---|---|---|
| Daniela | 1.62 | 52 | 46 | 54 | 8 | 14.81 | 19.81 |
| Gabriela | 1.48 | 38.3 | 21 | 38 | 17 | 44.74 | 17.48 |
| Helena | 1.58 | 54 | 49 | 54 | 5 | 9.26 | 21.63 |
| Carolina | 1.59 | 45 | 38 | 48 | 10 | 20.83 | 17.80 |
| Julia | 1.52 | 52.5 | 49 | 66 | 17 | 25.76 | 22.72 |
| Camila | 1.51 | does not know | 37 | 50 | 13 | 26.00 | ------- |
| Paula | 1.56 | 48 | 37 | 56 | 19 | 33.93 | 19.72 |

* Data on weight and height were reported by adolescents
** BMI was calculated based on the anthropometric data reported

Table 2. Anthropometric characteristics of the adolescents

### 3.2 The content of the interviews and signification units

With respect to the guiding question of how female adolescents with ED's perceive and experience their relationship with food, the analysis of the interviews brought out nine signification units, namely: what food represents, eating habits, foods that are no longer eaten, food that came to be consumed, the consumption of soft drinks, food choices, meal composition, the family's eating habits and healthy food.

#### 3.2.1 What food represents

The term food, in the vernacular sense, means: "1. What you eat or is suitable for eating. 2. Action of eating" (Ferreira, 1993, pp.131). But for the teenagers interviewed in this research, in most cases, food had a very different meaning, referring to something negative, as we found in the reports below:

"*Hum, well, torture.*" (Daniela)

"*It represented fear, so I was afraid.*" (Carolina)

"*I think it is a very bad thing.*" (Gabriela)

"*Escape, a decadence, drugs.*" (Helena)

For some of the teenagers interviewed, the food was an obligation, something that would take their freedom, described as follows:

"*It is necessary, mandatory, but I did not want it to be like this.*" (Julia)

"*If I were not forced to eat, perhaps it might be good.*" (Gabriela)

"*I feel freer when I do not eat.*" (Helena)

Others commented on the positive side of food:

"*While that is good. [...] The foods that you like.*" (Daniela)

"*Food that makes you feel good. [...] The food is good for me today, it's tasty.*" (Carolina)

With a view to what food represents to these teenagers, we can observe their eating habits.

### 3.2.2 Eating habits

The development of eating habits is influenced by several factors - physiological, psychological, sociocultural, economic - and occurs as the children grow, until the moment when consciously and independently they will choose the food that will be part of their diet. While a child, usually parents determine their food, but as they go to school and socialize with other children, they get to know other foods, preparations and habits (Bandeira et al., 2000).

During adolescence, due to the rapid physical growth and development, there is an increased need for nutrients, but at this stage there is also a change in food preferences, which puts these individuals at a nutritional risk group (Bandeira et al., 2000).

In the interviews that made up this study, we observed, from the adolescents, a concern with food control, both alone and with nutritional counseling, as described below:

"*Oh, now I'm going to eat, not now, I won't eat now, I'll wait a little longer, I have to wait some hours to eat breakfast, some hours and I'll have lunch, later in the afternoon I'll have a snack.*" (Camila)

"*Today I see that I was eating all wrong.*" (Carolina)

"*But I eat everything in the right quantity. [...] As I have nutritional counseling with a nutritionist I eat all kinds of food.*" (Paula)

"*So, you know, everything is under control. [...] I am on a diet with a nutritionist now.*" (Helena)

Some of their reports showed that they intended to adhere to a diet considered healthy by them:

"*I'm not a fan of vegetables or greens, or anything like this, I don't eat them. [...] Eating something lighter, though that's not what I like, you see!*" (Daniela)

"*I simply don't eat as much fat. [...] I like to eat fruits, watermelon. [...] I always eat fresh sandwiches (when I eat at the mall).*" (Gabriela)

*"Now I'm really on a diet [...] My meals were kind of reduced. [...] I eat enough fruit as well. [...] I am vegetarian so I have to eat soy and a lot of small protein bars."* (Helena)

However, this food considered healthy, is not always preferred by these adolescents, as shown by the following reports:

*"I was not eating food, I was eating bread, that's one thing I did not use to eat before, so. [...] I'm eating carbs more often now [...] I like pasta, junk, snacks."* (Daniela)

*"Like, I used to eat chocolate. [...] Sometimes I felt like eating a truffle and I did, but without feeling guilty."* (Carolina)

*"But I really like sweets, then I can eat sweets too, I can eat a small chocolate bar a day."* (Helena)

*"When I was little I used to eat a lot (fast food)."* (Gabriela)

It is also interesting to note that many of these teenagers interviewed stressed the fact that they are eating, according to the excerpts below:

*"But I'm eating, I'm not quitting food."* (Camila)

*"I eat everything."* (Gabriela)

*"But I eat [...] I eat everything I like, such as rice and beans every day."* (Paula)

*"Beats me, I eat."* (Helena)

*"I ate bread, I ate meat, rice, everything."* (Gabriela)

To proceed with the subject related to food, we may observe then, the foods that are no longer consumed by the adolescents interviewed.

### 3.2.3 Foods that are no longer eaten

Nutrition and diet play an important role in the development and maintenance of ED's, and should thus be taken into account during the treatment plans of such disorders.

People with these disorders have severe dietary restrictions, eating patterns and wrong eating habits due to a number of factors such as myths and false beliefs, feelings of incompetence to deal with food, fear of putting on weight (Alvarenga & Larino, 2002).

The main foods that are no longer consumed by the adolescents interviewed were those they considered "junk" - chocolate, for example - regardless of whether they liked it or not:

*"Chocolate. I like it so much, but I'm not eating. Mostly junk, like this, you know, I limit. [...] Candy, gum, chocolate."* (Camila)

*"Chocolate. [...] Popcorn, stuff like that, no way."* (Carolina)

*"I do not like them today (chocolate, candy, potato chips)."* (Gabriela)

Besides these, other foods such as bread, fruit and meat are no longer consumed, and these along with fried food have even been linked to negative points by some of the teenagers, as these reports show:

*"I do not eat fried food. I still feel sick of fries."* (Carolina)

*"I had stopped eating red meat. [...] I stopped eating fried food. [...] I keep thinking it will not do any good for my body."* (Paula)

*"I had stopped eating bread."* (Daniela)

*"I stopped eating fruit."* (Julia)

In ED's, the relationship with food is so distorted that sometimes it becomes difficult to even describe what they stopped eating, as it happened to this adolescent:

*"I can not say that I stopped eating a lot , I lost track of what I eat [...]. It looks like it's just food, there isn't much difference, [...] so I don't know exactly what I can tell you that I stopped eating, what I started eating, it's getting a little complicated."* (Helena)

In the study by Dunker & Philippi (2003), the types of food that were least consumed were soda, chocolate, pasta and potato chips, and those that they least liked were vegetables, meat and fat, consistent with what was found in our research about what was no longer consumed, with the exception of soda. We describe below, the type of food that started to be consumed.

### 3.2.4 Food that came to be consumed

Looking at the most consumed foods in the study by Dunker & Philippi (2003) among the students with symptoms of AN, we found the presence of some special foods, which by their own qualities , reflect the concern in making a balanced diet, having mainly a variety of fruits and vegetables. In the interviews of this survey we also found the approval of consumption of vegetables by some of the teenagers, whether they like it or not, as shown by the statements below:

*"Although I don't like them (vegetables), I have to learn to love them."* (Daniela)

*"Vegetable is one thing I learned to eat that I don't, I don't, I never realy liked it."* (Carolina)

*"One thing I started to eat that I didn't use to eat much is vegetable."* (Paula)

One of the adolescents surveyed also reported an increased consumption of sweets, as described below:

*"I started to eat more sweets"* (Helena)

In addition to these foods, the consumption of soda is also notable in the case of adolescents with ED's, as will be seen below.

### 3.2.5 The consumption of soft drinks

Excessive consumption of soft drinks by teenagers is a common problem across the globe (Bandeira et al., 2000), also occurring in adolescents with ED's, as noted in the statements below:

*"I woke up at 6 o'clock, then I didn't eat anything, I only had soda, my other addiction... So, it's normal, I didn't eat anything else. [...] I wake up and play on my computer, I'm always on my computer, you know, then I have a soda, anything, and it is hard for me to eat, you know."* (Daniela)

"*And a lot of Coke. I drink a lot of soda. By and large, two liters per day. In the morning if I wake up in the morning the first thing I do is drinking a Coke. At dawn, if I wake up and I'm thirsty, I have a Coke. [...] I don't drink water, only in the Coke. It's very rare that I drink water. Only when I take some medicine.*" (Julia)

We found that soft drink, for these teenagers, sometimes end up replacing meals or water itself, becoming thus one of the food choices made by adolescents. This process of food choice will be observed in the sequence.

### 3.2.6 Food choices

Several factors may be involved in the choice of food, both from signals originated in the brain or on the outer edge when out of habit (Bacaltchuk & Appolinário, 2005). In our study, some of the factors mentioned by the adolescents interviewed for the food choices were the amount of calories or what is less filling, as described below:

"*Usually I'm watching the calories. [...] I'm eating a snack, but I'm watching the calories right there, it's automatic.*" (Daniela)

"*Before, I used to look for less fattening food.*" (Julia)

"*I know what is more caloric, what is less caloric, so when I think I'm a little overweight, I know what I can eat.*" (Paula)

"*On the following day I do something else to eat, you know, not to eat the same again. [...] Not to get fat.*" (Camila)

In a study conducted by Lobera & Ríos (2009), where they analyzed the diets chosen by forty-four anorectic patients and thirty-four people without ED, they also found that anorectic patients have a lower fat intake than healthy people, and also the content of carbohydrates, proteins and fats were lower among these people.

Other factors mentioned about their food choices were the cravings, flavor, or taste, as testimonials below:

"*If I feel like eating something, I do, but then I feel guilty afterwards [...] I eat because I feel like eating it.*" (Julia)

"*I choose what I eat [...] according to my will.*" (Paula)

"*Mostly because of the taste too.*" (Daniela)

"*There is taste, then, there's that pleasant feeling of eating it.*" (Carolina)

Another food choice mentioned by the adolescents interviewed were salads and fruits, what matches with the study of Lobera & Ríos (2009), that showed that vegetables were chosen more often by these patients:

"*Sometimes I do not like salad so much, but I used to eat more salad, and less food.*" (Camila)

"*I'd eat a lot of fruit, I would drink juice. [...] I could eat bread, but not rice.*" (Gabriela)

"*My food choice is salad, I'm a vegetarian, I like salad and sweets. I don't know, I could eat it all day long.*" (Helena)

During episodes of binge eating that occur in ED's it is possible to happen considering food choices when these episodes are planned. But in most cases, they are not planned, so there is no choice of foods to be eaten (Devoraes & Fagundes, 2005), which can be confirmed by the testimonies below:

"*Oh, I don't choose (compulsion),whatever is there I eat, you know. [...] It is usually what I love.*" (Julia)

"*In binge, [...] that's when I usually eat, I'm hungry, so I'll eat it.*" (Helena)

One of the professionals needed in a team that works with people with ED's is a nutritionist. His role is closely linked with the factor of food choices, since the nutritional advice is important to clarify and demystify inappropriate beliefs as well as enabling the establishment of a proper relationship with food (Alvarenga & Larino, 2002). The statements below show the influence of this specialist in food choices on some of the adolescents interviewed:

"*The nutritionist who chooses. She also lets me choose, but I prefer her to choose because it is difficult, I don't know what I like.*" (Gabriela)

"*We (she and the nutritionist) tried to make a balanced menu, in the first month I followed a menu strictly, later we started adapting to make some modifications.*" (Paula)

"*I didn't know how to do this before I went to the nutritionist, I didn't know how to eat and stop feeling hungry.*" (Helena)

We can not unlearn that food choices are complex decisions related to social conditions, cultural traditions and irrational elements, and that eating is also a social activity and food is an emotional issue (Alvarenga, 2004). Furthermore, since the beginning of our lives, food is intertwined with emotions, symbolisms and socioeconomic and cultural influences. Thus, eating infers, for sure, in making choices. But it also involves establishing relationships, relating or not with models and values from the family or others , adapting well or poorly to the established standards and living with habits, schedules and several lifestyles (Eisenstein et al., 2000).

To carry on the issue of food choice, we describe the meals made by the adolescents interviewed, as well as the meal composition.

### 3.2.7 Meal composition

According to the Guia para Escolha de Alimentos[2] (Philippi, 1999), the eating habits of an individual should be distributed in six meals, arranged as follows: breakfast, morning snack, lunch, afternoon snack, dinner and evening snack. In our survey, the number of meals ranged from 3 to 8 a day. According to Philippi et al. (2000), breakfast should be between 6 and 9 o'clock and make up 25% of total calories of the day. The teenagers interviewed described their breakfast as follows:

"*In the morning I rarely have breakfast, I always wake up late to leave, or something like that, and when I sleep late I skip to lunch.*" (Daniela)

[2] Guide for the Choice of Food

"*I wake up by noon, I can not wake up early, I wake up and go straight to lunch.*" (Julia)

"*Oh, there's bread (one, one and a half rolls), coffee (one cup), normally like this.*" (Camila)

"*For breakfast I have a slice of bread with jam and light cheese and chocolate milk, coffee with milk.*" (Carolina)

"*There are crackers, bread, fruit and milk.*" (Gabriela)

"*For breakfast I always drink lots of coffee with milk, [...] toast with fruit, or a fruit, or yogurt.*" (Paula)

"*When I'm not on a diet, I have yogurt and a fruit. But now that I'm on a diet, during this last week I can choose between yogurt or a fruit. Just for me to lose weight.*" (Helena)

Thus, we observed that breakfast for the teens surveyed consists of food considered healthy. The mid-morning snack, also recommended, is not always done, but when it happens, it is also composed of food considered healthy, as evidenced by the statements below:

"*Then, sometimes, by 10 o'clock I have some light yogurt, still, everything is light, light yogurt.*" (Carolina)

"*Now I don't have morning snack anymore, I have it all together, I used to have it but now I have everything together.*" (Gabriela)

"*It's a fruit and some yogurt, or a cup of coffee and two pieces of toast, or a small cereal bar, then it depends on if my weight is okay, it depends.*" (Paula)

"*After breakfast I eat a fruit, or a cheese roll during the recess.*" (Helena)

Lunch should happen between 11 a.m. and 1 p.m., constituting 35% of total calories of the day - the largest meal of the day (Philippi et al., 2000). With respect to foods consumed for lunch by the adolescents surveyed, we highlight the following statements:

"*Usually I make noodles, [...] I have a bagel or something like that.*" (Daniela)

"*Rice, pasta, pretty normal food like that, you know, like meat, but if it's fatty then I have chicken, everything.*" (Julia)

"*But I eat whatever is there, like, beans, rice, meat, potatoes. [...] About three spoonfuls of rice, a little bit of beans. Just a little. A little bit of meat. [...] A little as well. Potatoes, a little, too.*" (Camila)

"*About three spoonfuls of rice, beans, then meat or chicken or fish and vegetables.*" (Carolina)

"*A fruit. [...] I am forced to eat meat, rice and beans. And a plate of salad.*" (Gabriela)

"*Brown rice, then I have fish once a week, [...] then once or twice a week I eat red meat, grilled steak, grilled chicken, roast chicken, beans and salad, a lot of salad.*" (Paula)

"*I have, I don't know, bread.*" (Helena)

These meals are often prepared by the adolescents themsemves, and this is a fairly common practice in ED's, and this was verified in their statements:

"*Usually I make noodles, my mom makes food, but I don't like to eat that.*" (Daniela)

*"There was some time that I wanted to prepare my lunch to take care of everything so that it was not fatty, or anything that would make me put on weight."* (Julia)

*"I usually do that (prepare the meals)."* (Camila)

Some of the teenagers interviewed "got rid of" food or made excuses for not eating, as shown by the following fragments:

*"Sometimes I don't have lunch."* (Daniela)

*"I'm not hungry ... I don't want to eat now."* (Julia)

*"I used to say I was not hungry."* (Paula)

*"I should prepare a plate of food, but I don't have time for that."* (Helena)

*"When I was in crisis, sometimes, I had lunch earlier, then I would be far away, or sometimes I didn't eat anything, I would give my food to the dog."* (Camila)

*"At that time I would hide it, I used to run away, I would find a way, I would go to the living room, I pretended to be watching television, I used to put little food on the plate, I would put it in the garbage, or would give it to the dog."* (Paula)

Otherwise, the food consumed - when consumed - was mostly in small amounts, as noted in the statements below:

*"I don't eat much at lunch. [...] It's the time I eat the least."* (Julia)

*"Oh, I eat very little, a little bit, like this."* (Camila)

The afternoon snack, when they have it, as well as in the morning, also consists of food considered healthy by the adolescents interviewed, according to their reports:

*"Sometimes I eat one thing or another. [...] A snack."* (Daniela)

*"In the afternoon I really don't eat anything. [...] It's very rare for me to eat anything in the afternoon."* (Julia)

*"As I work, I have lunch, then when I come back, I drink coffee."* (Camila)

*"I eat at 3 o'clock, before, I didn't use to eat anything, fruit salad or anything like that. Now I eat cookies, or something whole wheat and light, or Social Club™. [...] In college she (nutritionist) said that I had to eat a little bit, and then I drink coffee with milk. [...] Then at 6 o'clock I get home and have a milk and Ovaltine™ shake, which the reason is that the shake had to be placed in my meal because some time ago I lost (weight) again, a month ago."* (Carolina)

*"Milk, juice, crackers and fruit."* (Gabriela)

*"In the afternoon snack I repeat the morning snack, I make something. [...] At the 6 o'clock snack too, or I do the breakfast reversed."* (Paula)

*"There are two snacks, it's a small snack and a regular snack. I can put it all together when I'm on PMS, I can put it all together and eat, but then I don't know, fruit, yogurt, cookie, or bread, may be, there's a variety, like this. Then in a controlled amount."* (Helena)

Dinner should happen between 7 p.m. and 9 p.m., comprising, as breakfast, 25% of total calories of the day (Philippi et al., 2000). With respect to foods consumed for dinner, the following were the testimonies of the adolescents:

"*At night I have a simple snack. [...] Oh, bread, sometimes I add a sausage or margarine, something like that and bread, I don't eat a lot of stuff.*" (Daniela)

"*I usually eat wheat bread with cheese, ham, ricotta cheese and lettuce and tomato. It's healthier. [...] Usually I eat something breaded or a sandwich during break at school, or a bowl of açaí with banana.*" (Julia)

"*Then later at night I eat an apple or a cracker.*" (Camila)

"*Then, at 8 pm, when I have dinner, I eat a roll, salad with white cheese or with a chicken patty.*" (Carolina)

"*For dinner I have only milk and fruits.*" (Gabriela)

"*For dinner I make a sandwich, turkey breast, reduced-fat cheese or cottage cheese, bread, and maybe light bread or regular bread, salad, a cup of coffee, a cup of yogurt.*" (Paula)

"*Then I have dinner, usually soy burger, I need to eat it one a day.*" (Helena)

It is also recommended to have a third snack, commonly called supper, composing, like the other snacks, 5% of total calories of the day (Philippi et al., 2000). Some of the teenagers interviewed have this meal, as described in the statements below:

"*She (nutritionist) recommended that I eat supper, sometimes I eat it, sometimes I don't, because it is an apple or any fruit.*" (Carolina)

"*Supper is also milk and fruit.*" (Gabriela)

"*And for supper usually a cup of coffee with skimmed milk, a banana, it's always something like that.*" (Paula)

Looking at the descriptions of these meals made by the adolescents interviewed, we found that they actually have a very big concern in maintaining a healthy diet, they eat food that they consider healthy, although sometimes in small quantities or even skipping some meals. Two factors stood out about the weekends. First, waking up late and spending the rest of the day eating "crap", even though many of these teenagers interviewed said that they don't eat, changing thus the pace of all other days of the week, as evidenced by the statements below:

"*Then on Sunday I usually sleep until very late, sometimes it's even because of the medication I've been taking, so I sleep the whole day, I wake up at night. [...] I have a soda, [...] I just nibble something. [...] Sunday is a day that I don't eat. [...] A cracker.*" (Daniela)

"*But on Sunday I wake up late, sometimes I sleep until 3 pm on Sunday, then I wake up, I don't eat, otherwise I just eat any crap. [...] Ice cream or any dessert that is in the fridge or a piece of cake, or something like that, then at night I usually have a snack, Sunday is the day that I eat the least.*" (Julia)

On the other hand, a second factor stands out: some of the teenagers interviewed about their eating habits on the weekend claim to overeat or feel hungrier for they are idle, as shown by these statements:

"*Saturday I eat the most, [...] I wake up at noon, then I have lunch, then I spend the whole Saturday afternoon doing nothing, so I eat everything that comes up.*" (Julia)

"*Over the weekend I'm hungrier because there's nothing to do, I don't work.*" (Camila)

"*On the weekends if I stay at home, I end up getting upset, I end up eating too much.*" (Helena)

In addition to the meals, there are also the so-called "extras" that would be eating anything that is caloric and different than what they are used to eating in their daily diet , as exemplified in the story of this adolescent:

"*Jaque ( nutritionist) kind of forced me to eat an 'extra' during the week as well. An extra, anything like this, a piece of cake, or more over the weekend. [...] But it's so tricky, I always feel kind of guilty.*" (Carolina)

Once observed these meals contents, we will describe, then the perceptions of these teenagers about the eating habits of their families, as well as the influence of these habits on the eating habits of these adolescents. It is noteworthy to stress that the opposite may also occur: the eating habits of adolescents influencing the family's eating habits.

### 3.2.8 The family's eating habits

From birth, parents have a fundamental role in the development of the eating habits of their children, either by the type of food they offer to their children, or through the food concepts that they express, and all these factors influence the formation of eating habits of children . The way the family organizes their diet - the type, quantity and quality of food - may constitute a risk factor for developing ED's. But in addition, another factor that plays a central role is the relationship that the family establish with food (Cobelo, 2004).

According to a study hold by Prieto (2011), in which fifty-seven relatives of patients with ED participated, the feeding of relatives of these patients with ED wouldn´t be healthy either, being in general hypocaloric. The study also showed that when the feed of the patient is compared to the feed of the relative, not big differences are found. In our study most of the adolescents interviewed also found their way to eat similar to their families', as these statements show:

"*It is (the family's eating habits similar to hers). A lot of fat, my father is more concerned, you know, but my mother is not, well, she is not fat, but she feels like eating the same things as I do, a lot of pasta, she can't eat only one roll of bread for the afternoon snack, she's always overeating, and sometimes she also spends hours without eating, she eats very little, well, three meals, she wakes up in the morning, she does not eat in the morning, she eats lunch, she eats more for lunch, then she drinks coffee at 6 o'clock, she goes up to 6 p.m. with no food, and then at night she eats something, always a snack, some crap.*" (Julia)

"*My brother has always been into martial arts and this stuff, then he's already been into healthier food, as well, but he eats a lot, he eats a fried egg every day, but he makes a lot of physical activity then. [...] Back home everybody liked fried food like, my mom liked fried chicken. [...] Before we used to eat a lot of crap, like, yellow cheese, [...] my mother has always been a big fan of chocolate, sweets like this, always, always. [...] My father has always been into a more healthy diet, like, his plate, more than half of it is made of salad [...] he's been always like this, into fruits and lots of greens. I have always been interested in fruits, but I always tried to stay away from vegetables and salad, like, it would never be on my plate and now it is. [...] Sometimes my mother makes it for my father, because my father likes fried fish, and fried chicken."* (Carolina)

*"I think it was similar (the family's eating habits similar to hers), but it's not now. I try other ways, I try to eat as little as possible. [...] My family is descendant of Italians, then they're very into pasta and that stuff, so I try not to care much for it. But at home everyone likes to eat. The only problem is that as everybody likes to eat, they also love to compare, they say, 'Oh, because I eat salad, I eat this and I eat that which is good'. Everyone wants to show off saying they have the best nutrition, healthier, [...] I think that everyone at home has an aesthetic concern. [...] My mom's a little overweight, a little bit, she has hypothyroidism, which makes it worse."* (Helena)

Under a different aspect, but still on the same topic, some of the teenagers interviewed found their families' eating habits similar to their own way, differing only in quantity, as you can see in the statements below:

*"Aham (the family's eating habits similar to hers). [...] The amount does not. [...] My sister occasionally eats dinner , my grandmother has dinner, my uncle who lives with us too, but I kind of eat this little (I eat little, only a small fruit)."* (Camila)

*"Yes (the family's eating habits similar to hers).[...] No. It's not (eating less and less)."* (Gabriela)

*"It is. It's much like this (the family's eating habits similar to hers). My family always had the habit of eating lots of vegetables, having meals together at the table and, during the same hours. The only habits that they don't have and I adhered to are the snacks, you know."* (Paula)

Some of them also reported that their current eating habits were influenced by the family's eating habits:

*"Yes (the way her mother eats influenced her eating habits). Yes, because then I eat whatever she prepares. Then I ended up eating the same things as she does. I eat what she brings from the bakery, then I end up having the same eating habits as hers."* (Julia)

*"Aham (the way her family eats influenced her eating habits). [...] Like eating, always having bread for breakfast, you know, for lunch we always have rice, beans, you know, some meat. [...] It is more the type of food, the quantity, I've never been into eating too much. [...] They eat well, you know."* (Camila)

*"For breakfast I always have lots of coffee with milk, as it is one thing I really like, I think it's one thing I inherited from my mother."* (Paula)

There was, moreover, a report that according to the adolescent, her eating habits influenced the family's, making it healthier:

*"I kind of encouraged, forced, you know, my whole family to eat more baked, or broiled food. [...] My brother says that I helped to improve the nutrition of the whole family because I kind of encouraged everyone to eat healthier things, you know, I always prepare the salad and I do it myself, I do not let my mother make much fried food. [...] Today, because of me she (mother) kind of avoids having much fried food, she learned to eat salad. [...] Today I pick on her to have salad, I always prepare a lot of salad, then everyone, kind of, ended up helping one another. [...] Then the whole family helps one another so that nobody eats fried food. [...] I always make it for me and they end up eating, you know, there's no other way, broiled fish or grilled fish, so it's been really good, pretty good."* (Carolina)

Only one of the teenagers interviewed said she believes that her way of eating was not influenced by the dietary habits of her family, as described below:

"*No, I don't think so (the way her family eats influenced her eating habits). I used to eat everything when I was little, like, vegetables. [...] In my mom's opinion I used to eat everything that was brought to me.*" (Daniela)

And only one of the teenagers interviewed said she considers her eating habits different from her family's, as testimony below:

"*Aham (her family eating habitits is different from hers). [...] My father usually eats lunch alone in the living room, he likes to watch TV and this stuff, so then I have lunch with my mother. It's so fast, we don't even have time to look at each other.*" (Daniela)

The family's relationship with food is important because the timing of meals goes beyond its nutritional aspect. It is a time to share, beyond food, information, daily activities, messages, etc.. (Cobelo, 2004). According to Cordás et al. (1998), eating and emotions are closely related, so meals should be happen, whenever possible, with all family members, with set hours and a friendly and pleasant atmosphere.

### 3.2.9 Healthy food

To be considered a healthy diet it is necessary to be present a variety of foods according to the dietary habits, food availability and nutritional needs of each individual. It should also be considered the calorie intake and the inclusion of all macro and micronutrients in adequate quantities and proportions (Philippi & Alvarenga, 2004).

According to the Ministry of Health of Brazil (Brasil, MS, 2005) a healthy diet should be based on "dieting practices taking social and cultural significance of food as a basic conceptual foundation", having the main characteristics: the respect and appreciation to the culturally identified dieting practices, since food has different cultural meanings; access guarantee, taste and affordability, because contrary to what has been socially constructed, a healthy diet is not expensive and should be tasty, it is varied: so it can provide different nutrients that the body needs; it is colorful, to ensure the variety especially in terms of vitamins and minerals, it is harmonious, with regard to quantity and quality of food consumed to the extent of appropriate nutrition considering the cultural, affective and behavioral aspects, and it is safe: from the physical chemistry and biological contamination standpoint and possible health risks.

In the description of the adolescents interviewed, the concept of healthy food seemed to us much more restricted. This is how they described it:

"*Not much exaggerated, but not very restrained. [...] Eating a little of everything, at the set hours.*" (Daniela)

"*Eating fruit, which I don't do, maintaining set hours to eat, practicing exercise to contribute with the diet, and eating a little of each food group, you know, a little carbohydrate, a little of everything, so that..., to balance the diet very well, you know. I think it's essential, but it is the most difficult thing to do as well.*" (Julia)

"*Eating, but not eating too much, of course, avoiding lots of fried food, but eating modestly the things that you like, like, I eat potato chips, but only on the weekend, I eat chocolate, but only a little bit. But not quitting the things you like. But that's something I don't do.*" (Camila)

*"One that makes you feel good about yourself. Not only so, what's the use for a woman, who wants to lose weight, but the doctor tells her no, you will not lose weight because you have to eat this and this and that for days. Then the woman is going to be unhappy. This is not healthy. She will have that diet, her body will be healthy, but not her mind, which will not be satisfied with her . [...] Oh, I don't know, one that makes me not feel hungry. That's what I wanted. But yeah, I'm working on it."* (Helena)

We see thus that these adolescents have an understanding of the principles of a balanced diet, although in most cases, they have attitudes that do not correspond to this understanding, since, as it was previoulsy seen, eating goes beyond nutritional dimensions, also involving emotional factors, being both socioeconomically and culturally influenced (Alvarenga, 2004).

## 4. Discussion

In recent years, AN and BN have become important topics of discussion in the Brazilian and world media. Characters in soap operas of the main open TV channel in Brazil carrying pictures of AN and BN, headlines from the covers of magazines, newspapers and central theme of several shows, both on TV and radio, contributed to the increased audience flow.

This whole discussion brings a positive aspect: the dissemination of information about ED's by these vehicles of mass communication, because the earlier one detects an ED, the greater the chances of a good prognosis. As people's attention is called to the ED and the population becomes aware of its existence, symptoms and consequences, the more likely it is to be discovered in less time. Often seen as a teen mania, because of lack of information, the episodes reported by the media leads knowledge to the outsider public that AN and BN can kill.

In our research, we believe that the best people to provide information about ED's were the individuals affected by these diseases. Thus, in order to understand the meaning of the lived experience of people with ED's, particularly adolescent girls, we looked for them. This contact allowed us to know their experiences and feelings directly and indirectly related to their ED's.

Discovering *what* ED's are is not a very hard task, once there are numerous scientific articles and several books describing them. Our proposal was to show *how* these disorders are in the view of who is going through them.

In the contact with the interviewed teenagers, the availability to open the doors of their existence and share the history of their disorders and lives called our attention, even in the presence of suffering that emerged so many times in form of a deep silence or of tears that almost, or sometimes, were shed. The contact with these teenagers was enriching. The interviews allowed us to describe behaviors, attitudes, feelings and perceptions that guided our research.

An exacerbated concern with eating control is the common base of ED's, according to literature. This concern was also evidenced in our interviews, both with the teenagers that were having nutritional counseling and the ones that were not. There is still the intention of a diet considered healthy by them, which is not always their favorite, but it is, even though, adopted.

We observed in our interviews that eating choices are usually done according to the amount of calories or with what gains less weight, but, besides these, the flavor, taste and desire also influence this choice. Some testimonies showed us that choices are made according to the guidance of the nutritionists, emphasizing the importance of this professional in the success of the treatment. However, in the episodes of binge eating, we observed that there is no rule for choosing.

Regarding to the number of meals had by the teenagers in our research, they quoted between three and eight a day, being distributed in breakfast, morning snack, lunch, afternoon snack, dinner, night snack, supper and "extras". Most of the interviewed teenagers considered their way of eating similar to their family's; some that the family's way of eating is similar to their own way, being different only to the amount. Others that their current eating habit had influence from the family's eating habit and one of them that she has influenced the family's eating habit, making it healthier.

This research allowed us to contemplate ED's by the prism of the relation with the food, confirming how this relation is connected to emotional matters. It has also shown us how it is to live with ED's in the view of the teenagers, trying to see these disorders according to their understanding and feelings. And, despite the theoretical knowledge and clinical practice with people with ED's, this "intersection" between nutrition and psychology led us also to see something relatively popular with a new vision.

In addition, this study, during its execution, caused significant changes in both personal and professional aspects, opening questions for future consideration.

With regard to the method adopted in this study, we believe that the choice of qualitative methods, focused on a phenomenological approach, was confirmed in fact to be the most appropriate according to the proposed objectives. The method adopted allowed us access to the content in a profound way, not generalized nor interpretative, as described by Heidegger (1989) " to let that which shows itself be seen from itself in the very way in which it shows itself from itself ".

## 5. Final considerations

This research, as noted, sought to understand the meaning of the lived experience of ED's instead of explaining them, since through the adopted phenomenological perspective, it is the understanding of the phenomenon that enables us to cover a whole in its multiple dimensions. Thus, it provided us to show you how it is to live with ED's in the vision of each of the seven adolescents interviewed.

But we can not stop here: it is essential to have more studies on this topic, especially providing space to people with ED's who have so much to say. Of great importance also is the information and disclosures about these ED's, as well as about the appropriate treatments and the right professionals to help in these cases, in an attempt to prevent that the suffering of those affected go unnoticed and last for too long - or even worse - lead to a tragic outcome.

## 6. References

Alvarenga, M. & Larino, M. A. (2002). Terapia nutricional na anorexia e bulimia nervosas. *Revista Brasileira de Psiquiatria*, Vol.24, No.3, (December 2002)

Alvarenga, M. (2004). A mudança na alimentação e no corpo ao longo do tempo. *In:* Philippi, S. T. & Alvarenga, M. *Transtornos alimentares: uma visão nutricional,* Manole, Barueri

Amatuzzi, M. M. (1996). Apontamentos acerca da pesquisa fenomenológica. *Estudos de Psicologia,* Vol.13, No.1, pp. 5-10

Appolinário, J. C. & Claudino, A. M. (2000). Transtornos alimentares. *Revista Brasileira de Psiquiatria,* Vol.22, No.2, (December 2000)

Assumpção Junior, F. B. (2004). Prefácio. *In:* Busse, S. de R. (org.). *Anorexia, bulimia e Obesidade,* Manole, Barueri

Bacaltchuck, J. & Appolinário, J. C. (2005). Neurobiologia. *In:* Claudino, A. de M. & Zanella, M. T. *Guia de Transtornos Alimentares e Obesidade.* Manole , Barueri, pp. 3-23.

Bandeira, C. R. S. et al. (2000). Hábitos Alimentares na Adolescência. *Pediatria Moderna,* Vol.36, No.11, (November 2000), pp.724-734

Beumont, P. J. V. (2002). The clinical presentation of anorexia and bulimia nervosa. *In:* Fairburn, C. G. & Brownell, K. D. *Eating disorders and obesity: a comprehensive handbook.* (edition 2), The Guilford Press, Nova York

Brasil. Ministério da Saúde (MS). *O que é uma alimentação saudável? Considerações sobre o conceito, princípios e características: uma abordagem ampliada.* 26.11.2006, Available from:http://dtr2004.saude.gov.br/nutricao/documentos/o_que_e_alimentacao_saudavel.pdf

Castro, J.M. & Goldstein, S. (1995). Eating attitudes and behaviors of pre- and postpubertal females: clues to the etiology of eating disorders. *Physiology & Behavior,* Vol.58, No.1, pp. 15-23

Chipkevitch, E. (1995). A dimensão psicossocial. *Puberdade e adolescência: aspectos biológicos, clínicos e psicossociais,* Roca, São Paulo

Cintra, I. de P. & Fisberg, M. (2004). Mudanças na alimentação de crianças e adolescentes e suas implicações para a prevalência de transtornos alimentares. *In:* Philippi, S. T. & Alvarenga, M. *Transtornos alimentares: uma visão nutricional,* Manole, Barueri

Cobelo, A. W. (2004). O papel da família no comportamento alimentar e nos transtornos alimentares. *In:* Philippi, S. T. & Alvarenga, M. *Transtornos alimentares: uma visão nutricional,* Manole, Barueri

Conde, W. L. & Monteiro, C. A. (2006). Valores críticos do índice de massa corporal para classificação do estado nutricional de crianças e adolescentes brasileiros. *Jornal de Pediatria do Rio de Janeiro,* Porto Alegre, Vol. 82, No. 4

Coppe, Â. A. F. (2001). *A vivência em grupos de encontro: um estudo fenomenológico de depoimentos.* Dissertação (Mestrado), Universidade Federal do Rio de Janeiro.

Cordás, T. A. et al. (1998). *Anorexia e bulimia – o que são? Como ajudar?,* Artes Médicas, Porto Alegre

Cordás, T. A. (2004). Transtornos alimentares: classificação e diagnóstico. *Revista de Psiquiatria Clínica,* São Paulo, Vol.31, No.4

Cordás, T. A. & Salzano, F. T. & Rios, S. R. (2004). Os transtornos alimentares e a evolução no diagnóstico e no tratamento. *In:* Philippi, S. T. & Alvarenga, M. *Transtornos alimentares: uma visão nutricional,* Manole, Barueri

Devoraes, A. R. & Fagundes, U. (2005). Avaliação e orientação nutricional. *In:* Claudino, A. de M. & Zanella, M. T. *Guia de transtornos alimentares e obesidade,* Manole, Barueri

Dietz, W. H. (1990). You are what you eat - what you eat is what you are. *Journal of Adolescent Health*, Vol.11, pp. 76-81

DSM-IV-TR (2002). *Manual Diagnóstico E Estatístico De Transtornos Mentais* (4 edition rev.), ArtMed, Porto Alegre

Dunker, K. L. L. & Philippi, S. T. (2003). Hábitos e comportamentos alimentares de adolescentes com sintomas de anorexia nervosa. *Revista de Nutrição*, Campinas, Vol.16, No.1, (January - March 2003)

Eisenstein, E. & Coelho, K. & Coelho, S. & Coelho, M. (2000). Nutrição na adolescência. *Jornal de Pediatria*, Rio de Janeiro, Vol.76, s.3, pp. 263-274

Ferreira, A. B. de H. (1993). *Minidicionário da Língua Portuguesa* (3 edition), Nova Fronteira, Rio de Janeiro

Fischer, M. et al. (1995). Eating disorders in adolescents: a background paper. *Journal of Adolescent Health Care*, New York, Vol.16, No.6, pp. 420-437

França, C. (1989). *Psicologia fenomenológica: uma das maneiras de se fazer*, Editora da Unicamp, Campinas

Heidegger, M. (1989). *Ser e Tempo (Part I)*, Vozes, Petrópolis

Holanda, A. F. (2002). *O resgate da fenomenologia de Husserl e a pesquisa em psicologia.* Tese (doutorado) - Universidade Católica de Campinas

Holanda, A. F. (2003). Pesquisa Fenomenológica e Pesquisa Eidética. *In:* Bruns, M. A. T. & Holanda, A. F. *Psicologia e fenomenologia: reflexões e perspectivas*, Alínea, Campinas

Jauregui, L. I. & Bolanos R. P. (2009). Choice of diet in patients with anorexia nervosa. *Nutrición Hospitalaria*, V.24, No.6, pp628-687

Juste, M. (2004). *Quando comer é um problema.* 21.09.2004, Available from: http://revistagalileu.globo.com/Galileu/0,6993,ECT705249-1718,00.html

Martins, J & Bicudo, M. A. V. (2003). A *pesquisa qualitativa em psicologia: fundamentos e recursos básicos*, (3 edition), Centauro, São Paulo

Moreira, D. A. (2002). *O método fenomenológico na pesquisa*, Pioneira Thomson, São Paulo

Nunes, M. A. et al. (2003). Prevalence of abnormal eating behaviours anda inappropriate methods of weight control in young women from Brazil: a population-based study. *Eating Weight Disorders*, Vol.8, No.2, pp. 1-7

Philippi, S. T. (1999). Guia Alimentar para o ano 2000. *In:* Angelis, R. C. *Fome oculta: impacto para a população do Brasil*, Atheneu, São Paulo

Philippi, S. T. et al. (2000). Alimentação saudável na infância e na adolescência. *In.*: Silva. M. V. et al. *Curso de Atualização em alimentação para professores da rede pública de ensino.* Escola Superior de Agricultura Luiz de Queiroz (Esalq), Piracicaba

Philippi, S. T. & Alvarenga, M. (2004). Alimentação saudável: princípios e recomendações. *In:* Philippi, S. T. & Alvarenga, M. *Transtornos alimentares: uma visão nutricional*, Manole, Barueri

Prieto, I. R. (2011). Elección dietética de familiares de pacientes com transtornos de la conducta alimentaria. Transtornos de la Conducta Alimentaria, 13, pp.1384-1415

Vieira, V. C. R. & Priore, S. E. & Ribeiro, S. M. R. et al. (2002). Perfil socioeconômico, nutricional e de saúde de adolescentes recémingressos em uma universidade pública brasileira. *Revista de Nutrição*, Vol.15, No.3, pp. 273-282

World Health Organization (WHO). *BMI Classification.* 18.09.2006, Available from: http://www.who.int/bmi/index.jsp?introPage=intro_3.html

World Health Organization (WHO). *Child and adolescent health and development.* 11.10.2005, Available from: http://www.who.int/childadolescenthealth/OVERVIEW/AHD/adh_over.htm

# Part 4

# Treatment and Prevention of Eating Disorders

# 11

# Eating Disorders Treatment: An Integrative Model by Means of Narrative Counseling, Motivational Interviewing, and Traditional Approaches

Moria Golan
*Shahaf, Community Services for the Management of Weight-Related Problems, Tel Hai Academic College and School of Nutritional Sciences, Hebrew University, Israel*

## 1. Introduction

The devastating effect of eating disorders on health has led to their inclusion among the priority mental illnesses for children and adolescents identified by the World Health Organization (World Health Organization [WHO], 2005). Crude mortality rates for anorexia nervosa have ranged from 0 to 8% across studies, with a cumulative mortality rate of 2.8% (9 deaths for 318 patients followed an average of 11 years) (Keel & Brown, 2010). The overall mortality rate for anorexia nervosa is five times that of the same aged population in general, the highest of all psychiatric illnesses. Death from natural causes, such as cardiac arrhythmia and infection, is four times greater, and death from unnatural causes, such as suicide, eleven times greater than expected. Risk of successful suicide is particularly high: thirty-two times that in the same aged general population (Centre for Excellence in Eating Disorders, Facts and Figures, 2005). About 50% of anorexia nervosa patients/victims return to a normal body weight within six months of treatment. 25% maintain a low but stable weight, and the remaining 25% remain chronically ill or die (CEED, 2005). 76% of patients enrolled in a randomized controlled trial achieved remission by five-year follow-up (Keel & Brown, 2010).

The mortality rate for bulimia nervosa is estimated to be 0.4 (Keel & Brown, 2010). Close to 45% of the patients on average showed full recovery from bulimia nervosa, while 27% on average improved considerably, and nearly 23% on average had a chronic, protracted course. Crossover to another eating disorder at the follow-up evaluation in 23 studies amounted to a mean of 22.5% (Steinhousen & Weber, 2009). As with studies of anorexia nervosa, remission rates for follow-up studies of bulimia nervosa are lowest for those with the shortest duration of follow-up (27–28% at 1-year follow-up) and increase as duration of follow-up increases (up to 70% or more by 10-year follow-up) (Keel & Brown, 2010).

### 1.1 The unmet challenges reflected by eating disorders

Clearly, many people live with an eating disorder for many years, particularly those who purge. They come to terms with it because symptoms are perceived as being preferable to the alternative distresses, as explained by different theories.

### 1.1.1 "Self" theorists

"Self" theorists argue that patients with anorexia nervosa and bulimia nervosa cannot rely on human beings to fulfill their self-object needs. In Kohutian terms, they cannot expect that others will give up, even temporarily, their own interests and viewpoint for the sake of fulfilling their self-needs, such as regulation of self-esteem, calming, soothing, and vitalizing (Kohut, 1977). Instead, these patients rely on a substance, food (its consumption or avoidance), to fulfill these needs. Therapy progresses when the patient gives up the pathological preference for food as a self-object and begins to rely on human beings as self-objects, starting with the therapist. According to this theory, eating disorder patients feel and behave like selfless souls serving others' needs. Women with anorexia nervosa are liable to feel self-guilt whenever they find themselves promoting their own interests (Goodsit, 1977). Bulimic symptoms may be utilized, for example, to soothe painful and unacceptable feelings or to adapt to an environment in which the self is constantly subjected to painful and/or damaging experiences. Strober (1991) suggests that a genetically-based personality style of high stimulus-avoidance, low novelty seeking, and high reward dependence, rather than restrictive parental behaviors alone, inhibits the natural exploration necessary for normal self-development. Vitousek and Ewald (1993) suggest that both genetic and environmental factors contribute to the failure to develop a clear and stable set of positive selves, leading to an over-reliance on environmental cues to define the self and to feel noticed.

### 1.1.2 Ego theorists

Ego theorists argue that eating disorders serve as defense against reality. Bruch (1982) emphasizes ego weakness and interpersonal factors. Her basic theory is that anorexia nervosa is a struggle for self-respecting identity in the context of autonomy-inhibiting parents; it is the failures and impairments in ego development and functioning that are of particular interest. These include an arrested conceptual development, a nearly delusional disturbance in body image, which is symptomatic of a much wider misperception, and a striking sense of ineffectiveness. In extreme cases it is a mechanism to avoid any genuine connection with reality or any representation of reality and the fears and anxiety associated with it (Bion, 1959). Resisting treatment is actually a considerable investment in the patient's need to maintain control over his/her internal and external worlds and the objects within them (Williams, 1997), a way to remain immature, with no responsibilities, narrow views, and protection from life's demands.

### 1.1.3 Developmental theorists

Developmental theorists assert that during times of emotional turmoil and disturbing life circumstances, eating disorder symptoms reflect a defense against developmental challenges. Bruch (1982) proposes that the adolescent turns to body weight as a viable source of self-definition and as an arena in which to struggle for autonomy, competence, control, and self-respect. Bruch (1982) sees anorexia nervosa as developmental defect: as the girls grew older, they found that to continue to be well-behaved by their parents' standards, they had to remain little girls, both physically and psychically. Thus they found in stringent dieting a process that accomplished two important goals: it kept them little and gave them one thing over which they had sole control. When the girls reach menarche and should begin dating boys, they retract into a cage, and, by losing weight, pull themselves back from the brink of adulthood. Menstruation stops, if it had begun, and they throw themselves into physically demanding activities, usually athletics, which garner them much praise and admiration and provide a convenient excuse for avoiding boys. An ingenious solution, one that the perpetrators are usually surprised to find is not unique to themselves. Crisp (1980) views anorexia nervosa as a mechanism by which the patient regresses to a pre-pubertal shape, hormonal status, and experience to avoid the fears and conflicts associated with psychosexual maturing. Eating disorder symptoms—restricting, purging, compulsively overeating, always feeling fat—provide distraction from original sources of personal stress or key developmental tasks in adolescents (Bruch, 1982). The thinking imposed by eating disorders directs the mind to criticize the body, obsess about food, and draw attention to weight loss. rather than to explore distressing feelings. Thus the eating disorder is less about food and weight than about trying to "solve" one's problems in life. In some cases, for example, an eating disorder may serve as an excuse for social difficulties and as a means of escaping psychosocial pressures; in others it may serve to unite parents in a troubled marriage and as a means of getting "special treatment" because the child could not recognize or express his/her primary distress.

### 1.1.4 Regulation theorists

Regulation theorists claim that by refocusing one's attention onto weight, shape, and eating, one gains a sense of emotional control and a sense of accomplishment. People with bulimia nervosa attempt to elevate their mood by eating; purging allows them to avoid gaining weight. Unfortunately, the person with bulimia nervosa eventually realizes that the binges are out of control and begins to feel guilty and to dread eating. Eating no longer provides relief, but rather, induces negative emotions such as guilt. Purging may then relieve the guilt, as well as discharging anger. It is thus possible that purging eventually replaces bingeing as a means of tension reduction (Polivy & Herman, 2002). In fact, bulimia nervosa patients report reduced anxiety and depression following a binge/purge episode (Sanftner & Crowther, 1998; Steinberg & Shaw, 1997). Bulimic behavior has been proposed to result from unregulated affects. The anorexia nervosa patient achieves at least partial emotional gratification by avoiding food and achieving slimness. More recent theorists concur that an extreme need to control both eating and other aspects of behavior is a central feature of eating disorders (Fairburn et al., 1999). Gaining a sense of control and pride in one's ability to control one's eating combats the feeling of being taken over by thoughts of food or of lacking control of one's thoughts, eating, and weight (Serpell et al., 1999).

### 1.1.5 Social perspectives

Social perspectives identify the idealization of slimness and the societal disparagement of overweight as major contributing factors to women's weight and shape dissatisfaction and related self-disgust (Striegel-Moore, 1997).

Feminist researchers argue that the "eating disorder" is a reflection of young girls' unease with social roles approved in Western, patriarchal societies, where gender inequality still prevails. Disease creation, therefore, becomes a way of gender control (Malson, 1999). This interpretation is derived from Foucault's power philosophy (Foucault, 1988) and our understanding of AN as a disciplinary practice that medicalizes the body and is interpreted through interrelationships between knowledge, social practices, and institutional authority (Hepworth, 1999).

### 1.1.6 Family theorists

Family theorists discuss three main areas in relation to the etiology of eating disorders: the family system and its organization, the patient's entanglement in his/her parents' conflict, and control issues in the family. Family theories have been implicated not only in the maintenance of eating disorders but also in their development (Minuchin et al., 1978). Minuchin, from his family interaction perspective, stresses the self-sacrifice, loyalty, and protectiveness of patients with anorexia nervosa towards their parents ,[22] the same motives reviewed above from a self-psychological and cognitive sociological perspective. Minuchin furthermore emphasizes guilt as the underlying motivation for this self-sacrifice in the service of the family's needs. Ward et al. (2000), however, conclude that "many of these (family dysfunction) characteristics are regarded as secondary to the presence of an ill family member, rather than causative." Perhaps problems of identity and/or control are central to eating disorders, with the individual attempting to resolve these problems by investing emotionally and behaviorally in the pursuit of slimness. The family, of course, may contribute directly to problems of identity or control and may also suggest the solution, by emphasizing slimness as a panacea. Steiger et al. (1996) conclude that families (including so-called normal families) may transmit eating concerns, but without an additional vulnerability factor, family factors do not explain the emergence of an eating disorder.

### 1.2 What type of therapy may address these challenges?

The best outcomes are achieved with those whose condition is identified early and who receive appropriate treatment. The National Institute of Clinical Excellence (NICE) guidelines (2004) recommend that people with eating disorders should first be offered outpatient treatment and that inpatient care be used for those who do not respond or who present with high risk and few support resources. Day treatment plans provide an intermediate treatment model. Practice recommendations emphasize the importance of specialized care for the treatment of eating disorders (American Psychiatric Association [APA], 2006).

There has been extensive research on different types of therapeutic approaches to the treatment of eating disorders (APA, 2006). Practice recommendations emphasize the importance of specialized care for the treatment of eating disorders, but such care is not often accessible (APA, 2006). Moreover, as Treasure et al. point out, comorbidity for patients with eating disorders is the rule rather than the exception (Treasure et al., 2010). Interest is growing in a transdiagnostic approach to eating disorders, both within and outside the field of eating disorders, with suggestions they should be linked to the obsessive-compulsive and autistic spectrums or to anxiety and mood disorders. An intervention model that approaches illnesses from a transdiagnostic orientation, which addresses the dynamics and needs of comorbidities while treating the eating disorder effectively, has been proposed.

Pluralism, consumerism, mobility, and increasing access to news, entertainment, and other features of the post-modern world have brought multiple therapeutic approaches, as well. In specialized eating disorders units, we see patients who receive nutrition counseling and pharmacotherapy alongside interpersonal psychotherapy (IPT), cognitive behavioral therapy (CBT), dialectical behavioral therapy (DBT), psychodynamic therapies (PT), and family-based therapy (Maudsley), as well as motivational enhancement interviewing (MEI or MI) and even elements of narrative therapy delivered by 2-6 team members. The difference among programs lies mainly in the management or the spirit of the therapeutic environment created by the strategies and practices of the team members and the manager. Post-modern approaches such as narrative therapy and MI (motivational interviewing) encounter the traditional medical model, which imposes authority and discipline.

### 1.2.1 Narrative therapy

Narrative therapy was developed by Michael White and David Epston (White & Epston, 1989). Incorporating the gender power analysis of feminism, narrative therapy was significantly influenced by Michel Foucault (Foucault, 1988) and his analysis of power (White & Epston, 1989). Narrative therapy challenges the idea that expert knowledge belongs to the world of therapists and the medical model. It challenges the truths and alleged objectivity of these disciplines, instead taking up the ethic of collaboration and engaging in the practice of "co-research" (Epston, 1991, 2001). It explores factors that have contributed to the meanings the person has constructed about his/her life and experiences and identifies the person's knowledge about the influence of his/her eating disorder on his/her life. It also identifies knowledge about factors supporting or undermining that influence. The counselor explores unique ways in which eating disorder patients resist and challenge problematic behaviors we call "pro-eating disorders steps," such as eating less or deciding not to join friends because of eating or mood issues (Lock, et al., 2005).

In contrast, decisions such as eating regularly, are called "anti-eating disorders steps" or "unique outcomes," which are viewed as foundations and possibilities for further change. Maisel, Epston, and Borden (2005) posit that people experiencing eating disorders have accumulated "insider" knowledge about living with the eating disorder that is different from others, such as therapists, who do not have that experience. Michael White incorporates some of the ideas of Lev Vygotsky and his proposals on ways humans might be assisted to move in new directions in collaboration and through language. White explains the practice of scaffolding conversations using Vygotsky's ideas (White, 2007). He uses Vygotsky's idea of "the space moved through" to obtain a new outcome, the "Zone of Proximal Development." White claims that crossing this zone takes a person from what is known and familiar (but perhaps not useful) towards "what it is possible to know and do." The art of re-authoring conversations, which is the practice of narrative therapy, invigorates people's efforts to understand what is happening in their lives, what has happened, how, and what it all means. In this way, these conversations encourage a dramatic re-engagement with life and with history and provide options for people to inhabit their lives and their relationships more fully (White, 2005). Co-research is considered an important method in narrative therapy.

### 1.2.2 Motivational interviewing

Motivational Interviewing is a directive, patient-centered counseling style for eliciting behavior change by helping patients to explore and resolve ambivalence. Compared with nondirective counseling, it is more focused and goal-directed. The examination and resolution of ambivalence is its central purpose, and the counselor is intentionally directive in pursuing this goal. Rollnick et al. (2008) called the communication style often found in helpful counseling "guiding style." The guiding style involves an approach in which a patient and counselor work as a team. They "walk" together, but the practitioner points out routes and options, serving as a resource about what is possible, what others have done, and what the risks and benefits might be of each approach. By pointing out possible paths, the practitioner helps the patient to choose directions that best suit him or her (Rosenberg, 2009). In this style the implicit message is, "I'll help you solve this yourself." Motivational interviewing uses reflective listening in guiding the person to resolve ambivalence about behavior change (Rollnick et al., 2008).

Narrative and motivational counseling share reliance on patients' personal agency rather than on a relationship of power. This encourages collaboration, evocation, and autonomy, empowers people, and strives to help them avoid eating disorders and other dangerous behaviors.

To avoid blaming, narrative counseling uses externalization, a process of creating a linguistic space or a sense of separation between the person and the problem by engaging in conversations that position the self in relationship to thoughts, feelings, experience, and actions (White & Epston, 1989). Over time people with eating disorders come to believe that the disorder is part of their identity. Externalizing conversations begin a process of deconstructing the beliefs and ideas that fuel the problem, examining where these discourses are situated and how they exert an influence on the person's life, "deconstructing some of the 'truths' that persons have about their lives" (White, 1995). They create a linguistic and experiential space for the person to view the problem and his/her relationship with it from a different perspective (Madigan & Goldner, 1998). Instead of being immersed in the problem, "a person gains a reflexive perspective on their life, and new options become available to them in challenging the 'truths' that they experience as specifying them and their relationships" (White & Epston, 1989).

In a different way but with the same intentions, in motivational interviewing the therapist aims to avoid conflict, resist a righteous stance, and understand patients' motivation even if s/he does not agree with the resulting behavior. Motivational interviewing makes use of OARS (open ended questions, affirmations, reflections, and summarizing) to "dance" with ambivalence rather than confront patients.

Furthermore, both approaches focus on change. In motivational interviewing, enhancing self-change talk is a core component. The counselor strategically elicits change talk and consistently responds to it when offered. In narrative therapy, a counselor usually asks, "Where does this knowledge take you? In what way will you respond differently now that you have this knowledge?"

Both narrative and motivational interviewing counseling have been adopted in a variety of health care areas. The idea of "marrying" narrative counseling and motivation interviewing in the treatment of eating disorders is not unique to our model (Leichner, 2005). Leichner described a comprehensive eating disorders program delivered at British Columbia's Children's Hospital using Motivational Enhancement Interviewing (2005). This model is in essence a repackaging of several different therapeutic approaches based on the stages of change model developed by Prochaska and DiClemente (1986). It includes components of cognitive behavioral therapy, psycho-education, patient-centered therapy, and narrative therapy. The author emphasizes that active listening and other strategies have replaced the more coercive and confrontational methods used in the past to treat AN and related disorders. The effectiveness of integrating various therapies and approaches in the management of eating disorders is not surprising, as survey findings consistently show that clinicians tend to identify less with any one approach the longer they have been in the field. Experienced therapists tend to pick and choose from a variety of approaches in an effort to tailor treatment to the makeup and characteristics of the individual patient (Duncan et al., 1999). This is certainly appropriate for transdiagnostic comorbidities. Duncan et al. (1999) show that the patient's view of the presenting complaint, potential solutions, and ideas about the change process form a theory of change that can be used as the basis for determining "which approach, by whom, would be the most effective for this person, with that specific problem, under this particular set of circumstances."

The current manuscript is innovative because it presents a model that goes beyond Prochaska and Di Clemente's process of change model (Prochaska & DiClemente, 1986). It was first developed for parents who expressed their longing for an anchor, a sense of control and location, while battling their daughter's eating disorder. For them, we defined five phases along the journey to recovery as a guide map. We are aware of the risk of simplification of a most often complex reality when establishing therapeutic models due to the desire for certainty and comfort, as well as the risk of falling into the trap of "knowing." We are also aware of the spiral, as opposed to linear, nature of the change process.

## 2. Treatment program and principles

Shahaf is a community-based facility for the treatment of eating disorders in Israel that provides various level of treatment intensity. We work with the whole spectrum of weight-related problems including severe food restriction for weight loss, excessive exercise, and purging behaviors such as vomiting, binge eating, and chewing and spitting. Approximately fifty patients are in treatment at any one time.

Comorbidities such as depression, obsessive compulsive disorder, and self-injuring behaviors are very common among our patients, who are often self-disparaging, convinced life has no value, pessimistic about the future, and unable to initiate or experience enjoyment. All admissions are voluntary. Treatment plans are tailored to the needs of patients and their families, and treatment is delivered by a multidisciplinary team.

Since we view emotional dysregulation as the core problem in eating disorders, each patient is allocated to at least one type of therapy aimed at improving his/her regulation skills and enhancing change in emotional states (psychotherapy, art therapy, drama therapy, and biofeedback). Skills for regulating emotions are acquired in most psychotherapies. "Meaning making" as acceptance and change, active validating of the worth of the individual, and mindfulness skills to substitute sensual activities for food satiety are included in therapy. Parents are invited to participate in a psycho-educational support group where they receive information and emotional support from the group facilitators and other parents who share experiences and offer possible solutions. Nutrition counseling, family therapy, and other components of psychiatric management for patients with eating disorders are also important: the therapeutic alliance, coordinate care and collaboration with other clinicians, assessment and monitoring of symptoms and behaviors, and cognitive and behavioral techniques such as stimulus control procedures and strategies aimed at modifying rigid all-or-nothing thinking and perfectionism, are also central in this program.

In addition, during the course of an intensive treatment, 5% of patients receive between six to twelve hours per week of contact with clinical mentors. Clinical mentors are social workers, clinical dietician, and graduate level psychology students who are trained to connect with patients in an intensive, informal manner. Senior clinical psychologists supervise them once a week, individually and in a group. The mentors address the need for a holding and containing environment, as well as the presence of a strong and reliable emotional resource, countering the eating disorder voice and helping the patient voice his/her own values. They serve as meal companions and soothing figures, representing a healthy self-caring image, which counters maladapted patterns of interaction, cognition, and behaviors. Social skills training as well as leisure-time activities are encouraged. Further along in the recovery process, patients are encouraged to direct their hunger for relationships away from the mentors to new friendships.

In order to counter the patient's resistance to change and the power struggle that often occurs when treating eating disorders, the narrative language (White & Epston, 1989) is utilized toward treating symptoms. During narrative conversations, AN and BN are externalized, and people are encouraged to identify the ways in which the eating disorder has taken over their lives (e.g., via isolation, physical and emotional disappearance, engagement in self-policing, empty promises, etc.). The therapists then enlist patients to form a coalition against the illness to regain freedom, engaging in change rather than guilt or blame, which are often the dominant feelings among patients with eating disorders (Grieves, 1997). Treatment integrates narrative therapy, motivational intervening, dialectic behavior therapy, cognitive-behavioral therapy, bio-feedback, and dynamic approaches. Psychosocial interventions are chosen on the basis of a comprehensive evaluation of the individual patient, considering cognitive and psychological development, psychodynamic issues, cognitive style, comorbid psychopathology, patient preferences, and family situation. Thus, different pathologies receive different treatment strategies, but the conversation is always a collaborative, generative process mutually constructed between the therapist and the people seeking help.

## 3. The process of the journey from patient's denial to recovery

Below is a description of a five-phase process to facilitate recovery. The therapeutic relationship as well as the practices engaged in will be described, from the first meeting, through the formation of a strong joint coalition against the problem, and to the farewell.

### 3.1 Preliminary phase: Choosing a shelter of understanding

Preliminary Conversation: collaborative authoring the patient's entanglement in the disease network. During this phase the patient and his/her parents assess and choose the site of therapy. They look for a shelter of understanding, a place where they can trust the professional's expertise as well as attitude towards patients with respect to autonomy and hierarchy.

### 3.1.1 The first "intake" conversation

The first "intake" conversation is performed with the clinical director (Prof. Golan) and the patient, and later on the parents join for a second re-telling of the patient's story. This session is aimed at get to know the patient, his/her problem, and how the problem took over the person's life. During this first "intake" meeting, open-ended questions are used to explore the story of the patient's childhood, what kind of a child s/he was, and what characterized her/his friendships. A major thrust is to explore unfolding hints that the eating disorder might have taken advantage of and given an illusionary protection: regulatory issues, fears, desires, self-control issues, social difficulties, personality traits, family conflicts, and the presence of a defensive style (tendency to deny or avoid conflicts). We might reflect that the eating disorder symptoms (preoccupation, slimness) may be helping the youth to deflect other distresses.

In this session, externalizing conversation is used to position the illness outside the patient and to contradict most patients' perception that they are the problem, that there is a deficit or defect of some kind within them or within their family dynamics. When they are labeled "anorexics" or "bulimics," linguistics promotes the full assimilation of the eating disorder into their identity.

In narrative terms, the person is referred to as being totalized (Maisel et al., 2005) by the effects of the eating disorder. Self-blame and guilt often arise from these perceptions. During this conversation the patient starts to understand how the eating disorder and emotional issues are related. We gently unfold the development of the signs and symptoms of the eating disorder and teach the patient to identify the traces of the eating disorder by him/herself. Some may see/understand, and some may not. Some may see and then forget. We then ask the patient's permission to invite his/her parents into the room and to share with them the story of how *we* (s/he and I) understand the problem have developed.

We re-tell the birth of a sensitive child with sensitive self-regulation (as was expressed by the events that the patient has described) and how the eating disorder took advantage of this core issue. We repeatedly re-tell the story of how the eating disorder took advantage of the patient's difficulties (based on what s/he has told me) and explain how the eating disorder distracted him/her from resolving his/her problems and provided short-term relief. We add that s/he now seems to view the price as being too high.

The patient is now asked to describe why the price has become too high for him/her and what his/her goals are. What are his/her goals/aspirations/life objectives?

The different budgets that our facility offers are presented, and with the family we consider which level of intensity is appropriate for the patient's physical condition, occupational functioning, and other factors. When a patient feels understood and can trust the treatment provider, s/he is more ready to enter a meaningful bond and consider treatment as an option.

After the parents approve the reframed history of the problem, we set the treatment goals. The main priority of the therapeutic alliance is stressed, guiding the process of recovery towards those issues that have been identified as difficult for the patient (not necessarily diagnostic symptoms) and what the patient feels should direct the goals of treatment. We insist that the patient feel as if s/he is a valid, significant part of the therapeutic alliance and has a personal role in the recovery process, decreasing the patient's feeling of being "controlled" throughout the treatment process.

Because anorexia nervosa patients tend to see their disorder as an accomplishment rather than an affliction, they are unlikely to enter treatment to free themselves from their feelings of guilt and shame, which are the motivational source of an introjected regulation. As such, we would predict that those with anorexia nervosa display a lower level of introjected motivation to change compared with other eating disorder patients.

The primary goal is to reassure patients that their apprehensions will be carefully appraised in shaping the interventions undertaken, and that changes sought will be measured against their tolerance of the anxieties that may be triggered, so that risk of terminating treatment is minimized.

This therapeutic stance, in which the therapist is viewed as a consultant helping the patient and the family, with little difference in power among them, may encourage both patient and parents to work more collaboratively, rather than deferentially. The team, thereby, increasing their ownership of treatment and outcome and strengthening the therapeutic bond.

Moreover, using a combination of narrative and motivational interviewing skills that emphasize that the patient or family holds the solution rather than the problem helps to establish effective cooperative bonds.

### 3.2 Phase 1: from partial recognition to full acknowledgment

During the first phase of the journey, there is only partial recognition of the problematic status. Neither parents nor patient are fully engaged in treatment and the full impact of the disease is not recognized. Patients feel stressed by their eating disorder but also safe, as if they were in a "bunker." Thus, the counseling focuses on engaging and guiding towards acknowledgment of the disease.

Although during the intake session the patient may seem to understood the relationship between the eating disorder and emotional issues, when the program starts, denial returns; the patient becomes trapped once again in the belief that the eating disorder is his/her guardian, and "sings" the familiar melody: "I am healthy, I can put on weight by myself." Parents can be firm and overcome this potential impasse by reminding the patient of the elusive nature of his/her eating disorder and stating firmly that, as previously decided, s/he will start the program. They can remind him/her that treatment is the way to achieve what s/he wants above all else: his/her autonomy. The case manager forms a general therapeutic alliance with the patient but allows several exceptions from the formal form to model active listening and mutual respect (e.g., "at the moment, X prefers not to commit to gain the target weight rather than improve the weight status").

### Objectives

Objectives of this phase include the creation of a meaningful bond; comprehensive assessment (physical, nutritional, psychiatric, psychological, family dynamics, defense styles); the development of an alliance; and the beginning of physiological and emotional stabilization.

### Means

**Curiosity.** In order to create a meaningful bond, patients must experience therapists as caring people who honor their views, feelings, ideas, and resources. For example, therapist and patient can examine how change usually happens in the patient's life, paying particular attention to the sequence of events, the role the patient and others adopt in the initiation and maintenance of change, and the success or failure of any attempts to resolve the illness and other problems.

**OARS** (Open ended questions, Reflections, Affirmations, Summarizing). This involves assessing nutritional status and discussion with the patient about the impact of exhaustion on different areas of his/her life. The patient may be asked what bothers him/her most—e.g., growth, autonomy.

**Therapeutic alliance**. We take a clear stance against the problem with firm focus on behavioral goals and announce clear boundaries and rules (stages of independence and discussion about which decisions should be mutual and which should not in each stage). Staff should clearly communicate that they are not seeking to engage in control battles and are not trying to punish patients with aversive techniques. The role of the patient in the treatment process is equally important to that of the treatment team. In this sense, the patient is an active participant and is accountable for his/her actions in the quest for behavior change and improvement in his/her quality of life. Patients must honestly and accurately disclose information to the individual therapist and staff. Patients should make a sincere effort to report accurate information about the history of the disorder and present symptoms, behaviors, and any past relapses. Patients must make a concerted effort to participate actively in the treatment program as well as any recommended intervention outside of the treatment setting.

We agree to support the patients' autonomy as long as s/he makes decisions that serve his/her own good and do not nurture the eating disorder. This often depends on the degree to which the patient perceives his/her locus of control within the treatment structure. If the progress of recovery is slow, a decision may be made to increase the level of care within the setting. This decision should involve the patient, the family, and/or support persons, so that they are accountable for their actions and the facilitation of recovery.

**Validating environment.** Elements crucial to the creation of a validating environment include recognizing the complexity of problem- solving skills, encouraging the expression and sharing of emotion, and encouraging the patient to trust his/her own emotional and cognitive responses as valid interpretations of situational and individual events. It is important to keep in mind that for any individual case, certain elements of treatment are more difficult than others.

**Individualized identification of the primary "obstacles" to recovery**. Acknowledging that weight gain is frightening for most patients can strengthen the therapeutic alliance and decrease the likelihood that the patient will perceive the therapist or treatment team as just wanting to make him or her "fat," versus truly understanding the emotional aspects of the recovery process.

**Ongoing direct communication** between the healthcare professionals and family members is of utmost importance. Families need to be kept up-to-date on the process, progress, and plans during treatment. They need to be informed directly, not just through their child, in order to avoid misinterpretation and misunderstanding. When possible, it is advisable to talk to parents with the patient present, to ensure that everyone hears the same message. Information provided to parents or by parents without the youth's knowledge leads to secrecy that can interfere with treatment. Openness and trust are best promoted by sending copies of notes or assessments to the family or sending them updates in the form of letters.

**Externalizing questioning.** This emphasizes the influence of the eating disorder. It includes recognizing illness tactics, illusions, and "prices" (unmasking), alongside advantages.

The patient may be asked, "Do you feel some power, some force, trying to persuade you not to eat or to binge and, if so, what? For instance, a patient may describe thoughts such as: "I want to binge. I can't control myself." We try to externalize it, to emphasize these thoughts as the property of an external voice. So we say something like, "Can you tell me more about these thoughts that came to you? What else did they say?" And s/he might reply, "It will give you relief." Then the therapist reflects, "So the eating disorder promises relief." Then s/he might ask, "Does the voice of these thoughts always sound the same? If so, how would you describe it?"

Some people find these questions easy to answer, but others do not. Nonetheless, we continue to ask questions because it is vital that we find a way to externalize and personify the voice of craving. Once we have found a resonant way of externalizing the problem, a way that fits with the person, many options open up. This is the crucial first step. Some find it easier to invite the patient to draw the problem and then reflect on their drawing: "It's a confusing image if she seems a witch with a magic wand and at the same time a guardian who keeps you from harming yourself; no wonder you are ambivalent about her presence." After s/he has talked a bit more about his/her experience of the problem and the way it impacts him/her, and about the patient's voice and thoughts that influence decisions and behaviors, we try to come up with an experience-near definition of the problem.

The aims of this means are to recognize illness tactics and illusions; gain familiarity with the eating disorder characteristics; express curiosity about how life might be without the eating disorder; engage the patient or help him/her become aware of the impact of current physical status and eating habits on his/her social relationships. Questions that the therapist may ask a patient include: How does the eating disorder get the you to think about it more than you wants to? Other people told me that the eating disorder got them to believe that they are not in danger when in fact they are; is it the same in your case? Other people told me that the eating disorder caused them to be dishonest with themselves; how about you? From which of your values does your eating disorder attempt to separate you?

Generally, it is not difficult for people to describe the feelings they experience and how it operates or what tactics it uses to influence their thinking (frightening, exaggerating, totalizing). We then ask a series of questions to gain more information about the timing/context of these thoughts: When do these thoughts come to you most, in what situation?

**Seeing how the eating disorder is interfering with life.** We talk about all the different effects the problem is having on the patient's health, friendships, hopes, and dreams. We also talk about the eating disorder's strategies and tactics. Some of these can be very tricky. By exploring these in detail it becomes easier for the patient to become more alert and sensitive to the ruses and technologies of craving. Conversations address the connections between the patient's temper, perceptions, difficulties in self-regulation and self-control, and deficits in social skills or learning, and how being preoccupied with the eating disorder distracted and relieved the patient from these things.

Having discussed the tactics and effects of the craving, the person is then asked to evaluate these effects. In both motivational interviewing and narrative therapy, we seek to develop a distinction between the patient's current maladaptive state and a more adaptive alternative. This might be done in various ways:

**A "decision matrix"** of the relative pros and cons of either changing or accepting their status quo. Practitioners might share their concern and at the same time recognize the patient's reasons and fears associated with change. This functional analysis of the pros and cons of a belief or behavior has become part of cognitive behavioral therapy for bulimia nervosa (Wilson, 1997) and has been incorporated in the treatment of anorexia nervosa (Bruch, 1982).

**Cognitive therapy technique** to facilitate change using the Socratic method to help patients think through the advantages and disadvantages of a particular belief or behavior (Overholser, 1993).

**Motivational interviewing:** Discuss discrepancy between current behavior and values in life: "How does the eating disorder distance you from the value of honesty, which you emphasized is very important to you?"

**Narrative practice:** "How would you describe your relationship with the problem? Is it positive or negative relationship? Can you name this relationship?

Both motivational interviewing and the narrative approach are progress-oriented, and the therapist is always expected to ask, "Where will this knowledge take you?" This is the guiding style; change and growth must be supported by directing patients to think of a more adaptive alternative to their difficulties.

### 3.3 Phase 2: from acknowledgment to clear cognitive stance against the eating disorder – the turning point

When patients acknowledge that their life was totalized by the eating disorder, they know they should fight it. Still, knowing is not enough to overcome what is inconvenient and even painful. At this stage they progress due to their trusted figures (parents and therapists), like children who learn things not because they internalize the values, but because they internalize trust - the idea that the adults want their best.

Patients perceive the illness as harmful but at the same time as a necessary defense strategy against fatness. During this period they will eventually feel by themselves the incentives of feeling satiety and security, as well as the incentives of direct communication rather than acting out, and hopefully develop a sense of hostility towards the eating disorder.

### Objectives

The objectives of this phase include: progress in physiological stabilization; strengthening of the patient's stance against the illness; symptomatic improvement; facilitation of more anti-eating disorder steps; generation of a broad description of unique outcome, skills, and knowledge about the patient as a person (knowledge, skills, identity); and development of an alternative/preferred story about the patient's coping skills.

### Means

At this stage, in all treatment areas, we focus on mapping out anti- and pro-anorexia/bulimia nervosa thinking and behaviors in the different domains (food, social, personal, family) and explore how the person is influencing the problem. In family therapy we recognize familial dynamics that enabled the eating disorder to set in. These include the influence of culture, ethnicity, discourses, sensitivity, guilt, secrets, strangeness, splits, power relations, family structure, family communication, and values important to the family.

Expanding the patient's influence on the problem using reflection and amplification of unique outcomes (White, 2005). Unique outcomes are exceptions to the problem, events in which the patient's behavior cannot be predicted by the problem. In narrative counseling we use a range of questions that focus on exploring the patient's experiences during the last week of successfully avoiding or resisting pro-eating disorder temptation/steps such as craving, binging, vomiting, over exercising, and skipping meals. We invite the patient to describe in detail any situation in which s/he has been able to avoid, postpone, or resist such temptations: When was this? Where was s/he? Was s/he alone or with friends? Gradually, a picture of the situation emerges, and we ask further questions: What did you do at this time? What were you saying to yourself at the time? What were you saying to the temptation? In response s/he might say, "I was trying to watch a movie," *or* "I and had a long conversation with a friend, and this helped me forget or ignore the temptation."

We try to generate a broad description of the skills and knowledge that they were drawing on at the time. From the viewpoint of motivational interviewing, this process serves as affirmation. Once we have generated a rich description of one particular time they resisted the temptation, we then ask if they had any similar experiences. We try to recall other times they used similar strategies. The process gradually becomes easier.

**Identity formation.** We then ask what these stories of successful events tell the patient about him/herself as a person. In asking this sort of question we seek a name for an alternative plot, an alternative narrative about the patient's life and identity. Perhaps the patient might say, "Well, I am thinking that maybe I am not as hopeless as I first thought. Maybe I do not give in all the time, maybe I am quite determined… I am not sure about this… I had not thought about it in this way before this conversation… but yes, maybe I am kind of determined." The patient often expresses surprise at this point. S/he is used to understanding him/herself only in negative terms, but by slowly and carefully eliciting particular skills and knowledge that the patient has used to resist the craving, different conclusions about his/her identity become possible.

In order to develop it further, I invite the patient to give a name to this alternative story that describes his/her agency, even if limited at the moment. This storyline may be named a story of "overcoming" or "determination" or "not giving up." Once we have a name, we might ask, "What has made these acts of relinquishment possible? Do you have any past experiences that may have cultivated them? We seek some historical evidence to support the new story, and this part of the process is not so difficult. In narrative practice we call this process the art of re-authoring the alternative or preferred story. As it develops we might also ask, "How will this trait, or this ability to resist the problem, help you in the future?" We try to imagine how they can use the skills and qualities that we are describing to resist their current difficulties. These questions can be asked again and again.

**Cognitive behavioral therapy skills.** At this stage, some team members might use cognitive behavioral therapy tools in conjunction with narrative practices to develop alternative ways of obtaining a good physical feeling, enhancing performance, increasing the variety of food items, eating with friends, and reducing obsessive compulsive symptoms. OARS and eliciting change talks are used to support the patient's self-efficacy in these phases of the journey. The same process is conducted with the family. The unique outcome, when the family was not tempted by the eating disorder traps and adopted alternative dynamics, is explored.

### 3.4 Phase 3: against the "patient" status – delayed adolescence and rehabilitation phase

During this phase of the journey, patients acknowledge the incentives of satiety and understand that as long as they eat regular meals and take care of their physical health, they can concentrate, feel better, and sense the ability to have a normal social life. They still do not believe in their ego strength and their ability to be like other people and face the challenges of day-to-day life. Counseling focuses on enhancing self-efficacy and supporting patients' independence. This phase lasts as long as it takes the body and psyche take to "catch up" to the developmental stage of body and mind before the eating disorder began. It might be seen as delayed adolescence.

#### Objectives

The objectives of this phase include: increase in independence; improvement in self-regulation and self-control; improvement in coping skills; and improvement in social and occupational functioning.

#### Means

Motivational interviewing principles lie at the core of this phase, as patients fear the challenges of life. Resisting a righteous stance, expressing empathy, and communicating acceptance are the most important attitudes during this phase of the journey.

We Use a decisional balance sheet and develop a distinction between the patient's "ill status" and the possibility of being recovered (Miller & Rollnick, 2002). We occasionally use a series of "miracle questions" drawn from solution-focused therapy (Walter et al., 1992).

Elaboration questions are used to explore the patient's importance, confidence, and ability to move beyond the "sick" status using the staging rulers. Acknowledging, eliciting, responding, and summarizing change talk are all frequently used.

Conversations focus mainly on what works and monitoring progress in self-regulation, self-control, and coping skills. Self-identity, values, wishes, events, and other developmental steps achieved during the struggle against the illness are recognized. This is done mainly by paying attention to unique outcomes according to narrative practice, naming preferred stories of rebellion against the dictator of eating disorders and re-authoring the story of the individual identity according to what is explored in each session. In terms of MI practice, we use a guiding style to engage with patients, clarify their strengths and aspirations, evoke their own motivations for change, and promote autonomy of decision-making. When guiding conversations about identity and values, we continuously question how our cultural beliefs are shaping our assumptions about what sort of lives people ought to be living, in order to avoid imposing our values.

**External witness interviewing**. To affirm and amplify the patient's achievements, we engage in another narrative practice called outside witness interviewing. We engage in this practice once every three months with each patient and use it as a follow-up session with the parents. In this particular narrative practice the first author invites the patient and the parents to a follow-up session focusing on the change process. The setting, which includes three interviews, is explained: The first is between the patient and me, with parents serving as external witnesses (only listening). Then I interview the parents, and the patient serves as outside listener. Then we have a discussion that includes a letter from all therapists. Finally, I interview the patient, asking how s/he would like to name the current journey in the program and what the journey means to him/her. OARS are used throughout this 15-minute conversation. Then I interview the parents, who were instructed not to criticize or evaluate what they have just heard, but simply to pick a phrase or image that stood out for them. They are asked to associate this item with their personal life and values. Then they are asked to reflect how their parenting has contributed to the patient's achievements. We then read aloud what the therapists wrote about the journey the patient and his/her family have made as they see it, and what still remains to be done. I leave space for all participants to respond to what has been written and to fix the agenda for the next three months.

### 3.5 Phase 4: re-authoring life – regaining self-agency

When the whole person catches up on the process of true maturity, the individual resumes cooperativeness, self-directedness, and self-transcendence, which allow identity to integrate fully and thrive. In this phase of the journey it seems that the patient can live without symptoms but would rather not declare this yet. Treatment intensity is gradually reduced and counseling focuses on empowering the patient and outsider witness practices.

### Objectives

The objectives of this phase include: normalization of weight and eating behavior; improvement in obsessive compulsive disorder behaviors; acknowledgment of self-regulation and self-control; normalization of social and occupational functioning.

### Means

**Narrative practice - Statement of position map of unique outcome with food, friends, and family members.** Michael White suggests that the therapist build a scaffold via questions that encourage people to fill the gaps between the unique events that currently describe certain aspects of their relationship with food, friends, or family and their past experiences, values, and hopes. This scaffold assists people to mobilize their life experience and exercise their imagination and their meaning-making resources. As an outcome, the alternative story lines of people's lives are strengthened and more deeply rooted in history, the gaps are filled, and these story lines are clearly named (White, 2005). Through these conversations a new narrative is constructed in relation to the person's eating, who s/he is, what s/he wants, how s/he manages without an eating disorder, how s/he handles life, how the narrative of his/her social status is changing, and how the narrative of his/her functioning and abilities to free him/herself from the eating disorder is changing. Patients still do not feel secure and complete agency with respect to this new story and often try to silence the achievement in front of parents so as to avoid external pressures to reduce treatment intensity or to make more rapid progress.

**Definitional ceremony and outsider witnesses interviewing.** To affirm and amplify the patients' achievements we engage in the definitional ceremony metaphor practice rituals, which were drawn from the work of Barbara Meyerhof (Myerhoff, 1986) by Michael White, a cultural anthropologist, and have developed therapeutic applications of this metaphor. In this therapeutic field, people are given the option of telling/performing the stories of their lives before an audience of outsider witnesses. The outsider witnesses his/her response by retelling certain aspects of what has been heard. Definitional ceremony structures usually include multi-layered stories of people's lives using images or phrases that stood out in what was heard.

## 3.6 Phase 5: recovery and maintenance

As time passes, the patient's eating behaviors and weight status become normalized and stabilized in the long term. Other areas of life become normalized, as well. Treatment intensity is low. The patient experiences self-acceptance.

### Objectives

The objectives of this phase include the farewell process; gathering assessments and summaries, and relapse prevention strategies.

### Means

At this phase, the patient's file is summarized, as each therapist gathers the specific journey process with its specific tools. There is a collaborative summation meeting, and the setting of a follow-up plan.

| STAGE | Dietician Role, Treatment Focus | Psychotherapist Role, Treatment Focus | Family Therapist Role, Treatment Focus | Clinical Mentors Role, Treatment Focus |
|---|---|---|---|---|
| **Choosing Site** | Preliminary intake session with professional manager to understand collaboratively (using externalizing language) how problem has come into patient's life, what ED has taken from him/her, and how, towards helping patient and his/her family consider the treatment plan offered to them. | | | |
| **1**<br><br>**From partial recognition to full acknowledgment** | • Nutritional assessment<br>• Engaging patient with ED's impacts<br>• Therapeutic alliance<br>• Externalization of ED<br>• Exploring eating issues | • Psychological assessment<br>• Engaging patient with ED's impacts<br>• Therapeutic alliance<br>• Unmasking ED's intentions and tactics<br>• Naming the current relationships with ED and future wishes<br>• Exploring patient's wishes beyond ED (longings?)<br>• Recognizing the unwanted part of ED | • Parents only<br>• Psycho-education to foster recognition of illness' signs, illusions, traps, anti- vs. pro-ED parenting style<br>• Parents + patient<br>• Exploring losses in the family space due to ED<br>• Assessment of family dynamic<br>• Therapeutic contract<br>• Design treatment goals around values | • Therapeutic contract<br>• Common goal, mutual expectations<br>• Soothing meal companions, representing healthy self-caring image, which counters maladapted patterns of interaction, cognition, behavior<br>• Emphasizing creation of coalition to achieve patient's aims<br>• Reflecting pro- and anti-ED behaviors |
| **2**<br><br>**From acknowledg-ment to clear cognitive stance against eating disorder**<br><br>**Guiding towards turning points** | • Externalization and mapping out anti- and pro-AN/BN thoughts and behaviors<br>• Expanding patient's influence on problem<br>• Responsibility around food is between patient and family member or mentor | • Mapping out anti- and pro- AN/BN thoughts and behaviors related to emotional difficulties (*not* related to food)<br>• Recognizing elements enabling ED penetration and control: trait, personal, social status, cultural, and familial factors | • Mapping out anti- and pro- AN/BN behaviors in the family<br>• Recognizing familial dynamics enabling ED penetration<br>• Exploring unique outcomes in which family resisted the dominant story and performed anti-ED steps | • Continued externalization<br>• Monitoring anti-ED voice and behaviors<br>• Forming strong coalition reflecting in real time<br>• Helping patient overcome pro-AN/BN thoughts and behaviors |
| **3**<br><br>**Against the "patient" status** | • Expansion of options around physical goals<br>• Independence around food is encouraged<br>• Dietician's role gradually transfers to that of a witness, reflecting the changes patient experiences in different areas of life after gaining freedom from ED<br>• Using guiding style when noticing stiffness around food issues | • Monitoring progress in coping skills, recognition of self-identity values, wishes, events, other developmental steps achieved during struggle against illness, done mainly via focus on unique outcomes and the strength and values behind these events<br>• Selective reflections on advantages of healthy status and of self-care<br>• Discussing general coping skills, handling conflicts, social skills, self- | • Identification and expansion of options towards resistant stance against nurturing ED in particular and illness in general in family surroundings<br>• Monitoring unique outcomes, re-writing richer familial narrative story of stronger familial identity, wishes, and demeanors<br>• Emphasizing new continual demeanor to create, | • Focus on new occupations, relationships, and identity formed<br>• Mentor moves to passive place |

| STAGE | Dietician Role, Treatment Focus | Psychotherapist Role, Treatment Focus | Family Therapist Role, Treatment Focus | Clinical Mentors Role, Treatment Focus |
|---|---|---|---|---|
| **Choosing Site** | Preliminary intake session with professional manager to understand collaboratively (using externalizing language) how problem has come into patient's life, what ED has taken from him/her, and how, towards helping patient and his/her family consider the treatment plan offered to them. | | | |
| | | regulation, self-control issues, other conflicts | essentially, a new narrative and not a series of sentences | |
| 4<br><br>**Re-authoring life**<br><br>**Re-gaining self-agency** | • New narrative regarding food<br>• Focus on normalization of eating behavior<br>• Only when choices are independent and without intervention of the disorder are decisions transferred to patients<br>• Dietician takes role of witness to changes | • Re-writing a new narrative in relation to who I am, what I want, how I manage without ED, how I handle situation<br>• Exploring new ways to cope with these issues and why patients can be assured that ED has no reason to come into their life anymore | • Re-writing of the family identity<br>• Glorification of unique event and what it means in relation to the new family identity | • Parting from mentors<br>• Patients perceived as if almost normal, mature adolescents |
| 5<br><br>**Recovery and maintenance** | • Practicing normalization with eating behaviors and stabilizing long-term weight status<br>• Relapse prevention plan | • Treatment becomes overbearing – request for lower intensity<br>• Dealing with mourning over the years that were "lost" and parting<br>• Discussing separation issue | • Dealing with farewells<br>• In the family, developing the attitude toward separation as part of a process in which one opens, as a growth step, as a source of pride to parents | |

Table 1. Stages of engagement and recuperation from eating disorders (ED)

**Journey closure.** "And the day came when the risk to remain tight in a bud was more painful than the risk it took to blossom." (Anais Nin) The journey from denial to partial or full recovery witnesses a whole process of development in the therapeutic relationship between patient and therapist. At the same time, the therapists' knowledge, creativity, and insights grow remarkably, and a richer story for all parties is created. During the last few months of treatment, patients are invited for relapse preventions and follow-up sessions with the dietician, as needed.

## 4. Conclusion

Narrative and motivational counseling share reliance on patients' personal agency rather than on a relationship of power. Both encourage collaboration, evocation, and autonomy, empower people, and strive to help them take steps towards actualization of the values that are important to them. Both use unique communication skills to manage ambivalence and "dominant stories" often associated with chronic diseases. The advantages of integrating these approaches within traditional counseling offer some promise in tackling eating disorders with a transdiagnostic orientation, which addresses the dynamics and needs of comorbidities while treating the eating disorder effectively.

## 5. Acknowledgment

The author thanks Shahaf's team and patients for being part of this enthusiastic journey. Special thanks to Daria Uval, Rachel Bachner, and Rachel Wyner for their helpful comments.

## 6. References

American Psychiatric Association (2006). Practice Guidelines for the Treatment of Patients with Eating Disorders (Third Edition). *American Journal of Psychiatry*, Vol. 163, No. 7, (July 2006), pp. 4-54, ISSN 1535-7228

Bion, W. (1959). Attacks on Linking, In: *Melaine Klein Today: Developments in Theory and Practice,* E. Spillius (Ed.), pp. 87–101, Routledge, ISBN 0-415-00675-9, London, United Kingdom

Bruch, H. (1982). Anorexia Nervosa: Therapy and Theory. *American Journal of Psychiatry*, Vol. 139, pp. 1531-49, ISSN 1535-7228

Centre of Excellence in Eating Disorders. (2005). Facts and Findings, In: *About Eating Disorders*, 16.07.2011, Available from http://www.ceed.org.au/www/452/1001127/displayarticle/1001246.html

Crisp, A.H. (1980). *Anorexia Nervosa: Let Me Be*, Academic Press, ISBN 0-86377-383-4, London, United Kingdom

Duncan, B.L.; Hubble, M.A. & Miller, S.D. (1999). *The Heart & Soul of Change: What Works in Therapy?* American Psychological Association Press, ISBN 10: 155798557X, Washington, District of Columbia, USA

Epston, D. (2001). Archive of resistance: Anti-anorexia/anti-bulimia, Co-Research: The making of an alternative knowledge (Anti-anorexia/Anti-bulimia), Available from http://www.narrativeapproaches.com/antianorexia%20folder/AAcoresearch.pdf

Epston, D. (2001). *Catching up with David Epston: A Collection of narrative practice-based papers published between 1991 and 1996*, Dulwich Centre Publications, ISBN 0958667853, Adelaide, Australia

Fairburn, C.G.; Shafran, R. & Cooper, Z. (1999). Invited Essay: A Cognitive Behavioural Theory of Anorexia Nervosa. *Behaviour Research and Therapy*, Vol. 37, No. 1, (January 1999), pp. 1–13, ISSN990-1935:X

Foucault, M. (1988). Technologies of the Self: A Seminar with Michel Foucault, In: *Technologies of the Self,* L.H. Martin, H. Gutman, & P.H. Hutton (Eds.), 16-49, University of Massachusetts Press, ISBN-10: 0870235931, Amherst, Massachusetts, USA

Goodsit, A. (1977). Eating Disorders: A Self Psychological Perspective, In: *Handbook of Psychotherapy for Eating Disorders,* D. Garner & P.E. Garfinkel (Eds.), 55-82 , The Guilford Press, ISBN 1572301864, New York, New York, USA

Grieves, L. (1997). Beginning to Start: The Vancouver Anti-anorexia, Anti-Bulimia League. *Gecko: A Journal of Deconstruction and Narrative Ideas in Therapeutic Practice,* Vol. 2, pp. 78-88, ISSN 1328-2123

Hepworth, J. (1978). *The Social Construction of Anorexia Nervosa*. Sage, ISBN 0-7619-5308-6, London, United Kingdom

Keel, P.K. & Brown, T.A. (2010). On Course Update and Outcome in Eating Disorders. *International Journal of Eating Disorders,* Vol. 43, No. 3, (February 2010), pp. 195-204, ISSN 108-1098X

Kohut, H. (1977). *Preface to Psychodynamics of Drug Dependence,* In: *Psychodynamics of Drug Dependence,* J.D. Blaine & D.A. Julius (Eds.), pp. 64-71, Government Printing Office, ISBN 1568211570, Washington, District of Columbia, USA

Leichner, P. (2005). A New Treatment Approach to Eating Disorders in Youth. *British Columbia Medical Journal,* Vol. 47, No. 1, (January, February 2005), ISSN 08203946

Lock, A.; Epston, D.; Maisel, R. & de Faria, N. (2005). Resisting Anorexia/Bulimia: Foucauldian Perspectives in Narrative Therapy. *British Journal of Guidance and Counselling,* Vol. 33, No. 3, (September 2005), pp. 315-332, ISSN 0306-9885

Madigan, S.P. & Goldner, E.M. (1998). A Narrative Approach to Anorexia: Discourse, Reflexivity, and Questions, In: *The Handbook of Constructive Therapies: Innovative Approaches from Leading Practiti*oners, M. Hoyt (Ed.), Jossey-Bass Publishers, ISBN 0787940445, San Francisco, California, USA

Maisel, R.; Epston, D. & Borden, A. (2005). *Biting the Hand That Starves You: Inspiring Resistance to Anorexia/Bulimia,* Norton & Company, ISBN 10: 0393703371, New York, New York, USA

Malson, H. (1999). Women Under Erasure: Anorexic Bodies in Postmodern Context. *Journal of Community & Applied Social Psychology,* Vol. 9, No. 2, (March, April 1999), pp. 137-153, ISSN 1099-1298

Miller, W. & Rollnick, S. (2002). *Motivational Interviewing: Preparing People to Change,* The Guilford Press, ISBN 978-1-57230-563-2, New York, New York, USA

Minuchin, S.; Rosman, B.L. & Baker, L. (1978). *Psychosomatic Families: Anorexia Nervosa in Pathologies.* Duckworth, ISBN 089862469X, London, United Kingdom

Myerhoff, B. (1986). Life Not Death in Venice: Its Second Life, In: *The Anthropology of Experience,* V. Turner & E. Bruner (Eds.), 261-286, University of Illinois Press, ISBN: 0-252-01249-6, Chicago, Illinois, USA

National Collaborating Centre for Mental Health (2004). National Clinical Practice Guideline: *Eating Disorders: Core Interventions in the Treatment and Management of Anorexia Nervosa, Bulimia Nervosa, and Related Eating Disorders.* National Institute for Health and Clinical Excellence, 17.07.2011, Available from http://www.nice.org.uk/CG009

Overholser, J.C. (1993). Elements of the Socratic Method: I. Systematic Questioning. *Psychotherapy,* Vol. 30, No. 1, (Spring 1993), pp. 67–74, ISSN 0033-3204

Polivy, J. & Herman, C.P. (2002). Causes of Eating Disorders. *Annual Review of Psychology,* Vol. 53, No. 1, (February 2002), pp. 187–213, ISSN 0066-4308

Prochaska, J.O. & DiClemente, C.C. (1986). Towards a Comprehensive Model of Change, In: *Treating Addictive Behaviors,* W.R. Miller & N. Heather (Eds.), 27-3, Plenum Press, ISBN 0-306-45852-7, New York, New York, USA

Rollnick, S.; Miller, W.R. & Butler, C. (2008*). Motivational Interviewing in Health Care: Helping Patients Change Behavior,* The Guilford Press, ISBN 978-1-60623-821-9, New York, New York, USA

Rosenberg, D.B. (2009). *Building Motivational Interviewing Skills: A Practitioner Workbook,* The Guilford Press, ISBN 978-1-60623-299-6, New York, New York, USA

Sanftner, J.L. & Crowther, J.H. (1998). Variability in Self-Esteem, Moods, Shame and Guilt in Women Who Binge. *International Journal of Eating Disorders,* Vol. 23, No. 4, (May 1998), pp. 391–397, ISSN 0276-3478

Serpell, L.; Treasure, J.; Teasdale, J. & Sullivan, V. (1999). Anorexia Nervosa: Friend or Foe? *International Journal of Eating Disorders*, Vol. 25, No. 2, (March 1999), pp. 177–186, ISSN 0276-3478

Steiger, H.; Stotland, S.; Trottier, J. & Ghadirian, A.M. (1996). Familial Eating Concerns and Psychopathological Traits: Causal Implications of Transgenerational Effects. *International Journal of Eating Disorders*, Vol. 19, No. 2, (March 1996), pp. 147–157, ISSN 0276-3478

Steinberg, B.E. & Shaw, R.J. (1997). Bulimia as a Disturbance of Narcissism: Self-Esteem and the Capacity to Self-Soothe. *Addictive Behaviors*, Vol. 22, No. 5, (September, October 1997), pp. 699-710, ISSN 0306-4603

Steinhousen, H.C. & Weber, S. (2009). The Outcome of Bulimia Nervosa: Finding from One-Quarter Century of Research. *American Journal of Psychiatry*, Vol. 166, No. 12, (December 2009), pp. 1331-1341, ISSN 1535-7228

Striegel-Moore, R. (1997). Risk Factors for Eating Disorders. *Annals of the New York Academy of Sciences*, Vol. 817, No. 2, (May 1997), pp. 98–109, ISSN 6632-1749

Strober, M. (1991). Disorders of the Self in Anorexia Nervosa: An Organismic-Developmental Paradigm, In: *Psychodynamic Treatment of Anorexia Nervosa and Bulimia*, C. Johnson (Ed.), 354-373, The Guilford Press, ISBN 0898625505, New York, New York, USA

Treasure, J.; Claudino, A.M. & Zucker, N. (2010). Eating Disorders. *Lancet*, Vol. 375, No. 9741, (February 2010), pp. 583-593, ISSN 6736-0140

Vitousek, K.B. & Ewald, L.S. (1993). Self-Representation in Eating Disorders: A Cognitive Perspective, In: *The Self in Emotional Disorders: Cognitive and Psychodynamic Perspectives*, Z.V. Segal & S.J. Blatt (Eds.), 221-266, The Guilford Press, ISBN 0898622565, New York, New York, USA

Walter, J.; Peller, L. & Jane, E. (1992). *Becoming Solution-Focused in Brief Therapy*, Brunner/Mazel, ISBN 0-87630-653-9 , New York, New York, USA

Ward, A.; Ramsay, R.; Turnbull, R.; Benedettini, S. & Treasure, J. (2000). Attachment Patterns in Eating Disorders: Past in the Present. *International Journal of Eating Disorders*, Vol. 28, No. 4, (December 2000), pp. 370-276, ISSN 0276-3478

White, M. & Epston, D. (1989). Literate Means to Therapeutic Ends, Dulwich Centre Publications, ISBN 0731659899, Adelaide, Australia

White, M. (1995). Re-Authoring Lives: Interviews & Essays, Dulwich Centre Publications, Adelaide, Australia

White, M. (2005). Current Workshop Notes (updated 21st September 2010), Available from www.dulwichcentre.com.au

White, M. (2005). Maps of Narrative Practice, Norton & Company, ISBN 0393705161, New York, New York, USA

Williams G. (1997). Reflections on Some Dynamics of Eating Disorders: 'No Entry' Defenses and Foreign Bodies. *International Journal of Psychoanalysis*, Vol. 78, No. 5, (October 1997), pp. 927-941, ISSN 7578-0020

Wilson, G.T. (1997). Cognitive Behavioral Treatment of Bulimia Nervosa. *The Clinical Psychologist*, Vol. 50, No. 2, (Spring 1997), pp. 10-12, ISSN 0009-9244

World Health Organization (2005). Mental Health of Children and Adolescents. *Facing the Challenges and Finding Solutions*. World Health Organization, Geneva, The Netherlands

# 12

# Treatments for Eating Disorders: The Patients' Views

Tatiana Escobar-Koch[1], Claudia Cruzat Mandich[2] and Ramón Florenzano Urzúa[3]
[1]*Universidad de Chile*
[2]*Universidad Adolfo Ibañez*
[3]*Universidad del Desarrollo*
*Chile*

## 1. Introduction

Eating disorders (EDs) have generated increasing concern in the last decades, both in the mental health field and in the general public. They are amongst the most frequent chronic health problems in adolescents, and the mortality rate of Anorexia Nervosa (AN) is one of the highest of all psychiatric illnesses. Clinical experience has demonstrated that EDs tend to be highly resistant to different modalities of treatment, and outcomes tend to be relatively poor, especially for those who do not receive early specialized interventions (Treasure et al, 2005). One study showed that of a sample of patients with AN who received inpatient treatment, less than 30% showed a good outcome and almost 60% had a poor outcome (Salbach-Andrae et al, 2009). Moreover, adherence is often poor, resulting in patients abandoning treatment; it is not infrequent for them to enter into treatment programs numerous times, both inpatient and outpatient, only to abandon them again. This not only worsens their prognosis but also implies a significant loss of resources for Health Services.

In this context, the fact that relatively little is known about patients' subjective opinions about the treatments they receive becomes highly relevant: what aspects do they value the most? Which are the elements they value least and could contribute to them abandoning treatment? Which health services do they feel can best respond to their needs? Although EDs have been studied from different perspectives, this particular area has been neglected within ED research (Bell, 2003; Vanderlinden et al, 2007).

Another important aspect to consider is the frustration the treatment team experiences when patients abandon treatment despite the severity of their illness and the efforts that have been made to motivate them to adhere. However, previous research suggests that there are significant differences between aspects of treatment valued by providers and patients (de la Rie et al, 2008), and learning about the sufferer's perspective could contribute to developing interventions which may be more effective.

The aim of this study was to identify the views of Chilean patients who have received treatment for an ED about these treatments, including aspects they value and feel have helped them in their recovery as well as aspects they feel have hindered their recovery or been missing from their treatments. We felt it would be interesting to explore ED patients' views in Chile since, to our knowledge, no previous study on this topic has been undertaken in a South American country.

## 2. Method

This was a qualitative, exploratory study based on the principles of the Grounded Theory Model developed by Glaser and Strauss (1967). This methodology is especially appropriate to access subjective processes from the involved individual's perspective.

### 2.1 Inclusion criteria, recruitment and participants

Patients of the Salvador Hospital of Santiago, Chile (main public hospital for the Eastern Metropolitan Health Service of Chile) were contacted through key informants and invited to participate in the study. Inclusion criteria included having been diagnosed with an ED and having received or currently being in treatment for this condition in the Salvador Hospital. All patients who were contacted agreed to participate. The sample size was 10 patients. All participants were female, and their ages ranged from 16 to 47 years, with a mean age of 30.7 years. 6 of the participants had been diagnosed with Bulimia Nervosa, 3 with Anorexia Nervosa and 1 with Eating Disorder Not Otherwise Specified. All patients were currently receiving treatment for their condition.

### 2.2 Data collection and analysis

Semi-structured individual interviews were undertaken. Data were analyzed using open coding. After preliminary results had been obtained a focus group was held in order to corroborate the findings with the participants.

### 2.3 Ethical considerations

The study was approved by the Eastern Metropolitan Health Service's Ethics Committee.

All participants signed an informed consent document.

## 3. Results

The participants' views generated four main themes, each one including positive aspects which patients felt had helped them in their recovery as well as negative aspects which they felt had hindered their recovery or elements which had been missing from their treatments. Each of these is described below and quotes are provided which illustrate these findings in the patients' own words. Findings are summarized in table 1.

### 3.1 Personal and professional characteristics of care providers

The first theme involved personal and professional characteristics of care providers. In terms of personal qualities, participants valued health professionals who were empathetic, concerned, understanding, good listeners, and who they felt they could build a trusting relationship with:

| Theme | Valued Aspects | Non-Valued Aspects |
|---|---|---|
| 1. Personal and Professional Characteristics of Care Providers | | |
| Personal qualities | Empathetic, concerned, understanding, good listeners, trustworthy. | Lack of dedication and commitment, distant, difficult to trust, sending negative messages. |
| Professional qualities | Multidisciplinary team. | Lack of coordination and communication amongst team, lack of specialists in EDs, rotation of professionals, few appointments. |
| 2. Types of Interventions | | |
| Individual psychotherapy | Cognitive-behavioural techniques, help with expression and regulation of emotions. | ---------- |
| Treatments focusing solely on weight gain | ---------- | Lack of consideration for psychological and emotional aspects. |
| Pharmacological treatment | ---------- | Too much medication, "medication for everything". |
| Absolute bed rest | ---------- | Very restrictive. |
| 3. Support | | |
| From care providers | Constant support. | Lack of support during the night in the in-patient ward. Lack of communication between care providers and family members who constitute patients' stable support network. |
| From family members | Feeling supported and accompanied during the therapeutic process. | Lack of support from family members. |
| 4. Patient-Centered Care | Motivation, being able to participate in treatment plans. | Lack of an individualized approach to care, not being given all the information concerning treatments. |

Table 1. Results

*"The psychiatrist who is with me, ehh...we start to talk, and the first thing she says: I bet you don't get any sleep, with two babies, and I understand you, because I have twins, so it's like she empathizes right away, she, she inspires trust....so, those things, when one is sick and when one lacks things, are very important... all the other doctors, they have all been like...eh...particularly special with, with me, I've felt it like that... and that's the very thing that motivates me to want to keep coming. I don't know if it's a, what's it called, a characteristic of the people sick of bulimia and of anorexia, the lack of affection, the loneliness, and all that... the people who are going to dedicate themselves to this, give it importance, because one ehh, needs not the attention, but the understanding, because one doesn't accept oneself, and someone has to accept you so they can help you to, to learn" (Interview 5).*

*"...I notice 100% of concern for me [from the psychologist]. Because, in fact, when at times I missed [the appointment], he called me, what's wrong, and all that. So that is helpful, especially, for example, there were times when I didn't feel like going out, and...I didn't get up all day....so he understood me in that sense, he understood the fact that I missed once, because we reached the compromise that I wouldn't miss... more than three times..." (Interview 7).*

*"I cared a lot about my psychologist, for the reason that we were more, more than psychologist and patient, we were like friends, so I trusted him a lot, it was like really fun, I liked coming, and yes, I felt like closer to him, not just like a doctor who tells you OK: this, and this, but I felt more, more closeness" (Interview 8).*

*"All three listen to me. My psychologist...has helped me a lot with my, with relationships with my family, everything. The psychiatrist also, has learned to listen to me quite a bit..." (Interview 7).*

Regarding professional qualities of treatment providers which patients' felt had helped them in their recovery, they identified being treated by a multidisciplinary team conformed by psychiatrist, psychologist and nutritionist, who worked together, as positive:

*"What I most value, am grateful for, is having an entire team because if not...because I alone, I know I can't come out of this alone, I've tried and, and that's what I most find value in...I thank that I have an entire, that I have an entire team" (Interview 8).*

*"I'd never been in treatment before. And since one always heard that, I don't know, anorexia and bulimia didn't....in the public sector there wasn't much...much solution, I mean... but actually, from January until today I've realized that it's a, it's a multidisciplinary team, that that's why they sent me here.....yeah, because actually...everything goes like together with everything, I mean... everything is related" (Interview 3).*

*"...constant psychological and psychiatric support are needed... and well, and nutritionist, it's like a team more than anything, made up by a nutritionist, psychologist, psychiatrist" (interview 2).*

*"...there was a time when I passed out, I had, I fasted for two weeks, two whole weeks, I mean, and they wanted to hospitalize me and everything, and everyone knew, psychiatrist, psychologist, everyone knew. So I liked that, that they were all connected" (Interview 8).*

Participants also described certain negative aspects of care providers which they perceived as obstacles to their therapeutic process. On a personal level, they described feeling a lack of dedication and commitment from some professionals, and feeling distanced from them which made it more difficult to establish trusting relationships:

> *"I'm actually not happy with the doctor's care, not at all, I feel that… [he was lacking] dedication, because I feel that they are not very concerned… more than anything I think… I think what's missing, lets say, being more dedicated, eh, getting more involved, if I commit, lets say with the treatment, that it be mutual" (Interview 4).*

> *"I don't know, it's that I've always had the impression that psychiatrists make you feel that they know much more than what they know, you know? I feel that they are like square-minded people, that they don't look beyond what they want to see. I don't know, I see them like people that like, people that like feel superior quote unquote, like they know everything. So I never, for that reason I don't, I don't believe them much sometimes" (Interview 1).*

> *"…one of the things I feel… is the distance from the psychiatrist" (Interview 7).*

Participants also referred to receiving negative messages from some members of staff and how this stood in the way of their recovery:

> *" Ehh… well, constantly repeating that your weight is not healthy, that, that the bulimic attacks…or, for example, if I'm eating, eat everything, or because if not, after, don't go throw it away. Messages like that… the nurses…it was that many would comment: there goes XX to vomit her food… and I was just going to the bathroom. So being constantly, like they have you marked, like if she goes to the bathroom she's going to eliminate the food…it was like they were constantly repeating that, that you're not well, that you're sick, so they didn't.. they didn't give like any solution… it was like they were constantly emphasizing that you were sick, and that everything you did was to sabotage the treatment. That was, that was more than anything what bothers or what obstructs [the treatment]" (Interview 2).*

On a professional level, one cause for concern for participants was the lack of coordination and communication amongst the different professionals treating them, which meant they often had to tell the same things twice and which ultimately led them to lose their trust in the treatment team:

> *"…I think that sometimes they don't even read what the psychologist wrote…so, eh, I think that the two things don't connect, they are like disconnected […] they don't form a team, because in fact when, eh, when two appointments came together, almost at the same time, the psychiatrist and psychologist on Monday, psychiatrist at eleven and psychologist at one, I was waiting for the psychiatrist for a long time…finally it was one, and I was still waiting for the psychiatrist, so in that moment…I told him, you know what, my psychologist is waiting for me, and he said: which is your psychologist?... he didn't even know who my psychologist was, he didn't even know him, I mean I had to like introduce them….so there I noticed that there was no connection […] it's like a waste of time… because I have to tell the same thing twice, and sometimes important details are lost, that a psychiatrist should know or a psychologist should tell him….so I sometimes need for these details not to get lost because…one can also make a mistake in the sense of giving medication…that's what I think, that they should be more connected, more united, not so different" (Interview 7).*

> *"The doctor who sees me now…told me: the exams came out really well…and suddenly I see an internal medicine doctor coming… and he started telling me that I had problems in this, and that, OK, and then I said: but how? If the doctor told me everything was fine. So I don't understand it… so I thought that was strange, so if the doctor tells me it's fine, and the other doctor started telling me other things, and on the side the nurse tells me the exams were bad, then I don't know which of the three to believe, since the three are professionals…so, it made me*

> *angry…I didn't know who was telling me the truth…this is why I sometimes don't believe much in doctors, in psychiatrists"* (Interview 2).

Another thing which participants felt hindered their recoveries was that at times one of the professionals treating them had to leave and was replaced with someone new. This once again brought up trust issues for the patients, making them feel vulnerable, as if they were starting over or going backwards in their therapeutic process:

> *"What I feel that's like negative is that I'm not going to see my psychologist any more because he's a trainee psychologist and since he finished his training, I'm going to end up with another psychologist… it's like starting over, because it's really difficult for me to maintain trust with a psychologist, it's hard for me… [I had] a psychologist with whom I could go happily to therapy because I'm going to talk with the person I like so much… so I think that the fact that I'm no longer going to see him is negative for my treatment, because I'm going to have to start over with another psychologist. […] It's terrible because I had trust with my psychologist, which had been difficult to achieve…so, once again feeling like… vulnerable. Because one feels vulnerable in that sense… I feel vulnerable because… I have to tell the story again, I have to talk about the same things again, it's like I already know it by heart…. It makes me feel… as I said, vulnerable, because it…it makes me sad, this makes me sad because, I mean, again! And, like going backwards, and going backwards makes me melancholic. And that, I feel, is negative"* (Interview 7).

> *"I started off really well. I liked it, I had a good connection with the psychologist who, who saw me the first time, lets say, a good connection…the treatment was really good with her… she had to leave, and we started from scratch, the treatment gets totally lost… these changes like this, so sudden… from one psychologist to another, in the end for the patient… they don't achieve anything, I mean, everything you achieved, gets lost, because actually…lost work, I find, starting over, the psychologist has to get to know you again. So it's, it has been like going backwards, I find, the change. […] Don't change the, the doctors, the psychologists, it's starting over, it's starting from scratch, going backwards, it's delaying the…what had been accomplished, lets say, I feel that I got delayed. I got delayed"* (Interview 4).

Participants also mentioned that having few appointments with their psychiatrists, sessions being too short and appointments being cancelled by their care providers had a negative impact on their treatments:

> *"…to start, the interviews are really short and…we have had, from the time I arrived, really few appointments [with the psychiatrist] because there was one time that I didn't come, well that was my mistake, I gave notice and everything… after that every time I came, eh… which were like three, four months more or less, I had to be with the doctors who were on call, because, either he was sick, well, he could have been sick, no, I don't know, but he was sick so many times in a row that…it calls my attention. I think maybe he has lots of things to do… he could have been sick but not that long. I think that he had trips out of the country, then he came back, and those gaps, I feel it hasn't, hasn't been good"* (Interview 4).

> *"My doctor, I think, is quite concerned about me, but they are not there all day [in inpatient ward], the paramedics take care of me more than the doctors…that's the problem…"* (Interview 6).

Finally, in terms of professional characteristics of care providers, participants identified that one central aspect which was missing from their treatments was for it to be undertaken by professionals who are specialized in EDs:

*"I feel I need a professional who is specialized in what I have... [...] maybe I'm not in the right treatment. That's what's going on. That's why my father is now finding out about several centers which are specialized in eating disorders. So, he wants to find one that also convinces him. Because it turns out that no doctor can give him an explanation of why I am this way... [...] but it's so difficult because those specialized places, finally, are private. So, that's the problem, that not all people have the financial situation to... change it, to change, I mean, to get a more adequate treatment" (Interview 1).*

*"And the lack of nutritionist, which I think is fundamental. I think there should be a nutritionist here, who was in charge, lets say, of the area of eating disorders" (Interview 4).*

### 3.2 Types of interventions

A second theme which emerged from the participants' responses involved the types of interventions they received during the therapeutic process, among which individual psychotherapy was highly valued. Patients' described certain cognitive-behavioural techniques which they felt had helped them in their recovery, including having to fulfill certain tasks between sessions and working through a book with the help of their therapists:

*"What I have found to be fundamental, at least with the psychologist that, that I started with.... I vented with her...what I couldn't do on the outside, I did with her. She started making outlines, giving me tasks, lets say, [an] outline of mi diet... every week I would bring her the outline. We would see each other every week, from one week to the next, with appointments...the amount that I ate, what I ate, what I thought of before I ate, eh, the purges, what I did to revert the purges, eh, any observation, lets say, that was important, the help I could receive, the people who know about the problem, if I had observed if my family worried about me. That was the task, lets say. I thought it was really good" (Interview 4).*

*"...my psychiatrist gave me a task with a book I was reading, some chapters I had to read, and work through them about how this is produced, I mean seeing, for example, that if there is a situation, from that situation there is a thought, and that from the thought there is a consequence from that, and that emotions are involved. So she explains through all those things and little by little I have come to understand all that is happening to me, which was that... I felt lost" (Interview 2).*

*"...methods....for example, writing down everything you eat, and realizing what is good for you and what is bad for you. So all these things help you... [...] this book... the two psychologists who saw me here lent it to me...this little book 'Risk and Prevention of Anorexia and Bulimia'...the first time they lent it to me was specific: read from this page to this page, and this one, this one and this one, and we'll comment. The second time they lent it to me, they told me to read the whole thing. And then it captivated me because... I felt very identified...it speaks directly to you, to you as a patient. So, I think that, it makes you, makes you become aware that there are possibilities to get better" (Interview 5).*

Patients also highlighted the importance of individual psychotherapy in helping them recognize and learn to deal with their emotions, and understand how their difficulties in the expression and regulation of their emotions related to their ED behaviours:

*"...we have reached one of the important conclusions with the psychologist, that I suppress my emotions, the good ones and the bad ones, that's why I don't have a... positive concept of myself, because I don't see anything, I don't see anything good, and the bad I... I don't know if I enlarge*

> *it, but I do see it more clearly, so...that's what we are doing, learning to, to...feel, because one blocks oneself... in order to not have a bad time... one also prevents oneself from having a good time [...] I would like... [to] know the cause, why, why I'm like this...what happened before, although she tells me that actually many things have happened to me, which could be the cause of...but, above all, it's like a feeling of loneliness, on, on my part, from childhood" (Interview 5).*

> *"... I would tell her I feel this and she [the psychologist] tried to find a solution as to why I felt that... she made me understand why I felt what I was feeling... I find that that helped me, because it, it made me... see the things in which I was wrong" (Interview 9).*

> *"With him [the psychologist] we talk around forty-five minutes, and we talk about anxiety, specifically about anxiety...and how I feel, of...of why I feel that way...what I most think is how, how he has helped me to understand why I react in some ways... try to understand why I vomit, without there being a need to do so...it helped me a lot because no other psychologist or psychiatrist had made me understand why I was doing what I was doing, and in general he, eh, he was concerned with telling me why I was feeling that way, why I was so anxious, or why I vomited, because, eh, what it was that I felt before I vomited, and what it was that I felt after I vomited...he made me realize how I could stop this. Because I realized, OK, I'm very anxious, so I'm going to binge, to realize when I was going to binge, so, I'm going to binge, and stop in that moment. Say no. That like helped me...to listen to what was going on inside of me, why I did it, so, that for me, well, of all the things we talked about, I was very touched by some conversations that I had with him, so I left like meditating, and I meditated about this same thing every week, so, one of the things is to like realize that, for example, I vomited because...it was a way of like harming myself and not harming others, OK?, and several other things, and to try to stop this, that anxiety" (Interview 7).*

Regarding therapeutic interventions which patients felt had not helped them in their recovery, treatments that focused solely on weight gain, without considering psychological or emotional aspects, were mentioned, and the importance of an integrated approach to treatment from the very beginning was highlighted:

> *"...in neither [hospitalization] a clear objective was achieved, I mean the only thing they achieved was making me gain weight, because for them...with your low nutritional condition, you can't understand, you can't reason many things, so having...the normal adequate weight, with that they could start treatment. But they focused so much on weight that I never had like psychological support, nor anything... that could like help me or [allow me to] understand why this happened, none whatsoever...they said: OK, you are here in the inpatient ward and here we feed you and everything, and when you leave...only then your treatment for the eating disorder will begin which would be as an outpatient. I found that sort of, like I don't know, it didn't make sense because it was like if one is in a process and all they did to me was make me eat, eat like they had ordered them to do....all I had on my mind all day was food, food, food, so no one helped me to like guide, how to avoid that...so that was, more than anything, the treatment that really didn't work [...] because there's something else there, I mean, it's not just the issue of food" (Interview 2).*

In addition, pharmacological treatments appeared to be less valued by participants, and in some cases family members, than psychological interventions:

> *"I find that the medication...for the binge episodes has helped me, but the antidepressants haven't, I believe I have done it more on my own than with the medication, you understand? ... thanks to the psychologist I've been able to, lets say, eh, [advance] more than with the*

*antidepressant they give me, you understand? And that thing of... medication for everything, to sleep at night... I've stopped taking those... I stopped taking them on my own, I found them unnecessary and I've been able to sleep [...] I can't say everything has been bad... but I know that also a large part of this has been due to the psychological support and because I've done it, I've had the willpower, because on the other side I think that no, medication doesn't, doesn't do everything" (Interview 4).*

*"He [my father] believes, tells me that the only thing they are doing is intoxicating me with pills. On one hand he's right, because I take a lot of pills. I'm going to end up getting sick to my stomach, I don't know, but they are a lot of pills. I think that of all those who are here, I think that I am the one who takes the most pills" (Interview 1).*

Another intervention which participants described as having a negative impact on their recovery was absolute bed rest, which was perceived as a very restrictive measure:

*"...one knows that what they are saying is really for your own good, but sometimes they like, one tends to think they exaggerate greatly, and it's like they take away your freedom, for example I was here the first days in absolute bed rest. I mean, I couldn't move... so it's like, that all the time, if I got up: XX, to bed! So it was like really bothersome, because I said, but come on, I don't have that freedom that I want... being so locked up also anguished me...I also needed my freedom to be able to do my things" (Interview 2).*

*"...I don't agree much with their, with the measures they take...for example having me in bed without moving, or not walking, I find... I don't find it good for me" (Interview 1).*

### 3.3 Support

Patients' responses generated a third theme which had to do with the importance of feeling supported throughout the road to recovery. Receiving constant support from their care providers, feeling accompanied and contained by them was highly valued:

*"The containment, the containment which they enable you to have, I mean, that I don't feel alone. I don't feel like that I'm there, as yet another patient, like: lets feed her now and then she'll leave. It's like that containment that they are constantly concerned about me, constantly thinking about what's happening with me, I mean, even if they see me lying down too much, with a certain face of some emotion... they ask me what's the matter, that... they are always there...and that was what I felt I needed because before I felt like very alone, like very abandoned, to put it in some way. So now I feel like that containment and constant concern, and I feel I needed it" (Interview 2).*

*"Look, what I most highlight is, is like, the time, and the, I don't know if the interest, but...they take good care of you, at least the Doctor [names her psychologist]...the whole thing has actually felt quite nice. They have been like really fraternal... the nutritionist also, I mean I've felt like... I don't know if love, but... like, like they support you a lot" (Interview 3).*

On the other hand, participants mentioned the lack of support they felt during the night in the in-patient ward as a negative aspect of their treatment:

*"Here there are no nurses on call at night. If a patient becomes unwell at night a doctor has to see her, or the paramedics. But here the paramedics are not awake all night, they go to bed and sleep. So I say, what kind of...of what's it called...of rehabilitation centre is this?" (Interview 3).*

Feeling supported and accompanied by their family members during the therapeutic process was also valued by participants. One patient portrayed how helpful it was for her to feel supported by her husband, and the positive impact it had on her recovery:

> *"...I would often get up to eat at night... I would get anxiety... and do something to myself at night. Many times, when I was doing well with my husband, he would pretend to be asleep and was paying attention to see if I did it or not at night, and one time I got up, I told him I wasn't going to do it, I went and I did it, and he was paying attention, and he, he didn't tell me straight away, he talked to me about it later on. So that helped me a great deal, it was like a click, and after that I went a long time without getting up at night, it was a way of containing me and, a help, I felt that it was a really good detail" (Interview 4).*

However, later in the interview she described the feeling of loneliness that set in when she lost his support:

> *"I can't [vent] with my close family, eh, in this case with my husband I had done it at some point and I had had his support, but I feel that now there hasn't been much support, or he got bored, so, actually...he tells me that I follow him around, that I pursue him, and that... I'm sort of... obsessed with the problem, and in part I know he is somewhat right, but he also has to put himself in my shoes, I mean, what reasons there have been, and unfortunately, my life is based on this, it is bulimia... I think. I don't know what would happen... if we weren't together, maybe I could handle it better. I've thought about it. It's been so many years, but... it's like fear, actually, of ending up alone, something like that..." Interview 4).*

Finally, an aspect which patients mentioned as missing from their treatment was greater communication between their care takers and the family members who constitute their stable support network:

> *"... I would have liked, for example, every once in a while, [for my psychologist] to talk to my family. I mean, to talk to me, and later a couple of weeks could go by and he could talk to my mother and tell her how I was advancing... the thing is that my father doesn't really believe in this... my mother is the one who has been there with me always [...] so... I would have liked for the psychologist to talk to my family... [about] the behaviours I've had, or the changes, or what I could improve..." (Interview 8).*

### 3.4 Patient-centered care

The fourth theme that emerged from the participants' interviews involved the desire for patient-centered care. Patients identified that in order to truly be at the centre of their own treatment they needed to be motivated, to feel that it was possible to get better, and to take responsibility for their recovery, and they valued receiving this motivation from their care providers:

> *"What treatments have I received with the nutritionist? Ehh, more than anything, it's funny but it's like, it's more than anything a psychological treatment, because she says: you are, you are in charge of yourself now, you have to assume the responsibility for your recovery [...] when I arrived here, I arrived saying that I wanted to get better to save my children, to have them near me, to be well for them, but now I am starting to, to think, I'm still not convinced of this, but now I'm starting to think that it's good for me, it's good to do it for me. Not only for the children, [although] the children will also benefit, but it is something for me, and I think that is*

*very important because, with the little appreciation I have for myself, to start to do something for me… can change many things" (Interview 5).*

*"…if a patient with an eating disorder arrives to treatment like very unmotivated, I mean, that you can tell that [she has] zero interest in that, start motivating her little by little to a recovery… with positive messages, that she, that what she has is not, she's not a sick person, rather she has a sickness that can be healed and that is not forever. Or, if it will be there… during her life… that she can control it, that she will be able to get to a point where she will be able to control it, and live her life, because this really, takes away your life" (Interview 2).*

Participants described that once they were able to recognize their illness and become motivated to recover, they were able to leave the role of the "victim" and take a more active stance in their treatment, which they felt had positive repercussions for their recovery:

*"Look, I was meditating about this, and what I most value is that they made me realize things I had not realized, I don't know how to explain it, but it's like, talking to me about the illness as it is, clearly, not as a victim... it's like what helped me and I think I value a lot" (Interview 7).*

*"I think that more than anything I see how positive it has been to have recognized [the illness], because by recognizing the illness one can, one can help oneself, and one can be helped, while one doesn't recognize it one can't…it's up to me, that's very clear to me, it doesn't depend on anybody else's help, which they already gave me, and thank God it was positive, because I recognized [the illness], and I stopped dieting for a long time" (Interview 10).*

Feeling like they were able to participate in their treatment plans was also valued by participants:

*"… afterwards the doctor changed my medication, he told me that these were effective for the problem I have… but that I wasn't going to gain as much weight as with the ones he gave me at the beginning. Because I told him that I wasn't going to go any more because I was already gaining weight, I didn't want to continue any more, so he made a whole change [in the treatment]" (Interview 10).*

On the other hand, not being given all the information concerning their treatments was perceived as negative by participants, making them less willing to cooperate:

*"… the paramedic comes and gives me another pill, which I though was like strange, I didn't want to take it. Because first they have to ask me about things, or explain why they are giving me a pill" (Interview 1).*

*"[They should] explain a little bit the reasons for the restrictions" (Interview 3).*

Finally, patients expressed that an individualized approach to care, which focuses on the specific needs of each person, was missing from their treatments:

*"Me as, as a person, as ME, I would like to receive help for anorexia… I think that…that the patient has to be studied more and see which medication [is] effective that will really be good for the, the person, because we don't all have the same body, we don't all have the same mind" (Interview 9).*

*"We the patients are not all the same" (Focus group).*

*"They put us all in the same bag" (Interview 3).*

## 4. Conclusion

The objective of this study was to explore the views of Chilean patients who have received treatment for an ED about these treatments, in order to identify the aspects that patients value and feel have helped them in their recovery as well as the aspects they feel have hindered their recovery. The participants' responses centered around four main themes, which included positive and negative aspects of care.

The first theme involved personal and professional characteristics of care providers. On a personal level, participants valued care providers who were empathetic, understanding, concerned, and who they felt they could build a trusting relationship with, stating that this contributed to them liking their treatments and motivated them to "want to keep coming". On the other hand, care providers who were perceived as distanced from the patient, difficult to trust or uncommitted were evaluated negatively. These results are in line with previous findings which suggest that the quality of the therapeutic relationship is an important element of ED patients' satisfaction with their treatments (Bell, 2003; de la Rie et al, 2006; Escobar-Koch et al, 2010). Participants also described professional aspects of their care providers which they felt were negative and hindered the development of the therapeutic alliance: the little time available to them with their psychiatrists, the cancellation of appointments and the fact that professionals were at times replaced with others (due to the Salvador Hospital being a teaching facility), which patients expressed made it difficult to trust their treatment providers and made them feel as if they were "going backwards" in their recovery. This supports the notion that a positive therapeutic alliance may contribute to improving treatment adherence and outcomes (Federici & Kaplan, 2008; Gallop et al, 1994) and suggests that effort should be made to provide patients with a stable treatment team which emphasizes the development of the therapeutic relationship.

Regarding professional characteristics of care providers valued by participants, they described wanting to receive treatment from specialists in EDs. Previous studies suggest that ED literacy amongst clinicians who are not specialized in the treatment of these disorders is relatively poor. One study found that primary care physicians lacked knowledge about diagnostic symptoms, physical complications and epidemiology of EDs (Currin et al, 2009). Another study showed that health professionals with an interest in EDs but not specialized in this field did not have more knowledge about the risks and maintaining factors of these disorders than a group of patients or a sample of college students (Schmidt et al, 1995). This supports participants' views that treatment for EDs should be provided by specialists in order to ensure the best care possible.

The fact that it is difficult to access specialized treatment within the public health system was also pointed out by participants. Chile has a public health system which serves over 70% of the population, including the poorest people in the country (MINSAL, 2006). However, few specialized ED treatment centres exist within the public system, and patients are often treated in general psychiatric facilities. Accessing specialized private care is very costly and therefore impossible for many patients. A similar situation was described by a British study in which almost 40% of participants ended up paying for private care due to the lack of specialized treatment centres within the (public) National Health Service (Newton et al, 1993), and a recent study suggested that this lack of availability of public ED Services in the UK still exists (Escobar-Koch et al, 2010). These findings emphasize the importance of developing specialist ED services that are available to all patients and ensuring that financial constraints are not an obstacle to receiving adequate care.

Receiving treatment from a multidisciplinary team was also identified as a positive aspect of care by the participants of this study. Previous research has indicated that due to the complexity of these disorders treatment provision by a team of professionals, including psychiatrists, psychologists, experts in nutrition and social workers, is warranted, and periodical team meetings must be held to discuss each patient and agree on a treatment plan (Miranda-Sánchez, 2010). However, amongst the negative aspects of care, patients mentioned the poor coordination that sometimes existed between their treatment providers, including instances in which one health professional did not know who the other clinicians treating the patient were. This highlights the importance of not only having a group of different professionals available to provide treatment but also ensuring that they are organized and truly collaborate as a team.

The second theme which emerged from participants' responses referred to types of interventions received, and, in accordance with previous findings, individual psychotherapy was highly valued (Bell, 2003; Escobar-Koch et al, 2010; Rosenvinge & Klusmeier, 2000). Patients in this study highlighted the benefits of cognitive-behavioral techniques, in line with a recent study in which patients with bulimia nervosa and eating disorder not otherwise specified responded well to cognitive-behavioral treatments (Fairburn et al, 2009). Moreover, participants described how therapy had enabled them to understand the connection between their difficulties in expressing and regulating their emotions and their ED behaviours, and they valued help in learning "to listen to what was going on inside", in recognizing and dealing with their emotions. This supports the notion that Emotion-Focused Therapy, which promotes the processing and expression of emotional experience, may be beneficial for the treatment of EDs (Dolhanty & Greenberg, 2009).

Pharmacological interventions were less valued than therapy by participants in this study. This supports previous findings that medication alone does not seem to be an effective treatment for EDs, due at least in part to the fact that many patients suffering from these disorders are reluctant to accept such treatment (Halmi et al, 2005). Therapeutic interventions focusing exclusively on weight gain were also evaluated negatively, in line with previous research which has identified the importance of not limiting ED treatments to issues of food and weight (Bell, 2003).

A third theme generated by participants in this study stressed the importance of feeling supported by their treatment providers during the recovery process. It has been shown that strategies focusing on support are predictors of ED patients' satisfaction with their treatments (Clinton, 2001; Clinton et al, 2004), and it is therefore essential for ED services to provide constant support to their patients. Feeling supported by their families was also valued by participants, and they expressed concern about what they felt was insufficient communication between their care providers and their support network. Similarly, a study evaluating anorexia nervosa patients' treatment perceptions found that many of the participants felt that their parents had not received sufficient help to support their daughters (Halvorsen & Heyerdahl, 2007). These findings suggest that ED treatment teams should have regular sessions with their patients' families in order to provide information and guidance about how to best support them during the therapeutic process.

The final theme which stemmed from the participants' views involved their wish for patient-centered care. In accordance with previous findings, patients identified the need for an individualized approach to treatment (Boughtwood & Halse, 2010; Escobar-Koch et al, 2010; Schaffner & Buchanan, 2008). The importance of feeling motivated and taking responsibility for their recovery was also highlighted, and participants described how becoming motivated enabled them to take on an active role in their treatment which had a positive impact on their recovery. ED patients tend to be very ambivalent about treatment and often enter into it reluctantly, and this is associated with bad treatment adherence and high drop out rates (Feld et al, 2001). In this context, finding ways to increase ED patients' motivation becomes essential. Motivational interviewing, which stemmed from the idea that motivation is not a personality trait but rather arises from an interpersonal process (Miller & Rollnick, 1991), offers a such a possibility. Its goal is to improve patients' intrinsic motivation to change by helping them explore and resolve their ambivalence, emphasizing personal choice and responsibility, and it has been suggested that it could be successfully applied with ED patients (Treasure & Ward, 1997, Treasure & Schmidt, 2001).

In summary, this study explored the views of Chilean ED patients about their treatments, identifying aspects that are valued by them as well as elements which they consider to have had a negative impact on their recovery. Themes generated from their responses echoed several findings from previous research, such as the importance of the therapeutic relationship, the need for treatment to be provided by specialized multidisciplinary teams, the lack of availability of specialized treatment facilities, the preference for individual psychotherapy and treatments that don't focus exclusively on issues of food and weight, the importance of receiving support from treatment providers and family members during the process of recovery and the wish for patient-centered, individualized care. The central role of patient motivation during the therapeutic process was also highlighted. The main limitation of this study was its small sample size. The main strength was that it is, to our knowledge, the first study evaluating the views of ED patients in a South American country.

## 5. Acknowledgment

We would like to thank the patients who participated in this study for their valuable contribution, and the Salvador Hospital of Santiago, Chile for granting us access to these patients.

We would also like to thank the Eastern Metropolitan Health Service (Servicio de Salud Metropolitano Oriente) of Chile and the Universidad del Desarrollo for their financial support.

## 6. References

Bell, L. (2003). What can we learn from consumer studies and qualitative research in the treatment of eating disorders? *Eat Weight Disord*, Vol.8, No.3, pp.181-187.

Boughtwood, D. and Halse, C. (2010). Other than obedient: Girls ´ construction of doctors and treatment regimes for Anorexia Nervosa. *J Community & Appl. Soc. Psychol*, Vol.20, pp. 83-94, ISSN 1052-9284.

Clinton, D. (2001). Expectations and Experiences of Treatment in Eating Disorders. *Eat Disord*, Vol.9, pp.361-371, 1064-0266.

Clinton, D., Björck, C., Sohlberg, S. and Norring, C. (2004). Patient Satisfaction with Treatment in Eating Disorders: Cause for Complacency or Concern? *Eur Eat Disord Rev*, Vol.12, pp.240-246, ISSN 1072-4133.

Currin, L., Waller, G. And Schmidt, U. (2009). Primary care physicians´ knowledge of and attitudes toward the eating disorders: Do they affect clinical actions? *Int J Eat Disord*, Vol.42, No. 5, pp. 453-458, ISSN 0276-3478.

De la Rie, S., Noordenbos, G., Donker, M. and Van Furth, E. (2006). Evaluating the Treatment of Eating Disorders from the Patient's Perspective. *Int J Eat Disord, Vol.* 39, pp. 667-676, ISSN 0276-3478.

De la Rie, S., Noordenbos, G., Donker, M. and Van Furth, E. (2008). The quality of treatment of eating disorders: A comparison of the therapists' and the patients' perspective. *Int J Eat Disord*, Vol.41, No.4, pp. 307-317.

Dolhanty, J. And Greenberg, L. (2009). Emotion-focused therapy in a case of Anorexia Nervosa. *Clin Psychol Psychother*, Vol. 16, pp. 366-382, ISSN 1063-3995.

Escobar-Koch, T., Banker, J.D., Crow, S., Cullis, J., Ringwood, S., Smith, G., van Furth, E., Westin, K. and Schmidt, U. (2010). Service Users' Views of Eating Disorder Services: An International Comparison. *Int J Eat Disord*, Vol.43, pp.549-559, ISSN 0276-3478.

Fairburn, C., Cooper, Z., Doll, H., O´Connor, M., Bohn, K., Hawker, D., Wales, J. and Palmer, R. (2009). Transdiagnostic cognitive- behavioral therapy for patients with eating disorders: A two-site trial with 60-week follow up. *Am J Psychiatry*, Vol. 166, No. 3, pp. 311-319.

Federici, A. and Kaplan, A. (2008). The patient´s account of relapse and recovery in Anorexia Nervosa: A qualitative study. *Eur Eat Disord Rev*, Vol. 16, pp.1-10, ISSN 1072-4133.

Feld, R., Woodside, D.B., Kaplan, A.S., Olmsted, M.P. and Carter J.C. (2001). Pretreatment Motivational Enhancement Therapy for Eating Disorders: A Pilot Study. *Int J Eat Disord*, Vol.29, pp.393-400, ISSN 0276-3478.

Gallop, R., Kennedy, S. H. and Stern, D. (1994). Therapeutic Alliance on an Inpatient Unit for Eating Disorders. *Int J Eat Disord*, Vol.16, No.4, pp.405-410, ISSN 0276-3478.

Glaser, B. G. & Strauss, A. L. (1967). *The Discovery of Grounded Theory*. Chicago: Aldine Publishing Company, ISBN 1-884156-13-4.

Halmi, K., Agras, S., Crow, S., Mitchell, J., Wilson, T., Bryson, S. and Kraemer, H. (2005). Predictors of Treatment acceptance and completion in Anorexia Nervosa. Implications for future study designs. Arch Gen Psychiatry, Vol. 62, pp. 776- 781.

Halvorsen, I. and Heyerdahl, S. (2007). Treatment perception in adolescent onset anorexia nervosa: Retrospective views of patients and parents. *Int J Eat Disord*, Vol. 40, No. 7, pp. 629- 639, ISSN 0276-3478.

Miller, W.R. and Rollnick, S. (1991). *Motivational Interviewing. Preparing People to Change Addictive Behavior.* New York: Guilford Press, ISBN 1-57230-563-0.

MINSAL. *Objetivos Sanitarios Para la Década 2000-2010. Evaluación a Mitad de Período.* Santiago: Ministerio de Salud 2006.

Miranda-Sánchez, S. (2010). Anorexia nerviosa: Manejo nutricional en pediatría. *Bol Med Hosp Infant Mex*, Vol. 67, pp. 4-18.

Newton, T., Robinson, P. and Hartley, P. (1993). Treatment for Eating Disorders in the United Kingdom. Part II. Experiences of Treatment: A Survey of Members of the Eating Disorders Association. *Eat Disord Rev*, Vol.1, No.1, pp.10-21, ISSN 1072-4133.

Rosenvinge, J. H. and Klusmeier, A. K. (2000). Treatment for Eating Disorders from a Patient Satisfaction Perspective: a Norwegian Replication of a British Study. *Eur Eat Disord Rev*, Vol.8, pp.293-300, ISSN 1072-4133.

Salbach-Andrade, H., Schneider, N., Seifert, K., Pfeiffer, E., Lenz, K., Lehmkuhl, U. and Korte, A. (2009). Short-term outcome of anorexia nervosain adolescents after inpatient treatment: A prospective study. *Eur Child Adolesc Psychiatry*, Vol.18, pp. 701-704.

Schaffner, A. and Buchanan, L. (2008). Integrating evidence-based treatment with individual needs in a outpatient facility for eating disorderds. *Eating Disorders*, Vol.16, pp.378-392, ISSN 1064-0266.

Schmidt, U., Ali, S., Slone, G., Tiller, J. and Treasure, J. (1995). The Eating Disorders Awareness Test: A New Instrument for the Assessment of the Effectiveness of Psychoeducational Approaches to the Treatment of Eating Disorders. *Eur Eat Disord Rev*, Vol.3, No.2, pp.103-110, ISSN 1072-4133.

Treasure, J. and Ward, A. (1997). A Practical Guide to the Use of Motivational Interviewing in Anorexia Nervosa. *Eur Eat Disord Rev, Vol.*5, No.2, pp.102-114, ISSN 1072-4133.

Treasure, J. and Schmidt, U. (2001). Ready, Willing and Able to Change: Motivational Aspects of the Assessment and Treatment of Eating Disorders. *Eur Eat Disord Rev, Vol.*9, No.1, pp.4-18, ISSN 1072-4133.

Treasure, J., Tchanturia, K. and Schmidt, U. (2005). Developing a model of the treatment for eating disorder: Using neuroscience research to examine the how rather than the what of change. *Counselling and Psychotherapy Research*, Vol.5, No.3, pp.191-202, ISSN 1473-3145.

Vanderlinden, J., Buis, H., Pieters, G. and Probst, M. (2007). Which elements in the treatment of eating disorders are necessary 'ingredients' in the recovery process?—A comparison between the patient's and therapist's view. *Eur Eat Disord Rev, Vol.*15, No.5, pp.357-365, ISSN 1072-4133.

# 13

# Towards a Comprehensive Model of Recovery

Jan H. Rosenvinge and Gunn Pettersen
*University of Tromsø, Norway*

## 1. Introduction

Most people with eating disorders do recover, but they do so according to changing diagnostic criteria and the many different definitions of recovery and the recovery process appearing in the literature. The definitions of recovery rest on various assumptions about the nature of eating disorders and the nature of "normality", risk factor research as well as on targets for change and end points developed within specific therapeutic traditions.

Another reason why people recover for different reasons rests on the issue is whether symptom reduction is sufficient for recovery, or whether one should take into account more broad domains of functioning. The symptom reduction perspective may yield highly reliable judgements but may suffer from low clinical validity. The broader perspective may be clinically valid, but stands the risk of including aspects remotely related to a recovery from eating disorders and of being highly constricted by normative assumptions.

Scientific accounts of patient experiences of recovery represent an additional perspective to the treatment and outcome literature. This perspective also contains diversity. Moreover, a patient may feel improved or even recovered, and still measure up to clinical indications of a subclinical or even a clinical condition.

Both process and end points are important to reach an understanding of the complexity of recovery. Process has been a focus in experiential studies and end point mainly within the treatment and outcome research. Recovery may also involve a change in risk conditions that initiate and contribute to maintain the eating disorder. This perspective has received little attention in the research focus on recovery. Risk factor research has evolved significantly through the years and with increasingly interesting findings.

Indeed, to reach an understanding of the complexity of recovery there are many elements to integrate to grasp the complexity, but in fact there are few (e.g. Jarman & Walsh, 1999) who have attempted to accomplish such an integration

The focus of this chapter is to develop a comprehensive model for recovery, and to propose a scoring procedure that may bring about more consistent evaluations of recovery in clinical and research contexts. The chapter ends with some suggestions for future research and clinical practice.

## 2. Measuring recovery

In principle, there are four ways of approaching the issue of defining and measuring recovery from eating disorders. The *negation approach* defines recovery as the absence of diagnostic criteria for any form of eating disorders for a specified amount of time. This approach is clear-cut and easy to administer. It has an obvious value for clearly malicious clinical features, notably medical complications. Important disadvantages of this approach are the absence of positive criteria related to well-being, interpersonal relations, coping and quality of life.

Moreover, with this approach it is easy to overlook the dimensional, gradual and process-related nature of recovery and the continuous nature of many eating disorder symptoms in terms of their severity and frequency. This creates a blurred border between the statistically normal and the normatively defined pathology. Also, a heavy reliance on the absence of diagnostic criteria may introduce variability in research as the diagnostic criteria and the number of eating disorder diagnoses change significantly over time.

The *psychometric* approach defines recovery as scores on a normal population validated instrument measuring symptoms and psychologically relevant clinical issues. Technically then, recovery is defined as scores relative to a cut-off-score or as clinical significance defined as scores proximal to a normal population mean or a range.

This approach is well known for instance in the evaluation of weight normalisation, and opens for a statistical dimensionality as opposed to normative judgements about "normality". This approach is limited by instruments developed for screening purposes and not for the purpose of recovery evaluations and by the fact that too few instruments have been validated to report community sample's normative scores. Another limitation is the inability of catching the diversity of subjective meaning of recovery in various clinical settings.

The third approach is the *clinical* one, defining recovery relative to clinically relevant features. It uses a mixture of a negation approach to symptoms and a number of positive attributes of recovery. Recovery indicators may range from global and sometimes rather unsystematic evaluations to rather specific clinical attributes derived from theoretical and therapeutic approaches to eating disorders or to mental problems in general. Like the negation approach the clinical approach may blur the border to normality, and may sometimes differentiate poorly between recovery from eating disorders and conceptions of a good life in general.

In the *experiential* approach subjective experiences define being recovered or being in a recovery process. This perspective thus means allowing patients to launch their own understanding and experiences. Subjective experiences may catch features and nuances that are poorly captured by clinicians or by instruments. This approach then, may serve as an important correction to the negation approach in the sense that patients may experience being recovered or in a recovery process despite displaying eating disorder symptoms. Hence, change in symptom frequency may be important, but not critical for recovery or at least to the recovery process. Yet, the subjective nature of experiences does contain biases, notably by errors of memory and errors of attributions. Errors of attribution may be a result of a poor understanding of the impact of denial of illness or the intrinsic nature of many eating disorder symptoms. Using the experiential approach as an epistemological platform, however, the "bias" as a source of error is made irrelevant or non-existent through the rejecting of an "objective" reality and norm. As a consequence, some authors (e.g. Björk & Ahlström, 2008) equal the *feeling* of being recovered with *being* recovered regardless of changes according to "objective" measures.

Theoretically, the experiential approach fits well into research on subjective well-being (Diener, 2000) in the sense that subjective well-being does not presuppose a particular norm as to how people should live their lives. Rather, in this tradition one define domains or areas in life where satisfaction may be present in various degrees. If we "translate" this way of thinking to recovery, one may define recovery or the consequences of recovery in terms of *domain dominance*. On the other hand, recovery may not be equal to subjective well-being in the sense that experiential studies also reveal that being recovered also may imply facing grief, new responsibilities and a lot of challenges that the eating disorder served as a protection from.

## 3. Clinically derived elements of recovery

### 3.1 Existing indicators of recovery

Using the negation, the psychometric and the clinical approach several attempts have been made to define recovery (*e.g.* Couturier & Lock, 2006a, b; Dare *et al.*, 2001; Kordy et al., 2002; Olmsted et al., 2005; Rø *et al.*, 2005a,b; Vrabel et al.,2010). Here recovery is defined as percentage of patients 1) not meeting the diagnostic criteria for an eating disorder 2) without any symptoms of an eating disorder within a period of 8-12 weeks before examination, 3) above or below a specific cut-off score on a psychometric test, and 4) who achieve a defined reduction of specified symptom measures. Partial recovery may be understood as not fulfilling all the criteria or fulfilling only some criteria completely. However, less attention has been paid to the *validity* of such criteria.

Some studies however, (e.g. Noordenbos, 1989; 1992; Tozzi et al., 2003; Vanderlinden et al., 2007) have compared recovery preferences from patients and clinicians or experiences of elements in treatment contributing to recovery. Overall, small differences across such samples have been detected indicating good convergent and external validity. However, there are no attempts in this research to provide a meaningful scoring procedure.

An influential device to assess outcome is the Morgan- Russell assessment schedule (Morgan & Russell, 1975) later modified by Morgan & Hayward (1988). The original version captures symptom aspects, i.e. weight, food intake, and menstruation as well as family life, occupational status, sexual life and preferences as well as mental and socio-economic status. A composite score represents a psychometric measure of outcome, yet there are no indications of what score range that indicates recovery. Again the issue of validity may be raised as the instrument is highly vulnerable to normative biases from assumptions about "optimal" standards of living and quality of life. The stricter version of the Morgan-Russell instrument, however, covers only the symptom aspects. This on the other hand, may be restrictive, and some authors (e.g. Strober et al., 1997) even claim that the strict version only captures partial recovery.

Noordenbos & Seubring (2005) on the other hand, suggest 52 broader criteria for recovery within six domains, i.e. symptom reduction, body satisfaction, reduction of medical complications, self-image, emotional regulation and social functioning. The number of criteria is highly extensive and there are no attempts to use empirical methods of condensation and data reduction.

Integrating findings from patients, clinicians and researchers and using factor analyses and content analysis to address data redundancy Pettersen (2007) developed a set of multicomponent recovery features. They comprise a symptom reduction to approach normal variations, but also a change in the motives for symptoms and a change in the purposes of symptoms, e.g. to cope with stress or to regulate feelings and relations. Also, recovery was related to a change in the consequences that symptoms may bring about with respect to social functioning interpersonal relations, and the capacity to reflect on prospects and hopes for the future. Here then, recovery is defined both in terms of narrow and broad criteria, covering eating disorder symptoms as well as many psychological and interpersonal issues relevant to an understanding of the spectrum of recovery.

Despite some weaknesses, lists of items relevant to recovery represent a first step towards a comprehensive understanding of recovery. Further progress needs to overcome a problem of failure to provide knowledge accumulation usually encountered in experiential studies using qualitative methods. This may have the consequence that studies may reiterate previous studies in their findings rather than explicitly exploring more nuances of a more limited set of phenomena relevant for recovery.

Further progress also needs to overcome an overreliance on single factors at the cost of interaction effects. For instance, many single factors have been empirically derived from the field of risk and outcome, bur here there has been a movement from studying single factors to testing multidimensional models and the interaction of factors. Such a development is highly needed also to understand recovery as a state, but probably more likely as a process and an interaction between many factors which create good or vicious intrapsychic and interpersonal circles. Hence, a comprehensive model of recovery should consider elements based on findings from the risk factor research and the research on prognostic factors.

### 3.2 Risk factors

To understand recovery, we need to understand what one should recover from. The etiological factors are relevant. However, etiologic factors may be unknown or unclear. On the other hand, risk factors and prognostic factors are relevant, and in particular those that for some reasons may be modified.

*Biological factors* in terms of a significant heritability and findings related to factors associated with affective regulation and regulation of hunger and satiety (Chavez & Insel, 2007) are important to understand etiology. Interesting for the same reason is risk related to *family based premorbidity or comorbidity* of eating disorders like addiction or depression. However, as such factors may be difficult to change they may be less relevant in the pursuit of building an understanding of recovery.

*Personal history* refers to a number of risk factors that in the current context stand out as more relevant. These factors comprise a negative self-image, compulsivity and perfectionism, as well as adverse life events like adult abuse, poor social network, a critical family climate and effects of negative comments on body weight and composition, notably from parents or other adults (Fairburn et al., 1997; 1998; 1999). Risk is related to the presence of premorbid overweight, addictive disorder, anxiety disorder or a depressive disorder as well as *developmental risk factors* related to bonding and attachment (Perry et al., 2002; 2008), the resolving of which represented in terms of symptom reduction. Hence, in a recovery perspective such findings serve as an argument for including improvement of psychological issues beyond symptom reduction as well as improvement of the quality of close interpersonal relations and social functioning.

*Cognitive risk and maintaining factors* comprise the exaggerated beliefs about the need to control one's eating habits, shape and weight (Fairburn et al., 2003). Also included are errors of reasoning resulting in errors of causal attributions and interpretations, e.g. overgeneralisations, emotional reasoning, dichotomous reasoning and negative predictions. Repeated errors of reasoning and interpretations reflect core belief predominantly about oneself, as for instance being of no value, as disgusting, worthy of shame or as an individual with some kind of deficit. While such beliefs may fluctuate through many people's minds, eating disorder patients may be convinced that they are generally and basically true. Therefore, one may more or less consciously seek for their confirmation through interpretation of events and other people's behaviours, or in one's own way of behaving, e.g. through the abuse of food. Such risk and maintaining factors are highly relevant to recovery in terms of being possible to change, notably through evidence based cognitive therapy. Recovery from this perspective implies symptom reduction as a consequence of strategies to reduce the belief in the universal and general truth of negative core beliefs and the truth of the need to control eating, weight and shape.

*Behavioural and psychological risk factors* include dieting, not perhaps so much to be thin, but to feel emotionally empty (Patton et al., 1999; Fairburn et *al.*, 2005), personality (Ghaderi & Scott, 2000), notably harm avoidance, low self-directedness, and low (anorexia nervosa) and high (bulimia nervosa) levels of novelty seeking (Fassino et al., 2002), neuroticism (Bollen & Wojciechowski, 2004) related to affective dysregulation, and personality disorders (Bulik et al., 2006; Claes et al., 2006; Johnson et al., 2006).

*Vicious risk circles* represent a multilevel or multidimensional way of thinking that may help understand important challenges of recovery. Such way of thinking illustrates the interplay between psychological and interpersonal aspects and the need for a comprehensive recovery model to accommodate for the interplay and why recovery need to address the breaching of such vicious circles. Several studies lend empirical support to models of multiple risks related to illness development (e.g. Perry et al., 2008) or maintenance (e.g. Vrabel et al., 2010). For instance, sexual abuse in combination with an avoidant personality may occur and reduce the probability of recovery unless addressed in therapy. Moreover, abuse may seriously affect the strength of the negative cognitive beliefs. Also, repetitive parental criticism about appearance may reinforce poor self-esteem and negative core beliefs, elicit dieting and set in motion negative interpersonal circles resulting in burdens related to living with or close to a sufferer of eating disorders.

One example of a circle is the avoidant personality disorder and dysfunctional perfectionism creating low social interaction as well as personal insecurity. This may interact poorly with having parents who, due to their personality organisation or burdens, have poor care taking competence and less ability to provide support and social stimulation. Another example is when parents actually are applauding an introverted and inhibited way of being and when such way of being fits well with family values of avoiding conflicts and of being polite. In such a family climate, there is little room for real or imagined failures or shortcomings, and criticism may be experienced as a serious correction. Then, there is a huge potential for vulnerability for negative affects, strict emotional regulation and for developing ideas that at least the body can or shall be perfect. This may also represent a poor psychological protection against sociocultural pressures towards thinness, hazels during puberty as well as undue criticism about body appearance and body changes as a result of biological maturity or immaturity. The driving force in such vicious circles of undue perfectionism and avoidance is low self-esteem, and some authors (e.g. Waller, 2008) advocates that eating disorder symptoms may serve the same purpose as avoidance strategies in anxiety disorders.

Taken together, risk factors and an interactive understanding of such factors focus on *behavioural aspects, interpersonal relations, social functioning* and *psychological issues*. As most of these factors may be possible to change they may become relevant elements in an understanding of recovery.

### 3.3 Prognostic factors

Outcome studies searching for factors predictive of recovery or a failure to recover are taking a clinician or researcher perspective. Several reviews (e.g. Steinhausen, 2002) show that a majority of patients do recover fully (47%) or partially (34%) from eating disorders. Adolescents tend to fare better than adults, particularly if given outpatient treatment (Fisher, 2003). Increasing the duration of follow-ups generally tend to increase the percentage who recover, but also the risk for mortality (Arcelus et al., 2011). Variations in the proportions who recover have been detected (Couturier & Lock, 2006a). Some proportion variations may be accounted for with reference to variations in design, sample characteristics, size and statistical power, the duration of follow-up, dropout, and in procedures for data collection. Another and perhaps more important source of variation refer to *definitions of outcome and recovery*.

Recovery is repeatedly, yet not consistently related to an early age of onset, short duration of illness before treatment, a need for brief therapeutic intervention, no readmissions as well as a high educational and socioeconomic level (Steinhausen, 2002). Such factors may point to clinical severity as the underlying factor that needs to be addressed to accomplish recovery notably bingeing, vomiting and purgative abuse as well as extreme weight loss (Fichter et al., 2003; Steinhausen, 2002).

Furthermore, the journey of recovery may be longer and steeper given a high load of interpersonal problems (Fichter et al., 2003), notably with parents and family members (Berkman et al., 2007), and if daily life activities are hampered by compulsivity. Also, failure to recover is related to a passive rather than an active coping approach to problem solving (Fichter et al., 2003).

Previous and concurrent symptom disorders other than eating disorders are also related to a poor prospect of recovery. In particular such disorders comprise addictive problems (Berkman et al., 2007; Keel & Brown, 2010), alcohol abuse during follow-up (Keel *et al.*, 2003), obsessive-compulsive disorder and depression (Berkman et al., 2007).

Depression is highly indicated by the fact that the rate of suicide and suicide attempts is significantly more frequent than in the general population (Arcelus et al., 2011; Keel et al., 2003). The negative impact of such disorders generally increases with their clinical severity, notably if hospital treatment is required.

Psychiatric comorbidity is also related to personality disorders occurring in 60% of eating disorder patients and in almost three of four inpatients (Rosenvinge et al., 2000). Frequently observed are the avoidant, obsessive-compulsive and borderline disorder (Fichter et al., 2003; Råstam, 1992, Vrabel et al., 2010; Wentz, 2000).

However, comorbidity represents a challenge with respect to whether the comorbid condition is causally related to the eating disorder. A valid conception of recovery from an eating disorder should exclude the possibility of post hoc developed symptom or personality disorder that may be remotely associated with the eating disorder. A causal attribution should rest on prospective clinical and scientific follow-up investigations. In clinical settings these judgements may be unsystematic in nature and may rest on etiological assumptions. Hence, requiring absence or improvement in concurrent mental problems stands out as an uncertain element in a model of recovery. However, comorbid conditions may act as mediator or moderator variables.

## 4. Experientially derived elements of recovery

### 4.1 Ambivalence, engagement and commitment

Ambivalence to change relates to the cost and benefit of *change* and the cost and benefit of *illness*. The costs of illness related to eating disorders are represented by for instance a realisation of medical complications and lack of opportunities within educational, social and interpersonal domains of life. Benefits comprise psychological issues of feeling unique, receiving support and comfort or using the disorder to control emotions and relations. Costs and benefits may be invariably realised throughout the course of illness (Freedman et al., 2006) and may elicit mixed feelings due to human individual differences in personality traits like novelty seeking versus fear of the unpredictable. Such individual differences are related to experiences of costs and benefits of change per se.

Experiential studies (Pettersen, 2007; Pettersen et al. 2008; 2011) show that mixed feelings range from shame to pride. Shame is related to symptoms and compensatory and concealing strategies. Shame may be more profound than in many other clinical groups (Frank, 1991; Sanfther & Crowther, 1998), and may also predict more symptom severity (Burney & Irwin, 2000). Shame may foster ambivalence to change, i.e. a drive to recover to abolish shame counteracted by self-stigmatisations (Gowers & Shore, 1999) and the triggering of cognitive beliefs ("because I do shameful things, I am a shameful person, and a shameful person doesn't deserve treatment or to get well") resulting in a decaying motivation to seek help to recover (Hepworth & Paxton, 2007). In fact, individuals who feel shame and self-stigmatisation may continue doing the shameful behaviours as an unconscious wish to confirm the truth of the beliefs of being a shameful person.

Patients also report concomitant feelings of pride (McLeod, 1989). Pride includes feelings of being unique, physically attractive and being able to control the body and one's weight, being able to control other people's concern and attention. Such feelings and experiences are important forces that block a process of recovery. Understanding eating disorders as a control strategy also involves symptoms as an avoidance strategy for coming into contact with dysfunctional perfectionism and negative core beliefs (Waller, 2008) may foster a fear of new challenges without eating disorders, a resistance to give up symptoms and to explore alternative ways of coping and survival.

Most previous studies (e.g. Geller & Drab, 1999; Serpell et al., 1999; 2004) of patient's accounts of ambivalence to change and recovery have focused on the initial phases of illness. Here, ambivalence may be related to experiences of immediate benefits and rewards, a low recognition of longer term costs and burdens, fear of loosing benefits as well as rather unrealistic expectations about life without the eating disorder (Beresin et al., 1989; Nilsson & Hägglöf, 2006).

In later stages unrealistic expectations may have been tempered by experiences with life as less impacted by the eating disorder and the challenges one need to confront in the phase of remission. Moreover, as times go by, "benefits" may be outnumbered by accumulated experiences of the negative aspects (Pettersen et al., 2008). Recent studies (Pettersen et al., 2011) however, indicate that ambivalence may be present also in later stages of the recovery process.

In the later phases ambivalence and mixed feelings are less related to shame and pride and more to grief and reconciliation. Grief refers to the sadness of loosing unrealistic ideas about the carefree nature of life without the eating disorder as well as loosing the benefits from the eating disorder, but also the grief over irreversible events and losses, and over events that did *not* happen as a result of being preoccupied with eating disorder symptoms (Pettersen et al., 2011). Because patients in their later stages of recovery may have good reasons for their grief (e.g. irreversible losses), this low-tempered state of mind may represent a normal acquisition of reconciliation, and not necessarily a comorbid depressive condition or a pathological process. Hence, scores in a pathological range on measures of depression and general maladjustment may be false positives, and may contribute to a failure to acknowledge a process of recovery.

Some patient accounts describe change as some kind of decision (Hsu et al., 1992). In some cases a shift of focus may be more sudden as a consequence of realising that severe medical complications could occur and with a fatal outcome. Then an interest in existential issues of life and death, and hopes for the future may be stimulated (Nilsson & Hägglöf, 2006; Patching & Lawler, 2009). Recent studies (Pettersen et al., 2008, 2011) however, have questioned the notion of decision as a cognitive phenomenon (see section 6.3) and that it needs to be sudden. Rather, the term *engagement* may be more appropriate, picturing the change of focus as a gradual process. A gradual process may also explain why symptoms still persist despite a wish to change.

### 4.2 Changes in state of mind and focus of interest

Patients tend to report that recovery means a change of focus and focus of interest. This often implies starting an ongoing fight against negative thinking about oneself and the ability to tolerate negative affects (Federeci & Kaplan, 2008).

Related to improvement in negative self-perceptions is another marker of recovery - the ability to really care for oneself and providing self-comfort (Björk & Ahlström, 2008;

Pettersen et al., 2011). This is consistent with a finding that women who recover report that they are more able to accept and regulate affects like anger or grief and report a courage to express and talk about such affects (Federici & Kaplan, 2008). The most beneficial is when the courage of expression comprises close relations. An important end point of this fight against negative thinking is for many to realise that the origin of negative thoughts is projected perfectionism and undue self-expectations rather than expectations genuinely produced by other people (Nilsson et al., 2007; Patching & Lawler, 2009). A sign of a more fruitful end point then is to adopt a "good-enough" way of thinking (Lamoreux & Bottorff, 2005). As a consequence, one may also believe in the credibility of other people's positive comments about oneself.

In the later phases of illness, recovery is a matter of being reconciled (see section 5.1). Several studies of patient's accounts (e.g. Weaver et al., 2005; Rahkonen & Tozzi et al., 2003; Federici & Kaplan, 2008; Pettersen et al., 2011) report that patients being recovered equalised recovery as a movement away from being a trapped by the eating disorder and towards taking a more active role in designing daily life and the future.

### 4.3 Changes in self-image and experiences of identity

Changes in self-identity are an important aspect of recovery. "Finding me" as detached from "the eating disordered me" is a psychological and existential feature of recovery (Björk & Ahlström, 2008; Weaver et al., 2005) representing a change of focus from fat, appearance and the counting of calories to a search for meaning and purpose in life (D'Abundo & Chally, 2004; Matusek & Knudson, 2009). Many women describe recovery as being more than just an individual with a preoccupation with food calories and appearance (Lamoureux & Bottorff, 2005) or being preoccupied with the planning of binges and developing plans to conceal them (Pettersen et al., 2008). Recovered women thus tend to report a distance to the eating disorder, realising that it no longer help them to attain life goals and aspirations.

Finding an identity detached from the eating disorder represents a complex interplay between psychological states of mind and social relations. Social relations tend to mirror and confirm states of mind, and states of mind may "design" how other people respond to ways of behaving. Hence, being recovered highly depends on whether other people will confirm a self-presentation beyond being a former or current "case" of eating disorders (Pettersen & Rosenvinge, 2002; Weaver et al., 2005). However, this depends on the validity and credibility of the commitment to change (Rahkonen & Tozzi et al., 2003), and to rediscover own resources, interests or relations (Weaver et al., 2005) and to reduce self-loathing (Garrett, 1997) in order to being able to accept the positive reinforcement from other people as genuine (see section 4.2). Many former patients have described this as a way out of a life of avoiding anxiety and fear of failures through the dysfunctional perfectionism in terms of the preoccupation of being thin (Lamoureux & Bottorff, 2005).

### 4.4 Changes in social relations

Recovery has also been associated with a reduced feeling of being detached from others (Garrett, 1997), and the access to loving and supporting relations, where disclosure is possible without fear of being criticized or condemned (Federici & Kaplan, 2008; Weaver et al., 2005; Woods, 2004). Disclosure may then be helpful as a confirmation or validation of oneself as a human being and not just as an individual with an eating disorder (see section 4.3).

One change in social relations associated with recovery has been described as a "cleaning-up" process. This means to abandon relations that only serve the purpose of satisfying other people's needs, without stimulating hope and vitality (D'Abundo & Chally, 2004), or leaving turbulent and destructive relations to parents or partners.

This change is highly related to a change in psychological focus. Patient's account of recovery comprises a defocus on food, weight and calories, and in fact active attempts to redirect social relations and interpersonal conversations away from such a focus. In particular, the social support is elicited by redefining romantic and family relations, and to change one's behaviours in order to elicit other people's support. Moreover, activities and life events appearing independent of the eating disorder also seem important for recovery (Nilsson & Hägglöf, 2006; Pettersen & Rosenvinge, 2002; Tozzi et al., 2003), and may include completing education, get a job, establishing a romantic relationship or having children.

### 4.5 Treatment factors

At least with respect to bulimia nervosa and binge eating disorder, there is compelling evidence for the effect of many treatments, notably cognitive therapy, interpersonal therapy, family therapy and guided self-help (Fairburn & Harrison, 2003; Shapiro et al., 2007). Unfortunately, treatment effects could for many reasons not be equalised with recovery (Keel & Mitchell, 1997; Strober et al., 1997; Keel & Brown, 2010). Moreover, patient experiences of helpful elements of therapy may not concur with the therapeutic ideology or theory about therapeutic factors contributing to recovery.

Nevertheless, patient perspective studies (e.g. Pettersen & Rosenvinge, 2002; Rahkonen & Tozzi, 2005; Tozzi et al., 2003) provide compelling evidence that treatment do contribute to recovery or a recovery process.

A robust finding across samples is that patients tend to experience treatment contributing to recovery if it facilitates improvement in terms of *interpersonal relations* as well as a number of *psychological issues* (i.e. self-esteem, self assertion, body experience as well as problem solving skills and affect regulation (Noordenbos, 1992; Vanderlinden et al., 2007). Also important for recovery is patient's experiences of being included in decisions about treatment content, e.g. the speed of weight gain, number of daily meals or routines for physical exercise (D'Abundo & Chally, 2004). Being included such decisions may increase the autonomy required for facilitating intrinsic motivation to change (see section 5.3) and to start a recovery process (Federici & Kaplan, 2008). In accordance with psychotherapy research, patients also tend to highlight the facilitating impact of *g*-factors, i.e. experiencing the therapist as competent, empathic, warm, and respectful and appreciating the individuality of the patient, and interestingly not necessarily reflecting actual competence on eating disorders (Pettersen, 2007).

### 4.6 Non-helping factors

Few experiential studies have specifically asked patients about factors unrelated or negatively related to recovery. In general, findings tend to support a notion that such factors represent the opposite of positive factors. Hence, non-helping factors comprise being negatively judged by others, the feeling of being stigmatized, feeling of sadness, distress and hopelessness and being "stuck" as well as denying the severity of illness, being focused on food and meal times, and experiencing the benefits of the eating disorder outnumbering the negative aspects (Nordbo, 2010). Moreover, negative thoughts about one's body, one's self-worth and dignity have also been highlighted as aspects associated with a failure to recover (Federici & Kaplan, 2008).

## 5. Integration - towards a comprehensive understanding of recovery

### 5.1 Content aspects and end points

In the following, we suggest a comprehensive model that may integrate factors and features relevant for understanding recovery. The model makes a distinction between necessary and sufficient elements of recovery.

A *necessary element* for recovery comprises reduction in frequency of dieting, bingeing and compensatory behaviours approaching general population means, in addition to a weight normalisation. Also, there is a need for reduction of the belief in the truth of certain cognitive beliefs about the necessity of controlling eating, weight and shape. For a state of recovery it is not the frequency per se, but how much a given frequency is approaching normal variations in the population. This is clearly opposed to a negation approach. On the other hand, a negation approach is appropriate when judging recovery in terms of absence of medical complications or symptoms clearly disparate from statistically normal variations of behaviour frequency (e.g. vomiting or using laxatives for compensatory purposes).

The model suggests four domains, i.e. psychological issues, existential issues, as well as interpersonal and social aspects. Changes and recovery within the four domains may be regarded as *sufficient.*

Hence, a comprehensive model of recovery must include changes the four domains, but changes in the domains may not be a valid conception of recovery of *eating disorder* unless accompanied by symptom and core pathology changes On the other hand only measuring symptom reduction may miss important indices of recovery.

*Psychological aspects*

An overarching issue is to what extent the individual feels, and is clinically judged as being committed to challenge core beliefs and symptom frequency. Thus, recovery in this domain implies a gradual less belief in the truth of core beliefs, a reduction of dysfunctional perfectionism, the increment of subjective well-being, self-esteem and body acceptance and the improvement in coping strategies and problem solving strategies, i.e. by not involving the use of eating disorder symptoms to regulate or communicate emotions. Furthermore, psychological aspects include an understanding of why the eating disorder developed and what purposes it served.

*Social aspects*

Social aspects of recovery include the ability to take part in social activities or viewing such activities as true rewarding and not just to please others. Having an eating disorder often prevent taking part in such activities, and they are usually difficult and are avoided because such activities elicit feelings of being stigmatised, disgraced or simply the feeling of being fat. Moreover, in a recovered state, eating disorder symptoms do not occupy mind and attention in a manner that makes it difficult or demanding to attend school or work on a regular basis. Social aspects also include the ability to move around in the society in order to attend to personal and social need.

*Existential aspects*

Existential aspects relates to taking an interest in forming a personal future, seeking meaning and purpose of life beyond the pursuit of food, body and thinness, coming to terms with grief through reconciliation as well as reflecting about identity beyond the identity shaped by the eating disorder. Another psychological aspect is to feel able to fulfil own potential and not just to conform to expectations from others.

*Interpersonal aspects*

Recovery from an interpersonal point of view means that symptoms do not disrupt family and close relations. Disruption may take place through being so preoccupied with symptoms that relations cannot be attended, or being preoccupied with the concealing of symptoms to avoid contact with the fear of disgrace, rejection and stigmatisation. In the illness phase relations are often contaminated by charades and cover up stories, as well as mutual distrust, allegations or histories of other people's dysfunctional control of symptoms in the pursuit of caring. Interpersonal conflicts may still be present in a recovered state, but their origins are not related to eating disorders. Another aspect of recovery from an interpersonal point of view is to (re)establish relationships that serve to reinforce positive core beliefs and to elicit social support sometimes as a part of the "cleaning-up" process (see section 4.4).

*Symptom aspects and core beliefs*

Such aspects overlaps much with psychological issues, and comprise core eating disorder related cognitive beliefs about oneself-and about the need to control food intake, weight and shape, frequency of core symptoms, *i.e.* restrictive eating, overeating, vomiting, body checking, excessive exercising or laxative abuse, as well as weight status, general condition, and somatic complications. Cognitive beliefs may be rigid and resistant to the change needed in order to recover. Recovery from a symptom perspective implies that symptom frequency approaches normal population means, and that the individual report a significant drop in the believing of the truth of core beliefs. This is clearly an alternative to the negation approach (section 2.0), yet such an approach must be used to assess medical complications.

Figures 1 and 2 illustrate the interrelationship between the psychological, social, interpersonal and existential domains. Figure 1 intends to depict a situation or state where clinically significant symptoms of eating disorders "contaminate" the domains. In the illness phase then, symptom frequency may lower the amount and quality of social and interpersonal relations, it may affect the interpretation of inner states and events, as well as the interest in, or the thinking about existential issues. Experientially, this has been described as some kind of "carpet ". The carpet then, is the eating disorder symptoms. In addition to deprive and to reduce quality of relations, the carpet also serves the purpose of regulating relations (see section 3.1 and 4.2). Other dual functions (i.e. positive and negative purposes) are to disturb, distract as well as to dissociate or temper engagement and activity within the four domains. The dual functions are the psychological platform for the ambivalence to change and recovery discussed in section 5.3 below.

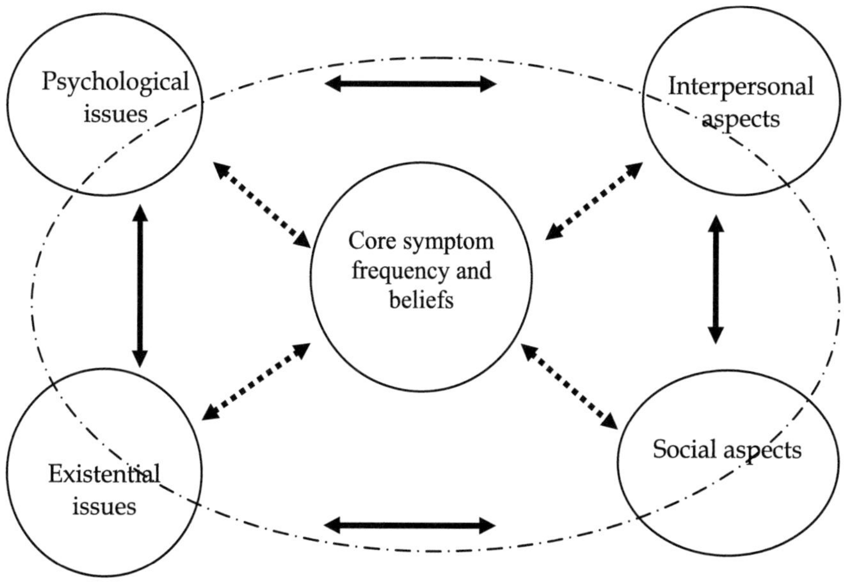


Fig. 1. The model of understanding recovery from eating disorders comprising the four domains (i.e. psychological issues, existential issues, interpersonal aspects and social aspects) and showing a state of non-recovery. Solid arrows indicate stable interrelations between the four domains (i.e. psychological issues, existential issues, interpersonal aspects and social aspects). Dotted arrows indicate how domains are influenced by core symptoms and beliefs. The dotted circle indicates how symptoms diffuse into the four domains.

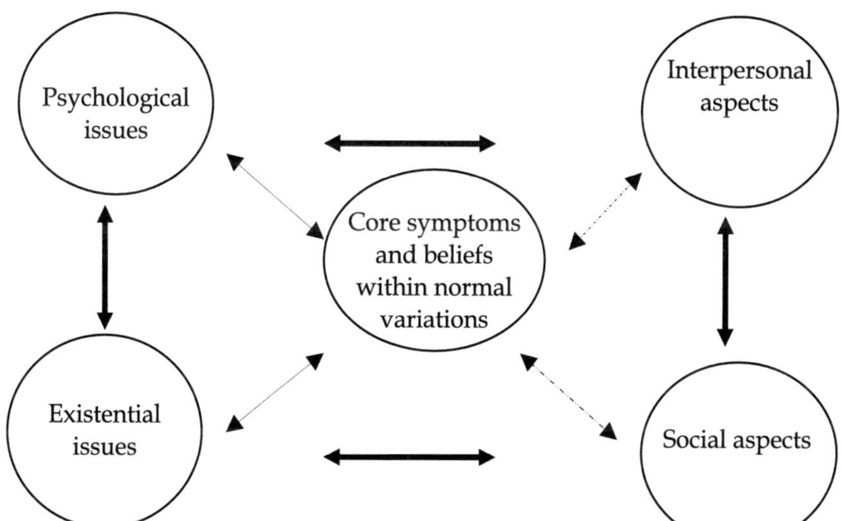


Fig. 2. The model of understanding recovery from eating disorders illustrating the relationship between model elements in a state of recovery. Solid arrows illustrate the stable interrelationship between the four domains (i.e. psychological issues, existential issues, interpersonal aspects and social aspects). Light dotted lines of various shapes indicate variations in the weak influence of core symptoms and beliefs on the four domains.

A life without an eating disorder still implies the need to confront challenges within the four domains. However, if the confronting strategy no longer comprises or are blurred or disturbed by a preoccupations with food, eating, shape and weight and believing in the need to control them, general challenges and problems may be more or less detached from the personal history suffering from eating disorders. Rather, they may be better accounted for as challenges of life. Lack of influence on the domains may indicate that symptoms no longer divert focus away from an engagement in existential, social and interpersonal issues, or that one's thinking and interpretation of issues related to these domains are not coloured by the eating disorder. Figure 2 illustrates a situation of recovery along this way of reasoning. Different shapes of the light dotted lines intend to illustrate that the impact of the inner circle aspects may be different on each of the four basic domains.

### 5.2 A composite scoring procedure

Apart from psychometrically validated instruments, scoring procedures are generally lacking in many attempts to generate lists of features relevant for evaluating recovery. Scoring procedures should be meeting several demands, like parsimony, construct validity and discriminative validity. Provisionally we suggest a scoring procedure inspired by the Global Assessment of Functioning Scale from the DSM-IV as follows:

0 no information

1-10 presence of medical complications, weight outside normal population range, symptom frequency fulfilling diagnostic criteria, dysfunctional core beliefs, low understanding of the need to change and a low commitment or engagement in making changes, concurrent low understanding of the need to change and a low commitment or engagement in making changes, and eating disorder symptoms grossly impairing all of the four domains

11-20 less medical complications, some extrinsic control over symptom frequency, but scores on measures of core psychopathology is within the clinical range

21-30 no medical complications, an understanding of alternatives to eating disorders in terms of coping, affect regulation and the prospect of a future without an eating disorder, no change in interpersonal relations or social functioning

31-40 a commitment to explore alternatives core beliefs about self image and about the truth of the need to control eating, weight and shape, starting to disclose symptoms to family or close friends

41-50 all changes comprised by scores comprising 11-40, and in addition, weight is within normal range, scores on measures of symptoms and core psychopathology approaching the normal population range, challenging core beliefs

51-60 as 41-50, and in addition that symptoms affect interpersonal relations and social functioning to a lesser degree, less need to control weight and shape as well as improved body acceptance.

61-70 as 51-60 but added that close relations are less disrupted by eating disorder symptoms and compensatory behaviours. Also close relations may be established without a reference to the eating disorder. The individual may feel grief related to being preoccupied with eating disorder and the related burdens, costs and lost opportunities.

71-80 as 61-70 but added improvement of concomitant problems related to anxiety, depression personality disorders, or abuse/trauma, better quality of interpersonal relations due to disclosure of symptoms and sustained symptom improvement

81-90 as 71-80 but added reconciliation related to grief, active reflections over existential issues, displaying hope and expectations for the future, and no unrealistically positive expectations about a future without the eating disorder, and social activities are not longer impossible or difficult because they are not longer disturbed by symptom behaviours like bingeing, or by feeling disgraced or simply fat.

91-100 as 81-90 but added that scores on measures of core psychopathology are within the normal population range, significant subjective well-being, a major change in core cognitive beliefs, interpersonal relations are not affected by eating disorder symptoms, if presence of other mental problems, they are not clearly attributable to the former eating disorder, as well as experiencing life as meaningful.

We also suggest that no change comprises scores 1-20, that being in a recovery process is indicated by scores 21-50, that partial recovery is indicated by scores 51-80 and that a full recovery will require scores from 81-100. This creates variability, but such variability may accommodate for the possibility of multiple facets of a state of recovery.

The model is multidimensional in content, but also with respect to levels of measurement outlined in section 2, i.e. a clinical, a psychometric, a negation and an experiential approach. Hence, validated rating scales and self-report instruments should be used to measure improvement or recovery with respect to symptoms and core beliefs, standard medical procedures should be used to determine the presence or absence of medical complications while recovery with respect to the four domains may be requiring a combination of all the levels of measurement.

### 5.3 Process elements and potentials for change

While change in core symptoms is necessary conditions for *recovery as a state*, commitment and motivation represents the necessary conditions for the *process of recovery*. Still it is important to notice that interventions aiming to increase motivation have a far less impact on recovery than the motivation that is created by taking part in evidence based treatments (Waller, 2011; Geller et al., 2011).

An influential motivational theory (Prochaska & DiClemente, 1982) posits a stage model starting with a stage of not recognising a problem, problem recognition, contemplating about pros and cons for change, an action stage and a feedback control loop of consolidating the changes. It stands out as rather self evident and the scheme has been used many psychological arenas where change is at focus, e.g. addiction problems and smoking cessation, but can be found in theories of identity development through adolescence (Marcia, 1966) as well as for eating disorders (Geller & Drab, 1999; Serpell et al., 2004). The model rests on recovery initiated by some kind of a cognitive decision and a weighting of immediate benefits (e.g. consolation, affect regulation, regulating of relations) against longer term costs (e.g. loss of quality of life). This kind of decision may be elicited through life event but as well as through therapy. A first sign of recovery then would be a commitment or a decision to explore new psychological frontiers. Such frontiers may be to seek an identity beyond being an eating disordered individual, to challenge the fear of stigmatisation when speaking openly about eating disorder symptoms and to challenge core beliefs. The effect is thus to break vicious circles of dieting, bingeing and purging. A problem with this theory is that although the succession of stages may seem logical and self-evident, patients actually may move back and forth in a very situation-dependent way (Waller, 2011). Another major problem is that being in an action stage does not tell us anything about whether the action (e.g. eating more to gain weight) is done for own purposes of gaining weight or for external reasons (e.g. to get out of the hospital) or just to please others.

The Self-Determination Theory (SDT) of motivation (Deci & Ryan, 2002) however, posits that motivators may be *intrinsic and extrinsic* and that the golden way to change is all therapeutic (and other) endeavours to make extrinsic motives become intrinsic. Apart from being a rather comprehensive theory, the extrinsic-intrinsic distinction is suitable for eating disorders where many symptoms may be intrinsically motivated and incorporated in lifestyle and because eating disordered individuals tend to make changes towards recovery for reasons not integrated in their true belief system. Hence, it has been argued (Vansteenkiste et al., 2005) that SDT may be a suitable overarching framework to understand change in eating disorders. SDT thus allows a focus on how to make externally motivated actions (introduced by for instance a therapist) intrinsic. This may be more efficient than to make the patient aware of illness costs and to just focus on or to search for intrinsic motivation to change, a motivation that may be absent or vague in the first place.

Intrinsically motivated behaviours are activities that are performed for their own sake and for pleasure or excitement. Within the model of recovery, a commitment and mental activity to explore new aspects of identity and aspirations about the future beyond being "an eating disorder individual" or being engaged in rewarding social activities may be intrinsically motivated. Extrinsic motivation on the other hand relates to instrumental behaviours relative to a specific purpose, governed by gaining an external reward, meeting external expectations or avoiding punishment. For instance keeping a normal weight through healthy eating habits can be extrinsically motivated by others, providing positive material or immaterial reinforcements. When reinforcement terminates, the behaviour however, will sooner or later drop in frequency as the behaviour is poorly integrated in the individual's structures of values and core beliefs.

One gateway to integration may be through mindfulness (Didonna, 2009), by which one may come into contact with suffering and the wish for another life than being an eating disordered individual. Another gateway would be to urge (extrinsic motivation) the individual to perform a non-enjoyable behaviour like adopting healthy eating habits. According to theories of attribution, cognitive dissonance and learning, the reward should be minimalistic and provided intermittingly. In this way, individuals turn to internal attributions, i.e. constructing an intrinsic motive as an explanation for doing the behaviour (healthy eating habits) because it is impossible to explain it as a response to a huge external reinforcer. Nevertheless, one may guard against oversimplifications in terms of overlooking fear of changes, strong intrapsychic and interpersonal symptom maintaining factors mediated or moderated by personality traits.

Personality traits may hamper, but in some cases also facilitate the recovery process, and there are individual differences across eating disorder diagnoses in how patients with eating disorders display facilitating personality factors (i.e. agreeableness, prosocial behaviours, resilience and control) or factors hampering recovery like neuroticism, dysregulative traits, harm avoidance, low novelty seeking, high persistence and low self-directedness (Claes et al., 2006; Fassino et al., 2002; Holliday et al., 2006). Obviously, facilitating personality traits may relate positively to the ability of acting according to ones own purposes or determination while harm avoidance and neuroticism may be more associated with reinforcement through extrinsic motivation. Hampering or facilitating personality traits has an additional process-related effect in terms of contributing to beneficial or vicious interpersonal circles that are vital for whether the outcome of the process is recovery or not.

Along with certain personality traits, poor prognostic factors and a failure to change their negative psychological impact reduce the probability to recover and the probability of developing an engagement and commitment to searching for alternatives to eating disorders and to replace drive for thinness with a drive for harmony, vitality and well-being. This comprise a failure to address sexual or other kinds of abuse, a failure to address anxiety, depression and personality disorders, notably of a borderline and avoidant form.

A longer duration of illness is generally associated with a poor prospect of recovery but this is not necessarily the same as to say that a shorter duration is beneficial. It may even be the case that it is not the duration per se that is important but to what extent the individual has a contact with feelings of suffering, whether symptoms and compensatory behaviours are integrated in one's lifestyle and value system, and whether one is able to consider the balance between the immediate rewards and the longer term consequences.

## 6. Implications

### 6.1 Research implications

The model is multidimensional to accommodate for the multidimensional nature of eating disorders. However, the model needs future statistical and clinical testing. Specifically there is a need to explore the interrelationship between the core aspects and the four general domains at various time points in a recovery process and the construct and discriminative validity. Another prospect for the future investigation is to study whether a mediating or a moderator model may best explain the nature of process elements related to motivation, engagement and commitment. Also the mediator or moderator role of personality factors, resiliency, symptom disorder (anxiety and depression) and personality disorder (avoidant and borderline) comorbidity and prognostic factors, notably the duration of illness should be investigated. It may be the case that some of these factors may strengthen or weaken the recovery process (a mediator model) or that recovery may take place only in the presence or absence of one of these factors (a moderator model).

In clinical work, focusing on promoting recovery, the model suggests that all the five domains should be targeted. Like in research on outcome and recovery, an evaluation of recovery in clinical settings should adopt a non-normative approach. For instance with respect to social functioning, the issue is how the individual experiences the quality of social interactions and the motivational source of such contacts and not for instance imposing a norm with respect to the number of contacts.

Similarly, in clinical work promoting recovery should address and change the frequency and duration of symptoms, but should equally much address subjective experiences of strategies to conceal symptoms in daily life interactions and to evaluate to what extent symptoms do not longer hamper social functioning, affect interpersonal relations, decrease engagement in the future and the experience of life with a purpose beyond the pursuit of thinness.

## 7. Conclusions

Recovery comprises both eating disorder features close to the diagnostic criteria as well as in many domains of life. It is important to avoid normative judgements based on conceptions of a "good life" as people do live their lives in many ways, think in many ways and act accordingly.

In this chapter a comprehensive model is suggested to conceive and assess recovery as a multidimensional phenomenon. In contrast to previous multidimensional measures (e.g. Morgan & Russell, 1975; Morgan & Hayward, 1998) the model intends to be non-normative in not specifying content or nature of domain changes or suggesting absence of symptoms with a distribution in the general population. Also a scoring procedure is proposed.

The model may hopefully contribute to a valid evaluation of recovery in clinical practice. Also, the model may inspire to a tighter integration of fields of research that may profit from mutual benefits. There is a need to bridge a gap between outcome research and patient experiences to understand elements of recovery. The present chapter is limited by the current research. Future research however, may focus on which aspects from the experiential research tradition that could be formally tested in prospective outcome research using multivariate methods, and how good prognostic factors may be elaborated and nuanced through experiential studies. Finally, factors that promote or characterise recovery should be integrated in treatment studies.

## 8. References

Arcelus, J., Mitchell, A. J., Wales, J. & Nielsen, S. (2011). Mortality rates in patients with anorexia nervosa and other eating disorders. *Archives of General Psychiatry*, 68 (7), pp. 724-731, ISSN 0003-990x.

Beresin, E. V, Gordon, C. & Herzog, D. B. (1989). The process of recovering from anorexia nervosa In: *Psychoanalysis and eating disorders,* Bemporad, J & Herzog, eds, New York, Guilford, pp. 101-130, ISBN 97-808-9862-3888.

Björk, T. & Ahlström, G. (2008). The patient's perception of having recovered from an eating disorder. *Health Care for Women International,* 29, (8-9), pp. 926-944, ISSN 0739-9332.

Berkman, N. D, Lohr, K. N. & Bulik, C. M. (2007). Outcomes of eating disorders: A systematic review of the literature. *International Journal of Eating Disorders,* 40 (4), pp. 293-309, ISSN 0276-3478.

Bollen, E. & Wojciechowski, F. L. (2004). Anorexia nervosa subtypes and the Big Five personality factors. *European Eating Disorders Review,* 12 (2), pp. 117-121, ISSN 1099-0968.

Bulik, C. M., Sullivan, P. F., Tozzi, F., Furberg, H., Lichtenstein, P, & Pedersen, N. L. (2006). Prevalence, heritability and prospective risk factors for anorexia nervosa. *Archives of General Psychiatry,* 63 (3), 305-312, ISSN 0003-990x.

Burney, J. & Irwin, H. J. (2000). Shame and guilt in females with eating disordered symptomathology. *Journal of Clinical Psychology,* 56 (1), pp. 51-61, ISSN 1097-4679.

Chavez, M. & Insel, T. R. (2007). Eating disorders: National Institute of Mental Health's perspective. *American Psychologist,* 62 (3), pp. 159-166, ISSN 0003-066x.

Claes, L., Wandereycken, W., Luyten, P., Soenses, B., Pieters, G. & Vertommen, H. (2006). Personality prototypes in eating disorder based on the Big Five. *Journal of Personality Disorders,* 20 (4), pp. 401-416, ISSN 0855-579x.

Couturier, J. & Lock, J. (2006a). What is remission in adolescent anorexia nervosa? A review of various conceptualizations and quantitative analysis. *International Journal of Eating Disorders,* 39 (3), pp.175-183, ISSN 0276-3478.

Couturier, J. & Lock, J. (2006b). What is recovery in adolescent anorexia nervosa? *International Journal of Eating Disorders,* 39 (7), pp.550-555, ISSN 0276-3478.

D'Abundo, M. & Chally, P. (2004) Struggling with recovery: Participant perspectives on battling an eating disorder. *Qualitative Health Research,* 14 (8), pp.1094-1106, ISSN 1049-7323.

Dare, C, Eisler, I, Russell, G., Treasure, J. & Dodge, L. (2001). Psychological therapies for adults with anorexia nervosa: randomised controlled trial of out-patient treatments. *British Journal of Psychiatry,* 178 (4), pp.216-221, ISSN 0007-1250.

Deci, E. L. & Ryan, R. M. (2002). *Handbook of self-determination research.* New York. The University of Rochester Press, ISBN 1-58046-108-5.

Didonna, F. (2009) *Clinical handbook of mindfulness.* New York: Springer, ISBN 978-0-387-09592-9.

Diener, E. & Lucas, R. E. (2000). Subjective emotional well-being. In: *Handbook of emotions,* eds. Lewis, M. & Haviland, J. M. 2nd edition, pp. 325-337. Guilford Press. New York, ISBN.

Fairburn, C. G, Norman P. A., Welch, S. L., O'Connor, M. E, Doll, H. A. & Peveler, R. C. (1995). A prospective study of outcome in bulimia nervosa and the long-term effects of three psychological treatments. *Archives of General Psychiatry,* 52 (4), pp.304-312, ISSN 0003-990x.

Fairburn, C. G., Welch, S. L, & Doll, H. A., Davies, B. A. & O'Connor, M. E. (1997). Risk factors for bulimia nervosa. *Archives of General Psychiatry,* 54 (6), pp.509-517, ISSN 0003-990x.

Fairburn, C. G, Doll, H. A. Welch, S., Hay, P. J., Davies, B. A. & O'Connor, M. E. (1998). Risk factors for binge eating disorder. A community-based, case-control study. *Archives of General Psychiatry,* 55 (5), 425-432, ISSN 0003-990x

Fairburn, C. G, Cooper, Z, & Doll, H. A. & Welch, S. (1999). Risk factors for anorexia nervosa. Three integrated case-Control comparisons. *Archives of General Psychiatry,* 56 (5), 468-476, ISSN 0003-990x.

Fairburn, C. G, Cooper, Z. & Zafran, R. (2003). Cognitive-behavioural therapy for eating disorders: a "transdiagnostic" theory and treatment. *Behavioural Research & Therapy,* 41 (5), pp. 509-528, ISSN 0005-7967.

Fairburn, C. G. & Harrison, P. J. (2003). Eating disorders. *Lancet,* 361 (9335), pp. 407-416.

Fairburn, C. G, Cooper, Z., Doll, H. A. & Davies, B. A. (2005). Identifying dieters who will develop an eating disorder: A prospective, population based *study. American Journal of Psychiatry,* 162 (12), pp. 2249-2255, ISSN 1535-7228.

Fassino, S., Abbate-Daga, G., Amianto, F., Leombruni, P., Boggio, S. & Rovera, G. G. (2002). Temperament and character profile of eating disorders: A controlled study with the Temperament and Character Inventory. *International Journal of Eating Disorders,* 32 (4), pp. 412-25, ISSN 0276-3478.

Federeci, A. & Kaplan, A. S. (2008). The patient's account of relapse and recovery in anorexia nervosa: a qualitative study. *European Eating Disorders* Review, 16 (1), pp. 1-10, ISSN 1099-0968.

Fichter, M., Quadflieg, N. & Rhem, J. (2003). Predicting the outcome of eating disorders using structural equation modeling. *International Journal of Eating Disorders,* 34 (3), pp. 292-313, ISSN 0276-3478.

Fisher, M. (2003). The course and outcome of eating disorders in adults and in adolescents: a review. *Adolescent Medicine State of the Art Review,* 14 (1), pp. 149-158.

Frank, E. S. (1991). Shame and guilt in eating disorders. American *Journal of Orthopsychiatry,* 61 (2), pp. 303-606, ISSN 1939-0025.

Freedman, G, Leichner, P., Manley, R., Sandhu, P. S. & Wang, T. C. (2006). Understanding anorexia nervosa through analysis of thematic content of letters in an adolescent sample. *European Eating Disorders Review,* 14 (5), pp. 301-307, ISSN 1099-0968.

Garrett, C. J. (1997). Recovery from anorexia nervosa: A sociological perspective. *International Journal of Eating Disorders,* 21 (3), pp. 261-272, ISSN 0276-3478.

Geller, J. & Drab, D. (1999). The readiness and motivation interview: a symptom-specific measure of readiness for change in the eating disorders. *European Eating Disorders Review,* 7 (4), pp. 259-278, ISSN 1099-0968.

Geller, J., Brown, K. E. & Srikameswaran S. (2011). The efficacy of a brief motivational intervention for individuals with eating disorders: a randomized control trial. *International Journal of Eating Disorders,* 44 (6), pp. 497-505, ISSN 0276-3478.

Ghaderi, A. & Scott, B. (2000). The Big Five and eating disorders: A prospective study in the general population. *European Journal of Personality,* 14 (4), pp. 311-323, ISSN 1099-0984.

Gowers, S. G. & Shore, A. (1999). The stigma of eating disorders. *International Journal of Clinical Practice,* 53 (5), pp. 386-392, ISSN 1742-1241.

Hepworth, N. & Paxton, S. J. (2007). Pathways to help-seeking in bulimia nervosa and binge eating problems: A concept mapping approach. *International Journal of Eating Disorders,* 40 (6), pp. 493-504, ISSN 0276-3478.

Holliday, J., Landau, S. & Treasure, J. (2006). Personality pathology among individuals with a lifetime history of anorexia nervosa. *Journal of Personality Disorders,* 20 (4), pp. 417-430, ISSN 0885-579x.

Hsu, L. K. G., Crisp, A. H. & Callender, J. S. (1992). Recovery in anorexia nervosa- the patient's perspective. *International Journal of Eating Disorders,* 11 (4), pp. 341-350, ISSN 0276-3478.

Jarman, M. & Walsh, S. (1999). Evaluating recovery from anorexia nervosa and bulimia nervosa: Integrating lessons learned from research and clinical practice. *Clinical Psychology Review,* 19 (7), pp. 773-778, ISSN 0272-7358.

Johnson, J. G., Cohen, P., Kasen, S. & Brook, J. S. (2006). Personality disorder trait evident by early adulthood and risk for eating and weight problems during middle adulthood. *International Journal of Eating Disorders,* 39 (1), pp. 1-9, ISSN 0276-3478.

Keel, P. K. & Mitchell, J. E. (1997). Outcome in bulimia nervosa. *American Journal of Psychiatry,* 154 (3), pp. 313-321, ISSN 1535-7228.

Keel, P. K. & Brown, T. A. (2010). Update on course and outcome of eating disorders. *International Journal of Eating Disorders,* 43 (3), pp. 195-204, ISSN 0276-3478.

Keel, P. K., Dorer, D., Kamryn, T., Eddy, K. T., Franko, D., Charatan, D. L. & Herzog, D. B. (2003). Predictors of mortality in eating disorders. *Archives of General Psychiatry,* 60 (2), 179-183, ISSN 0003-990x.

Kordy, H., Kramer, B., Palmer, R. L., Papezova, H., Pellet, J., Richard, M., Treasure, J. & COST Action B6. (2002). Remission, recovery, relapse, and recurrence in eating disorders: conceptualization and illustration of a validation strategy. *Journal of Clinical Psychology,* 58 (7), pp. 833-846, ISSN 1097-4679.

Lamoureux, M. M. H. & Bottorff, J. L. (2005). "Becoming the real me": Recovering from anorexia nervosa. *Health Care for Women International,* 26 (2), pp. 170-188, ISSN 0739-9332.

Leventhal, H., Meyer, D. & Nerenz, D. (1980). *The common sense representation of illness danger.* Eds S. Rachman. Contributions to medical psychology (vol. 2), Pergamon Press, ISBN, Oxford.

Marcia, J. E. (1966). Development and validation of ego identity status. *Journal of Personality and Social Psychology,* 3 (5), pp. 551-558, ISSN 0022-3514.

Matusek, J. A., & Knudson, R. M. (2009). Rethinking recovery from eating disorders: Spiritual and political dimensions. *Qualitative Health Research,* 19 (5), pp. 697-707, ISSN 1049-7323.

McLeod, S. (1989). *The art of starvation.* London: Virago. ISBN 0 86068 169 6

Morgan, H. G. & Russell, G. F. M. (1975). Value of family background and clinical features as predictors of long term outcome in anorexia nervosa: four-year follow-up study of 41 patients. *Psychological Medicine,* 5 (5), pp. 355-371, ISSN 0033 2917.

Morgan, H. G. & Hayward, A. E. (1998). Clinical assessment of anorexia nervosa: The Morgan-Russell outcome assessment schedule. *British Journal of Psychiatry,* 152 (3), pp. 367-371, ISSN 0007-1250.

Nilsson, K, Abrahamsson, E, Torbiornsson, A. & Hägglöf, B. (2007). Causes of adolescent onset anorexia nervosa. Patient perspectives. *Eating Disorders,* 15 (2), pp. 125-133 ISSN 1064-0266.

Nilsson, K, & Hägglöf, B. (2006). Patient perspectives of recovery in adolescent onset anorexia nervosa. *Eating Disorders,* 14 (6), pp. 305-311, ISSN 1064-0266.

Noordenbos, G. (1989). Improving the process of recovery of patients with anorexia nervosa. *British Review of Bulimia and Anorexia Nervosa,* 4 (1), pp. 17-31.

Noordenbos, G. (1992). Important factors in the process of recovery according to patients with anorexia nervosa. In: *The course of eating disorders. Long term follow-up studies of anorexia and bulimia nervosa,* eds, Herzog, W., Deter, H. C. & Vandereycken, W., pp. 304-322. Springer, ISBN 3-540-54036-9, London.

Noordenbos, G. (1998). Eating disorders in primary care: Early identification and intervention by general practitioners. In: *The prevention of eating disorders,* eds. Vandereycken, W. & Noordenbos, G., pp. 214-229, Athlone Press, ISBN 0 485 24014, London.

Noordenbos, G. & Seubring, A. (2005). Criteria for recovery from eating disorders according to patients and therapists. *Eating Disorders,* 14 (1), pp. 41-54, ISSN 1064-0266.

Nordbo, R. H. S. (2010). *Meaning and motivation in anorexia nervosa.* Doctoral dissertation, University of Oslo, ISSN 1504-3991.

Olmsted, M. P., Kaplan, A. S. & Rockert, W. (2005). Defining remission and relapse in bulimia nervosa. *International Journal of Eating Disorders,* 38 (1), pp. 1-6, ISSN 0276-3478.

Patching, J. & Lawler, J. (2009). Understanding women's experiences of developing an eating disorder and recovering: A life-history approach. *Nursing Inquiry,* 16 (1), pp. 10-21, ISSN 1440-1800.

Patton, G. C, Selzer, R. Coffey, C. & Carlin, J. B. (1999). Wolfe R. Onset of adolescent eating disorders: Population based cohort study over 3 years. *BMJ*, 318, pp. 765-768.

Pettersen, G. & Rosenvinge, J. H. (2002). Improvement and recovery from eating disorders – a patient perspective. *Eating Disorders*, 10 (1), pp. 61-71, ISSN 1064-0266.

Pettersen, G., Rosenvinge, J. H. & Ytterhus, B. (2008). The "double life" of bulimia: Patient experiences in daily life interactions. *Eating Disorders*, 16 (3), pp. 204-211, ISSN 1064-0266.

Pettersen, G., Wynn, R. Thune-Larsen, K-B. & Rosenvinge, J. H. (2011). Eating disorders: Challenges in the later phases of the recovery process. *Scandinavian Journal of Caring Sciences*, 25, pp. 12-18.

Pettersen, G. (2007). *Eating disorders, studies of understanding and recovery.* PhD-thesis, NTNU, Trondheim, Norway, ISBN 678-82-471-5451-9.

Perry, J. A., Silvera, D. H., Rosenvinge, J. H. & Holte, A. (2002). Are oral, obsessive, and hysterical personality traits related to eating patterns? A general population study of 6313 males and females. *Journal of Personality Assessment*, 78 (3), pp. 405-416, ISSN 0022-3891.

Perry, J. A., Silvera, D. H., Neilands, T. B., Rosenvinge, J. H. & Hanssen, T. (2008). A study of the relationship between parental bonding, self-concept and eating disturbances in Norwegian and American college populations. *Eating Behaviors*, 9 (1), pp. 13-24, ISSN 1471-0153.

Prochaska, J. O. & DiClemente, C.C. (1982). Transtheoretical therapy: Toward a more integrative model of change. *Psychotherapy: Theory Research and Practice,* 19 (2), pp. 276-288, ISSN 0033-3204.

Rahkonen, A. K. & Tozzi, F. (2005). The process of recovery in eating disorder sufferers' own words: An Internet study. *International Journal of Eating Disorders,* 37 (S1), pp. S80-S86, ISSN 0276-3478.

Rie, S, Noordenbos, G, Donker, M. & van Furth, E. (2007). The patient's view on quality of life and eating disorders. *International Journal of Eating Disorders,* 40 (1), pp. 13-20, ISSN 0276-3478.

Rosenvinge, J. H., Martinussen, M. & Østensen, E. (2000). The comorbidity of eating disorders and personality disorders. A meta-analytic review of studies published between 1983 and 1998. *Eating & Weight Disorders,* 5 (1), pp. 52-61.

Rø, O., Martinsen, E. W, Hoffart, A. & Rosenvinge, J. H. (2005a). Two-year prospective study of personality disorders in adults with longstanding eating disorders. *International Journal of Eating Disorders,* 37 (2), pp. 112-118, ISSN 0276-3478.

Rø, O., Martinsen, E. W., Hoffart, A., Sexton, H. & Rosenvinge, J. H. (2005b). The interaction of personality disorders and eating disorders: a two-year prospective study of patients with longstanding eating disorders. *International Journal of Eating Disorders,* 38 (2), pp.106-111, ISSN 0276-3478.

Råstam, M. (1992). Anorexia nervosa in 51 Swedish adolescents. Premorbid problems and comorbidity. *Journal of the American Academy of Child & Adolescent Psychiatry,* 31 (5), pp. 819-829.

Sanfter, L. J. & Crowther, J. H. (1998). Variability in self-esteem, moods, shame and guilt to eating disorder symptomathology. *Journal of Social & Clinical Psychology,* 14, pp. 315-324.

Serpell, L., Teasdale, J., Troop. N. & Treasure, J. (2004). The development of the P-CAN, a measure to operationalize the pros and cons of anorexia nervosa. *International Journal of Eating Disorders,* 36 (4), pp. 416-73, ISSN 0276-3478.

Shapiro, J. R., Berkman, N. D., Brownley, K. A., Sedway, J. A., Lohr, K. N. & Bulik. C. M. (2007). Bulimia nervosa treatment: A systematic review of randomised controlled trials. *International Journal of Eating Disorders,* 40 (4), pp. 321-336, ISSN 0276-3478.

Steinhausen, H. C. (2002). The outcome of anorexia nervosa in the 20th century. *American Journal of Psychiatry,* 159 (8), pp. 1284-1293, ISSN 1535-7228.

Strober, M., Freeman, R. & Morrell, W. (1997). The long-term course of severe anorexia nervosa in adolescents: survival analysis of recovery, relapse, and outcome predictors over 10-15 years in a prospective study. *International Journal of Eating Disorders,* 22 (4), pp. 339-360, ISSN 0276-3478.

Tozzi, F, Sullivan, P. F., Fear, J. L., McKenzie, J. & Bulik, C. M. (2003). Causes and recovery in anorexia nervosa: The patient's perspective. *International Journal of Eating Disorders,* 33 (2), pp. 143-154, ISSN 0276-3478.

Troop, N. A., Holbrey, A., Towler, R. & Treasure, J. (1994). Ways of coping in women with eating disorders. *Journal of Nervous and Mental Disease,* 182 (10), pp. 535-540, ISSN 1539-736x.

Waller, G. A. (2008). A 'trans-transdiagnostic' model of the eating disorders: A new way to open the egg? *European Eating Disorders Review,* 16 (3), pp. 165-172, ISSN 1099-0968.

Vanderlinden, J., Buis, H., Pieters, G. & Probst, M. (2007). Which elements in the treatment of eating disorders are necessary 'ingredients' in the recovery process? A comparison between the patient's and therapist's view. *European Eating Disorders Review,* 15 (5), pp. 357-365, ISSN 1099-0968.

Vansteenkiste, M., Souenes, B. & Vandereycken, W. (2005). Motivation to change in eating disorder patients: A conceptual clarification on the basis of self-determination theory. *International Journal of Eating Disorders,* 37 (3), pp. 207-219, ISSN 0276-3478.

Vrabel, K-A., Rø, Ø., Martinsen, E., Hoffart, A. & Rosenvinge, J. H. (2010). Co-occurrence of avoidant personality disorders and child sexual abuse predicts poor outcome in longstanding eating disorder. *Journal of Abnormal Psychology,* 119 (3), pp. 623-629, ISSN 0021-843-x.

Waller, G. (2011). The myths of motivation. *International Journal of Eating Disorders,* 43, doi: 10.1002/eat.20900, ISSN 0276-3478.

Weaver, K., Wuest, J. & Cilisca, D. (2005). Understanding women's journey of recovering from anorexia nervosa. *Qualitative Health Research,* 15 (2), pp. 188-192, ISSN 1049-7323.

Wentz, E. (2000). *Ten-year outcome of anorexia nervosa with teenage onset.* Doctoral dissertation, Goteborg University, ISBN 91-628-4011-8.

Wentz, E., Gillberg, C., Anckarsäter, H., Gillberg, C. & Råstam, M. (2009). Adolescent-onset anorexia nervosa: 18 year outcome. *British Journal of Psychiatry,* 194 (2), pp. 168-174, ISSN 0007-1250.

Woods, S. (2004). Untreated recovery from eating disorders. *Adolescence,* 39 (154), pp. 361-371, ISSN 0001-8449.

# 14

# Prevention of Eating Disorders: A Review

Ashley M. Kroon Van Diest and Marisol Perez
*Texas A&M University,*
*USA*

## 1. Introduction

Nearly 10% of young women experience clinical eating disorders (Lewinsohn et al., 2000), and an even greater amount of women experience subclinical eating disorders and risk factors association with eating disorders, such as body dissatisfaction. Eating disorders are associated with a number of negative physical and psychological consequences, increased risk of mortality, and are often severe and debilitating (Thompson & Stice 2001). Of the individuals who experience eating disorder symptoms and their negative consequences, less than 25% will receive treatment (Hudson et al., 2007; Johnson et al., 2002). For those that do receive treatment, treatment effects are limited with only 30% experiencing long-lasting symptom remission (Agras et al., 2000; Fairburn, 2002; Fairburn et al., 2009; Wilson et al., 2003), and approximately 20% drop out (Fairburn 2002). Treatment for eating disorders is also relatively expensive, and most insurance companies will not fund inpatient treatment for individuals with severe eating disorders (Shaw et al., 2009). Therefore, more efforts have been devoted to the development of effective programs for the prevention of eating disorders.

Many types of eating disorder prevention programs have been developed, with some programs producing lasting reductions in current or future eating disorder symptoms and risk factors (Stice, Shaw et al., 2007). This chapter will focus on the importance of the prevention of eating disorders, including features of successful prevention programs. Specific eating disorder prevention strategies covered within this chapter include dissonance based, mirror exposure, healthy weight, motivational interviewing, computer-administered cognitive-behavioral, and other strategies. Most of these strategies have been evaluated in controlled trials and have produced promising reductions in eating disorder symptoms and associated risk factors, with some programs having enough research evidence to be considered empirically supported interventions. Also, new preliminary information will be presented on the ability of prevention programs to create long-lasting systematic reductions in eating disorder symptoms and associated risk factors within large social organizations in order to increase the overall health and well being of members enrolled in the organization. The chapter will conclude with suggested directions for future research on prevention efforts and a brief overview of the eating disorder prevention literature.

## 2. Importance and clinical utility of prevention

Eating disorders are one of the most common psychiatric problems experienced by females (Lewinsohn et al., 2000) and are characterized by serious eating disturbances, such as fasting, purging, and binge eating, as well as excessive concern about body shape and weight. They are commonly associated with a number of medical complications including diabetes, hypertension, loss of teeth enamel, osteoporosis, decreased kidney functioning, gastrointestinal bleeding, malnutrition, bowel disease, infertility, stress fractures, obesity and cardiac arrest (Kaye et al., 2003; Keel et al., 2003; Mitchell & Crow, 2006). Eating disorders are also associated with psychosocial functional impairment, and are marked by chronicity and relapse (Fairburn et al., 2000; Newman et al., 1996; Thompson & Stice, 2001). Increased rates of mortality, suicide, future risk for onset of obesity, substance abuse, and mood, anxiety, and personality disorders are also seen in individuals with eating disorders (Becker et al., 1999; Birmingham et al., 2005; Carlat et al., 1997; Franko & Keel, 2006; Hudson et al., 2007; Johnson et al., 2002; Stice et al., 1999).

Prevalence rates of clinical and subclinical levels of eating disorders and associated risk factors have increased over the past several decades and are affecting individuals at younger ages (Feingold & Mazzella, 1998; Muth & Cash, 1997; Park, 2007; Stice 1994; Striegel-Moore & Franko, 2002). Approximately 61% of young adult females experience subclinical eating disorders, including binging and purging, and subclinical bulimia nervosa (Mintz & Betz, 1988), and 80-91% report dieting (Striegel-Moore et al., 1990). Males are also increasingly experiencing body dissatisfaction and subclinical eating disorders (Drummond, 2002; O'Dea & Abraham, 2002), and 5-10% of all individuals with clinical eating disorders are male (Carlat & Camargo, 1991; Lucas et al., 1991). This increase in prevalence rates, combined with societal pressures placed on individuals to be thin and a decrease in the ideal body weight promoted by society places individuals at greater risk for experiencing eating disorder risk factors such as thin-ideal internalization, self-objectification, and body dissatisfaction (Stice & Shaw, 1994), further increasing the risk for the development of eating disorders (Tiggemann, 2011). Eating disorder risk factors alone are impairing and can lead to both clinical and subclinical levels of eating disorders. Since research indicates that subclinical levels of eating disorders and associated risk factors can be just as impairing as clinical eating disorders (Hoffman & Brownell, 1997; Thompson et al., 1999), the prevention of subclinical eating disorders and associated risk factors is equally important as the prevention of diagnosable eating disorders.

The negative physical and psychological consequences associated with eating disorders, combined with the increase in prevalence rates of eating disorder symptoms and risk factors and the lack of success of treatment programs has made the development and evaluation of programs for the prevention of eating disorders essential. Prevention programs are designed to decrease current and future eating disorder symptoms and associated risk factors in order to reduce or eliminate the subsequent negative consequences. If prevention programs are effective, they can reduce rates of eating disorder symptoms and risk factors, potentially reducing the need for expensive treatment programs.

The clinical utility of prevention programs is reflected in the similarity between prevention and treatment, as the goal of prevention is to prevent the onset or exacerbation of a disorder. However, in order for clinicians to use eating disorder prevention programs in a variety of contexts, research on the effectiveness of these programs is necessary as effectiveness studies allow for the examination of generalizability, variability in participants and settings, and outcome of preventive effects of the intervention. Additionally, effectiveness studies can measure costs of implementing an intervention, including the cost savings of preventing the numerous negative outcomes associated with disordered eating, and practicability within community agencies.

## 3. Features of successful prevention programs

Research on prevention programs has identified several factors that may influence program effectiveness, such as program format, participant risk status, age of participants, type of interventionist, and number of sessions (Shaw et al., 2009; Stice, Shaw et al., 2007). Initial eating disorder prevention programs primarily used a psychoeducational or didactic format, but have since developed into interactive formats that focus on reducing eating disorder risk factors in order to subsequently reduce eating disorder symptoms (Stice, Shaw et al., 2008). These psychoeducational programs often primarily provide information about eating disorders including consequences of disordered eating behaviors and risk factors associated with the development of eating disorders (Killen et al., 1993; Moreno & Thelen, 1993; Paxton, 1993). Unfortunately, didactic formats are often less effective in changing attitudes and behaviors than interactive programs that actively engage participants and teach new skills, and alone may not be enough to alter any maladaptive behaviors (Stice & Shaw, 2004; Stice, Shaw et al., 2007; Stice et al., 2003). Therefore, many current prevention programs use more interactive formats which seem to increase program effectiveness.

Prevention programs can be categorized as universal, selective, or indicated (also known as primary, secondary, and tertiary), each depending on the risk status of participants (Gordon, 1983; Marchand et al., 2011). These categories may also influence effectiveness of prevention programs. Universal prevention programs target all individuals within a general population regardless of risk status while selective prevention programs only target individuals at high risk for developing eating disorder symptoms (Shaw et al., 2009; Stice, Shaw et al., 2007). Both universal and selective prevention programs aim to prevent the development of symptoms of a disorder. Indicated programs are aimed at individuals who already have symptoms of a disorder in order to prevent further increases in symptoms. Empirical evidence suggests that universal programs produce smaller effects than selective programs, with some universal prevention programs producing greater effects for the high risk participants than for the entire sample (Kaminski & McNamara, 1996; Killen et al., 1993; Stewart et al., 2001; Stice et al., 2004; Taylor et al., 2006; Weiss & Wertheim, 2005). Selective programs have also been found to produce larger effects for obesity and depression than universal programs (Horowitz & Garber, 2006; Stice, Shaw, & Marti, 2006). It is hypothesized that these differences in outcomes for individuals based on risk status is due to high risk individuals being more motivated to engage in prevention programs to reduce current distress, which may result in greater outcomes for these individuals. Additionally, participants who are low risk may have less room for improvement, resulting in smaller outcome effects.

Participant age also influences the effects of the intervention (Shaw et al., 2009). Programs with participants older than 15 years had larger effects than programs with participants younger than 15. This may be because programs are more effective when implemented during the peak risk period for the emergence of eating disorder symptoms, which has been identified as between the ages of 15 and 19 by prospective studies. Younger individuals may also have less insight and ability to apply the principles and skills learned throughout the program because they are still developing abstract reasoning skills. Additionally, lower levels of eating disorder symptoms in younger individuals may lead to lower effect sizes.

Outcomes of eating disorder prevention programs can also be influence by the type of interventionist. Research has found that prevention programs conducted by a trained interventionist are more effective than programs conducted by endogenous providers, such as teachers (Shaw et al., 2009; Stice, Shaw et al., 2007). This could be because endogenous providers may have other responsibilities that interfere with the delivery of the prevention program. While programs that are led by endogenous providers are less effective than programs led by trained interventionists, researchers have found that eating disorder prevention programs can be led by individuals who are trained on the protocol and are as effective as programs led by trained professionals (Becker et al., 2006; Becker, Bull et al., 2008; Perez et al., 2010). For example, Perez and colleagues (2010) implemented a dissonance based eating disorder prevention program in a sorority at a large public university led by peer facilitators who had undergone training from a doctoral level psychologist and found the program to be just as effective as programs facilitated by trained doctoral level psychologists.

The number of sessions used during the intervention has also been examined in order to determine if fewer sessions using the same materials are as effective as programs with a greater number of sessions. Researchers had postulated that more sessions would increase program effectiveness by increasing the length of time participants have to reflect on the program content between sessions as well as giving participants more time to practice the new skills learned during the program (Stice, Shaw et al., 2007).While previous researchers had concluded that brief single-session prevention programs were not sufficient to produce lasting attitudinal and behavioral change (Martz & Bazzini, 1999), it appears that programs with fewer sessions prove to be just as effective in reducing eating disorder symptoms and associated risk factors as longer programs containing multiple sessions (Stice, Shaw et al., 2007).

## 4. Eating disorder prevention strategies

Evaluations of current prevention programs are providing encouraging results. For example, a meta-analysis of eating disorder prevention programs revealed that 51% of eating disorder prevention programs reduced risk factors associated with disordered eating, and 29% reduced current or future eating disorder symptoms (Stice, Shaw et al., 2007). Some programs have produced reductions in eating disorder symptoms and associated risk factors that persisted through follow-up assessments. For example, Becker and colleagues (2005) evaluated the effects of a dissonance based prevention program in a college sorority and found that significant reductions in eating disorder symptoms and associated risk factors including body dissatisfaction and thin-ideal internalization were maintained at a 1-year follow-up assessment. These results from the same program conducted within a different sorority have been replicated by other researchers (Perez et al., 2010). Also, Low and colleagues (2006) examined the effects of a computer-administered prevention program that used a combination of interactive and psychoeducational techniques and found that significant reductions in eating disorder symptoms were maintained at an 8-month follow-up assessment. Other programs have reduced the risk of future onset of clinical and subclinical eating disorders (Stice et al., 2004). In fact, an evaluation of a computer based eating disorder prevention program conducted by Taylor et al., (2006) indicated that this program prevented the onset of eating disorders in high risk groups in addition to reducing weight and shape concerns.

These results support the benefits of eating disorder prevention programs. Research on prevention programs has resulted in the development of several different prevention strategies that utilize different formats and approaches to prevention. Some of these programs have been extensively researched and have gained empirical support, while others need further research in order to determine their effectiveness in preventing eating disorders. The main types of studies on prevention programs are presented in Table 1. Next, specific eating disorder prevention strategies will be discussed in detail including program format, different versions of the program, and research supporting the effectiveness of the program.

| **Types of Studies** |
|---|
| Dissonance based studies |
| Health weight based studies |
| Mirror exposure based studies |
| Motivational interviewing based studies |
| Computer-administered cognitive behavioral based studies |
| Other |

Table 1. Main types of studies.

### 4.1 Dissonance based

Dissonance based eating disorder prevention programs are one of the most extensively studied and empirically supported forms of eating disorder prevention (Stice, Shaw et al., 2008). Dissonance based interventions were developed using principles from Festinger's cognitive-dissonance theory (1957). Cognitive dissonance is a state in which incongruent thoughts, beliefs, or attitudes create psychological discomfort or tension (Brehm & Cohen, 1962; Festinger 1957). This discomfort may motivate individuals to change their thoughts, beliefs, or attitudes in order to restore a sense of internal consistency (Beauvois & Joule, 1999). Based on this theory, dissonance based eating disorder prevention programs seek to create dissonance in individuals about eating disorder risk factors such as thin-ideal internalization and body dissatisfaction. This is accomplished through a series of verbal, written, and behavioral exercises that encourage participants to critique a particular eating disorder risk factor in order to create dissonance. Dissonance based prevention programs have been used for preventing a variety of problems including obesity (Axsom & Cooper, 1985), snake phobia (Cooper, 1980), smoking onset (Killen, 1985), substance use (Barnett et al., 1996), substance abuse (Ulrich, 1991), and dating aggression (Schumacher & Slep, 2004).

Many current dissonance eating disorder prevention programs are based on the dual pathway model (Stice et al., 1996), an empirically supported etiologic model which suggests that sociocultural pressures to have a thin body promote thin-ideal internalization, which predicts body dissatisfaction, negative affect, and dieting. Body dissatisfaction, negative affect and dieting in turn foster eating disorder symptoms. Therefore, many current dissonance based eating disorder prevention programs attempt to create cognitive dissonance about the thin ideal, as it occurs early in the causal chain and can potentially lead to eating disorder symptoms. Once participants engage in counter-attitudinal activities in which they critique the thin-ideal proposed by society and voluntarily take a stance against it, they are more likely to become faced with an internal conflict between their own internalized acceptance of the thin-ideal and the arguments they generated to counter the pressures to attain this thin-ideal, therefore experiencing the psychological discomfort that results from cognitive dissonance. They may then be motivated to alter their own thin-ideal internalization in order to reduce or eliminate this discomfort. This reduction of internalization of the thin-ideal in turn leads to decreases in other eating disorder risk factors and eating disorder symptoms. Research on the effects of dissonance based prevention programs that target thin-ideal internalization has provided evidence that supports the idea that reductions in thin-ideal internalization mediate the effects of the change in body dissatisfaction and eating disorder symptoms (Seidel et al., 2009; Stice, Marti et al., 2011; Stice, Presnell et al., 2007), and should therefore be targeted first within prevention programs. However, a recent study on the integration of thin-ideal internalization and self-objectification within a dissonance based eating disorder prevention program revealed that thin-ideal internalization and self-objectification are equally predictive of one another in the causal chain of eating disorder development, suggesting that both variables should be targeted equally within prevention programs in order to further increase reductions in eating disorder symptoms and risk factors and sustain these reductions for longer periods of time (Kroon Van Diest & Perez, 2011).

The original dissonance based eating disorder prevention program developed by Stice and colleagues (2000) was designed to include three one-hour group sessions. During the first session, the thin-ideal was defined followed by discussions on the origin of the thin-ideal, how it is perpetuated, different sources of pressures encouraging women to conform to the thin-ideal, and who benefits from the thin-ideal. Participants were asked to write a one-page counterattitudinal statement about the costs associated with attaining the thin-ideal as homework to be discussed during the next session. The second session began with a review of the first session and a discussion of the homework assignment. Role plays were conducted allowing participants to attempt to dissuade each other from pursuing the thin-ideal. Participants were asked to engage in a mirror exposure task as homework, recording physical and non-physical characteristics they liked about themselves to be discussed during the next session. The third and final session began with a review of the previous session and a discussion of the mirror exposure homework activity. Discussions about difficulties in resisting the thin-ideal and how to overcome these difficulties, as well as ways participants may be unknowingly promoting the thin-ideal were conducted. The session concluded by encouraging participants to challenge themselves to engage in behavioral challenges relating to body image concerns. An expanded four one-hour session version of the same program was later developed (Stice, Shaw et al., 2008). Other versions of dissonance based eating disorder prevention programs have since been developed, including a two two-hour session format developed by Becker and colleagues (2005) developed for use in college sororities, a six 45-minute session format developed by Mitchell and colleagues (2007), and a one two-hour session format developed by Matusek and colleagues (2004). Manuals are available for each of the various versions.

Although there are slightly different formats for dissonance based eating disorder prevention programs, most current programs assign homework between sessions in order to increase the amount of time participants are engaging in activities that increase dissonance.

Also, most dissonance based programs minimize the use of didactic techniques, as they are less effective than interactive techniques in changing thoughts and behaviors (Stice & Shaw, 2004; Stice, Shaw et al., 2007; Stice et al., 2003). It is also common for dissonance based prevention programs to promote adaptive behavior by encouraging participants to model certain behaviors in groups during sessions as a form of strategic self-presentation. Some of the exercises used in dissonance based prevention programs are viewed as an opportunity to combat maladaptive cognitions through a cognitive-behavioral perspective, and group activities are often used to foster social support and group cohesion.

Other techniques used in dissonance based eating disorder prevention programs are less universal and have only been used by a small number of researchers. Specifically, incentive for participants to use the new skills they learn during sessions is increased through the use of motivational enhancement exercises, such as group discussions of the costs of body image concerns (Stice, Shaw et al., 2008). Also, input about the intervention has been collected from participants and facilitators during some trials in order to improve manuals and the program for future trials. For example, handouts conveying information about the program to younger participants were incorporated into the program based on feedback received in previous trials from individuals who have already participated in the intervention. While these techniques have been utilized by Stice and colleagues, it may prove beneficial for other groups of researchers assessing dissonance based eating disorder prevention programs to begin using these strategies as well which may increase program effectiveness.

Dissonance based eating disorder prevention programs have been thoroughly studied, mostly providing medium to large effect sizes in outcome. Numerous studies examining the efficacy of these programs have provided evidence of significant reductions in thin-ideal internalization, body dissatisfaction, and eating disorder symptoms in high risk adolescent girls (Stice et al., 2001; Stice, Marti et al., 2008; Stice et al., 2000; Stice, Shaw, Burten, et al., 2006; Stice et al., 2003), college women, and sororities (Becker et al., 2006; Becker, Bull et al., 2008; Perez et al., 2010). When compared to control groups, dissonance prevention programs have produced greater reductions in eating disorder symptoms and risk factors, such as body dissatisfaction, bulimic pathology and dietary restraint, future risk for onset of clinical and subclinical eating disorders and obesity (Becker, Ciao et al., 2008; Mitchell et al., 2007; Roehrig et al., 2006; Stice et al., 2003; Stice, Marti et al., 2008; Stice, Shaw et al., 2008; Wade et al., 2009), with some of these reductions continuing through a 3-year follow-up assessment (Stice, Marti et al., 2008; Stice et al., 2000; Stice, Shaw, Burton et al., 2006; Stice, Shaw et al., 2008). These results have been replicated in Hispanic, and Asian American samples, with no significant differences in outcomes when compared to a sample of White participants who had undergone the same intervention (Rodriguez et al., 2008). Dissonance prevention programs have also been found to reduce eating disorder symptoms and risk factors in dissemination research in college students (Becker, Bull et al., 2008; Becker et al., 2006; Perez et al., 2010), and high school students (Stice et al., 2009; Stice, Rohde et al. 2011).

### 4.2 Mirror exposure

Body dissatisfaction is commonly associated with eating disorders and has consistently been identified as a major risk factor for the development, maintenance, and relapse of eating disorders (Cash & Deagle, 1997; Fairburn, Peveler et al., 1993; Fairburn, Stice et al., 1993; Freeman et al., 1985; Killen et al., 1996; Post & Crowther, 1987; Ricciardelli et al., 1997; Stice,

2002). Therefore, prevention programs that focus on improving body image are important for reducing eating disorder symptoms. Mirror exposure exercises, a form of body exposure, are a central component to prevention programs targeting body dissatisfaction. For mirror exposure exercises, individuals are instructed to stand in front of a mirror while systematically looking at each part of their body for an extended period of time. Many mirror exposure techniques involve include verbal interaction including challenging and feedback from a therapist (Delinsky & Wilson, 2006; Key et al., 2002; Vocks et al., 2007).

While the procedure for mirror exposure is relatively uniform, there are different ways of completing a mirror exposure exercise; each with slightly different instructions for participants. Vocks and colleagues (2007) conducted mirror exposure exercises in two separate sessions lasting for 40 minutes in which participants were instructed on what body parts to look at. In contrast, Delinsky and Wilson (2006) asked participants to describe themselves from head to toe systematically rather than instructing them on which body part to look at. Participants were asked to refrain from dwelling on or skipping any body parts and using critical language. During the second session, participants were asked to select clothing to wear that would cause them to face their fears about their appearance while challenging them to be nonjudgmental towards themselves. Behavioral homework assignments designed to eliminate body monitoring and avoidance were also given between sessions. Other researchers have followed similar protocols with alterations in the length of each exposure session (Key et al., 2002).

Mirror exposure has also been included as a component within some dissonance based eating disorder prevention programs (Becker et al 2005; Perez et al., 2010; Stice et al., 2000). Mirror exposure was given as a homework assignment between sessions to increase the amount of time spent on the prevention program as well as to encourage discussion about the activity during the subsequent session. For the assignment, participants were instructed to stand in front of a full length mirror in as little clothing as they were comfortable wearing and no cosmetic products. While viewing themselves in the mirror, they were instructed to list all positive physical and non-physical attributes they like about themselves. During the second session of the program, a discussion was held where participants shared non-physical attributes they liked about themselves that they had identified during the exposure task.

Mirror exposure has also been used in conjunction with other forms of therapy for eating disorder treatment. For example, mirror exposure has been incorporated in cognitive-behavioral therapy for body dissatisfaction (Cash, 1997). Wilson (1999, 2004), has incorporated mindfulness training, a component of dialectical behavior therapy (Linehan, 1993), into cognitive-behavioral therapy that uses mirror exposure. Studies have supported the effectiveness of the use of mirror exposure in conjunction with cognitive-behavioral therapy (Butters & Cash, 1987; Cash & Lavallee, 1997; Grant & Cash 1995).

It has been suggested that the tendency of individuals with eating disorders to overestimate the size of their body (Cash & Deagle, 1997; Skrzypek et al., 2001) may be one of the underlying mechanism responsible for the effectiveness of mirror exposure techniques (Vocks et al., 2007). This is because individuals receive feedback about their true body size throughout the exposure technique, resulting in body acceptance and decreased fear of weight gain. In fact, several studies have shown that overestimation of body size can be reduced through mirror exposure techniques (Fernandez & Vandereycken, 1994; Norris, 1984; Rushford & Ostermeyer, 1997). A second hypothesized explanation for the effectiveness of mirror exposure is that this technique addresses negative feelings or affect the individual has about their body (Cash, 2004; Thompson et al., 1999). Individuals with eating disorders have been found to show greater increases in negative emotions towards their bodies than healthy controls when experiencing exposure to their bodies (Tuschen-Caffier et al., 2003). Therefore, it is suggested that with repeated exposure to one's body, negative emotions towards the body will be reduced through the habituation process. Research on the effect of mirror exposure in reducing negative emotions has supported this theory by indicating that negative affect or emotions towards the body was reduced through repeated mirror exposure exercises in individuals with eating disorders (Hilbert et al., 2002; Vocks et al., 2007). A final potential explanation for the effectiveness of mirror exposure techniques is that this exercise addresses negative body-related cognitions and assumptions associated with eating disorders, such as "I have to lose weight because I am too fat" (Cash & Deagle, 1997; Vocks et al., 2007). Studies have shown that individuals with eating disorders tend to have more negative cognitions about weight and shape when looking at themselves in full-length mirrors than healthy controls (Cooper & Fairburn, 1992; Hilbert & Tuschen-Caffier, 2005). This idea that mirror exposure leads to reductions in negative body-related cognitions has been supported in a study by Hilbert et al. (2002), who found that when body exposure was repeated on two separate days with patients with an eating disorder, negative cognitions were less frequent in the second session than in the first. However, cognitions were only measured one time during the entire exposure exercise in this study. Another study on the effectiveness of mirror exposure exercises in reducing negative cognitions conducted by Vocks et al. (2007), found that mirror exposure for 40 minutes did not reduce negative cognitions related to the body. The conflicting results from these studies suggests that further investigation is needed in order to determine if mirror exposure is effective in reducing negative cognitions about weight and shape associated with eating disorders.

Mirror exposure alone has been shown to be an effective way to reduce body image disturbances (Delinsky & Wilson, 2006). An examination of the effects of mirror exposure in a sample of undergraduate women indicated that mirror exposure produced a decrease in body image avoidance, weight and shape concerns, dieting and depression, and an increase in body satisfaction, with these improvements being maintained at a 1-month follow-up assessment (Delinksy & Wilson, 2006). Mirror exposure has also been found to enhance outcomes of obesity (Jansen et al., 2008) and eating disorder treatment (Key et al., 2002). Research on the effects of mirror exposure when used as a component in a dissonance based prevention program via a dismantling study indicated that mirror exposure moderates the effects of the prevention program (Ramirez et al., 2011). Additionally, participants who completed the mirror exposure assignment as part of the dissonance intervention showed higher body acceptance and body likability than participants who did not complete the assignment with these effects being sustained at a 1-year follow-up assessment. This evidence suggests that while mirror exposure alone can be an effective way to reduce body image disturbances and eating disorder symptoms, it may be more effective when used in conjunction with other techniques in a prevention program.

### 4.3 Healthy weight

In healthy weight eating disorder prevention programs, individuals are guided in creating permanent healthy lasting lifestyle changes, including lower fat intake and regular moderate exercise in order to achieve a healthy body weight and increase body satisfaction

(Matusek et al., 2004; Stice et al., 2001; Stice et al., 2003). Specifically, participants are educated about the importance of healthy eating practices and regular exercise. Differences between complete and incomplete nutrition, effective and ineffective dieting, and moderate and extreme forms of exercise, as well as dangers associated with poor eating behaviors are also highlighted. Participants are also given more detailed instructions on how to develop and maintain a healthy diet. Discussions on healthy lifestyle changes and relapse prevention are guided by facilitators at the end of this intervention.

The original healthy weight intervention, developed by Stice et al. (2001), was designed to incorporate three one-hour group sessions. In the first session, participants were informed that the purpose of the intervention was to help them create a healthy lifestyle that would incorporate a balanced diet and regular exercise which would result in weight control and body satisfaction. Participants then discussed their individual diet and exercise goals within the group. Goals were then reframed into a healthy weight management plan, including nutritional information in order to make dietary changes to achieve dieting goals. A homework assignment of developing an exercise plan to share during the next session was given at the conclusion of the first session. The second session began with a review of the previous session and a discussion of physical exercise and the development of regular exercise routines, including a review of each participant's plan developed for the homework assignment. The group then discussed possible problems with the plans, reasons for other programs failing, and ways to incorporate behavior modification techniques to maintain goals. Participants were asked to keep a food diary and set specific diet goals for the homework assignment that would be discussed at the next session. The third and final session began with a review of the second session, followed by participant reviews of problem areas identified while keeping the food diary. Problem areas with individual diet goals were also discussed. Factors that led to the failure of previous diet programs were discussed in order for participants to avoid these factors, as well as the inclusion of behavior modification techniques to maintain diet goals. The session was concluded with the presentation of additional nutritional information relevant to individual diet plans. This program has also been conducted using a single session format (Matusek et al., 2004), and a 4-session format (Stice et al., 2009), and has been disseminated by endogenous providers and professional facilitators.

This prevention strategy is more psychoeducational than interactive, as is mostly comprised of facilitators providing information and having group discussions on healthy lifestyle practices and includes less interactive group activities commonly used in other prevention programs. The healthy weight program was originally designed as a placebo control condition in a randomized trial examining the effectiveness of a dissonance based eating disorder prevention program and was not expected to produce significant reductions in eating disorder symptoms, partly due to the didactic format of the program (Stice et al., 2001). Since the program was designed only as a control condition, researchers were surprised to find that participants in the healthy weight program showed decreases in body dissatisfaction, dieting behaviors, negative affect, and bulimic symptoms. These results were similar to participants in the dissonance program, although effect sizes were smaller for the healthy weight group.

An 8-session version of this strategy facilitated by master's level graduate students has been evaluated as a treatment for individuals with clinical and subclinical bulimia nervosa (Burton & Stice, 2006). Results indicate that compared to a control group, individuals who participated in the treatment program showed significant decreases in bulimic symptoms and experienced some weight loss. Importantly, these results were observed at a 3-month follow-up assessment. This evidence suggests that healthy weight programs may also be used as a cost effective treatment for bulimia nervosa, as well as a form of prevention of eating disorders.

Studies have shown that this strategy decreases body dissatisfaction, dieting, negative effect, and eating disorder symptoms that are larger than reductions seen in wait list control groups (Matusek et al., 2004; Stice et al., 2001; Stice et al., 2003). These reductions have been found to persist through 1-year follow-up assessments (Stice, Shaw, Burton et al., 2006). Additionally, this program was found to reduce the onset of eating disorders and obesity at a 3-year follow-up (Stice, Marti et al., 2008). Research has also found that when reduced to a single session workshop rather than the multiple session approach previously used, the intervention still produced decreases in thin-ideal internalization, body dissatisfaction and disordered eating symptoms at a follow-up assessment (Matusek et al., 2004; Stice et al., 2001). While these effects are promising, they often have smaller effect sizes than other prevention programs, such as dissonance based programs. This supports research indicating that programs that are mostly psychoeducational in nature are less effective than interactive programs.

### 4.4 Motivational interviewing

Motivational interviewing, developed by Miller and Rollnick (2002), is a client-centered method used to enhance intrinsic motivation to change. This approach was created to enhance motivation for recovery in populations of individuals who are ambivalent about change, such as individuals with eating disorders. The primary goal of motivational interviewing is to encourage individuals to increase their readiness to change in an attempt to ensure that skill building will occur when the individual is most receptive to change. It is important for facilitators to be nonjudgmental, warm, and empathic, while showing genuine interest in the individuals' experience of the problem (Geller & Dunn, 2011).

Motivational interviewing has been used as a component in dissonance based eating disorder prevention programs (Stece, Shaw et al., 2008) and healthy weight eating disorder prevention programs (Stice, Presnell et al., 2011) to enhance motivation for behavioral change and maximize one's incentive to use the new skills learned during the intervention. For example, reviewing costs of body image concerns has been used as a motivational group activity within a dissonance based prevention program (Stice, Shaw et al., 2008), and motivational exercises of having participants identify benefits of striving for a healthy lifestyle and discuss positive benefits from the intervention were used in an obesity prevention program (Stice, Marti et al., 2008). Motivational interviewing has also been used in the treatment of eating disorders as an aid to clinicians in enhancing readiness for change and adapting interventions to a patient's current status of readiness to change (Stice, Shaw et al., 2008).

While a few program facilitators have incorporated motivational interviewing within some forms of prevention programs, the technique is not frequently used as a component within prevention programs. Also, no dismantaling studies have been conducted with prevention programs that incorporate motivational interviewing within them in order to determine what additional benefits motivational interviewing may provide. Therefore, little research on the effectiveness of motivational interviewing in preventing eating disorder symptoms exists. Most of the effectiveness research on the use of motivational interviewing and eating disorders has been with treatment rather than prevention, with preliminary evidence being promising (Cassin et al., 2008; Dunn et al., 2006; Feld et al., 2001; Treasure et al., 1999). It is possible that motivational interviewing could potentially be used for the prevention of disordered eating by motivating individuals to be willing to change certain risk factors they may be experiencing, such as thin-ideal internalization and body image dissatisfaction. However, like mirror exposure, motivational interviewing may produce the greatest reductions in eating disorder symptoms and associated risk factors when used in combination with other interventions such as dissonance based programs.

### 4.5 Computer-administered cognitive-behavioral

This strategy is a computer-administered prevention program that is modeled after self-help eating disorder treatment programs and based on cognitive-behavioral body dissatisfaction interventions (Butters & Cash, 1987). The program is designed to reduce body dissatisfaction and reduce weight and shape concerns in order to subsequently reduce eating disorder symptoms (Winzelberg et al., 1998). The program includes psychoeducational formats that provide information on eating disorders, healthy weight control behaviors, and nutrition, as well as interactive formats using an unstructured email support interchange that allows participants to express their emotional reactions to the program and interact anonymously with other participants.

The program is conducted as a structured 8-week intervention conducted via the internet. The program utilized interactive software that had text, audio, and video components. The program commences with a description of the development and consequences of eating disorders. Each week a primary focus was placed on improving overall body image, including discussions about cultural ideals of beauty, the role the media plays in cultural standards of beauty, and cognitive-behavioral strategies for improving body satisfaction. Participants were given mandatory and optional assignments to complete each week, such as on-line self monitoring journals and behavior change exercises. Participants were required to post a message to the discussion group each week regarding the psychoeducational material that was the focus of that week in addition to answering or commenting on at least one other message. Group discussions were designed to allow participants to receive and provide emotional support and discuss reactions to the program content. Participants who missed assignments or discussions were contacted via email and encouraged to complete the assignments.

Computer-administered eating disorder prevention programs are more cost effective than other forms of prevention programs (Winzelberg et al., 2000). They are also standardized and are more easily delivered than in-person programs, making them more easily disseminated. Computer-administered programs are also more flexible, allowing participants to use them at their own convenience without scheduling conflicts, and can be used frequently and for shorter time periods. Further, the interactive software utilized in current computer-administered prevention programs allows for a more personal experience and can be more easily tailored to meet individual needs. Evidence suggests that programs conducted without a therapist, such as computer-administered programs, based on cognitive-behavioral principles are effective in reducing symptoms in subclinical populations (Fairburn & Carter, 1997). While this program may be cheaper and easier to implement than other programs, the rate of attrition for this particular program may be higher than other programs (Winzelberg et al., 1998).

This strategy has successfully reduced eating disorder risk factors such as body dissatisfaction (Low et al., 2006). These results have been replicated in multiple trials conducted by the same lab group. When compared to control groups, participants showed significantly lower bulimic pathology and lower body dissatisfaction at an 8-month follow-up assessment. This program has also been found to significantly reduce eating disorder risk factors including weight and shape concerns, and the onset of eating disorders in participants with higher body mass indexes in at-risk college women (Taylor et al., 2006). While this program has produced reductions in body dissatisfaction and eating disorder symptoms, the effects are less than other prevention programs that are more interactive such as the dissonance based prevention programs.

### 4.6 Other prevention strategies

There are a few additional prevention strategies that have been developed, but with minimal empirical support. For example, Neumark-Sztainer and colleagues (1995) developed and evaluated a psychoeducational program that includes social-cognitive principles for behavior change that had minimal outcome effects. This program is a 10-session school based program facilitated by a health educator aimed at changing attitudes and behaviors about nutrition, weight control, improving body image and self image, and promoting greater control over social pressures regarding dieting and excessive eating. Significant reductions in weight control behaviors, dieting, and binge eating were observed at a 6-month follow-up, but these reductions were not sustained at the 2-year follow up. Also, no significant reductions in body dissatisfaction or negative affect were observed at any assessments.

A couple of other psychoeducational prevention programs have produced similar results. Stice, Orjada, and Tristan (2006), evaluated a 15-week psychoeducational college course on eating disorders and found that when compared to a control group, participants showed significantly greater reductions in thin-ideal internalization, body dissatisfaction, dieting and eating disorder symptoms at post-intervention and 6-month follow-up assessments. While these results are promising for a psychoeducational intervention, they have not been replicated by other researchers to provide additional support. Additionally, Stewart and colleagues (2001) evaluated a different psychoeducational program that addresses body dissatisfaction, societal pressures to be thin, changes associated with puberty, development of eating disorders, self-esteem, and dieting. This program produced small reductions in dietary restraint and attitudes about shape and weight at a post-intervention assessment, but these reductions were not maintained at the 6-month follow-up assessment.

Finally, McVey and Davis (2002) developed an interactive program conducted using peer-support groups. This 10-session program focuses on promoting critical media use, body acceptance, healthy weight control behaviors, and stress management skills. Evaluations of this program have indicated that this intervention produced increases in weight related esteem and decreases in dieting in middle school girls when compared to a control group at post-intervention and 3-month follow-up assessments. However, a subsequent evaluation of this program was unable to replicate these positive results (McVey et al., 2003).

## 5. Using prevention programs in social organizations to create systematic changes

Women routinely report feeling pressure to attain a thin-ideal body type from peers, family, and society (Perez et al., 2010). The use of social organizations to prevent eating disorders has been relatively unexplored but is an important avenue of future research. By implementing eating disorder prevention programs within social organizations, researchers and practitioners alike can create systemic changes in the organization's environment in addition to changes within individuals across time. For example, prevention programs can target the organization's views of the thin-ideal and change practices that enhance or maintain the thin-ideal, thereby reducing the peer pressure and environmental pressure women report. In addition, prevention programs that successfully reduce eating disorder risk factors in current members of the organization may also reduce risk factors for new incoming members of the organization. Social organizations can also assist in wide-spread dissemination of prevention programs.

College fraternities are an example of a social organization that can be conducive to the dissemination of eating disorder prevention programs. Previous research examining the implementation of dissonance based eating disorder prevention programs within college sororities has indicated that dissonance based programs can be effective in reducing eating disorder symptoms and associated risk factors within this particular form of social organization (Becker et al., 2005, 2006; Becker, Bull et al., 2008; Perez et al., 2010). In addition, research has found that naturalistic dissemination of a dissonance based eating disorder prevention program within a sorority can be effective at reducing eating disorder symptoms and associated risk factors (Perez et al., 2010). However, this research has yet to examine if the intervention was successful in creating systematic changes throughout the organization by creating an overall reduction in eating disorder symptoms in the members. Therefore, a dissonance based eating disorder prevention program implemented in a sorority at a large public university was examined to assess if the intervention was successful in creating systematic reductions in eating disorder symptoms throughout the organization.

To examine group-level change in eating disorder symptoms instead of individual change, a sorority at a large public university participated in a dissonance based eating disorder prevention program. During the first year, all current members of the sorority participated in the prevention program. During the second and third year, all incoming new sorority members participated in the eating disorder prevention program during their first semester as members of the sorority. All participants completed self-report questionnaires prior to the intervention (baseline), immediately after the intervention (post-intervention), 5 months later, and at 1 year follow-up. Because members participated in the program at different times based on the year they entered the sorority, longitudinal data was compared to examine the similarities between classes at certain time points. Specifically, the 5-month follow-up assessment for the Year 1members was conducted at the same time as the baseline assessment for Year 2 new members, and the 1-year follow-up assessment for Year 1 members overlapped with 5 month follow up for Year 2 and the baseline assessment for Year 3 new members.

The total sample included 212 participants: 125 members already enrolled in the sorority at the time the program was initiated, 49 new members recruited during the second year the program was ran, and 38 new recruits from the third year. Ages ranged from 18 to 22 (19.16 ± 1.16), with body mass indexes ranging from 16.18 to 26.66 (21.15 ± 1.98). Most participants identified as Caucasian (94.8%), followed by Hispanic (2.4%), Asian (.5%), Native American (.5%), and of mixed ethnicities (1.9%). Participants completed baseline, post-intervention, 5-month, and 1-year follow-up assessments throughout the course of the program. Eating disorder symptoms were assessed using the Eating Disorder Examination-Questionnaire (EDE-Q; Fairburn & Beglin, 1994). The EDE-Q is designed to measure individual's eating attitudes and behaviors over one-month and can be used to make tentative diagnoses of clinical eating disorders. Higher global scores indicate higher levels of overall eating disorder symptoms. Research on the EDE-Q has demonstrated good internal consistency for global scores, $a$ =.78 to .93, and test-retest reliability, $r$ = .81 to .94 (Luce & Crowther, 1999; Mond et al., 2004). Alphas for the current study were .94, .95, .93, and .95 for baseline, post-intervention, 5-month follow-up, and 1-year follow-up respectively.

All participants completed baseline assessment before beginning a dissonance based eating disorder prevention program that focuses on creating cognitive dissonance about both thin-ideal internalization and self-objectification. The program was led by peer facilitators that had been extensively trained by a doctoral level psychologist on the protocol for the prevention program. The intervention consisted of 2-hour group sessions in group format, with groups containing approximately 20 members. The first session began by defining the thin-ideal body image for women proposed by society, including discussions of the costs and origins of the thin-ideal, sources of pressures placed on women to obtain the thin-ideal, and the impact this has on women. The session concluded with a discussion of personal situations where members felt pressured to conform to the thin-ideal and ways to respond to these pressures appropriately. Participants were given a homework exercise of completing the mirror exposure task outlined in section 3.2. The homework assignment was then discussed at the beginning of the second session, by having participants share two non-physical qualities they like about themselves that they had identified during the mirror exposure exercise. This then became a discussion on the importance of focusing on non-physical qualities rather than physical appearance. Role plays where members attempted to prevent friends from pursuing the thin-ideal were conducted and discussions about ways women perpetuate the thin-ideal and ways women can resist pressures to conform to these standards were also included in the second session. TThe same assessments that participants completed at baseline were completed immediately following the intervention, as well as at 5-month and 1-year follow-up assessments.

The dissonance-based eating disorder prevention program was effective at reducing eating disorder symptoms and associated risk factors for new members from each year through 1-year follow-up. The details of these results are reported elsewhere (Perez et al., 2010). The figure below depicts the mean global EDE-Q scores for each year at each assessment time point. At Time 3, 5 and 7, where the members of each year overlap in assessment, there were no significant differences between the years. It is interesting to note that Year 1 recruited incoming new members (i.e., Year 2) that were similar to them in global eating disorder symptoms. At Time 5, Year 1 and Year 2 had virtually identical global EDE-Q scores, and recruited new members (i.e., Year 3) that were similar to them. At Time 7, Year 2 and Year 3 had very similar global EDE-Q scores. Thus, a pattern emerged where the eating disorder symptoms

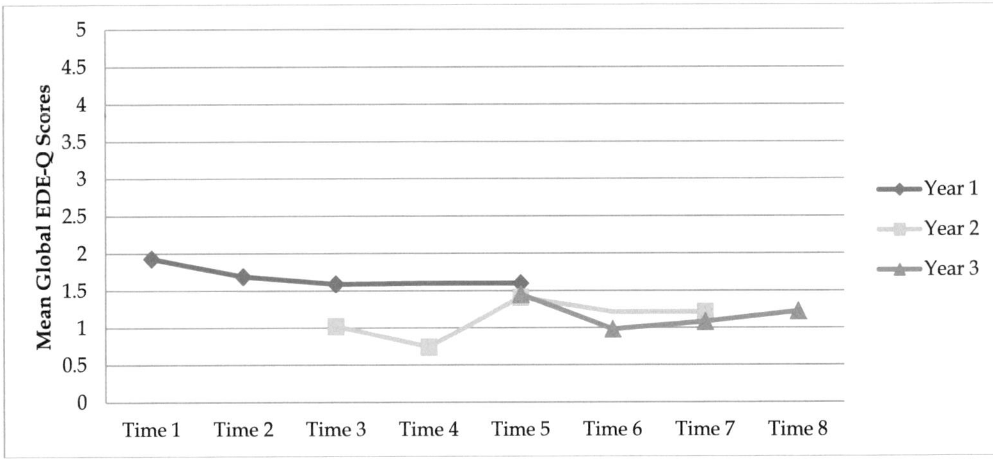


Fig. 1. Global EDE-Q scores for each year across time. *Note:* Time 1 - Baseline assessment for Year 1; Time 2 - Post intervention assessment for Year 1; Time 3 – 5 month follow up Year 1 and Baseline assessment for Year 2; Time 4 – Post intervention assessment for Year 2; Time 5 – 12 month follow up for Year 1, 5 month follow up for Year 2, and Baseline assessment Year 3; Time 6 – Post intervention assessment for Year 3; Time 7 – 12 month follow up for Year 2 and 5 month follow up for Year 3; Time 8 – 12 month follow up for Year 3.

of the incoming new members were similar to the eating disorder symptoms of the social organization as a whole. In addition, there seems to be a migratory convergence of eating disorder symptoms over time.

This preliminary evidence suggests that implementing eating disorder prevention programs within large social organizations such as sororities can be beneficial in creating long-term systematic changes throughout the organization. Eating disorder prevention programs that can be adapted to school settings, athletic organizations, dance teams, and other social structures may have an advantage of creating systemic change in addition to individual change. While this information is promising, this evidence is preliminary and requires replication. Further research is needed to increase the effectiveness of creating systematic reduction in eating disorder symptoms in large social organizations and sustaining these changes for longer time periods.

## 6. Conclusion

The field of eating disorder prevention has produced a number of encouraging advancements. Specifically, research on eating disorder prevention has produced several prevention programs that have successfully reduced current eating disorder symptoms and risk factors as well as the risk for future onset of eating disorder symptoms. These effects have also been replicated in multiple trials conducted by the same lab for some programs, and some program results have been replicated by independent labs. Certain programs have also been shown to be effective when delivered by endogenous providers in a variety of conditions. Additionally, several programs have been found to significantly outperform alternative interventions. For example, dissonance based programs that decrease attitudinal risk factors and healthy weight control programs were more effective than others. Also, preliminary evidence suggests that prevention programs may also help create systematic changes throughout large social organizations, further increasing the benefits of prevention programs.

While many current programs are producing promising effects, effect sizes for these results could be larger and more persistent (Shaw et al., 2009; Stice, Shaw et al. 2007). Further research needs to be conducted to determine what components of programs need to be adapted to increase the effectiveness of programs, as well as to sustain improvements made during the program for longer periods of time. Also, many examinations of the effects of prevention programs have not included a control group, which prevents researchers from determining if the effects are a direct result of the intervention or if they are actually due to regression to the mean or the passage of time. Researchers continuing to evaluate current prevention programs should address these limitations in order to refine these programs and increase the program effectiveness.

Overall, empirical evidence supports the effectiveness of several eating disorder prevention programs, with most programs decreasing current and future eating disorder symptoms and associated risk factors. More importantly, some of these effects have been sustained for extended periods of time. Some of these programs have also been successfully disseminated and are effective when facilitated by endogenous providers. As more research is conducted on eating disorder prevention programs, limitations of current programs can be reduced and program effectiveness can be further increased. Continued research on the prevention of eating disorders and efforts directed towards increasing effectiveness of prevention programs will assist in reducing the overall prevalence of eating disorders.

It is also important to examine prevention programs within diverse populations. Future research should examine the generalizability of these programs to individuals of other ethnicities, genders, and sexual orientations in order to determine if programs are effective within these populations. Although females are more likely than males to experience eating disorder symptoms and associated risk factors like thin-ideal internalization and self-objectification, men are still affected by body dissatisfaction and eating disorder symptoms and should therefore be included within studies evaluating the effectiveness of prevention programs (Hudson et al., 2007). Only one eating disorder prevention program in the last 20 years has included males (Yager & O'Dea, 2008), and this program was purely psychoeducational, and did not produce any significant reductions in eating disorder symptoms or risk factors (Rabak-Wagener et al., 1998). Therefore, more efforts need to be directed at examining the effectiveness of prevention programs in males, as well as other more diverse populations.

Finally, although extensive progress in prevention research on individual change has been made in the past decade, further research is needed on eating disorder prevention programs that can create systemic changes in social organizations. The ability to intervene at a systemic level allows for dissemination of prevention programs to greater numbers of individuals, and creates a healthier environment.

## 7. References

Agras, W. S., Walsh, T., Fairburn, C. G., Wilson, G. T., & Kraemer, H. C. (2000). A multicenter comparison of cognitive-behavioral therapy and interpersonal psychotherapy for bulimia nervosa. *Archives of General Psychiatry*, Vol.57, No.5, (May 2000), pp. 459-466, ISSN 0003-990X.

Axsom, D., & Cooper, J. (1985). Cognitive dissonance and psychotherapy: The role of effort justification in inducing weight loss. *Journal of Experimental and Social Psychology,* Vol.21, No.2 (March, 1985), pp. 149-160, ISSN 0022-1031.

Barnett, L. A., Far, J. M., Mauss, A. L., & Miller, J. A. (1996). Changing perceptions of peer norms as a drinking reduction program for college students. *Journal of Alcohol and Drug Education,* Vol.41, No.2, pp. 39-62, ISSN 0090-1482.

Beauvois, J. L., & Joule, R. V. (1999). A radical point of view on dissonance theory. In: *Cognitive dissonance: Progress on a pivotal theory in social psychology.* Harmon-Jones, E., & Mills. (Eds.), pp. 43-70, American Psychological Association, ISBN 1557985650, Washington, DC, US.

Becker, A. E., Grinspoon, S. K., Klibanski, A., & Herzog, D. B. (1999). Current concepts: Eating disorders. *The New England Journal of Medicine,* Vol.340, No.14, (April 1999), pp. 1092-1098, ISSN 0028-4793.

Becker, C. B., Bull, S., Chaumberg, K., Cauble, A., & Franco, A. (2008). Effectiveness of peer-led eating disorder prevention: A replication trial. *Journal of Consulting and Clinical Psychology,* Vol.76, No.2, (April 2008), pp. 347-354, ISSN 0022-006X.

Becker, C. B., Ciao, A. C., & Smith, L. M. (2008). Moving from efficacy to effectiveness in eating disorders prevention: The sorority body image program. *Cognitive and Behavioral Practice,* Vol.15, No.1, (February 2008), pp. 18-27, ISSN 1077-7229.

Becker, C. B., Smith, L., & Ciao, A. C. (2005). Reducing eating disorder risk factors in sorority members: A randomized trial. *Behavior Therapy,* Vol.36, No.3, pp. 245-253, ISSN 0005-7894.

Becker, C. B., Smith, L. M., & Ciao, A. C. (2006). Peer-facilitated eating disorder prevention: A randomized effectiveness trial of cognitive dissonance and media advocacy. *Journal of Counseling Psychology,* Vol.53, No.4, (October 2006), pp. 550-555, ISSN 0022-0167.

Birmingham, C., Su, J., Hlynsky, J., Goldner, E., & Gao, M. (2005). The mortality rate from anorexia nervosa. *International Journal of Eating Disorders,* Vol.38, No.2, (September 2005), pp. 143-146, ISSN 0276-3478.

Brehm, J. W., & Cohen, A. R. (1962). *Explorations in cognitive dissonance.* Wiley, New York, NY, US.

Burton, E., & Stice, E. (2006). Evaluation of a healthy-weight treatment program for bulimia nervosa: A preliminary randomized trial. *Behaviour Research and Therapy,* Vol.44, No.12, (December 2006). pp. 1727-1738, ISSN 0005-7967.

Butters, J. W., & Cash, T. F. (1987). Cognitive behavioral treatment of women's body-image dissatisfaction. *Journal of Consulting and Clinical Psychology,* Vol.55, No.6, (December 1987), pp. 889-897, ISSN 0022-006X.

Carlat, D. J., & Camargo, C. A. (1991). Review of bulimia nervosa in males. *American Journal of Psychiatry,* Vol.148, (July 1991), pp. 831-843, ISSN 0002-953X.

Carlat, D. J., Camargo, C. A., & Herzog, D. B. (1997). Eating disorders in males: A report on 135 patients. *American Journal of Psychiatry,* Vol.154, No.8, (August 1997), pp. 1127-1132, ISSN 0002-953X.

Cash, T. F. (1997). *The body image workbook: An 8-step program for learning to like your looks.* New Harbinger Publications, Inc, ISBN 1572240628, Oakland, CA, US.

Cash, T. F. (2004). Body image: Past, present, and future. *Body Image,* Vol.1, No.1, (January 2004), pp. 1-5, ISSN 1740-1445.

Cash, T. F., & Deagle, E. A. (1997). The nature and extent of body-image disturbances in anorexia nervosa and bulimia nervosa: A meta-analysis. *International Journal of Eating Disorders,* Vol.22, No.2, (September 1997), pp. 107-125, ISSN 0276-3478.

Cash, T. F., & Lavallee, D. M. (1997). Cognitive-behavioral body-image therapy: Further evidence of the efficacy of a self-directed program. *Journal of Rational-Emotive and Cognitive Behavior Therapy,* Vol.15, No.4, pp. 281-294, ISSN 0894-9085.

Cassin, S. E., von Ranson, K. M., Heng, K., Brar, J., & Wojtowicz, A. E. (2008). Adapted motivational interviewing for women with binge eating disorder: A randomized controlled trial. *Psychology of Addictive Behaviors,* Vol.22, No.3, (September 2008), pp. 417-425, ISSN 0893-164X.

Cooper, J. (1980). Reducing fears and increasing assertiveness: The role of dissonance reduction. *Journal of Experimental Social Psychology,* Vol.16, No.3, (May 1980), pp. 199-213, ISSN 0022-1031.

Cooper, M., & Fairburn, C. F. (1992). Thoughts about eating, weight and shape in anorexia nervosa and bulimia nervosa. *Behaviour Research and Therapy,* Vol.30, No.5, (September 1992), pp. 501-511, ISSN 0005-7967.

Delinksy, S. S., & Wilson, G. T. (2006). Mirror exposure for the treatment of body image disturbance. *International Journal of Eating Disorders,* Vol.13, No.2, (March 2006), pp. 108-116, ISSN 0276-3478.

Drummond, M. (2002). Men, body image and eating disorders. *International Journal of Men's Health,* Vol.1, No.1, (January 2002), pp. 89-103, ISSN 1532-6306.

Dunn, E. C., Neighbors, C., & Larimer, M. E. (2006). Motivational enhancement therapy and self-help treatment for binge eaters. *Psychology of Addictive Behaviors,* Vol.20, No.1, (March 2006), pp. 44-52, ISSN 0893-164X.

Fairburn, C. G. (2002). Cognitive-behavioral therapy for bulimia nervosa. In: *Eating disorders and obesity: A comprehensive handbook (2nd ed.),* Fairburn, C. G., & Brownell, K. D. (Eds.), pp. 302-308, US: Guilford Press, ISBN 1572306882, New York, NY, US.

Fairburn, C. G., & Beglin, S. J. (1994). Assessment of eating disorders: Interview or self-report questionnaire ? *International Journal of Eating Disorders,* Vol.16, No.4, (December 1994), pp. 363-370, ISSN 0276-3478.

Fairburn, C. G., & Carter, J. C. (1997). Self-help and guided self-help for binge eating problems. In: *Handbook of treatment for eating disorders.* Garner, D. M., & Garfinkel, P. E. (Eds.), pp. 494-499, Guilford Press, ISBN 1572301864, New York, NY, US.

Fairburn, C. G., Cooper, Z., Doll, H. A., O'Conner, M. E., Bohn, K., Hawker, D. M., Wales, J. A., & Palmer, R. L. (2009). Transdiagnostic cognitive-behavioral therapy for patients with eating disorders: A two-site trial with 60-week follow-up. *The American Journal of Psychiatry,* Vol.166, No.3, (March 2009), pp. 311-319, ISSN 0002-953X.

Fairburn, C. G., Peveler, R. C., Jones, R., Hope, R. A., & Doll, H. A. (1993). Predictors of 12-month outcome in bulimia nervosa and the influence of attitudes to shape and weight. *Journal of Consulting and Clinical Psychology,* Vol.61, No.4, (August 1993), pp. 696-698, ISSN 022-006X.

Fairburn, C. G., Stice, E., Cooper, Z., Doll, H. A., Norman, P. A., & O'Conner, M. E. (2003). Understanding persistence in bulimia nervosa: A 5-year naturalistic study. *Journal of Consulting and Clinical Psychology,* Vol.71, No.1, (February 2003), pp. 103-109, ISSN 0022-006X.

Feingold, A., & Mazzella, R. (1998). Gender differences in body image are increasing. *Psychological Science,* Vol.9, No.3, (May 1998), pp. 190-195, ISSN 0956-7976.

Feld, R., Woodside, D. B., Kaplan, A. S., Olmstead, M. P., & Carter, J. C. (2001). Pretreatment motivational enhancement therapy for eating disorders: A pilot study. *International Journal of Eating Disorders*, Vol.29, No.4, (May 2001), pp. 393-400, ISSN 0276-3478.

Festinger, L. (1957). *A theory of cognitive dissonance*, Stanford University Press, ISBN 0804701318, Palo AHo, California.

Fernandez, F., & Vandereycken, W. (1994). Influence of video confrontation on the self-evaluation of anorexia nervosa patients: A controlled study. *Eating Disorders: The Journal of Treatment and Prevention*, Vol.2, No.2, pp. 135-140, ISSN 1064-0266.

Franko, D. L., & Keel, P. K. (2006). Suicidality in eating disorders: Occurrence, correlates, and clinical implications. *Clinical Psychology Review*, Vol.26, No.6, (October 2006), pp. 769-782, ISSN 0272-7358.

Freeman, R. J., Beach, B., Davis, R., & Soylom, L. (1985). The prediction of relpase in bulimia nervosa. *Journal of Psychiatric Research*, Vol.19, No.2-3, pp. 349-353, ISSN 0022-3956.

Geller, J., & Dunn, E. C. (2011). Integrating motivational interviewing and cognitive behavioral therapy in the treatment of eating disorders: Tailoring interventions to patient readiness for change. *Cognitive and Behavioral Practice*, Vol.18, No.1, (February 2011), pp. 5-15, ISSN 1077-7229.

Gordon, R. (1983). An operational classification of disease prevention. *Public Health Reports*, Vol.98, No.2, (March 1983), pp. 107-109, ISSN 0033-3549.

Grant, J. R., & Cash, T. F. (1995). Cognitive-behavioral body image therapy: Comparative efficacy of group and modest-contrast treatments. *Behavior Therapy*, Vol.26, No.1, pp. 69-84, ISSN 0005-7894.

Hilbert, A., & Tuschen-Caffier, B. (2005). Body-related cognitions in binge-eating disorder and bulimia nervosa. *Journal of Social and Clinical Psychology*, Vol.24, No.4, (June 2005), pp. 561-579. ISSN 0736-7236.

Hilbert, A., Tuschen-Caffier, B., & Vögele, C. (2002). Effects of prolonged and repeated body image exposure in binge-eating disorder. *Journal of Psychosomatic Research*, Vol.52, No.3, (March 2002), pp. 137-144, ISSN 0022-3999.

Hoffman, J. M., & Brownell, K. D. (1997). Sex differences in the relationship of body fat distribution with psychosocial variables. *International Journal of Eating Disorders*, Vol.22, No.2, (September 1997), pp. 139-145, ISSN 0276-3478.

Horowitz, J. L., & Garber, J. (2006). The prevention of depressive symptoms in children and adolescents: A meta-analytic review. *Journal of Consulting and Clinical Psychology*, Vol.74, No.3, (June 2006), pp. 401-415, ISSN 0022-006X.

Hudson, J. I., Hiripi, E., Pope, H. G., & Kessler, R. C. (2007). The prevalence and correlates of eating disorders in the national comorbidity survey replication. *Biological Psychiatry*, Vol.61, No.3, (February 2007), pp. 348-358, ISSN 0006-3223.

Jansen, A., Bollen, D., Tuschen-Caffier, B., Roefs, A., Tanghe, A., & Braet, C. (2008). Mirror exposure reduces body dissatisfaction and anxiety in obese adolescents: A pilot study. *Appetite*, Vol.51, No.1, (July 2008), pp. 214-217, ISSN 0195-6663.

Johnson, J. G., Cohen, P., Kasen, S., & Brook, J. S. (2002). Eating disorders during adolescence and the risk for physical and mental disorders during early adulthood. *Archives of General Psychiatry*, Vol.59, No.6, (June 2002), pp. 545-552, ISSN 0003-990X.

Kaminski, P. L., & McNamara, K. (1996). A treatment for college women at risk for bulimia: A controlled evaluation. *Journal of Counseling and Development*, Vol.74, No.3, (January 1996), pp. 288-294, ISSN 0748-9633.

Kaye, W. H., Bulik, C., Thornton, L., Barbarich, N., & Masters, K. (2004). Comorbidity of anxiety disorders with anorexia and bulimia nervosa. *Archives of General Psychiatry,* Vol.161, No.12, (December 2004), pp. 2215-2221, ISSN 0002-953X.

Keel, P. K., Dorer, D. J., Eddy, K. T., Franko, D., Charatan, D. L., & Herzog, D. B. (2003). Predictors of mortality in eating disorders. *Archives of General Psychiatry,* Vol.60, No.2, (February 2003), pp. 179-183, ISSN 0003-990X.

Key, A., George, C. L., Beattie, D., Stammers, K., Lacey, H., & Waller, G. (2002). Body image treatment within an inpatient program for anorexia nervosa: The role of mirror exposure in the desensitization process. *International Journal of Eating Disorders,* Vol.31, No.2, (March 2002), pp. 185-190, ISSN 0276-3478.

Killen, J. D. (1985). Prevention of adolescent tobacco smoking: The social pressure resistance training approach. *Journal of Child Psychology, and Psychiatry and Allied Disciplines,* Vol.26, No.1, (January 1985), pp. 7-15, ISSN 0021-9630.

Killen, J. D., Taylor, C. B., Hammer, L., Litt, I., Wilson, D. M., Rich, T., Hayward, C., Simmonds, B., Kraemer, H., & Varady, A. (1993). An attempt to modify unhealthful eating attitudes and weight regulation practices of young adolescent girls. *International Journal of Eating Disorders,* Vol.13, No.4, (May 1993), pp. 369-384, ISSN 0276-3478.

Killen, J. D., Taylor, C. B., Hayward, C., Haydel, K. F., Wilson, D. M., Hammer, H., Kraemer, H., Blair-Greiner, A., & Strachowski, D. (1996). Weight concerns influence the development of eating disorders: A 4-year prospective study. *Journal of Consulting and Clinical Psychology,* Vol.64, No.5, (October 1996), pp. 936-940, ISSN 0022-006X.

Kroon Van Diest, A. M., & Perez, M. (2011). *Integrating thin-ideal internalization and self-objectification within eating disorder prevention for women.* Manuscript submitted for publication.

Lewinsohn, M. P., Striegel-Moore, R. H., & Seeley, J. R. (2000). Epidemiology and natural course of eating disorders in young women from adolescence to young adulthood. *Journal of the American Academy of Child and Adolescent Psychiatry,* Vol.39, No.10, (October 2000), pp. 1284-1292, ISSN 0890-8567.

Linehan, M. M. (1993). *Skills training manual for treating borderline personality disorder.* Guilford Press, ISBN 0898620341, New York, NY, US.

Low, K. G., Charanasomboon, S., Lesser, J., Reinhalter, K., Martin, R., Jones, H., Winzelberg, A., Abascal, L., & Taylor, C. B. (2006). Effectiveness of a computer-based interactive eating disorders prevention program at long-term follow-up. *Eating Disorders: The Journal of Treatment and Prevention,* Vol.14, No.1, (January 2006), pp. 17-30, ISSN 1064-0266.

Lucas, A. R., Beard, C. M., O'Fallon, W. M. & Kurland, L. T. (1991). 50-year trends in the incidence of anorexia nervosa in Rochester, Minn.: A population-based study. *American Journal of Psychiatry,* Vol.148, No.7, (July 1991), pp. 917-922, ISSN 0002-953X.

Luce, K. H., & Crowther, J. H. (1999). The reliability of the Eating Disorder Examination - self-report questionnaire version (EDE-Q). *International Journal of Eating Disorders,* Vol.25, No.3, (April 1999), pp. 349-351, ISSN 0276-3478.

Marchand, E., Stice, E., Rohde, P., Becker, C. B. (2011). Moving from efficacy to effectiveness trials in prevention research. *Behaviour Research and Therapy,* Vol.49, No.1, (January 2011), pp. 32-41, ISSN 0005-7967.

Martz, D., & Bazzini, D. (1999). Eating disorders prevention programming may be failing: Evaluation of two one-shot programs. *Journal of College Student Development,* Vol.40, No.1, (January 1999), pp. 32-42, ISSN 0897-5264.

Matusek, J. A., Wendt, S. J., & Wiseman, C. V. (2004). Dissonance thin-ideal and didactic healthy behavior eating disorder prevention programs: Results from a controlled trial. *International Journal of Eating Disorders,* Vol.36, No.4, (December 2004), pp. 376-388, ISSN 0276-3478.

McVey, G. L., & Davis, R. (2002). A program to promote positive body image: A 1-year follow-up assessment. *The Journal of Early Adolescence,* Vol.22, No.1, (February 2002), pp. 96-108, ISSN 0272-4316.

McVey, G., Lieberman, M., Voorberg, N., Wardrope, D., Blackmore, E., Tweed, S., et al.(2003). Replication of a peer support program designed to prevent disordered eating: Is a life skills approach sufficient for all middle school students ? *Eating Disorders: The Journal of Treatment and Prevention,* Vol.11, No.3, pp. 187-195, ISSN 1064-0266.

Miller, W. R., & Rollnick, S. (2002). *Motivational interviewing: Preparing people for change,* (2nd ed.), Guilford Press, ISBN 1572305630, New York, NY, US.

Mintz, L., & Betz, N. (1988). Prevalence and correlates of eating disordered behaviors among undergraduate women. *Journal of Counseling Psychology,* Vol.35, (October 1988), pp. 463-471, ISSN 0022-0167.

Mitchell, J. E., & Crow, S. (2006). Medical complications of anorexia nervosa and bulimia nervosa. *Current Opinions in Psychiatry,* Vol.19, No.4, (July 2006), pp. 438-443, ISSN 0951-7367.

Mitchell, K. S., Mazzeo, S. E., Rausch, S. M., & Cooke, K. L. (2007). Innovative interventions for disordered eating: Evaluating dissonance-based and yoga interventions. *International Journal of Eating Disorders,* Vol.40, No.2, (March 2007), pp. 120-128, ISSN 0276-3478.

Moreno, A. B. & Thelen, M. H. (1993). A preliminary prevention program for eating disorders in a junior high school population. *Journal of Youth and Adolescence,* Vol.22, No.2, (April 1993), pp. 109-124, ISSN 0047-2891.

Mond, J. M., Hay, P. J., Rogers, B., Owen, C., & Beumont, P. J. V. (2004). Beliefs of women concerning causes and risk factors for bulimia nervosa. *Australian and New Zealand Journal of Psychiatry,* Vol.38, No.6, (July 2004), pp. 463-469, ISSN 0004-8674.

Muth, J. L., & Cash, T. F. (1997). Body image attitudes: What difference does gender make ? *Journal of Applied Social Psychology,* Vol.27, No.16, (August 1997), pp. 1438-1452, ISSN 0021-9029.

Norris, D. L. (1984). The effects of mirror confrontation on self-estimation of body dimensions in anorexia nervosa, bulimia and two control groups. *Psychological Medicine: A Journal of Research in Psychiatry and the Allied Sciences,* Vol.14, No.4, (November 1984), pp. 835-842, ISSN 0033-2917.

Neumark-Sztainer, D., Butler, R., & Palti, H. (1995). Eating disturbances among adolescent girls: Evaluation of a school-based primary prevention program. *Journal of Nutritional Education,* Vol.27, pp. 24-31.

Newman, D. L., Moffitt, T. E., Caspi, A., Magdol, L., Silva, P. A., & Stanton, W. R. (1996). Psychiatric disorder in a birth cohort of young adults: Prevalence, comorbidity, clinical significance, and new case incidence from ages 11 to 21. *Journal of Consulting and Clinical Psychology,* Vol.64, No.3, (June 1996), pp. 552-562, ISSN 0022-006X.

O'Dea, J., & Abraham, S. F. (2002). Eating and exercise disorders in young college men. *Journal of American College Health,* Vol.50, No.6, (May 2002), pp. 273-278, ISSN 0744-8481.

Park, D. C. (2007). Eating disorders: A call to arms. *American Psychologist,* Vol.62, No.3, (April 2007), pp. 158, ISSN 0003-066X.

Paxton, S. J. (1993). A prevention program for disturbed eating and body dissatisfaction in adolescent girls: A 1 year follow-up. *Health Education Research,* Vol.8, No.1, (March 1993), pp. 43-51, ISSN 0268-1153.

Perez, M., Becker, C. B., & Ramirez, A. (2010). Transportability of an empirically supported dissonance-based prevention program for eating disorders. *Body Image,* Vol.7, No.3, (June 2010), pp.179-186, ISSN 1740-1445.

Post, G., & Crowther, J. H. (1987). Restricter-purger differences in adolescent females. *International Journal of Eating Disorders,* Vol.6, No.6, (November1987), pp. 757-761, ISSN 0276-3478.

Rabak-Wagener, J., Eickhoff-Shemek, J., & Kelly-Vance, L. (1998). The effect of media analysis on attitudes and behaviors regarding body image among college students. *Journal of American College Health,* Vol.47, (July 1998), pp. 29-35, ISSN 0744-8481.

Ramirez, A., Perez, M., & Becker, C. B. (2011). *The importance of body image exposure in dissonance-based eating disorder prevention programs.* Manuscript submitted for publication.

Ricciardelli, L. A., Tate, D., & Williams, R. J. (1997). Body dissatisfaction as a mediator of the relationship between dietary restraint and bulimic eating patterns. *Appetite,* Vol.29, No.1, (August 1997), pp. 43-54, ISSN 0195-6663.

Rodriguez, R., Marchand, E., Ng, J., & Stice, E. (2008). Effects of a cognitive dissonance-based eating disorder prevention program are similar for Asian American, Hispanic, and White participants. *International Journal of Eating Disorders,* Vol.41, No.7, (November 2008), pp. 618-625, ISSN 0276-3478.

Roehrig, M., Thompson, J. K., Brannick, M., & van den Berg, P. (2006). Dissonance-based eating disorder prevention program: A preliminary dismantling investigation. *International Journal of Eating Disorders,* Vol.39, No.1, (January 2006), pp. 1-10, ISSN 0276-3478.

Rushford, N., & Ostermeyer, A. (1997). Body image disturbance and their change with videofeedback in anorexia nervosa. *Behaviour Research and Therapy,* Vol.35, No.5, (May 1997), pp. 389-398, ISSN 0005-7967.

Schumacher, J., & Slep, A. (2004). Attitudes and dating aggression: A cognitive dissonance approach. *Prevention Science,* Vol.5, No.4, (December 2004), pp. 231-243, ISSN 1389-4986.

Seidel, A., Presnell, K., & Rosenfield, D. (2009). Mediators in the dissonance eating disorder prevention program. *Behaviour Research and Therapy,* Vol.47, No.8, (August 2009), pp. 645-653, ISSN 0005-7967.

Shaw, H., Stice, E., & Becker, C. B. (2009). Preventing eating disorders. *Child and Adolescent Psychiatric Clinics of North America,* Vol.18, No.1, (January 2009), pp.199-207, ISSN 1056-4993.

Skrzypek, S., Wehmeier, P. M., & Remschmidt, H. (2001). Body image assessment using size estimation in recent studies on anorexia nervosa: A brief review. *European Child and Adolescent Psychiatry,* Vol.10, No.4, (December 2001), pp. 215-221, ISSN 1018-8827.

Stewart, D. A., Carter, J. C., Drinkwater, J., Hainsworth, J., & Fairburn, C. G. (2001). Modification of eating attitudes and behavior in adolescent girls: A controlled study. *International Journal of Eating Disorders,* Vol.29, No.2, (March 2001), pp. 107-118, ISSN 0276-3478.

Stice, E. (1994). Review of the evidence for a sociocultural model of bulimia nervosa and an exploration of the mechanisms of action. *Clinical Psychology Review,* Vol.14, No.7, pp. 633-661, ISSN 0272-7358.

Stice, E. (2002). Risk and maintenance factors for eating pathology: A meta-analystic review. *Psychological Bulletin,* Vol.128, No.5, (September 2002), pp. 825-848, ISSN 0033-2909.

Stice, E., Cameron, R., Killen, J. D., Hayward, C., & Taylor, C. B. (1999). Naturalistic weight reduction efforts prospectively predict growth in relative weight and onset of obesity among female adolescents. *Journal of Consulting and Clinical Psychology,* Vol.67, No.6, (December 1999), pp. 967-974, ISSN 0022-006X.

Stice, E., Chase, A., Stormer, S., & Appel, A. (2001). A randomized trial of a dissonance-based eating disorder prevention program. *International Journal of Eating Disorders,* Vol.29, No.3, (April 2001), pp. 247-262, ISSN 0276-3478.

Stice, E., Fisher, M., & Martinez, E. (2004). Eating disorder diagnostic scale: Additional evidence of reliability and validity. *Psychological Assessment,* Vol.16, No.1, (March 2004), pp. 60-71, ISSN 1040-3590.

Stice, E., Killen, J. D., Hayward, C., & Taylor, C. B. (1998). Age of onset for binge eating and purging during late adolescence: A 4-year survival analysis. *Journal of Abnormal Psychology,* Vol.107, No.4, (November 1998), pp. 671-675, ISSN 0021-843X.

Stice, E., Marti, C. N., Rohde, P., & Shaw, H. (2011). Testing mediators hypothesized to account for the effects of a dissonance-based eating disorder prevention program over longer term follow-up. *Journal of Consulting and Clinical Psychology,* Vol.79, No.3, (June 2011), pp. 398-405, ISSN 0022-006X.

Stice, E., Marti, C. N., Spoor, S., Presnell, K., & Shaw, H. (2008). Dissonance and healthy weight eating disorder prevention programs: Long-term effects from a randomized efficacy trial. *Journal of Consulting and Clinical Psychology,* Vol.76, No.2, (April 2008), pp. 329-340, ISSN 0022-006X.

Stice, E., Mazotti, L., Weibel, D., & Agras, W. S. (2000). Dissonance prevention program decreases thin-ideal internalization, body dissatisfaction, dieting, negative affect, and bulimic symptoms: A preliminary experiment. *International Journal of Eating Disorders,* Vol.75, No.2, (March 2000), pp. 206-217, ISSN 0276-3478.

Stice, E., Orjada, K., & Tristan, J. (2006). Trial of a psychoeducational eating disturbance intervention for college women: A replication and extension. *International Journal of Eating Disorders,* Vol.39, No.3, (April 2006), pp. 233-239, ISSN 0276-3478.

Stice, E., Presnell, K., Gau, J., & Shaw, H. (2007). Testing mediators of intervention effects in randomized controlled trials: An evaluation of two eating disorder prevention programs. *Journal of Consulting and Clinical Psychology,* Vol.75, No.1, (February 2007), pp. 20-32, ISSN 0022-006X.

Stice, E., Rohde, P., Gau, J., & Shaw, H. (2009). An effectiveness trial of a dissonance-based eating disorder prevention program for high-risk adolescents. *Journal of Consulting and Clinical Psychology,* Vol.77, No.5, (October 2009), pp. 825-834, ISSN 0022-006X.

Stice, E., Rohde, P., Shaw, H., & Gau, J. (2011). An effectiveness trial of a selected dissonance-based eating disorder prevention program for female high school students: Long-term effects. *Journal of Consulting and Clinical Psychology,* Vol.79, No.4, (August 2011), pp. 500-508, ISSN 0022-2117.

Stice, E., & Shaw, H. (1994). Adverse effects of the media portrayed thin-ideal on women and linkages to bulimic symptomatology. *Journal of Social and Clinical Psychology,* Vol.13, No.3, pp. 288-308, ISSN 0736-7236.

Stice, E. & Shaw, H. (2004). Eating disorder prevention programs: A meta-analytic review. *Psychological Bulletin,* Vol.130, No.2, (March 2004), pp. 206-227, ISSN 0033-2909.

Stice, E., Shaw, H., Becker, C. B., & Rohde, P. (2008). Dissonance-based interventions for the prevention of eating disorders: Using persuasion principles to promote health. *Prevention Science,* Vol.9, No.2, (June 2008), pp. 114-128, ISSN 1389-4986.

Stice, E., Shaw, H., Burton, E., & Wade, E. (2006). Dissonance and healthy weight eating disorder prevention programs: A randomized efficacy trial. *Journal of Consulting and Clinical Psychology,* Vol.74, No.2, (April 2006), pp. 263-275, ISSN 0022-006X.

Stice, E., Shaw, H., & Marti, C. N. (2006). A meta-analytic review of obesity prevention programs for children and adolescents: The skinny on interventions that work. *Psychological Bulletin,* Vol.132, No.5, (September 2006), pp. 667-691, ISSN 0033-2909.

Stice, E., Shaw, H., & Marti, C. N. (2007). A meta-analytic review of eating disorder prevention programs: Encouraging findings. *Annual Review of Clinical Psychology,* Vol.3, pp. 207-231, ISSN 1548-5943.

Stice, E., Trost, A., & Chase, A. (2003). Healthy weight control and dissonance-based eating disorder prevention programs: Results from a controlled trial. *International Journal of Eating Disorders,* Vol.33, No.1, (January 2003), pp. 10-21, ISSN 0276-3478.

Stice, E., Ziemba, C., Margolis, J., & Flick, P. (1996). The dual pathway model differentiates bulimics, subclinical bulimics, and controls: Testing the continuity hypothesis. *Behavior Therapy,* Vol.27, No.4, pp. 531-549, ISSN 0005-7894.

Striegel-Moore, R. H., & Franko, D. L. (2002). Body image issues among girls and women. In: *Body image: A handbook of theory, research, and clinical practice.* Cash, T. F., & Pruzinsky, T. (Eds.), pp. 183-191, Guilford Press, ISBN 1572307773, New York, NY, US.

Striegel-Moore, R. H., Silberstein, L. R., Grunberg, N. E., & Rodin, J. (1990). Competing on all fronts: Achievement orientation and disordered eating. *Sex Roles,* Vol.23, No.11, pp. 697, ISSN 0360-0025.

Taylor, C. B., Bryson, S., Luce, K. H., Cunning, D., Doyle, A. C., Abascal, L. B., Rockwell, R., Dev, P., Winzelberg, A. J., & Wilfley, D. E. (2006). Prevention of eating disorders in at-risk college-age women. *Archives of General Psychiatry,* Vol.63, No.8, (August 2008), pp. 881-888. ISSN 0003-990X.

Thompson, J. K., Heinberg, L. J., Altabe, M., & Tantleff-Dunn, S. (1999). *Exacting beauty: Theory, assessment and treatment of body image disturbance.* American Psychological Association, ISBN 1557985413, Washington, DC, US.

Thompson, J. K., & Stice, E. (2001). Thin-ideal internalization: Mounting evidence for a new risk factor for body-image disturbance and eating pathology. *Current Directions in Psychological Science,* Vol.10, No.5, (October 2001), pp. 181-183, ISSN 0963-7214.

Tiggemann, M. (2011). Mental health risks of self-objectification: A review of the empirical evidence for disordered eating, depressed mood, and sexual dysfunction. In: *Self-objectification in women: Causes, consequences, and counteractions.* Calogero, R., Tantleff-Dunn, S., & Thompson, J. K. (Eds.), pp. 139-159, American Psychological Association, ISBN 143380798X, Washington, DC, US.

Treasure, J., Katzman, M., Schmidt, U., Troop, N., Todd, G., & deSilva, P. (1999). Engagement and outcome in the treatment of bulimia nervosa: First phase of a sequential design comparing motivation enhancement therapy and cognitive behavioral therapy. *Behaviour Research and Therapy,* Vol.37, No.5, (May 1999), pp. 405-418, ISSN 0005-7967.

Tuschen-Caffier, B., Vögele, C., Bracht, S., & Hilbert, A. (2003). Psychological responses to body shape exposure in patients with bulimia nervosa. *Behaviour Research and Therapy,* Vol.41, No.5, (May 2003), pp. 573-586, ISSN 0005-7967.

Ulrich, J. (1991). A motivational approach to the treatment of alcoholism in the Federal Republic of Germany. *Alcoholism Treatment Quarterly,* Vol.8, No.2, pp. 83-92, ISSN 0734-7324.

Vocks, S., Legenbauer, T., Wächter, A., Wucherer, M., & Kosfelder, J. (2007). What happens in the course of body exposure ? Emotional, cognitive, and physiological reactions to mirror confrontation in eating disorders. *Journal of Psychosomatic Research,* Vol.62, No.2, (February 2007), pp. 231-239, ISSN 0022-3999.

Wade, T., George, W. M., & Atkinson, M. (2009). A randomized controlled trial of brief interventions for body dissatisfaction. *Journal of Consulting and Clinical Psychology,* Vol.77, No.5, (October 2009), pp. 845-854, ISSN 0022-006X.

Weiss, K. R., & Wertheim, E. H. (2005). An evaluation of a primary prevention program for disordered eating in adolescent girls: Examining responses of high- and low-risk girls. *Eating Disorders: The Journal of Treatment and Prevention,* Vol.13, No.2, (March 2005), pp. 143-156., ISSN 1064-0266.

Welch, S. L., & Fairburn, C. G. (1994). Sexual abuse and bulimia nervosa: Three integrated case control comparisons. *American Journal of Psychiatry,* Vol.151, No.3, (March 1994), pp. 402-407, ISSN 0002-953X.

Wilson, G. T. (1999). Cognitive behavior therapy for eating disorders: Progress and problems. *Behaviour Research and Therapy,* Vol.37, No.1, (July 1999), pp. S79-S95, ISSN 0005-7967.

Wilson, G. T. (2004). Acceptance and change in the treatment of eating disorders: The evolution of manual-based cognitive therapy. In: *Mindfulness and acceptance: Expanding cognitive-behavioral tradition.* Hayes, S. C., Follette, V. M., & Linehan, M. M. (Eds.), pp. 243-260, Guilford Press, ISBN 1593850662, New York, NY, US.

Wilson, G. T., Becker, C. B., & Heffernan, K. (2003). Eating Disorders. In: *Child psychopathology (2nd ed.).* Mash, E. J., & Barkley, R. A. (Eds.), pp. 687-715, Guilford Press, ISBN 1572306092, New York, NY, US.

Winzelberg, A. J., Eppstein, D., Eldredge, K. L., Wilfley, D., Dasmahapatra, R., Dev, P., & Taylor, C. B. (2000). Effectiveness of an internet-based program for reducing risk factors for eating disorders. *Journal of Consulting and Clinical Psychology,* Vol.68, No.2, (April 2000), pp. 346-350, ISSN 0022-006X.

Winzelberg, A. J., Taylor, C. B., Sharpe, T., Eldredge, K. L., Dev, P., & Constantinou, P. S. (1998). Evaluation of a computer-mediated eating disorder intervention program. *International Journal of Eating Disorders,* Vol.24, No.4, (December 1998), pp. 339-349, ISSN 0276-3478.

# Part 5

## Nutritional Issues

# 15

# Nutritional Evaluation of Eating Disorders

Ruiz Prieto Inmaculada
*Behavioural Sciences Institute, Seville, Spain*

## 1. Introduction

Eating disorders comprise a group of psychiatric pathologies with an important organic impact, mainly caused by poor eating practices (Miján de la Torre et al., 2006).

In anorexia nervosa, there are a number of anatomical and physiological disturbances resulting from malnutrition. However, it is not usually found malnutrition in case of bulimia nervosa or eating disorders not otherwise specified (EDNOS) with tendency to bulimic behaviours, which can reach slightly higher than normal range of Body Mass Index (Loria & Gómez, 2010).

Nutritional status is the result between the income and metabolism of nutrients and the nutritional requirements in order to reach a proper growth and maintenance of the normal body's functions (Olveira et al., 2007). When there is not a suitable balance to meet body needs, a process of metabolic adaptation, with major impact on the nutritional status (Jen & Yan, 2011; Planas et al., 2002), begins.

When the income and metabolism of nutrients is not adequate to the body requirements (what means that there is a negative energy balance), the process of malnutrition begins, facilitating the outcome of eating disorders (Olveira et al., 2007; Planas et al., 2002).

Nutritional status assessment consists of data collection that reveals possible energy and protein deficiencies, as well as any other nutrient deficiency (Olveira et al., 2007).

There are two types of nutritional evaluation, individual and collective. Individual nutritional assessment aims to obtain a defined diagnosis of malnutrition and evaluate the impact of this malnutrition, identifying medical complications. Collective nutritional assessment aims to identify malnourished subjects with potential risk of malnutrition or to make an early detection of malnourished individuals (Lama et al., 2002; Olveira et al., 2007).

In this way, it would be able to qualify and quantify the malnutrition state, which will allow assessing the impact of bad dietary behaviours on the organism, identifying medical complications that can lead to hospitalization. Furthermore, it would be able to determine the nutritional requirements for a proper re-feeding and physical recovery of the subject by determine the appropriate nutritional intervention (Loria & Gómez, 2010).

To choose the appropriate nutritional intervention it has been used different methods to assess the nutritional status and eating habits. However, since there is no ideal information about collecting methods, it is recommended the use of several markers of nutritional status and dietary habits, to compare them with each other and over time. It is important to emphasize that as a greater number of methods used in the nutritional status assessment more information we will have to implement an individualized nutritional treatment, trying to make it more effective. However, as more collecting information methods are used more time and resources are needed (economic, material and professional). To sum up, methods should be chosen according to real possibilities (Planas et al., 2002).

Therefore, nutritional assessment should include medical and dietary history, physical examination, anthropometric measurements and laboratory analysis (Olveira et al., 2007).

## 2. Medical and dietary histories

Eating disorders are complex diseases with a high morbidity and mortality, involving somatic and nutritional impact as a result of poor eating practices (Carrard et al., 2011; Schebendach et al., 2008, 2011).

The etiology of these diseases is also complex and eating disorders have been defined as multifactorial disorders. That make it necessary to acquire as much information as possible in order to implement a complete treatment which includes medical care, nutritional intervention, psychological therapy and health care in order to decrease symptoms as well as to obtain a complete socio-cultural integration, self-care capacity and prevention of relapse or recurrence (Allen et al., 2011; Rosen, 2010; Schebendach et al., 2011).

Therefore, a complete medical history is essential to determine the nutritional status (Castro et al., 2000). It is the first part of the nutritional assessment and it is important to the establishment of the clinician-patient relationship (Huang, 2010).

Clinical interview should include diagnostic criteria for eating disorders and the evaluation of previous treatments (Rosen, 2010). Thus, data of filiation, personal and family disease history, survey of current knowledge about nutrition, bulimic episodes, compensatory behaviors, physical activity and/or exercise, menstrual history, disease awareness and motivation to change will be included in a complete medical history (Loria & Gómez, 2010).

Personal interviewing is considered the most reliable and valid information collecting method. However, in certain circumstances it is appropriate to obtain information from relatives, as well as the information provided by the person. In eating disorders several factors justify the surrogated interview, as well as the individual. These factors include, on one hand, ignorance of much of the data as well as the inability to express or identify relevant information. In adolescent and infancy period, parents tend to be responsible for the care and feeding of children, so patient does not have the information needed to complete the dietary history.

On the other hand, people with eating disorders hide, voluntarily or involuntarily, certain behaviors as well as temperamental and physical changes during the pathology. It makes necessary to compare the information provided by the patient with that provided by family members (Yago et al., 2002).

Medical history can be structured, semi-structured or free. Structured clinical history presents information to collect step by step. Generally, this type of interview offers closed answers, so the respondent does not provide additional information.

Semi-structured clinical history involves the most important aspects of eating disorders, although there is the possibility of extending the information according to the interviewer criteria.

Free medical history is totally flexible. It requires an experienced interviewer (with extensive knowledge about eating disorders), who can drive the patient's dialogue to obtain relevant clinical information.

In summary, the clinical history ensures that patient answers, provides security and control to the interviewer over the course of the interview, is flexible to recompile information allowing an individual interview which provides the maximum information that the subject is able to give, except the structured interview that is not flexible. Questions can be complex because the interviewer can solve subject's doubts. However, the realization of medical history requires time and high cost and requires a trained interviewer to maintain a neutral attitude, so that there is no bias in the answers of the respondent. In addition, the interviewer should be formed in the field of eating disorders so it could be collected relevant data to deal with this pathology (Planas et al., 2002; Reiter & Graves, 2010; Yago et al., 2002).

### 2.1 Personal data

Personal data are needed to identify and contact the patient, therefore it is useful to identify socio-familial context. It will collect name, address, age and date of birth, current occupation, studies, couple's relationships, members of the family and, if possible, relations between them. Phone number of the subject and any family member, e-mail address and any other necessary contact information should be written in the medical history. All of this provides a slight idea of family economic opportunities, relationships and family structure, job integration and interpersonal relationships (Jáuregui, 2006).

### 2.2 Personal medical history

There is a controversy about whether pregnancy and childhood data should be collected or not. However, in childhood period it would be appropriate to collect data on pregnancy, breastfeeding and growth that could explain the current nutritional status of the subject (Lama et al., 2002).

As consequence, characteristics and complications of pregnancy, such as intrauterine-malnutrition and alcohol, drugs or tobacco mother's consumption during pregnancy should be collected. Mothers' nutritional status during pregnancy and after childbirth and mothers' dieting in this time are collected in the medical history. Subsequently, some baby's characteristics will be collected such as weight, height and circumference of the newborn after childbirth. In addition, it must be picked up the period of breastfeeding, lasting and characteristics of this period, baby's appetite and behaviour during meals, mother-child relationship, as well as the food's introduction chronology and family meal introduction.

Additionally, personal medical history must include suffered diseases (especially those related to food), such as cardiovascular disease, diabetes, allergies or food intolerances. All of them must be supported by specific medical diagnosis.

Finally, it is essential to make a present's illness history which collect the triggering factors considered by the subject, previous diagnosis, evolution of the pathology, previous treatments, well-being of the patient related to the disease, changes in lifestyle, socio-cultural role of the disease, mental and emotional reaction of the patient with the illness (Jáuregui, 2006; Planas et al., 2002).

### 2.3 Family medical history

Taking into account the genetic component in the development of eating disorders as well as the tendency to maintain a certain weight, it is interesting to collect the history of family illnesses, especially related to eating disorders and psychological pathologies like depression, anxiety, personality disorders and organic illness such as cardiovascular disease, diabetes, cancer or obesity (Planas et al., 2002).

### 2.4 Nutritional interview

It is the main part of the clinical history for nutritional status assessment which not only collects the quantitative and qualitative characteristics of the subject's food intake but also the eating habits and the specific environment during meals (Loria & Gómez, 2010).

It should be taken into account that data provided by respondents are subjective, so the indicated eating habits might not be real (Yago et al., 2002).

Number of meals per day will show if there are restrictions for any of the recommended intakes (usually 5: breakfast, mid-morning, lunch, tea time and dinner), if so it can be seen which meal is restricted and why. With respect to meals' schedule, it is important to know if it is organized or not, rigid or flexible. A proper schedule is appropriate for metabolic activity, so these data are useful for the therapeutic approach. In addition, it could provide data on the possible evolution of the disease, because usually the more restrictive profile are organized and inflexible whereas those profiles of purging eating disorders tend to be erratic and very flexible (Loria & Gómez, 2010; Schebendach et al., 2008). Intakes' place register provides information if the person usually eats at home or regularly has out-home meals and provides information if intakes are made in a dining room or in any other room. If the person eats sitting, foot or lying down, so treatment based on postural corrections might be necessary to facilitate digestion and food intake. In addition, it is important to collect if intakes are performed accompanied by relatives or alone or if there is some entertainment while the person eats, which could prevent the detection of satiety signals.

Moreover, meals can be structured or disorganized. For lunch and dinner, it is necessary to know if they consist of a single course or two courses, if it is accompanied with bread, if dessert is often eaten and if dessert is eaten before or after meals. Although it would be answered if the person drinks while eating or otherwise reserves the drink for before or after the food intake. Usually, people with eating disorders have inaccurate cognitions about food and usually manifest them through altered eating behaviours (Jáuregui & Bolaños, 2010).

Preferences and food dislikes, as well as the reason for this must be collected in the nutritional interview. Also, it is appropriate to record preferences and dislikes in culinary techniques. It is interesting for a proper nutritional treatment to know the changes in food tastes of the person from the onset of the disease. It is important to know the personal assessment given to the food, if the person finds it something necessary, compulsory, pleasant, unpleasant and, especially, how the perception has changed of the food with the evolution of the pathology.

Hunger, satiety and appetite perceptions are altered so it is appropriate to collect the capacity of the differentiation of these sensations in people with eating disorders, as well as the perception of the quantities of food, why it is recommended to write down if the subject is responsible of its food, if it ends the amount served or if it returns to serve more quantity.

Many times patients suffering from an eating disorder are concerned about eating practices of their relatives and are dedicated to select, plan, buy and prepare food for the family. One of the consequences of malnutrition is the emergence of obsessions and occasionally also compulsions, so it is necessary to recognize rituals related to food and abnormal eating behaviors as hide, shredding or cutting food excessively (Jáuregui, 2006). Furthermore, nutritional survey must collect emotional irritability, anxiety or aggression when the person with eating disorder eats or before eating time and if eating with the family is avoided. The food survey should also include bowel habits (Loria & Gómez, 2010).

In addition, one of the factors present in the development and maintenance of eating disorders is the realization of restrictive diets to reduce weight so nutritional interview should contain information on the realization of such diets under supervision of professionals or at the sole discretion of the person (Kontic et al., 2010).

### 2.5 Bulimic episodes

It is very important to explore the presence of bingeing. Medical history oriented to nutritional status assessment in eating disorders must be based on the kind of food eaten and the approximate food intake volume to check whether the binge episodes are subjective or objective. Precipitating factors of the overeating, features, frequency and location as well as the feelings of the person who suffers them should be recognized (Kontic et al., 2010; Loria & Gómez, 2010).

### 2.6 Compensatory behaviours

To learn about the potential physical impacts of altered behaviors present in eating disorders it is necessary to register the presence of vomits as well as the use-abuse of laxatives, diuretics or drugs that promote weight loss.

Medical history must show the frequency, characteristics, and feelings of the subject before these purging behaviors as well as if the compensatory behaviours are linked to binge eating (Killen et al., 1986; Loria & Gómez, 2010).

### 2.7 Physical activity

Many people with eating disorders present severe hyperactivity focused on day-to-day tasks in an extreme way. However, physical exercise in order to loose weight is a typical behavior of eating disorders patients (Killen et al., 1986).

To perform an adequate dietetic treatment it is necessary to pick up the physical exercise practice as well as the daily physical activity (Bratland-Sanda et al., 2010). Excess or defect of physical activity may explain part of the energy balance, negative or positive, respectively.

In addition, it should be included the sleeping and resting habits, i.e. hours of sleep, if sleep is restful, resting at night, as well as there is resting after meals (Misra & Klibanski, 2010; Tong & D'Alessio, 2011).

### 2.8 Weight history

Medical history must collect the minimum and the maximum weights as well as the normal person's weight in order to obtain the amount of weight lost or weight gained and the period of time in which the weight has changed.

On the one hand, it is appropriate to examine whether the undernourished person tolerates weight gain and, on the other hand, if he/she would support that change. In addition, weight history covers the wish of the person to loose weight even when it is well nourished or malnourished (Jáuregui, 2006; Loria & Gómez, 2010).

### 2.9 Menstrual history

One of the metabolic adaptations present in patients with altered nutritional status is the involvement of the hypothalamus-pituitary-gonad axis, so it is necessary that clinical history collects information about menstruation characteristics, its regularity, menarche age, amenorrhea periods, sexual and reproductive function and use of oral contraceptives or hormone replacement therapy (Chou et al., 2011; Loria & Gómez, 2010; Misra & Klibanski, 2010).

### 2.10 Psychosocial history

The social impact of the pathology, interpersonal relationships, family relationships and couple relationships as well as leisure activities give relevant information to choose the appropriate nutritional intervention (Jáuregui, 2006).

### 2.11 Illness knowledge

It is essential to determine the patients' disease knowledge and motivational state to change, because if the patient does not recognize its altered behaviours as an illness it is very difficult to change them (Loria & Gómez, 2010). Therefore, when setting the nutritional treatment it is important to know if the person is motivated to change (von Wietersheim & Hoffmann, 2011).

## 3. Physical examination

As a result of malnutrition, certain dietary practices or compensatory behaviors, common in patients with eating disorders, different clinical signs and medical complications are usually developed, which can be distinguished by the simple observation of the patient, accompanied by certain measures (Olveira et al., 2007).

It should be noted that clinical manifestations that results from malnutrition depends on various factors such as age, sex and the evolution and severity of the eating disorder (Lama et al., 2002).

The observation of an emaciated or edematous aspect leads to suspect the presence of marasmus or kwashiorkor. These are two types of malnutrition, the first is a type of malnutrition by calorie deficiency and the second by protein deficiency (Loria & Gómez, 2010; Planas et al., 2002), and even there are mixed kinds of malnutrition. Eating disorders usually presents marasmus because they decrease daily energy intake reducing lipids and carbohydrates consumption but maintaining, to some extent, the protein intake (Loria & Gómez, 2010).

Observing skin abnormalities, dryness, swelling, dermatitis, skin atrophy, cyanosis of the sacral parts, livid distal extremities or body hair reflecting energy and nutritional deficiencies can be detected. Sometimes, it is possible to detect Acanthosis nigricans in people who binge, which makes suspect the existence of hyperinsulinism. Carotenodermia may appear as a result of hepatic metabolism alterations. Sometimes, people with eating disorders feel cold, particularly referred to their extremities. Pale mucous membranes may reflect anemia whereas the hair weakness may indicate protein deficiencies. Russell's sign as a result of self-induced vomiting, dental erosion, decay, discoloration of the teeth, tooth sensitivity, mouth dry, halitosis, cold sores or parotid gland hypertrophy can be found (Lama et al., 2002; Loria & Gómez, 2010).

Gastrointestinal signs may appear as delayed gastric emptying which tends to pursue with early satiety, constipation, diarrhoea, gastric dilatation, ulceration esophageal or gastric, haematemesis, colonic dysfunction or rectal prolapse (Lama et al., 2002; Loria & Gómez, 2010).

Sensory and reflexes capacity may decrease as the involvement of the nervous system because of the under nutritional status (Lama et al., 2002; Loria & Gómez, 2010).

## 4. Anthropometric measurements and body composition

Malnutrition induces changes in body composition, so assessing those changes would provide information on the nutritional status of the person (Bellido et al., 2002; Misra & Klibanski, 2010).

However, there are no ideal nutritional evaluation methods. On the one hand, malnutrition itself afflicts the determination of physical parameters. On the other hand, the values found with body measures are compared with reference values to determine the nutritional status of the person while these reference values are not always reliable for the person. The ideal is to compare the values obtained with the body composition measurement of the person with initial values of the own person to assess nutritional status change (Bellido et al., 2002).

Anthropometric parameters give information on the compartments and body structure through the measure of the size and proportions of the body (Bellido et al., 2002; Olveira et al., 2007).

Generally, anthropometric parameters are easy to obtain and are not very expensive but require specific materials such as clinical balance, stadiometer, skin folds and millimeter precision gauge. The collection of these measures requires trained personnel, especially for the obtaining of the skin folds and corporal perimeters (Bellido et al., 2002; Loria & Gómez, 2010).

### 4.1 Height, weight and body mass index

These are the measures most used in the assessment of nutritional status especially because the ease to obtain them. However, they are bit sensitive for the early detection of malnutrition (Loria & Gómez, 2010; Olveira et al., 2007).

They are indicators of lean and fat compartments, so that a weight lost or gain exaggerated in the adult is indicative of malnutrition, while the delay in growth and weight gain in children would be indicative of malnutrition (Olveira et al., 2007).

#### 4.1.1 Height

Height is measured using a millimeter precision stadiometer with the person's back to the vertical stem. The person must be barefoot, with the heels together, its arms relaxed and the position of its head should be one in which the auditory meatus and lower orbit eye are horizontal (Bellido et al., 2002; Loria & Gómez, 2010).

Sometimes the measure of the size cannot be carried out in a conventional manner, this would be the case of elderly or unable to stand or get straight youth. In this case, one can measure the height of the knee, while the patient is in supine decubitus with flexed knee forming a right angle with the leg and level planting at a right angle. Through predictive formulas, it is possible to find the height of people aged between 60-80 years:

$$\text{Height (cm)}: 64.19 - [0.04 \times \text{age (years)}] + [2.02 \times \text{height of the knee (cm)}] \quad (1)$$

$$\text{Height (cm)}: 84.88 - [0.24 \times \text{age (years)}] + [1.83 \times \text{height of the knee (cm)}] \quad (2)$$

1 Men height (Bellido et al., 2002; Olveira et al., 2007)
2 Women height (Bellido et al., 2002; Olveira et al., 2007)

If the person cannot maintain the bent leg, one can measure the length from the top edge of the patella to the lower edge of the external maleolo, and it is possible to calculate the size by using the formula:

$$\text{Height (cm)}: [\text{knee height- external maleolo (cm)} \times 1.121] - [0.117 \times \text{age (years)}] + 119.6 \quad (3)$$

$$\text{Height (cm)}: [\text{knee height- external maleolo (cm)} \times 1.263] + [0.159 \times \text{age (years)}] + 107.7 \quad (4)$$

3 Men height (Bellido et al., 2002; Olveira et al., 2007)
4 Women height (Bellido et al., 2002; Olveira et al., 2007)

#### 4.1.2 Weight

Weight must be assessed in a clinical scale with the patient in a straight position, look upwards and heels together. It should take place barefoot and with light clothing. It is appropriate that patients do not know the weight in order to not encourage unrest in eating disorders (Loria & Gómez, 2010).

This measure by itself has no value as determinant of nutritional status, however it is very suitable as a percentage of weight lost, percentage of ideal weight and as a follow-up of the evolution of the physical status of the person (Bellido et al., 2002; Loria & Gómez, 2010; Olveira et al., 2007).

Weight loses reliability when edema is present in the person (Loria & Gómez, 2010; Olveira et al., 2007).

#### 4.1.2.1 Ideal weight

There are tables of ideal weight depending on age, sex and complexion. This measure provides an overall idea of the nutritional status of the person. However, it should be noted that reference tables are not validated for the people we are trying to. However, weighing less than 10% of the ideal weight is considered underweight (Bellido et al., 2002; Loria & Gómez, 2010).

Furthermore, it is not appropriate to speak of ideal weight to a population that is especially concerned about their weight.

The percentage of ideal weight is calculated:

$$\% \text{ Ideal weight: [current weight (kg) / ideal weight (kg)] x 100} \quad (5)$$

5 Bellido et al., 2002

#### 4.1.2.2 Weight lost

Weight lost exceeding 10% of initial weight in a period less than six months is associated with alterations in body composition with high risk for complications, so it reflects an altered nutritional status (3.; Loria & Gómez, 2010). The same applies to serious weight lost exceeding 2% in a week, 5% in a month, and 7.5% in three months (Gil et al., 2002; Olveira et al., 2007).

However, these figures are not reliable with the presence of edema or the increase of the total body water, since it hides current lost of muscle mass and fat mass (Bellido et al., 2002).

To calculate the percentage of weight lost, the first thing is to estimate the usual weight that is the weight that the person usually has under normal circumstances and in a stable situation (Bellido et al., 2002).

$$\% \text{ Weight lost: [(usual weight (kg) - current weight (kg)) / usual weight (kg)] x 100} \quad (6)$$

6 Bellido et al., 2002; Loria & Gómez, 2010

### 4.1.3 Body Mass Index

Although the Body Mass Index (BMI) is related to the percentage of weight lost it is a little sensitive indicator to the early detection of malnutrition. It is estimated a 21% sensitivity and 95% specificity in the determination of malnutrition by BMI (Olveira et al., 2007).

It is calculated by a formula relating weight and height:

$$\text{BMI: current weight (kg) / current height}^2 \text{ (m)} \quad (7)$$

7 Bellido et al., 2002; Loria & Gómez, 2010; Olveira et al., 2007

The World Health Organization has determined ranges to indicate the nutritional status of adults until the age of 65 using Body Mass Index. In this way:

| BMI | Malnutrition |
|---|---|
| 18.5-24.9 | Well-nourished |
| 17-18.4 | Low malnourished |
| 16-16.9 | Moderated malnourished |
| <16 | High malnourished |

Table 1. Malnutrition degree based on the Body Mass Index according to the World Health Organization

However, although a BMI equal to 18.5 is considered as a lower limit of well-nourished people, usually people with a BMI lower than 20 already reflect some degree of malnutrition. From 18.5, each drop of one point of the BMI is associated with a decrease of 5% of body weight, in the same way that each point greater than 18.5 is associated with increase of 5% of body weight (Bellido et al., 2002; Loria & Gómez, 2010).

Nonetheless, BMI is not a good indicator of the nutritional status of persons under 18 years, due to the rate of growth and development, percentile with respect to the normal population will reflect the nutritional status in this period. The limitation of the use of percentile is the acquisition of reference tables validated in the study population (Lama et al., 2002; Nicholls et al., 2002; Olveira et al., 2007). It should be taken as normal the percentiles of 5-95, while focusing on the 50 percentile (Lama et al., 2002).

### 4.2 Skin folds

Being concerned that over 50% of total body fat is located in the subcutaneous tissue, the extent of skin folds is adequate to determine the fat depletion degree and fluctuations in body fat (Bellido et al., 2002; Loria & Gómez, 2010; Olveira et al., 2007).

However, the extent of skin folds presents some limitations such as low reproducibility, the need for trained personnel for its measurement and the necessity of assessment based on reference values (Olveira et al., 2007).

Skin fold must be assessed in the non-dominant side. It is estimated the approximate point where the measurement must be carried out and take the crease with thumb and index fingers of left hand separating the muscle layer through lateral movements.

Once caught the skin fold, it is placed the gauge of skin folds at the bottom of the fingers without releasing the fold to measure.

This measurement should be made three times and the average value of three measures will be used. For each measurement the process should start again. The gauge must not be removed since the skin fold is measured so not appear bruise by pressure.

Skin folds values are expressed in millimetres (Loria & Gómez, 2010).

#### 4.2.1 Tricipital skin fold

It is the skin fold most used in clinical practice.

Before proceeding to the measurement, the midpoint of the arm must be found, which is located at the average distance between the acromiun and olecranun. This fold is measured vertically, on the back of the arm, above the midpoint of the arm.

Arms must be relaxed and extended (Bellido et al., 2002; Loria & Gómez, 2010; Olveira et al., 2007).

### 4.2.2 Bicipital skin fold

It is measured the same way as the tricipital skin fold but in the anterior face of the arm (Bellido et al., 2002; Loria & Gómez, 2010; Olveira et al., 2007).

### 4.2.3 Subscapular skin fold

It is measured diagonally from the lower angle that forms the scapula. The arms should be relaxed and extended and the person must be by feet (Bellido et al., 2002; Loria & Gómez, 2010; Olveira et al., 2007).

### 4.2.4 Suprailiac skin fold

It is measured obliquely, in the midline of the front-top iliac crest. The person should be standing by feet and relaxed (Bellido et al., 2002; Olveira et al., 2007).

### 4.2.5 Body fat mass

It is the estimated percentage of total body fat mass through a combination of measurement of the different skin folds by comparison with reference tables or by predictive equations:

$$\text{\% Body fat mass: tricipital skin fold + bicipital skin fold + subscapular skin fold + front-top iliac skin fold} \quad (8)$$

8 Durnin y Womersley equation (Loria & Gómez, 2010)

However, there are many predictive equations to estimate body fat mass through the use of skin folds (Kehoe et al., 2011).

### 4.3 Body perimeters

TThey are measured by means of millimeter gauge.

Body perimeters are not very reliable measures since alterations in the hydration state, body composition and the presence of oedema influence their values.

Moreover, these measures have low reproducibility, on the one hand because they depend on much of the realise personnel and, on the other hand, because the interpretation of the results as an indicator of nutritional status must be based on reference tables, which are not usually appropriate for eating disorders (Bellido et al., 2002).

### 4.3.1 Waist-Hip perimeter

One of the most commonly used indices has been the waist-hip index, employed as an indicator of the location of adipose tissue in the body.

Thus, a central location of adipose tissue has been related to increased risk for cardiovascular disease and metabolic alterations.

However, there are several studies, which have not found a relationship between the waist-hip index and visceral adipose tissue. Moreover, this measure may be influenced by external to the adipose tissue factors (Bellido et al., 2002). So, today, it is not widely used.

Waist-Hip Index: waist (cm) / hip (cm) (9)

9 Gil et al., 2002

| | Central obesity | General obesity |
|---|---|---|
| Men | W-H I > 0.95 | W-H I ≤ 0.95 |
| Women | W-H I > 0.80 | W-H I ≤ 0.80 |

Table 2. Waist-Hip Index (W-H I)

### 4.3.2 Brachial circumference

Comparing the brachial circumference value with references tables related to a particular population results in proper information about the body fat mass and lean body mass, especially in terms of muscle mass (Bellido et al., 2002; Loria & Gómez, 2010; Olveira et al., 2007).

The professional has to find the average distance between the olecranun and acromiun and go around the arm with a millimeter gauge. The arm must be straight and relaxed and it must be measured in the non-dominant arm (Bellido et al., 2002).

#### 4.3.2.1 Muscular arm circumference

Using the measure of the tricipital fold (TF) and the brachial circumference (BC), the muscle circumference of the arm (MCA) can be estimated. However, the obtained value must be compared with reference tables to estimate whether the muscle circumference of the arm corresponds to the average of the population (Bellido et al., 2002; Loria & Gómez, 2010; Olveira et al., 2007) or not.

$$\text{MCA: } [0.314 \times \text{TF (cm)}] - \text{BC (cm)} \quad (10)$$

10 Bellido et al., 2002; Loria & Gómez, 2010; Olveira et al., 2007

#### 4.3.2.2 Arm muscle area

The arm muscle mass can be estimated using the value of the muscle circumference of the arm (MCA) and tricipital fold (TF) under the belief that the arm is circular:

$$\text{AMA: } [\text{MCA - TF (cm)}]^2 / 4 \quad (11)$$

11 Bellido et al., 2002; Loria & Gómez, 2010; Olveira et al., 2007

### 4.4 Body composition

To estimate the body composition, a set of sophisticated measures is needed. This is due to the difficulties of anthropometric measures, especially in people with diseases such as obesity or eating disorders, which usually have hidroelectrolytic and body compartments alterations (Bellido et al., 2002; Olveira et al., 2007).

In order to determine body composition many measurement's methods are based on the "four-compartments body model". The first level is the atomic level, consisting of those elements that compound the 98% of body weight, which are oxygen, carbon, hydrogen, nitrogen, calcium, phosphorus, potassium, sodium and chlorine. The second level is the molecular one and consists of four compartments: water, proteins, minerals and fat. The third level, called cell model, includes the cell mass, extracellular liquid, adipose tissue and skeletal tissue. The fourth level includes muscle and visceral mass, adipose tissue, and bones (Bellido et al., 2002; Olveira et al., 2007).

Approximately, it is estimated that water represents 60% of the total body weight of a norm-nourished human. The muscle mass is 15-20%, and fat mass is 20-25% and 30-35% in men and women respectively. Nevertheless, these values depend on the characteristics of the population (Olveira et al., 2007).

### 4.4.1 Bone densitometry

It is based on the Archimedes' principle which indicates that the volume of a body is equal to the volume of water that the body moves, dividing the body into two compartments, fatty and lean, and calculating the body composition according to the density of each compartment (Bellido et al., 2002).

This method is little used in determining body composition. Nevertheless, bone mineral densitometry is essential in eating disorders (Castro et al., 2000; Winston et al., 2008).

Nutritional deficiencies and hormonal alterations presented in patients with eating disorders, especially with a diagnosis of anorexia nervosa, lead the appearance of osteopenia or osteoporosis (Lawson et al., 2010).

It is very important the diagnosis and early treatment of these complications in order to normalize the bone mineral density level and to avoid large decreases in bone mass because although they improve with the re-nutrition, all the lost bone mineral density cannot be recovered. Subsequently, in order to check the evolution of bone mineral density recovery it is necessary to repeat this test during the treatment and not doing it only at the beginning as nutritional evaluation assessment (Mehler et al., 2011). However, it seems that men with osteopenia will recover all of the bone mineral density lost (Castro et al., 2002).

These complications are the most frequent and they are the most relevant among puberal and prepuberal adolescents (Turner et al., 2001).

### 4.4.2 Bioelectrical impedance

Bioelectrical impedance is a method to analysis body composition that is based on the resistance that provides water and body tissues to the course of an electric current determined by the water and electrolytes contained in the different body compartments (Bellido et al., 2002; Olveira et al., 2007; Talluri et al., 1999).

At low frequency current it reflects the extracellular fluid while at high frequency currents it penetrates in the intracellular layer and reflects the total body water. Lean mass is related to the total body water so that it can be calculated. Body fat mass is obtained subtracting the weight of the fat-free mass with respect to the total body weight.

Body composition is obtained through prediction equations for a specific population that take into account weight, age and sex of the person (Mika et al., 2004).

The possible errors derived from the estimation of body composition by bioelectrical impedance are similar to those obtained by means of the anthropometric methods so there seems to be no advantages in its use (Hannan et al., 1990). However, these mistakes are similar to those committed by other measurement methods that are more expensive and to some extent more difficult to realize (Hannan et al., 1990; Kerruish et al., 2002).

One advantage of the bioelectrical impedance is the determination of the intracellular and extracellular composition, one of the most sensitive indexes of the malnutrition's state (Talluri et al., 1999). In the estimation of the total body water the bioelectrical impedance is suitable (Scalfi et al., 1999) due to the existence of hydrolytic alterations in eating disorders. Usually, patients with anorexia nervosa have a high percentage of total body water that increases with the re-nutrition. Then total body water level normalizes (Mika et al., 2004; Mocanu et al., 1997; Vaisman et al., 1988).

Since the bioelectrical impedance measurement is based on the total body water resistance it is very sensitive to hydrolytic alterations. However, in people over-hydrated it would be estimated an increase in the basal metabolic rate autonomous of anabolism and upside down, in dehydrated people it would be estimated a decrease in the basal metabolic rate self-determined to catabolism. For this reason it seems that the estimation of body fat mass would be blighted by variations in body water (Birmingham et al., 1996). Generally, body composition methods overestimate body fat mass (Haas et al., 2009).

Otherwise, it does not seem that neither bioelectrical impedance analysis nor anthropometric measurements are reliable in people with BMI below 15 (Piccoli et al., 2005).

In contrast, during re-nutrition, body composition changes appear more frequently than weight changes so bioelectrical impedance reflects them (Mika et al., 2004; Olveira et al., 2007; Scalfi et al., 1999).

In summary, the reliability of body composition assessment by bioelectrical impedance analysis is ambiguous although the use of multi-frequency phase-sensitive bioelectrical impedance is appropriate to determine both the energy needs of patients with eating disorders and body composition. The phase-angle measurement does not use predictive formulas and it is used as an indicator of the intracellular and extracellular water and the integrity of cell membranes (Mika et al., 2004; Olveira et al., 2007).

Main advantages of this method are that it is a non-invasive, economic and quick method to determine body composition (Hannan et al., 1990; Mika et al., 2004).

In order to reduce bioelectrical impedance analysis' error it is appropriate to standardize a suitable protocol thus it requires that the person will be in supine position on a non-conductive surface, it must have members in a $45^{o}$ abduction, barefoot, fasting for more than two hours, not having made strenuous physical exercise in the last 24 hours, have urinated thirty minutes before the test and not have ingested alcohol, coffee, soft drinks with caffeine or chocolate in the last 24 hours. Also, the person may not be on premenstrual and menstrual period and not to use metal fittings during the test. The bioelectrical impedance must be at room temperature but not extreme (Loria & Gómez, 2010).

#### 4.4.3 Other methods

There are other methods of body composition analysis less used in the clinical practice of eating disorders because they are more costly and difficult to implement.

In addition most of them require specific materials and more time to realize.

##### 4.4.3.1 Isotopic methods

Isotopic methods are relatively simple techniques that consist of administering radioactive isotopes, typically deuterium ($^{2}H$), tritium ($^{3}H$) or oxygen-18 ($^{18}O$), to measure the dilution and thus calculate total body water and extracellular fluid. Subsequently, predictive formulas are used to find the fat mass and lean body mass.

Another method is the radiation measurement of an isotope of potassium ($^{40}K$) to mediate the total body potassium. This potassium isotope is directly associated with the fat-free mass so after getting its value one subtract the lean mass weight to the total body weight as fat mass is obtained.

They are methods that require specific devices that make them difficult to realize in the clinical practice (Bellido et al., 2002; Olveira et al., 2007).

##### 4.4.3.2 Absorciometry

Absorciometry analyses body composition by dividing the body into three compartments via the absorption of x-rays. It is especially important in determining bone mineral density in the presence of osteoporosis but it is an expensive method that requires complex equipment found only in certain hospitals (Bellido et al., 2002).

##### 4.4.3.3 Ultrasonography

Subcutaneous fat is measured through the application of perpendicular ultrasonic waves on the surface of the skin with ultrasonografic methods. Considering the clinical practice, it is a non-wide applicable technique due to its high cost (Bellido et al., 2002; Olveira et al., 2007). In addition, it does not seem an adequate application in eating disorders (DiVasta et al., 2007).

##### 4.4.3.4 Nuclear magnetic resonance

Nuclear magnetic resonance is a non-invasive and highly targeted technique focused on the first body level called atomic level. It measures the ability of atomic nuclei in the absorption of certain frequency energy when they are subjected to a magnetic field.

Due to its high cost and time required to realize, nuclear magnetic resonance has short interest in the clinical practice. However, it is a useful tool to determine changes in cellular metabolites without biopsies (Bellido et al., 2002; Olveira et al., 2007).

##### 4.4.3.5 Computerized axial tomography

Computerized axial tomography analyses body composition at the tissue level according to the density of different tissues. It is a very precise technique but little representative of nutritional status that would be appropriate to determine the visceral fat mass in very malnourished patients (Bellido et al., 2002; Olveira et al., 2007).

## 5. Laboratory analysis

Biochemical data are analysed to obtain information on the nutritional status and possible metabolic disturbances in eating disorders (Bellido et al., 2002; Loria & Gómez, 2010). However, it should be taken into account that the nutrients' serum level does not indicate their deposits' state, because that depends on the homeostatic regulation and food intake, as well as the individual malnutrition's adaptation (Loria & Gómez, 2010).

In explanation, biochemical parameters are little sensitive and little specific by determining the nutritional status as well as little reproducible.

However, it is often found a nearly normal biochemical profile in eating disorder patients. So it is rarely found hypoproteinaemia, albumin is usually normal and, occasionally, they are elevated serum cholesterol levels which leads to suspicion of alterations in lipid metabolism, commonly in those with eating disorders who have amenorrhea. Also, HDL-cholesterol values are usually high while triglycerides are usually low, possibly as a result of hipoestrogenism and decreased thyroid function. Sometimes there is hypoalbuminaemia at the beginning of the re-nutrition, which must be taken into account with respect to a possible refeeding syndrome (Olveira et al., 2007; Loria & Gómez, 2010).

Normocytic and normochromic anaemia can be found in malnourished eating disorder patients. Thus, the presence of ferropenic anaemia is rare because the absence of menstruation compensates the reduced iron's intake.

Lymphopenia and thrombocytopenia can appear in severe malnourished people.

### 5.1 Proteins

It is assumed that serum proteins decrease corresponds to a decreased hepatic synthesis, which may reflect the visceral protein mass depletion. However, in the amount of serum protein, factors as the rate of metabolism, protein degradation, hydration degree, concentration and amount of extracellular fluid or in hospitalized patients, administration of serum or plasma (Bellido et al., 2002; Olveira et al., 2007) play a relevant role.

As a consequence of metabolic adaptation and body composition alterations, protein synthesis markers are not useful in the determination of the nutritional status (Loria & Gómez, 2010) in eating disorder patients.

#### 5.1.1 Albumin

Albumin measurement is a nonspecific marker of nutritional status, which does not reflect acute nutritional changes as a result of its long half-life (18-20 days) and its high body pool (4-5 g/kg).

It is considered that 2.8-3.5g/dL plasma levels reflect slight malnutrition, 2.1-2.7g/dL reflect moderate malnutrition and $<$2.1g/dL indicates severe malnutrition. However, serum albumin decreases may reflect specific pathological states or homeostatic regulations (Bellido et al., 2002; Olveira et al., 2007).

Hipoalbuminaemia is not usually found (Bellido et al., 2002;Loria & Gómez, 2010; Olveira et al., 2007) even in anorexia nervosa.

### 5.1.2 Transferrin

Transferrin is an iron transporter protein. Despite its short half-life (8-10 days) and its low plasma pool (5g) is not a good indicator of nutritional status in patients with eating disorders. Its level may be altered as a result of specific pathologies and can be found elevated in the presence of iron deficiencies and with estrogenic treatment (Bellido et al., 2002; Olveira et al., 2007).

However, it is described that plasma level of 150-175mg/dL indicates slight malnutrition, plasma level of 100-150mg/dL indicates moderate malnutrition and plasma level <100mg/dL shows severe malnutrition (Bellido et al., 2002).

### 5.1.3 Pre-albumin

Prealbumin is a protein that binds to thyroxine (T3) so that is very sensitive to metabolic stress. It has a short half-life (2-3 days) and it is considered to be a good marker of acute nutritional changes but in eating disorders it is not very useful (Bellido et al., 2002; Olveira et al., 2007).

Normal values are estimated between 17 and 20mg/dL. Therefore, levels of 10-15mg/dL would indicate slight malnutrition; levels of 5-10mg/dL would indicate moderate malnutrition; and levels <5mg/dL would reflect severe malnutrition (Bellido et al., 2002; Olveira et al., 2007).

### 5.1.4 Retinol binding protein

Retinol binding protein presents a very short half-life (10 hours), which makes it a good marker of acute nutritional changes but it is very sensitive to stress. In addition, in eating disorders it is usually altered the level of vitamin A as a result of lipid metabolism alterations, which makes retinol binding protein be an non-good indicator of nutritional status (Bellido et al., 2002; Loria & Gómez, 2010; Olveira et al., 2007).

Its short half-life makes it a marker no useful enough for clinical practice. Even so, their plasma reference values are 2.6-7.6mg/dL (Bellido et al., 2002; Olveira et al., 2007).

### 5.1.5 Insulin-like growth factor 1 (IGF1)

Insulin-like growth factor coupled with its transport protein has a half- life of 3-18 hours, which makes it to have little clinical use. It depends on human growth hormone and the energy intake levels so that its value is usually altered in eating disorders (Loria & Gómez, 2010; Olveira et al., 2007).

### 5.1.6 Creatinine/height index

Creatinine/height index would serve as muscle mass depletion indicator although it depends on the kidney and liver function and it is altered by the use of diuretics and high-protein diets, which reduces its usefulness in the nutritional evaluation of eating disorders.

It has also a little clinical use index because it is necessary the collection of 24-hour urine during 3 consecutive days and, in addition, reference tables are necessary to evaluate it (Bellido et al., 2002).

### 5.1.7 Nitrogen balance

Nitrogen balance represents the difference between the ingested and the excreted nitrogen and it is used as an indicator of protein turnover.

In a healthy subject, nitrogen balance should be equal to zero. Thus, a nitrogen balance < 0 indicates a catabolic state or an inadequate protein intake. Nitrogen balance between 0 and 5 indicates a moderate level of catabolism while less than -5 values indicates a severe degree of catabolism. However, eating disorder patients often keep high-protein diets, which may hinder this parameter's validity (Bellido et al., 2002; Olveira et al., 2007).

A predictive equation that uses the urine ureic nitrogen as total ureic nitrogen is used to calculate nitrogen balance because the real value of total ureic nitrogen is very complex. In addition, this equation does not take into account the nitrogen's lost by skin and stool which is estimated to be between 2-3g (Bellido et al., 2002; Olveira et al., 2007).

$$\text{Nitrogen balance: (ingested protein g / 6.25) – (urine urea g + 4)} \quad (12)$$

12 Bellido et al., 2002; Olveira et al., 2007

### 5.1.8 Immunity test

Some alterations with regards to the lymphocyte population and hypersensitivity have been observed in malnourished people. However, eating disorder patients rarely suffer infections till the last evolutional stages of the disease, which could be due to cortisol, cytokines and leptin alterations (Bellido et al., 2002; Loria & Gómez, 2010; Olveira et al., 2007).

#### 5.1.8.1 Account and lymphocyte function

It is considered normal a number of lymphocytes > 1500cells/mm$^3$. A lymphocytes account between 1500-1200cells/mm$^3$ could indicate a slight malnutrition. A range between 1200-800cells/mm$^3$ usually reflects a moderate malnutrition, and a severe malnutrition may be reflected by < 800cells/mm$^3$.

In addition, lymphocyte function usually decreases (Bellido et al., 2002; Loria & Gómez, 2010; Olveira et al., 2007).

#### 5.1.8.2 Delayed hypersensitivity

It is not a specific test to know the nutritional status since it can be influenced by many factors.

Delayed hypersensitivity consists of injecting different antigens intra-skinny, which the subject has been previously sensitized. The immune system acts and shows a skin's induration of > 5mm during the subsequent 24-72 hours.

In malnutrition states this reaction is committed (Bellido et al., 2002; Olveira et al., 2007).

## 6. Determination of energy requirements

Before the nutritional approach in eating disorders, it is essential to estimate the energy requirements of the subject according to his/her nutritional status (Klein et al., 2011) that would be beneficial to normalize the weight (Krahn et al., 1993).

In anorexia nervosa, the re-nutrition period is very dangerous because high energy intakes can trigger altered physiological responses, which can lead to a refeeding syndrome (Birmingham et al., 2005; Forman-Hoffman et al., 2006). Therefore, a progressively increase in the diets' energy density is required (Birmingham et al., 2005; Cuerda et al., 2005; Gentile et al., 2010; Scalfi et al., 2001; Schebendach et al., 1995).

Nutritional requirements are directly related to the basal metabolic rate, which is often diminished in anorexia nervosa and augmented in bulimia nervosa (Hlynsky et al., 2005; Nicholls et al., 2002; Russell et al., 2001; Scalfi et al., 2010; Schebendach et al., 1997; Sedlet et al., 1989). However, anorectic patients tend to present high respiratory coefficient and induced thermogenesis, which may explain the high weight reduction in emaciated patients and the difficulties to recovery and maintain a healthy weight (Russell et al., 2001).

Similarly, it is necessary to determine the energy requirements in eating disorder patients with overweight/obesity (Kushner & Drover, 2011).

There are different methods to determine the energy requirements: empirically, using predictive equations, indirect calorimetry and bioelectrical impedance (Schebendach et al., 1995).

### 6.1 Empirical method

It consists of the prescription of a well-known energy diet and it is based on the evolution of the nutritional status and the presence of symptoms related to the refeeding syndrome. Taking into account these two factors, changes in the energy density of the initially prescribed diet will be introduced.

In clinical practice this is the gold standard to determine the energy requirements (Schebendach et al., 1995). In addition, it seems the most appropriate method to determine the energy requirements to gain weight since there is no other method to quantify it (Birmingham et al., 2005). In overweight or obese patients it is usually indicated some restrictive diets because there are no specific guidelines to determine the energy requirement for the weight normalization (Kushner & Drover, 2011).

### 6.2 Predictive equations

After the empirical method to determine the energy requirements in eating disorders, this is the second most used one in clinical practice due to its speed and ease (Loria & Gómez, 2010).

Different types of predictive equations can be used, although all of them have an error rate, and only some of them have been validated to be applied in eating disorders (Kushner & Drover, 2011).

#### 6.2.1 Harris-Benedict equation

Harris-Benedict equation is used to determine the basal energy expenditure in healthy adults (BEE) expressed in kilocalories per day (Scalfi et al., 2010). This formula is not adequate to estimate the energy requirements in eating disorders, obesity or adolescents although it is the most commonly used in clinical practice (Klein et al., 2011; Scalfi et al., 2010).

It seems that this equation overestimates the energy requirements in undernourished people while it underestimates the energy requirements because eating disorder patients increase the energy requirements during re-nutrition (Cuerda et al., 2005; Krahn et al., 1993; Marra et al., 2002; Schebendach et al., 1997). It only appears to be appropriate when the weight normalization and stabilization in eating disorders (Forman-Hoffman et al., 2006).

However, even taking into account the error, its application does not seem to be very wrong (Schebendach et al., 1995).

$$\text{Men BEE: } 66.47 + [13.75 \times \text{weight (kg)}] + [5 \times \text{height (cm)}] - [6.75 \times \text{age (years)}] \quad (13)$$

$$\text{Women BEE: } 665.1 + [9.56 \times \text{weight (kg)}] + [1.85 \times \text{height (cm)}] - [4.68 \times \text{age (years)}]$$

13 Harris-Benedict equation (Loria & Gómez, 2010)

### 6.2.2 Owen equation

Owen equation appears to be appropriate to estimate the basal energy expenditure (BEE) in healthy Caucasian women and women who practice restrictive diets (Siervo et al., 2003).

It seems adequate to calculate the basal metabolic rate in anorectic patients since the beginning of treatment until the normal weight restoration (Forman-Hoffman et al., 2006).

$$\text{Men BEE: } 879 + [10.2 \times \text{weight (kg)}] \quad (14)$$

$$\text{Women BEE: } 795 + [7.18 \times \text{weight (kg)}]$$

14 Owen equation (Loria & Gómez, 2010)

### 6.2.3 Miffin-St. Joer equation

Similarly to Owen predictive equation it is appropriate to calculate the basal metabolic rate in anorexia nervosa since the beginning of treatment until several weeks of re-nutrition (Forman-Hoffman et al., 2006).

$$\text{Men BEE: } 5 + [10 \times \text{weight (kg)}] + [6.25 \times \text{height (cm)}] - [5 \times \text{age (years)}] \quad (15)$$

$$\text{Women BEE: } 161 + [10 \times \text{weight (kg)}] + [6.25 \times \text{height (cm)}] - [5 \times \text{age (years)}]$$

15 Miffin-St. Joer equation (Loria & Gómez, 2010)

### 6.2.4 World Health Organization (WHO), Food and Agriculture Organization (FAO) and United Nations Organization (ONU) equations

Like the rest of predictive equations they usually overestimate the basal energy expenditure in eating disorders (Cuerda et al., 2005; Marra et al., 2005).

### 6.2.5 Schebendach equation

It is the only equation focused on anorexia nervosa, which is a correction of the Harris-Benedict predictive equation that allow to be applied it in adolescents with anorexia nervosa. However, it is not appropriate for anorectic patients over than 18 years (Marra et al., 2005; Scalfi et al., 2010).

| Age (years) | Malnourished level | |
|---|---|---|
| | Men | Women |
| 0-3 | [60.9 x weight (kg)] - 54 | [61.0 x weight (kg)] - 51 |
| 3-10 | [22.7 x weight (kg)] + 495 | [22.5 x weight (kg)] + 499 |
| 10-18 | [17.5 x weight (kg)] + 651 | [12.2 x weight (kg)] + 746 |
| 18-30 | [15.3 x weight (kg)] + 679 | [14.7 x weight (kg)] + 496 |
| 30-60 | [11.6 x weight (kg)] + 879 | [8.7 x weight (kg)] + 829 |
| > 60 | [13.5 x weight (kg)] + 487 | [10.5 x weight (kg)] + 596 |

Table 3. Basal Energy Expenditure (kilocalories per kilogram)

$$\text{BMR (kJ/day)} = 148.3 + 91.5 \times \text{weight (kg)} \tag{16}$$

16 Schebendach equation (Scalfi et al., 2001)

### 6.3 Indirect calorimetry

Indirect calorimetry is a non-invasive and low-cost method used to determine the basal metabolic rate that provides information to raise an adequate nutritional intervention and monitoring eating disorder patients (Dragani et al., 2006; Hlynsky et al., 2005; Scalfi et al., 2010; Schebendach et al., 1995).

It is appropriate for both patients with anorexia nervosa and with bulimia nervosa, as well as for binge eating disorder patients (Cuerda et al., 2005; Schebendach et al., 1995).

In addition, the continuous metabolic changes faced by people with eating disorders justify the use of this method (Schebendach et al., 1997). Furthermore the additional use of anthropometric measurements allows the adaption of the nutritional therapy to the patient's evolution (Dragani et al., 2006).

### 6.4 Bioelectrical impedance

Bioelectrical impedance is appropriate to calculate the basal metabolic rate in anorexia nervosa taking into account its limitations as a result of hydration alterations (Marra et al., 2005).

## 7. Food choice in eating disorder patients and relatives

### 7.1 Food choice in eating disorders

It is difficult to learn about eating habits in eating disorder patients especially because the usual data collection system has been based on the amount of intake and not on the quality of the food choice in these people (Banna et al., 2010). Nowadays, a low nutritional variety is associated with a poor prognosis of the pathology (Loria et al., 2009; Schebendach et al., 2008; Steinhausen et al., 2002).

One analysis of the dietary choice in patients with eating disorders shows a trend to choice little varied, low energy density menus with protein excess and fat deficiencies (Jáuregui & Bolaños, 2009; Loria et al., 2009; Loria & Gómez, 2010; Schebendach et al., 2008; Steinhausen et al., 2002).

It seems that people with anorexia nervosa tend to maintain certain dietary behaviors and to modify others following the usual patterns of the socio-cultural context (Jáuregui & Bolaños, 2009).

Moreover, there are differences in the intake of the different food groups. It seems that people with bulimia nervosa choose less bread and cereals than patients with anorexia nervosa, although people with anorexia nervosa choose less bread, cereals, meat, sausages, fatty, and fried foods, than people without eating disorders do (Jáuregui & Bolaños, 2009; van der Ster Wallin et al., 1995).

### 7.2 Relatives food choice's influence in eating disorder patients

Originally relationship between family and eating disorders has been studied on the basis of family relationships and family structures or genetics. However, it is increasingly more remarkable that food attitudes, implementation of physical activity and self-care, even health knowledge in relatives influence directly on behaviour and cognitions in their children (Hendrie et al., 2011).

Eating habits, as well as different foods tastes start to develop since the early childhood. It is believed that babies are born with a natural ability to control intake depending on their energy needs. This ability is developed and maintained over time through adequate education and training, however, it is lost when the baby is not able to learn to distinguish hunger and satiety sensations. For example while artificial bottled eating (Gregory et al., 2010; Ruiz, 2011; Savage et al., 2007).

Furthermore, parents act as a behavioral eating pattern (modelling) for their children, being responsible to choose different foods, elaborate and provide them while feeding and socialize the child in the eating behaviour, which should be maintain during its lifetime. So parents influence children's future preferences. So similar food preferences and intakes characteristics are distinguished between mothers and their children as discovering more frequently daughters that make energy restrictive diets when their mothers are chronic dieters and intake's control problems in daughters whom parents also have (Brunstrom et al., 2005; Ruiz, 2011). It seems that when children are overweight or obese their parents act restricting and controlling their feeding thus promoting hidden intakes in the absence of hunger (Faith et al., 2008).

In this way, certain emotional relations with food appear depending on the mother's behavior and displays of affection received by the mother from breastfeeding. Even more it seems as negative factors in the eating disorders development, those families, which give too much importance to weight, caloric intake value, families where one parent is a chronic dieter, those in which parents have intake's control problems and those with unstructured meals (Ruiz, 2011).

Emotional eating is a complex set of behaviors and cognitions involved in the development and maintenance of eating disorders (Ricca et al, 2011).

Benefits of relatives' inclusion in the treatment of patients with eating disorders are well described in order to provide them with strategies for management of the pathology and as support in the acquisition of new habits of life (Cairns et al., 2007; Ruiz, 2011; Treasure et al.,

2011). However, it have not been studied the benefits of carrying out nutritional education and healthy habits acquisition in relatives of eating disorder patients (Ruiz, 2011).

Generally, relatives' food choice trend to be low caloric diets with protein and fat excess but carbohydrate deficiency. Lipid profile in dietary choice of relatives of eating disorder patients seems to be unbalanced, with saturated and monounsaturated fatty acids excess, cholesterol excess and polyunsaturated and essential fatty acids deficiency. In addition, it presents under contribution to the requirements of calcium, magnesium, zinc, iodine, fluorine, folic acid and vitamin D and does not comply with the recommendations of food consumption frequency. This shows that dietary choice of relatives of patients with eating disorder does not constitute a healthy food choice pattern (Ruiz, 2011).

Nevertheless, it should be taken into account that food choice depends on the population and more studies are needed to obtain more consistency data.

## 8. Questionnaires

The difficulty of collecting information about food habits and cognitions justify the use of questionnaires (Olveira et al., 2007).

### 8.1 24-hour dietary recall

The 24-hour dietary recall is the most used method for the current intake's nutritional evaluation as its ease and low cost needs to implementation (Greger & Etnyre, 1978; Yago et al., 2002). Generally, it requests the patient to fill out the survey with all the food eaten and beverages drank during the last 24 hours.

It provides information on the amount, type of food consumed, elaborating methods used, ingredients of the dish made and hours of consumption to know the intakes' structure (Anselmo et al., 1995; Yago et al., 2002).

Nevertheless, it must be noted that the reliability of this questionnaire is affected by the memory capacity of the patients, its capacity of description and its concern about the intake so that greater attention paid to food greater capacity to complete the questionnaire adequately. The 24-hours dietary recall is usually fulfilled by mothers, in case of children under 12 years old (Anselmo et al., 1995).

If the patients know previously that it is going to make this questionnaire and the presence of the interviewer may vary the characteristics of the diet written down so it results somewhat healthier than it was, really. Foods most frequently omitted in the 24-hour recall are sauces and condiments.

It is very important that the interviewer is trained in nutrition especially to estimate the ingested quantities.

Advantages of 24-hour recall are that it does not modify the usual intake of the respondent and that it is a fast, simple, low-cost method, as it requires little effort by the respondent. However, it does not provide information about eating habits since it only includes one day and depends on the ability of memory and expression capacity of the patient. The 24-hour recall shows a higher energy intake than the real although its adequacy to the real intake is intermediate between that reflects the dietary record and food frequency intake's questionnaire (Prentice et al., 2011). It is a validated nutritional assessment method but the estimation of nutrient intake should not be based on it (Greger & Etnyre, 1978).

The less reliable data obtained from the 24-hour recall is the portion of food intake, vegetables being the worst reflected amounts (Souverein et al., 2011). In addition, the amount of intake often appears overestimated in malnourished children (Anselmo et al., 1995).

### 8.2 Dietary record

The dietary record consists of writing down the meals and drinks ingested over a period of time ranging from 1 to 7 days. Data should be described carefully and completely, structured in five meals per day and including all the food used in the preparation of a dish. In this way, the dietary record shows the food frequency consumption, meals' structures, diet variety and quality of dietary choice (Yago et al., 2002).

The ingested amounts can be estimated by different methods. It can be estimated by double weight, in explain weigh food to eat and then weigh leftovers. Also, the amount of food intake can be estimated by recording the usually cooking measurement used, in example a spoon, a plate, a saucepan, or a ladle (Yago et al., 2002).

In anorexia nervosa the dietary record shows a higher energy intake than real but it reflects properly lipid and caloric profile and micronutrient consumption (Hadigan et al., 2000). Food attitudes affect the appropriateness of the dietary record's registration. Thus, in obese people that restrict their food intake the questionnaire shows lower energy than the real while it resembles reality in those with emotional intake or large numbers of intakes away from home, in restaurants (Vansant & Hulens, 2006). Furthermore, women's dietary records show lower energy intake than real more frequently than men (Asbeck et al., 2002).

Nonetheless, the weekly intake registered in the dietary record fits adequate with the energy requirements obtained by indirect calorimetry (Vansant & Hulens, 2006).

During childhood, the reliability of the dietary records is related with the cognitive ability, and girls usually have greater skill at any age, probably by being more aware with food (Smith et al., 2011).

The advantages of this questionnaire are the possibility of nutritional current intake assessment and knowledge of the nutritional habits. Disadvantages are the potential bias made in the implementation of the register, the requirement of a high collaboration and the possibility of habits' modification (all proving that the intake must be evaluated by a professional). Double weighing registration requires a high effort but is the most exact while the estimate record there may be an error in the estimation (Gil et al., 2002).

### 8.3 Food frequency questionnaires

A food frequency questionnaire aims to obtain the frequency of consumption of the different foods or groups of them.

It does not offer quantitative information about the intake, nor provides knowledge about the eating habits of the person who complete the questionnaire (Taylor et al., 2009).

However, it provides global information referring to large periods of intake (Yago et al., 2002).

Anyway, the questionnaire can be quantitative when moreover to frequency of consumption it shows the amount of food ingested, semi-quantitative when the list of foods expresses the amount of the ration or qualitative which does not include the amount of food or portion size (Yago et al., 2002). Of all the most used is the semi-quantitative food frequency questionnaire which is suitable for groups of food consumption (Vázquez et al., 2011).

Some of the advantages of this questionnaire are its low cost, the short time required to complete it, the ease of encoding data and, finally the fact that it does not change the eating habits of the patient. However, its reliability depends on the memory and synthesis capacity of the user and the information provided is limited because it depends on the list of foods that the questionnaire presents. Nevertheless, this list of foods also provides an advantage because one can select groups or types of food on the basis of the nutrient or nutrients on which want to get more information. For this reason, this type of questionnaires must always be validated (Yago et al., 2002).

One of the most important aspects in the nutritional treatment of patients with anorexia nervosa is to ensure an adequate consumption of calcium and vitamin D to encourage correct bone mineralization improving or preventing the onset of osteopenia. In relation to this, a questionnaire of frequency of food intake that determines the amount of calcium and vitamin D in these patients has been validated (Taylor et al., 2009).

In clinical practice, a way to obtain reliable and complete information about the patient's intake is to combine data obtained through a questionnaire of frequency food intake, with a 24-hour dietary recall and various nutritional markers which are mentioned above (Freedman et al., 2011).

### 8.4 Food craving inventory

The experience of the craving involves behavioural and emotional aspects as well as cognitive. So it would be the feeling of a high desire to eat a certain type or group of food with great difficulty to resist (Jáuregui et al., 2010).

This feeling is very present in eating disorders and appears to be related with other psychopathological aspects like depression or anxiety issues. However, craving should not be understood as a feeling characteristic of eating disorders because it appears in the general population.

Even so, craving has been related to the presence of bulimia nervosa or purging-type eating disorders. Correlating the food craving inventory with other eating disorder inventories one gets relationship between craving and bulimia, although it must be taken into account that not all people who crave manifest overeating episodes. It is appropriate to use the food craving inventory in patients with obesity and binge eating disorder who shows greater desire for sweet food (White & Grilo, 2005).

Craving relates to bulimia nervosa, binge eating disorder or obesity. Moreover it is associated with premenstrual syndrome and seasonal affective disorder. Also, food craving inventory correlates with a high concern about weigh, awareness-raising by the food restriction, fear of gaining weight and body dissatisfaction which are characteristic factors of eating disorders (Jáuregui et al., 2010).

Data obtained in relation to restrictive diets and hunger with presence of craving are ambiguous, existing studies that confirm the relationship while others finding it not to exist (Jáuregui et al., 2010).

Then, women experience more craving than men although there are differences in the type of food they desire. Thus, women show greater attraction for sweets and *-trans* fats which is especially observed in foods such as chocolate, while men prefer high caloric density food or fast food and saturated fat. There are no differences according to sex in the attraction of carbohydrates and proteins.

The Spanish version of the Food Craving Inventory has undergone some changes in the list of foods and food types deleted because they were not object of craving in that socio-cultural context (Jáuregui et al., 2010).

### 8.5 Irrational food beliefs scale

The irrational food beliefs scale measures cognitive distortions, attitudes and unhealthy beliefs in relation to food (Osberg et al., 2008). These cognitions and behaviors are associated to thoughts about weight or body image and related to phobias, stress and internalization of the current body aesthetic model (excessively thin), all present in eating disorders. Furthermore, these cognitions help to keep the intake of low-calorie diets as a means to regulate weight and food intake (Jáuregui & Bolaños, 2010).

The questionnaire has two factors, one of irrational beliefs associated with cognitive distortions, beliefs and attitudes to food altered and one of rational beliefs which is associated with healthy eating based on recommendations of current nutritional guidelines (Jáuregui & Bolaños, 2010).

Irrational food beliefs are associated to bulimic symptoms like overeating or impulses control as well as the realization of low-calorie diets in obese population (Jáuregui & Bolaños, 2010; Osberg et al., 2008).

### 8.6 Food choice questionnaire

The acquisition of healthy eating habits begins in a good food choice. Socio-cultural level influence food choice as well as personal preferences so it will influence food choice, the inhabited country, ethical aspects, socio-economic level or sensory aspects of food, among other things.

The presence of psychopathology affects the food choice and it is related to a higher level of irrational ideas relative to food. As greater irrational ideas related to food greater ready-to-eat food would be chosen. Concern about weight, tendency to have a muscular body low in fat and preference for low energy density foods does not appear only in women as men show great concern for that which shows that cultural qualities influence food choice.

### 8.7 Eating attitudes test

The objective of the Eating Attitudes Test is to know attitudes relative to food in patients with anorexia nervosa.

The original version features 40 items while there is an abbreviated version of 26 items, which has a high correlation with the original (Castro et al., 1991; Garner & Garfinkel, 1979; Garner et al., 1982; Mateos et al., 2010; Orbitello et al., 2006).

This questionnaire shows high specificity and sensitivity to recognize people with characteristics of anorexia nervosa or bulimia nervosa although it is not sensitive to distinguish between anorexia nervosa and bulimia nervosa (Castro et al., 1991; Garner & Garfinkel, 1979; Garner et al., 1982).

However, it shows three main factors, one shows food restriction and does not display differences between anorexia nervosa and bulimia nervosa. A second factor indicates bulimia and concern for food, and a third factor reflects self-control related to food and perception of social concern about weight gain. It seems that people with anorexia nervosa score lowest in factor 2 and highest in factor 3 than people with bulimia nervosa (Castro et al., 1991; Garner et al., 1979; Garner et al., 1982).

An advantage of this questionnaire is the sensitivity to symptomatic changes reaching normal scores in patients who suffered anorexia nervosa and that do not currently suffer (Castro et al., 1991; Garner et al., 1979; Garner et al., 1982).

## 9. Difficulties in the registration of the ingested food quantities and knowledge of dietary habits: new technologies

One of the most difficult data to obtain reliably with the food survey is the amount of food ingested. There are various methods to estimate the food quantity consumed although there is not an ideal measure.

The use of standardized rations is not appropriate because it depends on the geographical area and even in the cooking utensils employed in each house (Yago et al., 2002).

Usually the amount of food ingested has been estimated through cooking utensils employed, in example spoon, plate, glass, and so on. And then, a professional trained in the field of food is responsible for estimating the real amount ingested. So it is a method of very low-cost and easy but unreliable especially in eating disorders where the ingested amounts are very altered (Yago et al., 2002).

Another method is the uses of 3D models or measurement photographs but these is not appropriate in clinical practice and less in eating disorders taking into account the difficulties in their perception of the amount of food (Yago et al., 2002).

Estimate the amount consumed in grams by the person is not valid in the nutritional survey insofar it is usually an elevated error in the estimation (Yago et al., 2002).

Double weighing method, in explain, weighing food to served on the plate before eating and then weigh the leftovers, is very reliable. However, it is not recommended for patients with eating disorders, which are already quite concerned about the amount and volume of food they eat. Furthermore, it is a costly method by the time it requires (Loria & Gómez, 2010; Yago et al., 2002).

Nonetheless, it is complex to collect information on the personal eating habits since methods of collecting information, in example the dietary record always have an error that they depend on the capabilities of the person who completes it (Matthiessen et al., 2011).

Currently, the reliability of the data collected increases in terms of amount of food ingested and eating habits through the use of digital photography and video.

The combination of estimating dietary record with digital photographs of meals, before and after eating them to assess the amount served and leftovers, is a suitable method to learn about eating habits of the person and it has shown internal reliability (Matthiessen et al., 2011).

Moreover, displaying behaviors and reactions, both of people suffering from eating disorders as of their families, are very helpful when it comes to know eating habits and behaviors altered during meals. It could prove helpful in guiding the nutritional treatment of patients with eating disorders (Cairns et al., 2007).

## 10. Conclusions

Nutritional evaluation consists of data collection to determine the nutritional status of the patient.

The knowledge of the malnutrition's characteristics permits to evaluate the impact in the organism of the unhealthy diet patterns in eating disorders, as well as to determine the nutritional requirements for a proper physical recovery.

However, there is no ideal nutritional status assessment's method as it is recommended to compare different systems.

Nevertheless, it should be taken into account that the more number of methods used are, the more will be the time and cost to complete the nutritional evaluation of the patient.

Summarising, the information collecting methods should be chosen according to their real possibilities but getting as more information as possible in order to make the nutritional treatment individualized and more effective.

Therefore, a complete medical history is essential to obtain information about the patient. It should include personal data, personal medical history, family medical history, nutritional interview and it should be focused on the eating disorders diagnostic criteria as bulimic episodes, compensatory behaviours, physical activity, weight history, menstrual history, psychosocial history and illness knowledge.

However, medical history would provide subjective information so physical examination and body composition measurements are needed to complete the nutritional evaluation.

Physical examination is based in well-known clinical signs and medical complications caused by unhealthy diets. It depends on the age and sex of the patient even the severity of the pathology and the type of malnutrition. In anorexia nervosa malnutrition is usually marasmus because of the daily energy intake restriction.

Body composition measurements are difficult and anthropometric measurements or body composition sophisticated systems can be applied.

Anthropometric measurements are skin folds and body perimeters measures that provide information on the nutritional status of the patient by comparing its values with reference tables or by predictive equations. Eating disorders deal with the problem that malnutrition influences the determination of the physical parameters and neither reference tables nor predictive equations are validated in such people.

Body Mass Index is one of the anthropometric measures more used in clinical practice because its ease to do. Nonetheless, it is a little sensitive measure of malnutrition and it is not adequate in people under 18 years old. Tricipital skin fold is also very used in the clinical practice.

In eating disorder patients bone mineral densitometry is necessary to know the mineralization state of the bones and to monitoring the bone mass recovering.

It results ambiguous the use or not of bioelectrical impedance in the body composition determination in eating disorders. However, it should make the same error rate than anthropometric measures and it is easily to realize. Nevertheless, multi-frequency phase-sensitive bioelectrical impedance seems to be adequate in eating disorders because it deal with hydrolytic alterations of these patients.

There are other body composition measurement methods but they are not used in clinical practice because of their high cost.

Laboratory analyses are not very proper nutritional evaluation markers because it is usually found an almost normal biochemical profile in eating disorder patients.

Something else in the nutritional evaluation of eating disorder patients is the energy requirements' determination. The empirical method is the most used in clinical practice followed by predictive equations methods. However, there are no predictive equations validated in eating disorders, except the Schebendach, but it is only validated in adolescents with anorexia nervosa. Furthermore, there are no predictive equations to know the energy requirements to gain or lose weight, if it is necessary.

Indirect calorimetry is a good method to know the basal metabolic rate in eating disorders and multi-frequency phase-sensitive bioelectrical impedance is a good predictor in anorexia nervosa.

Nowadays, it is not only important to know the intake quantity. The quality of food choice is a good profile marker in eating disorders. Moreover, parental eating behaviours may affect the nutritional choice and preferences of their children so it would be appropriate to know about the eating habits in relatives of patients.

To complete the nutritional evaluation, some questionnaires providing information on the amount and type of food eaten, presence and intensity of craving and irrational food beliefs are used in eating disorder patients. The same applies to attitudes relative to food in anorexia nervosa patients.

Finally, the combination of 24-hour recall, dietary record and questionnaire of frequency of food intake besides digital photograph and video provides reliably information about the amount of food ingested and eating habits.

## 11. Acknowledgement

I would like to thank Ignacio Jáuregui for his excellent teaching methods focused in eating disorders as well as patients and their relatives for allow me to learn more and more about these disorders.

## 12. References

Allen, KL., Fursland, A., Watson, H. & Byrne, SM. (2011). Eating disorder diagnoses in general practice settings: comparison with structured clinical interview and self-report questionnaires. *Journal of Mental Health*, Vol.20, No.3, pp. 270-280, ISSN 1360-0567

Anselmo, Mt., Gomes, C., Barros, FC. & Petrucci D. (1995). Twenty-four-hour recall overestimates the dietary intake of malnourished children. *The Journal of nutrition*, Vol.125, No.4, (April 1995) pp.880-884, ISSN 1541-6100

Asbeck, I., Mast, M., Bierwag, A., Westenhöfer, J., Acheson, KJ., Müller, MJ. (2002). Severe underreporting of energy intake in normal weight subjects: use of an appropriate standard and relation to restrained eating. *Public health nutrition*, Vol.5, No.5, (October 2002) pp. 683-690, ISSN 1475-2727

Banna, JC., Vera, LE., Kaiser, LL. & Townsend, MS. (2010). Using qualitative methods to improve questionnaires for Spanish speakers: assessing face validity of a food behavior checklist. *Journal of the American Dietetic Association,* Vol.110, No.1, (January 2010) pp.80-90, ISSN 1878-3570

Bellido, D., Carreira, J. & Martínez, M. (2002). Análisis de la composición corporal, In: *Tratado de Nutrición*, Gil, A., pp. 149-192, Editorial Panamericana, ISBN 84-88336-43-8, España

Birmingham, CL., Hlynsky, J., Whiteside, L. & Geller, J. (2005). Caloric requirement for refeeding inpatients with anorexia nervosa: the contribution of anxiety exercise, and cigarette smoking. *Eating and weight disorders*, Vol.10, No.1, (March 2005) pp. e6-9, ISSN 1590-1262

Birmingham, CL., Jones, PJ., Orphanidou, C., Bakan, R., Cleator, IG., Goldner, EM. & Phang, PT. (1996). The reliability of bioelectrical impedance analysis for measuring changes in the body composition of patients with anorexia nervosa. *The International journal of eating disorders*, Vol.19, No.3, (August 1996) pp. 311-315, ISSN 1098-108X

Bratland-Sanda, S., Sundgot-Borgen, J., Rosenvinge, JH., Hoffart, A. & Martinsen, EW. (2010). "I'm not physically active - I only go for walks": physical activity in patients with longstanding eating disorders. *The International journal of eating disorders*,Vol.43, No.1, (January 2010) pp. 88-92, ISSN 1098-108X

Brunstrom, JM., Mitchell, GL. & Baguley, TS. (2005). Potential early-life predictors of dietary behaviour in adulthood: a retrospective study. *International journal of obesity*, Vol.29, No.5, (May 2005) pp. 463-474, ISSN 1476-5497

Cairns, JC., Styles, LD. & Leichner, P. (2007). Evaluation of meal support training for parents and caregivers using a video and a manual. *Journal of the Canadian Academy of Child and Adolescent Psychiatry*, Vol.16, No.4, (November 2007) pp. 164-166, ISSN 1719-8429

Carrard, I., Crépin, C., Rouget, P., Lam, T., Golay, A. & van der Linden, M. (2011). Randomised controlled trial of a guided self-help treatment on the Internet for binge eating disorder. *Behaviour research and therapy*, Vol.49, No.8, (August 2011), pp. 482-491, ISSN 1873-622X

Castro, J., Lázaro, L., Pons, F., Halperin, I. & Toro, J. Predictors of bone mineral density reduction in adolescents with anorexia nervosa. *Journal of the American Academy of Child and Adolescent Psychiatry*, Vol.39, No.11, (November 2000) pp. 1365-1370, ISSN 1527-5418

Castro, J., Toro, J., Lázaro, L., Pons, F. & Halperin, I. (2002). Bone mineral density in male adolescents with anorexia nervosa. *Journal of the American Academy of Child and Adolescent Psychiatry*, Vol.41, No.5, (May 2002) pp. 613-618, ISSN 1527-5418

Castro, J., Toro, J., Salamero, M. & Guimera, E. (1991). The Eating Attitudes Test: Validation of the Spanish version. *Psychological assessment*, Vol.7, No.2, pp. 175-190, ISSN 1040-3590

Chou, SH., Chamberland, JP., Liu, X., Matarese, G., Gao, C., Stefanakis, R., Brinkoetter, MT., Gong, H., Arampatzi, K. & Mantzoros, CS. (2011). Leptin is an effective treatment for hypothalamic amenorrhea. *Proceedings of the National Academy of Sciences of the United States of America*, Vol.108, No.16, (April 2011) pp. 6585-6590, ISSN 1091-6490

Cuerda, MC., Ruiz, A., Moreno, C., Iriondo, MT., Velasco, C., Bretón, I., Camblor, M. & García, P. (2005). Study of energy expenditure in anorexia nervosa: agreement between indirect calorimatry and several equations. *Nutrición hospitalaria*, Vol.20, No.6, (November-December 2005) pp. 371-377, ISSN 1699-5198

DiVasta, AD., Ringelheim, J., Bristol, SK., Feldman, HA. & Gordon, CM. (2007). Skeletal measurements by quantitative ultrasound in adolescents and young women with anorexia nervosa. *The Journal of pediatrics*,Vol.150, No.3, (March 2007) pp. 286-290, ISSN 1097-6833

Dragani, B., Malatesta, G., Di Ilio, C. & De Cristofarok P. (2006). Dynamic monitoring of restricted eating disorders by indirect calorimetry: a useful cognitive approach. *Eating and weight disorders*, Vol.11, No.1, (March 2006) pp. e9-14, ISSN 1590-1262

Faith, MS., Storey, M., Kral, TV. & Pietrobelli, A. (2008). The feeding demands questionnaire: assessment of parental demand cognitions concerning parent-child feeding relations. *Journal of the American Dietetic Association*, Vol.108, No.4, (April 2008) pp. 624-630, ISSN 1878-3570

Forman-Hoffman, VL., Ruffin, T. & Schultz, SK. (2006). Basal metabolic rate in anorexia nervosa patients: using appropriate predictive equations during the refeeding process. *Annals of clinical psychiatry*, Vol.18, No.2, (April-June 2006) pp. 123-127, ISSN 1547-3325

Freedman, LS., Schatzkin, A., Midthune, D. & Kipnis, V. (2011). Dealing with dietary measurement error in nutritional cohort studies. *Journal of the National Cancer Institute*, Vol.103, No.14, (June 2011) pp. 1086-1092, ISSN 1460-2105

Garner, DM. & Garfinkel, PE. (1979). The Eating Attitudes Test: an index of the symptoms of anorexia nervosa. *Psycholycal Medicine*, Vol.9, No.22, pp. 273-279, ISSN 0033-2917

Garner, DM., Olmsted, MP., Bohr, Y. & Garfinkel, PE. (1982). The Eating Attitudes Test: psychometric features and clinical correlates. *Psychological Medicine*, Vol.12, pp. 871-8, ISSN 0033-2917

Gentile, MG., Pastorelli, P., Ciceri, R., Manna, GM. & Collimedaglia, S. (2010). Specialized refeeding treatment for anorexia nervosa patients suffering from extreme undernutrition. *Clinical nutrition*, Vol.29, No.5, (October 2010) pp. 627-632, ISSN 1532-1983

Greger, JL. & Etnyre, GM. (1978). Validity of 24-hour dietary recalls by adolescent females. *American journal of public health*, Vol.68, No.1, (January 1978) pp. 70-72, ISSN 1541-0048

Gregory, JE., Paxton, SJ. & Brozovic, AM. (2010). Maternal feeding practices, child eating behavior and body mass index in preschool-aged children:a prospective analysis. *International Journal of Behavioral Nutrition and Physical Activity*, Vol.28, No.7 (June 2010) pp. 55, ISSN 1479-5868

Haas, VK., Kohn, MR., Clarke, SD., Allen, JR., Madden, S., Müller, MJ. & Gaskin, KJ. (2009). Body composition changes in female adolescents with anorexia nervosa. *The American journal of clinical nutrition*, Vol.89, No.4, (April 2009) pp. 1005-1010, ISSN 1938-3207

Hadigan, CM., Anderson, EJ., Miller, KK., Hubbard, JL., Herzog, DB., Klibanski, A. & Grinspoon, SK. (2000). Assessment of macronutrient and micronutrient intake in women with anorexia nervosa. *The International journal of eating disorders*, Vol.28, No.3, (November 2000) pp. 284-292, ISSN 1098-108X

Hannan, WJ., Cowen, S., Freeman, CP. & Shapiro, CM. (1990). Evaluation of bioelectrical impedance analysis for body composition measurements in anorexia nervosa. *Clinical physics and physiological measurement*, Vol.11, No.3, (August 1990) pp. 209-216, ISSN 0143-0815

Hendrie, GA., Coveney, J. & Cox, DN. (2011). Defining the complexity of childhood obesity and related behaviours within the family environment using structural equation modeling. *Public health nutrition*, Vol.2, (August 2011) pp. 1-10, ISSN 1475-2727

Hlynsky J, Birmingham CL, Johnston M, Gritzner S. (2005). The agreement between the MedGem indirect calorimeter and a standard indirect calorimeter in anorexia nervosa. *Eating and weight disorders*, Vol.10, No.4, (December 2005) pp. e83-87, ISSN 1590-1262

Huang, CM. & Hsieh, CJ. (2010). Treating bulimia nervosa: a nurse's experience using cognitive behavior therapy. *Hu li za zhi The Journal of Nursing*, Vol.57, No.2, (April 2010) pp. S29-34, ISSN 0047-262X

Jáuregui, I. & Bolaños, P. (2009). Choice of diet in patients with anorexia nervosa. *Nutrición Hospitalaria*, Vol.24, No.6, (May 2009) pp. 682-687, ISSN 0212-1611

Jáuregui, I. & Bolaños, P. (2010). Spanish version of the irrational food beliefs scale. *Nutrición Hospitalaria*, Vol.25, No.5, pp. 852-859, ISSN 0212-1611

Jáuregui, I. (2006). *La imagen de una sociedad enferma: anorexia, bulimia, atracones y obesidad* (1st Ed.), Grafema, ISBN 84-934225-9-2, España

Jáuregui, I., Bolaños, P., Carbonero, R. & Valero, E. (2010). Psychometric properties of the Spanish version of Food Craving Inventory (FCI-SP). *Nutrición Hospitalaria*, Vol.25, No.6, pp. 984-992, ISSN 0212-1611

Jen, N. & Yan, AC. (2010). Syndromes associated with nutritional deficiency and excess. *Clinics in dermatology*, Vol.26, No.6, (November-December 2010), pp. 669-685, ISSN 1879-1131

Kehoe, SH., Krishnaveni, GV., Lubree, HG., Wills, AK., Guntupalli, AM., Veena, SR., Bhat, DS., Kishore, S., Fall, CH., Yajnik, CS. & Kurpad, A. (2011). Prediction of body-fat percentage from skinfold and bio-impedance measurements in Indian school children. *European journal of clinical nutrition*, (July 2011) ISSN 1476-5640

Kerruish, KP., O'Connor, J., Humphries, IR., Kohn, MR., Clarke, SD., Briody, JN., Thompson, EJ., Wright, KA., Gaskin, KJ. & Baur, LA. (2002). Body composition in adolescents with anorexia nervosa. *The American journal of clinical nutrition*, Vol.75, No.1, (January 2002) pp. 31-37, ISSN 1938-3207

Killen, JD., Taylor, CB., Telch, MJ., Saylor, KE., Maron, DJ. & Robinson, DN. (1986). Self-induced vomiting and laxative and diuretic use among teenagers. Precursors of the binge-purge syndrome?. *The journal of the American Medical Association*, Vol.255, No.11, (March 1986) pp. 1447-1449, ISSN 1538-3598

Klein, CJ., Villavicencio, SA., Schweitzer, A., Bethepu, JS., Hoffman, HJ. & Mirza, NM. (2011). Energy prediction equations are inadequate for obese Hispanic youth. *Journal of the American Dietetic Association*, Vol.111, No.8, (August 2011) pp. 1204-1210, ISSN 1878-3570

Kontic, O., Vasiljevic, N., Jorga, J., Jasovic-Gasic, M., Lakic, A. & Arsic, A. (2010). Presence of different forms of compensatory behaviours among eating disorder patients. *Srpski arhiv za celokupno lekarstvo*, Vol.138, No.5-6, (May-June 2010) pp. 328-332, ISSN 0370-8179

Krahn, DD., Rock, C., Dechert, RE., Nairn, KK. & Hasse, SA. (1993). Changes in resting energy expenditure and body composition in anorexia nervosa patients during refeeding. *Journal of the American Dietetic Association*, Vol.93, No.4, (April 1993) pp. 434-438, ISSN 1878-3570

Kushner, RF. & Drover, JW. (2011). Current Strategies of Critical Care Assessment and Therapy of the Obese Patient (Hypocaloric Feeding): What Are We Doing and What Do We Need to Do?. *Journal of parenteral and enteral nutrition*, Vol.1, (August 2011), ISSN 0148-6071

Lama, RA., Codoceo, RE. & Morais, A. (2002). Valoración del estado nutricional en el niño, In: *Tratado de Nutrición*, Gil, A., pp. 81-116, Editorial Panamericana, ISBN 84-88336-43-8 , España

Loria, V. & Gómez, C. (2010). *Manual teórico-práctico de Educación Nutricional en Trastornos de la Conducta Alimentaria* (1st Ed.), EDIMSA, ISBN 978-84-7714-337-6, Madrid, España

Loria, V., Gómez, C., Lourenço, T., Pérez, A., Castillo, R., Villarino, M., Bermejo, L. & Zurita, L. (2009). Evaluation of the utility of a Nutrition Education Program with Eating Disorders. *Nutrición Hospitalaria*, Vol.24, No.5, (September-October 2009) pp. 558-567, ISSN 1699-5198

Marra, M., De Filippo, E., Signorini, A., Silvestri, E., Pasanisi, F., Contaldo, F. & Scalfi, L. (2005). Phase angle is a predictor of basal metabolic rate in female patients with anorexia nervosa. *Physiological measurement*, Vol.26, No.2, (April 2005) pp. S145-152, ISSN 1361-6579

Marra, M., Polito, A., De Filippo, E., Cuzzolaro, M., Ciarapica, D., Contaldo, F. & Scalfi, L. (2002). Are the general equations to predict BMR applicable to patients with anorexia nervosa? *Eating and weight disorders*, Vol.7, No.1, (March 2002) pp. 53-59, ISSN 1590-1262

Mateos-Padorno, C., Scoffier, S., Polifrone, M., Martínez-Patiño, MJ., Martínez-Vidal, A. & Zagalaz, ML. (2010). Analysis of eating disorders among 12-17 year-old adolescents in the island of Gran Canaria. *Eating and weight disorders*, Vol.15, No.3, (September 2010) pp. e190-194, ISSN 1590-1262

Matthiessen, TB., Steinberg, FM. & Kaiser, LL. (2011). Convergent validity of a digital image-based food record to assess food group intake in youth. *Journal of the American Dietetic Association*, Vol.111, No.5, (May 2011) pp. 756-761, ISSN 1878-3570

Mehler, PS., Cleary, BS. & Gaudiani, JL. (2011). Osteoporosis in anorexia nervosa. *Eating disorders*, Vol.19, No.2, (March 2011) pp.194-202, ISSN 1532-530X

Miján, A., Pérez-García, A., Martín, E. & de Mateo, B. (2006).Is an integral nutritional approach to eating disorders feasible in primary care? *British Journal of Nutrition*, Vol.96, No.1, (August 2006), pp.82-85, ISSN 0007-1145

Mika, C., Herpertz-Dahlmann, B., Heer, M. & Holtkamp, K. (2004). Improvement of nutritional status as assessed by multifrequency BIA during 15 weeks of refeeding in adolescent girls with anorexia nervosa. *The Journal of nutrition*, Vol.134, No.11, (November 2004) pp. 3026-3030, ISSN 1541-6100

Misra, M. & Klibanski, A. (2010). Neuroendocrine consequences of anorexia nervosa in adolescents. *Endocrine development*, Vol.24, No. 17, (November 2010) pp. 197-214, ISSN 1662-2979

Mocanu, V., Zbranca, E., Colev, V. & Estour, B. (1997). An analysis of the evolution of body compartments in anorexia nervosa--the bioelectrical impedance method. *Revista medico-chirurgicală a Societății de Medici și Naturaliști din Iași*, Vol.101, No.3-4, (July-December 1997) pp. 83-90, ISSN 0048-7848

Nicholls, D., Wells, JD., Singhal, A. & Stanhope, R. (2002). Body composition in early onset eating disorders. *European journal of clinical nutrition*, Vol.52, No.9, (September 2002) pp. 857-865, ISSN 1476-5640

Olveira, G. (2nd Ed.). (2007). *Manual de Nutrición Clínica y Dietética*, Ediciones Díaz de Santos, ISBN 978-84-7978-806-3, España

Orbitello, B., Ciano, R., Corsaro, M., Rocco, PL., Taboga, C., Tonutti, L., Armellini, M. & Balestrieri, M. (2006). The EAT-26 as screening instrument for clinical nutrition unit attenders. *International journal of obesity*, Vol.30, No.6, (June 2006) pp. 977-981, ISSN 1476-5497

Osberg, TM., Poland, D., Aguayo, G. & MacDougall, S. (2008). The Irrational Food Beliefs Scale: development and validation. *Eating behaviors*, Vol.9, No.1, (January 2008) pp. 25-40, ISSN 1873-7358

Piccoli, A., Codognotto, M., Di Pascoli, L., Boffo, G. & Caregaro, L. (2005). Body mass index and agreement between bioimpedance and anthropometry estimates of body compartments in anorexia nervosa. *Journal of parenteral and enteral nutrition*, Vol.29, No.3, (May-June 2005) pp. 148-156, ISSN 0148-6071

Planas, M., Pérez-Portabella, C. & Virgili, N. (2002). Valoración del estado nutricional en el adulto, In: *Tratado de Nutrición*, Gil, A., pp. 117-148, Editorial Panamericana, ISBN 84-88336-43-8, España

Prentice, RL., Mossavar-Rahmani, Y., Huang, Y., Van Horn, L., Beresford, SA., Caan, B., Tinker, L., Schoeller, D., Bingham, S., Eaton, CB., Thomson, C., Johnson, KC., Ockene, J., Sarto, G., Heiss, G. & Neuhouser, ML. (2011). Evaluation and Comparison of Food Records, Recalls, and Frequencies for Energy and Protein Assessment by Using Recovery Biomarkers. *American journal of epidemiology*, Vol.15, (July 2011), ISSN 1476-6256

Reiter, CS. & Graves, L. (2010). Nutrition therapy for eating disorders. *Nutrition in Clinical Practice*, Vol.25, No.2, (April 2010) pp. 122-136, ISSN 1941-2452

Ricca, V., Castellini, G., Fioravanti, G., Lo Sauro, C., Rotella, F., Ravaldi, C., Lazzeretti, L. & Faravelli, C. (2011). Emotional eating in anorexia nervosa and bulimia nervosa. *Comprehensive psychiatry*, (May 2011) pp. 25, ISSN 1532-8384

Rosen, DS. (2010). Identification and management of eating disorders in children and adolescents. *Pediatrics*, Vol.126, No.6, (December 2010) pp. 1240-1253, ISSN 1098-4275

Ruiz I. (2011). Elección dietética de familiares de pacientes con trastornos de la conducta alimentaria. *Trastornos de la conducta alimentaria*, Vol.13, (May 2011) pp. 1384-1415, ISSN 1699-7611

Russell, J., Baur, LA., Beumont, PJ., Byrnes, S., Gross, G., Touyz, S., Abraham, S. & Zipfel, S. (2001). Altered energy metabolism in anorexia nervosa. *Psychoneuroendocrinology*, Vol.26, No.1, (January 2001) pp. 51-63, ISSN 1873-3360

Savage, JS., Fisher, JO. & Birch, LL. (2007). Parental influence on Eating Behavior: Conception to Adolescence. *The Journal of law, medicine & ethics*, Vol.35, No.1, (Spring 2007) pp. 22-34, ISSN 1748-720X

Scalfi, L., Marra, M., Caldara, A., Silvestri, E. & Contaldo, F. (1999). Changes in bioimpedance analysis after stable refeeding of undernourished anorexic patients. *International journal of obesity and related metabolic disorders*, Vol.23, No.2, (February 1999) pp. 133-137, ISSN 0307-0565

Scalfi, L., Marra, M., De Filippo, E., Caso, G., Pasanisi, F. & Contaldo, F. (2001). The prediction of basal metabolic rate in female patients with anorexia nervosa. *International journal of obesity and related metabolic disorders*, Vol.25, No.3, (March 2001) pp. 359-364, ISSN 0307-0565

Schebendach, J., Golden, NH., Jacobson, MS., Arden, M., Pettei, M., Hardoff, D., Bauman, N., Reichert, P., Copperman, N. & Hertz, S. (1995). Indirect calorimetry in the nutritional management of eating disorders. *The International journal of eating disorders*, Vol.17, No.1, (January 1995), pp. 59-66, ISSN 1098-108X

Schebendach, JE., Golden, NH., Jacobson, MS., Hertz, S. & Shenker, IR. (1997). The metabolic responses to starvation and refeeding in adolescents with anorexia nervosa. *Annals of the New York Academy of Sciences*, Vol.28, No.817, (May 1997) pp. 110-119, ISSN 1749-6632

Schebendach, JE., Mayer, LE., Devlin, MJ., Attia, E., Contento, IR., Wolf, RL. & Walsh, BT. (2008). Dietary energy density and diet variety as predictors of outcome in anorexia nervosa. *The American Journal of Clinical Nutrition*, Vol.87, No.4, pp. 810-816, ISSN 1938-3207

Schebendach, JE., Mayer, LE., Devlin, MJ., Attia, E., Contento, IR., Wolf, RL. & Walsh, BT. (2011). Food choice and diet variety in weight-restored patients with anorexia nervosa. *Journal of American Dietetic Association*, Vol.111, No.5, pp. 732-736, ISSN 1878-3570

Sedlet, KL. & Ireton-Jones, CS. (1989). Energy expenditure and the abnormal eating pattern of a bulimic: a case report. *Journal of the American Dietetic Association*, Vol.89, No.1, (January 1989) pp. 74-77, ISSN 1878-3570

Smith, AF., Baxter, SD., Hardin, JW., Guinn, CH. & Royer, JA. (2011). Relation of Children's Dietary reporting accuracy to cognitive ability. *American journal of epidemiology*, Vol. 173, No.1, (January 2011) pp. 103-109, ISSN 1476-6256

Souverein, OW., de Boer, WJ., Geelen, A., van der Voet, H., de Vries, JH., Feinberg, M. & Van't Veer, P. (2011). Uncertainty in intake due to portion size estimation in 24-hour recalls varies between food groups. *The Journal of nutrition*, Vol.14, No.7, (July 2011) pp. 1396-1401, ISSN 1541-6100

Steinhausen, HC. (2002). The outcome of anorexia nervosa in the 20th century. *The American Journal of Psychiatry*, Vol.159, No.8, (August 2002) pp. 1284-1293, ISSN 1535-7228

Talluri T., Lietdke, RJ., Evangelisti, A., Talluri, J. & Maggia, G. (1999). Fat-free mass qualitative assessment with bioelectric impedance analysis (BIA). *Annals of the New York Academy of Sciences*, Vol.20, No.873, (April 1999) pp. 94-98, ISSN 1749-6632

Taylor, C., Lamparello, B., Kruczek, K., Anderson, EJ., Hubbard, J. & Misra, M. (2009). Validation of a food frequency questionnaire for determining calcium and vitamin D intake by adolescent girls with anorexia nervosa. *Journal of the American Dietetic Association*, Vol.109, No.3, (March 2009) pp. 479-485, ISSN 1878-3570

Tong, J. & D'Alessio, D. (2011). Eating disorders and gastrointestinal peptides. *Current opinion in endocrinology, diabetes, and obesity*, Vol.18, No.1, (February 2011) pp. 42-49, ISSN 1752-2978

Treasure, J., Whitaker, W., Todd, G. & Whitney, J. (2011). A description of multiple family workshops for carers of people with anorexia nervosa. *European eating disorders review*, Vol.6, (July 2011), ISSN 1099-0968

Turner, JM., Bulsara, MK., McDermott, DM., Byrne, GC., Prince, RL. & Forbes, DA. Predictors of low bone density in young adolescent females with anorexia nervosa and other dieting disorders. *The International journal of eating disorders*, Vol.30, No.3, (November 2001) pp. 245-251, ISSN 1098-108X

Vaisman, N., Corey, M., Rossi, MF., Goldberg, E. & Pencharz, P. (1988). Changes in body composition during refeeding of patients with anorexia nervosa. *The Journal of pediatrics*, Vol.113, No.5, (November 1988), pp. 925-929, ISSN 1097-6833

van der Ster Wallin, G., Norring, C., Lennernäs, MA. & Holmgren, S. (1995). Food selection in anorectics and bulimics: food items, nutrient content and nutrient density. *Journal of the American College of Nutrition*, Vol.14, No.3, (June 1995) pp. 271-277, ISSN 1541-1087

Vansant, G. & Hulens, M. (2006). The assessment of dietary habits in obese women: influence of eating behavior patterns. *Eating disorders*, Vol.14, No.2, (March-April 2006) pp. 121-129, ISSN 1532-530X

Vázquez, C., Alonso, R., Garriga, M., de Cos, A., de la Cruz, J., Fuentes-Jiménez, F., Salas-Salvadó, J. & Mata, P. (2011). Validation of a food frequency questionnaire in Spanish patients with familial hypercholesterolaemia. *Nutrition, metabolism, and cardiovascular diseases*, Vol.22, (June 2011), ISSN 1590-3729

Von Wietersheim, J. & Hoffman, C. (2011). Comparison of instruments assessing the readiness to change in patients with anorexia nervosa. *Zeitschrift für Psychosomatische Medizin und Psychotherapie*, Vol.57, No.1, pp. 62-76, ISSN 1438-3608

White, MA. & Grilo, CM. (2005). Psychometric properties of the Food Craving Inventory among obese patients with binge eating disorder. *Eating behaviors*, Vol.6, No.3, (June 2005) pp. 239-245, ISSN 1873-7358

Winston, AP., Alwazeer, AE. & Bankart, MJ. (2008). Screening for osteoporosis in anorexia nervosa: prevalence and predictors of reduced bone mineral density. *The International journal of eating disorders*, Vol.41, No.3, (April 2008) pp. 284-287, ISSN 1098-108X

Yago, MD., Martínez, E. & Mañas, M. (2002). Métodos para la evaluación de la ingesta de alimentos, In: *Tratado de Nutrición*, Gil, A., pp. 35-74, Editorial Panamericana, ISBN 84-88336-40-3, España

# 16

# Nutritional Treatment in Eating Disorders

Patricia Bolaños Ríos
*Institute of Behavioral Sciences, Seville, Spain*

## 1. Introduction

Eating Disorders (ED) are complex and fundamentally psychological disorders with a rendering in the eating behavior, in which multiple alterations are produced (Jáuregui, 2006). These disorders are characterized by an unusual nutritional pattern and cognitive distortions relating to foods and body weight which produce serious nutritional alterations and medical complications (Martínez & Gómez, 2004).

Eating behavior is determined by nutritional aspects and others such as the economy, the availability, the weather, the culture or the mass media (Jáuregui, 2006). Consequently the dietary approach is essential within the action protocol for eating disorders. The nutritional treatment should consider all cited factors to modify the altered eating behavior. This part of the treatment must be carried out by a nutritionist, who should be part of an interdisciplinary team. The interdisciplinary team ought to be made up of doctors, psychologists, nutritionists and nurses, among others. These professionals are required in order to treat medical, psychological and nutritional aspects which converge in an eating disorder. All members of this team must maintain a constant communication about the patient evolution (Sayag & Latzer, 2002).

In the current literature, concrete and precise guidelines which constitute the action protocols to treat the medical and psychological aspects in eating disorders can be found. However, the same is not occurring for the nutritional treatment. The nutritional treatment is indispensable to treat eating disorders but only its importance has been considered recently.

To establish general rules to be applied in the nutritional treatment of eating disorders is possible. However, the nutritionist must always consider each individual case and the treatment should be personalized according to the nutritional state, the age, the clinical and nutritional histories, the psychosocial situation and the attitude to the disease and the treatment of the patient (Waisberg & Woods, 2002).

The family of the patient with an eating disorder has a fundamental role in the effectiveness of the nutritional treatment. To give the family clear patterns is required, emphasizing the need for meals as a relaxed social event. The nutritionist should teach the family to distinguish problems regarding meals from irrelevant aspects like "During this week, once my daughter left a little of legumes in the dish" (Jáuregui, 2006).

## 2. The nutritional treatment

Regardless of the intervention area needed, the nutritional team functions in eating disorder units are (Iglesias et al., 2004):

a. The nutritional state assessment.
b. The diagnosis of organic sequelae and related illness.
c. The treatment of malnutrition and other possible nutritional deficiencies.
d. The treatment of the presented organic complications.
e. Nutritional education for patients and their families.

When patients who start the treatment in an eating disorder unit are malnourished, the nutritional treatment is indispensable because of the cognitive and affective alterations which are caused by the malnutrition make the psychological treatment impossible or hardly difficult (Fernández & Turón, 1998; Iglesias et al., 2004).

When nutritionists have collected the information and obtained the diagnosis, they must establish the nutritional treatment of which the main aims are (Iglesias et al., 2004): getting an adequate nutritional state, obtaining an organized, well-balanced and sufficient food intake and avoiding the appearance of medical complications.

## 3. Intervention areas

Generally, the eating disorder units are coordinated by a psychiatrist who establishes the general points of the treatment and manage the rest of the interdisciplinary team (Chinchilla & Padín, 1996). This team must be present in the eating disorder units during the whole process of the treatment because a "forced" weight gain without psychological support is not recommended (Cheryl, 1999).

The indicated nutritional treatment for each patient with eating disorder depends on the therapeutic context where the patient is treated (Jáuregui, 2006).

The intervention areas for the eating disorder treatment are the following (Iglesias et al., 2004; Jáuregui 2006):

### 3.1 Outpatient treatment

This intervention area is very recommendable to keep the normal social, family, school or professional life of patients as long as their nutritional and psychological state allows it (Iglesias & Gómez, 2002). Nutritionists will try to correct any biological alteration suffered by the patient. Then, they will work with the patient to modify wrong nutritional habits towards healthier nutritional patterns by means of the nutritional education.

The outpatient treatment is suggested for initial clinical manifestations with mild or moderate symptomatology. Considering Fernández & Turón (1998) the following contraindications exist for the outpatient treatment:

- Low motivation for the treatment that makes unlikely an adequate treatment adherence.
- A very marked low weight.
- The recurrent failures of previous outpatient treatments.

- Family conflicts which maintain the disorder.
- Lack of family support.
- Organic or psychopathological reasons for the admission.

The nutritional treatment:

The body mass index is the most used parameter to follow up the weight recovery. A normal body mass index ranges between 18.5 and 25. In this context, the nutritionist has to explain to the family nutrition and behavioral patterns which make possible meals in a correct way (Jáuregui, 2006). Procedures to modify the behavior with programs of operational conditioning with positive and negative reinforcement are the most effective (Saldaña, 2001). This treatment can last a minimum period of one or two years. In order to obtain an effective nutritional treatment, the nutritionist should not only consider the patient but the family members must be taken into account. Working with them is very important (Russell et al., 1987), so as to indicate clear guidelines and actuation rules for different situations which can crop up. In addition, the nutritionist, by means of this work with the family, can modify wrong acquired habits in the family unit towards more healthy patterns through the nutritional education.

At the beginning of the nutritional treatment, patients with an eating disorder are provided with a life - plan which includes dietary and behavioral patterns. This life plan must comprise: basic rules for a normal nutrition, control of the bathroom, rest periods, possible restrictions in scholar or labor schedules, other activities, pharmacological prescription and further indications.

The above-mentioned life-plan contains as a first point the chapter nutrition where dietetic rules are specifically established for patients. Taking into account the patients' nutritional state, their diet may be either based on the families' meals respecting some general nutritional recommendations or consist of a diet prescribed by the nutritionist according to the specific needs of each patient. The caloric value of such diet can vary between 1000 up to 3000 kcal, divided into five categories, increasing each one by 500 kcal. These diets are also recommended wherever the nutritional habits of the family are resulting to be unhealthy and the family members refuse to adapt their habits to the recommendable nutritional patterns. However, the nutritionist will avoid the use of programmed diets which delay the patient integration in a normal diet (Iglesias et al., 2004). If patients are suffering from malnutrition, oral protein-calorie supplements or a special milkshake on the basis of cereals and fruits will be prescribed to patients and this last one can be prepared at home. However, the recommended quantity of water is, for all types of diets, between 1.5 to 2 liters per day. The total water intake of patients must be controlled in order to avoid the potomania like a compensatory behavior.

If patients are allowed to follow the family-diet, some general rules for a normal diet are explained in order to modify wrong nutritional habits of patients towards healthier patterns, which patients should acquire and maintain after their recovery. These rules are exposed in this chapter as follows.

Patients should have five daily intakes consisting of: breakfast, midmorning snack, lunch, afternoon snack and dinner.

It is important to offer variety in every meal in order to obtain a complete and well-balanced diet.

The breakfast ideally is composed of a dairy product (e.g. full milk), a portion of the group of farinaceous (bread or cereals) and a piece of fresh fruit (can be natural juice too).

The midmorning and afternoon snacks may include nuts and dried fruit, cereals, fruits, dairy products, sandwiches and occasionally pastry.

The lunch and the dinner necessarily must consist of two courses each, in order to include as much as possible of the groups of foods with a correct frequency and should be followed by a piece of fruit. Both meals need to be accompanied by a portion of bread. The liquid preferably will be water, the ideal quantity being one to three glasses. Soft drinks and packed juices should be avoided generally, whatever diet is followed. Alcoholic drinks are strictly forbidden.

Light, skimmed and integral products are forbidden unless a pathology requires their consumption. In order to avoid the excessive intake of simple sugars, goodies are not allowed.

Patients cannot make any choice with respect to the food, neither to the quality nor the quantity. In fact, the portions will be served by the person in charge of the patient, who will always be present during the patient's meals. When the dished are served, the responsible person must retire any type of container like trays or serving dishes. Generally all meals should be carried out at home, this allows patients to better obey to all rules accordingly.

In a recent study (Jáuregui & Bolaños, 2009), when a control student group decided on their diet, the food intake was 2123.94±220.61 kcal/day but in eating disorder patients it was 1815.74±508.38 kcal/day. The food intake of patients also was deficient in niacin, $B_{12}$ vitamin, sodium, zinc, phosphorous, copper and selenium. With respect to the food groups, the diet was deficient in bread and cereals, sausages, sweets or fried foods and the more frequent group was vegetables.

During the meals, patients cannot have any distraction as watching TV, talking on their mobile phone or playing with their computer. The family must avoid conversation topics based on foods, body image, weight, diets or the eating disorder itself as well as arguments during meals. The responsible person must control patients when they eat but in a relaxed way to avoid an unpleasant situation.

Patients ought to eat in a correct way: using cutlery adequately, sitting down right or respecting the established dishes order. Patients will not leave the table until the end of the meal (González et al., 2001).

The second aspect considered in the life plan is the control of the bathroom. Patients cannot enter the bathroom until nineteen minutes after meals. In addition, they must be accompanied at all times. This control is very necessary in order to avoid the practice of physical activity (e.g. in the shower) or the use of compensatory behaviors (vomiting, laxatives and diuretics).

Nowadays is very frequent to have a scale at home. Many patients with ED often weigh. Therefore, is very important to remove the scale with the purpose of patients cannot know their weight, because this data can harm the evolution of patients.

The nutritionist should indicate the recommended rest periods too. After meals, patients must not carry out any activity, it's to say, they have to rest. The rest periods may be on sofa or on bed, depending on the nutritional state of the patient. The advisable time to rest is half an hour after breakfast, midmorning and afternoon snacks and an hour after lunch and dinner. As during meals, in the rest periods, patients should not have any distraction (television, mobile phone or computer).

With the intention that patients acquire regular times of meals and rest periods, the nutritionist specifies a schedule for each patient, which assures the compliance of the nutrition and rest guidelines. The night's sleep must last eight hours in an approximate way.

The next point to treat is the school and working schedules. Taking into account the nutritional state of the patient, the nutritionist will can restrict theses schedules in order to facilitate a correct evolution of the patient. The professional will indicate if the scholar or labor activities will be maintained on full-time or partial-time. In cases of patients with a severe malnutrition these activities can be void. Also the dedicated time to study or work should be specified.

Then, consider others activities that patients can carry out is important. In this case, depending on the nutritional state of the patient, the nutritionist should think about the possibility to walk or practice some type of sport. If the patient is suffering malnutrition all type of physical activity must be forbidden. When the patient is at school age, indications about the subject "Physical Education" in the syllabus and the physical activities implemented must be given, considering, again, the nutritional state of the patient.

The sixth item listed in the life plan, which does not correspond to the work of the nutritionist, is the medication. The prescribed medication should be indicated by a psychiatrist. This data must be known by the nutritionist in order to consider the possible effects about the appetite or the weight changes that can be produced.

Finally, in the life plan, the nutritionist details others general indications. With the aim to ease the correct compliance of food standards, the kitchen must be controlled or closed considering each case in particular. This arrangement is necessary to avoid that patients cook their own meals, throw food, peck or binge. When the control of the kitchen is not enough, the family will proceed to close the door with a padlock or a door lock. With the bathroom, the same guidelines will be applied. The aim of controlling or closing the bathroom is to avoid that patients can practice physical exercise or use compensatory techniques such as vomiting, laxatives or diuretics. These are the causes for which patients must not enter the bathroom after meals and they always should shower before meals. Another recommendation in relation with the bathroom is that patients should be always accompanied.

Another indication very important is that patients must be go out without money not even credit cards, at least the responsible person should control the money that patients have got and spend. This aspect is necessary in order to avoid that patients can buy foods, diuretics or laxatives, among others.

With the aim to get a greater control respecting meals and compensatory behaviors, the person in charge of the patient must review, with a regular frequency the room, the handbag or backpack with the intention of find money, foods, diuretics or laxatives that the patient can hide. This is only possible after having obtained the consent of the patient.

Nowadays out-home meals are very frequent, and this acquires importance especially among adolescents, that search more autonomy in their nutrition. This reason justifies that patients should eat at home and they must be always accompanied by some member of the family and the whole family ought to eat together, if possible. When the patient follows the family-diet, the person that plans the menu and cooks has not got any type of restriction considering foods and culinary techniques, but this person must respect the nutrition rules explained by the nutritionist during the first visit. The nutritionist must clarify that this person should not give in to the requests of the patient relating to meals because patients have not a correct criterion to decide.

The frequent outputs night among adolescents must be avoided because both uncontrolled meals and insufficient rest times could arise. On the other hand, this habit facilitates the alcohol consumption among adolescents in an early way. The alcohol consumption, as explained in the first point of life plan, must be excluded during the treatment.

Traditionally foods are placed in the kitchen. However, to find food in the sitting room, in the rooms or in the bathroom is not unusual at the present. Therefore, the nutritionist ought to try that the family provides all food only in a room. The person in charge for the purchase should buy the essential and necessary.

The patients with eating disorders buy their own food, look all nutrients that these foods contain and cook their own meals. With the aim of get a better efficacy in the nutritional treatment, patients should not plan the weekly menu, or choose, buy and cook food or enter the kitchen when meals are being prepared.

Finally, the last indication in this chapter is the recommended time for meals. Patients have a maximum time for eat in order to maintain a regular meal schedule. These times are twenty minutes for breakfast, midmorning and afternoon snacks and forty minutes for lunch and dinner.

In addition to the abovementioned aspects, when the nutritionist proposes the patient the family-diet, the recommended frequency of food consumption is explained, including all groups of food: bread and cereals 3 times a day, rice and pasta 2-4 times a week, legumes 2-3 times a week, potatoes 2-3 times a week, fish 4-5 times a week, meat 3-4 times a week, eggs 3-4 times a week, dairy 4-5 times a day, vegetables 1-2 times a day (a portion should be raw, e.g. a salad) and fruits 2-3 times a day. On the other hand sweets and ice cream as well as fried food are included, and their frequency depends on the nutritional state of the patient. Generally the recommended frequency is 1-2 times a week for sweets and ice cream and the same for fried food.

From the first visit, patients must write food records and take digital photographs of meals (before and after eating) with the intention of controlling the quality and the quantity of food in an exact way. At first, appointments are given weekly and this frequency is modified according to the patient evolution. The nutritionist will carry out a complete anthropometric assessment in each visit. The nutritional treatment is especially based on the nutritional education with patients and their families. Currently, patients and families express irrational food beliefs which the nutritionist must treat with them. These beliefs can be assessed by means of different instruments [i.e., the Irrational Food Beliefs Scale (Jáuregui & Bolaños, 2010)]. When the nutritionist ignores these beliefs, the nutritional treatment efficacy decreases and the relapse risk increases. It is necessary to take into account that many eating disorder patients compose their diets by means of these irrational beliefs.

In this intervention area as well as in the rest of them the nutritionist should try to obtain the patients confidence and assume the responsibility of their control weight. Increasing the amount of foods gradually is very important to avoid the association between a best food intake and a sudden weight increase.

The dietetic-nutritional education tries to support and increase basic knowledge of eating disorders and their nutritional treatment, modify wrong nutritional habits, give tools to patients who can create their own diet in a healthy way and get a stable and normal weight by them. A nutritional intervention program includes basic topics like food groups and their nutritional composition, explanations for irrational food beliefs, nutritional guidelines, information on culinary techniques, and dietary strategies to modify the wrong nutritional habits and eating behavior (Muñoz et al, 2004).

### 3.2 Day hospital

This intervention is an intermediate step between the outpatient and hospital treatments. There are two possible therapeutic modalities according to the number of hours that patients stay at the unit: complete and limited stay. In this case an intensive interdisciplinary treatment is given to patients who are not strayed from their social and family contexts. The day hospital provides patients with greater control of their nutritional state and eating behaviors than the outpatient treatment. This treatment modality is recommended for patients who have received an outpatient treatment without adequate outcomes or who had required a hospital treatment but still present a serious symptomatology at the end of this treatment. Also, this treatment modality is used as a temporary pre-hospitalization treatment and for patients who have a family environment with recurrent conflicts and lack of family support (Jáuregui, 2006).

According to Kaplan & Olmsted (1997), the contraindications are:

- Organic state with indication of admission.
- Psychiatric reasons.
- Serious toxic substance dependence or abuse.

With shortened inpatient hospitalizations many patients require long term care for their recovery which the day treatment programs can provide. This option eases the correct development of children and adolescents (Dancyger et al., 2003).

The nutritional treatment maintain the general objectives of the outpatient treatment but others are included (Iglesias et al., 2004): the nutritional state control, the recovery of a normal weight, the suppression of compensatory behaviors, the eating behavior and food intake observation, the meals and rest periods control by specialized monitors, meals in group, nutritional education for patients and families, medical control and psychological support.

Some patients need nutritional supplements (Imbierowicz et al., 2002), but these measures must be provisional and these will be applied during a short time (Mejia et al, 1994).

### 3.3 Hospitalization

This intervention area is recommended when the outpatient treatment or the day hospital have failed or the nutritional and health states are severe and other therapeutics alternatives are not possible. The nutritional and psychiatric units must indicate the admission by mutual agreement. This treatment involves the normalization of eating behavior, medical complications treatments, psychotherapy and family support (Jáuregui, 2006).

When nutritional reasons are key aspects for this decision the most important objectives are:

- The organic balance recovery.
- The improvement of associated medical complications.
- The treatment of the nutritional alterations.
- The recovery of a normal weight.
- The introduction of a normal oral diet.

The admission criteria in patients with anorexia nervosa are (Jáuregui, 2006):

- Weight loss > 25-30% and vital risk produced by medical complications. In these cases the responsible department is internal medicine. If the patient suffers lower weight loss and has medical complications without vital risk, the responsible department is psychiatry.
- Psychopathological complications.
- Family crisis.
- The outpatient treatment is not possible or the patient has had an inadequate response to it.

The admission criteria in patients with bulimia nervosa are, according to Yates (Turón, 1997):

- Repeated failures of the outpatient treatment.
- Substance abuse/dependence.
- Severe binge episodes and vomits.

The nutritionist carries out the control of patients' weight every morning. Patients are weighed before breakfast, after urinate, barefoot and with underwear, and their back to the scales. Patients should not know their weight in order to ease their psychological recovery. Also nutritionists collect the complete information about the eating behavior of patients. They establish an adequate nutritional plan, which can include nutritional supplements and artificial nutrition if it is necessary (Gómez et al., 1999).

The nutritionist must be present at patient meals where parents are too. At this moment the nutritionist can work with patients and families by means of the nutritional education, in order to get the maintenance of correct nutritional habits after admission.

The nutritional treatment will start with oral nutrition if it is possible. At first, a hypocaloric diet is indicated in proportion to the nutritional state of the patient and the food intake will be increased during the hospital stay until a normal diet. The use of nutritional supplements must be provisional because patients usually create habituation towards this supplement and then, the suppression is difficult (Iglesias et al., 2004). The nutritionist avoids the refeeding syndrome with gradual increase of the food intake. The most frequent alterations caused by the refeeding syndrome are: hypophosphatemia, hypokalemia, hypomagnesemia, thiamine deficiency, glucose metabolism alterations and extracellular water increase (Birmingham et al., 1996).

### 3.4 Domiciled hospitalization

This treatment modality avoids the admission in many cases. The domiciled hospitalization is very effective if correct selection criteria of patients and families are applied and adequate action protocols are used. This type of medical care is similar to the offered by a hospital but patients are in their own house during the treatment. Patients and their families should undertake to fulfill in a strict way the therapeutic indications of a well delimited in time and specified in objectives program. This intervention area is recommended for malnourished patients without serious medical and psychiatric complications, after recurrent failures of outpatient treatments or as a previous or posterior step to the admission. The inclusion criteria are (Jáuregui, 2006):

- Diagnosis of anorexia or bulimia but not patients with severe course and very impulsive symptoms.
- Body mass index higher than 14.
- Organized and available family.
- Good patient disposition.
- Previous unsuccessful outpatient treatments.

The therapeutic objectives with respect to the physical aspects are three: the recovery of an acceptable body mass index, which will permit the outpatient treatment (higher than 18), the introduction of correct nutritional habits and the suppression of purgative or other compensatory behaviors. This treatment modality allows working with families some maintainer attitudes for the eating disorder like inadequate served amount of foods, recurrent arguments and conflicts between patients and their families or their irrational food beliefs (Jáuregui, 2006).

Generally, the domiciled hospitalization duration is from six to eight weeks approximately. Shorter domiciled hospitalizations are performed with bulimic patients to correct purgative behaviors and relapses. Patients have two appointments a week to control the weight and the therapeutic fulfillment by the interdisciplinary team. The calorie intake and the allowed activities are modified according to the weight and the patient attitude by the nutritionist. When patients do not improve notably in two weeks the admission will be indicated (Jáuregui, 2006).

The first phase begins with the retirement of all reinforcement to increase its value. This phase comprises the total rest in bed and the privation of any type of activity. The nutritionist gives the nutritional and behavioral guidelines to parents (the life plan). The duration of this phase can be from three to seven days. In the second phase, the nutritionist introduces some reinforcement according to the treatment fulfillment and the weight evolution (music, reading or phone calls among others). During the third phase more significant reinforcements are included like receiving a visit, going for a walk or studying. The partial resumption of normal activities takes place during the fourth phase and in their totality are introduced in the fifth and last phase, before starting the outpatient treatment (Jáuregui, 2006).

The nutritionist should not include reinforcements immediately and new reinforcements are preferable to an increased availability of an obtained reinforcement in previous weeks.

## 4. Nutritional treatment in anorexia nervosa

A patient with anorexia nervosa is characterized by body image distortion and weight fear. These aspects involve food restriction, physical exercise and compensatory behaviors in order to get the desired weight loss (Jáuregui, 2006).

Behavioral changes are observed with respect to foods. Patients restrict their food intake (they select certain foods to eat and limit the amount of these foods). In general, patients limit carbohydrates, lipids and proteins in keeping with this order. Nutritional rituals are frequent like drinking water before meals, cooking their foods themselves, eating slowly or quickly, cutting up foods in a particular way, crumbling, throwing or hiding foods, serving the amount of foods themselves or eating the different ingredients of a dish in a specific order and separately, among others. These rituals show obsessive characteristics of these patients (Jáuregui, 2006).

Another typical symptom to consider in the nutritional treatment is the hyperactivity. Patients use strategies in order to increase the energy consumption like walking constantly, doing exercise every day, standing up during meals, studying or reading standing, going up and down stairs, doing the housework, avoiding the rest after meals or sleeping a short time, among others (Jáuregui, 2006).

Before and during meals, arguments and protests with respect to the quality and quantity of foods are recurrent creating a tense environment which affects the family dynamics. In relation with this, patients avoid any social event where foods are present (Jáuregui, 2006).

Anorexia nervosa entails the appearance of medical complications, some of them potentially severe like osteoporosis, refeeding derived complications and cardiac arrhythmia. Most of these complications are reversible after weight recovery. In order to obtain this objective, to emphasize the importance of an interdisciplinary team is necessary, where the medical-psychiatric, psychological and nutritional treatments are essential to get the successful patient's recovery (Mehler & Krantz, 2003).

The objectives of the outpatient treatment relating to nutritional aspects are (American Dietetic Association, 2001): The recovery of a healthy minimum weight, the normalization of nutritional patterns, the establishment of a normal perception of hunger and satiety and the correction of biologic and psychological repercussions of malnutrition.

During the treatment these patients can communicate binge episodes and the use of compensatory behaviors that can be the result of their restrictive food intake (Rock & Curran-Celentano, 1996).

The nutritional education in this intervention area is essential to work the common and numerous irrational beliefs of these patients. Usually patients with anorexia nervosa classify foods in "good" "bad" "permitted" and "forbidden". This classification leads patients to exclude high-calorie foods and include vegetables and fruits frequently due to these foods are considered by them as healthy (Affenito et al., 2002; Stoner et al., 1996).

The first objective of the nutritional treatment in malnourished patients is to stop the weight loss and then the gradual weight gain. At first, a food intake of 800-1200 kcal a day can be prescribed (Marcason, 2002) that the nutritionist will increase according to the nutritional state of the patient, until a food intake of 3000 kcal a day in some cases (Russell et al., 1998). The nutritionist avoids the refeeding syndrome through this gradual increase of the patient food intake (Krahn et al., 1993).

## 5. Nutritional treatment in bulimia nervosa

Patients with bulimia nervosa have a pathological concern about body shape and weight. The most important symptom in bulimia nervosa is the binge eating, whose definition is an excessive food intake (in comparison with any normal person in similar conditions) in a short period of time (minutes or hours) with the feeling of control loss. The binge eating finishes because the patient feels satiety and abdominal pain, has not available foods or is surprised during the episode. After binge eating, patients feel guilt, anxiety or sadness, which leads them to compensatory behaviors. These behaviors can be purgative (self-induced vomiting, laxatives, diuretics and enemas) or not (fasting or excessive physical exercise). During binge episodes, patients ingest all type of foods depending on the availability, but in general they prefer high-calorie foods, which patients exclude from their normal diet (Jáuregui, 2006). The nutritionist must know the moment with more frequency of binge episodes of each patient.

There are patients with anorexia nervosa who communicate binge episodes. Usually, these patients refer to "subjective bingeing", that is, patients ingest a small amount of an excluded food like two squares of chocolate (Jáuregui, 2006) but their feelings are similar to those emotions described by bulimic patients.

Patients with bulimia nervosa usually suffer overweight or obesity despite the used compensatory behaviors. The total ingested amount of foods during a binge episode is not eliminated by means of vomiting. Therefore, a part of the ingested energy, that can be 1200 kcal in a binge episode, is absorbed in the first portions of the alimentary tract (Martínez & Gómez, 2004). Some patients maintain a normal weight because they combine bingeing and compensatory behaviors with calorie restrictions. The nutritional treatment aims to normalize the nutritional patterns as well as to eliminate or reduce the binge episodes and the existing compensatory behaviors (American Dietetic Association, 2001).

The nutritionist should not use hypo-caloric diets since these can facilitate the binge eating continuity. Therefore, the considered recommendations are: the suppression of binges eating, the modification of wrong nutritional habits by means of the nutritional education and the practice of physical exercise.

## 6. Patients with eating disorders and associated overweight or obesity

Some patients with bulimia or binge eating disorder are overweight or obese (Bolaños & Jáuregui, 2010). The nutritional education is essential for these patients. The fundamental aspects that the nutritionist will need to treat include promotion of healthy habits, acquisition of a complete and well-balanced diet, and regular practice of physical exercise (Bolaños, 2009). The nutritionist, with the nutritional education, modifies the eating behavior towards healthier patterns (Loria et al., 2009).

The trend toward the normalization of the associated excess weight and obesity has been observed after the nutritional intervention in these patients (Loria et al., 2009). A main purpose of this intervention is to teach the existing differences among hunger, appetite, satiety, and craving. A nutritional education program improves eating behaviors, bulimic episodes (binge eating and compensatory behaviors), irrational food beliefs, and self-control of food choices (Loria et al., 2009).

These patients need an interdisciplinary treatment (Martínez & Gómez, 2004). In many cases obesity is linked with psychosocial aspects (Jáuregui, 2006) and the "emotional ingest" (Martínez & Gómez, 2004). Therefore, a hypocaloric diet can be damaging to these patients because it could maintain binge eating (Martínez & Gómez, 2004), and an excess of weight. Establishing goals is critical for these patients. This aspect must be considered also with respect to physical exercise: most of these persons do not exercise regularly. Thus, this activity must be increased gradually.

On the other hand, the diet must include all foods. If patients like sweets, for example, and nutritionists forbid these foods, patients can feel craving for them and they can go into binge eating. Frustration could make patients leave the treatment. Therefore, high-calorie foods must be limited but not forbidden.

These patients must have regular mealtimes, sit-down to eat, remove the serving dish once courses are served, avoid distractions during meals, eat with family, plan the weekly menu, avoid buying foods (patients should write a list of the foods and have the exact quantity of cash if necessary), write a list of activities which help avoid pecking and avoid alcohol consumption (Jáuregui, 2009; Muñoz et al., 2004).

Patients with eating disorders who are overweight or obese must complete food records and take meals' photos, in order to modify the quality and amount of foods, if necessary.

## 7. General aspects about the nutritional treatment

### 7.1 Nutritional habits in adolescents

During childhood, people acquire the nutritional habits, which will be maintained throughout life. These habits will determine persons' nutritional state and consequently their health. Considering the duration of this period, the family plays an important role since children tend to imitate attitudes and behaviors which they observe in the context where they live. However, in the adolescence these habits can undergo alterations given that adolescents require a greater autonomy than children respecting meals. Adolescents start deciding the aspects with respect to their nutrition and influences of peers and mass media increase at this age.

Many adolescents acquire feeding styles without any type of information. An example is the vegetarianism. A teenager can be vegetarian because a peer is also vegetarian, the vegetarianism is in fashion or this teenager wants to be simply different. As a result, the lack of information can produce the appearance of nutritional deficiencies which can influence the adolescents' development in a significant way.

Vegetarian adolescents and young adults ingest a bigger quantity of fruits and vegetables and have a smaller risk for overweight or obesity than no vegetarian. However researchers have observed that vegetarian adolescents and young adults have an increased risk for binge eating with loss of control, and former vegetarians have high risks for extreme unhealthful weight-control behaviors (Robinson-O`Brien et al., 2009). For this reason any feeding style acquired for patients with an eating disorder, which does not meet with the nutritional recommendations, must be forbidden during the treatment. When the treatment finishes and patients have a correct information with respect to the nutritional habits they can decide with a correct criterion if they want to continue with the previous feeding style or not.

### 7.2 Exercise and eating disorders

Due to the relationship between the development of eating disorders and some sport practices, this subject must be taken into account. In case of women, the "female athlete triad" is known. This condition includes an altered eating behavior, amenorrhea and osteoporosis. The female athlete can suffer one, two or the three components of the triad. This must be considered in the medical examination performed so as to detect possible cases of eating disorders in an early way and avoid potentially more serious consequences. When a female athlete is diagnosed of eating disorder, the nutritional treatment should be aimed at the recovery of medical complications. These complications are the result of an excessive physical exercise level and the adaptation to a negative energy balance (Mendelsohn & Warren, 2010). Taking into account these data, this type of patients must completely abandon the sport activities at a competitive level. However, a difference with others patients with eating disorders is that an athlete patient can practice physical exercise but in a lower intensity way and the exercise should be completely different from the patient practiced. The nutritionist will control the caloric intake of the patients and will give them clear rules of physical exercise in order to avoid a sudden weight recovery in these patients, a fact that could harm their psychological recovery.

### 7.3 Food craving in eating disorder patients

Patients with anorexia nervosa live extremely worried about the consequences of their behaviors (Wagner et al., 2007). This fact produces the loss of the patients' ability to distinguish if they like a specific food or not, so many patients are not able to enjoy while eating because they only think about the consequences after eating this food. This aspect is expressed by patients with phrases like "I do not think if I like a food or not, I simply eat", "I'm not able to enjoy when I eat" or "I loved the chocolate before, but now I know the big quantity of calories that the chocolate has got, therefore it make me feel sick!". This problem may be treated by the nutritionist, by means of visual-analogue scales (color, texture, smell, taste, temperature or presentation of meals). These scales make the patient think about the food in order to give a score for each scale. Patients will acquire, again, the ability to distinguish the food that they like or not and they can learn to eat in a non mechanical way with this easy task.

The food craving, that is the intense desire to eat and specific food, is frequently felt by patients with eating disorders. Instruments like the Food Craving Inventory are used to evaluate the food craving. Generally, patients with anorexia nervosa get low scores because of the rejection of all food and especially to those which can generate a feeling of pleasure.

However, high scores are frequent in patients with bulimia nervosa, binge eating disorder or overweight/obesity. These patients express an intense desire for certain foods and after that, they can peck or binge and then use compensatory behaviors depending on patients and the context where they are. The nutritionist can face the patients' food craving by using imaginative, visual, olfactory or tactile stimuli. In a study (Gutiérrez-Maldonado et al., 2006), researchers showed six virtual contexts to thirty women with eating disorders: a living-room (neutral situation), a kitchen with high-calorie food, a kitchen with low-calorie food, a restaurant with high-calorie food, a restaurant with low-calorie food and a swimming-pool. Results revealed that virtual reality instruments are useful to simulate daily situations, which can produce anxiety and depression in patients. The highest levels of state anxiety and depression were obtained with the contexts where high-calorie food appeared.

On the other hand, the nutritionist can indicate the following instruments to induce an increase in food craving: to imagine and write situations respecting meals, to show meals and supermarket shelves' pictures, to give food to patients who can handle, smell or savor them. Then the nutritionist provides patients with the Food Craving Inventory and they should complete it. With the obtained scores, the nutritionist should indicate some guidelines to include the food craving-related foods in the patients' normal diet. This facilitates the loss of emotional value that these patients attach to these foods. In addition, the nutritionist is specific about strategies that patients can use in order to avoid eating these foods, depending on the patient and the context: going out for a walk without cash or credit cards, avoiding buying the necessary foods for the weekly menu at this moment and especially no going alone (the nutritionist can entrust someone this task), avoiding going into the kitchen, making a phone call, listening to music, reading a book, working with the computer or watching television.

## 7.4 New technologies for the nutritional education in eating disorders

Apart from the patients' weight monitoring the nutritionist should supervise the nutrition through weekly food records. All days of a week with the five recommended daily intakes (breakfast, midmorning snack, lunch, afternoon snack and dinner) appear in each food record. Patients have to write all food that they ingest in the section of the corresponding intake. At lunch and dinner, patients should specify the first and second courses, the bread intake, the drink they have with the meals and the dessert. If patients miss a meal, they should trace a line in the corresponding section for that intake. In addition, the section "Others" is included in the food record, where patients can show foods that they eat between meals or situations which have a relation with meals like binges eating, using of compensatory behaviors, different emotions (anxiety, depression or food craving, among others), circumstances surrounding the meals that patients want to treat, the alcohol consumption or the outputs night. As well patients have to indicate for each meal the time at which they eat. The nutritionist can know if patients have a regular mealtimes or not with these data. Nutritionists advise patients with eating disorders and diabetes mellitus to write the glycemia levels, because this data will help them to give recommendations when these levels are not correct. As mentioned above, out-home meals are very frequent at the present time; therefore patients must made known whenever they eat out and if they are accompanied by a family member or not.

Most of persons are not aware of the quantity of food that they ingest per day, especially per week, since the nutrition has become a mechanical action that few people stop to think. Besides showing the weekly diet of patients, writing the food record eases the nutritional treatment since patients are really aware of their food intake when they write the food records. This makes the guidelines' fulfillment easier by patients because they know that their intake will be assessed. In fact, generally parents of anorexia nervosa patients highlight a slight increase of the quantity of food that patients ingest since they write the food record for first visits. Patients with bulimia nervosa or binge eating disorder express a decrease in the frequency of binge eating and compensatory behaviors or in the quantity of ingested food during each binge eating for the reason that they should note down all ingested food in the food record. Something similar to this occurs with overweight and obesity patients who appreciate a decrease in their food intakes. These patients usually demonstrate their surprise in this way: "I was not aware on all foods that I can get to eat during a binge eating". Writing food records also affects parents because they make an effort to carry out a more varied and well-balanced diet, expressed truth by patients during first visits with phrases like: "This week we are surprised about meals because my mother has cooked meals which I did not remember, for example lentils. My diet has being more varied than ever!" This detail helps the nutritionist to establish priorities with the aspects to treat by means of the nutritional education in the eating disorder patients' families.

The use of food records causes a problem because these are not very precise. With food records, the nutritionist can know the food consumption frequency but not the exact ingested quantity of food by patients, therefore wrong portion estimations may be produced. When food records were used as only instrument for know about the food ingest, the therapeutic context was the scenario for continuous arguments which did not let the nutritionist treat real problems that could have happened in the course of the week. Confrontations between patients and their family were frequent because they did not agree on the described quantity of food that patients had ingested. Normally, anorexia nervosa patients point to large and even excessive amounts of food served in the dish whereas binge eating disorder or obesity patients indicate quite the opposite. On the other hand, occasionally parents describe the served amount of food accurately but the nutritionist can detect a certain degree of visual distortion in others cases when they describe these amounts as small or big when these are really normal. For this reason the nutritionist can recommend digital photos before and after meals (to see the served amount of food and the leftovers when the patient finishes eating) in order to know the real intake of patients. The family member who accompanies patients at meals should take a photograph of all foods that patients ingests in each meal, for example, at lunch, the first and second courses, the piece of bread, the dessert, the drink and the necessary cutlery must be placed in a tray and then, the responsible person can take a photo of this tray. The same applies to other meals. The presence of cutlery is necessary to help the nutritionist to interpret the served amount of food as accurately as possible. In cases of special meals where an established first course does not exist because this is made up of appetizers, a family member must serve out the food in the dish of patients in order to avoid having an adverse effect on their psychological evolution and this makes the photo of the patients' dish possible. With this type of photos, the nutritionist can work with patients on difficulties and emotions which they can feel in special meals (with friends, family or workmates for example). Usually parents ask: "when my daughter does not leave any leftover, is it necessary to take the picture?" The photo is always necessary because "any leftover" according to parents could mean very small amounts of food which patients leave with some intention: "I am calm when I leave a little of food on my plate". This is an example of "insignificant details" that parents do not explain to the nutritionist who can detect it by means of the photo. At the beginning of the treatment lots of parents and patients are reluctant to photograph meals; however they change their mind by observing the efficacy of this instrument for the nutritional treatment.

Fig. 1. Patients with anorexia nervosa at the beginning of the treatment. These photos show the served amount of food and the leftovers when patients finish eating.

Fig. 2. Patient with anorexia nervosa after six months of treatment.

In addition to the demonstrated usefulness to show the real amount of food, the nutritionist can make use of photos to observe the meals' presentation and improve it, if necessary. Eating is an easier task for patients with an appropriate meals' presentation. Taking a meal's photo improves the presentation right from the start because the responsible persons show a great interest in the meals' appearance, given that this photo will see by a person beyond the family. This is one of the consequences of the lack of importance that the nutrition has at present. Generally, people do not pay attention to the meal presentation but this issue has a great influence on the nutritional evolution of patients. Usually, responsible persons for the meal presentation do not take any pain to satisfy the eyesight, which is particularly important for the nutrition of children, the elderly and eating disorders patients. Sometimes, eating disorder patients, as well as a normal person would make, express great efforts to eat given the lack of interest showed by family member responsible for cooking, for example: a meat croquette whose size was equivalent to five normal croquettes since the mother did not like cooking, a burnt omelet or a fried fillet without any previous preparation with eggs, flour or breadcrumbs, that is to say, from the butcher's shop to the deep fryer directly.

Fig. 3. These photos show that meals' presentation must be included in the nutritional education.

The nutritionist stresses the importance of a pleasant meal presentation because this detail makes the confrontation between patients and the fearsome foods easier. The same happens when patients have a varied diet, for example, any normal person would prefer a first course of pasta and a second course with five meatballs instead of an only dish with thirteen meatballs. With meals' photos, nutritionists assess the context where patients eat and they also establish different aspects which the family must change. Observing computers, ironing, the car keys, books, mobile phones, pets...with foods on the table is very frequent. These things distract patients during meals and create an inappropriate environment to eat. The room where patients eat is also noticed with the photo, a detail that family members do not remark generally. However, bearing this data in mind is necessary because lots of patients with eating disorders usually eat in their bedroom, even in the bathroom. Patients must eat with their family in a common room which is assigned to this action. Patients will not eat in their bedroom or in the bathroom in order to avoid creating unhappy memories and experiences with foods throughout the whole house. With this recommendation patients have got reserved rooms where they can be if they feel food craving for example.

Furthermore, the digital photos are used to examine the nutritional habits of patients' family. Sometimes it happens that patients, thanks to the nutritional treatment, are the only member of the family who has a varied and well-balanced diet. Lots of patients' parents do not know the influence of their acquired nutritional habits on the nutritional treatment of patients and patients consider these habits as normal. For these reasons, this problem is not explained by patients or the family. In the meals' photos of patients, the rest of the table appears often. The nutritionist can see soft drinks, dishes with lots of sausages, crisps (as fundamental food at meals), excessive consumption of fried foods, alcohol bottles, goodies, sweets, fast food and great amounts of foods thanks to these pictures. The presence of these foodstuffs at meals can have an adverse effect on patients' evolution, who could consider the complete, varied and well-balanced diet as a treatment instead of nutritional habits which should be acquired and maintained throughout the life to ensure a good nutritional and health state. Therefore, the nutritionist works with families by means of the nutritional education to modify wrong attitudes and behaviors towards healthier nutritional patterns.

Additionally unhealthy nutritional habits are identified in meal photos but not in food records because there are lots of details regarding meals which patients do not write despite the fact that the nutritionist explains the way in which the food record should be completed to both the patient and the family. A clear example in this regard could be the inaccurate annotation of dairy products. Normally, when patients ingest any dairy product, they write "yoghurt". Firstly, patients must indicate if the yoghurt is composed of fruits, enriched with fiber or skimmed and the yoghurt characteristics like the taste. Afterward patients ought to distinguish the different dairy products in the food record because these have different nutritional compositions one each other. Another example is the explanation for the type of ingested fruit by patients, who usually indicate "fruit" as a rule. However, the nutritionist needs to know the specific type of fruit in order to assess the variety of this food group. In addition, there are groups of foods, which patients do not write down in a correct way (e.g., fish). Moreover many patients do not know the type of fish that they ingest, they do not distinguish the different foods of this group; therefore they write "fish" in the food record. The same occurs with the meat but to a lesser extent. These doubts are clarified with digital photos because the nutritionist sees them on the computer with the patients and their food records and all doubts can be explained at the moment.

Fig. 4. These photos are the result of the nutritional education. A good presentation eases the nutritional treatment.

Likewise, patients' families forget to mention anomalous eating attitudes of patients which the nutritionist observes in digital photos like crumbling foods, leaving always leftovers, peeling fruits in a particular way, mixing foods (for example the salad with lentils), using out of the ordinary plates and cutlery (anorexia nervosa patients who use small plates and cutlery, for example), among others. Finally, when out-home meals are allowed taking into account the patients' evolution, photos are again recommended to show them. Patients are uncomfortable taking a meal photograph out home, but the nutritionist needs these photos to evaluate the ability to choose of patients in a different context. If patients are not accompanied by any family member, photos reveal the patients' choices without family supervision.

Patients like using their photos and they pose the weekly doubts and problems about meals easily. Photos of some patients can be used as examples for others patients and their families.

During the nutritional treatment the nutritionist advises the family to modify the amounts of food which are served to patients, if necessary. The increase or decrease of these amounts should be progressive until patients get their recommended intake. With food records as only used instrument, responsible persons had to weigh foods in order to serve the indicated quantity but this aspect usually causes anxiety in many patients. However, with digital photos, these small changes are indicated to the family by means of meal photos each week. Meal photos are required throughout the nutritional treatment because if patients do not show their photos during several weeks, when they provide the nutritionist with their photos again, the nutritionist observes the decline in the quality of their nutritional intake.

Usually parents emphasize that patients have many obsessions with respect to meals. The digital video is suggested with the aim to face these obsessions. This instrument consists of recording patients while they are eating (all meals for a whole day). Patients may be uncomfortable during the recording but this tool demonstrates the patients' attitudes and behaviors during meals accurately. Through the digital video, the nutritionist can observe if patients: sit down adequately, employ the cutlery correctly or not (there are patients who use the fork for lentils, for example), respect the established order for the dishes of meals, eat bread during or at the end of meals, drink water before, during or after meals, cut up foods themselves or these are prepared by some family member (and the same for fruits), watch TV, speak with their family while they eating, stock the cutlery in their mouth right, slice the bread or crumble it, leave leftovers and the way which they do it (on the edge of the plate or in the broth or soup for example), fill the spoon or the fork with foods or not (there are patients who eat chickpeas in pairs). The nutritionist also examines the position acquired by patients on the table, the presence of objects which distract patients, the time used by patients for eating and the way in which they organize themselves, their expressions and feelings (repugnance or disgust, anger, sadness or anxiety for example) and how they eat (in a mechanical or pleasant way).

The nutritionist makes a list of nutritional objectives with all things observed in meal photos and digital videos which patients must carry out.

### 7.5 The current families of eating disorder patients

Nutritionists must know their tasks and be clear with families of eating disorder patients with respect to them because their work does not involve acquiring the role of mother or father. This explanation can be unnecessary for someone who is aware of the parents' responsibilities. Nevertheless, the fact that a nutritionist, in this case, acquires part of these obligations relating to patients is very frequent in the comfortable current society. From the first visit, when the life plan is explained, the next expressions are very frequents between the families: "You have told me that the whole information about the treatment is known by my son but...are you sure? If not I prefer my son to enter again and know all rules with you because I'm afraid of him". "A rule of the treatment is avoiding the outputs night, how has my daughter reacted to this? We will have an argument for this reason when we arrive at home so we will not fulfill this rule". The lack of authority of parents is more worrying every time, in such a way that they are not able to carry out the required treatment for an eating disorder. Currently, a life plan based on regular hours of meals and rest, the prohibition of alcohol consumption and the control of the bathroom, cash, credit cards and bedroom involves a very radical change of the family dynamics. In many cases, parents expect that psychiatrists, psychologists and nutritionists work out the lack of discipline of some patients using the eating disorder treatment. The nutritional treatment helps parents with all aspects with regard to the disorder, but not with their children's manners. Arguments, raising one's voice, slams and insults are recurrent among the family members, even on the surgery. In these cases patients know the strategy to get their purpose, to sum up, the non-fulfillment of the nutritional treatment decreasing its efficacy. Some parents modify the rules of the treatment to avoid bad reactions by the patient but this means a lower efficacy of the treatment again.

The lie has always had an important role in eating disorders concerning patients. However, nowadays the interdisciplinary team also evaluates the parents versions due to they lie about the patient evolution to avoid confrontations with their children. In some cases, parents speak to patients about the information that they will say by mutual agreement. Nonetheless, working with an interdisciplinary team make possible to detect details concealed from patients and families because of lies are twisted when they relate them again and again. Some examples: (patient) "We went to the beach the last weekend. I missed meals and I ate an only dish at lunch and dinner" (mother) "The last weekend we went to the beach, but do not worry about the nutritional treatment because my daughter carried out the recommended five intakes and even we ate set meals to have two courses with bread and dessert!" In this case, mother lied to avoid a reprimand by the nutritionist; (patient) "I do not understand the loss of weight this week. I have fulfilled the treatment rules, for example I have not missed any intake and not even I have had a night out" (father) "I do not believe the loss of weight! Sincerely, there is something I have to tell you about my daughter...she has missed all midmorning snacks and some afternoon snacks and she have had two night outs. I allowed her to fail to fulfill these rules. It upsets me sad to see her with these meals (she is overwhelmed) and without night outs. She is a very good daughter! We agreed on this lie but I did not imagine the loss of weight". In this case the nutritionist can realize that father is not aware of the eating disorder.

Another topic in fashion is the "parents-friends", which does not ease the nutritional treatment fulfillment: "We have a very good relationship; my mother/father is as a friend". Parents must think that both are very different concepts and their union is not recommendable, especially for the treatment. Imposing regular hours of meals and rest on patients or avoiding the snack intake between meals are difficult rules when the nutritionist listens: (mother) "The last weekend I had a night out with my daughter. We arrived at four o'clock and I made her eat sausages and chocolate to avoid a loss of weight!". Finally, this mother told the nutritionist this information because her daughter lost weight.

For the abovementioned reasons, the nutritionist should always clarify what issues are included in the nutritional treatment and explain the parents' responsibilities with respect to the patients with eating disorders to get greater effectiveness.

## 8. The nutritional education

The nutritional education is a fundamental part in the nutritional treatment of patients with eating disorders. Many acquired habits come from the family-unit. In addition to the current need for nutritional education, the nutritionist needs to consider patients' families to be able to improve the efficacy of the nutritional treatment.

Nutritionists explain the importance of healthy habits modifying the wrong attitudes and involving all family members. The family must complete food records and take photos of the meals. With these instruments, nutritionists can modify family behaviors such as meal structure, meal presentation, or evaluate the drinks associated with meals. However, families are often not interested in modifying nutritional or lifestyle habits. Families do not think about the importance of nutrition on health or the influence that these habits can have on the recovery of the patient.

A persistent problem expressed by patients during the nutritional treatment is the comparison with other family members: "I do not understand why I need five intakes a day and my sister does not"; "I need more time to eat than other family members because they only have a course without bread or dessert"; "With all these rules I am a weirdo in my family"; "When I finish the treatment, will I be able to eat like the rest of my family or I will carry out these nutrition rules forever?" Patients may consider the nutritional treatment patterns like a needed treatment to recover and not like habits that they should acquire and maintain throughout their lives.

Patients must learn to eat. This objective is difficult when, for example, parents ingest bread with sausages or siblings ingest fast food in each meal, family members peck frequently, miss meals or eat a small amount of foods and anxiously look for chocolate thereafter. Nutritionists try to make the family understand that the nutritional treatment is focused on the recovery of the patient and the improvement of nutritional habits of all other family members.

When the family accepts the changes from the beginning, the patient's treatment is more efficient and the family members perceive the positive influence of correct nutritional and lifestyle habits on their health status and the patient's recovery.

In other cases, patients' families have a negative attitude: "I am sorry but I will not change my habits because of my son/daughter. I am not ill, my health is perfect. Therefore I do not need the positive influence of nutrition changes".

Nutritionists should avoid extreme attitudes such as situations where family members try to eat the same food as the patient, considering quality and quantity. Many parents eat the same amount in order to avoid comparisons by their children, the patients, but this can pose a significant problem. Nutritionists should clarify that their nutritional needs are different due to their age differences and the specifics of the individual situation. Parents must acquire healthy nutritional habits but they must eat appropriate amounts. When they imitate the amount of foods of the patients, they could suffer from an excessive intake, with problems such as obesity, diabetes, hypertension, hypercholesterolemia, or hypertriglyceridemia, among others. They should understand that the acquisition of correct nutritional habits helps the patient but this does not mean the same quantity also applies to other family members.

Nutritionists encourage healthy habits among families by means of the nutritional education. Programs of nutritional education for families of patients with eating disorders must include informative sessions and keeping food records and taking photos of meals by relatives or friends. Nutritionists, using the informative sessions, will explain about different groups of foods, their nutritional properties and their representation in the habitual diet, difference among hunger, satiety, and craving, guidelines to organize the weekly menu, selection and purchase of foods, different culinary techniques, organization of time to buy and cook, location of foods within the kitchen, behavioral rules about meals, new cookbooks, irrational food beliefs, importance of regular mealtimes, positive influence of physical exercise, link between emotions and nutrition, rules for eating out, and consequences of fast-food and pecking between meals, among other nutritional issues.

The food choice is the main factor that determines the habitual diet. There are different instruments, like the Food Choice Questionnaire (Jáuregui & Bolaños, 2011) used by nutritionists to know what influences the food choices of the person who is responsible for the nutrition at home, such as price, health issues, weight control, mood or familiarity, among others. With these data, nutritionists can work with families in order to modify the aspects that determine the food choice in order to develop a healthier diet.

The informative sessions can be carried out individually or grouping different families. The food records completed by the patients' families are very useful for the group sessions. They explain the food records, analyze them, and must be able to identify wrong and correct nutritional habits, giving nutritional recommendations if necessary, keeping in mind what they have been taught. Nutritionists are always present during these sessions. When families attend sessions regularly nutritionists can observe how they improve their nutritional habits and emphasize the positive influence on their health (weight control, improvement in mood or in pathologies like diabetes, hypertension or hypercholesterolemia) as well as on the nutritional treatment of patients. These aspects encourage other families to modify wrong behaviors towards healthier patterns.

## 9. Conclusion

Eating disorders are characterized by multiple anomalies in the eating behavior, which can produce serious nutritional and medical complications. Therefore, a nutritional treatment must be included in the action protocol for eating disorders, by means of nutritionists who work within interdisciplinary teams.

The nutritional treatment for eating disorder patients must include patients and their families. With respect to patients, nutritionists must analyze each individual case in relationship with the diet, the physical exercise, the regular daily activity (at school or at work) and the rules about the control of food intake (money issues, time at the bathroom or bedroom, or outside of home, among others). All patients must complete food records and take photos of the meals. With these instruments nutritionists can establish goals, related to the structure of meals, amounts, water intake, physical exercise, or the inclusion of "forbidden" foods by the patient. All proposed changes by the nutritionist must be gradual and progressive, regardless of diagnosis. Nutritionists must always take into account that they treat persons, and therefore the emotions, feelings and fears must always be considered. Each patient needs a different treatment pace, which needs to be explained to families who try to speed up the treatment.

To improve the efficacy of the nutritional treatment with eating disorder patients, nutritionists can use new technologies like digital photos or videos. These instruments facilitate some aspects of the treatment like documentation of the exact amount of food needed by the patient, meals' presentation, detection of rituals carried out by patients, and observation of nutritional habits of families.

Nutritionists consider families in the nutritional treatment of eating disorder patients in order to avoid any contact of the patient with food between meals and to ease the fulfillment of the rules. When families have correct nutritional habits, the patient's recovery is positively influenced by them. Therefore, an important issue in the nutritional treatment is the nutritional education with patients and families, in order to modify wrong nutritional habits towards healthier patterns.

## 10. References

Affenito SG., Dohm FA., Crawford PB., Daniels SR. & Striegel-Moore RH. (2002). Macronutrient intake in anorexia nervosa: the National Heart, Lung, and Blood Institute Growth and Health Study. *J Pediatr*, 141, 5, Nov, 701-705, ISSN 1097-6833.

American Dietetic Association. (2001). Position of the American Dietetic Association: nutrition intervention in the treatment of anorexia nervosa, bulimia nervosa, and eating disorders not otherwise specified (EDNOS). *J Am Diet Assoc*, 101, 7, Jul, 810-819, ISSN 1878-3570.

Birmingham CL., Alothman AF. & Goldner EM. (1996). Anorexia nervosa: refeeding and hypophosphatemia. *Int J Eat Disord*, 20, 2, Sep, 211-213, ISSN 1098-108X.

Bolaños P. (2009). Evolución de los hábitos alimentarios. De la salud a la enfermedad por medio de la alimentación. *Trastornos de la Conducta Alimentaria*, 9, May, 956-972, ISSN 1699-7611.

Bolaños P. & Jáuregui I. (2010). Sobrepeso y obesidad en los trastornos de la conducta alimentaria. *Rev Esp Nutr Comunitaria*, 16, 2, Abr-Jun, 83-89, ISSN 1135-3074.

Rock CL. (1999). Nutritional and medical assessment and management of eating disorders. *Nutr Clin Care*, 2, 6, Dec, 332-343, ISSN 1523-5408.

Chinchilla A. & Padín JJ. (1996). Estructura funcional de las unidades de trastornos de la conducta alimentaria, anorexia nerviosa y bulimia nerviosa en los servicios de Psiquiatría, In: *Guía teórico-práctica de los trastornos de la conducta alimentaria: anorexia nerviosa y bulimia nerviosa,* Chinchilla A., Masson, ISBN 978-84-458-0317-2, Barcelona.

Dancyger I., Fornari V., Schneider M., Fisher M., Frank S. & Goodman B et al. (2003). Adolescents and eating disorders: an examination of a day treatment program. *Eat Weight Disord*, 8, 3, Sep, 242-248, ISSN 1590-1262.

Fernández F. & Turón VJ. (1998). *Trastornos de la alimentación: Guía básica de tratamiento en anorexia y bulimia*. Masson, ISBN 84-458-0746-3, Barcelona.

Gómez C., De Cos AI. & González B. (1999). Trastornos de la conducta alimentaria, In: *Tratado de Nutrición,* Hernández M. & Sastre A., Díaz de Santos, ISBN 84-7978-387-7, Madrid.

González I., Pérez J. & Peinó R. (2001). Anorexia y bulimia nerviosa, In: *Trastornos alimentarios,* Diéguez C. & Yturriaga R., McGraw Hill Interamericana, ISBN 978-84-486-0431-8, Madrid.

Gutiérrez-Maldonado J., Ferrer-García M., Caqueo-Urízar A, Letosa-Porta A. (2006). Assessment of emotional reactivity produced by exposure to virtual environments in patients with eating disorders. *Cyberpsychol Behav*, 9, 5, Oct, 507-513, ISSN 1557-8364.

Iglesias C. & Gómez C. (2002). Trastornos de la conducta alimentaria y obesidad, In: *Fisiopatología aplicada a la nutrición*, Planas M. & Pérez-Portabella C, 1ª Ed, Mayo, ISBN 978-84-961-2256-7, Barcelona.

Iglesias C., Gómez C., de Cos AI. & Castillo Rosa. (2004). Papel del médico nutriólogo en las unidades de trastornos de la conducta alimentaria, In: *Nutrición y Metabolismo en Trastornos de la Conducta Alimentaria*, Miján de la Torre A., pp. 493-505, Glosa, ISBN 84-7429-192-5, Barcelona.

Imbierowicz K., Braks K., Jacoby GE., Geiser F., Conrad R., Schilling G., et al. (2002). High-caloric supplements in anorexia treatment. *Int J Eat Disord*, 32, 2, Sep,135-145, ISSN 1098-108X.

Jáuregui I. (2006). *La imagen de una sociedad enferma: anorexia, bulimia, atracones y obesidad* (2ª Edición). Grafema, ISBN: 84-934225-9-2, Barcelona.

Jáuregui I. (2009). *El pequeño gran libro de la alimentación. Cómo comer para sentirte bien* (1ª Edición). Almuzara, ISBN 978-84-92573-55-4.

Jáuregui I. & Bolaños P. (2009). Choice of diet in patients with anorexia nervosa. *Nutr Hosp*, 24, 6, Nov-Dec, 682-687, ISSN 1699-5198.

Jáuregui I. & Bolaños P. (2010). Spanish version of the Irrational Food Beliefs Scale. *Nutr Hosp*, 25, 5, Sep-Oct, 852-859, ISSN 1699-5198.

Jáuregui I. & Bolaños P. (2011). What motivates the consumers' food choice? *Nutr Hosp(accepted)*. ISSN 1699-5198.

Kaplan AS. & Olmsted MP. (1997). Partial hospitalization, In: *Handbook of Treatment for Eating Disorders*, DM. Garner & PE. Garfinkel, 2nd ed., pp. 354-360), Guilford Press, ISBN 978-15-723-0186-3, New York.

Krahn DD., Rock C., Dechert RE., Nairn KK. & Hasse SA. (1993). Changes in resting energy expenditure and body composition in anorexia nervosa patients during refeeding. *J Am Diet Assoc*, 93, 4, Apr, 434-438, ISSN 1878-3570.

Loria V., Gómez C., Lourenço T., Pérez A., Castillo R., Villarino M. et al. (2009). Evaluación de la utilidad de un Programa de Educación Nutricional en Trastornos de la Conducta Alimentaria. *Nutr Hosp*, 24, 5, Sep-Oct, 558-567, ISSN 1699-5198.

Marcason W. (2002). Nutrition therapy and eating disorders: what is the correct calorie level for clients with anorexia? *J Am Diet Assoc*, 102, 5, May, 644, ISSN 1878-3570.

Martínez C. & Gómez P. (2004). Tratamiento dietético en los trastornos de la conducta alimentaria, In: *Nutrición y Metabolismo en Trastornos de la Conducta Alimentaria*, Miján de la Torre A., pp. 289-303, Glosa, ISBN 84-7429-192-5, Barcelona.

Mehler PS. & Krantz M. (2003). Anorexia nervosa medical issues. *J Womens Health (Larchmt)*, 12, 4, May, 331-340, ISSN 1931-843X.

Megía A., Gil Canalda I., Luna R., Herranz L., Weisz P., Bacaicoia A., et al. (1994). Nuestra experiencia en el tratamiento nutricional de la anorexia nerviosa (1989-1991). *Nutr Hosp*, 9, 6, Nov-Dec, 399-406, ISSN 1699-5198.

Mendelsohn FA. & Warren MP. (2010). Anorexia, bulimia, and the female athlete triad: evaluation and management. *Endocrinol Metab Clin North Am*, 39, 1, Mar, 155-167, ISSN 1558-4410.

Muñoz M., Aranceta J. & García-Jalón I. (2004). *Nutrición aplicada y dietoterapia* (2ª Edición). EUNSA, ISBN 84-313-2196-2, Navarra.

Robinson-O'Brien R., Perry CL., Wall MM., Story M. & Neumark-Sztainer D. (2009). Adolescent and young adult vegetarianism: better dietary intake and weight outcomes but increased risk of disordered eating behaviors. *J Am Diet Assoc*, 109, 4, Apr, 648-655, ISSN 1878-3570.

Rock CL. & Curran-Celentano J. (1996). Nutritional management of eating disorders. *Psychiatr Clin North Am*, 19, 4, Dec, 701-713, ISSN 1558-3147.

Russell GF., Szmukler GI., Dare C. & Eisler I. (1987). An evaluation of family therapy in anorexia nervosa and bulimia nervosa. *Arch Gen Psychiatry*, 44, 12, Dec, 1047-1056, ISSN 1538-3636.

Russell J., Baur L., Beumont P., Byrnes S. & Zipfel S. (1998). Refeeding of anorexics: wasteful not willful. *Lancet*, 352, 9138, Oct, 1445-1446, ISSN 1474-547X.

Saldaña C. (2001). Tratamientos psicológicos eficaces para trastornos del comportamiento alimentario. *Psicothema*, 13, 3, Jul-Sep, 381-392, ISSN 0214-9915.

Sayag S. & Latzer Y. (2002). The role of the family physician in eating disorders. *Int J Adolesc Med Health*, 14, 4, Oct-Dec, 261-267, ISSN 0334-0139.

Stoner SA., Fedoroff IC., Andersen AE. & Rolls BJ. (1996). Food preferences and desire to eat in anorexia and bulimia nervosa. *Int J Eat Disord*, 19, 1, Jan, 13-22, ISSN 1098-108X.

Turón VJ. (1996). *Trastornos de la alimentación. Anorexia nerviosa, bulimia y obesidad*, Masson, ISBN 978-84-458-0550-3, Barcelona.

Wagner A., Aizenstein H., Venkatraman VK., Fudge J., May JC., Mazurkewicz L. et al. (2007). Altered reward processing in women recovered from anorexia nervosa. *Am J Psychiatry*, 164, 12, Dec, 1842-1849, ISSN 1535-7228.

Waisberg JL. & Woods MT. (2002). A nutrition and behaviour change group for patients with anorexia nervosa. *Can J Diet Pract Res*, 63, 4, Winter, 202-205, ISSN 1486-3847.

# Enteral Nutrition as a Life-Saving Treatment in Patients with Severe Anorexia Nervosa

Maria Gabriella Gentile
*Eating Disorder Unit, Niguarda Hospital, Milan, Italy*

## 1. Introduction

Anorexia Nervosa is a serious, potentially life-threatening illness characterized by severe malnutrition, with abnormally low body weight (BMI <17.5 kg/m$^2$ or body weight at least 15% below the expected value), an intense fear of weight gain, and an undue emphasis on weight and shape in self-evaluation. Amenorrhea (i.e. loss of three consecutive menstrual cycles) is currently required for the diagnosis, but often is hidden by contraceptive drugs. Anorexia nervosa can cause significant clinical complications in every organ system, particularly relevant in adolescents in the growing and developing body with slowing in linear growth, impaired bone mineral accretion, structural and functional damage of the brain. Most of these complications are reversible if there is a timely restoration of body weight, since weight restoration is associated with concomitant decrease in anorectic symptoms and an improvement in physical and cognitive function (American Academy of Pediatrics. Committee on Adolescence. Identifying and treating eating disorders. Pediatrics, 2003; American Dietetic Association, Nutrition intervention in the treatment of eating disorders, 2011; American Psychiatric Association. Work Group on Eating Disorders. Practice Guideline for the treatment of Patients with Eating Disorders. 2006; Beumont, 2004; Eating Disorders. Core Interventions in the treatment and management of anorexia nervosa, bulimia nervosa and related eating disorders. National Institute for Clinical Excellence, 2004).

Weight restoration is also a prerequisite for psychotropic interventions and effective use of psychotherapeutic therapy (Eating Disorders. Core Interventions in the treatment and management of anorexia nervosa, bulimia nervosa and related eating disorders. National Institute for Clinical Excellence, 2004; Stanga et al., 2007).

Moreover, we also must consider that anorexia nervosa patients display the highest death rate of all mental illnesses and a relevant part of mortality has to be attributed to undernutrition.

If undernutrition is severe, patients are at high risk, and medical complications affect virtually every organ system. Severely undernourished patients, if not appropriately treated with a specialized in-patient care program, may present cardiovascular, metabolic complications, and abnormalities in brain functions, and it is not infrequent for these complications to require treatment in intensive care units, thus extending hospitalisation time and consequently increasing costs (Golden & Meyer, 2004; Gentile et al., 2008).

Severe and protracted undernutrition nearly always leads to marked changes in body spaces (e.g. intra-extracellular water), in body masses (e.g. potassium, phosphate, magnesium overall and compartmental stores), in equilibrium relationships between bodily spaces, concentrations and in feedback mechanisms which are set at new-pathological levels of functioning. These changes set the body at risk of refeeding syndrome, i.e. the disturbances caused by a too rapid / or unbalanced refeeding which the deranged bodily system just referred to be unable to support (Mehanna et al., 2008).

Several guidelines, papers and reviews provide guidance for medical and nursing staff managing patients with severe undernutrition and/or at risk of refeeding syndrome. There are also many reports of medical complications in refeeding anorexia nervosa patients (Stanga et al., 2008; Marinella et al., 2005; Hearing, 2004; Birmingham, 2008).

So, caring for severely starved patients with anorexia nervosa and re-starting nutrition commands close monitoring seeking for early signs or symptoms of refeeding and specialized care operating, within a timely plan, both at a physical (first) and emotional level (successively), the final goal being to restore a healthy, self managing person to her/his family and social environment (Gentile et al., 2010).

Until now there has been no category A evidence for treatment of anorexia nervosa, but international guidelines and society position papers agree in defining the best treatment as a multidisciplinary, comprehensive and rigorous process conducted by a team of medical, nutritional, mental health and nursing professionals, experienced in the evolution and treatment of eating disorders (American Academy of Pediatrics. Committee on Adolescence. Identifying and treating eating disorders. Pediatrics, 2003; Eating Disorders. Core Interventions in the treatment and management of anorexia nervosa, bulimia nervosa and related eating disorders. National Institute for Clinical Excellence, 2004).

Usually Centres that treat inpatient anorexia nervosa who have moderate or severe degrees of undernutrition use a combination of behavioural techniques, cognitive restructuring and a progressive structured program of oral caloric intake to achieve the goal of weight restoration. In the more complicated cases i.e. patients with extreme undernutrition and life threatening weight loss or patients unwilling to take dietary treatment or refusing oral intake, artificial nutrition has been utilized (Table 1).

| |
|---|
| Patient with severe malnutrition (BMI ≤ 13 $Kg/m^2$) disposed to intake less than 100% of the caloric needs or patients with body weight not increasing |
| Patient with BMI between 13 -15 $Kg/m^2$ showing a reduction of measured resting metabolic rate more than 30% of exstimated basal metabolic rate according to Harris Benedict formula. |
| Patient unwilling to take dietary treatment or refusing any oral intake but accepting only Artificial Nutrition. |

Table 1. Criteria for life-saving intervention with artificial nutrition in anorexia nervosa patients

Although it has always been stressed how crucial nutritional rehabilitation is in these patients, where only few studies are reporting the use of artificial nutrition in anorexia nervosa patients. Enteral nutrition and parenteral nutrition are both used in nutritional

| Reference | City/ Country | Source of case detection | Diagnostic criteria | Study period | Sample used to calculate the incidence | Incidence (per 100 000 population) | Total number of cases |
|---|---|---|---|---|---|---|---|
| Williams & King (1987) | London (England) | Psychiatric admissions register | Unspecified | 1972-1981 | All (♀)<br>♀ (10-64 years) | Between 1.4 and 2.0<br>Average annual increase: 2% | Unspecified |
| Nielsen (1990) | Denmark (nationwide) | Nationwide psychiatric admissions register | ICD-8 | 1973-1987 | All (♀)<br>All (♂) | 1.90<br>0.17 | N(♀)= 744<br>N(♂)= 63 |
| Willi et al. (1990) | Zurich (Switzerland) | Medical and psychiatric records (public and private health services) | Clinical | 1956-1958<br>1963-1965<br>1973-1975<br>1983-1985 | ♀ (12-25 years) | 0.38<br>0.55<br>1.12<br>1.43 | N(♀)= 10<br>N(♀)= 17<br>N(♀)= 38<br>N(♀)= 48 |
| Hall & Hay (1991) | Wellington (New Zealand) | Interview in the first admission of patients with eating disorders | DSM-III | 1977-1986 | All (♀+♂)<br>♀ (15-29 years) | 5.0<br>33.9 | N(♀)= 162<br>N(♂)= 8 |
| Hoek et al. (1995) | Netherlands (nationwide) | General medical practitioners were trained to diagnose eating disorders | DSM-III-R and DSM-IV | 1985-1989 | All (♀+♂)<br>All (♀)<br>♀ (15-19 years) | 8.1<br>14.7<br>79.6 | N(♀)=55<br>N(♂)= 5 |
| Turnbull et al. (1996) | England | Primary care registers | Clinical | 1988<br>1994 | ♀ (10-39 years)<br>♀ (10-39 years)<br>Age- and gender-adjusted | 18.5<br>18.1<br>4.2 | Unspecified<br>N(♀)=100 |
| Currin et al. (2005) | England | Primary care registers | Clinical | 2000 | ♀ (10-39 years)<br>Age- and gender-adjusted | 20.1<br>4.7 | N(♀)=51 |
| Milos et al. (2004) | Zurich (Switzerland) | Medical records | DSM-III-R | 1983-1985<br>1993-1995 | Total (♀+♂)<br>♀ (12-25 years)<br>Total (♀+♂)<br>♀ (12-25 years) | 1.43<br>16.44<br>1.17<br>19.72 | N(♀+♂) = 48<br>N(♀+♂) = 41 |

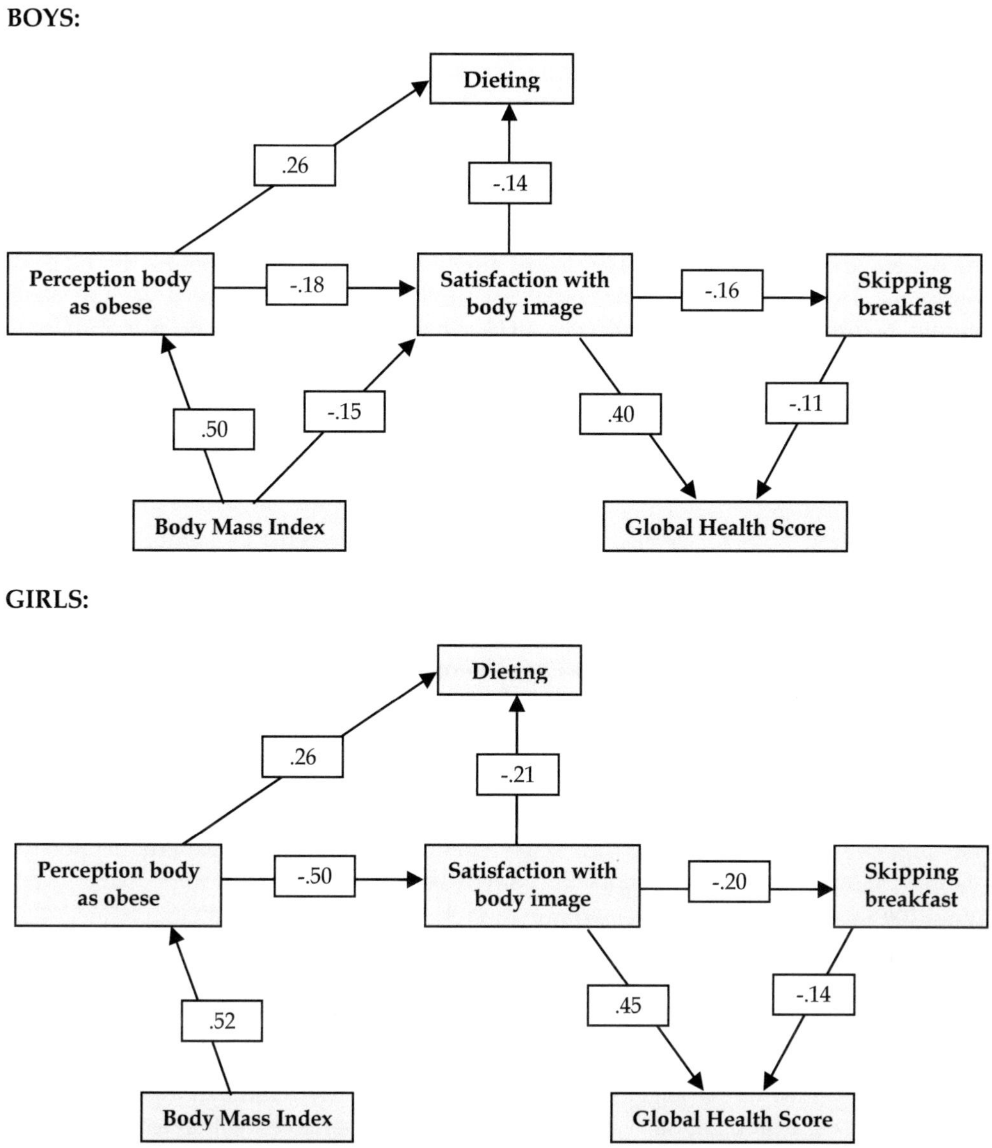

rehabilitation of severe anorexia nervosa patients (Paccagnella et al., 2006; Robb et al., 2002; Tonoike et al., 2004; Zuercher et al., 2003; Gentile et al., 2008; Gentile et al., 2010).

Given the recognised difficulties in conducting randomized clinical trials in patients with anorexia nervosa, evidence-based guidelines for enteral and parenteral nutrition are lacking. If we apply the international guidelines for the use of artificial nutrition ("if guts work you must use it") also in those anorexia nervosa patients who require life-saving intervention with artificial nutrition, we must choose enteral nutrition while parenteral nutrition should be considered only for very rare patients with impaired intestinal function (Lochsa et al., 2006; Bankhead et al., 2009) (Table 2).

| |
|---|
| Enteral tube feeding should be considered in people who are malnourished and have inadequate or unsafe oral intake and a functional accessible gastrointestinal tract.<br>**Reducing contamination**<br>Use of sterile, non-manipulated closed systems for enteral tube feeding administration and good hygiene, along with routine microbial surveillance reduce contamination associated with preparation. The use of closed system enteral administration set has been demonstrated to be safe for 24 hours.<br>**Enteral formula stability**<br>The stability of each component of an enteral tube feeding formula is important to maintaining the product's integrity and the patient's nutrition status.<br>**Selection of Enteral Access Devices**<br>In general gastric access relies on a functional stomach free of delayed gastric emptying obstruction or fistula. Small bowel feedings are most appropriate for patients with gastric outlet obstruction gastroparesis, pancreatitis and in those with known reflux and aspiration of gastric contents. Enteral access devices inserted via the nasal routes are usually placed for short-term use in the hospitalized patient. |

Table 2. Indication for enteral tube feeding and practice recommendation

Enteral feeding must be closely monitored and regulated via a electronically operated pump. Nasogastric feeding is the preferred procedure in many eating disorders units, because it is a safe and simple non surgical procedure that can be performed also by nursing staff. Compared with other methods of refeeding nasogastric feeding has a lower risk of complications and is cost-efficient.

The aim of this retrospective cohort study is to describe our experience with the use of enteral tube feeding for gradual correction of severe undernutrition in anorexia nervosa patients according to main international guidelines for the use of artificial nutrition and to available studies and clinical experience that support the effectiveness of enteral nutrition in weight restoration.

## 2. Patients and methods

### 2.1 Patients

We treated 122 (118 females, 4 males) inpatients, referred to the Eating Disorders Unit of Niguarda Hospital and affected by severe undernutrition due to anorexia nervosa (according to the Diagnostic and Statistical Manual of Mental Disorders, 2000), treated with nasogastric enteral nutrition. The observation period was from May 1999 to January 2011.

### 2.2 Measurements

#### 2.2.1 Anthropometry and resting metabolic rate

Body weight was recorded to the nearest 100 g, using a standard physician's weight scale with patient wearing only underwear (without shoes). Height was determined to the nearest 0.5 cm on a standard stadiometer.

Resting gas exchange was measured by open circuit, indirect calorimetry (Sensor Medics) for 30 minutes. Before each measurement, the system was re-calibrated using a reference gas mixture of 95% $O_2$ and 5% $CO_2$.

## 3. Treatment

Our multidisciplinary treatment consist in:

a. Behavioural and psychological therapy for patient and their parents.
b. Nutritional rehabilitation to restore weight correcting biological and psychological consequences of undernutrition.

Usually caloric intake levels were established beginning with indirect calorimetric measurements because resting energy expenditure is the main component of daily expenditure particularly in severely malnourished patients.

For severely malnourished patients, our nutritional rehabilitation program includes temporary supplementation with liquid food supplements, or - in life-threatening situations - temporary nasogastric feeding.

In our experience, enteral nutrition is necessary only in a minority of inpatients with a relevant degree of malnutrition and for a limited period of time. Enteral nutrition must always be integrated in a multidisciplinary approach, and managed by an expert team. In order to reduce gastric discomfort, it is usually administered via a nasogastric feeding tube and consists of a polymeric diet free of lactose and gluten, with a high degree of calories, a high nitrogen, complete fluid formula. The flow rate is maintained constant with a pump, during all infusion time (Table 3).

Enteral nutrition was used until the patients were no longer at life-risk and they started to collaborate with the treatment, increasing oral food amounts to a significant amount.

Dietary management was devised to achieve also behavioural modifications, patients were encouraged - not forced to eat enough to restore their weight.

Vitamin supplementation started just before feeding and continued during refeeding days.

Electrolyte levels were measured and if necessary supplemented. Phosphate supplements were administered unless blood levels were above normal values.

### 3.1 Data analysis

Data were analyzed with the SAS PACKAGE (Release 8.2 by SAS Institute Inc. Cary NC USA, 2002). The results are reported as means ± Standard Deviations or frequencies and percentages. Changes in body weight and body mass indexes at admission and those after enteral nutrition treatment were tested with the sign test for paired data. The hypothesis of

| | | |
|---|---|---|
| **Formula** | | |
| Calorie dense | 1,7 - 2 Kcal/ml | |
| **Delivery site** | | |
| Route | Access | |
| Gastric | Nasogastric | |
| **Method of Administration** | | |
| Method | | |
| Pump - assisted | Rate | |
| | Initial | 20 - 30 ml/h |
| | Advance to goal of | 40 - 50 ml/h or more if tolerated, start with a 24-hour per day and proceed with a drop infusion for 18-12-8 hours per day if tolerated. |
| **Other indications** | | |
| Flush the feeding tube with indicated amount of water every 6 - 8 hours | | |
| No interruption of oral feeding if it is accepted | | |
| **Monitoring** | | |
| Check gastric residual volume according individual necessity | | |
| Observe for abdominal distension, nasogastric tube site and assessment at least twice a day | | |
| **Weight daily** | | |

Table 3. Specific enteral nutrition protocol for Anorexia Nervosa patient

no difference between the body weight and the body mass index at admission and after enteral nutrition treatment was rejected by a $p < 0.0001$ for both variables.

## 4. Results

One hundred twenty-two patients were eligible for the study. Mean BMI was 13.1 ± 1.6 kg/m$^2$ and the mean age was 23.7 ± 9.7 years. A summary of patients' anamnestic, demographic and clinical characteristics are reported in Table 4.

| | Mean | S.D. | Range |
|---|---|---|---|
| Number of patients | 122 | | |
| Age at reported onset/diagnosis of Anorexia Nervosa | 18.8 | 6.7 | ( 10.0 – 42.0) |
| Duration of disease (months) | 54.4 | 64.1 | ( 2 - 356) |
| Age at beginning of enteral nutrition treatment (years) | 23.7 | 9.7 | (10 - 64) |
| Body Mass index (kg/m$^2$) at beginning of enteral nutrition | 13.1 | 1.6 | (9.7 – 18.6) |
| Body weight (kg) at beginning of enteral nutrition | 34.4 | 6.2 | (19.5 – 63.8) |
| Height (cm) | 162 | 0.1 | (137 - 185) |
| Estimated resting metabolic rate (Kcal/24 h) | 1166 | 120.5 | (826 - 1724) |
| Measured resting metabolic rate (Kcal/24h) | 860 | 160.5 | (580 - 1356) |
| % difference versus estimated basal metabolic rate according to HB formula | -25.7 | 12.3 | (-47 - 9) |

[a] Values are means ± SDs, range in parenthesis

Table 4. Anamnestic, demographic and clinical data of Anorexia Nervosa patients treated by Enteral Nutrition [a]

We observed a clinically significant reduction in measurement resting metabolic rate (- 25.7 ± 12.3%) respect to estimated basal metabolic rate according to Harris Benedict formula.

Table 5 presents the results of 122 anorexia nervosa patients treated with enteral nutrition. These patients continued to be treated by enteral nutrition till the achievement of BMI 16.4 ± 1.35 kg/m$^2$ (t=1). Mean body weight increased from 34.4 ± 6.2 kg to 43 ± 0.5 kg after 96 ± 91 days of enteral nutrition treatment with a mean enteral caloric supply of 1378 ± 261 Kcal; oral diet was never stopped. Patients and dieticians, together, selected a menu each day. Dieticians helped patients choose their own meals and provided a personalized, structured meal plan, which ensured nutritional adequacy and the inclusion of all major food groups.

Nasogastric tube feeding was continuously delivered over 24 h daily for the first 20-30 days, using feed pumps also to reduce gastric discomfort; as clinical conditions improved we proceeded with a drop infusion of 18-12-8 hours per day. We used a caloric dense completely fluid-formula diet, high nitrogen with protein intake of 1.63 ± 0.3 g/kg/body weight.

| | T = 0 | T =1 | T =2 |
|---|---|---|---|
| N | 122 | | |
| Body weight (kg) | 34.4 ± 6.2 | 43.0 ± 5.5 [a] | 47.4 ± 7.4 |
| Body mass index (kg/m$^2$) | 13.1 ± 1.6 | 16.4 ± 1.35 [a] | 18.0 ± 2.5 |
| Duration Enteral Therapy (days) | | 96 ± 91 | |
| Enteral feeding regimen Kcal/day | | 1378 ± 261 | |
| Amount of fluid enteral diet ml/day | | 707 ± 181 | |
| Amount of fluid enteral diet ml/hour | | 29 ± 8 | |
| Caloric dense amount Kcal/ml | | 1.9 ± 0.2 | |
| Protein g/day | | 56.1 ± 13.9 | |
| Protein g/kg Body weight | | 1.63 ± 0.3 | |
| Δ weight (kg) | | 8.7 ± 4.4 | 12.8 ± 7 |
| Δ weight /month (Kg) | | 3.6 ± 2.0 | 0.7 ± 1.0 |

T=0 onset of Enteral Nutrition Treatment, T=1 at end Enteral Nutrition Treatment,
T=2 at the last out patient check after 599 ± 670 days
[a] significantly different from t=0

Table 5. Clinical variables of 122 anorexia nervosa inpatient treated by enteral nutrition

We started slowly and we gradually increased the caloric intake during the first week to avoid refeeding syndrome.

## 5. Conclusion

Enteral nutrition was well tolerated and in those inpatients with severe, life-threatening undernutrition did not present any major complications, neither gastrointestinal complications such as diarrhea, vomiting, nor metabolic alterations such as hypoglycemia or hypophosphoremia nor hepatic malfunction.

If enteral feeding is integrated in a psychotherapeutic, empathic medical, nursing and dietitian approach the patients initially oppose it, but then, their compliance and co-operation is generally reasonable.

We choose to use enteral nutrition because we considered parenteral nutrition is more dangerous for developing a refeeding syndrome, and we agreed that parenteral nutrition should not be necessary for nutritional rehabilitation in Anorexia nervosa patients unless there is significant gastrointestinal dysfunction. In the group of 122 patients we never used it. In more severe patients we used infusion of 5-10% glucose fluid delivered during 24 hours a day until the metabolic alterations improved. The caloric intake was very gradually advanced in the first weeks to prevent the refeeding syndrome in those patients who are considered to be in high risk of refeeding syndrome. Prevention of refeeding syndrome is of crucial importance. The refeeding syndrome, a potentially lethal complication of refeeding the malnourished patient, can result in potential metabolic and pathophysiological complications, which can affect the cardiac, respiratory hematological, hepatic and neuromuscular systems leading to clinical complications and even death.

We choose to start with a 24 hour continuous flow supplement to reduce gastric discomfort, diarrhea and metabolic alterations, and only when the undernutrition was partially corrected, we gradually reduced the infusion time.

Our results seem to provide strong support for using a highly structured program for treating patients with severe anorexia nervosa; highly specialized eating disorder inpatient treatment is more effective and acceptable than standard psychiatric care, also the use of artificial nutrition and dietary management alone are both unacceptable as a primary interventions and ineffective as a form of relapse prevention, the overall conclusion is that therapies should have a full cooperation of the multidisciplinary medical and psychological teams specialized in eating disorders treatment.

## 6. Acknowledgment

The author would like to thank all the members of multidisciplinary team for their high professional work.

The author acknowledges the Fondazione FOBAN (obesity, bulimia, anorexia, nutrition) which supported the preparation of this manuscript.

## 7. References

American Academy of Pediatrics. (2003). Committee on Adolescence. Identifying and treating eating disorders. *Pediatrics*, 111(1): 204-211.

American Dietetic Association. (2011). Nutrition intervention in the treatment of eating disorders. *J Am Diet Assoc*, 111: 1236-1241.

American Psychiatric Association. (2006). Work Group on Eating Disorders. Practice Guideline for the treatment of Patients with Eating Disorders. *DOI. 10.1176/appi.books.9780890423363.138660.*

Bankhead, R., Boullata, J., Brantley, S., Corkins, M., Guenter, P., Krenitsky, J., Lyman, B., Metheny. N.A., Mueller, C., Robbins, S.& Wessel, J. (2009). Enteral nutrition administration. In: A.S.P.E.N. enteral nutrition practice recommendations. *JPEN J Parenter Enteral Nutr*, 33: 149-58.

Beumont, P., Hay, P., Beumont, D., Birmingham, L., Derham, H., Jordan, A., Kohn. M., McDermott, B., Marks, P., Mitchell, J., Paxton, S., Surgenor, L., Thornton, C.,

Wakefield, A. & Weigall, S. (2004). Royal Australian and New Zealand College of Psychiatrists Clinical Practice Guidelines Team for Anorexia Nervosa. Australian and New Zealand clinical practice guidelines for the treatment of anorexia nervosa. *Aust N Z J Psychiatry* Sep; 38(9):659-70.

Birmingham, L. (2008). Managing Eating Disorders: The Refeeding Syndrome. *The Canadian Journal of Diagnosis*, 85-89.

Gentile, M.G., Manna, G.M., Ciceri, R. & Rodeschini, E. (2008). Efficacy of inpatient treatment in severely malnourished anorexia nervosa patients. *Eat Weight Disord*, 13: 191-7.

Gentile, M.G., Pastorelli, P., Ciceri, R., Manna, G.M. & Collimedaglia, S. (2010). Specialized refeeding treatment for anorexia nervosa patients suffering from extreme undernutrition. *Clin Nutr*, 29:627-632.

Golden, N.H. & Meyer, W. (2004). Nutritional rehabilitation of anorexia nervosa. Goals and dangers. *Int J Adolesc Med Health*, 16: 131-44.

Hearing, S.D. (2004). Refeeding Syndrome. *BMJ*, 328: 908-9.

Lochs H., Allison, S.P., Meier, R., Pirlich, M., Kondrup, J., Schneider, St., van den Berghe, G. & Pichard, C. (2006). Introductory to the ESPEN Guidelines on Enteral Nutrition: Terminology, Definitions and General Topics. *Clinical Nutrition*, 25:180–186.

Marinella, M.A. (2005). Refeeding Syndrome and Hypophosphatemia. *J Intensive Care Medicine*, 20: 155-59.

Mehanna, H.M., Moledina, J. & Travis, J. (2008). Refeeding syndrome: what it is, and how to prevent and treat it. *BMJ*, 336: 1495-98.

National Institute for Clinical Excellence, (2004). Eating Disorders. Core Interventions in the treatment and management of anorexia nervosa, bulimia nervosa and related eating disorders. *www.nice.org.uk*

Paccagnella, A., Mauri, A., Baruffi, C. et al. (2006). Application criteria of enteral nutrition in patients with anorexia nervosa: Correlation between clinical and psychological data in a "lifesaving" treatment. *J Parenter Enter Nutr*, 30:231–239.

Robb, A.S., Silber, T.J., Orrell-Valente, J.K. et al. (2002). Supplement nocturnal nasogastric refeeding for better short-term outcome in hospitalised adolescent girls with anorexia nervosa. *Am J Psychiatry*, 159: 1347–1353.

Stanga, Z., Field , J., Iff, S., Stucki, A., Lobo, S.N. & Allison, S.P. (2007). The effect of nutritional management on the mood of malnourished patients. *Clin Nutr*, 26: 379-82.

Stanga, Z., Brunner, A., Leuenberger, M., Grimble, R.F., Shenkin, A., Allison, S.P. & Lobo, D.N. (2008). Nutrition in clinical practice - the refeeding syndrome: illustrative cases and guidelines for prevention and treatment. *Eur J Clin Nutr*, 62: 687-94.

Tonoike, T., Takahashi, T., Watanabe, H., Kimura, H., Suwa, M., Akaho. & Itaku, Y. (2004). Treatment with intravenous hyperalimentation for severely anorectic patients and its outcome. *Psych Clin Neurosci*, 58: 229–235.

Zuercher, J.N., Cumella, E.J., Woods, B.K., Eberly, M. & Carr J.K. (2003). Efficacy of voluntary nasogastric tube feeding in female inpatients with anorexia nervosa. *JPEN J Parenter Enteral Nutr* Jul-Aug; 27(4):268-76.